Y0-BDH-338

The Theory and Experience of
Economic Development

The Theory and Experience of Economic Development

Essays in Honor of Sir W. Arthur Lewis

Edited by
MARK GERSOVITZ, CARLOS F. DIAZ-ALEJANDRO,
GUSTAV RANIS and MARK R. ROSENZWEIG

London
GEORGE ALLEN & UNWIN
Boston   Sydney

George Allen & Unwin (Publishers) Ltd,
40 Museum Street, London WC1A 1LU, UK

George Allen & Unwin (Publishers) Ltd,
Park Lane, Hemel Hempstead, Herts HP2 4TE, UK

Allen & Unwin, Inc.,
9 Winchester Terrace, Winchester, Mass. 01890, USA

George Allen & Unwin Australia Pty Ltd,
8 Napier Street, North Sydney, NSW 2060, Australia

First published in 1982

British Library Cataloguing in Publication Data

The Theory and experience of economic development.
   1. Lewis, *Sir* W. Arthur   2. Economic
development – Addresses, essays, lectures
I. Gersovitz, Mark   II. Lewis, *Sir* W. Arthur
330.9   HD82

ISBN 0-04-330323-4

Library of Congress Cataloging in Publication Data

Main entry under title:
   The Theory and experience of economic development.

1. Economic development – Addresses, essays, lectures.
2. Economics – Addresses, essays, lectures. I. Gersovitz,
Mark. II. Lewis, W. Arthur,
(William Arthur), 1915– .
HD82.T47   338.9   82-3910
ISBN 0-04-330323-4   AACR2

Set in 10 on 12 point Times by Pintail Studios Ltd, Ringwood, Hampshire
and printed in Great Britain by Mackays of Chatham

Contents

Preface   *page* vii

1   On W. Arthur Lewis's Contributions to Economics
    by Ronald Findlay   1

2   W. Arthur Lewis: an Appreciation
    by Jagdish N. Bhagwati   15

PART ONE   THE DUAL ECONOMY

3   Lewis and the Classicists
    by Gustav Ranis and John C. H. Fei   31

4   The Pattern of Shift of Labor Force from Agriculture,
    1950–70
    by Simon Kuznets   43

5   Food Price Inflation, Terms of Trade and Growth
    by Lance Taylor   60

6   Alternative Theories of Wage Determination and
    Unemployment: the Efficiency Wage Model
    by Joseph E. Stiglitz   78

7   Agricultural Development, Education and Innovation
    by Mark R. Rosenzweig   107

8   Uncertainty, Information and the Inflation Tax in
    Poor Countries
    by Mark Gersovitz   135

PART TWO   THE OPEN ECONOMY

9   Unequal Exchange in a Lewis-Type World
    by Pranab K. Bardhan   157

10 Protection and Growth in a Dual Economy
    by Ronald Findlay   173

11 Lessons of Experience under Fixed Exchange Rates
    by Arnold C. Harberger and Sebastian Edwards   183

12 Currency Baskets and Real Effective Exchange Rates
    by William H. Branson and Louka T. Katseli   194

13   Negotiating International Economic Order
     by Goran Ohlin   *page* 215

PART THREE   COST BENEFIT AND PLANNING

14   General Equilibrium Theory, Project Evaluation and
     Economic Development
     by T. N. Srinivasan   229

15   The Economics of Pollution Control
     by Partha Dasgupta   252

16   Planning and Dual Values of Linearized Nonlinear
     Problems: a Gothic Tale
     by William J. Baumol   275

**PART FOUR   ECONOMIC HISTORY AND HISTORY
              OF THOUGHT**

17   Economic Growth and Stagnation in the United Kingdom
     before the First World War
     by Sir Alec Cairncross   287

18   The Cyclical Pattern of Long-Term Lending
     by Charles P. Kindleberger   300

19   Inter-Country Diffusion of Economic Growth, 1870–1914
     by Lloyd G. Reynolds   313

20   Latin America in Depression, 1929–39
     by Carlos F. Diaz-Alejandro   334

21   Indian Industrialization before 1945
     by Ian M. D. Little   356

22   The Rise and Decline of Development Economics
     by Albert O. Hirschman   372

Publications by W. Arthur Lewis   391

List of Authors and Their University Affiliations   395

Author Index   396

Subject Index   400

Preface

As have very few other economists, W. Arthur Lewis has been personally responsible for creating a dominant framework used by many others in a given subdiscipline of economics. In 'Unlimited labour' he presented a general equilibrium model of the economy with key insights focused on the interaction among its principal components. Part of the strength of Lewis's formulation is its continuous calling forth of additional efforts to refine the detailed workings of each piece of the model and then to investigate the empirical and operational behavior of the whole. What began with a simple assumption about surplus labor has continued to grow into a vast literature on how agriculturalists make decisions under a wide variety of circumstances and on how this affects the overall growth prospects of the economy. The basic strength of Lewis's model is that it has provided us with the all-important scalpel with which to initiate the general inquiry into a vital issue, even if the specific instrument has been substantially modified over time – witness the huge volume of research on land tenure and decision-making in agriculture; witness also the central role of the Lewis two-sector formulation in understanding growth, unemployment and distribution in LDCs.

The basic model of 'Unlimited labour', is, of course, only part of W. Arthur Lewis's contribution to the study of economic development. His other work includes the theory and practice of cost–benefit analysis and planning, the analysis of the economic history of the countries of the South, and of the relationship of the developing countries to the international economy. It is small wonder, then, that it has been impossible in this volume to adequately reflect the large scope of W. Arthur Lewis's contributions to economic development, not to speak of his work on education, on industrial organization, on public administration, or on the politics of development. Nor can this selection of papers testify to his frequent involvement in public affairs as advisor to governments and international organizations.

Our initial intent in organizing this volume was to recognize Arthur Lewis's many contributions on the occasion of his retirement from Princeton University. Since then that still-impending event has been supplemented in our minds by a number of at least equally important happenings: his sixty-fifth birthday, the award of the Nobel Prize in Economics and his nomination to the presidency of the American Economic Association. Historical foresight now permits us, his colleagues, students and friends, to dedicate this volume to him in recognition of all these happy and well-merited occasions.

The first section of the book is devoted to a discussion of aspects of W. Arthur Lewis's work on economic development and economic history. Ronald Findlay's paper begins with a short biographical sketch and then proceeds to discuss the dual economy and Lewis's model of the terms of trade. Jagdish Bhagwati treats these two themes from a complementary perspective but also pays special attention to Lewis's work on planning, politics and history.

Part One, on the dual economy, focuses on a number of problems in the development of a closed economy. Gustav Ranis and John Fei discuss the role of unlimited labor in models of development. In the next paper Simon Kuznets analyzes the transfer of labor from the agricultural to the nonagricultural sector. Then Lance Taylor examines the determination of the domestic terms of trade and food price increases. The following paper by Joseph Stiglitz looks at the efficiency wage theory of labor markets in LDCs, especially as it pertains to urban unemployment. Mark Rosenzweig analyzes the connection between technological diffusion in agriculture and education and other aspects of rural labor markets. The section ends with a discussion by Mark Gersovitz of inflation's role in financing government investment in situations of uncertainty.

Part Two examines problems of development in an economy trading with the rest of the world. Pranab Bardhan provides an interpretation of Arthur Lewis's model of the terms of trade between the poor and the rich countries. Ronald Findlay analyzes the impact of import substitution on growth when capital goods are obtained from abroad. The next two papers discuss aspects of international finance and development. Arnold Harberger and Sebastian Edwards concentrate on the connection between domestic policies and exchange rate performance during the recently abandoned regime of fixed parities. William Branson and Louka Katseli examine strategies for LDCs in the newly dawning world of floating currencies. This section closes with Goran Ohlin's analysis of the political economy of multilateral negotiations and the new international economic order.

Part Three consists of papers on cost–benefit analysis and planning. T. N. Srinivasan provides a critical survey of what has been learnt in both these fields. Partha Dasgupta looks at the environmental effects of development, a recent area of growing concern. William Baumol's examination of the implications of the linearization assumption for planning exercises is an important call for caution in the use of these models.

Part Four, on economic history, begins with papers that are relatively international and comparative in perspective and proceeds to studies focused on a single region or country. The first two papers discuss the pattern of growth in the industrial countries and the consequences for the less developed. Sir Alec Cairncross concentrates on the causes of the British climacteric, while Charles Kindleberger examines the historical determinants of international investment. Next, Lloyd Reynolds compares the early modern economic history of a number of poor countries, emphasizing common and contrasting experiences. The paper by Carlos Diaz-Alejandro analyzes the response of the Latin

American countries to an extreme form of external stimulus – the Great Depression. Then, Ian Little examines a number of economic controversies associated with the history of India under British rule. Through its reflections on some of the subdiscipline's failings, the final paper by Albert Hirschman provides an antidote to any hubris possibly generated by the preceding papers.

1

On W. Arthur Lewis's Contributions to Economics

RONALD FINDLAY

A major concern of economics in our time has been the problem of economic development, the achieving of a sustained increase in per capita incomes of the millions of people living in the so-called Third World. The urgency of this issue has led economists in the past three decades to return to the 'inquiry into the nature and causes of the wealth of nations' that they had abandoned during the previous century for the investigation of the allocation of given resources and the stabilization of employment and income. Among the many distinguished economists who have contributed notably to this recently revived field the pre-eminent figure is Professor W. Arthur Lewis of Princeton University. The purpose of the present chapter is to describe and evaluate the nature and significance of his contribution.

I

Lewis was born on the island of St Lucia in the British West Indies in 1915. He studied at the London School of Economics, obtaining his doctorate in 1940, and taught there for several years after the war. His first three books were written during this period. *Economic Survey, 1919–1939* (1949) began as a course of lectures to provide students with some background knowledge of the period but, as he says in the preface, it grew from this humble origin into 'an over-ambitious attempt to interpret the inter-war years in the setting of world economic history'. This concern with 'world economic history' has remained with Lewis throughout his career, as witnessed by the fact that his last book, published three decades later, is devoted to the evolution of the world economy from 1870 to 1913. One of the main strengths of his work on development economics is that he has never considered the problems of the LDCs (less developed countries) in isolation but always in the context of the world economy as a single interdependent system.

Also dating from this period is *Overhead Costs* (1949), a collection of essays dealing with the application of price theory to problems of industrial organization and public utilities. The chapter on the 'two-part tariff' for the pricing of electricity and telephone services provided a definitive analysis of this scheme.

There is also a very interesting model of 'competition in retail trade' which considers the question of the optimal number of retail stores. The solution proposed, in terms of balancing economies of scale against customer convenience in having a larger number of outlets to purchase from, anticipates the work done only very recently by Lancaster and others on optimal product variety. The third book of this London period was *Principles of Economic Planning* (1949), an early discussion of the subject.

The time Lewis spent at the London School of Economics can be thought of as preparatory to his work on development economics, which began after he moved to Manchester, where he occupied the Stanley Jevons Chair of Political Economy. With Harry Johnson and Ely Devons there at the same time the bleak northern city, home and symbol of the Industrial Revolution, must have been a stimulating environment, as one can gather from the many exciting papers that appeared in *Manchester School* during the mid-1950s. His two most famous works, the celebrated article on 'Economic development with unlimited supplies of labour' (*Manchester School*, May 1954) and the magisterial treatise on the *Theory of Economic Growth* (1955) were written during this decisive period of his career.

The treatise is much broader in scope than the title indicates. It not only discusses capital accumulation, technical progress and population growth, but also the bearing upon these of geography, social structure, religious and cultural values, political institutions and the psychology of human motivation. While much of the attention is concentrated on the LDCs, the book is concerned with the problems of economic growth and social change at such a basic level that it has relevance for societies at all stages of development. Since the purpose of the book was to provide a synthesis of existing knowledge bearing on the subject, rather than to put forward any novel theories or views, we shall not attempt to summarize and comment upon its contents. Attention should be drawn, however, to the fact that in the appendix Lewis asks and effectively answers the profound question 'is economic growth desirable?' long before critiques of 'growth mania' became fashionable. He says quite bluntly that the benefit of economic growth is *not* that it increases happiness, since there is no evidence at all for this, but that it increases the scope for choice by giving man greater control over his environment, thereby increasing his freedom. Also, well before the rise of 'women's liberation', he wrote these words: 'It is open to men to debate whether economic progress is good for men or not, but for women to debate the desirability of economic growth is to debate whether women should have the chance to cease to be beasts of burden, and to join the human race.'

Since 1963 Lewis has been at the Woodrow Wilson School of Public and International Affairs at Princeton University, USA, where he now occupies the James Madison Chair of Political Economy. He has also held several important administrative positions in the West Indies and has been an advisor to many African countries and to the UN and World Bank. While at Princeton, he published an authoritative textbook on *Development Planning* (1966) and edited a volume of essays by his students on *Tropical Development,*

1880–1913 (1970). He has also published three sets of public lectures, each notable for the manner in which a wide-ranging subject is treated in a brief space. The 1969 Wicksell Lectures and the 1978 Janeway Lectures will be considered below in relation to the main line of his research on trade and development.[1] The Whidden Lectures on *Politics in West Africa* (1965) deal with the crucial issues of the relations between democracy and development in the West African context. In addition to being a valuable contribution to political science, these lectures are memorable for the unequivocal commitment to liberal values displayed by the author and his scorn for the pretensions of the one-party state. It should be required reading for the many advocates of 'dictatorship for development' among Western intellectuals.

II

In terms of Isaiah Berlin's well-known classification of thinkers into 'hedgehogs' and 'foxes' Lewis is indubitably a hedgehog. His one big idea is set forth in the 1954 article on 'Economic development with unlimited supplies of labour'. His own subsequent work, and in fact a large part of the literature of development economics, can to a large extent be seen as an extended commentary on the meaning and ramifications of this central idea. Few other instances come readily to mind of an entire field being so dominated by a single paper. In view of its importance, and the controversy with which it is still to some extent surrounded, it will be necessary to devote considerable space to an examination of its contents.

There have been, broadly speaking, three alternative approaches to economics. These are the Classical, the Keynesian and the Neoclassical. The Marxist approach is, for present purposes, similar to the Classical and so will not be considered separately. The Keynesian situation is one in which output is constrained not by any supply factor, either labor or capital, but by a lack of effective demand. The remedy for this, especially in the midst of a deep depression, is clear, though these days we are not so confident of what to do when the economy is closer to full employment. At full employment both labor and capital are scarce, and the Neoclassical approach determines the rewards to both factors (or any number, if different types of labor and capital are distinguished) on the basis of the marginal productivity principle. Lewis regards this approach as the relevant one for developed industrial economies, with integrated labor markets, operating under conditions of reasonably full employment and utilization of capacity. For LDCs, however, he considers it more appropriate to return to the Classical method of postulating a real wage rate for unskilled labor that is determined by social convention, not 'subsistence requirements' in any biological sense. He thus conforms to the Sraffa or Cambridge view of the real wage as being exogenous for the LDCs but not for the developed countries.

The LDC he regards as a 'dual economy', divided into a 'capitalist' and a 'traditional' sector. In the 'traditional' sector labor is considered as being essentially self-employed, as in peasant family farms or petty trade, or as consisting of service occupations of various sorts such as domestic servants, feudal retainers, and the like. The motive for employment, whether of one's self or family members, or in hiring others, is essentially consumption. In the 'capitalist' sector, on the other hand, the motive for employment is to generate profit, which is the source of investment and, thus, of greater employment in the future. Lewis here explicitly invokes Adam Smith's distinction between 'productive' and 'unproductive' labor and his interpretation of Smith on this point corresponds to that of the important doctrinal study by Myint (1948, ch. 5), who argues that Smith's preferences for the former arose not from any 'materialistic fallacy', but from a desire to promote growth over stagnation. Needless to say, the 'capitalist' employer in this sense can be the state itself and the model can apply quite well to the USSR in the 1920s and 1930s as well as to the Asian communist countries of today.

The exogenously given real wage in the 'capitalist' sector exceeds alternative earnings available in the 'traditional' sector, so that employment in the former sector is constrained by demand and not by supply. It is in this sense that he speaks of 'unlimited supplies' of labor. Given the wage and technology, profit maximization determines the capital–labor ratio and the rate of profit, while the size of the capital stock determines the level of employment in the 'capitalist' sector. Lewis is also Classical in assuming that all wages are consumed and that profits are the only source of savings. The rate of growth in his model is, therefore, equal to the product of the rate of profit and the propensity to save out of profits, just as in the von Neuman model or the Kaldor–Robinson Cambridge theory. The demand for labor can expand faster than the growth of population without driving up the real wage, because peasant agriculture, the urban underemployed and increasing female labor-force participation form a labor reservoir which can be drawn on for a considerable time. It is only when this reservoir is exhausted that there is an integrated labor market with a uniform wage determined endogenously by demand and supply, at which point the economy is developed and the Neoclassical approach comes into its own.

The economic history of England is consistent with this model, since the real wage rate was virtually constant for two generations from 1780 to 1840, the classic era of the Industrial Revolution. It is possible that other instances can be found. In contemporary developing economies, however, real wage rates generally appear to have been rising. For skilled labor of various kinds this is only to be expected, since the supply is limited in the short run. The capital stock, fixed at each instant but expandable over time, is interpreted to include both 'human' and 'physical' capital. The differentials obtained by skilled labor, just like the quasi-rents of particular types of physical capital, provide the inducement to expand the supply of these inputs by education and training. The average wage will therefore rise if the demand for skilled labor increases faster than for unskilled labor, as one might expect to occur during the process of economic development. Thus, it is only if the real wage rate for unskilled labor rises that a problem appears of whether the Lewis or the Neoclassical view of the labor market in developing countries is the appropriate one.

It is consistent with the spirit of Lewis's approach to have a perfectly elastic supply of labor over the relevant range at each instant at a given real wage, while allowing this wage to rise over time as a result of exogenous forces such as union pressure or government intervention. For the Neoclassical approach to be valid, the rise in the real wage must be due to excess demand at the original level of wages. This is difficult to reconcile with the widespread existence not only of rural and urban underemployment, but of open urban unemployment throughout most of the less-developed world, which has been increasing not only absolutely, but relatively to the size of the labor force.[2] A plausible hypothesis is that the real wage rises at the same rate as productivity increases, leaving the rate of profit constant. The extensive literature associated with the popular Harris Todaro (1970) model of urban unemployment follows Lewis in postulating an exogenously fixed real wage in the urban sector, above alternative rural earnings, which induces a flow of migration equilibrated by the probability of unemployment in relation to the urban–rural wage differential.

Lewis regards the purpose of his model as attempting to explain 'the central problem in the theory of economic development', which for him is 'to understand the process whereby a community which was previously saving and investing 4 or 5 per cent of its national income or less, converts itself into an economy where voluntary saving is running at about 12 or 15 per cent of the national income or more'. His model accounts for this fact not by a rise in the propensity to save out of any given type of income, but as a result of an increase in the share of profits brought about by the relative expansion of the 'capitalist' sector. As Chenery and Syrquin (1975) point out, the econometric results of a number of studies have tended to confirm this basic hypothesis, that 'saving rises relatively to the national income because the incomes of the savers increase relatively to the national income'.

The origins of the 'capitalist' sector are outside the scope of the model, as are the determinants of the rate of technological change and the propensity to save out of profits. These would obviously depend upon the particular historical circumstances of each country and upon broader social and cultural forces that are beyond the scope of economics as a discipline.[3] Once this process has started, for whatever reason, growth in the economy as a whole accelerates even if the growth rate of the 'capitalist' sector is constant, since it is higher than in the rest of the economy. Under these conditions, the growth rate would be continually increasing but at a decreasing rate, since it is bounded from above by the growth rate of the 'capitalist' sector itself.

Eventually, however, the conditions of unlimited supply of labor must come to an end. Growth can then be regarded as being governed by a Neoclassical-type model, with an integrated labor market and a fixed saving rate. Initially, the growth rate of capital exceeds the natural rate of growth (population growth plus labor-augmenting technical change). The growth rate therefore decelerates in this phase, asymptotically approaching the natural rate by which it is bounded from below.

The two models in combination therefore yield the prediction of a 'long swing' in the rate of growth, rising from a level of near zero toward a limit set by the growth rate of the 'capitalist' sector and then falling toward a lower bound determined by the natural rate, the Lewis model governing the first phase and the Neoclassical model the second. The cross-section data conforms to this prediction, since growth rates plotted against per capita levels show an inverted U-shaped pattern, with low growth in the very poor countries such as Bangladesh, Burma and Nepal, very high growth rates in middle-income countries such as Brazil, Korea and Taiwan and growth at around 3 or 4 per cent in the rich countries such as Germany and the USA. On a time-series basis the experience of several mature countries may also correspond to this pattern, but the picture is not so clear since there has probably been a secular increase in the rate of technological progress itself.

III

As we have seen, the relationship between Lewis and the Neoclassical approaches is one of complementarity in accounting for the characteristic features of 'modern economic growth'. They are not alternative hypotheses attempting to explain the same phenomena. The complementarity is explicitly recognized both by Lewis himself and by Solow, Swan and other distinguished Neoclassical writers such as Meade and Hicks. Taking employment as given and determining the wage, or taking the wage as given and determining employment, are two limiting polar cases each of which may have its own appropriate sphere of application with respect to time and place.

Why, then, the extensive controversy surrounding Lewis's model? Much of it has been generated by some of his asides in the 1954 article concerning labor and its renumeration in the rural sector. It seems to have been a widespread impression that his model required 'disguised unemployment' in the rural sector in the sense of zero marginal productivity. As Lewis points out, he explicitly denied this in his original paper, although he frequently used his particular special case in illustrations and examples and believed it to hold in certain parts of the world such as India, Egypt and Jamaica. Thus, even if this phenomenon is shown to be empirically unsustained, his model is not thereby reduced to inapplicability, since all that he means by 'unlimited supplies' is an excess supply of labor at an exogenously given wage.

Part of the criticism arises from the view that his model attempts to make the real wage in the 'capitalist' sector endogenous, by treating it as determined explicitly as some function of the alternative earnings available in the rural sector. A popular scenario is cultivation by peasant families owning their own land who share the total product equally between members, so that the average product in peasant agriculture becomes the wage to the 'capitalist' sector. This can yield a perfectly elastic supply curve if land is abundant in the peasant sector, so that average and marginal product coincide. In this case the Lewis model and the Neoclassical model of the labor market become identical. It is 'unlimited supplies' of land which creates 'unlimited supplies' of labor to the 'capitalist' sector in this instance. This is an interesting example to consider, since it can be applied to a wide range of historical cases when there is a variable extensive margin or moving frontier – as in the USA, where the floor to industrial wages was provided by what labor could earn with 'forty acres and a mule' until the close of the nineteenth century.

In the case of the densely populated LDCs of today, however, land is a scarce factor in the rural sector, so that average product exceeds marginal product, with both diminishing in response to increases in labor input. Under these circumstances the supply curve of labor to the 'capitalist' sector would be upward sloping, if the wage were endogenously determined on the basis of either marginal or average productivity in agriculture. This would be the case even if there were 'disguised unemployment' in the rural areas, since a withdrawal of labor leaving total output constant would raise the per capita share of those remaining. Thus, 'disguised unemployment' in agriculture, by itself, is neither necessary nor sufficient for the horizontal supply curve of labor to the 'capitalist' sector, though it is compatible with it.

Though it is not essential to his model, Lewis is clearly a believer in the widespread existence of the phenomenon of zero marginal productivity of labor in the densely populated LDCs. By 'labor' he clearly meant 'men' and not 'manhours', since he says in his original article that the phenomenon arises when 'the family holding is so small that if some members of the family obtained other employment the remaining members could cultivate the holding just as well (of course they would have to work harder: the argument includes the proposition that they would be willing to work harder in these circumstances)'. He also points out, in the next sentence, that it is 'not by any means confined to the countryside' and cites a whole range of urban examples such as the market stalls all competing for the same volume of business that a fraction of them could handle just as well. It is, therefore, surprising to find how devastating the profession apparently found Jacob Viner's observation that it was impossible to conceive of a farm of any kind on which it would not be possible to raise output by more careful seed selection, planting, weeding, harvesting and gleaning.[4] The importance of the distinction between labor in the sense of 'bodies' and labor in the sense of 'work' is crucial in connection with the logic of the concept of 'disguised unemployment'. Given the number of workers, output could be increased if each works a little harder (positive marginal product of 'manhours'), but the additional returns may be so meager as not to be worth the extra effort. If some workers are removed, however, the remaining ones may find it worth while to maintain the same labor input and, hence, output as before (zero marginal product of 'men'). This response is shown to be perfectly consistent with 'rational choice' by individuals in a valuable formal analysis by Sen (1966) and in an extensive subsequent discussion by Lewis (1972) himself, though a restriction of constancy over a relevant range has to be placed on the trade-off between leisure and consumption.

This is not the appropriate place to review the extensive debate on whether and to what extent there actually is 'disguised unemployment' in the agricultural sectors of any LDCs. Both the early 'estimates' of 25 per cent in India and the apparent refutations such as the T. W. Schultz example of the 1918 influenza epidemic leading to a decline in farm output have to be interpreted with some care.[5] On the whole, however, it does appear that the early optimism about the enormous latent development potential represented by 'disguised unemployment' on a massive scale was exaggerated. This is damaging to the Nurkse (1953) and Rosenstein-Rodan (1943) theories of breaking out of the 'vicious circle' of poverty by means of a 'big push' but not, as pointed out earlier, to Lewis's approach, since he does not attempt to explain how and why development gets started. He confines himself to the analysis of the logistic process of transition from a traditional to a mature industrial economy.

Space also does not permit much discussion of the many contributions by others who have extended Lewis's work. Jorgenson (1961) presents an alternative approach to the 'dual economy' that is more Neoclassical in spirit. Fei and Ranis (1964) provide an elaborate discussion of dualism and the transition in terms of various phases. There has also been a lot of work on the appropriate shadow price of labor and choice of techniques for development projects in an economy where the real wage exceeds the marginal product of labor in agriculture, including monographs by Dobb (1960) and Sen (1960). Much of this work has been absorbed into the influential manuals of cost–benefit analysis for practitioners in developing countries prepared by Little and Mirrlees (1969) for the OECD and by Dasgupta, Marglin and Sen (1972) for UNIDO. The problem of the terms of trade between the two sectors of the dual economy has also given rise to an extensive literature, which connects with the fascinating debates between Bukharin and Preobrazhenski in the USSR, in the 1920s on 'primitive socialist accumulation', described by Erlich (1960). This issue has been discussed in terms of inter-temporal planning models by Hornby (1968), Bardhan (1970) and Findlay (1973). A Ramseyan optimal saving model of the dual economy is provided by Dixit (1968). Lewis's framework has also been fruitfully applied to many historical episodes, including an analysis by Kindleberger (1967) of Europe's postwar growth, stressing the role of 'unlimited supplies' of labor from the less-developed regions of the south.

IV

This section surveys Lewis's ideas on the trade-development nexus, a subject of crucial importance in view of the fact that the development process is influenced in so many ways by the movement of goods, factors and technology across national boundaries. While he has many pertinent observations on the relation between trade and growth in his treatise and in his textbook on development planning, his most original insights are contained once again in that wonderfully seminal 1954 paper, in the brief section on the open economy. By contrast with the long first section on the closed economy, this part of the paper has largely been neglected, in spite of his further development of the same ideas in the widely praised 1969 Wicksell Lectures. This no doubt reflects the unfortunate separation between trade theory and the study of economic development, in spite of Marshall's well-known observation on the link between the two.

In the 1954 paper Lewis independently advances the argument first made by the Romanian writer Manoilesco (1931), that protection is justified in LDCs on the ground that wages in industry are excessive in relation to agriculture. In Lewis's analysis the marginal product of labor in manufactures is equated with the average product in food, because of sharing within peasant families, whereas the social optimum requires it to be equal to the marginal product, which is less. There is consequently a case for intervention in the price mechanism to expand the output of manufactures and contract the output of food. The Manoilesco argument was revived by Hagen (1958), and pursued further by Bhagwati and Ramaswami (1963) and Johnson (1965) in the context of the theory of optimal intervention. It is readily shown that a wage subsidy to manufacturing is the ideal or 'first-best' intervention, while an output subsidy is 'second best'. A tariff will have the right effect in raising the output of manufactures but it restricts consumption, and hence on balance may either raise or reduce welfare in comparison with no intervention at all. Lewis did not examine the issue of how best to intervene, but clearly appeared to support tariffs over *laissez faire* under the circumstances considered.

Another model given in the 1954 paper and expanded upon in the Wicksell Lectures is more original and interesting than the one related to the Manoilesco argument, and leads to completely different policy recommendations. This is a simple but ingenious Ricardo–Graham model in which there are two regions and three goods, with each region producing two goods, one of which is common to both. Thus one region, the north, produces steel and food, while the south produces coffee and food, both regions consuming all three goods. Each region has a linear transformation curve for the two goods it produces, so that the relative prices of both steel and coffee are determined in terms of food, purely from the supply side. The terms of trade between the two regions are therefore determined purely by relative labor productivities in food, independently of demand conditions, because of the assumption of linearity. Thus if 1 labor produces 1 food or 1 coffee in the south, while 1 labor produces 5 food or 1 steel in the north, the commodity terms of trade will be 5 coffee for 1 steel and the double factoral terms of trade will be 5 units of southern labor for 1 unit of northern labor. This divergence of the double factoral terms of trade from unity, for which the Marxist writer Emmanuel (1972) has coined the emotive expression 'unequal exchange', is therefore explained by Lewis in terms of the disparity in labor productivity in *food*, reflecting the continuance of traditional methods in the south and the application of modern science in the form of mechanization and chemical fertilizers in the north.

The model can be applied to analyze the trend in the terms of trade over time if some realistic assumptions are made about productivity changes. Productivity in steel would be expected to increase faster than in coffee, which should lead to the prediction of *improving* terms of trade for the south, other things being equal. But, as Lewis points out, the relevant comparison is between the productivity trends for steel and food in the north, and for coffee and food in the south. In the Wicksell Lectures he cites data indicating convincingly that productivity in steel grows more slowly than in food in the north, while productivity in coffee grows faster than in food in the south. Hence the price of steel rises relative to the price of coffee, so that the commodity as well as the double factoral terms of trade turn against the south over time. He is thus able to provide a rigorous and elegant argument for a modified form of the thesis of secular deterioration of the terms of trade, more familiarly associated with the names of Prebisch (1950) and Singer (1950).[6]

Notice that nothing is altered in this model, if we substitute textiles for coffee. The development of labor-intensive manufactured exports is thus not regarded by Lewis as an appropriate strategy for LDCs in the long run, since he considers it to be a perpetuation of comparative advantage based on low-wage labor, reflecting low productivity in the subsistence sector. The strategy he recommends is therefore one of raising productivity in *food*, through investment in physical and human capital, technological change and government assistance. Since the LDCs are now becoming increasingly larger net importers of food, the strategy is one of import substitution, but on a quite different front from the emphasis on manufactures usually associated with this strategy.

At this point there is an apparent conflict between the original model, model A, stressing the relative expansion of the 'capitalist' sector as the path of development, and the present one, model B, which emphasizes the importance of raising the level of productivity in the 'traditional' sector. Thus on the basis of model B, he argues that in exporting manufactures instead of primary products to the rich countries, the LDCs merely 'exchange one dependence for another', whereas if they concentrate on raising productivity in food, they would be able to raise the wage level and improve the terms of trade. In the context of model A, however, he spoke of 'the Charybdis of real wages rising because the subsistence sector is more productive', leading to a fall in the profit rate and hence in the expansion of the 'capitalist' sector. The main reason for these apparent contradictions is that model A is dynamic but closed, while model B is open but static. Appropriate frameworks to consider alternative development strategies such as export of manufactures or import substitution in food can only be provided by dynamic models of open dual economies, examples of which can be found in the work of Hornby (1968), Bardhan (1970), Inada (1971) and Findlay (1973, pt 2). The right policy for each country to pursue would depend upon a complex set of constraints, both internal and external, and upon inter-temporal social preferences. Models A and B simply do not have enough structure to enable valid policy conclusions to be derived from them.

Lewis's writings reflect a rather deep-rooted and pervasive skepticism about the effectiveness of trade as an 'engine of growth'. Perhaps this is due to the experience of living through the Depression of the 1930s and his later study of its devastating effects in *Economic Survey, 1919–1939*. Thus, although statements like 'the planner neglects foreign trade at his peril' can frequently be found in his writings, he on the whole favors development oriented toward the home market, and his 'balanced growth' strategy is designed with this end in view. Imbalance between supply and demand in the various sectors of a growing economy lead to trade deficits and sharp changes in relative prices that are potentially disruptive, because of their consequences on the distribution of incomes.

In his Adam Smith Bicentenary essay he says that the Industrial Revolution offered the rest of the world two options – to imitate Britain by having one's own technological revolution, or to trade with her by exchanging primary products for the manufactured goods produced by the new methods.[7] Taking the trade option is easier but the true 'engine of growth' has to be internal, and can only be installed by having an industrial and associated agricultural revolution of one's own. As Myint (1948) argues in his incisive comment on this essay, the contrast here between the two options is overdrawn. Instead of being alternatives, trade and technological imitation can mutually reinforce each other, and have done so, most notably in the case of Japan but also more recently in the cases of Korea and Taiwan. The present pragmatic leaders of China appear to recognize this fact as well. It is, of course, true that trade by itself is not sufficient to transform a backward country into a modern developed one, and may possibly even raise obstacles in the form of enhancing the political power of 'feudal' landowners linked to the export sector, for example. However, in the context of the LDCs of today there is ample evidence of a positive association between trade and growth, as may be gathered from the valuable surveys of empirical work in this area by Little, Scitovsky and Scott (1970), Diaz-Alejandro (1975) and Bhagwati (1978).

V

Lewis's stature and authority as a student of the economic problems of the contemporary LDCs largely stems from the fact that he has always looked at these problems in the context of the evolution of the world economy as a whole. This has naturally required a deep knowledge of the economic history of the developed economies, which he calls the 'core' of the world economy, and of its relations with the 'periphery'. While in *Economic Survey, 1919–1939* he largely drew upon the work of others in presenting his interpretation of those years, he subsequently devoted much of his own scholarly efforts to the field of quantitative economic history. Though his name has never been associated with 'cliometrics', he should certainly be regarded as a pioneer in this field, especially in the light of his 1952 article on 'World production, prices and trade, 1870–1960', where he constructed and estimated a simple econometric model of world production and trade in manufactures, food and primary products. His work on the history of the world economy has culminated in his latest book *Growth and Fluctuations, 1870–1913* (1978). This is a truly remarkable work, which only Lewis himself could have written. No one else possesses the combination of qualities needed to write it, which are acute theoretical insights, vast historical knowledge and painstaking labor in the collection and analysis of statistical data. The result is a combination of theory, history and statistics that only a Schumpeter could match. The 'engine of growth' is located in the expansion of manufacturing in the four 'core' countries – the United Kingdom, France, Germany and the USA. The strong but irregular beat of this engine is measured for each country and compared, and there are fascinating analyses of trends and cycles in output and prices. The decline of the United Kingdom and the rise of Germany and the USA to world industrial leadership is a major theme of this aspect of the work.

The engine of growth sent its 'pulsations' to the rest of the world. Lewis concentrates on the contrasting effects on two groups of countries, the tropical regions containing most of the LDCs of today, and the temperate 'regions of recent settlement' such as Australia, New Zealand, Canada and Argentina. While the role of both these regions was to export primary products to the 'core' in exchange for manufactures, there was a fundamental difference between them. The temperate zone of the 'periphery' was populated by migrants from Europe, and consequently the wage level there had to be sufficiently high to provide a European standard of living for unskilled labor. In the tropics, on the other hand, wages were held at subsistence levels by 'unlimited supplies' of Indian and Chinese coolie labor. The difference in wage levels for unskilled labor in the two regions in the 1880s was of the order of nine to one, reflecting the difference between European and Asian labor productivities in food. This meant that exporters of wool, wheat, meat and dairy products had very favorable commodity and factoral terms of trade, while exporters of coffee, tea, sugar, rubber and jute had very unfavorable terms. This, of course, had fateful consequences on the size of the domestic market and the prospects for industrialization and import substitution in these two zones of the 'periphery'.

This link between migration, terms of trade and industrialization is but one example of Lewis's extraordinary ability to connect apparently isolated phenomena into a rationally coherent whole, in which theory and history, past and present, illuminate each other. In his hands economic history ceases to be a pedestrian 'application' of received doctrine to some previous episode of a particular national economy, and economic theory ceases to be a sterile exercise in formal logic without spatio-temporal coordinates that relate it to human experience. His contribution to economics transcends the study of the problems of the LDCs themselves. He alone has had the vision, the courage and the fortitude to devote a career, in an age of increasing specialization dedicated to the principle of discovering more and more about less and less, to no less a theme than the structure and evolution of the world economy during the last century.

Chapter 1: Notes

This paper originally appeared in the *Scandinavian Journal of Economics*, vol. 82, no. 1 (1980), pp. 62–76. The editors would like to express their appreciation to the *Scandinavian Journal* for permission to reprint this paper.
1 These have been published as Lewis (1969) and Lewis (1978a).
2 See Turnham (1971), for evidence.
3 There is, however, an extensive discussion of these issues in *Theory of Economic Growth*.
4 See Viner (1970).
5 See, for example, Myrdal (1968, appendix 6), Wellisz (1968) and Bhagwati and Chakravarty (1969), for critical appraisals of theory and evidence.
6 See Findlay (1981), for a more detailed analysis of the Lewis model and its relation to the work of Prebisch, Singer and others on the terms of trade.
7 See Lewis (1976).

Chapter 1: References

Bardhan, P. K. *Economic Growth, Development and Foreign Trade* (New York: Wiley, 1970).
Bhagwati, J., *Anatomy and Consequences of Exchange Control* (Cambridge, Mass.: Ballinger, 1978).
Bhagwati, J. and Chakravarty, S., 'Contributions to Indian economic analysis: a survey', *American Economic Review*, vol. 59, no. 4, (1969), pt 2, pp. 2–73.
Bhagwati, J. and Ramaswami, V. K., 'Domestic distortions, tariffs and the theory of optimum subsidy', *Journal of Political Economy*, vol. 71, no. 1 (1963), pp. 44–50.
Chenery, H. B. and Syrquin, M., *Patterns of Development, 1950–1970* (London: Oxford University Press, 1975).
Dasgupta, P., Marglin, S. and Sen, A. K., *Guidelines for Project Evaluation* (New York: United Nations, 1972).
Diaz-Alejandro, C. F., 'Trade policies and economic development', in P. B. Kenen, ed., *International Trade and Finance* (Cambridge: Cambridge University Press, 1975), pp. 93–150.
Dixit, A. K., 'Optimal development in the labor surplus economy', *Review of Economic Studies*, vol. 35, no. 101 (1968), pp. 23–34.
Dobb, M. H., *An Essay on Economic Growth and Planning* (London: Routledge & Kegan Paul, 1960).
Emmanuel, A., *Unequal Exchange* (New York: Monthly Review Press, 1972).
Erlich, A., *The Soviet Industrialization* (Cambridge, Mass.: Harvard University Press, 1970).
Fei, J. C. H. and Ranis, G., *Development of the Labor Surplus Economy* (Homewood, Ill.: Irwin, 1964).
Findlay, R., *International Trade and Development Theory* (New York: Columbia University Press, 1973).
Findlay, R., 'Fundamental determinants of the terms of trade', in S. Grassman and E. Lundberg, eds, *Past and Prospects of the Economic World Order* (London: Macmillan, forthcoming).
Hagen, E., 'An economic justification of protectionism', *Quarterly Journal of Economics*, vol. 72, no. 4 (1958), pp. 496–514.
Harris, J. R. and Todaro, M. P., 'Migration, unemployment and development: a two-sector analysis', *American Economic Review*, vol. 60, no. 1 (1970), pp. 126–42.
Hornby, J. N., 'Investment and trade policy in a dual economy', *Economic Journal*, vol. 78, no. 309 (1968), pp. 96–107.

Inada, K., 'Development in monocultural economies', *International Economic Review*, vol. 12, no. 2 (1971), pp. 161–85.

Johnson, H. G., 'Optimal trade intervention in the presence of domestic distortions', in R. E. Caves, H. G. Johnson and P. B. Kenen, eds, *Trade, Growth and the Balance of Payments* (Chicago: Rand McNally, 1965), pp. 3–34.

Jorgenson, D. W., 'The development of a dual economy', *Economic Journal*, vol. 61, no. 282 (1961), pp. 309–34.

Kindleberger, C. P., *Europe's Post-War Growth* (Cambridge, Mass.: Harvard University Press, 1967).

Lewis, W. A., *Economic Survey, 1919–1939* (London: Allen & Unwin, 1949a).

Lewis, W. A., *Principles of Economic Planning* (London: Allen & Unwin, 1949b).

Lewis, W. A., *Overhead Costs* (London: Allen & Unwin, 1949c).

Lewis, W. A., 'World production, prices and trade', *Manchester School*, vol. 20, no. 2 (1952), pp. 105–38.

Lewis, W. A., 'Economic development with unlimited supplies of labor', *Manchester School*, vol. 22, no. 2 (1954), pp. 139–91.

Lewis, W. A., *Theory of Economic Growth* (London: Allen & Unwin, 1955).

Lewis, W. A., *Politics in West Africa* (London: Allen & Unwin, 1965).

Lewis, W. A., *Development Planning* (London: Allen & Unwin, 1966).

Lewis, W. A. *Aspects of Tropical Trade* (Stockholm: Almqvist & Wiksell, 1969).

Lewis, W. A. (ed.), *Tropical Development, 1880–1913* (London: Allen & Unwin, 1970).

Lewis, W. A., 'Reflections on unlimited labor', in L. E. DiMarco, ed., *International Economics and Development* (New York: Academic Press, 1972), pp. 75–96.

Lewis, W. A., 'The diffusion of development', in T. Wilson and A. S. Skinner, eds, *The Market and the State* (London: Oxford University Press, 1976), pp. 135–56.

Lewis, W. A., *The Evolution of the International Economic Order* (Princeton, NJ: Princeton University Press, 1978a).

Lewis, W. A., *Growth and Fluctuations, 1870–1913* (London: Allen & Unwin: 1978b).

Little, I. M. D. and Mirrlees, J. A., *A Manual of Industrial Project Analysis in Developing Countries* (Paris: OECD, 1969).

Little, I. M. D., Scitovsky, T. and Scott, M. F., *Industry and Trade in Some Developing Countries* (London: Oxford University Press, 1970).

Manoilesco, M., *The Theory of Protection and International Trade* (London: King, 1931).

Myint, H., *Theories of Welfare Economics* (Cambridge, Mass.: Harvard University Press, 1948).

Myrdal, G., *Asian Drama* (New York: Twentieth Century Fund, 1968).

Nurkse, R., *Problems of Capital Formation in Underdeveloped Countries* (Oxford: Blackwell, 1953).

Prebisch, R., *The Economic Development of Latin America and its Principal Problems* (New York: United Nations, 1950).

Rosenstein-Rodan, P. N., 'Problems of industrialization of Eastern and South-Eastern Europe', *Economic Journal*, vol. 53, nos 210–211 (1943), pp. 202–11.

Sen, A. K., *Choice of Techniques* (Oxford: Blackwell, 1960).

Sen, A. K., 'Peasants and dualism with and without surplus labor', *Journal of Political Economy*, vol. 64, no. 5 (1966), pp. 425–50.

Singer, H. W., 'The distribution of gains between investing and borrowing countries', *American Economic Review*, vol. 40, no. 2 (1950), pp. 473–85.

Turnham, D., *The Employment Problem in Less Developed Countries: A Review of Evidence* (Paris: OECD, 1971).

Viner, J., 'Reflections on the concept of disguised unemployment', reprinted in G. M. Meier, ed., *Leading Issues in Development Economics* (London: Oxford University Press, 1970), pp. 151–5.

Wellisz, S., 'Dual economies, disguised unemployment and the unlimited supply of labour', *Economica*, vol. 35, no. 137 (1968), pp. 22–51.

2

W. Arthur Lewis: an Appreciation

JAGDISH N. BHAGWATI

Principal Scientific Achievements

Arthur Lewis's principal achievements can be classified into three major categories: political economy; historical analysis; and modeling developmental problems. These are not exclusive categories and, indeed, one of the most attractive aspects of Lewis's work, which has led to its profound impact, is that the three interact so well. Thus, his model of development with unlimited supply of labor builds on Classical economic thought, uses empirical insights into the developmental process, combined with keen perception of the institutional peculiarities of the overpopulated poor countries. None the less, while I shall stress these interacting dimensions wherever appropriate, I shall utilize the threefold classification to evaluate Lewis's work.

Political Economy

It is perhaps appropriate to begin with the much broader, rather than narrowly technical, aspect of Lewis's major achievements, since he is primarily in the tradition of political economy. Here, the major impact that he exercised on the economic thinking of his generation, right after the war, has been through his important work, *The Principles of Economic Planning*, published as early as 1949. This book was extremely influential and is generally regarded as a classic in the field. In contrast to the polemical argumentation of Hayek concerning the inevitable disaster to be incurred by 'planning', Lewis came up with the significant distinction between 'planning by direction' and 'planning through the market', a distinction whose importance has been underlined by the sad experience of many countries (not exclusively the underdeveloped) since the Second World War.

Arthur Lewis's general preference for planning through the market, developing the case for it as also for the conditions under which the market would need to be supplemented by intelligent state action, is based on subtle and scientific argumentation, as will be detailed below. But its humanistic basis is aptly illustrated by the beautiful story of Lewis telling Balogh, the apostle of planning by direction: 'Tommy, the difference between your kind of socialism and mine is that when *you* think of socialism, you think of yourself as being behind the counter whereas when *I* think of socialism, I think of myself as being in front of it.'

The book contains several classic formulations of the case against planning by direction, which have not been improved upon since by anyone in either content, or elegance of style. It is best to let Lewis speak for himself:

> There is ... a formidable case against planning by direction, and in favour of using the market.
>
> In the first place, the central planner, who issues the directions, cannot hope to see and provide for all the consequences of his actions. The economic system is exceedingly complex. If you plan to increase the output of watches you must at the same time plan to increase the output of everything complementary to watches, i.e. everything used with watches or in making watches, and to reduce the output of all substitutes for watches and the constituents of substitutes. Now no single person can make a complete list of all the complements and substitutes of watches or decide what will be all the economic effects of having more watches. And even if he could make a list for watches, he would need also to make a separate list for each of the complements and substitutes, each of which has to be planned, and again separate lists for each of their complements and substitutes, and so on. It is because of this complexity that the fulfilment of plans by direction is always so unsatisfactory. Thousands of engines are produced, but they have to be stored through shortage of ball bearings or of screws. In planning by direction the result is always a shortage of some things, and a surplus of others. Planning through the market (e.g. the state placing an order for watches, or paying a subsidy) handles all this better because, in any sphere that is affected by the decision to have more watches, the flow of money and the adjustment of prices acts as a 'governor', turning on or off automatically without any central direction.
>
> Secondly, and for the same reason, planning by direction has to be inflexible. Once the planners have made the thousands of calculations that are necessary to fit the plan together, and have issued their directions, any demand that any of the figures be revised is bound to be resisted. The plan once made must be adhered to simply because you cannot alter any part of it without altering the whole, and altering the whole is too elaborate a job to be done frequently. The price mechanism can adjust itself from day to day, the flow of money alters, and prices and production respond; but the economy planned by direction is inflexible. (pp. 16–17)

Remember, these words were written in 1949, way before the onset of Liebermanism in the USSR, or the overwhelming documentation and analysis of the errors of centralized planning in developing countries such as India, Pakistan, Ghana and Egypt in several recent studies by the OECD and NBER on foreign trade and industrialization strategies of the developing countries since the war![1]

But Lewis foresaw not only the practical impossibility of efficient central planning, thanks to informational problems and the inflexibility of centralized procedures. He also saw clearly a number of other deficiencies which were far more difficult to perceive ahead of the failures that would eventually plague planning by direction. Thus, if one reads on, Lewis warns of three deleterious consequences, all of which are now familiar to students of planning systems:

To the inflexibility and errors of planning by direction we must add its tendency to be procrustean. It is hard enough to step up the output of watches if there is only one kind of watch; if there are two kinds of watch it is more than twice as hard, and it gets progressively harder the more different types of watch there are. Central planners in consequence are always tempted to excessive standardisation, not because they think that standardisation is good for the public, but because it simplifies their job. Standardisation is frequently an engine of progress; but it is also frequently the enemy of happiness, and in foreign trade it is in many lines fatal to success.

Related to this is the stifling effect of direction on enterprise, and this is a consideration of the utmost importance in a country like the United Kingdom. This is a country which lives by foreign trade. We built up this trade by being first in the field of mass production of standard commodities. But today other nations are as good as we are at this game, if not better, and we can hold our own only if we are constantly in the vanguard pioneering new ideas; inventing new goods and processes, trying them out on the market, adjusting rapidly in accordance with consumer reaction, and so on. None of this can be foreseen, and so none of this can be planned from the centre. The future of the country depends on bold and free entrepreneurship; on people with new ideas being free to back them against all opposition, to get what resources of capital, labour and raw materials they need without bureaucratic hindrance, and to test out the market for themselves. Any form of planning which prevents this permanently, or for long periods, will be the ruin of Great Britain.

And finally, the more one tries to overcome the difficulties of planning by direction, the more costly planning becomes in terms of resources. We cannot plan without knowledge, so we must have elaborate censuses, numerous forms and an array of clerks. We cannot issue thousands of licences rapidly without thousands of clerks. The better we try to plan, the more planners we need. The Soviet Census returns over 800,000 'economists', who are mostly administrative staff connected with planning. The price mechanism does the same job without this army of economists, who are thus released for useful work in the mines and the potato fields. To be sure, the market economy also has its army of hangers-on, who contribute to profit making rather than to production, its contact men, sales promoters, stockbrokers and the like, but they are not as essential to it as are the planners to planning. (pp. 18–19)

The scientific strength of Lewis lies not merely in these remarkable perceptions of the major economic implications of planning by direction, but also in his characteristic ability to extend his arguments to the political sphere. Thus, on the political effects of planning by direction, he argued cogently that:

> On account of its complexity, planning by direction does not increase, but on the contrary diminishes democratic control. A plan cannot be made by 'the people' or by parliament or by the cabinet; it has to be made by officials, because it consists of thousands of details fitted together. Its results are embodied in thousands of administrative orders and decisions, of which parliament and ministers can have only the briefest knowledge, and which provide innumerable opportunities for corrupting the public service. The more we direct from the centre the less the control that is possible. When the government is doing only a few things we can keep an eye on it, but when it is doing everything it cannot even keep an eye on itself. (p. 19)

These few samples of Lewis's analysis of planning by direction could be amplified by his many other splendid insights, for instance, into the consequences of price control without measures to augment supplies, and the all-too-important distinction that he draws between general and particular shortages and the radically different measures necessary to deal with either. The work, therefore, has deservedly the status of a classic. Falling between the literary and theoretical styles of Hayek, on the one hand, and Lange, Lerner, Durbin and other writers on the viability of efficient centralized planning, on the other hand, Lewis seems to combine the immediate realism and relevance of his analysis with a firm grasp of the basic analytical issues raised by the problems, thus dominating the works of both these classes of writers of his vintage in terms of its impact on a whole generation of economists interested in planning problems.

Indeed, it is most important to stress that, while Lewis did not use formal modeling and arguments based on such analysis as is to be found in modern theoretical articles, his arguments go straight to the heart of the matter, avoid the tedium of excessive focus on one narrow aspect of the many dimensions of the problem at hand, and his pithy and terse writing is always precise and analytically strong. Thus, we have in Lewis the rare spectacle of an economist who is always a pleasure to read and learn from, since Lewis combines his style, shrewd insights and wisdom with a superb grasp of the economic principles pertinent to the problem at hand.

Lewis's ability to cut through a lot of fog and get to the heart of a problem, and then to apply common sense, wisdom and historical insights creatively to its resolution, is evident in most of his writings. I find particularly apt illustration of it, however, in his *Politics in West Africa*, the 1965 Whidden Lectures. This work is probably unknown to many economists and may not appear pertinent to an evaluation of Lewis's scientific achievements *qua* economist.

However, I mention it because it illustrates well the qualities that I have listed above, while also underlining his broader interests and, in particular, his ability to bring an economist's tools and insights to bear on political problems: thus demonstrating the range of economics. The lectures are based on his advisory missions to West African countries and are addressed to exploring, and essentially dismissing, the arguments for single-party government in these countries. They make a cogent case for a multiparty democratic system, but recommend proportional representation and coalition government in favor of the Anglo-Saxon rule of 'first-past-the-post'. The insights of a sophisticated practitioner of economic science are evident in the lectures; one beautiful passage illustrates this well:

> Politicians like to be thought of as heroes, but in fact they are just like other men. All of us have mixed motives. We want to serve our fellow men, and to earn their respect and gratitude for great achievement; at the same time we need money, power and prestige to fulfill our personalities. Economic philosophers insist that it is absurd to devise an economic system on the assumption that men are motivated mainly by a desire to serve; on the contrary, the function of a good economic system is to transmute into social benefit the drive for personal gain which keeps the system going. This is achieved (or sought) by a system of controls which tries to ensure that money can be made only by serving the public: only by offering the market what it wants. Business men seek constantly to escape these controls; strengthening the market to prevent manipulation is one of the continuing tasks of economic democracy. The same applies to political systems. Politicians, like business men, are motivated by the desire for money, power and prestige as well as by the desire to serve. A good political system assumes that politicians are ordinary men, and seeks through its control to ensure that politicians can fulfill their personal ambitions only by serving the public. A political system whose functioning depended on the altruism of politicians would be just as much an absurdity as an economic system depending upon the altruism of business men. The essence of political democracy is that the politicians are subordinate to the public, in whom are vested the fundamental rights of free criticism, opposition and dismissal. A political system in which the public surrenders these rights to a political party must have the same evil results as an economic system in which the market is subordinated to a guild of business men. (pp. 62–3)

Admittedly, Lewis here is to be distinguished from Kenneth Arrow, who brilliantly extended economic argumentation to political philosophy. But the arid and theological nature of current social-choice theory, which has seduced the talents of an unduly large number of young theorists since Arrow's pioneering work, makes Lewis's lectures appear far more refreshing, insightful and relevant to political concerns of the societies we live in than the writings of Arrow's humorless followers in the theory of social choice.

Historical Analysis

Rivalling his mastery of political economy is Lewis's considerable ability to look at historical events and draw out valuable lessons. In fact, his creative insights with the greatest scientific impact – principally the 'models' that I review in the next section – have come from his historical sense and also from his familiarity with the history of (Classical) thought. But while this will be evident from the next section, I intend to underline two other things here: first, Lewis's legitimate claim to having been one of the earliest economic historians that ushered in the 'new economic history'; and, secondly, the profound way in which Lewis can use historical insights to turn around one's way of looking at problems. Let me turn to each of these two aspects of Lewis in turn.

I believe that Lewis's *Economic Survey, 1919–1939* (which, like nearly all his major works, has gone into several impressions), published originally in 1949, defines with two other books of similar vintage the beginning of the new economic history. The other two works are Walt Rostow's *British Economy in the Nineteenth Century* (1948) and Robin Matthews's *A Study in Trade Cycle History: Economic Fluctuations in Great Britain, 1833–1842* (1954). Compared to Clapham and other predecessors, these works represented a great seachange: the level of sophistication in the use of complex and subtle economic argumentation put these economic historians into a separate class and made economic history an appropriate subject for the labors of gifted economists, rather than historians. (I *am* aware that the present-day cliometricians like to trace the origins of the new economic history to the Conrad–Meyer articles of slavery and to the works of Fogel, Fishlow, Temin, and others, who resorted to econometrics utilizing primarily the tools of modern general-equilibrium theory. However, I think that this is too narrow a conception. Surely, the important change was the application of sophisticated economic analysis to historical research, rather than the application of some specific tools or models! Once the use of economic argumentation and ideas at the best professional level had begun marking a departure from works which betrayed a rather poor grasp of economic ideas of the time, it was surely inevitable that econometrics, general-equilibrium theory, and for that matter modern macrotheoretic models would all get into the act, transforming economic history dramatically.) Written primarily as a review of the developments of the interwar years, it weaves them together very nicely, always seeking to cast light on events by resort to economic theorizing. Again, I find in this work many insights that should startle one because of their aptness in light of what transpired later. Thus, for example, Lewis writes of the lessons of interwar experience with trade barriers in terms that seem quite prophetic in light of the postwar experience with protectionism before and after the OPEC upset the long period of relative stability in the developed countries during the mid-1950s through the 1960s:

We are left, therefore, with the conclusion that the level of obstacles to international trade will depend on whether or not measures are adopted to promote stability. If such measures are not taken, countries will insist on the right to control their currencies and their tariff policies, and to make bilateral arrangements; international trade will be viewed with suspicion, as one of the ways in which depression is transmitted from country to country, and its level will be low. But if stability is assured – and it can be, and sooner or later must be – the principal incentive to the creation of obstacles to international trade will be removed, and, men being by and large and in the long run reasonable, international trade will once more be valued and cultivated, and the experience of the 1930's will prove to have been only a passing phase in economic history. The prospects are not too bad. The U.S.A., whose fluctuations dominate the world economy, has learnt much since 1929. Agricultural prices can no longer topple catastrophically, because the parity formula puts a floor to them, and nearly all responsible Americans now seem to agree that it is the duty of their government to pursue a budgetary policy which will minimise industrial fluctuations. The world will yet see many slumps; but it is unlikely to repeat the horrors of the 1930's.

If reasonable stability is assured, the barriers to international trade will be relaxed. Movements in the volume of trade will then depend on the working out of long term trends in world economic development. (p. 175)

Lewis's ability to look at problems in a refreshing and stimulating manner, thanks to his historical sense, is underlined by several of his other papers. I would illustrate with but one example. Thus, in his 1976 paper on 'Development and distribution' in the Hans Singer *festschrift*, Lewis is writing about a subject that has received already a great deal of academic attention. But in contrast to the absurdly mechanical and naïve statistical manipulations of recent writers which have become an in-joke in the profession, Lewis begins with the historical insight that developmental theorists have traditionally maintained that growth is an inegalitarian process and that this was so in the Classical models of Smith, Ricardo and Marx. He typically turns then to sketching a framework to examine the process which related development to distribution, beginning with the effects of growth in 'enclaves' surrounded by traditional activities, tracing the effects of development on the traditional activities and then the evolution of distribution within the enclave itself. The 'enclave' notion is really insightful, since it is quite general. For Lewis correctly argues that:

Development must be inegalitarian because it does not start in every part of an economy at the same time. Somebody develops a mine, and employs a thousand people. Or farmers in one province start planting cocoa, which will grow only in 10 per cent of the country. Or the Green Revolution arrives, to benefit those farmers who have plenty of rain or access to irrigation, while offering nothing to the other 50 per cent in drier regions. There may be one such enclave in an economy, or several; but at the start development enclaves include only a small minority of the population. (p. 26)

A number of interesting hypotheses to test emerge from this essay, as also important insights such as the misleading character of Gini coefficients (or, for that matter, the new Atkinson measure of inequality) when estimated for an entire economy, rather than for the enclave and the traditional sectors separately, for example. Here then we have, in my judgment, an ideal example of how Lewis's ability to think of developmental issues in the context of historical processes and, indeed, to reflect his acute historical sense can be illuminating and exciting for other economists.

The next section, where I sketch the influential models of Lewis on development, will contain yet added examples of the power of Lewis's historical perceptions and nothing need be added here itself on this theme. However, I should note here Lewis's celebrated book, *The Theory of Economic Growth* (1955), for to many economists it may represent one of his major achievements. It exhibits at many places rich historical and political-economic insights. In many ways, this work nicely complements the briefer, 'model'-oriented and profoundly influential contributions that Lewis has managed to develop elsewhere. I turn to these now.

Modeling Developmental Problems

While the preceding discussion underlies Lewis's 'broader' scientific contributions to economics, I turn to his narrowly scientific work, where he has attempted 'modeling' developmental problems in the customary, professional manner of modern economists. In my view, these attempts (two, and no more) have been so profoundly influential that, on their strength alone, Lewis may be considered legitimately to be a major figure in economics.

At the outset, however, it should be stressed that the modeling by Lewis is *not* exactly in the manner of a modern theoretical piece. It is more in the nature of a 'grand design' where relationships are sketched with a broad brush, with a number of important ideas woven in at different places, and 'models' of the narrow type lie within easy reach of the serious theorist. An excellent analogy is provided by Bertil Ohlin's work: his great work on the theory of international trade does *not* contain a well-specified model with logically derived theorems, but it still sketches effectively the outlines of the modern theory of international trade and was 'transmuted' into the Heckscher–Ohlin theory essentially by the alchemy of Paul Samuelson who 'extracted' from it the model that led to the celebrated theorems on factor price equalization, on the effects of protection on real wages, and so on. Identically, Lewis's work has had a simply profound impact on the thinking of an entire generation of developmental economists via his 1954 *Manchester School* piece on economic development with unlimited-supply-of-labor. This pathbreaking paper actually contains two differentiable (but not unrelated in Lewis's own arguments) models: one for closed economies, and the other containing his thoughts on the terms of trade of tropical countries which he has subsequently pursued further in his Wicksell (1961) and Janeway (1977) lectures, for example, and which is only presently coming into its own and is likely to prove every bit as important and influential as the closed-economy model that I first proceed to discuss.

The closed-economy model was absurdly simple. It was based on dualism: between the traditional, peasant, or informal sector which was characterized by elastic supply of labor at a constant subsistence-determined real wage, which then became available to a 'capitalist' sector, where the surplus over the real wage would accrue primarily as profits which, in turn, were reinvested to generate growth in the economy. While Lewis did consider the determination of profits with some sophistication, for instance, whether profits would grow or not as a proportion of national income as a reflection of technological and behavioral conditions, basically the story was unfolded in terms of the real wages rising as increasing supply of labor at a constant real wage was eliminated and the supply price of labor rose and, therefore, the rate of invest-ment and growth rate of national income would decelerate. Implicit in the Lewis account was perhaps the Classical notion of the stationary state: with increasing real cost of labor replacing the increasing resort to infertile land as the villain of the piece.

That this 'model' is insightful is testified to by the number of eminent historians who have found it useful to analyze economic growth processes in terms of Lewis's model. The great economic historian of Japan, Ohkawa (1964), has illuminated Japanese growth with its aid; Kindleberger (1967) has looked at postwar European growth in terms of it; many professional analyses of the unskilled immigration into Europe and of illegal immigration into the USA have drawn upon Lewis's concepts quite freely (and, in fact, Lewis had himself a detailed discussion, again years ahead of its time, of the role of immigrant labor once his basic model was opened up to the international economy); Sukhamoy Chakravarti (1974) has examined the Indian growth process since 1950 in terms of it; and there are doubtless many such examples.[2]

But, quite aside from this scientific impact, the model has generated an immense literature on models of dualistic growth by professional theorists such as Jorgenson, Fei and Ranis, Dixit, and others, as testified to by the few major references that I have singled out at the end of this essay.[3] The dominance of this model over other writings in the field of developmental economics is to be explained simply by the fact that Lewis was the only developmental economist of that great generation (which includes Ragnar Nurkse and Rosenstein-Rodan as the other two major figures) to have produced a *descriptive* model of the growth process which could challenge the new generation of young growth theorists. Thus, Lewis-inspired growth theorists have constituted an impressive subset of the theorists who turned to the analysis of growth models with the take-off of the Harrod–Domar–Solow contributions which have been reviewed in the well-known Hahn–Matthews (1964) survey in the *Economic Journal*.

But Lewis's paper also anticipated and inspired a great deal else in developmental thinking. First, he brought into focus the possibly different institutional feature of the traditional peasant sector in the developing countries. Nearly all of the later research on this question, regarding whether there is average-product pricing on family farms and its impact on the supply function for labor migrating to the urban sector (for instance, Lewis explicitly noted that the assumption of average-product pricing on the farm could lead to a rising supply price of labor in the presence of even surplus labor, if the supply price was set by the average product on the farm), is essentially a matter of tidying up Lewis's basic observations. Secondly, now that the 'informal sector' in the urban areas, which constitutes essentially the urban counterpart of the traditional sector in the rural areas, has shot into prominence, it is useful to note (as indeed the recent researchers on the subject have not failed to note) that Lewis explicitly described this sector as such and listed it among the reasons why the supply of labor at a constant real wage would materialize in the traditional societies of Asia. The modern-day researchers are largely filling out again Lewis's early observations. Thirdly, Lewis noted the possibility of surplus labor, though here the credit should go to Rosenstein-Rodan's wartime *Economic Journal* (1943) article, from which evidently Lewis and Nurkse (in his celebrated 1953 *Problems of Capital Formation* book) must have picked it up. Again, Lewis, as also Nurkse, correctly noted that, if surplus labor was to be removed without change in output on the farm, then the remaining people on the farm would have to work harder (and may not): an original insight which led to later work elaborating how the choice between leisure and income would determine the resulting impact on farm production. Fourthly, and finally, while Lewis himself did not extend his essential analysis in the direction of normative prescriptions, the dualistic models inspired by him have led to both static and dynamic analyses of the resulting implications for optimal policy intervention. Thus, for example, the theorists of trade and welfare have noted the case for protection of manufactures that may follow from Lewis-type dualism, where the marginal product in capitalist manufacturing exceeds the marginal product in traditional agriculture, since the latter is below the average product on the farm that is equated to the manufacturing wage; and others have extended the analysis of optimal tariffs and capital mobility tax-cum-subsidies to the case where labor supply is elastic at a constant real wage.

In short, to date, the 1954 *Manchester School* article, judged according to its marginal product as required by the Austrian theory of value, is one of those rare achievements for which any economist should gladly swap at least ten theoretical papers in the leading professional journals! The theory of development would have been vastly poorer, if Lewis had not written it; and what more could one say in favor of it?

But, tucked away at the end of this classic paper is the kernel of another model that explains the terms of trade between the poor and the rich countries which, for the simple reason that the unlimited-supply-of-labor at a constant real wage was such a beautifully neat assumption for growth-theoretic analysis, somehow got lost soon after. However, Lewis himself has returned to it time and again, as in his Wicksell and Janeway lectures, and it is only now coming into its own. For, of late, many well-trained economists around the world have come to ask the question as to why the terms of trade are what they are, this being a basic issue in the current debates on the New International Economic Order. And Lewis's 'model', which I will presently outline, asks this question – the subject of influential but opaque writings by Emmanuel and of rather obscure but beautifully stimulating writings by Prebisch, for example – with superb effect and is destined to have substantial influence. Findlay at Columbia is currently working on it, and other trade theorists are also greatly interested in it, so that I foresee professional economists reacting to variants of it for a variety of analytical problems.

I shall sketch only the outlines of it since, as with the unlimited-supply-of-labor 'model', we are dealing here with broadly sketched arguments, with what I called a 'grand design'. Lewis envisages the terms of trade between the tropics and the temperate zones, the 'poor' and the 'rich' countries, as being determined *à la* a three-commodity model with two 'countries' producing (in its basic version) one common commodity, 'food', and each country specialized in producing one of the remaining two goods. If then the 'tropics' produce steel and the 'temperate' areas produce coffee, the labor productivity per head in Lewis's Ricardian model may be put down as:

	steel	food	coffee
in temperate	3	3	–
in tropics	–	1	1

The terms of trade between coffee and steel are, in this simplest version of the Lewis model, linked by the productivity in food in the two areas.

Lewis has used this basic model to argue why, despite trade growing rapidly for the tropics in the nineteenth century, there were limited income gains and the world got divided into the rich temperate zone and the poor tropics. For a rise in the productivity in commodities (coffee) exported by the tropics would, in this model, be fully reflected in deterioration in their terms of trade (*vis-à-vis* steel). Additionally, Lewis has argued that the 'effective' labor productivity in food was set for the tropics by the immigrant, indentured labor from China and India: therefore, at an admittedly low level; whereas that for the temperate zone by the migration of higher-productivity Europeans. The nineteenth-century pattern of high opportunity cost European migration to the temperate zone and low opportunity cost Chinese and Indian migration to the tropics thus, in this Lewis model, explains why the tropics had the poor terms of trade that have bothered many economists. In Lewis's own elegant words:

> The factoral terms available to the tropics, on the other hand, offered the opportunity to stay poor at any rate until such time as the labour reservoirs of India and China might be exhausted. A farmer in Nigeria

might tend his peanuts with as much diligence and skill as a farmer in Australia tended his sheep, but the return would be very different. The just price, to use the medieval term, would have rewarded equal competence with equal earnings. But the market price gave the Nigerian for his peanuts a 700 lbs. of grain per acre level of living, and the Australian for his wool a 1600 lbs. per acre level of living, not because of differences in competence, nor because of marginal utilities or productivities in peanuts or wool, but because these were the respective amounts of food which their cousins could produce on the family farms. This is the fundamental sense in which the leaders of the less developed would denounce the current international economic order as unjust, namely that the factoral terms of trade are based on the market forces of opportunity cost, and not on the just principle of equal pay for equal work. And of course nobody understood this mechanism better than the working classes in the temperate settlements themselves, and in the U.S.A. They were always adamant against Indian or Chinese immigration into their countries because they realised that, if unchecked, it must drive wages down close to Indian and Chinese levels. (p. 14)

Concluding Observations

I have indicated above the most appealing aspects of Arthur Lewis's work from the standpoint of scientific achievement. Judged by his best work, Lewis stands sufficiently ahead in the front ranks of his profession to have deserved recognition by the Nobel Prize Committee. His influence on work in developmental problems can be fully anticipated to endure.

Chapter 2: Notes

This is a slightly edited version of a paper prepared for the Nobel Prize Committee. The suggestions of the editors of the present volume, in regard to stylistic changes, were very valuable. The Nobel Prize Committee's permission to publish the present paper is gratefully acknowledged.

1   See, in particular, the synthesis volume for the OECD project: Little, Scitovsky and Scott (1970); and the two NBER synthesis volumes: Bhagwati (1978) and Krueger (1978).
2   See Ho (1972) on Taiwan.
3   See the citations of Jorgenson (1961; 1966; 1967; 1969); Kelley, Williamson and Cheetham (1972); Dixit (1973); Fei and Ranis (1963; 1964); McIntosh (1975); Niho (1976); Ranis and Fei (1961); Sato and Niho (1971); and Zarembka (1970; 1972).

Chapter 2: References

Bhagwati, J., *The Anatomy and Consequences of Exchange Control Regimes*, NBER (Cambridge, Mass.: Ballinger, 1978).

Chakravarti, S., *Reflections on the Growth Process in the Indian Economy*, Foundation Day Lecture (Hyderabad: Administrative Staff College of India, 1974).

Dixit, A., 'Models of dual economies', in J. A. Mirrlees and N. H. Stern, eds, *Models of Economic Growth* (New York: Wiley, 1973), pp. 325–52.

Fei, J. C. H. and Ranis, G., 'Innovation, capital accumulation and economic development', *American Economic Review*, vol. 53, no. 3 (1963), pp. 283–313.

Fei, J. C. H. and Ranis, G., *Development of the Labor Surplus Economy: Theory and Policy* (Homewood, Ill.: Irwin, 1964).

Findlay, R. E., *International Trade and Development Theory* (New York: Columbia University Press, 1973).

Hahn, F. and Matthews, R. C. O., 'A survey of growth theory', *Economic Journal*, vol. 74, no. 296 (1964), pp. 779–902.

Ho, Y., 'Development with surplus population – the case of Taiwan: a critique of the classical two sector model, à la Lewis', *Economic Development and Cultural Change*, vol. 20, no. 2 (1972), pp. 210–35.

Jorgenson, D. W., 'The development of a dual economy', *Economic Journal*, vol. 71, no. 282 (1961), pp. 309–34.

Jorgenson, D. W., 'Testing alternative theories of the development of a dual economy', in I. Adelman and E. Thorbecke, eds, *The Theory and Design of Economic Development* (Baltimore, Md: Johns Hopkins University Press, 1966), pp. 45–60.

Jorgenson, D. W., 'Surplus agricultural labour and the development of a dual economy', *Oxford Economic Papers*, vol. 19, no. 3 (1967), pp. 288–312.

Jorgenson, D. W., 'The role of agriculture in economic development: classical versus neoclassical models of growth', in C. R. Wharton, ed., *Subsistence Agriculture and Economic Development* (Chicago: Aldine, 1969), pp. 320–48.

Kao, C. H. C., Anschel, K. R. and Eicher, C. K., 'Disguised unemployment in agriculture: a survey', in C. K. Eicher and L. W. Witt, eds, *Agriculture and Economic Development* (New York: McGraw-Hill, 1964), pp. 129–44.

Kelley, A. C., Williamson, J. G. and Cheetham, R. J., *Dualistic Economic Development* (Chicago: University of Chicago Press, 1972).

Kindleberger, C. P., *Europe's Postwar Growth: The Role of the Labor Supply* (Cambridge, Mass.: Harvard University Press, 1967).

Krueger, A. O., *Liberalization Attempts and Consequences*, NBER (Cambridge, Mass.: Ballinger, 1978).

Lewis, W. A., *The Principles of Economic Planning* (London: Allen & Unwin, 1949a).

Lewis, W. A., *Economic Survey, 1919–1939* (London: Allen & Unwin, 1949b).

Lewis, W. A., 'Economic development with unlimited supplies of labour', *Manchester School*, vol. 22, no. 2 (1954), pp. 193–7.

Lewis, W. A., *The Theory of Economic Growth* (London: Allen & Unwin, 1955).

Lewis, W. A., 'Unlimited labour: further notes', *Manchester School*, vol. 26, no. 1 (1958), pp. 1–32.

Lewis, W. A., *Politics in West Africa* (London: Allen & Unwin, 1965).

Lewis, W. A., *Development Planning: The Essentials of Economic Policy* (London: Allen & Unwin, 1966).

Lewis, W. A., *Aspects of Tropical Trade, 1883–1965*, Wicksell Lectures (Stockholm: Almqvist & Wicksell, 1969).

Lewis, W. A., 'Development and distribution', in A. Cairncross and M. Puri, eds, *Essays in Honor of Hans Singer* (New York: Holmes & Meier, 1976), pp. 26–42.

Lewis, W. A., *The Evolution of the International Economic Order*, Janeway Lectures (Princeton, NJ: Princeton Universtiy Press, 1978).

Little, I. M. D., Scitovsky, T. and Scott, M. Fg., *Industry and Trade in Some Developing Countries*, OECD (London: Oxford University Press, 1970).

McIntosh, J., 'Growth and dualism in less developed countries', *Review of Economic Studies*, vol. 42, no. 131 (1975), pp. 421–33.

Matthews, R. C. O., *A Study in Trade Cycle History: Economic Fluctuations in Great Britain, 1833–1842* (Cambridge: Cambridge University Press, 1954).

Niho, Y., 'The role of capital accumulation in the industrialization of a labor-surplus economy', *Journal of Development Economics*, vol. 3, no. 2, (1976), pp. 161–9.

Nurkse, R., *Problems of Capital Formation in Underdeveloped Countries* (Oxford: Blackwell, 1953).

Ohkawa, K., 'Concurrent growth of agriculture with industry: a study of the Japanese case', in R. N. Dixey, ed., *International Exploration of Agricultural Economics* (Ames, Iowa: Iowa State University Press, 1964), pp. 201–12.

Ranis, G. and Fei, J. C. H., 'A theory of economic development', *American Economic Review*, vol. 51, no. 4 (1961), pp. 533–65.

Rosenstein-Rodan, P. N., 'Problems of the industrialization of Eastern and South-Eastern Europe', *Economic Journal*, vol. 53, nos 210–11 (1943), pp. 202–11.

Rostow, W. W., *The British Economy in the Nineteenth Century* (Oxford: Clarendon Press, 1948).

Sato, R. and Niho, Y., 'Population growth and the development of a dual economy', *Oxford Economic Papers*, vol. 23, no. 3 (1971), pp. 418–36.

Zarembka, P., 'Marketable surplus and growth in the dual economy', *Journal of Economic Theory*, vol. 2, no. 2 (1970), pp. 107–21.

Zarembka, P., *Toward a Theory of Economic Development* (San Francisco: Holden Day, 1972).

Part One

The Dual Economy

3

Lewis and the Classicists

GUSTAV RANIS AND JOHN C. H. FEI

Introduction

The recent revival of concern with development in the so-called 'overseas territories', after 150 years of virtual neglect, will undoubtedly be recorded some day as one of the transcendental events of the postwar era. This phenomenon undoubtedly had much to do with fundamental changes in the political map of the world. But the 'academic scribbler' who will be among those most remembered in that context will just as undoubtedly be the man being honored in this volume. Both by means of his sometimes neglected encyclopedic contribution, *The Theory of Economic Growth* (1955), which managed to touch virtually every base and yet convey important insights, and via his celebrated 'Unlimited supplies of labor' articles (1954 and 1958), Arthur Lewis has been heavily responsible for imbuing this subject of inquiry with renewed respectability and intellectual vigor. His contributions to a deeper understanding of history, of development planning, of North–South relations, even of the philosophical underpinnings of growth as a desirable objective, are many – and have been expounded by Bhagwati and Findlay, earlier in this volume. But what we would like to focus on here is Lewis's major single intellectual contribution seen in the context of both its Classical roots and its modern analytical extensions.

That central idea, the notion of a dualistic economy, with its traditional sector containing a pool of surplus labor setting labor-supply conditions for the capitalistic sector is, indeed, almost annoyingly simple – thus, uniquely elegant. In that sense it reminds us very much of the consumption function which occupies a similar central role in the Keynesian system. Few of our own contemporaries, indeed, have demonstrated anything approaching the same 'feel' for analyzing history with the help of simple analytical constructs without which all the heavy equipment of modern-day economics may in the end yield very little. Lewis belongs to a tradition of basically literary economists, which is unfortunately about to become an endangered species.

Both in the choice of subject matter, and in the method of analysis, Arthur Lewis is clearly more comfortable in the company of the Classicists. But while it is generally recognized that he deserves major credit for reintroducing us to the Classical tool-kit, it is our contention that he deserves even more credit for applying those tools to a really rather different problem, and in a rather different historical and analytical context. We will also conclude that not all of the voluminous literature to which his seminal contribution gave rise has been fundamentally constructive.

Lewis and the Classicists: Roots and Differences

In evaluating Lewis's contribution in leading us back into the Classical fold we will find it helpful to relate it to Simon Kuznets's idea of modern economic growth. According to Kuznets (1966), the industrial revolution which spread through Western Europe in the last quarter of the eighteenth century was a major event marking off rather sharply two major phases of growth, that of a long historical epoch of agrarianism which preceded it, and that of modern economic growth which followed. The characteristics of modern economic growth include the systematic application of science and technology to industrial production, an acceleration of growth, major structural change and the diffusion of the process across countries.

As is well known, the so-called stylized facts of modern economic growth seemed to first take hold in England, then spread to the Continent, from there to some of the late-comer countries, including Germany, the USA, Japan and Russia during the nineteenth and early twentieth centuries. Only after the Second World War, with the exception of some earlier Latin American cases, did the so-called developing countries begin their own efforts to reach the modern growth epoch.

Lewis's writings, like much of the work of the so-called contemporary development economists, is really directed toward an understanding of transition growth through which societies endeavor to move between the sharply contrasting regimes of agrarian colonialism and modern economic growth. Such a period may last approximately fifty years, as in the case of England between 1775 and 1825, or the case of Japan between 1870 and 1920. Over the three postwar decades a number of Third World countries have similarly registered a major try at achieving successful transition.

These two historical efforts, one in the 'West' and one in the 'South' are very relevant to our discussion of Lewis and the Classical tradition, for the obvious reason that theories relevant to any such change are likely to develop during any such period of upheaval. Smith, Ricardo and Malthus's growth theory was developed at the end of the eighteenth century, as was Lewis's during the past thirty years. While the physiocrats described the more or less constant rules of the game during the long agrarian epoch, and growth theorists in the post-Keynesian tradition described behavior in the steady state of advanced industrial societies, the Classicists and Lewis were really engaged in analyzing the transition process from one to the other, if from a somewhat different perspective.

One major difference is that Lewis's analysis is really heavily based on the existence of organizational dualism which, in the case of successful transition, ultimately yields to organizational one-sector homogeneity. While Lewis does not employ this terminology, his two sectors, the traditional and the capitalistic, are essentially marked off by differences in their institutional/organizational behavior – one emphasizing sharing rules of distribution, the other competitive rules under profit maximization. In the case of the Classicists, on the other hand, such a differentiation is not made, largely because they wrote under the influence of the world as they saw it, namely, one which was heavily agricultural but also capitalistic. The Classicists were essentially production-oriented and worried about the inability of the agricultural sector to overcome the drag of Malthusian population pressures and, thus, generate the savings required for the sustained growth of non-agricultural activity.

A second difference may be noted with respect to the identification of evolutionary subphases of growth during the transition period. In the Classical context we encounter the famous long-run stagnation thesis toward which the system is gravitating, with an essentially heavily pessimistic pall covering the proceedings. Looking back over more than 9,000 years of settled agricultural life under the long agrarian epoch the Classicists clearly saw nonagricultural activity as little more than a temporary 'blib' on the body-economic. While they discussed industrial activity – and Smith, more than the others, perceived a certain potential dynamism there, associated with economies of scale – the focus of most of the analytics was the land; and the predominant view was that the land was not about to lose its dominant grasp over the economic fate of mankind. The preponderantly pessimistic conclusions of the Classical school can be traced in large part to this essentially agrarian, one-sector view of the world, especially when that one sector's own prognosis was not viewed as favorable.

For Lewis, quite in contrast, the definition of different phases of growth is crucial, because he is essentially engaged in depicting the metamorphosis of the system from a preponderantly traditional to a preponderantly capitalistic set of rules of the game. This, plus the fact that he is basically optimistic about the outcome, marks him off sharply from his Classical mentors. He, of course, had the benefit of hindsight provided by almost two centuries of successful transition growth in the now-advanced countries of the world. But it was his general view not only that the contemporary developing economy, like its predecessors, could move from a predominantly traditional to capitalistic organization via a turning-point landmark, but also that the chances of achieving such a goal, that is, for the continued spread of the modern growth phenomenon, were substantial.

There are unfortunately, few, if any, development economists who have studied the Classical writers as carefully as Arthur Lewis has. Because of his dusting off of analytical tools which had fallen into disuse and his contribution to the revival of interest in the age-old problem of development, the facile assumption has often been made that Lewis simply accepted and then built upon the Classical foundations. In fact, however, while no one will deny Lewis's Classical roots, the differences we have already briefly noted above are as important, and instructive, as the common heritage. They are based on at least three factors, all relating to Lewis's historical advantage: the benefit of being able to take into account actual global experience since the last quarter of the eighteenth century; a different view of the role and importance of science and technology; and a different conceptual and practical view of capital formation.

The Classical economists were writing at the time of a great flurry of a new kind of economic activity, in textiles, in textile machinery, and so on, organized under a mass-production factory system. It focused attention for the first time on nonagricultural activities and on the so-called urban employment problem which might accompany development. This break with the relative tranquillity of the agrarian society of the Middle Ages and with the regularities of a well-understood system as portrayed in the physiocrats' *tableau économique*, led them, however, to believe that this was but a transient deviation from the norm, rather than a fundamental change in the rules of the game. Their basic conclusion was that the new urban-centered activities would not turn out to be a permanent feature and that agriculture would continue as the mainstay, namely, that sooner or later England would probably revert to the type of peaceful agrarianism which was part and parcel of contemporary Europe's historical experience.

They were, of course, proved wrong in this overall prediction, partly because of Engels's Law, but mainly because they underestimated the potentialities of science and technology in overcoming what they believed to be a system's overwhelming natural resource constraints. That the (not always causally clear) interaction between science and technology would not only render the predictions for longer-term agricultural stagnation irrelevant, but prove a major feature of sustained non-agricultural growth, was, of course, difficult to anticipate. How could they know, as Lewis did, observing the world many years later, that the flurry of industrial activity being observed was really more than a temporary departure but marked the arrival of the modern growth epoch.

Lewis's relative optimism on the possibility of reaching the promised land of modern growth stands in sharp contrast. The fact that his was basically a dynamic theory taking the economy through various subphases of growth has usually been ignored. His famous unlimited-supply-of-labor diagrams really indicated two phases, the first characterized by the relative constancy of the real wage, and the second by a substantial increase in the real wage. The essential message that cut through all this was that a labor-surplus economy can be successful when it ultimately experiences a metamorphosis from one to the other state in its transition to modern growth. The fact that the economy is likely to throw off its initial economic/geographic constraints, with technology change overcoming demographic pressures over time, and evolve into a situation where the real wage can increase in a sustained fashion, is clearly an optimistic view and a far cry from the long-run stagnation thesis in the Classical tradition.

Lewis's greater faith in the power of science and technology to overcome not only the initial unfavorable endowment situation, but also rising population pressures over time, is clearly related to his adoption of a more realistic and modern concept of capital accumulation. While the Classical school still focused heavily on agriculture and on the circulatory or wages-fund type of capital accumulation, Lewis accepted the view that fixed capital, represented by machinery, plant and equipment, and so on, is likely to be more important and, moreover, essential for 'carrying' the new processes and product designs resulting from the advances of science and technology. Finally, the successful demographic transition of Western Europe provided evidence that population growth, while a formidable obstacle – and presumably much more so in more overpopulated regions impacted by modern health and sanitation methods – could be overcome by the forces of capital accumulation and technology change. It is really small wonder that, in the light of past 'Western' performance, Lewis could favorably assess the prospects for success in the postwar 'Southern' transition effort.

Lewis's unlimited supply curve of labor, first only gently and then steeply sloping, constitutes, moreover, more than just an optimistic prediction. It constitutes at the same time an important behavioristic hypothesis with large operational significance. An approach to real wage constancy in the first phase really represents behavioral tools which simplify the analysis of the functional distribution of income, always an integral part of growth theory, especially when growth is thought of as of the savings-pushed variety. Classical economists envisioned an increasing dosage of labor and capital, as a wages fund, applied to a fixed amount of land and leading to diminishing marginal productivity and an ever-increasing rental share. In the Classical, especially the Ricardo, world this rental share is wasted in consumption by the labor aristocracy, while the rate of return to labor-cum-capital keeps falling steadily. When it finally comes to the battle between labor and capital, since the wages are kept constant by institutional forces, the rate of return to capital must decline. Hence, with profits as the exclusive source of savings, stagnation inevitably results. In this way the constancy of the real wage in the hands of the Classical economists is a simplifying hypothesis integral to the theory of the functional distribution of income. It is needed as the foundation of Classical capital accumulation and growth theory.

There is little doubt that the constancy of the real wage plays a similar role in the Lewis system. The simplifying assumption about the real wage leads to a simple version of functional distribution theory and of savings, and inevitably to the turning point and phase two. Before the turning point, the constancy of the real wage implies natural austerity contributing favorably to the generation of a larger volume of profits and thus savings, thus in turn rendering the arrival of the turning point more likely. Once the elastic supply curve of labor ends and the real wage begins to increase markedly, the rules of functional distribution and the rules of savings, as Lewis puts it, begin to change. In this fashion, the same view of the functional distribution of income problem commits Lewis to arrive at a more optimistic vision of successful transition growth which, unlike the Classical thesis, is in fact fully borne out by the contemporary facts in many of the more successful labor-surplus contemporary LDCs, for example, the East Asian 'Gang of Four'.

Lewis and the Classicists: Extensions and Controversy

By proudly accepting his Classical heritage Professor Lewis also inherited what appear to some modern economists two flaws within the system, namely, the aforementioned ambiguity about dualism itself, and the indeterminacy of real wages. These 'flaws' have proven a source of unnecessary misunderstanding and irritation, but also at times a blessing in disguise, as they have led to some helpful clarifications and extensions of the debate and advanced our understanding of the development problem. We, finally, turn to a more detailed illustration of this general point.

The term 'dualism' is one of the more overburdened and misused terms in economics, as well as in anthropology and sociology. When Professor Lewis speaks of dualism or a two-sector world, he starts with the simple coexistence of two production sectors, which differ in organizational rules only. To others, including many of Lewis's followers, dualism meant specifically a division into agricultural and nonagricultural activities, in a mode familiar to analytical economists in the two-sector, Neoclassical trade theory context. Lewis's organizational dualism as between a traditional and a capitalistic sector may or may not completely map into the notion of agricultural and nonagricultural sectors. The capitalistic sector is characterized by contractual hiring of labor in order to maximize profits, while the production unit in the traditional sector coincides practically with the household decision-making unit containing members glued together by kinship or some other non purely economic relations. The distinction between noneconomic and economic arguments is drawn much more sharply in modern economics, the essential point being that the particular commodities produced is not what constitutes the essential ingredient in the dichotomy, while the method of organization as between traditional and capitalistic certainly is.

By modern standards the Classical growth model is, of course, ambiguous with respect to dualism. The very fact that overall economic stagnation was traced to the shortage of land relative to population betrays the fact that agricultural production is viewed as the dominant production sector and that the nature of the product centrally matters. The urban-centered industrial production story is, thus, really marginal and relatively unimportant in most Classical writings. Modern economists presenting the Classical model to a group of graduate students, in fact, often feel somewhat uncomfortable, because the formal operational relationships between the dominant agricultural and the nondominant nonagricultural sectors (presumably both capitalistic in organization) are not clearly spelled out. It seems quite clear, however, that to the Classical economist the agricultural production sector was also the capitalistic sector in the sense of Arthur Lewis, that is, the tripartite division of labor of Smith, with capitalist farmers renting land from the aristocracy and hiring labor, is as close a representation of the profit-maximizing capitalistic method of organization *à la* Schumpeter as one can find.

It is, thus, not an accident that both the Classical theory and the development theory of Lewis encompass notions of institutional economics, if we may designate concentration on the method of organization of production in this fashion. For transition growth as distinct from epochal growth involves two dimensions of evolution: the way resources are utilized, and the way methods of organization are modified. This second consideration may be trivial for an economy already in the modern growth epoch.

Mature socialist economies differ from mature capitalist economies in the type of production organization they have chosen, but in either case they stay relatively put and are judged by their ability to solve complex issues of modern production. The difference between Lewis and the Classical school, however, is that while the latter did not concern themselves with organizational evolution, just as they did not concern themselves with technological change, the evolution of organizational choices really lies at the heart of the division of production sectors into capitalistic and traditional and is central to the Lewis turning-point thesis.

If pushed to the logical extreme, the arrival of the turning point is really the result of a race between capital accumulation, represented by an upward shift through time of the marginal product curve $M_0M_1M_2$ in Figure 3.1 to determine the amount of labor absorbed $E_0E_1E_2$, and so on, and the amount of labor available, related to the initial labor surplus and to population growth, represented by the population-growth curve shown in the lower diagram along P_0P_0'. Labor absorption finally catches up with labor supply at the turning point, when the reservoir (represented by the horizontal gap between the labor-force growth curve and the capitalistic-sector employment path) is exhausted, at point T. While Professor Lewis himself abhors such dynamic formulism, he nevertheless makes it clear that it was the savings-pushed growth of this type that was the essential driving force for solving the development problem. In this sense, in spite of the claim of many of his critics, he has never, in fact, neglected agriculture or emphasized industrial expansion as the main savior. His is an operational dualism, which emphasizes the crucial role of the traditional sector in generating the necessary savings to enable the race between population growth and labor absorption to be won.

Professor Lewis is, of course, aware of the fact that the meaningfulness of the postulation of two sectors hinges on its operational significance. On the surface there are two 'constant' wage rates, for the capitalistic sector w, and for the traditional sector w', represented by the two horizontal lines in Figure 3.1,

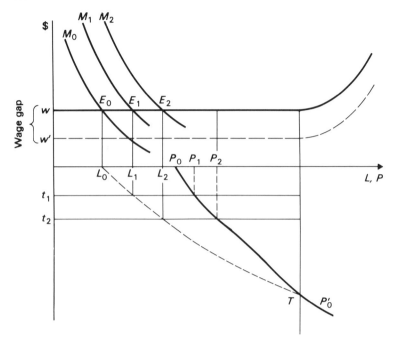

Figure 3.1

such that there is a wage gap *ww'*, which attracts labor into the capitalistic sector provided employment opportunities can be found. Beneath the surface, 'the non-capitalistic sector serves for a time as a reservoir from which the capitalist sector draws labor' (Lewis, 1972, p. 76). We may quickly add that because of the demographic transition, this pool is also continuously being augmented. Thus the unlimited supply of labor which at a given wage rate *w'* is available to the capitalist sector will, for some time, exceed the demand. This is really all Professor Lewis needs for his purposes, namely, the analysis of transition growth in the context of a functional income-distribution-determined and savings-pushed growth. The reservoir of labor in his dualistic model corresponds to disguisedly unemployed labor in all kinds of occupations, for example, retail services, distribution, and so on, and is explicitly not restricted to the agricultural sector. Dynamically speaking, the reservoir is fed by population growth, as well as determined by the size of the initial pool of underemployed in all such activities.

Lewis's unlimited-supply-of-labor condition, like Keynes's consumption function, represents a key behavioral assumption on which many others have been able to build. One apparently innocent extension of Professor Lewis's work, in fact, may represent a potentially very important departure, namely, that of substituting or augmenting his organizational dualism with product dualism. In the realm of substitution there exists a long tradition of two-sector models in the economics literature as illustrated by the well-known Neoclassical two-sector model of international trade and other Neoclassical models applied to development. Some such models involve food and clothing, a two-commodity specification *à la* Ricardo and Heckscher–Ohlin, with the emphasis on inter-sectoral resource allocation and taking into consideration both production and consumer-preference conditions. More generally, in addition to inter-sectoral commodity flows, such models can focus on inter-sectoral relations including migration and capital mobility.

Once product dualism is added, rather than simply replacing organizational dualism, we have a potentially much richer broth, permitting us to analyze important inter-sectoral issues in the context of development phasing. Lewis himself still seems not fully aware of this distinction: other writers with different purposes have made different divisions. A now popular division is between industry and agriculture (Lewis, 1972, p. 76). The point is that Lewis's own purposes might well have been better served by superimposing product dualism explicitly on his organizational dualism. The reason for this is that inter-sectoral analysis really must lie at the heart of a meaningful dualistic development theory. As Kuznets's modern economic growth concept indicates, the speed, spread and structural changes of an economy focus our attention on inter-sectoral changes of the product type. When the contemporary LDC, on the other hand, attempts its transition from agrarianism to modern growth, the key structural change is, in fact, the anticipated growth of the capitalist non-agricultural sector at the expense of the traditional agricultural sector as proxied by labor allocation and/or the percentage contribution to value added. The two sectors are, however, neither organizationally symmetrical in the input–output sense, nor in the product content sense. In fact, the impediments to reaching the turning point center on the commercialization of the agricultural sector as a prerequisite. All essential inter-sectoral issues, not only the inter-sectoral allocation of labor but also inter-sectoral commodity and financial markets, represent crucial links for determining the success of the transition growth process.[1] We need to be in a position to analyze the full range of interactions between the two sectors. This forces one to move beyond organizational dualism and to incorporate important aspects of product dualism as well.

It must, of course, be recognized that the attempt to capture the full interplay of the two sectors with a focus on both types of dualism also requires delving more deeply into the behavioristic equations which need to be postulated in order to determine the magnitude of these various flows over time. Any such deterministic model is certainly not Lewis's cup of tea, but he is happy to let others furrow the field he has laid out. What he does find somewhat annoying is the persistent questioning by those who want to build such models based on a fully determined real wage in agriculture. This touches on a sensitive nerve, because the question appears to be so basic to the thesis of unlimited-supply-of-labor, and yet Professor Lewis and his followers cannot provide a coherent, rigorous answer which will satisfy modern analytical economists: 'The model *does not* attempt to derive the conventional wage: as in the Classical system, this depends not only on productivity but also on social attitudes.' Lewis barely conceals his irritation when he states that

> whether marginal productivity is zero or negligible is not at the core of fundamental importance to our analysis. It was probably a mistake to mention marginal productivity at all, since this has merely led to an irrelevant and intemperate controversy. (Lewis, 1972, p. 77)

Almost by definition, any 'institutional explanation' of the level of real wages can never satisfy the card-carrying theorist. But the key point is that much of the controversy between the so-called Classical and Neoclassical positions on this very point may really constitute a misdirected search for concreteness. The persistent challenges by modern analytical economists concerning a coherent and rigorous determination of the real wage have stimulated the search for the construction of a rural real-wage theory down to the present time, taking into account many specific micropeculiarities of rural organization and tenure arrangements.[2] Many arguments have focused on the attempts to demonstrate that the marginal productivity of labor is not, in fact, zero, namely, that the real wage may, in fact, simply not be as high as the marginal productivity of labor.[3] Others have tried to explain the empirical fact of a gently sloping real wage by elaborate assumptions on the agricultural production function within a basically Neoclassical context.[4]

The real wage, in fact, really has three basic elements of significance. From the point of view of factor rewards, it has distributional significance. This, when combined with assumed Classical savings behavior, attributes savings mainly to income from property and can be fully explored in the context of a one-sector growth model. It also has allocation significance, an aspect which is fully explored in general equilibrium theory, namely, in relation to the equalization of wage rates among production sectors as a key condition for allocative efficiency. In this respect the allocation significance of the real wage is manifested in the context of any two-sector model. The notion of an unlimited-supply-of-labor model as developed by Professor Lewis refers mainly to the distributional significance of wages. However, when the notion of unlimited supplies of labor is extended to a two-sector world, with product dualism superimposed, the wage rate takes on an additional allocative significance, since it is the main regulator of the allocation of the labor force, as well as of the determination of the terms of trade and of inter-sectoral exchange in the context of a mixed economy. Inter-sectoral labor, commodity and financial markets become crucial and the food/nonfood content of the two sectors assumes its own special importance within a general equilibrium context.

A third and final element of significance of the real wage relates to its impact on technology, an issue especially – but not exclusively – sensitive in the non-agricultural sector of a dualistic economy. This is another big subject, related both to technology choice, given relative-factor prices, and to the inducement of technology change in one direction or another depending on the expectations with respect to future relative-factor price movements. While Harris and Todaro (1970) have analyzed the wage and expected employment in the industrial or capitalistic sector as the regulators of the inter-sectoral rate of labor migration, other extensions have included a focus on the closely related inter-sectoral commodity and financial markets and on the size and direction of induced innovative activity.

Lewis knows, as well as his critics, that once one abandons the marginal productivity theory of the real wage, one is hard put to construct a credible alternative; this is true even for the advanced countries where institutional forces and attitudes toward collective bargaining also play a role. It is easy enough to construct arguments and alternative models for the determination of the real wage. But after the model is constructed, one also has the right to ask the following question: if an already relatively abundant labor force is being augmented very rapidly by population increase and/or by labor-saving technology change, is it not true that, in whatever system is adopted, the real wage is not likely to be rising very much over a considerable period of time? If that is so, and there is presumably no basic disagreement here, empirically speaking, Professor Lewis, one suspects, would be perfectly happy to accept whatever theory one might want to construct leading to the relative constancy of the real wage over a considerable stretch of historical time.[5] In his work he was simply assuming that those basic conditions are met − which freed him to focus his analysis on the issues he really cared about, the distribution of income, and the process by which a 5 percent saving rate gradually yields to a 12 percent saving rate as the capitalistic sector exerts its increasing dominance in the course of transition growth.

Almost three decades have passed since the theoretical construct of unlimited-supplies-of-labor first made its appearance. As with all ideas, it did not emerge full-blown from the brow of Zeus, but had its antecedents; much additional construction, some glittery, some faulty, has since been added, and much controversy has swirled about the edifice. But no one will dispute that it has been and remains impossible to write about development without reference to Arthur Lewis's contribution. It has become part of the precious and unavoidable core of the profession, rising above disagreements, extensions and polemics.

Chapter 3: Notes

1 See, for example, Fei and Ranis (1964).
2 For example, the work of Bardhan, Srinivasan, and Rosenzweig.
3 This, rather than the conceptually, as well as statistically, unlikely event of zero is certainly what most of Lewis's followers had in mind, and on paper.
4 See, for example, Kelley, Williamson and Cheetham (1972).
5 In this sense, we may note again the analogy with the Keynesian consumption function. We all know its operational significance as lying at the heart of Keynes's system, that is, aiming

at the determination of income with the help of the multiplier. It was much later that analytical economics began to explore the precise behavioristic foundations of the consumption function, for example, whether it rests on the foundations of the Slutsky equations, generally on the work of Patinkin, and to what extent other than income factors affect consumer behavior. To Keynes, such theoretical niceties were also somewhat secondary, his main objective being the use of the consumption function for a larger analytical purpose, rather than complete agreement on its derivation.

Chapter 3: References

Fei, J. C. H. and Ranis, G., *Development of the Labor Surplus Economy* (Homewood, Ill.: Irwin, 1964).

Harris, J. and Todaro, M. P., 'Migration, unemployment and development: a two-sector analysis', *American Economic Review*, vol. 60, no 1 (1970), pp. 126–42.

Kelley, A. C., Williamson, J. G. and Cheetham, R. J., *Dualistic Economic Development* (Chicago: University of Chicago Press, 1972).

Kuznets, S., *Modern Economic Growth: Rate, Structure and Spread* (New Haven, Conn.: Yale University Press, 1966).

Lewis, W. A., 'Economic development with unlimited supplies of labour', *Manchester School*, vol. 22, no. 2 (1954), pp. 137–91.

Lewis, W. A., *The Theory of Economic Growth* (London: Allen & Unwin, 1955).

Lewis, W. A., 'Unlimited labour: further notes', *Manchester School*, vol. 26, no. 1 (1958), pp. 1–32.

Lewis, W. A., 'Reflections on unlimited labour', in L. E. DiMarco, ed., *International Economics and Development* (New York: Academic Press, 1972), pp. 75–96.

4

The Pattern of Shift of Labor Force from Agriculture, 1950–70

SIMON KUZNETS

Introduction

The comprehensive estimates by the International Labor Office of the industrial structure of the labor force distinguish three major sectors: agriculture, including forestry, fisheries and hunting; industry, including mining, manufacturing, construction, water, power and light utilities; and services, comprising all the other branches, ranging from transport, storage and communication to trade, finance, business services, personal services and government services.

Our interest here is in the *pattern* of the decline in the share of labor force in agriculture, a decline that was widespread from 1950 to 1970 – the two decades covered so far by the ILO estimates. Because the treatment of the female labor force varies widely among regions and countries, particularly for female workers in agriculture, we use the estimates for the share of the male labor force alone. While parallel calculations show that the patterns derived from the share of the *total* labor force in agriculture would differ only in detail, we thought it best to limit the statistical evidence here. It is not feasible to appraise critically the validity of the ILO estimates. We accept them as referring to approximate orders of magnitude, acceptance implying that the findings suggested by the estimates merit discussion and probing.

Pattern of the Decline in the Share of Male Labor Force in Agriculture, in Relation to the Initial Share

The pattern of the declines in the share of the male labor force in agriculture during 1950–70 in relation to the initial share in 1950, is clearly conveyed in Table 4.1. As we move from countries in which the initial share of the agricultural sector is high to those with appreciably lower shares, the absolute decline in the share (let alone the relative drop) widens. In the decade 1950–60, the decline was less than 3 percentage points for countries with an initial share in agriculture of over 90 percent, and reached a peak of 8·8 points for the group with an initial level of the share in agriculture of about 46 percent. And if

Table 4.1   *Proportions of Male Labor Force in Agriculture (1950) and Changes over 1950–70: Selected Sequences of Eleven Country Moving Averages, 1950 Ranking*

Sequence	%age proportion (1950) (1)	Decline, %age points (1950–60) (2)	%age proportion (1960) (3)	Decline, %age points		%age proportion (1970) (6)
				(1960–70) (4)	(1950–70) (5)	
1 5–15	92·9	2·8	90·1	3·3	6·1	86·8
2 25–35	84·3	3·8	80·5	3·8	7·6	76·7
3 45–55	76·3	5·0	71·3	6·0	11·0	65·3
4 65–75	66·8	5·1	61·7	7·0	12·1	54·7
5 85–95	55·4	6·5	48·9	8·6	15·1	40·3
6 95–105	46·1	8·8	37·3	9·3	18·1	28·0
7 105–15	33·2	5·8	27·4	7·0	12·7	20·4
8 115–25	23·2	5·6	17·6	5·6	11·2	12·0
9 121–31	16·7	4·7	12·0	3·9	8·7	8·0

Notes:
The entries in the vertical stub are the order numbers of the countries included in each of the selected eleven country averages – taken from an array of all 131 countries in declining order of the share of male labor force in agriculture in 1950.

The averages are unweighted arithmetic means. The totals may show slight discrepancies because of rounding.

The total number of countries, including residual groups in some regions, was 131 – covering both less and more developed countries, market economies and communist units, in short, world coverage.

Source:
The table is based on table 28, p. 62 of *Labour Force, 1950–2000: Estimates and Projections*, Vol. VI, 2nd edn (Geneva: International Labour Office, 1977), Methodological Supplement. It was supplemented to cover a wider selection, using appendix table C, pp. 118–20 in the same source.

we continue with the group formed by the 1950 rankings, the decline from 1960 to 1970, which amounts to 3·3 percentage points for the highly agricultural countries in line 1, reaches a peak of 9·3 percentage points for the group with the initial share in agriculture at the 46 percent level. The absolute magnitude of the decline then diminishes as we move to countries in which the initial share of agriculture is lower. The pattern suggests a parabolic curve, the latter describing the movement of the absolute declines on the y-axis, as we shift on the x-axis from the high to the low initial shares of male labor force in agriculture, the peak point being reached in the neighborhood of 50 to 40 percent.

This pattern is derived from a cross-section comparison for a large group of countries, including subgroups that, for our analytical purposes, should be excluded. One such subgroup comprises the communist countries, in which the distinctive character of the economic-growth policies may yield sharp declines in the share of labor in agriculture, regardless of how high or low the initial share may be – within the relevant range from 90 to 40 or 30 percent. Another subgroup are those less developed countries (LDCs) that may benefit from oil (or similarly valuable natural resources exploitable for the benefit of the host nation) – and for many of these, declines in the share of labor in agriculture were dramatically different from those shown by the other LDCs. Also, national units that are tiny, and there has been an increasing number of them in recent years, may be subject to erratic behavior. For all of these reasons, we decided to check the pattern so clearly indicated in Table 4.1, by selecting countries with 1 million or more population in 1950, excluding communist units and those appreciably affected by oil export possibilities. We arrayed these countries separately within each of three major less developed regions, and added the more developed region that would provide, within the regional array, countries at the lower ranges of initial shares in agriculture (Table 4.2).

Table 4.2 includes, in the three less developed regions, groups of countries in which the initial, 1950, share of labor force in agriculture ranges from 96 to about 64 percent — with the odd small group in Temperate South America (line 13) with an initial share of only 33 percent. The significant finding is that the arrays, within each of the three less developed regions, show a rise in the magnitude of the decline — as we move down from the initially high shares of labor in agriculture. We fail to observe here the drop that follows the rise, because with the single exception of Latin America, we miss the groups with an initial, 1950, share level that would be past the peak of the parabolic pattern referred to in connection with Table 4.1. In other words, lines 1–12 of Table 4.2 confirm the presence, among those countries that are less developed market economies, of the rising phase of the pattern revealed for a far more heterogeneous population of countries in Table 4.1.

The confirmation of the declining phase of the pattern of Table 4.1 is provided by the countries covered in lines 14–18 — the dominant majority of which would be classified as more developed countries.[1] These countries cover, at least in the 1950 rankings, the range of initial shares of male labor in agriculture that extends over the declining phase of the parabolic pattern. A glance at the movement of the declines in the shares in lines 14–18 shows the large magnitude of the average declines in line 14 (with an initial share of over 50 percent) and the sharp drop in these declines as we move to the low initial levels of the share in line 18.

Table 4.2 relates to eighty-nine countries, rather than the 131 countries covered in Table 4.1. But at least thirty countries, and possibly a few more, in the larger total would be classified as either communist (centrally planned), or oil export units. Table 4.2 omits some important and relevant units, particularly Japan among the industrial countries, some of the closely associated rapidly growing LDCs such as South Korea and Taiwan, South Africa, and the like. But for our purposes, it is sufficient to show that the parabolic pattern so clearly indicated in Table 4.1 would hold even if we were to limit our universe to market economies, less and more developed. We can then retain the general features of the pattern in Table 4.1, while discussing the behavior of market economies at different levels of industrialization — as revealed by shares of male (and most likely also total) labor force in agriculture.

Table 4.2　Decline in Percentage Share of Male Labor Force in Agriculture: Selected Countries in One Developed and Three Less Developed Regions, 1950–70 (1950 Ranking)

	% age proportion (1950) (1)	Decline (1950–60) (2)	% age proportion (1960) (3)	Decline (1960–70) (4)	(1950–70) (5)	% age proportion (1970) (6)
			Less Developed Regions			
East and Southeast Asia						
1　1–5	85·2	2·3	82·9	2·9	5·2	80·0
2　6–10	66·0	4·1	61·9	4·7	8·9	57·2
Africa, excluding South Africa						
3　1–5	95·8	2·5	93·3	3·6	6·1	89·7
4　6–10	92·1	3·5	88·6	3·9	7·4	84·7
5　11–15	89·6	3·8	85·8	3·6	7·4	82·2
6　16–20	86·0	3·8	82·2	4·2	8·0	78·0
7　21–25	79·5	5·0	74·5	4·6	9·6	69·9
8　26–30	71·4	5·3	66·1	5·5	10·8	60·6
Latin America						
9　1–4	80·6	2·5	78·1	5·4	7·9	72·7
10　5–8	72·0	2·8	69·1	7·4	10·2	61·7
11　9–12	65·1	4·4	60·7	5·9	10·3	54·8
12　13–16	63·7	5·1	58·6	7·8	12·9	50·8
13　17–19	33·1	4·1	29·0	6·2	10·3	22·8
			Developed Region (Noncommunist Europe and Overseas Offshoots)			
14　1–4	52·3	6·1	46·2	14·3	20·4	31·9
15　5–8	38·3	8·0	30·2	10·6	18·6	19·6
16　9–12	26·6	7·4	19·2	7·3	14·8	11·9
17　13–16	20·5	5·6	14·9	4·0	9·6	10·9
18　17–20	13.0	4·7	8·3	3·2	7·9	5·2

Notes:

Only countries with about 1 million or more of population in 1950 were included. Communist countries were excluded, limiting the group to the market economies. Units affected by being major (in terms of their economy) oil exporters were also excluded. So were units like Hong Kong and Singapore, being essentially urban enclaves within a larger economic sphere.

Within each of the four regions, the countries were arrayed in descending order of the share of male labor force in agriculture in 1950. The numbers in the vertical stub are the order numbers of the countries within each of the four arrays. Then, for the successive groups within each region, unweighted arithmetic means of the 1950 percentage shares of male labor force in agriculture, the 1960 and the 1970 shares (columns 1, 3 and 6) were computed – as well as unweighted means of the declines in columns 2, 4 and 5. The averages will not fully check because of rounding.

The identity of the individual countries included (in declining order of the share in column 1 within each of the four regions) is as follows:

line 1　Nepal; Bangladesh; Afghanistan; Thailand; Burma;
line 2　India; Philippines; Pakistan; Malaysia; Sri Lanka;
line 3　Niger; Chad; Rwanda; Mali; Upper Volta;
line 4　Madagascar; Malawi; CAR; Ethiopia; Ivory Coast;
line 5　Uganda; Sudan; Tanzania; Somalia; Burundi;
line 6　Togo; Guinea; Benin; Kenya; Cameroon;
line 7　Zambia; Senegal; Liberia; Zaire; Angola;
line 8　Sierra Leone; Ghana; Tunisia; Morocco; Egypt;
line 9　Haiti; Honduras; Nicaragua; Dominican Republic;
line 10　Guatemala; El Salvador; Bolivia; Colombia;
line 11　Panama; Brazil; Paraguay; Mexico;
line 12　Costa Rica; Ecuador; Jamaica; Peru;

Findings and Implications

Let us return now to Table 4.1 and, using its parameters as rough approximations to those in the group of market economies, consider aspects of the findings that were not discussed so far. The first impression that deserves noting is the enormously wide range in the share of labor force in agriculture – from well above 90 percent in the least industrialized countries to well below 10 percent in the industrial countries. It leads one to wonder whether the agricultural sector, while bearing the same title in all these countries, is at all comparable as between countries at extreme positions in the range. Still, we should assume that there are sufficient elements of comparability to warrant the comparison, if only to make it possible to discover the important differences that may still be found.

Secondly, given the two phases of the pattern in Table 4.1, it will be noted that for the less developed countries, in the range of shares of the labor force in agriculture from 93 down to 46 percent (lines 1–6 of Table 4.1), the declines over the period 1950–70 *widened* the differences among the less and more industrialized countries. The range was 46·8 percentage points in 1950; 52·8 points in 1960; and 58·8 points in 1970 (see columns 1, 3 and 6). By contrast, for the more developed countries, associated with the declining phase of the pattern in Table 4.1, that is, in the range from 46 percent of the labor force in agriculture down to less than 10 percent (lines 6–9), the declines over 1950–70 *narrowed* the differences: the range was 29·4 percentage points in 1950; 25·3 points in 1960; and 20·0 points in 1970. Of course, such a comparison implies that the countries do not shift from the less developed to the more developed category, despite the decline in the share of labor force in agriculture – an assumption tenable only for the shorter run.

Thirdly, recent cross-section comparisons of share of labor force in agriculture and per capita product all indicate close and markedly negative association between the two. A comparison (Kuznets, 1971, table 28, p. 200) including some fifty-nine countries, with per capita GDP for 1958 and the share of labor force in agriculture about 1960, shows a decline in the latter from 80 percent in the lowest income group (of about $72 per capita) to 12 percent in the top income group (with about $1,500 per capita). A more

---

line 13   Chile; Uruguay; Argentina;
line 14   Spain; Portugal; Greece; Finland;
line 15   Ireland; Italy; Norway; France;
line 16   Denmark; Austria; Sweden; Canada;
line 17   New Zealand; Switzerland; Australia; The Netherlands;
line 18   Germany (FR); USA; Belgium; United Kingdom.

Source:
The basic source for the data on individual countries used here is the same as that used for Table 4.1: see Vol. I, for Asia; Vol. II, for Africa; Vol. III, for Latin America; and Vol. IV, for the developed region.

elaborate analysis, based on a larger number of countries (over ninety-three) utilizing time-series data for them within the span 1950–70, and fitting a variety of regression equations, estimates the 'predicted' values of the share of labor in *primary* production (agriculture and mining, but most predominantly agriculture) for a range of income levels (per capita GNP, US dollar 1964) from $70 to about $1,500, the share of the labor force declining consistently from 71·2 to 15·9 percent (Chenery and Syrquin, 1975, table 3, pp. 20–21).

Given the close negative association between the share of labor force and per capita product of the country or group of countries, it seems reasonable to argue that a more *moderate* decline in the labor share in the A sector characterizing the groups with the initially high shares implies a *smaller* rise in per capita product than that for the less developed market economies with initially lower share of the labor force in agriculture. In other words, the finding of the *widening* over 1950–60 and 1960–70 in the differences among the less developed economies in the share of labor force in agriculture, discussed above, is translated into a *widening* of per worker (or per capita) income differentials among the groups of less developed countries in the array associated with the rising phase of the pattern found in Table 4.1. The higher share of labor in agriculture groups which are initially also the lower per capita product groups, showing moderate declines in the labor force shares, would presumably show also the lower rates of increase in per capita product.

Partial, yet significant, support for this inference is provided in Table 4.3. Here, we have again a group of seventy-two less developed market economies, omitting the oil exporters, purely urban enclaves (such as Hong Kong and Singapore) and a few countries for which national product data were not available. These countries are grouped throughout by the share of male labor force in agriculture in 1960; and one should first note that the negative association between the magnitude of declines in the share during 1960–70 and the level of the initial share is quite similar to that observable for the much larger and more heterogeneous group in Table 4.1 (see columns 3 and 4, lines 1–6 of that table, in comparison with columns 1 and 2, lines 9–13 of Table 4.3). In Table 4.1 the declines associated with 1960 shares ranging down from 90 to about 37 percent move from 3 percentage points to roughly 4, 6, 7, 8·6 and 9; in Table 4.3 the analogous declines move from 3 to 3·6, to 5·6, to 6·8 and, finally, to 9·2.

It is with this array of MLFA shares and declines that we associate, in columns 3 and 4 of Table 4.3, the growth rates of GNP per capita, and the roughly estimated initial levels of GNP per capita in 1960. The growth rates are for 1960–76, a sixteen-year span, while the changes in MLFA shares are over a decade; but one may doubt that the broad association shown would be much changed with recalculation of growth rates in per capita GNP to relate to a shorter span. The entries given now in columns 2 and 3, lines 9–13 show a significant positive correlation between magnitude of decline in the MLFA share over 1960–70 and the growth rate in per capita GNP over 1960–76. Also there is the expected negative association between the levels of the MLFA

Table 4.3   *Grouping of Less Developed Market Economies by Share of Male Labor Force in Agriculture (MLFA), for Comparison with Level and Growth Rate of GNP per Capita (1976 US Dollar)*

	%age proportion, MLFA (1960) (1)	Decline in column 1 (1960–70) (2)	Growth rate, per year, GNP per capita (1960–76) (3)	GNP per capita (1976 US dollar)	
				(1960) (4)	(1976) (5)
Successive sequences, nine countries each					
1 1–9	92·7	3·0	0·94	124	144
2 10–18	87·7	3·7	1·52	191	243
3 19–27	83·8	3·6	1·37	159	198
4 28–36	76·5	5·0	2·22	352	500
5 37–45	70·6	6·1	2·12	220	308
6 46–54	64·3	8·8	3·26	469	783
7 55–63	57·3	4·7	3·07	422	684
8 64–72	39·9	9·2	3·17	881	1,452
Sequences above, averaged					
9 1–9	92·7	3·0	0·94	124	144
10 10–27	85·8	3·6	1·44	175	221
11 28–45	73·6	5·6	2·17	286	404
12 46–63	60·8	6·8	3·16	456	733
13 64–72	39·9	9·2	3·17	881	1,452

Note:
The GNP data used for columns 3–5 were taken from table 1, pp. 76–7, *World Development Report, 1978* (Washington, DC: World Bank, 1978). This table presents data on GNP per capita in 1976 US dollars, and on the growth rate, percentage per year, for 1960–76, in GNP per capita in 1976 US dollars, for ninety-two less developed (low- and middle-income) countries. We selected seventy-two countries, omitting the communist economies, the oil exporters, the city enclave units (such as Hong Kong and Singapore) and the few units for which data were incomplete. In terms of 1976 per capita GNP, the seventy-two countries ranged from $70 for Bhutan, to $2,920 for Spain.

For these seventy-two countries we used the shares of male labor force in agriculture in 1960 and 1970, provided in the source used for Table 4.1, above (table A, pp. 105–7, for 1960; and pp. 111–13, for 1970). The countries were arrayed by decreasing share of male labor force in agriculture in 1960, and grouped into eight sequential groups of nine countries each. The entries in columns 1–2, lines 1–8 are unweighted arithmetic means of the shares in 1960 and of the declines (percentage points) from 1960 to 1970.

The growth rates in column 3 are similarly unweighted arithmetic means of those for the individual countries included in each of the eight sequential groups; and so are the unweighted means of 1976 GNP per capita in column 5. Those in column 4 were extrapolated from the eight means in column 5 by applying the average growth rates in column 3, cumulated over sixteen years and carried backwards from 1976 to 1960.

The entries in lines 9 and 13 are identical with those in lines 1 and 8, respectively. Those in lines 10–12 are unweighted means of the entries in lines 2–3, 4–5 and 6–7, respectively. The calculations for the MLFA shares used shares to two decimal places, and the averages were rounded off.

shares in 1960, in column 1, and the approximate levels of GNP per capita in 1960, in column 4.

To be sure, the association is subject to a few exceptions when we deal with the more detailed groups in lines 1–8; and, more important, association is not causation. It would be impermissible to argue that the declines of the MLFA share were small *because* the initial MLFA shares were high, among the poorer LDCs; and that the *small* declines in the MLFA shares *caused* low rates of growth in per capita GNP. A more realistic and plausible approach would be to argue that the economic and social characteristics of less developed market economies at high levels of the MLFA share were such as to make it difficult to attain a high growth rate in per capita or per worker product, and the latter being the consequence, it also impeded a substantial decline in the share of labor in agriculture. Yet the association noted is of both interest and value, because it draws our attention to the character of the socioeconomic structures within which the pattern of movement of labor from agriculture indicated by Tables 4.1, 4.2 and 4.3 is embedded.

Fourthly, we turn to the last aspect of the pattern to be noted explicitly – its possible effects on inequality in product per worker between agriculture (A) and the other (I + S) sectors, and hence possibly, at further remove, on inequality in income per worker or per capita. The effects to be considered are specifically of the conspicuous rise and fall in the magnitude of the changes in the shares of male labor force in the two sectors, as we move from the high initial shares of the A sectors to about 37 percent (in 1960) and down to 12 percent (see Table 4.1, columns 3 and 4). To illustrate these possible effects we are forced to use assumptions, with whatever loss of realism they imply. But stating these assumptions and considering their possible limitations could, in itself, be useful in suggesting the significant connections.

The first step is to view the decline in the share of MLF in the A sector, and the corresponding rise in the share in the I + S sector, as 'migration' – a change in the sectoral attachment either of workers within their working lifespan, or in the new generation of workers compared with the older, or in both. The change may or may not involve migration in space, although the likelihood of such migration would be substantial, considering the dominance of rural locus for the A sector and the dominance of the urban locus for the I + S sector.[2] But it is a change that means a group of *new*comers in the I + S sector, whereas such new migrants would be absent or scarce in the labor force of the A sector.

Identifying the net change in the share of MLF in the A and I + S sectors as the migration component, as we do in Table 4.4 (see columns 3 and 5 of panel I), implies an assumption. It is to the effect that the rates of increase (natural increase combined with the change in male specific labor force participation rates) are, say, over the decade 1960–70, the same for the 1960 male labor in the A and the I + S sectors. If these rates of increase are *unequal*, for instance, if the rate is higher for the 1960 labor force attached to the A sector, the migration or shift segment, of newcomers to the I + S sector, would be larger than now stated in Table 4.1 (and hence in Table 4.4). No firm evidence is available for recent years on this point, particularly if we recognize that the data would be needed separately for the groups of countries at different levels of socioeconomic development associated with the different initial levels of the share of MLF in the A or I + S sectors. We decided not to illustrate the effects of variant assumptions on this aspect of sectoral shift in labor force, to avoid complicating unduly the presentation in Table 4.4.[3]

The next set of assumptions refers to differentials in per worker product between the two major sectors. In Table 4.4 we used two variants, with differences in product per worker of 2 to 1 and 3 to 1, both in favor of the I + S sector. And most importantly, we assumed that either of these ratios, once adopted, was the same for the nine groups of countries that we distinguished, and that differed so much with respect to the share of labor force in the A sector and to the associated economic characteristics.

It is difficult to judge the validity of these assumptions. The 2 to 1 and 3 to 1 ratios used were suggested by the empirical evidence in the two sources referred to in references 2 and 3, above. In my 1971 study the ratios ranged from 4 at the lower income levels to 1·4 at the upper income levels, with the middle of the range at somewhat over 2 (1971, table 31, p. 209). In the much larger sample in the Chenery–Syrquin monograph, the inter-sectoral ratio (labor force in the primary sector, agriculture and mining, and in the other sectors) of product per worker, at 2·26 in the poorest countries, with the total labor force share in the primary sector of 71·2 percent, rises to a peak of 2·64 at higher income levels with the labor force shares in the primary sector at 49 and 44 percent, respectively; and then declines to 2·10 at the next-to-highest income group, with total labor force share in the primary sector of 25 percent. It is only in the top income group, with the primary labor force share of 16 percent, that the inter-sectoral product per worker ratio drops to 1·30 (see Table 3, pp. 20–1). One can, thus, suggest that in the range of the share of the labor force in the A sector from 70 to 25 percent, the inter-sectoral ratio moved within a range from 2·1 to 2·6; and to that extent there is an element of realism in the illustrative assumptions in Table 4.4.

The third important assumption relates to the product differential to be assigned to the recent migrants (RM) segment. For Table 4.4, we assumed that the per worker product of the new migrant segment, at the end of the decade during which the migration occurred, would be the same as the per worker product in the A sector at the end of the decade but no larger. This implies that the migrant subgroup sustains a rise in per worker product equal to that of the sector from which it came; but the results would be only partly affected by more favorable assumptions concerning the per worker product of that segment so long as it remains much lower than the product per worker of the 'old-timers' (OT) – a term we use for members of the I + S labor force who have been attached to that sector for a long time, or descended from the latter. We complete the step by adding the assumption that by the end of the *second* decade after migration, when the length of stay with the I + S sector extends roughly to a decade and a half, the migrant subgroup would be fully assimilated to the point of generating an average product equal to that of the 'old-timers'. The result is that, say, in 1970 only the migrant segment of the immediately preceding decade is to be considered – there being no separate effect of the migrant subgroups of the decade 1950–60 or of earlier decades. The assumption is clearly unrealistic in implying a rapid rate of rise in per worker product of the migrant segment; but its results are suggestive, if in reality there is a marked movement upward in per worker product of in-migrants a decade to a decade and a half after migration. Table 4.4 applies to

Table 4.4   *Effects of Decline in Share of MLF in Agriculture (1960–70) on Inter-Sectoral Inequality in Product (P_1 and P_2) Per Worker in 1970 (Data from Table 4.1)*

Panel I. %age Shares in MLF and in Product (P_1P_2), Total MLF and MLF in the (I + S) Sector, 1970

Successive Sequences from Table 4.1	(A) (1)	%age Shares in Total MLF (I + S) Total (2)	Recent migrants (3)	Old-timers (4)	%age Shares in (I + S) Recent migrants (5)	Old-timers (6)
5–15						
1 MLF	86·8	13·2	3·3	9·9	25·0	75·0
2 P_1 (113·2)	76·7	23·3	2·9	20·4	12·4	87·6
3 P_2 (126·4)	68·7	31·3	2·6	28·7	8·3	91·7
25–35						
4 MLF	76·7	23·3	3·8	19·5	16·3	83·7
5 P_1 (123·3)	62·2	37·8	3·1	34·7	8·2	91·8
6 P_2 (146·6)	52·3	47·7	2·6	45·0	5·45	94·55
45–55						
7 MLF	65·3	34·7	6·0	28·7	17·3	82·7
8 P_1 (134·7)	48·5	51·5	4·5	47·0	8·7	91·3
9 P_2 (169·4)	38·55–	61·45+	3·5	57·95	5·7	94·3
65–75						
10 MLF	54·7	45·3	7·0	38·3	15·45	84·55
11 P_1 (145·3)	37·6	62·4	4·8	57·6	7·7	92·3
12 P_2 (190·6)	28·7	71·3	3·7	67·6	5·2	94·8
85–95						
13 MLF	40·3	59·7	8·6	51·1	14·4	85·6
14 P_1 (159·7)	25·2	74·8	5·4	69·4	7·2	92·8
15 P_2 (219·4)	18·4	81·6	3·9	77·7	4·8	95·2
95–105						
16 MLF	28·0	72·0	9·3	62·7	12·9	87·1
17 P_1 (172·0)	16·3	83·7	5·4	78·3	6·45	93·55
18 P_2 (244·0)	11·5	88·5	3·8	84·7	4·3	95·7
105–115						
19 MLF	20·4	79·6	7·0	72·6	8·8	91·2
20 P_1 (179·6)	11·4	88·6	3·9	84·7	4·4	95·6
21 P_2 (259·2)	7·9	92·1	2·7	89·4	2·9	97·1
115–125						
22 MLF	12·0	88·0	5·6	82·4	6·4	93·6
23 P_1 (188·0)	6·4	93·6	3·0	90·6	3·2	96·8
24 P_2 (276·0)	4·35	95·65	2·0	93·65	2·1	97·9
121–131						
25 MLF	8·0	92·0	4·0	88·0	4·35	95·65
26 P_1 (192·0)	4·2	95·8	2·1	93·7	2·2	97·8
27 P_2 (284·0)	2·8	97·2	1·4	95·8	1·4	98·6

Notes:

Panel I, lines 1, 4, 7, 10, 13, 16, 19, 22 and 25: taken directly, or computed from Table 4.1, columns 6 and 4. No assumptions are involved except in viewing the decline in the share of MLF in agriculture in 1960–70 as net migration (change) over the decade from the A to the I + S sectors (see discussion in text).

Panel I, lines 2, 5, 8, 11, 14, 17, 20, 23 and 26: calculated on the assumption that the ratio of product per male worker in the I + S sector to product per male worker in the A sector is 2 : 1, the ratio held the same for the groups of countries at different levels of the initial or terminal share (for discussion of this assumption, see text). The entry in parentheses in the vertical stub for each group is the index for the total product for country group, that for MLF in each group being 100.

Panel I, lines 3, 6, 9, 12, 15, 18, 21, 24 and 27: calculated on the assumption of a ratio of product per male worker in the I + S sector to product per male worker in the A sector of 3 : 1. The entries in parentheses are indexes of the total product for each country group, that for MLF in each group being 100.

Panel II. *Measures of Disparity* (TDM), *Product Per Worker*

	For Total MLF *and* P				*For* MLF *and* P *in* (I + S)		
	TDM	Ratio RM *to*	Column 1 x	TDM (A)–RM–OT	TDM	Weight (I + S)*in*	Column 5 x
Successive Sequences	(A)–(I +S) (1)	MLF *in* (A) Column 2 (2)	Column 2 (3)	*directly* (4)	RM–OT (5)	*Total* (6)	Column 6 (7)
			For P_1				
28 5–15	20·2	0·038	0·8	21·0	25·2	0·132	3·3
29 25–35	29·0	0·050	1·4	30·4	16·2	0·233	3·8
30 45–55	33·6	0·092	3·1–	36·6	17·2	0·347	6·0
31 65–75	34·2	0·128	4·4	38·6	15·5	0·453	7·0
32 85–95	30·2	0·213	6·4	36·6	14·4	0·697	8·6
33 95–105	23·4	0·332	7·8	31·2	12·9	0·720	9·3
34 105–15	18·0	0·343	6·2	24·2	8·8	0·796	7·0
35 115–25	11·2	0·467	5·2	16·4	6·4	0·880	5·6
36 121–31	7·6	0·500	3·8	11·4	4·3	0·920	4·0
			For P_2				
37 5–15	36·2	0·038	1·4	37·6	33·4	0·132	4·4
38 25–35	48·8	0·050	2·4	51·2	21·7	0·233	5·1
39 45–55	53·5	0·092	4·9+	58·5	23·2	0·347	8·1
40 65–75	52·0	0·128	6·6	58·6	20·5	0·453	9·3
41 85–95	43·8	0·213	9·3+	53·2	19·2	0·597	11·5
42 95–105	33·0	0·332	11·0	44·0	17·2	0·720	12·4
43 105–15	25·0	0·343	8·6	33·6	11·8	0·796	9·4
44 115–25	15·3	0·467	7·1+	22·5	8·6	0·880	7·6
45 121–31	10·4	0·500	5·2	15·6	5·9	0·920	5·5

Panel II: the disparity measures in columns 1, 4 and 5 are obtained by comparing the percentage shares in male labor force and in product P_1P_2, and adding the differences, signs disregarded (see brief discussion of measure in the text). The needed percentage shares are in panel I (columns 1 and 2, for the measure in column 1 here; columns 1, 3 and 4, for the measure in column 4 here; columns 5 and 6, for the measure in column 5 here).

The proportions in column 2 are those of the share of the RM segment in male labor force (column 3, panel I, lines relating to MLF) to the percentage share in the A sector (column 1 of panel I, lines relating to MLF). The product of this ratio by the TDM in column 1 of panel II should yield the absolute addition to the TDM due to separate treatment of the RM component (see text); and the sum of columns 1 and 3 should yield the TDM in column 4. The slight discrepancies are due to rounding.

The proportions in column 6 are those of the 1 + S sector in total male labor force in 1970, and appear as percentage shares in column 2 of panel I, lines 1, 4, 7, 10, 13, 16, 19, 22 and 25.

As the discussion in the text indicates, the product of columns 5 and 6 should yield, for the variant P_1, the magnitudes of the decline in the percentage share of the male labor force in agriculture over the decade 1960–70. For variant P_2, the product in column 7 should yield the same magnitudes of the decline, multiplied by the fraction $\frac{4}{3}$ (see text).

the labor and product shares in 1970 and, thus, to the movements from 1960 to 1970; but the results for 1960 and the movements from 1950 to 1960 would be similar. Also the results do not depend on the specific values of the initial shares and changes in them, so long as the general pattern familiar to us now prevails.

The gist of the assumptions stated, and the expediency reasons for adopting them being obvious enough not to require elaboration, we can now note the findings in Table 4.4. With panel I of the table needed largely to derive the disparity measures appearing in panel II, we can concentrate on the latter and attempt to list the findings seriatim. These disparity measures are the sums of differences between two variables in the associated percentage shares, signs disregarded.[4]

(1) While our main interest in Table 4.4 is in the effects of *change* in MLF shares in the two main sectors A and I + S, that is, essentially of what we designate as recent migrants (the RM segment), it is relevant to begin with the effects of the assumed inter-sectoral product per worker ratios on the total (or weighted) sectoral disparities at the different levels of the sectoral shares. These measures appear in column 1 of panel II and convey a similar pattern of differences in associated disparities of the two variants P_1 and P_2, despite the wider amplitude of the disparities for P_2. The sectoral disparities widen as we shift from the high shares of sector A countries to about the middle range (87 to 55, or 40 percent) and then narrow appreciably as the share of the labor force in the A sector dwindles rapidly.

This pattern of total disparities in product per worker, with its rise and decline, column 1 of panel II, is of interest, because it is a necessary result of the conditions set − a two-sector model in which the initially high share of the lower income sector in labor force continuously declines, and the ratio of per worker product in the rising sector to that in the declining sector remains at the same level. To illustrate: the TDM of 20·2 in line 28, column 1 can be seen as *double* the difference between 86·8 and 76·7 in column 1, lines 1 and 2 (panel I), with 76·7 derivable as the ratio 86·8 : 1·132. The *difference* between 86·8 and 86·8 : 1·132 can be rewritten as the *product* of two components: 86·8 (component A) and (0·132 : 1·132) or 0·1166 (component B) − the former determined by the movement of the share of labor force in agriculture, the latter being moved by the complementary changes in the share of labor force in the I + S sector. As we shift from one sequence to the next in panel I, component A declines by ever-increasing fractions, which in and of itself would reduce the TDM; while at the same time component B would be rising, but at diminishing rates, which by itself would raise the TDM. As a consequence, the TDM for this two-sector case would be increasing, so long as the relative rise in the B component exceeds the relative decline in the A component; and would start to decline when, inevitably, the *proportional* rise in the B component, being slowed down by the rise in the I + S share, begins to fall short of the A component.

The comment just made will perhaps be more telling, if illustrated by the data from Table 4.4. In Table 4.5, supplementary to Table 4.4, we calculate the two components, for four pairs of contiguous sequences in panel I of Table 4.4; and demonstrate how the continuously widening drop in the share of the labor force in agriculture (component A) is first more than offset by the rise in component B, and then results in a decline in the total disparity measure.

The illustration also reveals why, with a wider inter-sectoral disparity in product per worker in the P_2 variant, the point of shift from rising to declining TDMs occurs at a higher level of the A share than for the P_1 variant. And it is easy to infer from the illustration what changing or different levels of the ratio of per worker product in the I + S sector to that in the A sector would mean for the levels and movements of the resulting TDMs. Finally, while both Tables 4.4 and 4.5 use specific data for the decade 1960–70 and for 1970, similar

Table 4.5   *Illustration of Changes in the Two Components that Determine the Total Weighted Disparity in Per Worker Product for the* A *and* I + S *Sectors, Four Pairs of Contiguous Sequences from Table 4.4*

Successive Sequence	Component A (1)	Component B_1 (2)	TDM_1 (3)	Component B_2 (4)	TDM_2 (5)
1 5–15	86·8	$\frac{0\cdot132}{1\cdot132}$ 0·1166	20·2	$\frac{0\cdot264}{1\cdot264}$ 0·2089	36·2
2 25–35	76·7	$\frac{0\cdot233}{1\cdot233}$ 0·1890	29·0	$\frac{0\cdot466}{1\cdot466}$ 0·3179	48·8
3 Line 2/ line 1	0·884	1·621	1·43	1·522	1·35
4 45–55	65·3	$\frac{0\cdot347}{1\cdot347}$ 0·2576	33·6	$\frac{0\cdot694}{1\cdot694}$ 0·4097	53·5
5 65–75	54·7	$\frac{0\cdot453}{1\cdot453}$ 0·3118	34·2	$\frac{0\cdot906}{1\cdot906}$ 0·4753	52·0
6 Line 5/ line 4	0·838	1·210	1·02	1·160	0·97
7 85–95	40·3	$\frac{0\cdot597}{1\cdot597}$ 0·3738	30·2	$\frac{1\cdot194}{2\cdot194}$ 0·5442	43·8
8 95–105	28·0	$\frac{0\cdot720}{1\cdot720}$ 0·4186	23·4	$\frac{1\cdot440}{2\cdot440}$ 0·5902	33·0
9 Line 8/ line 7	0·695	1·1199	0·78	1·0845	0·75
10 105–15	20·4	$\frac{0\cdot796}{1\cdot796}$ 0·4432	18·0	$\frac{1\cdot592}{2\cdot592}$ 0·6142	25·0
11 115–25	12·0	$\frac{0\cdot880}{1\cdot880}$ 0·4681	11·2	$\frac{1\cdot760}{2\cdot760}$ 0·6377	15·3
12 Line 11/ line 10	0·588	1·0562	0·62	1·0383	0·61

Notes:
B_1 and TDM_1 designate the B component and the total disparity measure for the P_1 variant. B_2 and TDM_2 are the B component and the total disparity measure for the P_2 variant.

The A component relating to male labor force alone, is the same for the P_1 and P_2 variants.

All the data on the components are from Table 4.4, panel I.

Column 3 is derivable as the product of entries in columns 1 and 2. Column 5 is derivable as the product of entries in columns 1 and 4. Entries in columns 3 and 5, lines 3, 6, 9 and 12 are also the ratios of the TDMs in lines 2, 5, 8 and 11 to those in lines 1, 4, 7 and 10.

results would be found for any set of sequences in which the share of the labor force in agriculture would be consistently declining over the range from over 90 down to less than 10 percent, while its per worker product would be consistently below that in the I + S sector by a constant or near-constant ratio over the range.

(2)   When we distinguish the RM segment, and deal with three divisions – the A sector, the RM segment within the I + S sector and the OT group, which we obtain by subtraction – the sectoral product per worker disparity (column 4 of panel II) becomes consistently and significantly larger than that for the two sectors in column 1 of panel II. The reason is that we derive the OT subgroup

of the I + S sector as a segment of the labor force with invariably higher per worker product than is true of the total I + S sector – thus, creating necessarily a wider product per worker disparity. This conclusion is inevitable, once we assume that the per worker product for the recent migrants into the I + S sector is below the per worker product for the old-timers while the ratio of per worker product in the total I + S sector to that in the A sector remains the same (whether it be 2 : 1 or 3 : 1).

In line with the distinction of the two components that determine the magnitude of the TDM for two sectors, particularly as illustrated in Table 4.5, there is an alternative way of deriving and viewing the absolute addition of the TDM resulting from the separation of the RM segment within the I + S sector. This can be viewed as *adding* a fraction to the A component, while retaining all other terms, a fraction that is formed by the proportion of the RM segment to the terminal share of the labor force in the A sector. These proportions, which appear in column 2 of panel II, can then be applied to the product of the two components (which multiplied by 2 constitute the TDM for the two-sector case) – and this would yield, as indicated in column 3 of panel II, the correct addition to the TDM in column 1 to derive that in column 4. One interesting aspect of this demonstration is the emphasis on the continuous rise in the *proportion* of the agricultural labor force that is lost in the decline, as we shift from the highly agricultural to the highly industrialized countries.

However derived, the absolute addition to the TDMs in column 1 of panel II of Table 4.4, due to the separation of the RM segment within the I + S sector, is naturally a function of the magnitude of the absolute magnitude of that segment. Consequently, the pattern of movements of this absolute addition in column 3 of panel II is a faithful reproduction, in timing, of that in the absolute declines of the labor share in the A sector rising from low magnitude in the 5–15 sequence, reaching a peak in the 95–105 sequence and then declining sharply. Thus, in absolute terms, the disparity measure is widened by the inclusion of the RM segment most in those countries in which this migration component is absolutely greater.

(3) In turning now to the effect of the RM segment on inequality in product per worker *within* the I + S sector we find that the disparity so contributed diminishes fairly steadily (except in the movement from the 25–35 to the 45–55 sequences) as we shift from the countries with very low I + S shares to the more industrialized countries (see column 5 of panel II). The result is one that could be expected, since a shift of 3·3 percentage points to the I + S sector in a country group in which the *total* share of this sector is 13·2 percentage points, means an RM segment equal to a *third* of the OT group; whereas even a major shift of 9·3 percentage points for the 95–105 sequence is about one-seventh of the much larger OT group of 62·7 (see lines 1 and 16 of panel I). Indeed, the large relative magnitude of the influx into the I + S sector of the least industrialized countries may, in itself, suggest reasons why the *absolute* magnitude of the influx is so limited.

Still, the introduction of the migrant segment into the I + S sector does result in a significant widening of intra-sector disparities in product per worker. In viewing the latter as part of total disparities within the countrywide labor force this intra-I + S sector disparity should be weighted by the share of that sector in total labor force. When we do this in columns 6 and 7 of panel II, we find that the *weighted* contribution of the migrant segment to per worker in-equalities within the I + S sector reproduces precisely the pattern that we found repeatedly in Table 4.1 and the other tables. This identity of the pattern in column 7 of panel II with those of changes in the shares of labor force in the A sector is a necessary result of the assumptions used in Table 4.4 and the procedure based on them. This can be illustrated by the data in Table 4.4, panel I, for the first sequence, that of 5–15; but the illustration holds also for each of these and similar sequences.

For P_1, the entry of 25·2 in line 28, column 5 is the difference between the entries in column 5 of lines 1 and 2, 12·6 percentage points, multiplied by 2. But the 12·6-points difference is that between 3·3 : 13·2 and 2·9 : 23·3, the latter in turn being derived from $(3\cdot3 : 113\cdot2)/(26\cdot4 : 113\cdot2)$. The 12·6 difference can then be written as that between 3·3 : 13·2 and 3·3 : 26·4. This yields one-half of 3·3, which multiplied by 2 yields 3·3 in column 7 – the value *identical* with the percentage-point decline in the share of the A sector.

For P_2, the entry of 33·4 in line 37, column 5 is the difference between 25·0 and 8·3, lines 1 and 3, column 5, or 16·7 multiplied by 2. But the 16·7-points difference is that between 3·3 : 13·2 and 3·3 : 39·6, which is two-thirds of 3·3. If we multiply the result by 2, we secure $\frac{4}{3}$ of 3·3, or 4·4 – the entry we find in lines 37, column 7. It follows that all entries for P_2 in column 7 would, allowing for rounding errors, approximate $\frac{4}{3}$ times the comparable entries in column 7 for the P_1 variant.

Concluding Comments

Our discussion dealt with the statistical evidence on the shift of the male labor force from agriculture to the other I + S sectors, for less developed and more developed market economies, for the two decades 1950–70 – utilizing the world-wide estimates of the ILO. This evidence revealed a distinctive pattern, in which the absolute magnitude of the declines in the labor force share in agriculture was quite small for the highly agricultural countries with initial high shares in the A sector; widened appreciably as we moved to the more industrialized countries among the less developed, with the initial shares of labor force in agriculture down to about 40 to 30 percent; and then narrowed again as we considered the industrialized, more developed countries with lower initial shares in the A sector. The different levels of shares of the labor force in agriculture were significantly and negatively associated with levels of product per capita or per worker; and among the less developed market economies, differences among the subgroups in the magnitude of the shift of labor force from agriculture were significantly and positively associated with differences in growth rates of per capita product. It follows that among the less developed countries, the poorer and more agricultural countries showed a smaller shift out of agriculture and a lower growth rate of per capita product than the middle- and upper-middle-income, less developed countries, which showed a greater shift of labor force out of agriculture and higher rates of growth of per capita product.

We also explored, with the help of simple but roughly realistic assumptions, the total disparity in per worker product between the A and I + S sectors in countries at different levels of industrialization (as indicated by shares of labor force in the two sectors). The findings can be briefly stated. First, for the two-sector model, without considering the changes in the share over the decade, total (weighted) disparity in product per worker was narrow for countries with very high shares of the A and very low shares of the I + S sectors; widened as the shares of labor force in the A sector approached the middle levels; and then narrowed again as the shares of the A sector declined to low levels (and those of the I + S sector rose to high levels). Secondly, the segregation of the decline in the share of the labor force in the A sector, viewed as a recent migration (RM) segment within the I + S sector, widened the total disparity measure (TDM) for the A − I + S comparison, the absolute additions to this measure following faithfully the pattern of absolute declines in the share of labor force in agriculture, associated with the different initial levels of these shares. And the separation of the RM segment within the I + S sector, contributed also to intra-sectoral differences in product per worker within that sector, which when weighted by the share of I + S sector in the total labor force, again followed the pattern of declines in the shares of labor force in agriculture associated with different initial levels of these shares. It follows that the widening of disparity in product per worker among the major sectors, and within the I + S sector, was greater for groups of middle- and higher-income LDCs than either among the low-income LDCs, or among the more developed market economies. But it should be stressed that these findings relate to only a part of the total inequalities in product per worker: the two other components of overall differences in product per worker, those within the A sector and those within the I + S sector were not considered, except for the distinction of the RM segment within the latter.

An acceptable explanation of the findings just summarized would require a critical appraisal of the ILO estimates, particularly for the poorer LDCs, in which the statistical bases are weak and the concept of attachment of the labor force to a sector may be much more ambiguous than in higher-income LDCs or in more developed countries in which the labor force is more distinctly specialized. It would also call for tested analysis of aspects of structural change and growth that were either dealt with here by assumption, or were not considered at all (for instance, the effect of the movement of labor from agriculture on the inequality in per worker product within the A sector). These and other lines of further exploration cannot be pursued here; and the discussion remains an exploratory probing of a limited aspect of recent economic growth experience.

Chapter 4: Notes

1 The World Bank (1979, table 1, pp. 126–7) classifies seventeen out of the twenty countries used in lines 14–18 as industrial countries. Only Spain, Portugal and Greece (included by us in the group in line 14) are classified as the upper range of the 'middle-income' group within nonindustrial countries.
2 See in this connection, United Nations (1980, ch. V, pp. 68–71).
3 For the pre-First World War decades in the currently developed countries, the rates of natural increase of the urban population were so much lower than those in the countryside that the implicit migration component in the rural–urban distribution of the labor force must have been appreciably greater than that obtained as net change in the percentage shares. But it is not clear that similar differential rates of natural increase between the cities and countryside are true of the LDCs in the post-Second World War decades. And such urban–rural differentials are not a fully relevant guide here.
4 For a recent brief discussion of this measure, see Kuznets (1976, pp. 12–13). We use the sum of differences, signs disregarded, as an index of disparity. It would be more comparable to the familiar Gini coefficient if the sum were divided by 200, the maximum limit which the total disparity can approach. Thus, the entry of 20·2 in line 28, column 1 would become 0·101. In that form, the disparity measure is a crude approximation to a Gini coefficient, lower than the latter for cases with more than two classes but yielding comparable differences. For only two classes, the two measures would be identical.

Chapter 4: References

Chenery, H. and Syrquin, M., *Patterns of Development, 1950–1970* (London: Oxford University Press, 1975).
Kuznets, S., *Economic Growth of Nations: Total Output and Production Structure* (Cambridge, Mass.: Harvard University Press, 1971).
Kuznets, S., 'Demographic aspects of the size distribution of income: an exploratory essay', *Economic Development and Cultural Change*, vol. 25, no. 1 (1976), pp. 1–94.
United Nations, *Patterns of Urban and Rural Population Growth* (New York: United Nations, 1980).
World Bank, *World Development Report, 1979* (Washington, DC: World Bank, 1979).

5

Food Price Inflation, Terms of Trade and Growth

LANCE TAYLOR

The relationships among the agricultural terms of trade, income distribution and growth have always been central to the economic-development literature, with the contributions of Arthur Lewis standing out. And in the more specifically Latin American tradition of the structuralist school, food supply rigidities are paramount among the root causes of inflation in the long run. This chapter attempts to integrate and clarify these two strands of analysis, by extending a recently proposed short-run model for the terms of trade to deal with questions of accumulation and growth.[1] The model treats agricultural output as being strictly limited by resources (capital and land) in the short run, while there is excess capacity and mark-up pricing in the nonagricultural sector. The conjunctural story revolves around responses of the agricultural price and nonagricultural output to shocks to the system. Since both sectors are treated on the same footing (though with different behavioral rules), the model best refers to a semi-industrialized country where a mixture of overall labor surplus and Keynesian behavior in the nonagricultural economy may reasonably be expected to obtain.

In the longer run, more output from agriculture requires more resources, specifically capital goods produced only by the nonagricultural sector. Once installed, capital cannot be moved. Thus patterns of growth follow the assignment of new productive capacity, determined in turn by conditions of saving and demand for investment and consumption goods. Higher saving is associated with higher rates of profit along Lewis and Cambridge lines. Inflation enters the system when workers bid up the money wage and prices in response to real-wage reductions induced by increases in the economywide saving rate to support potentially faster growth. Under nonrestrictive or passive monetary policy, it is perfectly possible for the economy to come to a steady state with a nonzero secular inflation rate, Conflicting claims between workers for a real wage and entrepreneurs for an 'adequate' profit rate underlie the inflationary process. Long-term patterns of inflation and growth would be further influenced in most countries by speculative holding of land and/or foodstocks in anticipation of capital gains, though this is a complication only briefly touched upon here. Rather, the emphasis is on how conflicting claims to product interact with real factors in determining the inter-sectoral terms of trade and the rate of growth.

In what follows, section 1 sets out the short-run model, with its solution and comparative statics worked out in section 2. The saving and consumption demand side of the corresponding growth model is presented in section 3, and details about the terms of trade, conflicting claims and the inflationary process in section 4. Steady-state growth in an economy where expansion of the agricultural sector has an upper limit is analyzed in section 5, and then the restriction is lifted in section 6. The last section gives a summary of the main results, emphasizing that policies aimed at achieving higher growth rates go hand-in-hand with inflation, high food prices and a low real wage.

(1) Output and Terms of Trade in the Short Run

Nonagriculture (or the N sector) resembles industry and urban services in most market economies by operating with chronic excess capacity. Under such circumstances, mark-up pricing along the lines urged by Kalecki (1971), Sylos-Labini (1957), and others, necessarily applies. The N sector price P_N is given by

$$P_N = (1 + \tau)wb_N \qquad (5.1)$$

where τ is the mark-up rate (assumed constant for simplicity), w is the money wage, and b_N is the labor–output ratio. The quantity wb_N represents prime cost, from which price is determined via the mark up.

Income flows generated by the N sector can be decomposed as

$$P_N X_N = wL_N + r_N K_N = wb_N X_N + r_N K_N \qquad (5.2)$$

where X_N is the level of output, K_N is the capital stock and r_N is the quasi-rent or gross return to capital. It is easy to solve for r_N from 5.1 and 5.2 as

$$r_N = \tau wb_N X_N/K_N \qquad (5.3)$$

so that nonagricultural quasi-rents go up when output rises relative to the level of capacity defined by K_N. To avoid entangling the algebra with a maze of elasticities of substitution and factor shares, the labor–output ratio b_N is treated as constant and independent of prices in the foregoing equations, but the basic result in 5.3 would go through (albeit in nonlinear fashion), if factor substitution were allowed.

As opposed to the N sector, agriculture (or the A sector) is resource-limited: supply does not respond to price or other incentives in the short run. Implicitly we assimilate land with capital, so that sustained output increases can come only from investment activities such as land-clearing, mechanization and works for irrigation. Available employment opportunities in the A sector are also limited by its capital, in terms of full-time equivalent jobs. (For macroeconomic purposes here, we do not go into details about how full-time jobs may be split among numerous part-time employees.) Finally, we treat agriculture as largely capitalistic in the sense that different agents receive different payment flows. As we will see in detail below, workers receive wages and use them for consumption of both types of goods. Landlords and capitalists receive rentals on land and capital, which they either save, or expend on consumption of the non-agricultural good. Another model could be constructed in which 'peasants' receive all agricultural income, but for brevity we do not pursue that option here.

Agricultural output X_A is determined by the land-cum-capital stock K_A,

$$X_A = a_A K_A \tag{5.4}$$

where a_A is the output–capital ratio. A sector employment follows directly as

$$L_A = b_A X_A = a_A b_A K_A \tag{5.5}$$

with b_A as the labor–output ratio. From these equations, the quasi-rent on capital in agriculture is

$$r_A = a_A (P_A - w b_A) \tag{5.6}$$

on the assumption that full-time equivalent workers in the two sectors receive the same money wage w.

To close the model, we have to bring in demand. To capture in crude fashion the implications of Engel's Law, total demand for agricultural (or food) products from wage income can be assumed to take the form

$$\text{value of workers' demand for food} = (L_A + L_N)(\alpha w + \phi P_A).$$

Here, workers are assumed to have real demand ϕ for the agricultural good, independent of prices and income. In addition, they devote a fraction α of wages to purchase of food. Their A-sector budget share is $\alpha + (P_A \phi / w)$, which declines as per worker income w goes up. This formulation can readily be seen to be an application of the linear expenditure system proposed by Stone (1954). In what follows we concentrate on the case in which $\phi = 0$ (so that the income elasticity of food demand is equal to one), but will indicate how results are modified when Engel's Law truly applies.

If recipients of capital incomes do not consume agricultural products (a simplification that saves one or two parameters), the supply–demand balance for the sector takes the form:

$$P_A X_A = (L_A + L_N)(\alpha w + \phi P_A). \tag{5.7}$$

With X_A and L_A fixed in 5.7 by available capital, it is clear that the agricultural price P_A will be determined by nonagricultural workers' spending, or

L_N $(aw + \phi P_A)$. Their employment level L_N follows from N sector output X_N, which responds to aggregate demand. To get to the details, we will work through the nonagricultural supply–demand balance, which takes the form:

$$P_N X_N = P_N I + (L_A + L_N) \left[(1 - \alpha)w - \phi P_A\right] + (1 - s) (r_A K_A + r_N K_N).$$

(5.8)

On the right side, demand is made up of investment $P_N I$, workers' purchases of the nonagricultural good and consumption by profit recipients. The latter save a fraction s of their income, and consume the rest in the form of N sector goods.

The savings–investment equation in this model when all markets clear can be derived directly from the supply–demand balances 5.7 and 5.8 and the income decompositions 5.2 and 5.6. Almost needless to say it takes the form

$$P_N I = s(r_N K_N + r_A K_A).$$

(5.9)

Investment is totally financed by income from capital in the two sectors. For use below, 5.9 can be expressed in terms of P_A and X_N as

$$X_N = \frac{1 + \tau}{s\tau} I + \frac{a_A B_A K_A}{\tau b_N} - \frac{a_A K_A P_A}{\tau w b_N}.$$

(5.10)

(2) Solution and Comparative Statics

The model as stated is easy to solve. The agricultural price and employment terms in the N-sector demand–supply balance 5.8 are determined from A-sector equilibrium 5.7 and the supply conditions 5.4 and 5.5. With substitutions from these expressions, 5.8 can be solved to get X_N. The outcome takes the form

$$X_N = \frac{w(1 + \tau)}{s\lvert w(\tau + \alpha) + P_A \phi \rvert} I + \frac{(1 - \alpha)w - P_A \phi}{b_N \lvert w(\tau + \alpha) + P_A \phi \rvert} a_A b_A K_A$$

(5.11)

where the mark-up rule 5.1 has been used to eliminate terms in P_N.

Equation 5.11 basically states that nonagricultural output rises in response to investment I and consumption demand by agricultural workers as determined by employment from the available capital stock K_A. The usual multiplier process induced by these two sources of demand gives rise to the specific form of the result.

In the simpler case when $\phi = 0$, 5.11 becomes

$$X_N = \frac{1 + \tau}{s(\tau + \alpha)} I + \frac{1 - \alpha}{b_N(\tau + \alpha)} a_A b_A K_A.$$

(5.12)

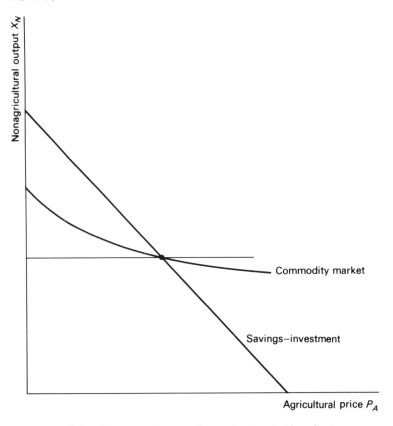

Figure 5.1   *Output and price determination in the short run.*

The short-run equilibrium is determined as in Figure 5.1. The savings–investment line corresponds to equation 5.10 and shows that investment can be met by different combinations of saving by sector. N-sector saving rises with X_N and A sector saving with P_A. The implication is that the two variables trade off inversely as saving supply adjusts to investment demand.

The commodity-market schedules show different (P_A, X_N) combinations that clear the market for the nonagricultural good. When $\phi = 0$, X_N is independent of P_A from 5.12 and its level is fixed along the horizontal line by investment I and the agricultural capital stock K_A. With a positive value of ϕ, X_N is a declining function of P_A as shown by the commodity-market curve, or equation 5.11. The inelastic portion of workers' food demand acts as a fixed charge on the system, reducing X_N as P_A goes up. Nonagricultural output response is damped by Engel's Law.

From the algebra and the diagram, comparative statics in the short run can be derived directly. The results go as follows:

(*a*) An increase in investment I shifts up the intercepts of both curves on the vertical axis. Comparison of 5.10 and 5.12, however, shows that the commodity-market intercept shifts less. The outcome is an increase in X_N via the multiplier process. The agricultural price goes up, because extra N sector employment adds to food demand which can only be rationed by an increase in its price.

(b) An increase in the mark-up rate τ creates both additional demand for non-agricultural products, and potential saving supply. If X_N is relatively high (specifically if it exceeds I/s), the latter effect is stronger and the rising mark up would lead to falling X_N and P_A in the usual Keynesian way. Such an outcome always occurs with $\phi = 0$. On the other hand, a high value of ϕ means that workers devote a rapidly increasing share of their consumption budget to food as its price P_A goes up. The corresponding decline in their nonagricultural demand might be offset by increased spending on 'luxuries' if profit incomes go up. Both X_N and P_A could rise in response to a higher mark-up rate. This finding recasts the debate between Malthus and Ricardo as to whether landlords' rents stimulated or retarded aggregate demand. In the present formulation, the answer depends on how consumption from wage income is allocated between the sectors, following Engel's Law.

(c) Because of the mark-up pricing rule, N sector demand is independent of the wage w, since any wage increases are passed along into the price P_N and real purchasing power of all agents over nonagricultural products is not affected. Similarly, P_A rises proportionately to w, also to keep everyone's real income unchanged.

(d) Increases in the consumption parameters α and ϕ both reduce N sector demand, and shift down the commodity market curve in Figure 5.1. The net outcome is a reduction in X_N and an increase in P_A.

(e) In another taste shift, an increase in the savings propensity s will reduce X_N along standard multiplier lines. Since food products are consumed by N sector employees, a reduction in demand from that source leads to a lower P_A.

(f) The effects of a consumer food subsidy can be modeled by replacing P_A with the quantity $(P_A - z)$ wherever it appears in 5.11, as well as adding the quantity zX_A to exogenous spending flows. The new term z represents the subsidy rate relative to the agricultural producer's price. An increase in z shifts up the commodity market curve in Figure 5.1, which would lead to more N-sector output and a lower agricultural price. At the same time, the subsidy represents negative saving and an increase causes the saving–investment line to slide up, tending to reduce X_N and increase P_A. On balance, the effect is to raise both variables. Indeed, P_A goes up by more than the increase in z and consumer food prices rise, because the expansionary effect of the subsidy raises employment overall. The increment in food demand can only be held back by a rise in the consumer price. Were additional saving created from some source to 'finance' the cost of the subsidy, it would reduce the consumer price. For example, food imports or a tax on mark-up incomes would do the trick.

(g) A sudden increase in the agricultural capital stock K_A reduces potential saving by increasing the agricultural wage bill, but at the same time raises demand for nonagricultural commodities and also agricultural supply. The last shift leads unambiguously to a lower agricultural price. When ϕ is zero and N-sector demand does not depend on P_A, X_N must rise. With a positive ϕ, the upward shift of the savings–investment line corresponding to the saving effect leads to a falling X_N along the commodity-market curve in Figure 5.1. The outcome is more nonagricultural output and a reduced agricultural price.

Stabilization policy in the economy considered here can be pursued along various lines. Higher profit or income taxes would in effect raise s, if the receipts were saved. Lower agricultural prices and nonagricultural output would be the result. Effective price controls in the N sector would reduce the mark up τ, causing deflation if Engels effects are strong, or an economic expansion if not. More agricultural capital (or an increase in its productivity) would stimulate output and reduce food prices, but both variables would rise with investment spending or government demand. If the aim of these policies is to hold down the cost of food, in most cases an output contraction would be an associated political cost. We will see shortly that this dilemma carries over into the long run.

(3) Growth in the Two–Sector Model

Extension of the model to deal with economic growth requires several steps. The first is to recognize that the short-run specification includes two equations that must hold along any growth path – the saving–investment balance 5.9 and an equilibrium condition for one commodity market, say, the agricultural sector as in 5.7. With these equations satisfied, the N sector will also be in equilibrium by Walras's Law.

When transformed to growth rates, 5.7 and 5.9 involve five variables. These are as follows. Growth rates of the two capital stocks:

$$g_A = \dot{K}_A/K_A \text{ and } g_N = \dot{K}_N/K_N.$$

Profit rates deflated by the cost of new capital goods:

$$i_A = r_A/P_N \text{ and } i_N = r_N/P_N.$$

The ratio of capital stocks in the two sectors:

$$\lambda = K_A/K_N.$$

In steady-state growth, if it is actually attained, these five variables reduce to three, that is,

$$\lambda, g_A = g_N = g \text{ and } i_A = i_N = i$$

where g and i are a growth and profit rate pair corresponding to a steady state. Also from its definition λ changes over time according to the differential equation

$$\dot{\lambda}/\lambda = g_A - g_N \tag{5.13}$$

so that $\dot{\lambda} = 0$ is a necessary condition for the existence of a steady state.

Our approach to solving the model is to set up and analyze the growth equivalents of 5.7 and 5.9 in this section. In sections 5 and 6 we add sectoral investment functions and use them together with the results here to reduce the whole system to a revised version of 5.13, which turns out to be a differential equation in λ alone. Standard stability and comparative dynamic analysis can then be applied to the real side of the economy. How real changes interact with inflation, can be analyzed using results developed in section 4.

By substituting 5.6 into 5.7, we can rewrite the agricultural supply–demand balance as:

$$r_A a_A K_A = (\alpha w + \phi P_A)L_N + (\alpha w + \phi P_A - w)a_A b_A K_A.$$

This equation states that the quasi-rent in agriculture is increased when there is higher food demand (net of payments to agricultural workers $wa_A b_A K_A$) on the right-hand side. Noting that $I = \dot{K}_N + \dot{K}_A$ and $L_N = b_N X_N$ we can substitute from 5.11 to get another expression for r_N. Dividing by $P_N K_N$, gives the result

$$i_A \lambda = \frac{\alpha w + \phi P_A}{s|(\alpha + \tau)w + \phi P_A|}(g_N + \lambda g_A) - \frac{\tau a_A b_A}{(1 + \tau)b_N}\frac{(1 - \alpha)w - \phi P_A}{(\alpha + \tau)w + \phi P_A}. \tag{5.14}$$

In special cases when $\phi = 0$, 5.14 becomes far simpler:

$$i_A \lambda = \frac{\alpha}{s(\tau + \alpha)}(g_N + \lambda g_A) - \frac{\tau a_A b_A}{(1 + \tau)b_N}\frac{(1 - \alpha)}{(\tau + \alpha)}. \tag{5.15}$$

This equation is basically still a supply–demand balance, and shows that i_A, the profit rate in agriculture, will be driven up as the growth rate in either sector gets bigger. An increase in the ratio of agricultural to nonagricultural capital ($\lambda = K_A/K_N$) will increase food supply and pull i_A down. As is clear from 5.14, things get more complicated when $\phi > 0$, and some of the details are sketched below.

The other relationship between growth and profit rates is easy to get. Dividing 5.9 by $P_N K_N$, gives the equation

$$g_N + \lambda g_A = s(i_N + \lambda i_A). \tag{5.16}$$

Growth in at least one sector can be faster, if the savings rate or either profit rate goes up.

Since they are most easily characterized, we focus on steady states. With $\phi = 0$, the demand–supply and savings–investment equations 5.15 and 5.16 respectively reduce to

$$i\lambda = \frac{\alpha}{s(\tau + \alpha)}(1 + \lambda)g - \frac{\tau a_A b_A}{(1 + \tau)b_N}\frac{1 - \alpha}{\tau + \alpha}\lambda \tag{5.17}$$

and

$$g = si. \tag{5.18}$$

Equation 5.17 shows that across steady states the economywide profit rate responds positively to faster growth and lower concentration of capital in agriculture, just as in 5.15. In 5.18 a higher profit rate is associated with faster growth, along Cambridge lines. Let

$$\mu = \lambda/(1 + \lambda) = K_S/(K_S + K_G)$$

so that μ is the share of agricultural capital in the total stock. Then by substituting 5.18 in 5.17, we can get an expression for i as:

$$\left(1 - \frac{\tau + \alpha}{\alpha}\mu\right)i = \frac{a_A b_A \tau}{(1 + \tau)b_N}\frac{(1 - \alpha)}{\alpha}\mu. \tag{5.19}$$

We can solve graphically for i using the solid lines in Figure 5.2, so long as the term in parentheses multiplying i on the left side of 5.19 is positive. This condition is equivalent to $\lambda/(1 + \lambda) = K_S/K_S + K_G < \alpha/(\tau + \alpha) < 1$, or else $\lambda = K_S/K_G < \alpha/\tau$. In either version, a steady state cannot exist, if the share of agricultural capital grows too large. If this contingency does not arise, then an increase in λ will shift up the horizontal line for the right side of 5.19 in Figure 5.2, and make the slope of the line for the left side of 5.19 less steep. The outcome of the increase in the agricultural share of total capital stock is a higher profit rate i. Other comparative dynamic exercises can be pursued, but we defer them for consideration in sections 5 and 6, below.

Much this same analysis goes through when ϕ moderately exceeds zero and the income elasticity of food demand is less than 1, but the details are more complex. To understand what happens, first, note that we can solve from 5.6 for the agricultural price P_A as

$$P_A = w\left[\frac{(1 + \tau)b_N}{a_A}i_A + b_A\right]. \tag{5.20}$$

Substituting this expression into 5.14 and assuming a steady state, gives the

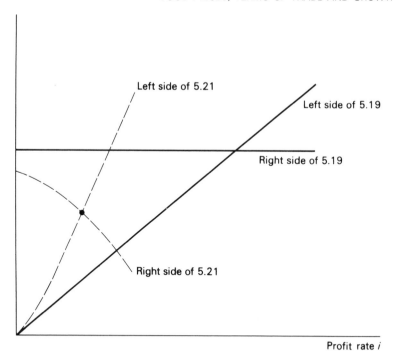

Figure 5.2   Determination of the steady-state profit rate when the income elasticity of demand for agricultural products equals 1 (full lines) or is less than 1 (broken lines).

profit rate as

$$\left[1 - \frac{\tau + \alpha + \phi\Delta}{\alpha + \phi\Delta}\mu\right]i = \frac{\tau a_A b_A}{(1 + \tau)b_N}\frac{1 - \alpha - \phi\Delta}{\alpha + \phi\Delta}\mu \qquad (5.21)$$

where Δ is the bracketed term on the right side of 5.20. The graphical solution is given by the broken lines in Figure 5.2. For given parameters and a given value of μ, a positive value of ϕ leads to a lower profit rate in steady state. Due to Engel's Law, there is less demand pressure on scarce agricultural capital as income goes up. The terms of trade are lower and as a consequence the profit rate falls off too.

(4) Terms of Trade and Inflation

With apparatus now developed, it is easy to talk about the terms of trade P_A/P_N. Division of equation 5.20 for P_A by 5.1 for P_N shows that the terms of trade are given by

$$\frac{P_A}{P_N} = \frac{(1 + \tau)b_N i_A + a_A b_A}{(1 + \tau)b_N a_A} . \tag{5.22}$$

Clearly, P_A/P_N rises with an increase in the agricultural profit rate i_A.

To bring in inflation, we assume with Lewis that workers have a desired real consumption wage R^*, set by societal standards and opportunities for productive work in the subsistence sector. With workers' postulated consumption patterns, their actual real wage R is most naturally defined by the true cost of living index corresponding to the linear expenditure system, which takes the form

$$R = \frac{w - (1 - \alpha)\phi P_A}{P_A^\alpha P_N^{1-\alpha}} = \frac{1 - (1 - \alpha)\ \phi[(1 + \tau)b_N\ (i_A/a_A) + b_A]}{[(1 + \tau)b_N]^\alpha\ [(1 + \tau)b_N(i_A/a_A) + b_A]^{1-\alpha}} \tag{5.23}$$

where the unpleasant expression after the second equality follows via substitution from 5.1 and 5.20. It shows that the real wage is a strictly declining function of i_A. Suppose that when R drops below the desired real wage R^*, workers press for money wage increases. The relevant differential equation is

$$\dot{w} = f(R^* - R) \tag{5.24}$$

where $f(\ )$ has a positive derivative. But by our assumptions increases in w are passed along into price increases, which do not influence i_A in 5.23. Hence, the real wage will not change until other factors adjust to increase R. One such adjustment could be a reduction in i_A; another would be a decline in λ. Until such changes occur, the economy will undergo inflation, brought on by conflicting claims for real wage and profit income. Moreover, equations 5.22–5.24 together show that the inflation will be sharper when the terms of trade are high. This is a proposition that would be interesting to test.[2]

(5) Steady States under Restricted Agricultural Growth

By now, it is well known that there are several customary ways to add restrictions to close a set of equations like 5.17 and 5.18 and characterize a steady state. Moreover, the qualitative behavior of the growth model is determined by the chosen closing rule.[3] Two such rules are adopted in this chapter, which seem realistic in the context. In this section we explore the case in which agricultural growth is limited to the rate $\bar{g}_A$ by absorptive capacity and similar constraints. This hypothesis corresponds to the stylized fact that agricultural output rarely grows for an extended period by more than a few percent per year.

To simplify the presentation, we concentrate on the case when $\phi = 0$ and

Engel's Law does not apply (but the same general results go through for moderately positive values of ϕ). The characteristics of steady growth can be easily illustrated if 5.14 and 5.15 are solved explicitly for sectoral profit rates under constant growth. To save space, define a new parameter $\theta = (1 - \alpha)a_A b_A/(1 + \tau)(\tau + \alpha)b_N$. Then the profit rates are

$$i_N = \frac{\tau(1 + \lambda)g}{s(\tau + \alpha)\lambda} + \theta\lambda \tag{5.25}$$

and

$$i_A = \frac{\alpha(1 + \lambda)g}{s(\tau + \alpha)\lambda} - \theta. \tag{5.26}$$

A next step is to eliminate λ between these equations and solve for i_N in terms of i_A. After some manipulation we get:

$$i_N = \frac{[(\tau + \alpha)\theta + \tau i_A]g}{s(\tau + \alpha)(i_A + \theta) - \alpha g}. \tag{5.27}$$

This expression shows that i_N is a declining function of i_A, when g is held constant. This result is essentially a restatement of the short-run saving–investment trade-off between X_N and P_A, illustrated in Figure 5.1. For a given rate of growth, the total saving required in the economy is prescribed. A higher profit rate and more saving from one sector requires the other to generate lower profits and save less. This relationship is sketched as the market-equilibrium curve in Figure 5.3.

At the same time steady states will have *equal* profit rates – the 45° line for investment equilibrium in Figure 5.3. And with profit rates determined along the 45° line we can solve for the equilibrium capital–stock ratio below. In the steady state illustrated by the diagram there are relatively high terms of trade and inflation, since the equilibrium level of i_A lies above the inflation-line value that would make R from equation 5.23 equal to the workers' desired real wage R^*.

From the form of equation 5.27 it is clear that faster agricultural growth $\bar{g}_A$ will drive up i_N for a given i_A. As a consequence the market equilibrium line in Figure 5.3 will shift up, increasing the steady-state profit rate as a higher economywide level of saving is required to support more investment for growth. One immediate consequence of the rightward movement of i_A is a faster rate of inflation. More rapid growth accelerates price increases from conflicting claims, as structuralist economists always point out. The same finding goes through when there is labor-augmenting technical change, if the desired real wage rises along with the residual, as seems likely to be the case. A one-shot increase in the A-sector output–capital ratio a_A would reduce the steady-

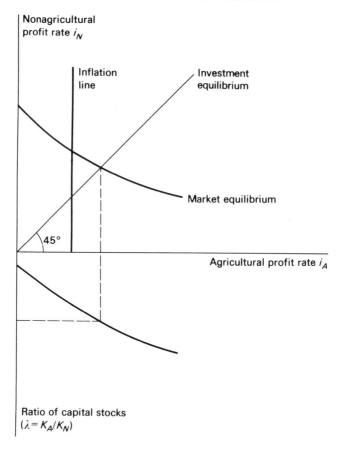

Figure 5.3   Determination of the profit rate and agricultural capital share in a steady state limited by the growth of agricultural capital stock.

state profit rate and inflation, but the empirical evidence suggests that there are limits to reductions in the agricultural capital–output ratio that can take place.[4] Once established, a positive association between growth and inflation is not easy to wipe out.

   To analyze the impacts of possible policy shifts, we can vary other parameters in equation 5.27. An increase in the saving rate will reduce the profit rate required to sustain a constant rate of growth – this can be seen more directly from 5.18. As long as agricultural growth keeps up, contractionary fiscal policy will reduce inflationary pressure. One can similarly show that a higher value of α will increase the profit rate and inflation, by directing demand toward the growth-limited agricultural sector. The effects of an increase in the mark-up rate τ are more complex. When φ is equal to zero, an increase in τ has no effect on profit rates but reduces the real wage from equation 5.23. As a consequence, the rate of inflation goes up. When ϕ exceeds zero and Engels's Law applies, a higher mark-up rate increases demand for nonagricultural products and the profit rate i_N. (The possible fall in aggregate demand from a higher τ that occurs in the short run is ruled out by the agricultural-determined rate of growth in this section's version of the steady state.) When equilibrium is reestablished, the gap between the actual and desired real wage is higher than when $\phi = 0$. Engel's Law exacerbates the inflationary impacts of higher mark ups. The other way round, price controls to reduce mark ups look like an effective anti-inflationary device.

A final policy to consider is implementation of food subsidies. As discussed in section 2, a subsidy increase would raise both X_N and P_A in the short run; in the long run the impact would be a higher profit rate along the steady growth path. There would also be a fall in the real wage, if the consumer food price rose in response to the subsidy, as seems likely to be the case. This unfavorable response could be offset by food subsidies operating *together* with price controls for the N sector. Success of this joint policy would depend on its ability to reduce inflation by changing the income distribution, while maintaining aggregate demand.

Stability of Figure 5.3 equilibrium depends on the investment function. The most straightforward specification is based on the idea that N-sector entrepreneurs aim for the A-sector growth rate, unless there is a profit-rate spread to which they react with a coefficient $1/v$:

$$g_N = g_A + (1/v)(i_N - i_A). \tag{5.28}$$

For an example of how equation 5.28 guarantees stability, suppose that the economy is initially in a steady state but that the consumption parameter α rises. From equations 5.25 and 5.26, i_A will rise and i_N fall. With a positive response coefficient v in 5.28, g_N will decline, and from 5.13, the capital-stock ratio λ will begin to rise. Stability comes in from an easy algebraic demonstration that this incipient increase in λ will raise the difference $i_N - i_A$, and thus increase the growth rate g_N. From 5.13, the higher g_N will cut back on the growth in λ, and finally lead to a steady state corresponding to the new value of α. With variation in details, this same stability argument goes through for other parameter shifts and shocks.

(6) Unrestricted Steady Growth

If agriculture can expand at any speed, then the growth rate will depend on how active investors' animal spirits really are. To illustrate the possibilities, assume that both sectors have the same investment function, given by:

$$g_j = g_0 + (1/v)(i_j - i_0), \quad j = A, N. \tag{5.29}$$

The parameter g_0 is a base growth rate, for which entrepreneurs aim. They will invest more if potential profits exceed some reference rate i_0, perhaps defined by monetary factors through the banking system. The general form of equation 5.29 is useful in the analysis of growth models, and follows Tobin (1961).

With no supply-side restrictions, the growth model formally resembles a Keynesian system in the short run. Under an investment function like 5.29, it will expand at a constant rate, if an increase in the steady-state profit rate i stimulates saving more than the investment response. A stability argument like the one sketched above shows that this will be the case when $(1/v)$ in equation 5.29 is less than the saving rate s, or $sv > 1$. A diagrammatic presentation appears in Figure 5.4. Growth rises with the profit rate along the saving-supply line corresponding to equation 5.18. The less-steep, steady-state investment-

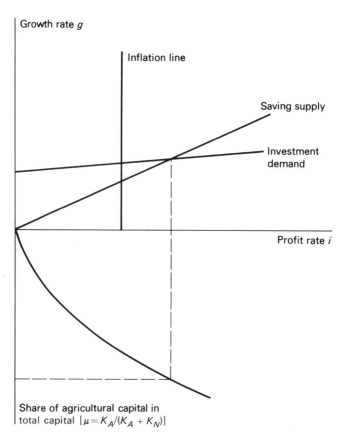

Figure 5.4   *Determination of the growth rate, profit rate and agricultural capital share from the investment function in an unrestricted steady state.*

demand function $g = g_0 + (1/v)(i - i_0)$ cuts this line from the left. Steady growth occurs at a point where

$$g = \frac{s}{sv - 1}(vg_0 - i_0). \tag{5.30}$$

From Figure 5.4, it is clear that more active investor response to profit incentives will steepen the slope of the investment line, leading to higher profit rates, faster inflation and more rapid growth. The same outcomes would also stem from a higher base growth rate g_0. Indeed, the response coefficient of g to g_0 is $sv/(sv - 1)$, which exceeds 1. If g_0 is pegged to population growth, then a more rapidly growing population will have a *higher* rate of increase of income per head. When there are no resource limits on food supply expansion, the traditional secular stagnationist argument in favor of rapid population growth seems to hold. Regrettably, the more rapid income growth is associated with a lower real wage from 5.23; in this sense Malthusian arguments are right.

In this model long-run restrictive monetary policy would bid up the alternative interest rate i_0. The investment-demand line would shift down, slowing growth and inflation rate at the same time. Speculation in land or foodstocks would also slow long-run growth through a similar means. Assume that speculation becomes more tempting as the inflation rate is higher. The impact would be to raise the reference interest rate i_0 in the investment function 5.29. But we know from the discussion in section 4 that inflation is sharper when the agricultural profit rate i_A is higher – hence, i_0 is an increasing function of i_A. Modifying equation 5.30 to take this effect into account, shows that steady-state growth is slower as speculative bidding up of the interest rate is stronger. Governments interested in rapid growth would do well to keep speculative commodity demands under control. Returning to more conventional policies, note that profit taxes would also slow growth and the inflation rate, by increasing s and rotating the savings supply line to the left. Note that in this model as opposed to the previous one, long-run contractionary policies affect the real side of the economy by reducing the growth rate along with the rate at which prices increase.

Finally, the lower quadrant of the diagram shows that the agricultural share in total capital stock is an increasing function of the steady-state profit rate i. The same phenomenon appears in Figure 5.3, when λ is treated as a function of i along the 45° line. The exact form of these relationships depends on all parameters of the model as in equation 5.21. The main point is that both show agriculture playing a larger role in the economy when the growth rate is high. The model illustrates why the traditional economists' advice to lay emphasis on agriculture has a basis in fact. The fact is that agriculture is resource-limited in the short run, and needs real investment to grow.

(7) Summary

Several models are developed in this chapter, but all focus on a few basic themes. These are:

(*a*)   agricultural supply is inelastic in the short run, and requires new capital formation to continue growing in steady state;

(*b*)   saving comes from both sectors, and in the short run nonagricultural output and the agricultural price adjust in part to bring saving in line with investment demand; a similar adjustment occurs in the long run, with sectoral profit rates playing the accommodating roles;

(*c*)   conjunctural food-price increases and secular inflation are both related to high profit rates and favorable agricultural terms of trade; there is a clear economic conflict between workers who consume food, and capitalists who control its means of production.

Under such circumstances, there is a strong inflationary bias in the system. Contractionary fiscal and monetary policies can reduce food-price levels in the short run and hold down inflationary pressures as well. At the same time, they reduce employment and real growth. Food subsidies are counter-productive, in that they stimulate food demand which can only be rationed by a rising consumer price. Price controls on nonagricultural goods are potentially a more effective instrument, except in a case where Malthus-style luxury-goods consumption from profit incomes, in fact, stimulates aggregate demand. By holding down producers' mark ups, price controls can in principle go together with food subsidies to shift the income distribution in such a way as to reduce inflationary pressure. However, profit recipients would resist this sort of change. On the ground of political economy, the consistent application of a joint price-control–food-subsidy policy can by no means be assured.

Finally, the overall rate of growth may well be limited by absorptive capacity and other constraints on the expansion of agricultural supply. If these restrictions do not bind, then growth depends on the vitality of investment demand. In a basically surplus labor situation, growth in income per capita may, in fact, be higher when investors respond to an overall rapid rate of population increase. If there are no restrictions on how fast food supply can expand, traditional Malthusian arguments do not apply directly. At one step's remove, however, they are very important, since faster growth is always associated with a lower real wage. Only capitalists benefit from more buoyant animal spirits in the long run. Workers simply pay the inflationary cost.

Chapter 5: Notes

I am grateful to Amit Bhaduri for comments on a previous draft, and to the National Science Foundation for research support under grant number SES-7914208.

1 For full details of the short-run story, see ch. 5 in Taylor (1979); Chichilnisky and Taylor (1980); Cardoso (1981).
2 The inflation model here follows Lara-Resende (1979) and Cardoso (1981). The latter works with lagged adjustment of both the wage and agricultural price, and ends up with an inflationary steady state in which the agricultural sector has permanent excess demand. Her formulation approaches the one here when the characteristic adjustment speed of wages is markedly slower than that of food prices, as appears empirically to be the case.
3 For example, see Sen (1963); Darity (1979); Taylor and Lysy (1979); Marglin (1982).
4 For evidence, see Kuznets (1966).

Chapter 5: References

Cardoso, E. A., 'Food supply and inflation', *Journal of Development Economics* vol. 8, no. 3 (1981), pp. 269–84.

Chichilnisky, G. and Taylor, L., 'Agriculture and the rest of the economy: macro-connections and policy restraints', *American Journal of Agricultural Economics*, vol. 62, no. 2 (1980), pp. 303–9.

Darity, W. A., Jr, *The Simple Analytics of Growth, Distribution and the Cambridge Saving Equation* (Austin, Texas: University of Texas, 1979).

Kalecki, M., *Selected Essays on the Dynamics of the Capitalist Economy* (Cambridge: Cambridge University Press, 1971).

Kuznets, S., *Modern Economic Growth* (New Haven, Conn./London: Yale University Press, 1966).

Lara-Resende, A., 'Inflation, growth and oligopolistic pricing in a semi-industrialized economy: the case of Brazil', unpublished Ph.D dissertation, Massachusetts Institute of Technology (1979).

Marglin, S. A., *Growth, Distribution and Prices* (Cambridge: Cambridge University Press, 1982).

Sen, A. K., 'Neo-classical and neo-Keynesian theories of distribution', *Economic Record*, vol. 39, no. 1 (1963), pp. 53–64.

Stone, R., 'Linear expenditure systems and demand analysis: an application to the pattern of British demand', *Economic Journal*, vol. 64, no. 255 (1954), pp. 511–27.

Sylos-Labini, P., *Oligopoly and Technical Progress* (Cambridge, Mass.: Harvard University Press, 1957).

Taylor, L., *Macro Models for Developing Countries* (New York: McGraw-Hill, 1979).

Taylor, L. and Lysy, F. J., 'Vanishing income redistributions: Keynesian clues about model surprises in the short run', *Journal of Development Economics*, vol. 6, no. 1 (1979), pp. 11–30.

Tobin, J., 'Money, capital and other stores of value', *American Economic Review (Papers and Proceedings)*, vol. 51, no. 1 (1961), pp. 26–37.

6

Alternative Theories of Wage Determination and Unemployment: the Efficiency Wage Model

JOSEPH E. STIGLITZ

Introduction

Wages in different sectors (different locations, industries, or firms) have been observed to differ markedly from one another. This may be because the quality of labor in the different sectors differs; but it may also be the case that a worker of a given quality who happens to obtain a job in one sector (firm) will obtain a higher wage than a similar individual who obtains a job in another sector. In conventional competitive equilibrium theory, such a situation could not persist; the fact that it does requires explanation and its consequences – in particular, the unemployment to which it gives rise – need to be taken into account in any analysis of policy. That is the purpose of this chapter.

I focus my discussion on the wage differentials existing between urban and rural sectors in a less developed economy, partly because this provides a setting in which these wage differentials and their consequences are so evident. But it should be apparent that most of what I say is, with minor modifications, applicable to labor markets in developed economies as well.

The basic argument of this chapter is that it pays firms to pay higher wages, because higher wages, up to a point, lead to lower labor costs; the 'optimal' wage may differ in different sectors, leading different sectors to pay different wages.[1] Although the alternative theories presented have this much in common, they differ in the explanation of why higher wages lead to lower labor costs; at least three views suggest themselves:

(1) higher wages lead to lower quit rates;[2]
(2) higher wages lead to greater productivity on the job;
(3) higher wages lead the firm to obtain a higher-quality labor force.

For convenience, I shall refer to the first as the 'labor-turnover model' (or hypothesis), the second as the 'efficiency wage–productivity model' and the third as the 'efficiency wage–quality' model.

It is important to distinguish among these alternative reasons, because the effect of various governmental policies (for instance, wage subsidies) may depend critically on what determines the level of wages. In particular, I showed in Stiglitz (1974c) that earlier discussions in the development literature may have led to seriously misleading conclusions concerning the desirability of wage subsidies and the relationship between the urban wage and the shadow price of labor. These earlier studies contended that because there was unemployment in the urban sector ('surplus labor'), the opportunity cost of hiring an additional worker was zero.[3] They ignored the effect of the policy on the wages paid in the urban sector and on the induced migration from the rural to the urban sector and the consequent unemployment. In the simplest model I showed that, if the unemployment rate remained unchanged, then the opportunity cost of hiring laborers was precisely the urban wage. The desirability of various governmental policies depended critically on what effect they had on the unemployment rate; this in turn was determined by the urban-rural wage differential. Whether, for instance, a wage subsidy raises the urban wage (thus increasing the unemployment rate) depends critically on whether the wage subsidy is 'shifted' in the sense that some part of the benefits accrue to the workers in the form of higher real wages; and whether the wage subsidy is shifted depends critically on one's theory of the determination of wages and the form which the wage subsidy takes. For example, for the labor-turnover model, I showed that an *ad valorem* wage subsidy is partially shifted, leading to higher unemployment rates. The shadow price of labor is, however, just equal to the urban wage. The results presented here are equally destructive of much of the folklore of development economics, but differ markedly from those of the 'labor turnover model':

(1) In the efficiency wage–productivity model, an *ad valorem* wage subsidy leaves the wage unaffected, and the optimal wage subsidy is $1/(1 + \xi)$, where ξ is the elasticity of labor supply to the urban sector.

(2) In the efficiency wage–productivity model, the opportunity cost of a laborer employed by the government is equal to $w_u\xi/(1 + \xi)$, where w_u is the urban wage. If, as is conventionally postulated, there is a very elastic supply of laborers from the rural sector to the urban sector (as there would be if the urban sector is very small), then the optimal *ad valorem* subsidy is small and the opportunity cost is approximately equal to the urban wage.

(3) If the government directly controlled the manufacturing sector, it would pay exactly the same wage as the market economy does, but would hire more laborers.

(4) A technical improvement which, at each level of wages increases the productivity of a worker, could not only lead to greater unemployment, but also lower national output.

(5) In the efficiency wage model with capital mobile between the sectors, the shadow price of labor is less than the urban wage. Similarly, the impos-

ition of a wage subsidy lowers the unemployment rate and raises net national income. These results should be contrasted with those obtained in the labor-turnover model, where we established that a wage subsidy would increase the unemployment rate.

(6) In the efficiency–quality model, the wage paid in the market economy is too high; if the productivity of the marginal migrant exceeds that of the average migrant, the level of employment is too low, but in the converse case, the level of employment is too high. To correct these distortions, requires a specific wage *tax* combined with an *ad valorem* wage subsidy.

(7) In the efficiency–quality model, the opportunity cost of hiring an additional worker may be either greater, or less, than the urban wage.

(8) Although the opportunity cost of the government's hiring additional laborers exceeds that conventionally assumed in the literature, the distributional implications are less significant. Consequently, the effect on investment is smaller. For instance, in the case of an infinitely elastic labor supply schedule to the urban sector, additional urban employment may have no effect at all on aggregate consumption.

Whether one believes the precise assumptions employed in the models presented here, they do cast considerable doubt on the widespread presumption that shadow prices for labor are considerably less than the urban wage and that as a consequence wage subsidies are desirable.

The Efficiency Wage–Productivity Model

The Basic Model

It is often argued that the efficiency of a worker is an increasing function of the wage he receives;[4] we let $\lambda(w)$ represent the efficiency of a worker receiving a wage w, and we assume that λ has the shape depicted in Figure 6.1: initially there are increasing returns to increasing the wage, but eventually diminishing returns sets in.

There are several alternative explanations of why efficiency (productivity) should increase with the wage; in very poor LDCs, nutritional considerations are probably dominant, but in more developed economies, morale and incentive effects are undoubtedly important.[5]

Firms pay a wage which minimizes labor costs per efficiency unit,[6] that is,

$$\min_{\{w\}} w/\lambda(w).$$

This implies that

$$\lambda'(w^*) = \lambda(w^*)/w^*. \tag{6.1}$$

The solution to equation 6.1 is referred to as the *efficiency wage* (see

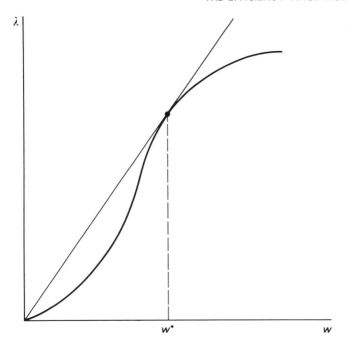

Figure 6.1 *Efficiency wage.*

Figure 6.1). Efficiency wage considerations may be important in both the rural and urban sectors; but there is no reason that the efficiency–wage function should be the same in the two sectors (since the nature of the work performed is so different, as are the environmental factors which affect the effect of wages on productivity). Thus, the wages paid in the two sectors may differ markedly. Here, we simplify by assuming that efficiency is independent of the wage in the rural sector.[7]

Let Q_u and Q_r be output in the urban and rural sectors, respectively; output in each sector is a function of the labor inputs,

$$Q_u = F(\lambda(w)L_u), \quad F' > 0 \quad F'' \le 0 \qquad (6.2)$$

and

$$Q_r = G(L_r) \quad G' > 0 \quad G'' \le 0 \qquad (6.3)$$

where L_u and L_r are employment in the urban and rural sectors, so $\lambda(w)L_u$ is the effective labor supply in urban employment.

We assume that the country in question is a small country, trading both urban and rural output at international prices; we normalize our units so the price of each is unity.[8]

The wage in the rural sector is just equal to (the value of) its marginal product,[9]

$$w_r = G'(L_r) \tag{6.4}$$

and similarly, in the urban sector,

$$w_u = \lambda(w)F'(\lambda(w)L_u). \tag{6.5}$$

But as we noted earlier, the urban wage is just the efficiency wage

$$w_u = w^*. \tag{6.6}$$

Finally, we must describe how labor becomes allocated between the urban and rural sectors. We let $\bar{L}$ be the total labor supply, N_u the total number of job-seekers in the urban sector and U the unemployment rate; then

$$L_r + N_u = \bar{L} \tag{6.7}$$

and

$$1 - U = L_u/N_u. \tag{6.8}$$

Under a variety of assumptions concerning the hiring behavior of firms and migration decisions of individuals, it can be shown that migration equilibrium requires that the expected wage in the urban sector equals the wage in the rural sector. The expected wage is just equal to the nominal wage times the probability of being hired, L_u/N_u[10]:

$$w_u^e = (1 - U)w_u = \frac{L_u w_u}{N_u} = w_r. \tag{6.9}$$

We can now describe the equilibrium. Given the efficiency wage w^*, equation 6.5 determines the demand for labor in the urban sector L_u^*:

$$L_u^* = \frac{1}{\lambda(w^*)} F'^{-1}(w^*/\lambda(w^*)). \tag{6.10}$$

Substituting equations 6.4 and 6.7 into 6.9, we obtain

$$G'(\bar{L} - N_u)N_u = w^*L_u^* \tag{6.11}$$

which can be solved uniquely for N_u (or equivalently L_r).

Comparative Statics
In this section we consider briefly the effect of a number of changes in the parameters of the model on the equilibrium. First, note that an increase in the

labor supply $\bar{L}$ has no effect on the urban wage, but does lead both to a lower rural wage (if there is diminishing returns to labor), and a higher unemployment rate. Secondly, an increase in the capital stock in the urban sector, which would lead to an increase in urban employment, will lead to a lower level of unemployment, a lower unemployment rate and a higher rural wage. Similarly, a change which leads to higher agricultural productivity, and a higher wage in the rural sector, will lower the unemployment rate but still leave the urban wage and urban employment unchanged.

Consider now what happens if the efficiency wage–productivity relationship should change. Labor could become more efficient at every wage rate (say, as a result of better schooling or a labor-augmenting technical innovation), but the efficiency wage could be increased; this would lead to an increase in the unemployment rate. Let us decompose a (small) change in the wage–productivity relationship into a change in the productivity, keeping the efficiency wage fixed, and a change in the efficiency wage, keeping productivity fixed.

Differentiating equation 6.5 with respect to λ, holding w^* fixed, we obtain

$$\left. \frac{\lambda}{L_u} \frac{\partial L_u}{\partial \lambda} \right|_{w^*} = \eta_u - 1 \qquad (6.12)$$

where $\eta_u = -F'/F''\lambda L_u =$ the elasticity of demand for labor in the urban sector. Thus, an increase in productivity leads to a decrease or increase in demand for labor as the elasticity of demand is less than or greater than unity.

The effect of this on *unemployment* can be directly calculated from equation 6.11, which we rewrite for convenience as

$$xG'(\bar{L} - L_u x) = w^* \qquad (6.13)$$

where $x = 1/(1 - U)$. Then

$$\frac{\partial \ln x}{\partial \ln L_u} = \frac{x^2 G''}{G' - xL_u G''} \frac{L_u}{x}$$

$$= -1/|(L_r \eta_r/N_u) + 1| = -\frac{1}{1 + \xi} \qquad (6.14)$$

(using equation 6.9) where $\eta_r = -G'/G''L_r =$ elasticity of demand for labor in the rural sector and $\xi = d\ln N_u/d\ln w_u^e =$ elasticity of supply of laborers to the urban sector. Thus, the unemployment rate is increased or decreased depending on whether urban employment is increased or decreased, in other words, depending on whether the elasticity of demand for labor is greater or less than unity. For a Cobb–Douglas production function $\eta_u > 1$, so a technical improvement always leads to increased employment, a higher unemployment rate and a larger number of unemployed individuals.

As a result of the increased unemployment rate, *a technical change could actually make the economy worse off.* Let Q be total national output:

$$Q = Q_u + Q_r. \tag{6.15}$$

Then, recalling that $Q_r = G(\bar{L} - L_u x)$

$$\left.\frac{\partial Q}{\partial \lambda}\right|_{w*} = F'L_u + \left(F'\lambda - \frac{G'}{1-U}\right)\frac{dL_u}{d\lambda} - G'L_u\frac{dx}{d\lambda}$$

$$= \frac{w_u L_u}{\lambda}\left(1 + \frac{\eta_u - 1}{1 + \xi}\right) > 0 \tag{6.16}$$

where we have made use of the migration equilibrium condition (so $F'\lambda = G'/1 - U$) and equations 6.12 and 6.14. At a fixed wage, technical change increases national output.

The effect of a change in the efficiency wage $w*$, keeping $\lambda(w)$ constant (at the efficiency wage), is more easily analyzed. Again, differentiating 6.5, we obtain

$$\left.\frac{w*}{L_u}\frac{\partial L_u}{\partial w*}\right|_\lambda = -\eta_u \tag{6.17}$$

and from equation 6.13

$$\frac{w*}{1/1-U}\frac{d(1/1-U)}{dw*} = \frac{\partial \ln x}{\partial \ln L_u}\frac{\partial \ln L_u}{\partial \ln w*} + \frac{\partial \ln x}{\partial \ln w*} = \frac{\xi + \eta_u}{1 + \xi} > 0. \tag{6.18}$$

As a result

$$\left.\frac{dQ}{dw*}\right|_{\lambda*} = \left(F'\lambda - \frac{G'}{1-U}\right)\frac{\partial L_u}{\partial w*} - G'L_u x\frac{d\ln x}{dw*} = -L_u\frac{\xi + \eta_u}{\xi + 1} < 0 \tag{6.19}$$

an increase in the efficiency wage leads to a lowering of national income.

A technical change will always lead to a lowering of labor costs, that is, of $w*/\lambda(w*)$, but may be associated with either a lower or a higher efficiency wage. Thus, any particular technical change may be associated with either an increase or decrease in unemployment, unemployment rate and national output.

Second-Best Optimality
We now compare the market equilibrium, already depicted, with the equilibrium which would emerge were the government to control the wage rate

and urban unemployment; we assume, however, that the government cannot control migration, and it is for this reason that we call the equilibrium a second-best optimum. We assume also that the government is interested in maximizing national income, that is,

$$\max_{\{L_u, N_u, w\}} Q = F(\lambda(w)L_u) + G(\bar{L} - N_u)$$

subject to the migration constraint, that

$$N_u G'(\bar{L} - N_u) = L_u w. \tag{6.20}$$

Straightforward calculations yield the result that

$$\lambda'(w^0) = \lambda(w^0)/w^0$$

and

$$F'\lambda = \frac{w^0 \xi}{1 + \xi}.$$

The government would, in fact, pay the efficiency wage – the same wage that the private market pays – but it would hire laborers up to the point where the marginal product of labor equals the urban wage times $\xi/(1 + \xi)$. *If the elasticity of labor supply to the urban sector is very large, then the market economy is approximately a second-best optimum.*

Calculation of Opportunity Cost of Labor

What is the consequence of the government hiring one additional laborer (in a situation where it does not directly control urban employment in the private sector)? Let L_g be government employment. The only modification to the model already presented is that we now write the migration equilibrium condition as

$$(L_u + L_g)w^* = G'(\bar{L} - N_u)N_u$$

where it is now understood the L_u refers to employment in the private urban sector. Since government employment will leave unaffected L_u and w^*, we have

$$\frac{dN_u}{dL_g} = \frac{w^*}{-G''N_u + G'} = \frac{w^*\xi}{G'(1 + \xi)} = \frac{\xi}{(1 - U)(1 + \xi)}$$

so that the opportunity cost of hiring one additional laborer is

$$-\frac{dQ}{dL_g} = \frac{w_r \xi}{(1 - U)(1 + \xi)} = \frac{w_u \xi}{1 + \xi}.$$

Again, if the elasticity of labor supply to the urban sector is large, then the opportunity cost is approximately the urban wage.

Ad Valorem Wage Subsidy

The equilibrium described in the section on second-best optimality can be attained in a private-market economy by the imposition of an *ad valorem* wage subsidy. An *ad valorem* wage subsidy leaves the wage rate unaffected, since

$$\min \frac{w}{\lambda(w)}$$

has exactly the same solution as

$$\min(1 - \tau) \frac{w}{\lambda(w)}$$

where τ is the *ad valorem* subsidy. The subsidy does lead firms to hire more workers:

$$\lambda F' = w_u(1 - \tau)$$

from which we immediately infer that

$$1 - \tau = \frac{\xi}{1 + \xi}$$

or

$$\tau = \frac{1}{1 + \xi}.$$

The Efficiency–Wage Quality Model

Firms often claim that they pay high wages as a means of recruiting a higher-quality labor force.[11] In a world of perfect information, firms would be unconcerned about the quality of labor: an individual who was twice as productive would receive twice the wage and there would be no gain to the firm. But with imperfect information, this is no longer true. However, the social returns from a firm in the urban sector obtaining a higher-quality labor force are very different from the private return; the social returns (the increase in national output) only arise from the sorting out of individuals according to comparative advantage, that is, in having workers who have a comparative advantage in urban employment working in the urban sector. If there is imperfect information, wages may not accurately reflect opportunity costs of the marginal individual hired in the urban sector. The firm is only concerned with the relation between the wages it pays and the quality of labor it obtains, not with opportunity costs and comparative advantage. As a result, the market economy is likely not to be efficient.

The model[12] we analyze in this section is very similar to that presented in the previous section, except now the quality (productivity) of those employed in the urban sector depends on the mix of those applying for jobs. For the ith firm, this depends on the wage it offers w_i; the wage offered by other firms $\bar{w}$ and the total number of job-seekers N_u:

$$\lambda_i = \lambda(w_i, \bar{w}, N_u). \tag{6.21}$$

For a given value of N_u and $\bar{w}$, λ_i is assumed to have the shape of Figure 6.1. The important assumption of the analysis is that any firm cannot identify who is more productive, who is less productive: all that it knows is the *average* quality mix of those who apply for a job (or who accept a job) paying a wage w. On the other hand,

$$\frac{\partial \lambda_i}{\partial \bar{w}} < 0.$$

If other *urban* firms increase their wage, relative to the given firm, the workers it succeeds in recruiting will be less productive.

Each firm is sufficiently small that it ignores its effects on N_u and $\bar{w}$ and hence, just as in the previous section, chooses its wage to

$$\min_{\{w\}} w/\lambda \tag{6.22}$$

so

$$\lambda_{w_i}(w_i, \bar{w}, N_u) = \lambda_i/w_i. \tag{6.23}$$

In equilibrium, of course, if all urban firms have the same λ_i function and pay the same wage,[13]

$$w_i = \bar{w}.$$

For simplicity, we write

$$\bar{\lambda}(w, N_u) \equiv \lambda_i(w, w, N_u)$$

where we write

$$\bar{\lambda}_w = \partial \lambda_i / \partial w_i$$

and

$$\bar{\lambda}_w^* = \frac{\partial \lambda_i}{\partial w_i} + \frac{\partial \lambda_i}{\partial \bar{w}}.$$

Where there is no ambiguity, we drop the subscripts on w_u. Equilibrium in this economy is, thus, fully described by the three following equations.

(a)   Firms choose a wage to minimize labor costs:

$$\bar{\lambda}_w(w_u, N_u) = \bar{\lambda}(w_u, N_u)/w_u. \tag{6.24}$$

(b)   Firms hire workers to the point where the wage equals the value of the marginal product:

$$\bar{\lambda}(w_u, N_u)F'|\bar{\lambda}(w_u, N_u)L_u| = w_u. \tag{6.25}$$

(c)   Workers migrate to equate the expected urban wage to the rural wage:

$$w_r N_u = w_u L_u. \tag{6.26}$$

Here w_r is the (rural) wage of the *marginal* migrant. We assume, in other words, that the marginal migrant assumes that he has a chance of obtaining employment equal to the average applicant; this is consistent with our hypothesis that the firm is unable to differentiate among those workers who apply to it.

Equations 6.24–6.26 are three equations in the three unknowns, w_u, L_u and N_u. We depict the solution diagrammatically in Figure 6.2. Differentiating equation 6.24, and using the second-order condition we see that [14]

$$-\frac{\mathrm{d}\ln w_u}{\mathrm{d}\ln N_u} = \left(\frac{\bar{\lambda}_{N_u} N_u}{\bar{\lambda}} - \frac{\bar{\lambda}_{wN_u} N_u}{\bar{\lambda}_w} \right) \Bigg/$$

$$\left(\frac{\partial^2 \lambda_i / \partial w_i^2 + \partial^2 \lambda_i / \partial \bar{w} \partial w_i}{\bar{\lambda}_w} + \frac{1}{\bar{\lambda}} \frac{\partial \lambda_i}{\partial \bar{w}} \right) w_u < 0 \tag{6.27}$$

provided

$$\bar{\lambda}_{wN_u} \leq 0 \tag{6.28}$$

and

$$\bar{\lambda}_{N_u} \geq 0 \tag{6.29}$$

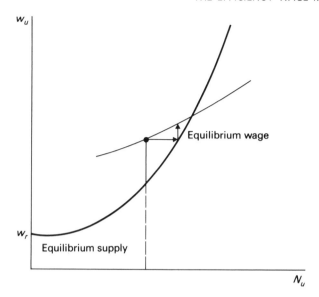

Figure 6.2   *Equilibrium in the efficiency-wage quality model.*

that is, increased urban migration not only increases average productivity in the urban sector (since the most marginal workers are those who migrate first) but also reduces the marginal return to increasing the wage. (Later, we shall present a simple model which satisfies inequalities 6.28 and 6.29.) If inequalities 6.28 and 6.29 are satisfied, as N_u increases, the equilibrium wage rises.

On the other hand, from 6.25 and 6.26,[15] assuming for simplicity that w_r is constant,

$$\frac{\text{d}\ln N_u}{\text{d}\ln w_u} = \frac{(1 - 1/\eta_u)(1 - \bar{\lambda}^*_{w_u} w_u/\bar{\lambda})}{(1 - 1/\eta_u)\, \bar{\lambda}_{N_u} N_u/\bar{\lambda} - 1/\eta_u}. \tag{6.30}$$

At w^*_u (the solution to 6.24), the numerator has the sign of $1 - 1/\eta_u$. (Since $\lambda^*_{w_u} = \dfrac{\partial \lambda_i}{\partial w_i} + \dfrac{\partial \lambda_i}{\partial \bar{w}}$ and $\dfrac{\partial \lambda_i}{\partial w_i} = \lambda/w$; from 6.28, $\dfrac{\partial \lambda_i}{\partial \bar{w}} < 0$.) The sign of the denominator is ambiguous. If a firm hires an additional worker, it induces migration and, under our assumptions, this increases the average productivity of those applying for jobs. Hiring an additional worker reduces the value of the marginal product of labor, but the indirect effect may partially offset this. Equations 6.25 and 6.26 together can be thought of as the supply function of laborers to the urban sector; given each value of w_u, it represents the equilibrium allocation of laborers between the urban and rural sector. As we increase w_u from a low level, we increase the productivity of workers in the urban sector by more than the wage increment, so that the cost of an effective labor unit is reduced. Thus, provided the elasticity of demand for labor is greater than unity, the number of individuals hired in the urban sector increases; moreover, the increase in w_u increases the unemployment rate, so total urban population increases even more rapidly. The equilibrium is depicted in Figure 6.2. The natural dynamics implies that, for stability, the equilibrium wage equation is flatter than the equilibrium labor-supply function to the urban sector.

Second-Best Optimality

The market equilibrium differs from what the government would have done both in the number of workers hired, and in the wages paid. We assume, as before, that the government wishes to maximize national income. Since some of the workers who apply for jobs and obtain them are infra-marginal, the opportunity cost of labor will, in general, be less than the wage. We let $\bar{B}(N_u)$ represent the mean opportunity cost of those applying for an urban job when there are N_u urban job-seekers. Clearly, individuals will not apply unless the urban expected wage exceeds the rural wage, so

$$\bar{B}(N_u) \lessgtr w_u^e = w_r \tag{6.31}$$

as the marginal migrant's opportunity cost is greater or less than that of infra-marginal migrants. Moreover, as we raise the urban wage and induce more migration, we induce more productive workers to migrate from the rural sector. Thus

$$\bar{B}'(N_u) > 0. \tag{6.32}$$

Maximizing net national output then entails

$$\max_{\{L_u, N_u, w_u\}} F(\bar{\lambda}(w_u, N_u)L_u) - \bar{B}(N_u)N_u \tag{6.33}$$

subject to the constraint that

$$N_u w_r = L_u w_u. \tag{6.34}$$

The first-order conditions yield

$$\frac{w_r F' \bar{\lambda}}{w_u} - (\bar{B} + \bar{B}'N_u) + L_u F' \left(\bar{\lambda}_{N_u} + \bar{\lambda} \frac{w_r'}{w_r} \right) = 0 \tag{6.35}$$

$$L_u F' \left(\bar{\lambda}_w^* - \frac{\bar{\lambda}}{w_u} \right) = 0. \tag{6.36}$$

To see more clearly the contrast between the market equilibrium and the second-best optimum, we rewrite 6.35 and 6.36 as

$$F'\bar{\lambda}/w_u = \frac{(\bar{B} + \bar{B}'N_u)/w_r}{1 + \bar{\lambda}_{N_u}N_u/\bar{\lambda} + w'_rN_u/w_r}$$

(6.37)

$$\frac{\bar{\lambda}^*_w}{\bar{\lambda}} w_u = 1.$$

(6.38)

There are three important differences between the market and the second-best optimum:

(1)   The market takes the cost of labor in the urban sector as w_u; the government recognizes that this is an overstatement of the opportunity cost of workers hired.

(2)   The market ignores the fact that as it hires more workers, it induces more migration, and this tends to increase the average quality of those applying to itself and all other firms and increases the *average* opportunity cost of the migration.

(3)   In the market economy, each firm takes the wages of other firms as given; thus, the quality of workers it obtains depends in part on its wage relative to the wages paid by other urban firms. The government, on the other hand, is concerned with the effect of the general level of urban wages on the quality of the work force. Thus, in determining the optimal wage, in the symmetric case, the government sets

$$\frac{\partial \lambda_i}{\partial w_i} + \frac{\partial \lambda_i}{\partial \bar{w}} = \lambda_i/w$$

(6.39)

while the firm sets

$$\frac{\partial \lambda_i}{\partial w_i} = \lambda_i/w.$$

(6.40)

From equation 6.38, it is thus clear that, at any given level of N_u, the market sets the wage too high, except in the limiting case where $\partial \lambda_i/\partial \bar{w} = 0$. There is some presumption, moreover, that at each level of wages, the market hires too few workers. Since the opportunity cost is less than the wage, the numerator of the left-hand side of 6.37 is less than (or equal to) unity, provided B' is not too large; moreover, the denominator is greater than unity, because migration raises both w_r and λ. Under our assumptions, increasing the number of job-seekers increases their average quality and increases the rural wage. It is clear, of course, that it is possible that there may be excessive employment in the urban sector, if for instance the initial migrants are those who are most skilled in the urban sector. This would be the case, if those who had the lower rural wages were the most skilled in the urban sector (an unlikely situation); or if those for whom the effective costs of migration were the lowest, were those most adapted to urban life and therefore had the highest productivity in the urban sector.

To obtain more precise results, we need to make explicit assumptions about the characteristics of the population. Assume a fraction $H(b)$ have a rural productivity coefficient less than b. Thus, if the least productive workers migrate,[16] rural output when a fraction $H(\hat{b})$ of the population has migrated is

$$Q_r = G\left(\left(\int_{\hat{b}}^{\infty} bh(b)\, db\right)L\right) \tag{6.41}$$

where $h = H'$, and

$$\bar{L}H(\hat{b}) = N_u. \tag{6.42}$$

The wage of the marginal worker is

$$w_r = G'\big| \cdot \hat{b}. \tag{6.43}$$

For the subsequent discussion, we shall assume G' is constant, and we choose our units so it equals unity. (The more general case is a straightforward extension.) Thus,

$$B(N_u) = \int_0^{\hat{b}} bh(b)\, db / H(\hat{b}). \tag{6.44}$$

Straightforward calculations[17] establish that

$$B + B'N_u = w_r. \tag{6.45}$$

Although the opportunity cost of the set of workers hired by any firm is less than the wage paid, the opportunity cost of the *marginal* individual induced to migrate to the urban sector is the rural wage. Thus, under these conditions, the market always leads to underemployment in the urban sector. The precise calculation of the magnitude of the bias depends on the specification of the λ_i function.

The derivation of the λ_i function is fairly complicated. We illustrate it with a simple example. Let us postulate that the productivity of a worker at the ith firm depends both on his general ability at urban jobs, and how well-matched his specific abilities are to the requirements of the job. The latter, in turn, depends on the size of the applicant pool, among which the firm has to choose. For simplicity, let us assume that individuals can only apply to one job, are risk-neutral, know the wages offered by the firm before they apply, but do not know how well their skills match the requirements of the firm until after they apply. The queues at each firm will then adjust, so that the expected wage from applying to each firm is identical:

$$w_i^e = \frac{L_i}{N_i} w_i \qquad (6.46)$$

where L_i is the number of jobs offered by the firm, N_i the number of applicants at the ith firm. The average *general* ability of those applying at all firms is the same. If the individual with productivity b in the rural sector has a general ability of a in the urban sector, the average general ability of those applying in the urban sector is just

$$A(N_u) = \int_0^{\hat{b}} a(b)h(b)db/H. \qquad (6.47)$$

For simplicity, let us assume that we can represent total ability as simply the product of general ability and specific ability. Specific ability depends on the size of the applicant pool (per job). Since

$$w_i^e = w_j^e \qquad (6.48)$$

from 6.46, this implies that specific ability is just a function of w_i/w_r, where w_r is the rural wage of the *marginal* migrant, that is,

$$w_r = \hat{b}.$$

We, thus, write

$$\lambda_i = A(N_u)\phi(w_i/\hat{b}). \qquad (6.49)$$

It is immediate that the market will, for each value of N_u, set the correct wage. However,[18]

$$F'\lambda \gtrless w_u \quad \text{as } A \gtrless a \qquad (6.50)$$

that is, as the average ability of those applying is greater or less than the marginal ability. If productivity in the urban and rural sectors are positively correlated, then since the marginal migrant's productivity in the rural sector exceeds that of the average, so too in the urban; thus, the marginal return to hiring workers in the urban sector exceeds the average return. On the other hand, if the marginal migrant's productivity is less than that of the average, just the converse holds.

Note that because the level of employment changes, the actual wage paid in the second-best optimum will differ from that in the market solution; in particular, in our example, if productivities are positively correlated, then the optimal wage will exceed the market wage. The market rate of unemployment will, however, be optimal.

On the other hand, with an additive specification of the productivity function

$$\lambda_i = A + \phi$$

if urban and rural productivities are positively correlated, the market unemployment rate can easily be shown to be too high.

Although in this simple example, the market wage, for each level of employment, is optimal, it is easy to modify the productivity function to show that, in general, it will be too high. Assume, for instance, that workers apply to several firms. The number of applicants (per job) at each firm will still be a function of the wage paid. Now, however, some of the individuals who are found to have the specific skills that are well suited for the given firm will also receive offers from other firms. Thus, the fraction of offers which the firm makes which are accepted will be a function of the wage it offers, relative to the wages offered by other firms. (If different workers have different evaluations of the nonpecuniary characteristics of the firm, this function will be a smooth one; by raising its wages slightly over that of its competitors, it will not, in fact, induce all workers to accept its offers.) Thus, if

$$g(w_i/w)$$

is the percentage of offers accepted, we can write the productivity function as

$$A\phi[(w_i/b)g(w_i/\bar{w})].$$

Now, firms believe that increasing the wage has two effects: it increases the length of the queue and it increases the probability of acceptance; but the latter gain is only at the expense of other firms. The government (in the symmetric equilibrium) takes $w_i = \bar{w}$.

Government Policies

It is clear from equations 6.37 and 6.38 that to induce firms to behave optimally, the government must use both *ad valorem* and specific wage taxes/subsidies. In particular, to induce firms to lower the wage, it imposes a specific wage subsidy and then, to induce firms to hire more workers, it provides an *ad valorem* wage subsidy (the latter, as before, leaves the wage paid unchanged).

The shadow price of labor may be calculated (using 6.33) by noting that (from 6.34)

$$L_u = \frac{N_u w_r}{w_u} - L_g. \tag{6.51}$$

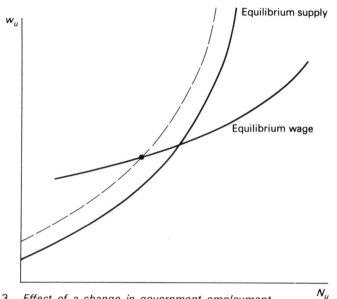

Figure 6.3   *Effect of a change in government employment.*

Differentiating $F - \bar{B}N_u$ and using 6.34 and 6.51 we obtain

$$-\frac{\mathrm{d}(F - \bar{B}N_u)}{\mathrm{d}L_g} = w_u + F'\lambda_u \frac{\mathrm{d}(w_r/w_u)}{\mathrm{d}L_g} + F' \frac{\mathrm{d}\bar{\lambda}}{\mathrm{d}L_g}.$$

If w_r/w_u remained unchanged (so the unemployment rate was unaltered), and if the mean productivity of those hired in the urban sector were unchanged, then the shadow wage would just equal the urban wage.

Turning to Figure 6.3 we note that a change in L_g leaves unaffected the equilibrium-wage curve (equation 6.24) but shifts the equilibrium labor-supply function. At a given level of N_u, if the elasticity of demand for labor exceeds unity, an increase in L_g necessitates an increase in w_u for 6.25 to hold. As a result, the equilibrium level of N_u and the equilibrium level of w_u fall. However, if the efficiency wage is not very sensitive to N_u, then the unemployment rate falls. Moreover, the decrease in N_u leads to a decrease in $\bar{\lambda}$. Hence, there would appear to be some presumption that the shadow wage is less than the urban wage, although perhaps not significantly so. Moreover, if the elasticity of demand for labor is less than unity, precisely the same arguments lead to the conclusion that the shadow price of labor exceeds the urban wage.

Capital Mobility

The basic principle of second-best economics – that a distortion in one market has important ramifications in other markets – is sufficiently widely known that it should come as no surprise that it is in general desirable to impose taxes and/or subsidies on capital in the different sectors. Moreover, the shifts in the allocation of capital induced by, say, the government's hiring one more worker in the urban sector, have secondary effects on the allocation of labor which may be sufficiently large to affect the shadow price of labor in a significant way. The detailed calculations of the shadow prices and optimal taxes and subsidies are elaborate, so we only illustrate the methodology for the case of the efficiency–productivity wage model.

Equilibrium

We assume a constant return to scale production function in the urban sector [19]

$$Q_u = Y^u(K_u, L_u) = L_u y_u(k_u) \tag{6.52}$$

where K_u is capital employed in the urban sector, and

$$k_u = \frac{K_u}{L_u} \tag{6.53}$$

is the capital intensity.

As before, firms in the urban sector pay the efficiency wage w^*. Hence,

$$w^* = w_u = y_u(k_u) - k_u y'_u(k_u) \tag{6.54}$$

which can be solved for the equilibrium capital–labor ratio k_u^*; this in turn immediately determines the rate of return on capital ρ,

$$\rho^* = y'_u(k_u^*). \tag{6.55}$$

Since output in the rural sector is a function of labor, capital and land, it is not reasonable to assume a constant returns to scale production function in labor and capital; since land is assumed fixed, we can write

$$Q_r = Y^r(K_r, L_r) \tag{6.56}$$

where K_r is capital in the rural sector.

Equilibrium requires the following.

(a)   Equality of rate of return on capital:

$$Y_K^r = \rho^*. \tag{6.57}$$

(b)   Rural wage equal expected urban wage:

$$Y_L^r = \left(\frac{L_u + L_g}{N_u}\right) w^*. \tag{6.58}$$

(c)   Capital and labor be allocated either to the rural or urban sectors:

$$K_r + K_u = \bar{K} \tag{6.59}$$

$$L_r + N_u = \bar{L}. \tag{6.60}$$

The equilibrium may now be easily described. First, we make use of the fact that the capital–labor ratio in the urban sector is given to rewrite equation 6.59 to read

$$K_r = \bar{K} - L_u k_u^*. \tag{6.61}$$

Then 6.58 may be thought of as defining the supply of labor to the urban sector as a function of urban employment

$$\left. \frac{d\ln N_u}{d\ln L_u} \right|_{w^*} = \frac{1 + mK_u/K_r - L_g/(L_u + L_g)}{1 + \varepsilon N_u/L_r} \tag{6.62}$$

where

$$\varepsilon = - \frac{Y_{LL}^r L_r}{Y_L^r}$$

and

$$m = \frac{Y_{KL}^r K_r}{Y_L^r}.$$

As urban employment increases, labor is drawn out of the rural sector.

On the other hand, equation 6.57 defines (with 6.61) pairs of values of rural employment and urban employment for which the capital market is in equilibrium. As urban employment increases capital is drawn out of the rural sector, raising the return on the remaining capital; for equilibration, some labor must migrate from the rural sector:

$$\left. \frac{d\ln N_u}{d\ln L_u} \right|_{p=p^*} = -\frac{Y_{KK}^r K_u}{Y_{KL}^r N_u}. \tag{6.63}$$

For a Cobb–Douglas production function with shares of labor and capital of β_L and β_K,

$$\left. \frac{d\ln N_u}{d\ln L_u} \right|_{w^*} = \frac{1 + \beta_K K_u/K_r - L_g/(L_u + L_g)}{1 + (1 - \beta_L)N_u/L_r}$$

while

$$\left. \frac{d\ln N_u}{d\ln L_u} \right|_{p^*} = \frac{1 - \beta_K}{\beta_L} \frac{L_r}{N_u} \frac{K_u}{K_r} > 1, \quad \text{provided} \quad \frac{K_u}{N_u} > \frac{K_r}{L_r}$$

The intersection of the two curves defined by equations 6.57 and 6.58, both of which are upward-sloping, is an equilibrium (see Figure 6.4). There is some presumption that the capital-market clearing curve 6.57 is steeper than the labor-market equilibrium curve. For the Cobb–Douglas case with $L_g = 0$, this requires that

$$\frac{(1 - \beta_K)}{\beta_L} \frac{K_u/K_r}{N_u/L_r} > \frac{1 + \beta_K K_u/K_r}{1 + (1 - \beta_L)N_u/L_r}$$

or

$$(1 - \beta_K)\frac{K_u}{K_r} + (1 - \beta_K - \beta_L)\frac{K_u}{K_r}\frac{N_u}{L_r} > \beta_L \frac{N_u}{L_r}.$$

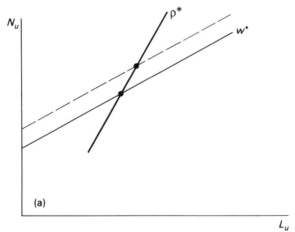

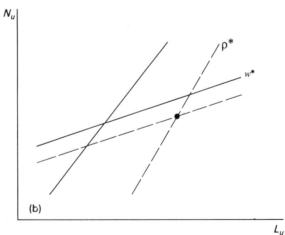

Figure 6.4   *Equilibrium with capital mobility. (a) Effect of increased government employment. (b) Effect of wage subsidies.*

If the urban sector is relatively capital-intensive and the equilibrium unemployment rate is not too high, so

$$\frac{K_u}{K_r} > \frac{N_u}{L_r} = \frac{L_u}{(1-U)L_r}$$

this inequality will clearly be satisfied. This, we assume; the assumption is important in determining the relationship between urban wages and shadow prices.

Shadow Wages Rates

We now calculate the effect of an increase in government employment on private output; we assume that the government does not divert directly any capital from the private sector, but that its hiring decision will have an effect on capital allocation. Since capital has the same (value of) marginal productivity in both sectors, the reallocation of capital will not have any direct effect on national output; but it will induce, in turn, migration. The higher level of government employment will imply that, for each value of L_u, there is a larger number of urban residents. Thus, in Figure 6.4, the labor-market curve shifts up. Thus, both the level of urban employment and the number of urban job-seekers increases. In the appendix to this chapter, we show that none the less the unemployment rate decreases:

$$\frac{dU}{dL_g} < 0.$$

It is immediate that

$$-\frac{d(Q_u + Q_r)}{dL_g} = \frac{Y_L^r}{1-U} - \left\{ Y_L^u - \frac{Y_L^r}{1-U} \right\} \frac{dL_u}{dL_g}$$

$$-(Y_K^u - Y_K^r)\frac{dK_u}{dL_g} + Y_L^r \frac{N_u}{1-U}\frac{dU}{dL_g}$$

$$= w_u \left(1 + N_u \frac{dU}{dL_g} \right) < w_u$$

The *opportunity cost is less than the urban wage.*

Optimal Wage Subsidies

As we noted earlier, an *ad valorem* wage subsidy has no effect on the wage paid to workers in the urban sector; its only effect in this model is to reduce the capital intensity:

$$y(k_u^*) - ky'(k_u^*) = (1 - \tau)w^*.$$

Hence, the choice of an optimal *ad valorem* subsidy is equivalent to the choice of an optimal value of k_u^*.

Let us rewrite equations 6.57 and 6.58 as

$$Y_K^r(\bar{K} - k_u L_u, \bar{L} - N_u) = \rho^* \tag{6.64}$$

$$N_u Y_L^r(\bar{K} - k_u L_u, \bar{L} - N_u) = w^* L_u. \tag{6.65}$$

For each value of N_u, equation 6.64 can be solved uniquely for $k_u L_u$. Hence, a decrease in k_u increases L_u. Similarly, at a fixed value of N_u, a decrease in k_u increases the LHS of equation 6.65, so that right-hand side is less than the left-hand side. An increase in L_u to the point where $k_u L_u$ is unchanged leaves Y_L^r unchanged, but now the RHS exceeds the LHS. Hence, both curves are shifted to the right, but the capital-market curve more than the labor-market curve. This implies that L_u is increased. N_u is increased, but it always does so less than L_u. Hence, unemployment is reduced

$$\frac{dU}{dk_u} > 0.$$

(See the appendix to this chapter.) Hence:

$$\frac{d(Q_u + Q_r)}{d\tau}\bigg|_{\tau=0} = (Y_K^u - Y_K^r)\frac{dK_u}{d\tau} + \left(Y_L^u - \frac{Y_L^r}{1 - U}\right)\frac{dL_u}{d\tau}\bigg|_{U=\bar{U}} - Y_L^r L_u \frac{dx}{d\tau}$$

$$= -Y_L^r L_u \frac{dx}{d\tau} > 0.$$

A wage subsidy increases national income.

Aggregate Savings, the Distribution of Income and Labor Migration

The traditional development literature has focused on the effect of employment on the distribution of income and, hence, on the level of aggregate savings; even if the opportunity cost of labor were zero, it has been argued, the shadow price of labor is positive. Whatever is paid out in wages is consumed, and therefore not available for investment. Thus, an increase in employment lowers savings and, since the shadow price of savings exceeds that of consumption, the shadow price of labor exceeds its direct opportunity costs. But in the labor-migration model we have formulated, hiring one additional worker has absolutely no effect on the total income of workers, provided the rural wage does not change. For total wages are equal to rural wages plus urban wages:

$$W = w_r L_r + w_u L_u$$

but expected urban wages equal rural wages,

$$\frac{w_u L_u}{N_u} = w_r.$$

Substituting, we obtain

$$W = w_r(L_r + N_u) = w_r \bar{L}.$$

The only effect on consumption of hiring more workers arises through the effect on rural wages. Thus, not only has the traditional model underestimated the opportunity cost of labor, it has overestimated the importance of employment for aggregate savings. Obviously, if there is an increase in government employment, financed by a tax on private-sector profits, then there may be an important effect on investment and saving.

Extensions, Modifications and Alternatives

The models formulated in this chapter are highly idealized: yet most of the results appear to be quite robust. Among the extensions we have investigated are: (a) disaggregating the urban sector, allowing for the existence of a 'murky' urban sector, into which those in the urban sector who do not succeed in obtaining employment go (shoeshine boys and newspaper vendors); (b) disaggregating the labor market to allow for different skill levels; (c) disaggregating the rural sector to allow for rural manufacturing; (d) taking into account the evaluation of the nonpecuniary benefits (or costs) of urban versus rural living. None of these seems to have a serious effect on our analysis. The effect of the murky sector on shadow prices is negligible; the shadow price of skilled labor is even more likely to exceed its wage than for unskilled labor (even when the marginal skilled person is hired at an unskilled job). Allowing for rural manufacturing and taking into account amenity values, may have an effect on the elasticity of supply of labor from the rural to the urban sector (the former likely increasing it; the latter likely decreasing it), but leaves the analysis otherwise unaffected.

There are at least two other models of wage determination in LDCs which should briefly be mentioned. One of them is a variant of the models developed here – that where the wage affects productivity through morale effects (see Stiglitz, 1973b). Although the descriptive properties of such a model are similar to those analyzed here, its analysis is more complicated for two reasons: first, it is likely that the effort supplied by an individual is a function of his wage relative to the whole wage distribution and, thus, even when all firms are identical, there may be a whole wage distribution (not just a single urban wage); second, if the wage the individual receives relative to other wages affects productivity, it presumably also affects welfare and this needs explicitly to be taken into account. An individualistic welfare analysis of the kind employed here is not possible.

The other model is a variant of the Cambridge savings model, implicitly employed in much of the development literature. Assume investment $\bar{I}$ is fixed; a fraction s_π of profits (and none of wages) is saved; and the capital market in the urban sector is separate from that in the rural sector. Then, for savings to equal investment,

$$\bar{I} = s_\pi(F(L_u) - w_u L_u)$$

and, if firms are profit-maximizers,

$$F'(L_u) = w_u.$$

Thus, the savings equals investment condition and the wage equals marginal productivity condition jointly determine the urban wage and employment, independently of the rural wage:

$$\bar{I}^*/s_\pi = F(L_u^*) - F'(L_u^*)L_u^*,$$

$$w_u = F'(L_u^*).$$

If the equilibrium urban wage exceeds the rural wage, there is induced migration and unemployment. This model, although plausible in several respects, has one most implausible implication: the reason for the excessively high wage is insufficient investment (an excess of savings), which is contrary to what is usually assumed to be the case in most LDCs. Hence, if the government hires additional laborers in the urban sector, financed by a profits tax, the wage *falls*, unemployment is reduced and, indeed, the opportunity cost can be shown to be negative.

Concluding Remarks

This chapter has formulated several alternative models of the economy which lead to wage differentials (here, between the urban and rural sectors): unemployment acts as an equilibrating mechanism. The models analyzed here are perfectly competitive; indeed, in the first model (the efficiency wage–productivity model), there is no market imperfection; in the second, there is imperfect information, but in the welfare analysis we have contrasted how well the market economy does with the given information structure with how well a government-managed urban sector could do with precisely the same information structure. Yet the results of the models differ markedly from those of traditional competitive analysis; in particular, the market allocation lacks the usual optimality properties. Perhaps more important is the suggestion that our intuition, developed in the context of the first-best analysis of traditional competitive models, may go seriously awry in the analysis of the implications of alternative policies for dealing with unemployment. Our analysis has at least called into question the widespread presumption that in LDCs shadow wages are significantly lower than market wages for unskilled labor, and that a wage subsidy would be desirable.

Although we have focused our discussion on the implications of this class of model for LDCs, these models (particularly the efficiency wage–quality model) are equally applicable to more developed economies; there, they have important implications of macroeconomic policy and the optimality of the natural unemployment rate – questions we shall pursue elsewhere.

Appendix

We rewrite equations 6.57 and 6.58 as:

$$Y_K^r|\bar{K} - k_u L_u, \ \bar{L} - (L_g + L_u)x| = \rho^*$$

$$xY_L^r|\bar{K} - k_u L_u, \ \bar{L} - (L_g + L_u)x| = w^*$$

where, as before

$$x = \frac{1}{1 - U}.$$

Totally differentiating, we obtain

$$\begin{bmatrix} -Y_{KK}^r k_u - Y_{KL}^r x & -Y_{KL}^r L_u \\ -xY_{LK}^r k_u - Y_{LL}^r x^2 & Y_L^r - xY_{LL}^r L_u \end{bmatrix} \begin{bmatrix} dL_u \\ dx \end{bmatrix} = \begin{bmatrix} Y_{KK}^r L_u \\ Y_{LK}^r L_u x \end{bmatrix} dk_u$$

$$+ \begin{bmatrix} Y_{KL}^r x \\ Y_{LL}^r x^2 \end{bmatrix} dL_g$$

so

$$\frac{dx}{dk_u} = \frac{x^2 L_u A}{A x K_u - Y_L^r(Y_{KK}^r k_u + Y_{KL}^r x)}$$

and

$$\frac{dL_u}{dk_u} = -\frac{L_u^2 A x - Y_{KK}^r Y_L^r L_u}{A x K_u - Y_L^r (Y_{KK}^r k_u + Y_{KL}^r x)}$$

$$\frac{dx}{dL_g} = \frac{-A k_u x^2}{A x K_u - Y_L^r (Y_{KK}^r k_u + Y_{KL}^r x)} < 0$$

$$A = Y_{KK}^r Y_{LL}^r - (Y_{KL}^r)^2 > 0$$

(by concavity of the production function). Hence, in the normal case where a wage subsidy increases urban employment ($dL_u/dk_u < 0$), it also decreases the unemployment rate. Similarly, an increase in L_g decreases the unemployment rate.

Chapter 6: Notes

This chapter represents a revision and extension of part of a paper originally written while the author was a research fellow at the Institute for Development Studies, University of Nairobi (1969–71) under a grant from the Rockefeller Foundation. Subsequent work on the paper has been supported by the National Science Foundation and the Ford Foundation. The author is indebted to his colleagues at the IDS for many helpful discussions; in particular he would like to thank G. E. Johnson and L. Smith. Part of that paper appeared as Stiglitz (1974c).

1 It is, of course, possible to have wage dispersion even without these differences among sectors; see Stiglitz (1974b; 1976a).

2 See, for instance, the labor-turnover model presented in Stiglitz (1974a).

3 A notable exception is Harberger's (1971) paper. Many of these earlier studies also argued that since the shadow price of investment exceeded that of consumption, and since hiring an additional worker increased the level of consumption, the shadow price of labor was positive, but less than its wage. The calculated changes in consumption were seriously in error, because they too ignored the effects of the policy on wages and migration. In one limiting case, where both the rural and urban wages remained unchanged, in the simple migration model of Harris–Todaro (1970) and Stiglitz (1974b) there is no change in the aggregate level of consumption; see below.

4 The purpose of this section is not to argue for the validity of the wage–productivity hypothesis, but rather to consider its consequences. For a further discussion of the model see Leibenstein (1957), Stiglitz (1976b) and Mirrlees (1975).

5 The morale interpretation has been discussed briefly by Stiglitz (1974c). If there were no unemployment, if all firms paid the same wage and if it were costly to monitor workers, all workers would shirk. The threat of being fired would not be effective; the workers could obtain an equally good job elsewhere. See Calvo (1979) and Shapiro and Stiglitz (1982) have explored a similar model.

6 The firm pays this wage, provided it can obtain labor at that wage; the implications of this qualification will be apparent shortly.

7 Alternatively, we can assume that the wage in the rural sector exceeds the efficiency wage. If workers in the urban sector remit funds to the rural sector, at a rate which depends on the wage differential, then the efficiency wage in the urban sector will depend on the rural wage; see Stiglitz (1974c). One of the essential differences between the labor-turnover model and the efficiency–wage model is that, in the former, turnover costs are a function of relative wages. In the model presented in the next section productivity at any firm is assumed to be a function of the wages paid by all other firms. The extension of the present model to a more general specification of the productivity function is left as an exercise for the reader.

8 For an extension of many of the results to a closed economy, see Stiglitz (1977).
9 The analysis can be easily extended to the case where the wage in the rural sector equals the average product; see Stiglitz (1981).
10 The notion that the unemployment rate would serve as an equilibrating device when factor prices did not adjust was presented in an appendix to Akerlof and Stiglitz (1969). The basic equilibrium condition 6.9 was also derived there. In Stiglitz (1974c) alternative derivations of 6.9 are presented and generalizations of 6.9 are considered and developed. To keep our focus on the central issue of alternative theories of wage determination, we shall employ the basic migration-equilibrium condition 6.9 throughout this chapter.

The application of this notion to LDCs is due to Todaro (1968) and Harris and Todaro (1970).
11 The model presented here is closely related to that of Stiglitz (1976a).
12 It should be obvious that the model may be considerably generalized without affecting the qualitative results; however, the form presented here is sufficiently general for developing the points we wish to raise.
13 There may, of course, be a wage distribution; see for example, Stiglitz (1976b).
14 The second-order condition assures that $\partial^2 \lambda_i / \partial w_i^2 < 0$. Although $\partial^2 \lambda_i / \partial w_i \partial \hat{w}$ may be positive, we assume the direct effect $\partial^2 \lambda_i / \partial w_i^2$ is larger in absolute value.
15 Substituting 6.26 into 6.25, we obtain

$$\bar{\lambda}(w_u, N_u) F' \left(\bar{\lambda}(w_u, N_u) \frac{w_r N_u}{w_u} \right) = w_u$$

Differentiating, we obtain 6.30.
16 In general those who have the lowest reservation wage need not be the first to migrate, if there is any uncertainty about obtaining employment, since individuals of different abilities may have different attitudes towards risk.

17
$$B' = \frac{(\hat{b} - B)h}{H} \frac{d\hat{b}}{dN_u}$$

$$w_r' = \frac{d\hat{b}}{dN_u} = \frac{1}{Lh}.$$

18
$$\bar{\lambda}_{N_u} = \left[\frac{(a - A)h\phi}{H} - \frac{A\phi' w_i}{\hat{b}^2} \right] \frac{d\hat{b}}{dN_u}.$$

Hence the RHS of 6.37 is (using 6.38)

$$1 \bigg/ \left[1 + \frac{(a - A)\phi}{A\phi} - \frac{\phi' w H}{\phi \hat{b}^2 h} + \frac{H}{hb} \right] = \frac{A}{a}.$$

19 Without loss of generality, we let $\lambda(w^*) = 1$.

Chapter 6: References

Akerlof, G. A. and Stiglitz, J. E., 'Capital, wages, and structural unemployment', *Economic Journal*, vol. LXXIX, no. 314 (June 1969), pp. 269–81.
Calvo, Guillermo, 'Quasi-walrasian theories of unemployment', *American Economic Review*, vol. 69, no. 2 (May 1979), pp. 102–7.
Calvo, Guillermo and Phelps, E. S., 'Appendix: employment contingent wage contracts', in Karl Brunner and Allan H. Meltzer, eds, *Stabilization of the Domestic and International*

Economy, Vol. 5, Carnegie-Rochester Conference Series on Public Policy, *Journal of Monetary Economics*, Supplement (1977), pp. 160–68.

Harberger, A., 'On measuring the social opportunity cost of labour', *International Labour Review*, vol. 103, no. 6 (June 1971), pp. 559–79.

Harris, J. E. and Todaro, M., 'Migration, unemployment and development: a two-sector analysis', *American Economic Review*, vol. 60, no. 1 (1970), pp. 126–42.

Leibenstein, H., *Economic Backwardness and Economic Growth* (New York: Wiley, 1957).

Mirrlees, J., 'A pure theory of underdeveloped economies', in L. A. Reynolds, ed., *Agriculture in Development Theory* (New Haven, Conn.: Yale University Press, 1975).

Salop, S. C., 'Wage differentials in a dynamic theory of the firm', *Journal of Economic Theory*, vol. 6, no. 3 (August 1973), pp. 321–44.

Shapiro, C. and Stiglitz, J. E., 'Equilibrium unemployment as a worker discipline device', (Woodrow Wilson School, Princeton University, 1982, mimeo.).

Stiglitz, J. E., 'Approaches to the economics of discrimination', *American Economic Review*, vol. 62, no. 2 (1973a), pp. 287–95.

Stiglitz, J. E., 'Alternative theories of wage determination and unemployment in l.d.c.'s: II. The efficiency wage model', Cowles Foundation Discussion Paper No. 357 (March 1973b), revised Oxford (January 1977).

Stiglitz, J. E., 'Theories of discrimination and economic policy', in G. M. von Furstenberg, ed., *Patterns of Racial Discrimination* (Lexington, Mass.: Lexington Publishing Co., 1974a), pp. 5–26.

Stiglitz, J. E., 'Equilibrium wage distributions', IMMSS Technical Report No. 154, Stanford University (1974b); forthcoming in *Economic Journal*.

Stiglitz, J. E., 'Alternative theories of wage determination and unemployment in L.D.C.'s: the labor turnover model', *Quarterly Journal of Economics*, vol. 88, no. 2 (1974c), pp. 194–227.

Stiglitz, J. E., 'Prices and queues as screening devices in competitive markets', IMMSS Technical Report No. 212, Stanford University (August 1976a).

Stiglitz, J. E., 'The efficiency wage hypothesis, surplus labor and the distribution of income in l.d.c.'s', *Oxford Economic Papers*, vol. 28, no. 2 (1976b), pp. 185–207.

Stiglitz, J. E., 'Some Further Remarks on Cost Benefit Analysis', in H. Schwartz and R. Berney (eds), *Social and Economic Dimensions of Project Evaluation*, (Inter-American Development Bank, 1977), pp. 254–82.

Stiglitz, J. E., 'The structure of labor markets in L.D.C.'s', in R. Sabot, ed., *Migration and the Labor Market in Developing Countries* (Boulder, Co: Westview Press, 1981).

Todaro, M., 'An analysis of industrialization, employment and unemployment in less developed countries', *Yale Economic Essays*, vol. 8, no. 2 (1968), pp. 331–402.

Todaro, M., 'A model of labor migration and urban unemployment in less developed countries', *American Economic Review*, vol. 59, no. 2 (1969), pp. 38–48.

Weiss, A., 'Job queues and layoffs in labor markets with flexible wages', *Journal of Political Economy*, vol. 88, no. 3 (1980), pp. 526–38.

7

Agricultural Development, Education and Innovation

MARK R. ROSENZWEIG

Introduction

Agricultural productivity is a significant determinant of the terms of trade faced by a country in international markets (Lewis, 1978) and agricultural development plays a central role in all scenarios of overall economic development. The most important agents of agricultural productivity gains are rural farmers, who, whatever the source of the technical advances, must utilize and adopt innovations in order for the technical progress to be embodied in realized output. An important question in the study of economic development is what characteristics of farmers, the new technologies and rural markets are associated with more rapid or more efficient transformations of technological advances into higher food productivity. A related issue is the income distributional consequences associated with technology adoption within the rural sector.

An important hypothesis, advanced by Nelson and Phelps (1966), Schultz (1975) and Welch (1970), among others, is that education serves to augment skills in allocating resources in settings in which information is scarce or costly to acquire, namely, in situations of change. This hypothesis has received support chiefly from empirical studies of US agriculture.[1] However, while a large number of studies of developing-country agriculture have looked at the roles of farmers' education in augmenting output, for given input levels (as summarized in Lockheed *et al.*, 1981) there have been few studies of technology adoption among LDC farmers.

The US studies would appear to suggest that among rural farmers the more educated would be the ones who would be the first to utilize any potentially available and profitable new technologies. Moreover, it would appear that if it is true that farmers with higher levels of education are more likely to be using the latest or most advanced (profitable) practices, the education-allocative skill hypothesis would be supported. In this chapter we show that both of these propositions may not be correct, even if we assume away relationships between education, risk-aversion, or preferences. It is demonstrated that, even if education does in fact lower costs of technology adoption, more educated farmers may be less likely than their less-educated counterparts to be using the new technology, and that the more educated farmers may be the 'innovators', even if schooling is not associated with higher dynamic allocative skills.

The source of the ambiguity characterizing the adoption-education association is the extensive participation by farmers in the labor market, an important but often overlooked characteristic of rural labor markets in developing countries in south Asia and Africa (Helleiner, 1975), as well as in the USA. As a consequence of the dual role of most farmers as agricultural decision-makers and as employees, it is demonstrated that the association between farmer innovation and farmer education will depend on the labor bias of the new technology, on credit-market characteristics and on the extent to which education reaps a return in the labor market. Because of the latter, the screening role of education, if any, can thus affect the observed correlation between education and resource allocations on the farm.

To ferret out the roles of education in adoption, we develop a model of farmer behavior in the context of a 'perfect' credit market, and then a segmented credit market. The model is used to show the necessary technology, labor and credit-market circumstances and information required for testing the hypothesis that education is *associated* with skills in allocating resources in a dynamic setting based on observations on farmer adoption behavior. As a byproduct of this analysis, tests for credit-market segmentation are also derived as are implications for the effects of wealth, farm scale and nonfarm earnings on innovation. We then demonstrate the conditions under which the hypothesis that schooling actually improves allocative skills can also be tested, based on the revealed schooling investment of farmers. In the last section of the chapter we examine empirically the adoption of new grain varieties by Indian farmers in the early stages of the 'green revolution'. The results suggest that the labor bias of the green revolution technology as well as the rewarding of education in the rural labor market masks a significant association between the education of farm wives and innovation, while evident credit-market segmentation accounts for a large proportion of the association between the schooling of the farmer and the likelihood of adoption. Finally, estimates indicate that Indian farmers behave with respect to schooling investment as if schooling improves allocative abilities where information is scarce and valuable.

Education and Technology Adoption: the Short Run

The technology adoption process in the short run is characterized by farmers with fixed levels of education E and ability μ, transforming a new set of exogenously provided innovations into realizable productivity gains. Let Z represent the resources – capital, information inputs utilized in adopting the new technology, γ the level of effective innovation used to augment farm production and I the rate of flow of new technologies. Then the farm-specific adoption function can be written as

$$\gamma = \gamma(Z, I; E, \mu), \ \gamma_i > 0, \ \gamma_{ij} > 0, \ \gamma_{ij} < 0 \quad i, j = Z, I, E, \mu \quad i \neq j.\,^2$$
(7.1)

In the green revolution case I could represent the rate at which new grain varieties become available, Z the resources expended in learning about and how to use them as well as new complementary inputs – fertilizer and irrigation facilities – and γ the package of new practices to be combined with conventional factors of production (land and labor) to produce farm output. It is assumed that (a) the greater the flow of innovations I, for given Z investments, the greater is the level of the productivity-enhancing innovation γ, and (b) increases in such investments make a given innovation flow more effective in augmenting output.

The hypothesis that education facilitates adoption of new technologies given available resources is represented by the positive cross partials involving E in expression 7.1. There are two difficulties in testing this hypothesis. The first is that the γ function is difficult to estimate directly, because of absent input information; inferences must be drawn, therefore, from measures of actual productivity gains or from price-conditioned alterations in factor-input use which reflect the behavior of the farmer. The second difficulty arises from farmer heterogeneity in inherent unobserved abilities μ, which may be correlated with schooling attainment. A positive correlation between schooling and ability may arise, for example even if schooling does not augment an individual's productivity, if it is known that schooling serves as an indicator to potential employers of the level of μ, as a 'screening' device. In the context of both US and Indian agriculture, in which at least one-half of farm operators receive off-farm earnings,[3] the operation of the market for labor skills is thus not irrelevant to the detection of on-farm educational productivity.

To see these points, differentiate 7.1 with respect to E:

$$\frac{d\gamma}{dE} = \gamma_Z \left(\frac{dZ}{dE} + \frac{dZ}{d\mu} \frac{d\mu}{dE} \right) + \gamma_E + \gamma_\mu \frac{d\mu}{dE}.$$
(7.2)

Expression 7.2 shows that the association between educational attainment and γ, or the productivity gains associated with γ (defined below), depend on the association of E with μ. Indeed, two extreme cases which are *observationally* identical are contained in 7.1; the first is characterized by schooling being totally unproductive but correlated with μ, that is,

$$\frac{d\gamma}{dE} = \left[\gamma_\mu + \gamma_Z \frac{dZ}{d\mu} \right] \frac{d\mu}{dE}.$$
(7.3)

In the second schooling and ability are uncorrelated, but schooling is productive:

$$\frac{d\gamma}{dE} = \gamma_E + \gamma_Z \frac{dZ}{dE}. \tag{7.4}$$

Expression 7.2 also indicates that the correspondence between the sign of the education–adoption association depends on whether more able (higher μ or E or both) farmers utilize more or less adoption inputs. It is thus possible that the association between farmer education and adoption will be quite weak or negative, even if the education cross partials in 7.1 are strong and positive if more able farmers use less adoption inputs.

Since the association between γ and E cannot evidently be used to ascertain whether education augments preexisting adoptive skills or is merely a proxy for innate ability, we first examine the conditions under which the association between farmer schooling attainment and technology adoption yields unambiguous information on the education *or* ability cross partials in the unobserved γ function, the 'structural' education effects, whatever their source. In the next section we then show how the extreme hypothesis embodied in 7.3, that schooling does not improve adoptive skills, can be tested.

Why might farmers with higher levels of schooling, if schooling is associated with greater efficiency in new technology adoption, tend to be less innovative? Is it possible that more educated farmers might be more innovative, even if there are no differences by E in adoptive efficiency? We now show with the use of a simple model that the answers depend on the labor 'bias' of the available technology, the roles of education in production (in addition to technology adoption) and the characteristics of the labor and credit markets.

Technology Bias and the Labor Market

Assume that on a typical farm the operator supplies time both to farming, and to the labor market, and that the planning horizon is two periods. In period 1, new technologies I become available which are then used, after transformation through 7.1, in production period 2. The present value of farm profits π over the two periods is given by

$$\pi = \Gamma(L_1, K; E, \mu) - L_1 W - pZ + \beta|\Gamma(L_2, K, \gamma; E, \mu) - L_2 W| \tag{7.5}$$

where $\beta = (1 + r)^{-1}$.

The Γ functions are assumed to have the usual Neoclassical properties, where L_i is farm labor time in period i, K is fixed farm size, W is the market wage rate, p is the price of the innovation input Z and r is the cost of capital.

Note that education E as well as the innovation variable appear in the second-period production function. For given γ, schooling may enhance or be associated with greater productivity of the labor and land inputs. There are thus two dynamic education roles: the dynamic-allocative role of education embodied in the adoption function 7.1, which relates chiefly to efficiencies in the decoding of new information and the acquisition of new inputs, and the managerial role which pertains to the allocation of traditional inputs in production, given the *new* technology package. As will be shown below, observation of farmer adoption behavior cannot distinguish between such roles; both, however, are important only in a dynamic setting. The package of new technology represented by the scalar variable γ may also alter the productivities of land and labor in addition to directly augmenting total output. The effect of the new inputs on labor productivity will be shown to play an important role in the association between schooling and adoption.

Initially, it is assumed that all future outcomes are known with certainty by both the farmer, and potential lenders of capital. Thus, r is independent of income or wealth and of the extent of borrowing; these latter assumptions are relaxed in the next section. Given labor-market participation, the intertemporal income constraint facing the farm is

$$F = \pi + W[(1 - l_i) + \beta(1 - l_i)] + V = x_1 + \beta x_2 \qquad (7.6)$$

where l_i is 'leisure' time in period i, and V is the discounted stream of nonearnings or nonfarm asset income.

Assume that the farmer maximizes utility over the two periods, given by 7.7,

$$U = U(l_1, x_1) + U(l_2, x_2) \qquad (7.7)$$

subject to 7.1, 7.5 and 7.6. The first-order conditions for an optimum are then

$$U_{x1} = U_{x2}\beta^{-1} = \lambda \qquad (7.8)$$

$$U_{l_1}\lambda^{-1} = U_{l_2}(\beta\lambda)^{-1} = W \qquad (7.9)$$

$$\Gamma_{L1} = \Gamma_{L2} = W \qquad (7.10)$$

$$\beta\gamma_z\Gamma_\gamma = p. \qquad (7.11)$$

Expressions 7.8 and 7.9 are the conventional two-period utility maximization conditions for 'dated' leisure time and consumption goods; expressions 7.10 and 7.11 are the conventional profit-maximizing conditions for labor-input use and for the optimal utilization of the innovation inputs, respectively. Because of the assumption that all goods (and capital used to finance innovation) can be bought and/or sold at a fixed price, input use is evidently independent of the preference orderings embodied in the utility function 7.7. Thus, both wealthy (high V), and poor (low V), farmers who are otherwise identical are equally efficient and innovative; with Z being used up to the point where the last discounted addition to second-period profit from increased technology adoption equals the price of Z. The production and consumption spheres are separable in this variant of the model.

As equation 7.2 indicates, the associations between E and γ depends in part on the relationship between education and the demand for the Z inputs utilized in adoption. Total differentiation of the first-order conditions 7.10 and 7.11 yields this relationship for the optimizing farmer, given by:

$$\frac{dZ}{dE} = -\Psi^{-1}\left[\Theta + \gamma_Z\Gamma_{L_2L_2}^{-1}\left\{\left(\frac{\partial W}{\partial E} - \Gamma_{L2E}\right)\Gamma_{\gamma L2} - \gamma_E(\Gamma_{\gamma L2})^2\right\}\right]$$
(7.12)

where

$$\Psi = \Gamma_{L_2L_2}^{-1}|(\gamma_{zz}\Gamma_\gamma + \gamma_Z^2\Gamma_{\gamma\gamma})\Gamma_{L2L2} - (\gamma_Z\Gamma_{\gamma L2})^2| < 0$$

and

$$\Theta = \gamma_{ZE}\Gamma_\gamma > 0.$$

Embodied in 7.12 are terms reflecting (a) the effects of both education, and the new technology on the productivity of labor time in second-period production, Γ_{L2E} and $\Gamma_{L2\gamma}$, respectively, (b) the association between the market wage received by the farmer and his schooling $\partial W/\partial E$ and (c) the first (γ_E) and second (γ_{ZE}) education partials of the adoption function 7.1. Two pathological cases are contained in 7.12. In the first assume that education is not associated with either higher productivity in agricultural technology adoption, or in production, but that more educated farmers receive higher wages in the market. Then, from 7.4, the relationship between γ and E is:

$$\frac{d\gamma}{dE} = -\gamma_Z^2\Psi^{-1}\Gamma_{\gamma L2}\Gamma_{L_2L_2}^{-1}\partial W/\partial E.$$
(7.13)

In this case the sign of the relationship between technology adoption and education will depend only on whether or not the technology is complementary to ($\Gamma_{\gamma L2} > 0$), or substitutes for labor time ($\Gamma_{\gamma L2} < 0$). If the latter characterizes the technology, more educated farmers would appear to be more 'innovative', but only because the new technology allows them to substitute away from farm production to work in better-paying off-farm employment, not because of higher adoptive efficiency. Thus, it is possible that educational differentials in technology adoption among US farmers exposed to mechanical innovations during the period 1920–50 may be much more evident than those observed among farmers in developing countries exposed to high-yielding grain varieties, because of the opposite labor bias characterizing the two technological innovations, not because of cross-cultural differences in the quality of schooling.

In the second extreme case assume that, for fixed farm size, use of the new technology leaves unaltered the marginal product of labor ($\Gamma_{\gamma L2} = 0$). Then 7.12 reduces to:

$$\frac{d\gamma}{dE} = -\gamma_2 \Psi^{-1} \Theta + \gamma_E \tag{7.14}$$

that is, the sign of the education–adoption association solely reflects the signs of the education (or ability) cross partials in the adoption function, differential skills in adoption.

An intermediate case, also yielding an unambiguous relationship between the sign of $d\gamma/dE$ and the cross partials in 7.1, is one in which either (a) schooling and labor productivity in production as well as wages are uncorrelated with schooling, or (b) both wages and labor productivity on the farm are increased by the same amount when schooling rises ($\Gamma_{L2E} = \partial W/\partial E$). Under these assumptions, 7.12 becomes

$$\frac{d\gamma}{dE} = -\gamma_Z \Psi^{-1} (\Theta - \gamma_Z \gamma_E (\Gamma_{\gamma L2})^2 / \Gamma_{L2L2}) + \gamma_E \tag{7.15}$$

which is positive if, and only if, education and adoption skills are positively associated.

In the absence of direct estimates of the 'effects' of education in production or in adoption, can unambiguous inferences be derived in the 'agnostic' case given by 7.12? Given that part of the ambiguity in 7.12, results from the wage–education association, parceling out this latter effect helps reduce the ambiguity. The wage–constant education–adoption relationship is given by

$$\left.\frac{d\gamma}{dE}\right|_{dW=0} = -\gamma_2 \psi^{-1} |\theta - \gamma_Z \Gamma_{L2L2}^{-1} (\Gamma_{L2E} \Gamma_{\gamma L2} + (\Gamma_{\gamma L2})^2 \gamma_E| + \gamma_E \tag{7.16}$$

The sign of 17.16 depends only on the sign of the effect of the new technology on the productivity of labor in agricultural production. If 7.16 is positive, then at least *some* of the dynamic efficiency 'effects' of education or γ_E must be positive whatever the sign of $\Gamma_{\gamma L2}$; education and adoptive or dynamic managerial efficiency must be positively associated. If education and both adoptive or productive efficiency are unrelated, as in the first pathological case, the wage–constant education–adoption association 7.16 (although not the gross association 7.12) will also be zero. Finally, if 7.16 is negative or zero, then $\Gamma_{\gamma L2}$ must be negative; the technology must be labor-replacing or else the hypothesis concerning adoptive efficiency must be rejected.

Equation 7.16 suggests that it is likely that no inference about the dynamic efficiency role of education can be made in the absence of knowledge of the technology *labor* bias. Fortunately, the direction of the relationship between the exogenous flow of innovations I and the demand for labor L_2, given by

$$\frac{dL_2}{dI} = \Psi^{-1}\Gamma_{\gamma L2}\left(\sigma\gamma_I + \frac{\gamma_{zI}\Gamma_\gamma}{\Gamma_{L2L2}}\right) \tag{7.17}$$

where

$$\sigma = \gamma_{zz}\Gamma_\gamma + \gamma_z^2\Gamma_{\gamma\gamma} < 0$$

corresponds to the sign of $\Gamma_{L2\gamma}$ and is independent of the roles of education. If 7.17 is positive – the technology increases the demand for labor – and the wage–constant relationship between education and adoption 7.16 is zero or negative, then the hypothesis that schooling and adoptive efficiency are positively associated can be rejected.

In summary, the simple association between farmer education and adoption can lead to erroneous inferences about the true efficiency effects of education, even ruling out ability bias, without accompanying information about the labor 'bias' of the new technology, and without knowledge of the associations between the market wages of farm operators and their education. Thus, whether in a given setting more educated farmers tend to more readily or extensively adopt new technologies will depend on the extent to which skills associated with education are rewarded in the labor market and on the type of technology made available to farmers.

Risk and the Cost of Capital

In this section we introduce more realistic capital market assumptions into the model and ascertain how the previous conclusions are altered. We also establish a test of credit-market 'segmentation'. Given that technology adoption is an investment process which consumes resources for deferred returns, the cost of capital to finance such investments is not an unimportant constraint on innovation. The uncertainties associated with weather variability and the evident absence of crop insurance mean that, even if the new technology leaves risk unaltered and information asymmetries are absent, any transactions costs associated with defaulted payments to lenders will make investments which are self-financed out of farm profits less costly than those financed through the credit market. Thus, the capital costs will not be independent of the farmer's income or of the size of the technology investment.

The (negative) association between income and financing costs creates an additional potential role of education in technology adoption not captured in the previous section. To the extent that education augments income independently of innovation, schooling attainment will be negatively associated with the capital costs of investments in new technologies. If, for example, more educated farmers receive higher wages in the labor market they would, *ceteris paribus*, have more (lower cost) funds with which to finance innovation.

Moreover, since realized income is a function of leisure (or *total* work effort = farm plus off-farm labor) which is conditioned by tastes, education may also influence innovation costs, through altering attitudes toward off-farm work. Note that this suggests that the presence of risk may result in a relationship between education, income and innovation, but not necessarily because education or income is related to farmers' attitudes toward or perceptions of risk. It is sufficient that market borrowing costs reflect risk (default losses) such that income and capital costs are correlated and that education affects labor–leisure choice.

To analyze the implications associated with relaxing the assumption that capital cost r is invariant to farmer characteristics and investment levels in the context of the model developed in the previous section, assume that the determinants of r are farm size, the farmers exogenously given financial or other assets, the farmer's wage and the amount of Z goods purchased, such that

$$r = r(Z, K, V, W) \; r_l < 0, \; l = K, V, W; \; r_2 > 0, \; r_{2l} < 0. \quad (7.18)$$

The assumption embodied in 7.17 that the level of r is a function of the exogenous variables determining income, rather than of realized income, simplifies the analysis by abstracting from the possibility that preference orderings condition capital costs by influencing labor supply. The critical assumptions are that for given amounts of investment Z true borrowing costs are lower for farmers with more assets and with higher-paying off-farm jobs and that such costs rise as the amount of investment in innovation Z increases. The problem of identifying whether schooling augments adoptive skills or merely reflects preference orderings with respect to risk and/or leisure is considered in the next section.

Maximization of 7.7 subject to 7.1, 7.6 and 7.18 yields first-order conditions 7.8 through 7.10 unaltered. The optimal level of Z, however, is given by:

$$\beta |\gamma_Z \Gamma_\gamma - \beta r_Z \pi'| = p. \quad (7.19)$$

Comparison of 7.19 with 7.11 indicates that there is an additional negative offset to the marginal gains to investment in Z, reflecting the rise in capital costs with increments to Z. Thus, the existence of exogenous production risk and transactions costs in credit markets reduces the level of innovation compared to a setting in which borrowing costs are independent of the source of financing.

The dependency of credit costs on farm resources and investment levels does not appreciably alter the wage-conditioned association between education and technology adoption; however, the education–adoption 'effect' inclusive of a wage–education correlation is affected due to the wage impact on the cost of borrowing. The effect of a wage rate change on the level of adoption γ, given by,

$$\frac{d\gamma}{dW} = -\gamma_z \Psi^{*-1} \left[\frac{\Gamma_{\gamma L_2}}{\Gamma_{L_2 L_2}} \gamma_z - \beta(\gamma_z \Gamma_\gamma r_W - r_z L_2 + \pi'(r_{ZW} - 2\beta r_z r_W)) \right]$$

(7.20)

where

$$\Psi^* = \Psi - 2 \cdot \beta^2 (r_z \gamma_z \Gamma_\gamma - \pi'(\beta r_z^2 - r_{ZZ})) < 0$$

and π' is second-period profit, consists of two additive effects: the first bracketed term reflects the interaction between the productivity of labor and the new technology (the factor 'bias'), and is negative (positive) if the technology is complementary to (substitutes for) labor; the second term embodies the wage–credit cost effects, of which all but the last term is positive. Thus, the inverse relationship between credit costs and income tends to make the wage effect on technology adoption more positive; as a consequence, the education association gross of the wage, if there is a positive schooling–wage association, can be positive even in the absence of adoptive efficiency effects or technology bias. Moreover, the greater the farmer's labor input L_2, the stronger is the (positive) credit component in the wage effect.

Because the wage rate–adoption association reflects both the technological factor bias, and any wage or income–credit relationship, a possible test for the latter can be performed if the direction of the labor bias can be established. We have already shown that the response of labor demand to the introduction of the new technology unambiguously reveals the sign of the labor bias, expression 7.17; it can be readily shown that this is true under the more general credit-market assumptions discussed here. Thus, if the new technology is labor-using, increases the demand for labor, but higher-wage farmers tend to exhibit higher levels of adoption, for given levels of schooling, the hypothesis that income and credit costs are independent can be rejected.

If the wage–adoption and labor–demand effects are not of the same sign, identification of credit–income effects from the wage rate relationship is not possible. However, confirmatory evidence can be obtained from the association between asset income and adoption, which can only arise as a consequence of credit–income association, as shown in:

$$\frac{d\gamma}{dV} = \gamma_z \Psi^{*-1} \beta | r_V \gamma_z \Gamma_\gamma + \pi'(r_{ZV} + 2\beta r_V r_z) |.$$

(7.21)

Expression 7.21 also indicates that wealthier farmers would be greater 'innovators' if, and only if, the credit cost increases associated with incremental investments in technology adoption are sharply curtailed by increases in the availability of own funds; if $|r_{ZV}| > |2(1 + r)^{-1} r_V r_Z|$.

While, as expression 7.21 shows, the profit-maximizing level of adoption and other resource allocations within the production section of the farm household should not be influenced by the level of financial asset income, *unless* there are disparities in internal and market credit costs, the association between farm size K and the level of adoption γ reflects both credit-market characteristics and the underlying production technology. The relationship between farm size and γ is given by:

$$\frac{d\gamma}{dK} = -\gamma_Z \Psi^{*-1} \left[\gamma_Z \left(\Gamma_{\gamma K} - \frac{\Gamma_{KL2} \Gamma_{\gamma L2}}{\Gamma_{L2L2}} \right) \right.$$

$$\left. - \beta \left(\gamma_Z \Gamma_\gamma r_K + V_Z \Gamma_K + \pi'(r_{ZK} - 2\beta r_Z r_K) \right) \right] \quad (7.22)$$

and can be seen to depend on whether the new technology is land-using ($\Gamma_{K\gamma} > 0$) or land-saving ($\Gamma_{K\gamma} < 0$), on the labor bias ($\Gamma_{\gamma L2} \gtrless 0$), on the degree of complementarity between the fixed factor and labor ($\Gamma_{KL2} \gtrless 0$) and on the income–credit cost association. The farm-size–innovation association thus also differs according to the market and technological contexts in which new technologies are offered to farmers. This contextual ambiguity characterizing the relationship between farm size and innovation is reflected in the empirical literature on agricultural innovation. For example, Singh (1971) finds a positive association between farm acreage and an index of modernization, based on farm-level data from the Jaunpur district in India, while Mangahas, as reported in Nerlove and Press (1973), finds a significant negative effect of farm size on the adoption of high-yielding grain varieties in the Philippines. Finally, Huffman (1976) does not find any significant association between farm scale and allocative efficiency as reflected in the response of US farmers to changes in fertilizer prices.

Education and Technology Change: the Long Run

In the previous sections we have shown that the sign and magnitude of the gross or simple association between the schooling level of farm operators and the adoption of new technologies will vary (a) according to how well developed markets are both for skills associated with schooling and for credit, and (b) with the direction of technological labor bias. As a consequence, supplementary empirical explorations of the effects of technology change on the demand for labor and of wage rate and financial asset effects on technology adoption were shown to be required in order to isolate any association between the schooling of farmers and their efficiency in technology adoption and/or utilization. It was also demonstrated, however, that evidence of such an association cannot provide full support for the hypothesis that schooling actually improves dynamic allocative skills, only that more skilled adoptors are more educated or possibly less leisure-oriented.

In this section we seek to obtain a test of the causal relationship between educational level and allocative skill by examining farmer behavior in a longer-run context, in which the level of education can be altered in response to the flow of new technologies. The issue addressed here is whether it is possible to infer from the educational investment behavior of heterogeneous farmers expectations regarding the usefulness of schooling in allocating farm inputs in a dynamic environment.

Assume that farmers know with certainty all the efficiency effects, *if any*, of education in the adoption and utilization of new inputs and practices and can choose the level of education which maximizes utility over the (two-period) planning horizon. If the cost per unit of schooling is P_E, then the new budget constraint for the farmer is

$$F = \pi + W[(1 - l_1) + \beta(1 - l_2)] + V = x_1 + Ep_E + \beta x_2. \quad (7.23)$$

If, as in the first model, the discount rate is invariant to behavior, maximization of 7.7, subject to 7.1, 7.5 and 7.23, yields identical first-order conditions to 7.8–7.11 plus a first-order condition for the optimal investment in schooling,

$$\beta(\Gamma_\gamma \gamma_E + \Gamma_E) + (H_1 + \beta H_2)\partial W/\partial E = p_E \quad (7.24)$$

where $H_i = 1 - l_i - L_i$, that is, off-farm work in period i.[4] The right-hand side of expression 7.24 consists of two terms representing the potential sources of income gain associated with educational investment: from adoptive γ_E and managerial Γ_E efficiency and from market-wage $\partial W/\partial E$ effects. Because the level of off-farm work H_i or leisure chosen l_i affects the returns from educational investments rewarded in the market, the longer-run model is somewhat complicated, since the l_i enter the utility function. However, as this complication – namely, that preference orderings are not irrelevant to the returns to schooling – does not alter the predictions that can be derived from the model, we assume for simplicity that market labor supply is totally inelastic, consistent with the evidence (for males) from both developing and developed countries (Rosenzweig, 1980).

Will farmers' schooling investment response to the introduction of technical change reveal their perceptions about the productivity of education in facilitating technology adoption? First, consider, as before, the polar case in which schooling is assumed not to augment allocative skills (all cross partials involving education in the profit or adoption functions are zero), but higher wages are paid to the more educated. This may come about, for example, if those farmers who are more able find it less costly to attend school, so that employers can use schooling as an ability screen, or if schooling augments skills that are only useful in off-farm work. The effect of an exogenous change in the flow of innovations I on optimal schooling investment is then given by,

$$\frac{dE}{dI} = [\Gamma_{L1L1}\phi^{-1}(\gamma_Z\gamma_{ZI}\Gamma_\gamma - \gamma_I\alpha)]\Gamma_{L2\gamma}\frac{\partial W}{\partial E} = \Phi_1\Gamma_{L1L1}\phi^{-1} \qquad (7.25)$$

where $\alpha = \gamma_{ZZ}\Gamma_\gamma^2 + \gamma_Z^2\Gamma_{\gamma\gamma}$ and ϕ is the determinant of the relevant bordered Hessian matrix. As can be seen, exposure to technical change will influence the educational investments of farmers, even if schooling is expected to do nothing to facilitate the use of new technologies if education augments off-farm earnings $\partial W/\partial E > 0$. The direction of the effect, moreover, as before, depends on whether or not the technology displaces labor (the sign of $\Gamma_{L2\gamma}$), since the bracketed term in 7.25, from second-order conditions, is negative. Thus, if the technology substitutes for (complements) labor, optimal schooling investment increases (decreases) to equalize the productivity of labor time in farm and off-farm activities.

Schooling investment also responds to the pace of technical change, however, when education is expected to improve allocative abilities. To see this, assume that the technology leaves the marginal product of labor unaffected, $\Gamma_{L2\gamma} = 0$. In this case an increase in the rate of flow of new technology will unambiguously increase schooling, as can be seen from

$$\frac{dE}{dI} = -\Gamma_{L1L1}\phi^{-1}|\psi\Gamma_{L2L2}(\gamma_I\Gamma_{E\gamma} + \gamma_{EI}\Gamma_\gamma^2)$$

$$-\gamma_{ZI}\Gamma_\gamma\Gamma_{L2L2}(\gamma_{ZE}\Gamma_\gamma^2 + \gamma_Z\Gamma_{\gamma E})| = \Phi_2\phi^{-1}\Gamma_{L1L1} > 0. \qquad (7.26)$$

In the general case, given by

$$\frac{dE}{dI} = \Gamma_{L1L1}\phi^{-1}\{\Phi_1 - \Phi_2 - (\Gamma_{\gamma L2})^2|\gamma_Z\gamma_I(\gamma_{ZE}\Gamma_\gamma^2 + \gamma_Z\Gamma_{\gamma E})$$

$$+ \gamma_E(\gamma_{ZI}\Gamma_\gamma\gamma_Z - \gamma_I\alpha)| + \Gamma_{L2\gamma}\Gamma_{L2E}(\gamma_Z\gamma_{ZI}\Gamma_\gamma - \gamma_I\alpha)\} \qquad (7.27)$$

the results parallel exactly those pertaining to the education–innovation associations of the previous section, except that the educational *investment* responses cannot be due to skill heterogeneity. From 7.25, 7.26 and 7.27, it is easy to show that (a) if the technology is labor-augmenting, then from expression 7.25 $\Phi_1 > 0$, and 7.27 cannot be positive, unless education is expected (by farmers) to augment allocation productivity; (b) if the technology is labor-augmenting, schooling investments by farmers who allocate their time to the labor market could be lower where exposure to technologies is most rapid, even though schooling is useful in production; and (c) schooling investment will increase in response to *labor-replacing* technical change whether or not schooling enhances allocative skills.[5]

Empirical application: the 'Green Revolution' in India

The results of the last two sections indicated that as long as farmers have some attachment to the labor force, little can be learned about the allocative roles of education based on either farmer adoption or schooling investment behavior in an environment in which agricultural technical change is biased away from labor, as in US agriculture. On the other hand, unambiguous inferences can be made about the associations between education and allocative efficiency, as well as about farmers' perceptions of the worth of schooling in actually enhancing allocative skills where the technological innovations do not reduce the demand for labor. In such a setting it was shown that (a) if more educated farmers, *ceteris paribus*, tend to adopt the available innovations more readily, and (b) if farmers exposed to more rapid rates of technical change tend to increase their investments in schooling, then the hypothesis that schooling does not improve dynamic allocative skills can be rejected.

In this section we examine empirically the relationship between agricultural technology adoption and education in rural India during the early years of the 'green revolution'. The Indian setting is particularly ideal for studying the interactions between wage rates, credit markets, schooling and innovation for a number of reasons. First, the technology associated with the green revolution – based on the availability of new, higher-yielding seed varieties – is unlikely to be labor-saving, allowing a strong test of the education–innovation skill hypothesis. Secondly, a large majority of Indian farmers participate in the labor market – a 1971 nationality probability sample from rural India (Rosenzweig, 1982) suggests that over 65 percent of farm-operator households received wage or salary income, evidently because of the small size of Indian farms. Indeed, approximately 62 percent of Indian farms are less than 6 hectares; on these 77 percent of farmers receive wage or salary income. The extensive labor-market participation of Indian farmers thus allows the investigation of the role of the labor market in technology adoption.

A third feature of the Indian green revolution experience facilitating the identification of the role of schooling in technology adoption is that the Indian government introduced the technology selectively across Indian districts beginning in the early 1960s (1961–4). Thus, Indian households were exposed differentially to new agricultural practices in a close approximation to a natural experiment in which the rate of technology change is varied randomly across households. This programme, the Intensive Agricultural District Programme (IADP), however, was *not* randomly allocated; one district from each Indian state was chosen to receive technical assistance and supplies of the relevant inputs on a continuing basis according to governmental perceptions of potential 'success' (Evenson and Kislev, 1975). Any assessment of the behavioral effects of differential exposure to technological progress based on this programme's effects thus must take into account the selection criteria.

Tests of the roles of education in technology adoption will be performed using data from the third round of a national sample survey of 4,115 rural households in India, collected in three rounds during 1968–71 by the National Council of Applied Economic Research. These data are unique in providing information on a large number of socioeconomic characteristics of rural families, such as education and wage rates, as well as production information for farm households, including the use of high-yielding grain varieties. Moreover, the location of the households is provided, enabling the identification of those farmers exposed to IADP. The empirical analysis will proceed in the following order: first, we will discuss the treatments of the programme-selection problem which will be used in all the subsequent analyses. Next, we will ascertain if higher educational attainment is rewarded in the labor market, whatever the cause of these rewards, and whether the 'green revolution' technology, introduced in the early 1960s, reduced or increased the demand for labor. In the following section, we look at the determinants of technology adoption, with attention to the 'effects' of farmer's education, wage rates, farm size and nonlabor earnings. Finally, we compare the differential school-enrollment rates of farm and nonfarm households as functions of exposure to IADP in order to extract information on farmers' perceptions of the productivity of education during a period of technical progress.

Estimating Programme Effects

Before performing the analyses described, it is necessary to deal with the non-random selection of IADP districts. The following equations outline the problem:

$$IADP_t = X_1\beta_1 + u + \varepsilon_{1t} \tag{7.28}$$

$$Y_{t+10} = X_{2t+10}\beta_2 + bIADP + \mu + \varepsilon_{2t+10} \tag{7.29}$$

where $Y = \{\gamma, E\}$; cov $(\varepsilon_1, \varepsilon_2)$, cov (u, ε_i), cov $(u, x_i) = 0$. In equation 7.28 the selection of IADP districts at time t (1961–4) is based on a set of observed variables X_1 at time t, a vector of time invariant unobserved (to the investigator) random variables u and a period-specific random error term ε_1. Equation 7.29, technology adoption and schooling investment by farmers at time $t + 10$ (1971), is also a function of the unobserved u, the introduction of IADP and a vector of observed variables X_2 at time $t + 10$, in addition to a random error ε_2.[6] The problem in estimating the effect of IADP on adoption or schooling investment is that IADP is correlated with the unobserved u, that is, time-invariant district-specific factors such as climate, soil quality, farmers' attitudes toward change which influence technology adoption may have been used in part as the criteria for programme allocation. Thus, neither b nor the coefficient vector β_2 would be estimated consistently unless the programme-selection 'rule' 7.28 is taken into account.

Two estimation procedures are used to obtain consistent estimates of the β_2. In the first, variables representing the X_{1t}, are used to estimate 7.28. Predicted values of IADP based on these estimates are then employed in the adoption and schooling equation 7.29. In this procedure a dummy variable representing whether or not a district was selected for the programme was regressed against a set of district characteristics potentially influencing district choice extracted from the 1961 Indian Census and other data sources (see Rosenzweig and Evenson, 1977). The relevant variables could be found for sixty-eight of the eighty-eight districts represented in the survey data, including all eleven of the IADP districts.

Table 7.1 reports the results from these regressions, estimated using ordinary least squares (for the subsequent analysis) and maximum likelihood logit; where LAND = average landholdings (acres), DIST = the Kuznets ratio of landholding inequality, NLAND = proportion of households without land, IRR = percentage of land irrigated, PROD = rupee value of production per acre, FACTRY = number of factories per household, SCALE = proportion of factories employing ten or more workers, LITM(F) = male (female) literacy rate, rural population ages 15–44 and ENRM(F) = male (female) school enrollment rate (ages 5–14). The results suggest that districts with large factories and characterized by greater landholding inequality, but not higher levels of agricultural productivity, were selected for the programme. The IADP districts also appear to be characterized by marginally higher levels of irrigation and literacy rates, but by lower average holdings of land. While these results could be interpreted in a number of ways, it is only necessary for the purposes at hand that some of the set of 1961 district-level variables chosen influence programme allocation but not adoption; that is, belong in X_{1t} but not in X_{2t+10}, such as FACT and SCALE. The predicted values of IADP, based on the OLS estimates of Table 7.1 (which are consistent) will be orthogonal to the unobserved factor u, allowing consistent estimates of the determinants of technology and schooling investment.

A second estimation strategy which yields consistent estimates of the effect if IADP exploits the time invariance of the unobserved u and the fact that the programme, where introduced, did not exist prior to 1961. If the adoption or schooling equation 7.29 has the same structure in 1961 (when IADP = 0), then consistent estimates of the β_2 and b can be obtained by first differencing, that is, by estimating the equation

$$Y_{t+10} - Y_t = (X_{2t+10} - X_{2t})\beta_2 + b(\text{IADP} - 0) + \varepsilon_{t+10} - \varepsilon_t.$$

$$(7.30)$$

In using this 'fixed effect' estimation technique, both the β_2 and b in 7.29 can be correlated with the fixed effect u. However, the β_2 can only be estimated for variables which vary over time – during the period 1961–71. This procedure thus cannot be used to obtain estimates of the effects of the farmers' schooling attainment on adoption or on wage rates, since the schooling of adult farm operators is not likely to change in the ten-year period. However, schooling investment – enrollment rates of the young – can change before and after the introduction of IADP. The fixed-effect procedure employing measures of 1971

Table 7.1 OLS and Maximum Likelihood LOGIT Estimates:
Selection of IADP Districts,
1961 District Data

Independent Variable	OLS	LOGIT
LAND	−0·0108	−0·297
	(1·97)	(1·97)
DIST	0·0110	0·165
	(2·87)	(2·58)
NLAND	0·0023	0·0596
	(0·55)	(1·05)
IRR	0·0024	0·0208
	(0·97)	(0·72)
PROD	−0·0021	−0·0280
	(1·50)	(1·69)
FACTRY	0·906	8·830
	(2·95)	(2·52)
SCALE	0·060	0·682
	(4·43)	(2·95)
LITM	0·0027	0·0508
	(0·34)	(0·45)
LITF	0·0153	0·208
	(1·11)	(1·04)
ENRM	0·0032	0·098
	(0·59)	(1·12)
ENRF	−0·0103	−0·197
	(1·15)	(1·51)
Constant	−1·195	−23·51
		(2·59)
F	21·49	
χ^2		32·56
n	68	68

and 1961 enrollment rates as well as the two-stage procedure will thus be used (and compared) to discern whether farmers increased their schooling invest-ment in response to the introduction of new agricultural technologies through the IADP programme.

Wages Rates, Education and the Green Revolution

The extensive participation by Indian farmers in the labor market means that, as we have seen, the association between education and market earnings, if any, can importantly affect the relationship between education and adoption depending on the labor bias of the technology. Given some rewards paid to the more educated through the market, the direction of the technological labor bias will in part determine the direction of the association between education and innovation as well as optimal schooling investment in the presence of technology change. To ascertain both the labor bias, if any, of the technology associated with the green revolution, and if more educated rural workers receive higher market earnings, we estimate daily-wage functions for rural (farm and nonfarm) males and females aged 20–65 who participated in the labor market at any time during 1971, based on reported market earnings and market days worked. To correct for the potential selectivity bias arising from the nonmarket participation of some farm males (one-half of the sample farm households)[7] and some females (two-thirds of the total sample), the two-stage correction procedure suggested in Heckman (1979) is used. The wage-equation estimates are:

$$\ln W_M = 0.822 + 093\text{EDH} - 0.0008\text{AGE} + 0.040\text{POPVIL} + 0.225\text{FACTRY}$$
$$ (0.016) \quad\quad (0.016) \quad\quad\quad (0.006) \quad\quad\quad\quad (0.069)$$

$$+ 10.117\text{WEATHER} + 0.172\text{IADP} + 0.665\lambda \quad \bar{R}^2 = 0.255 \quad n = 732$$
$$ (0.055) \quad\quad\quad\quad (0.072) \quad\quad (0.100)$$

$$\text{S.E.E.} = 0.410$$

$$\ln W_F = 0.686 + 0.58\text{EDW} + 0.011\text{AGE} + 0.057\text{POPVIL} + 0.266\text{FACTRY}$$
$$ (0.034) \quad\quad (0.016) \quad\quad\quad (0.007) \quad\quad\quad\quad (0.079)$$

$$+ 0.031\text{WEATHER} + 0.092\text{IADP} + 0.483\lambda \quad \bar{R}^2 = 0.232 \quad n = 438$$
$$ (0.063) \quad\quad\quad\quad (0.61) \quad\quad (0.111)$$

$$\text{S.E.E.} = 0.372$$

where $\ln W_M (\ln W_F)$ = natural logarithm of male (female) daily wage rate, *EDH(EDW)* = schooling attainment, in years, for males (females), AGE = age, in years, POPVIL = total population of village, WEATHER = crops not adversely (1) or adversely (0) affected, IADP = *predicted* value of programme presence based on Table 7.1 equation, λ = inverse of Mills ratio based on probit market participation regression (see Heckman, 1979). These estimates indicate that (a) both men and women who have higher levels of schooling receive higher wage rates in the labor market, and that (b) for given worker characteristics, wage rates are higher where the 'green revolution' technologies were more intensively introduced. This latter finding is consistent with the hypothesis that the green revolution technology increased the demand for labor, is a labor-augmenting technology (equation 7.17). Both the education and programme effects on wage rates are significantly smaller for women than for men, however. Male wage rates increase by over 9 percent for each year of additional education, females by only 5.8 percent; male wage rates are over 17 percent greater where IADP was introduced, female wage rates are 9.2 percent greater.[8]

From expression 7.19, 7.12 and 7.16 of the model, the wage-rate results suggest that, *in the absence of credit-market segmentation*, (a) where wage rates are higher, the green revolution technology will be less profitable, if hired labor cannot be easily substituted for family labor and thus the technology will be adopted less readily, and (b) the gross education–adoption association will be less positive than the wage–constant education–adoption (partial) association and will only be positive at all if education is associated with higher adoptive and/or allocative efficiency.

Adoption, Education and the Market for Credit

In this section we look at the determinants of the adoption by farm households of green revolution high-yielding varieties to see if a positive association between education and innovation can be identified, to test for the importance of credit-market segmentation, and to ascertain if the labor bias of the green revolution technology affects adoption behaviour as predicted by the model. The sample of households used for this analysis consists of cultivating households residing in the sixty-eight districts with the relevant 1961 data and in which the heads were aged 20–65, a total of 1,082 'farm' households.

Because the measure of adoptive efficiency is dichotomous, taking on the value of 1 if high-yielding varieties (HYV) are used and 0 if not, we assume that the probability of using the new grains in the jth farm household P_j is determined according to the logistic function

$$P_j = (1 + e^{-a - \Sigma \beta_i x_{ij} + \varepsilon_j})^{-1} \tag{7.31}$$

where the x_i are the independent variables assumed to influence adoption and a and β are the parameters to be estimated. Equation 7.31 can be transformed into a linear equation in the x_i by solving for the natural logarithm of the odds ratio:

$$L = \ln(P_j/(1 - P_j)) = a + \Sigma \beta_i x_{ij} + \varepsilon_j. \tag{7.32}$$

The parameters in 7.32 can be estimated using maximum-likelihood techniques and will have desirable asymptotic properties.

The estimating equation determining the level of innovation, as measured by HYV use is:

$$L = a + \beta_1 EDH + \beta_2 EDW + \beta_3 LAND + \beta_4 NEARN + \beta_5 ELEC$$

$$+ \beta_6 BANK + \beta_7 AES + bIADP + \sum_{k=8}^{9} \beta_k WAGE_k + \varepsilon \tag{7.33}$$

where *EDH, EDW* are the schooling attainment levels (in years) of the farm head and spouse, representing the most important sources of farm labor, *LAND* is net cropped area; *NEARN* is household nonearnings income, and *ELEC, BANK* and *AES* are dummy variables which take on the value of 1, if the *village* in which the family resides is electrified, contains a bank or credit union, or contains an agricultural extension programme, respectively. The $WAGE_k$ are the predicted daily wage rates of the head and spouse based on the equations of the previous section and *IADP* is the predicted programme variable obtained from the estimates of Table 7.1.

Based on the prior analysis, segmentation of the credit market can be discerned from the coefficients of *BANK* and *NEARN*. The coefficient of the variable *BANK*, included to reflect regional differences in the cost of capital, would be expected to display a positive sign if the cost of credit significantly influences HYV adoption and bank credit is cheaper than loans obtained from informal sources. From equation 7.21, moreover, if self-financing is the cheapest source of credit, the coefficient of the nonearnings income variable *NEARN* should also be positive. Land size, from 7.22, should be positively associated with adoption as well, given the labor-using nature of the HYV technology and assuming that land and labor are complementary inputs, whether or not the credit market is segmented. The direction of the effects of the wage rates on adoption will depend, however, on the relative importance of credit segmentation (expression 7.20).

Of the other variables included in 7.33, *ELEC* is proxy for the price of an input complementary to innovation; Singh (1971) has noted that electricity, available to only a third of the households in the sample, is an important input for irrigation systems; given complementarities between irrigation and HYV, this variable should be positively associated with the adoption of the new grain varieties. The *AES* and *IADP* variables might be expected to have differential effects on the adoption of high-yielding varieties. The agricultural extension programmes had been in existence in India for several decades prior to the introduction of the high-yielding grains and thus may be associated with more traditional techniques. The IADP programme, however, was designed specifically to encourage use of nontraditional methods; it would be expected to significantly raise levels of HYV use.

Table 7.2 reports the estimates of three variants of the adoption equation 7.33. In the first column wage rates are omitted for comparison to the conventional or gross education–adoption estimates from other studies. In this specification, the coefficient of the male head's educational attainment is positive and statistically significant, while that of the head's wife's schooling level is very small and not statistically significant. As was shown, however, these education associations are biased, due to their evident correlation through the labor market with the omitted wage variables. The labor-using character of the HYV technology would suggest that the education coefficients are biased downward. However, the estimates in Table 7.2 also suggest the presence of significant credit-market segmentation: the presence of a bank in the village increases the probability of HYV adoption by 21 percent;[9] more importantly, farmers with greater financial as well as land wealth appear also to be significantly more likely to be innovators, suggesting that 'internal' financing is less costly than market capital. Because higher wage earnings are thus likely to be associated with lower investment costs, and higher wage rates make the adoption of labor-using HYV less profitable, the net effect of the wage on HYV adoption cannot be signed *a priori*.

Table 7.2   *Maximum Likelihood* LOGIT *Coefficient Estimates: Adoption of High-Yielding Varieties*

Independent Variables (Mean)	(1)	(2)	(3)
EDH (5·98)	0·198	0·092	—
	(3·27)*	(1·61)	
EDW (0·98)	0·094	0·213	—
	(1·20)	(2·17)	
EDH1	—	—	1·506
			(3·52)
EDH2	—	—	0·185
			(0·56)
EDH3	—	—	0·671
			(2·16)
EDH4	—	—	0·738
			(2·09)
EDW1	—	—	−0·070
			(0·13)
EDW2	—	—	0·611
			(2·86)
EDW3	—	—	0·139
			(0·29)
EDW4	—	—	−0·018
			(0·02)
LAND (11·31)	0·025	0·026	0·027
	(3·99)	(4·04)	(3·80)
WAGEM† (3·26)	—	0·097	0·080
		(5·93)	(4·73)
WAGEF† (1·95)	—	−0·187	−0·097
		(4·50)	(2·31)
NEARN x 10^{-3} (0·097)	0·452	0·455	0·218
	(2·47)	(2·31)	(1·95)
ELEC (0·32)	1·139	1·010	0·840
	(6·37)	(5·21)	(3·93)
BANK (0·64)	1·108	1·090	1·147
	(5·77)	(5·45)	(4·94)
AES (0·51)	−0·318	−0·296	−0·214
	(1·91)	(1·74)	(1·63)
IADP† (0·25)	0·517	1·002	0·951
	(2·86)	(4·11)	(3·46)
Constant	−3·219	−3·547	−3·954
	(13·30)	(11·73)	(10·11)
χ^2	155·14	201·38	178·70
n	1,082	1,082	836‡

*Asymptotic *t* ratios in parentheses.
†Predicted value; see text.
‡Random sample from 1,082 households; see text.

The predicted wage rates for the household head and his wife are entered in the specification reported in column 2 of Table 7.2. The coefficients of the education variables are altered significantly. With the wage rates included, the coefficient of the wife's education doubles in size and becomes statistically significant at the 1 percent level; that of the household head is more than halved and barely retains statistical significance. The differential biases are explained by the opposite signs of the head and wife wage effects on adoption – higher male wage rates are associated with a greater probability of adoption, while higher female wage rates are associated with a smaller likelihood of HYV use. Expression 7.20 of the model suggests that the evident dominance of the credit–wage effect for the household head compared to the wife may be due to the greater market participation of farm males – the magnitude of the (positive) credit–wage effect depends on the level of market labor supply, unlike the (negative) labor–cost component. Thus, given imperfect substitutability between family and hired labor, the labor-using nature of the green revolution technology appears to mask a significant association between the education of farm wives and agricultural innovation when the effect of education on wage rates is not taken into account. On the other hand, the lower finance costs faced by male farmers with high-wage off-farm employment opportunities evidently accounts for a significant proportion of the gross male education–adoption association.

Because the schooling–innovation association net of wage-rate effects may be nonlinear, in the third column the singulate years of schooling variables are replaced by dummy variables representing levels of schooling, where $EDH(W)1$ = completed primary education or below, but some schooling, $EDH(W)2$ = above primary but below matriculation, $EDH(W)3$ = matriculation or its equivalent and $EDH(W)4$ = college graduate or above. This specification, estimated on a random subsample of households from the 1,082 household sample in order to meet computational constraints, indicates that for males *all* but the schooling levels above primary but below matriculation contribute significantly and positively to innovation, with the initial schooling years providing the greatest effect. These estimates suggest, for example, that the probability that a farm has adopted HYV is 28 percent higher, if the farm operator has received some primary education than if he is totally unschooled, controlling for the wage effects of schooling. Moreover, farms with wives who have attained schooling levels beyond primary are 11 percent more likely to have adopted the new grain varieties, controlling for market wage rates. Of the other variables, farms in IADP areas and in villages with electrification are 17 and 15 percent more likely, respectively, to be using the HYV, while farmers exposed to a village-level extension programme (AES) are 4 percent less likely to have adopted the new technology.

Investment in Schooling and the Green Revolution

The results described in the previous section suggest that the level of innovation on Indian farms, measured by the adoption of high-yielding varieties, is positively associated with the schooling levels of the farmer *and* his wife, given wage rates and other variables representing costs and constraints on allocative activities. As demonstrated in the theoretical section, this result implies that allocative efficiency, but not labor-market screening, via labor costs or credit-market effects, is responsible for the observed relationship between education and innovation but does not rule out the possibility of schooling attainment being a proxy for 'innate' entrepreneurial ability. In this section the schooling investment test for this latter proposition is implemented by ascertaining if farm households in areas characterized by more intensive and continuous exposure to new farm inputs, that is, in IADP districts, respond by increasing the schooling of their children (male and female), as would occur if schooling was expected to enhance allocative efficiency in the absence of a technology bias (expression 7.26). Given the finding that the HYV technology is labor-using, a strong test of the hypothesis that schooling augments allocative skills is established, since, from 7.25, in the absence of these effects, schooling would be *less* profitable where such technologies are adopted. We also exploit another dimension of the data by simultaneously examining school investment behavior in *landless* or nonfarm households, who would not be expected to derive direct benefits from improved allocative skills in the presence of technical change.[10]

To investigate the determinants of schooling investment at the household level using the microdata, it is necessary to construct a measure of schooling investment which simultaneously takes into account differences in the size and age structure of households and the problem that not all children will have completed their schooling at the time of the survey. As one measure, based on child schooling attainment, the mean schooling levels by single years of age for boys and girls aged 5–14 in the total sample are computed. The schooling-age gradient is then used to standardize the schooling levels of children within each household. The measure obtained, which represents relative schooling investment EDI, computed separately for boys and girls, is given by:

$$EDI_{kj} = \sum_{i=1}^{nj} \frac{ED_{ixkj}}{\overline{ED}_{ixk}} \cdot n_j^{-1} k = m, f, x = 5 \ldots 14 \qquad (7.34)$$

where $\overline{ED}_{ixk}$ = the mean population schooling level of children of sex k aged x; ED_{ixkj} = the actual level of schooling attainment of child i of sex k aged x in household j; and h_j = the total number of children aged 5–15 in household j. EDI will be less (more) than 1, if a family schools any child (or all children) below (above) average levels, independent of age, sex-composition and number of children. The measure will be biased (toward 1) by the presence of any children who have not completed school but will reflect the higher school investment levels of the household, if these children are already at levels higher than the 'norm' for their age group.

To take into account the bias associated with district selection, we utilize both the two-stage procedure used in the adoption–regression equations which relies on the estimates of Table 7.1 and the fixed-effects technique described in equation 7.31. To utilize the latter, district-level enrollment rates for males and females aged 5–14 were computed for the sixty-eight districts represented in the household sample based on the 1961 Census data. These rates, divided by the relevant sex-specific mean rates for all sixty-eight districts in 1961, were subtracted from the sample, 1971 district-mean EDI indices for farm and nonfarm households and regressed against a dummy variable representing whether or not the district was in the IADP programme. Estimates of the IADP effects using the two-stage procedure were based on regression specifications similar to the adoption equation 7.33, except that the district-level child wage was also included as a 'cost' of schooling and in the nonfarm subsample, the farm-related variables ELEC and LAND are omitted. There are, thus, eight samples used in this analysis: two household-level subsamples consisting of farm households with at least one boy aged 5–14 or one girl aged 5–14 ($n = 615$ and 576, respectively), two nonfarm household subsamples with boys and girls aged 5–14 ($n = 264$ and 242) and four district-level 'samples' consisting of sixty-eight observations corresponding to the sex-specific enrollment rates in farm and nonfarm households.

The IADP coefficients for all subsamples estimated using ordinary least squares (OLS), the two-stage and the fixed-effect procedures are reported in Table 7.3. Table A in the appendix to this chapter contains all the coefficient estimates obtained from the farm and nonfarm household subsamples. The results indicate that whichever estimation technique is used, school enrollment rates appear to be significantly higher for both boys and girls in *farm* households exposed to the new grain varieties through the IADP programme. Male and female enrollment rates are 23 to 27 percent and 45 to 50 percent higher, respectively, as a result of the programme, despite the fact that the technology evidently increases the demand for farm labor and that schooling increases the value of nonfarm employment.

In contrast to the results for farm households, among landless households, when IADP district selection is taken into account, sex-specific enrollment rates are not significantly higher in areas subject to the flow of grain variety innovations, whether or not wage rates are 'held constant'.[11] Moreover, although the OLS estimate of the IADP effect on the school index of nonfarm boys is statistically significant and positive, *Wu* tests reject the hypothesis that

Table 7.3   *Effects of* IADP *on Schooling Investment in Farm and Nonfarm Households*

	Farm		Nonfarm	
Estimator	*Male*	*Female*	*Male*	*Female*
OLS	0·223	0·485	0·267	0·090
	(2·47)*	(5·58)	(2·13)	(0·53)
Instrumental Variables	0·269	0·509	0·133	0·043
	(2·47)	(6·88)	(0·82)	(0·19)
Fixed effect	0·226	0·451	0·077	0·149
	(2·48)	(5·21)	(0·56)	(0·76)

*t values in parentheses.

the IADP variable is uncorrelated with the residuals in all of the enrollment and adoption equations. The use of the two-stage and first-difference procedures is thus warranted. Evidently, it is the expected gains associated with allocative decision-making, which do not accrue to hired workers, which accounts for the greater schooling investment in farm families exposed to the new technologies. Finally, consideration of credit-market segmentation suggests that schooling investment on farms might be increased where technical change is most rapid in order to augment (wage) income and thus lower the costs of financing investments in innovation. However, the significantly smaller labor-market participation rates of females compared to males would suggest that the schooling investment response for males would be significantly greater than that for females, if credit motivations were dominant. The results in Table 7.3 reject this implication.

Concluding Remarks

This chapter has been chiefly concerned with identifying the characteristics of farmers which facilitate the development of agriculture through technology transfer. It was shown that the roles of farmers in most developing countries as both manager-entrepreneurs and employees could result in (a) the rejection of new (labor-using) technologies by more educated farmers, despite advantages of education in environments characterized by information scarcity, or (b) the ready adoption of (labor-saving) technologies by the more educated, in the absence of any allocative educational advantages, to better exploit nonfarm employment opportunities. Whether formal education appears to be a complementary input to the importation (as opposed to the development) of new technologies thus depends on rural-labor and credit-market characteristics as well as the input biases of the transferred technology.

Data from rural India, describing the period when imported high-yielding grain varieties were recently introduced, were used to test whether education is associated with costs of adoption. It was found that more-educated Indian farmers (and farms with more-educated farm wives), despite the labor-using nature of the technology and the positive returns to schooling in the rural nonfarm sector, did appear to adopt HY varieties more readily. Moreover, in areas exposed on a continuing basis to new hybrid seeds, farm but not nonfarm households appeared to increase investments in the schooling of their male and female offspring, to act as if there were a higher pay-off to education in a dynamic setting. This latter phenomenon suggests an overlooked distributional consequence of the 'green revolution'. The differential in the school investment response to flows of new techniques between farm households and rural nonfarm families, reflecting the confinement of dynamic allocative returns to agricultural decision-makers, implies that earnings inequality between landed and landless families may grow each generation if agricultural technical change persists, unless the returns to schooling also rise in the nonfarm sector.

Appendix

Table A   *Instrumental Variables Regression Coefficients: Male and Female Schooling Attainment Indices, Children Aged 5–14, Farm and Nonfarm Households*

Independent Variables	Farm		Nonfarm	
	Male	Female	Male	Female
EDH	0·283	0·223	0·333	0·360
	(8·91)*	(7·62)	(8·54)	(6·55)
EDW	0·208	0·201	0·058	0·095
	(4·58)	(5·24)	(1·16)	(1·36)
LAND	−0·0061	−0·0045	—	—
	(1·98)	(1·47)		
WAGEM†	−0·0052	0·0086	−0·0025	−0·0029
	(0·95)	(1·62)	(0·39)	(0·32)
WAGEF†	−0·0042	−0·022	0·0104	0·045
	(0·36)	(2·11)	(0·74)	(2·40)
WAGEC	−0·016	−0·0078	−0·134	−0·173
	(0·30)	(0·16)	(1·89)	(1·75)
NEARN x 10^{-3}	0·103	0·049	0·032	0·135
	(1·72)	(0·82)	(0·18)	(0·47)
BANK	0·091	0·102	0·0021	−0·218
	(1·21)	(1·41)	(0·02)	(1·50)
EDINST	0·250	0·196	0·088	0·191
	(1·69)	(1·49)	(0·47)	(0·80)
AES	0·091	0·057	—	—
	(1·19)	(0·77)		
IADP†	0·269	0·509	0·133	0·043
	(2·47)	(6·88)	(0·82)	(0·19)
Constant	0·226	0·065	0·454	0·346
$\bar{R}^2$	0·258	0·303	0·370	0·383
SEE	0·876	0·812	0·753	1·030
F	18·80	20·92	16·45	15·96
n	615	596	264	242

*t values in parentheses.
†Instrumental variable; see text.

Chapter 7: Notes

This paper has benefited from the comments of T. Paul Schultz and Finis Welch on a preliminary draft. Research support was provided by the US Agency for International Development under Order No. AID/otr-1432.

1 T. W. Schultz (1975) summarizes this literature.
2 Note that the process of technology adoption is independent of farm scale; the returns to such informational investments, however, may not be. See below.
3 Approximately half of US farm operators reported off-farm earnings in 1964 according to the 1964 *Census of Agriculture*. On Indian farmers, see below.
4 It is assumed, for simplicity, that education and the level of preinnovation output in period 1 are independent. All output gains thus accrue in the second period. This assumption does not affect subsequent results.
5 The positive association between school enrollment rates in US agriculture and technical change, reported in Rosenzweig (1977), may be due wholly to farmers' reactions to the labor-saving nature of the technology (Binswanger, 1975). Schooling investment is increased in this

context, not necessarily because of its value on the farm, but because education may enhance the prospects of 'redundant' offspring in nonfarm pursuits.

6 Some of the X_1 and X_2 variables may be the same.

7 The market participation rate of male farmers in the sample is lower than that for India as a whole, because the NCAER sampling scheme was designed to oversample large landowners. The participation rate of male farm heads, computed using the sample weights, is 65 percent; all empirical results are from the unweighted sample.

8 The premiums paid to educated rural workers appear to occur exclusively in nonfarm jobs, which are more likely to be held by the more educated. Restriction of the sample to agricultural wage workers, as in Rosenzweig (1980), reduces the education coefficients to insignificance.

9 The effect of a unit change in any independent variable x_i on the probability of HYV adoption can be approximated from the Logit parameter estimates by the formula $\delta P/\delta x_i = b_i(\bar{P})(1 - \bar{P})$, where $\bar{P}$ is the sample mean proportion of HYV-users.

10 Ram (1976) finds, on the basis of 1961 and 1971 farm data from 150 districts in India, that total output and value added are positively associated with the educational level of the farmer; neither measure is significantly related to the schooling of hired laborers, who are presumably not involved in allocative decisions.

11 The IADP coefficients obtained using the fixed-effect estimation technique may not be unbiased due to the omission of other time-varying variables, in particular wage rates. Work is now underway to construct district-level time series of sex-specific agricultural wages. However, it is not clear why any potential bias in these estimates should result in the differential farm and nonfarm IADP effects, which are also observed net of wage-rate differences using the two-stage technique.

Chapter 7: References

Binswanger, H. P., 'The measurement of technical change biases with many factors of production', *American Economic Review*, vol. 64, no. 6 (1974), pp. 964–76.

Evenson, R. E. and Kislev, Y., *Agricultural Research and Productivity* (New Haven, Conn.: Yale University Press, 1975).

Heckman, J., 'Sample selection bias as specification error', *Econometrica*, vol. 47, no. 1 (1979), pp. 153–61.

Helleiner, G. K., 'Smallholder decision-making: tropical African evidence', in L. G. Reynolds, ed., *Agriculture in Development Theory* (New Haven, Conn.: Yale University Press, 1975), pp. 27–52.

Huffman, W. E., 'Allocative efficiency: the role of human capital', *Quarterly Journal of Economics*, vol. 91, no. 2 (1977), pp. 59–79.

Lewis, W. A., *The Evolution of the International Economic Order* (Princeton, NJ: Princeton University Press, 1978).

Lockheed, M. E., Jamison, D. T. and Lau, L. J., 'Farmer education and farm efficiency: a survey', *Economic Development and Cultural Change* (1982, forthcoming).

Nelson, R. R. and Phelps, E. S., 'Investments in humans, technological diffusion and economic growth', *American Economic Review*, vol. 56, no. 3 (1966), pp. 69–75.

Nerlove, M. and Press, S. J., *Univariate and Multivariate Log-Linear and Logistic Models* (Santa Monica, Calif.: RAND publication R-1306-EDA/NIH, December 1973).

Ram, R., 'Education as a quasi-factor of production: the case of India's agriculture', Office of Agricultural Economic Research, Paper No. 76:12 (1976).

Rosenzweig, M. R., 'Farm family schooling decisions: determinants of the quantity and quality of education in agricultural populations', *Journal of Human Resources*, vol. 12, no. 1 (1977), pp. 71–91.

Rosenzweig, M. R., 'Neoclassical theory and the optimizing peasant: an econometric analysis of market family labor supply in a developing country', *Quarterly Journal of Economics*, vol. 94, no. 1 (1980), pp. 31–55.

Rosenzweig, M. R., 'Determinants of wage rates and labor supply behavior in the rural sector of a developing country', in H. Binswanger and M. R. Rosenzweig, eds, *Rural Labor Markets in Asia: Contractual Arrangements, Employment and Wages* (New York: Agricultural Development Council, 1982).

Rosenzweig, M. R. and Evenson, R. E., 'Fertility, schooling and the economic contribution of children in rural India: an econometric analysis', *Econometrica*, vol. 45, no. 5 (1977), pp. 1065–80.

Schultz, T. W., 'The value of the ability to deal with disequilibria', *Journal of Economic Literature*, vol. 13, no. 1 (1975), pp. 827–46.

Singh, S., *Modernisation of Agriculture* (New Delhi: Heritage Publishers, 1971).

Welch, F., 'Education in production', *Journal of Political Economy*, vol. 78, no. 1 (1970), pp. 25–59.

8

Uncertainty, Information and the Inflation Tax in Poor Countries

MARK GERSOVITZ

Introduction

Most literature on the inflation tax considers the effects of inflation occurring at a steady rate and with the perfect foreknowledge of market participants.[1] To the extent that variability in the inflation rate is discussed, it is usually considered indicative of monetary mismanagement. In this chapter I show that an unpredictable inflation tax may be optimal given the constraints on the revenue-raising powers and expenditure requirements of poor-country governments. This consideration affects the way in which inflation should be used to finance infra-structure, a recurrent topic in Arthur Lewis's writings most fully explicated in Lewis (1954).

The model assumes that the individuals in the economy derive satisfaction from the consumption of a private good and of a public good. The sole aim of government policy is to maximize the expected utility of the average consumer by providing the optimal quantity of the public good subject to certain constraints. The first restriction is that the government must plan its expenditure on the public good before the level of output is known, and it is costly but possible to deviate in either direction from this plan. This assumption is especially relevant to LDCs where much of government expenditure is on goods and services (Prest, 1972), generally involving projects of relatively long duration. This situation contrasts with the relative importance of transfers in developed-country budgets which, political opposition aside, are more easily adjusted than are the programs of LDC governments.

After the level of output is determined, the government raises revenue via an inflation tax and decides whether to adjust the level of government expenditure. Other methods of taxation have been excluded from the model[2] for analytical convenience, but could be incorporated, and would be set before the realization of income. This sequence emphasizes the fact that the inflation tax is undoubtedly the most easily adjustable form of taxation.[3]

The actions of the government in raising revenue in response to any realization of output lead to a corresponding rate of inflation. It is assumed that consumers know the random distribution of output and, therefore, the distribution of rates of inflation. Thus, consumers are rational in the sense of Muth (1961).

Given any distribution of inflation rates, consumers determine optimal holdings of real-money balances subject to a transactions technology. In deciding on the optimal distribution of inflation rates, the government takes into account this behavior of the average consumer.

Although consumers are rational, the government may still have an advantage over private agents in obtaining information about the occurrence of any particular state of nature. For instance, the government is likely to know first about surprise costs of government projects and consequent changes in the need for revenue. Similarly, the government may know the countrywide quality of a harvest before individual farmers. Any asymmetry of information means that the government can implement an increase in the money supply before consumers know the state of nature. An important and paradoxical result of this model is that the expected utility of the average *risk-averse* consumer can be higher, if the government can withhold information about the particular realization of income. Consumers are then left to make their decisions knowing only the distributions of income and the rate of the inflation tax. Particular examples are given where no information is better than full information. These results imply that *inflation may be more harmful when it is more predictable*.

A number of parameters influence the expected value and variability of the optimal inflation rate in this model. The most important are: the variability of output, the costs of adjusting government expenditure, the return on stores of value other than money and the dependence of utility on the two types of goods. The role of these structural parameters in determining the behavior of the rate of inflation lend support to a structuralist perspective[4] on inflation in LDCs, despite the traditional monetarist mechanism of price increase embodied in the model.

Section 1 of this chapter presents a brief overview of the salient features of Latin American inflation. Section 2 develops the formal model. Section 3 discusses the relationship between the parameters of the model and the behavior of the inflation rate. Section 4 addresses the issue of the optimal amount of information for the government to provide the private economy. Section 5 presents concluding remarks emphasizing the place of this chapter in the monetarist–structuralist debate.

(1) Quantitative Aspects of LDC Inflation

Before developing the theoretical model, it is worthwhile underlining the potential importance of the issues by examining some benchmark figures on average rates of inflation and the variability and predictability of the rate. Table 8.1 presents some statistics on the inflation rate[5] in a number of South American countries, and for comparison, the USA. Three facts emerge from this comparison:

(*a*)   As is well known, almost all these countries have experienced average inflation rates well in excess of the US rates.

Table 8.1   *Statistics on the Inflation Rate, 1950–77*

Country	Mean	SD	SE	SE/SD
US	3·49	3·01	2·47	0·82
Argentina	58·86	89·53	75·48	0.84
Bolivia	31·23	45·28	35·82	0·79
Brazil	31·09	19·36	11·05	0·57
Chile	80·61	122·65	57·59	0·47
Colombia	12·63	8·93	8·93	1·00
Ecuador	46·13	218·95	226·77	1·04
Paraguay	18·22	26·51	22·61	0.85
Peru	13·00	11·84	6·07	0·51
Uruguay	39·90	32·97	24·94	0·76
Venezuela	2·82	3·28	2·60	0·79

(*b*)   The variability of these rates has been much higher in these LDCs than in the USA. For several countries, the standard deviation of the inflation rate has exceeded the mean.

(*c*)   The predictability of inflation has also been much lower in some of these LDCs than in the USA. Column 3 of Table 8.1 gives the standard error of the regression of the inflation rate on a constant, inflation-lagged one period and inflation-lagged two periods. The ratio of the standard error to the standard deviation (column 4) is one measure of the fraction of variability that cannot be predicted by the simple ARIMA model. Ecuador provides a spectacular example of unpredictable inflation with the standard error exceeding the standard deviation (possible because the two calculations use different degrees of freedom).

The inflation equations were also estimated with inflation-lagged three years as an additional independent variable and with a first-order autocorrelation parameter. For most countries, neither of these additions was statistically significant. The picture presented in Table 8.1 is also consistent with the evidence presented by Logue and Willett (1976).

While the biggest contrast is between the USA and South American experience, there are also wide contrasts within the LDC group. Compare, for instance, the variability and predictability of inflation in Bolivia, Brazil and Uruguay where the average rate was roughly similar. The theoretical framework developed in this chapter provides hypotheses about why some countries may have opted for more variable rates of inflation. The model is also used to discuss the welfare implications of less predictable inflation.

(2) A Model of the Inflation Tax under Uncertainty

Output y_θ is assumed to be a random variable dependent on the state of nature θ occurring with probability π_θ. For simplicity, there are two states of nature, $\theta = 1$ and 2, and one representative consumer who acts as though he were one of many identical individuals. The representative consumer chooses x, the proportion of each period's output which is not marketed. The remaining amount of output is sold to private firms, which can costlessly store output, for the available money supply m_0 at price $p_{0,\theta}$. Therefore, the price level is given by

$$p_{0,\theta} = \frac{m_0}{(1-x)y_\theta}. \tag{8.1}$$

At the end of the period, the consumer spends the proceeds from the sale of $(1-x)y_\theta$ on repurchasing output from the storage firms. At this time, the government also makes purchases by printing additional money Δm_θ. The condition that total money demand equal the total value of supply determines the price at the end of the period $p_{1,\theta}$:

$$p_{1,\theta} = \frac{m_0 + \Delta m_\theta}{(1-x)y_\theta}. \tag{8.2}$$

The decision on how much output to reserve for home storage and how much to sell and repurchase is based on the trade-off between the costs of physical depreciation $\delta[x]$ and the inflationary loss of purchasing power. This notion is developed formally in what follows and is one representation of the many different ways that inflation causes individuals to incur real costs by reducing their use of money. Since the storage firms store output costlessly, the social optimum if lump-sum taxation could be substituted for the inflation tax would have x and $\delta[x]$ both zero. Real government revenue is given by

$$R_\theta = \frac{\Delta m_\theta}{p_{1,\theta}} = \hat{p}_\theta(1-x)y_\theta \tag{8.3}$$

where

$$\hat{p}_\theta \equiv (p_{1,\theta} - p_{0,\theta})/p_{1,\theta}.$$

The individual obtains utility from consumption of a public good g_θ, provided by the government and from consumption of a private good c_θ:

$$U_\theta = u[g_\theta] + v[c_\theta]. \tag{8.4}$$

The utility function is assumed separable to facilitate analysis but this assumption is not critical. Private consumption is given by

$$c_\theta = xy_\theta - \delta[x]y_\theta + p_{0,\theta}(1-x)y_\theta/p_{1,\theta}. \tag{8.5}$$

The first term represents the quantity of output which is not marketed. The second term gives total physical deterioration on storage of the nonmarketed part of output. The percentage rate of depreciation $\delta[x]$ increases with the percentage of total output which is withheld. The specific form of $\delta[x]$ used throughout this chapter is

$$\delta[x] = \delta_0 x + \delta_1 x^2/2 \tag{8.6}$$

with δ_0 and $\delta_1 > 0$. The final term of expression 8.5 gives the part of consumption made possible by repurchases at the end of the period and implicitly includes the effect of the inflation tax. Equation 8.5 can be simplified as

$$c_\theta = \{1 - \delta[x] - \hat{p}_\theta(1 - x)\}y_\theta. \tag{8.7}$$

The individual chooses x to maximize his expected utility given 8.7 and his information about y_θ, g_θ and $\hat{p}_\theta$. In this section I discuss two alternative assumptions about this information. The first assumption is that the consumer knows θ and, therefore, y_θ, g_θ and $\hat{p}_\theta$ when choosing x (*full information*). The alternative assumption is that the consumer knows only the probability distribution of θ, y_θ, g_θ and $\hat{p}_\theta$ when choosing x (*no information*).

With full information, the consumer chooses a different x conditional on each value of θ, x_θ, to maximize equation 8.4 subject to 8.7. The first-order condition is given by

$$v'[c](-\delta_0 - \delta_1 x_\theta + \hat{p}_\theta)y_\theta = 0 \tag{8.8}$$

so that, if $0 \le x_\theta \le 1$,

$$x_\theta = \frac{\hat{p}_\theta - \delta_0}{\delta_1} \quad \theta = 1, 2. \tag{8.9}$$

With foreknowledge, no cash balances are held unless $\hat{p}_\theta < \delta_0 + \delta_1$. Furthermore, there is a maximum amount of revenue which can be raised in state θ, independent of the revenues raised in other states of nature. Substituting from 8.9 into 8.3, and maximizing R_θ with respect to $\hat{p}_\theta$, yields

$$\hat{p}_\theta^* = \left(\frac{\delta_0 + \delta_1}{2}\right). \tag{8.10}$$

Thus, the revenue-maximizing rate of inflation is well defined for this transaction model. As is well known, this maximum revenue is given where the elasticity of money demand is one (Friedman, 1971).

Without any information on θ the consumer chooses one value of x to maximize

$$EU = E\{u[g] + v[c]\} \tag{8.11}$$

subject to 8.5 giving the first-order condition

$$E\{v'|c|(-\delta_0 - \delta_1 x + \hat{p})y\} = 0. \tag{8.12}$$

Equation 8.12 implies

$$x = \frac{E\{v'|c|(\hat{p} - \delta_0)y\}}{E\{v'|c|\delta_1 y\}}. \tag{8.13}$$

Under these conditions, $\hat{p}_\theta > \delta_0 + \delta_1$ does not imply $x = 1$. Only if $\hat{p}_\theta > \delta_0 + \delta_1$ for all states of nature, is it necessarily true that $x = 1$ and no money balances are held.

The contrast between the way x is determined under complete information and no information has important implications for policy. Variability in income and consequently in government revenues may be more easily dealt with if private agents have imperfect knowledge of θ. Consider a situation where a severe shortfall in income lowers the revenues from a given inflation rate and, in a more elaborate model, the revenues from other taxes. If individuals are immediately aware of the shortfall in income, x is determined by 8.9 and the maximum possible revenue may be quite low. Any attempt to raise increased revenue by an even higher $\hat{p}_\theta$ is defeated by individuals' movement out of real balances. Yet, the shortfall in revenues, by jeopardizing almost-completed projects, may have particularly severe effects.

Now consider a situation where the government is able to print money and spend it without individuals' having knowledge that a state associated with a high shadow price of revenue has occurred. A high $\hat{p}_\theta$ in one state is only partially reflected in state θ, because agents make money-holding decisions before a realization of the state, and at that stage, a particular state has only a probability of occurrence. Money balances decrease in all states as a consequence of the increase in inflation in any one state, of course, since decisions are made rationally. But withholding information about y_θ does give the government the opportunity to transfer inflation tax revenues across states of nature.

On the other hand, the withholding of information increases uncertainty from the individual's point of view and one might expect that this loss offsets the gains just mentioned when consumers are risk-averse. Recent literature on monetary policy and rational expectations (for instance, Barro, 1976) has concluded that it is optimal to reveal all information to private agents. Indeed, these authors view the revelation of information as a substitute for policy. Sections 3 and 4 of this chapter will demonstrate that it need not be optimal to reveal all information to the private agents.

The government maximizes the expected utility of private consumers through decisions made both before and after the realization of θ. The government commits itself *ex ante* to a project of size G. Once θ is known to the government, changes in the size of projects can be made, but only at a cost C which depends on the deviation of actual expenditure g from planned expenditure G. The cost of adjustment is given by

$$C = C|g_\theta - G| \tag{8.14}$$

where $C|0| = 0$, $-1 < C'|z| < 0$ for $z < 0$ and $C'|z| > 0$ for $z > 0$. Any choice of g implies a rate of inflation $\hat{p}$ via the government's budget constraint:

$$g_\theta + C|g_\theta - G| = R_\theta \tag{8.15}$$

and equation 8.3. This structure of the model represents the long gestation period of government projects with the need to raise revenues while the project is in progress.

If the private agents have full information, then G is chosen so that

$$\frac{\partial EU}{\partial G} = E\left(\frac{u'C'}{1 + C'}\right) = 0 \tag{8.16}$$

since $dc_\theta/dx_\theta = 0$ from 8.8. Because $u' > 0$, this condition requires C' to be positive in one state and negative in the other, so that g_θ exceeds planned G in one state and falls short of it in the other state. The additional first-order con-ditions are

$$\frac{\partial EU}{\partial \hat{p}_1} = \pi_1 y_1 \left\{ \frac{u'}{1 + C'} \left((1 - x_1) - \hat{p}_1 \frac{\partial x_1}{\partial \hat{p}_1} \right) - v'(1 - x_1) \right\}_{\theta=1} = 0 \tag{8.17}$$

and

$$\frac{\partial EU}{\partial \hat{p}_2} = (1 - \pi_1) y_2 \left\{ \frac{u'}{1 + C'} \left((1 - x_2) - \hat{p}_2 \frac{\partial x_2}{\partial \hat{p}_2} \right) - v'(1 - x_2) \right\}_{\theta=2} = 0 \tag{8.18}$$

where u' and v' and C' are evaluated at $\theta = 1$ and 2 in equations 8.17 and 8.18, respectively, as indicated at the end of the braces.

In the case where private agents have no information about the actual θ, the first-order conditions are given by:

$$\frac{\partial EU}{\partial G} = E\left(\frac{u'C'}{1 + C'}\right) = 0 \tag{8.19}$$

$$\frac{\partial EU}{\partial \hat{p}_1} = \pi_1 y_1 \left\{ \frac{u'}{1 + C'} \left((1-x) - \hat{p}_1 \frac{\partial x}{\partial \hat{p}_1} \right) -v'(1-x) \right\}_{\theta=1}$$

$$-(1-\pi_1) y_2 \left\{ \frac{u'}{1 + C'} \left(\hat{p}_2 \frac{\partial x}{\partial \hat{p}_1} \right) \right\}_{\theta=2} = 0 \tag{8.20}$$

$$\frac{\partial EU}{\partial \hat{p}_2} = -\pi_1 y_1 \left\{ \frac{u'}{1 + C'} \left(\hat{p}_1 \frac{\partial x}{\partial p_2} \right) \right\}_{\theta=1}$$

$$+ (1-\pi_1) y_2 \left\{ \frac{u'}{1 + C'} \left((1-x) - \hat{p}_2 \frac{\partial x}{\partial \hat{p}_2} \right) -v'(1-x) \right\}_{\theta=2} = 0. \tag{8.21}$$

Equation 8.19 implies, as did 8.16, that g_θ exceeds G in one state and falls below it in the other state. Equations 8.20 and 8.21 indicate the interdependence of optimal rates of inflation for each state of nature. This result contrasts with the independence of inflation rates implied by 8.17 and 8.18.

(3) Comparative Static Simulations

The model developed in the preceding section has the structure of an optimal tax problem (see, for instance, Sandmo, 1976). Agents maximize utility with respect to those variables directly under their own control, taking as given the variables under government control. This first stage of maximization yields a rule relating agents' decisions to variables under government control and to exogenous parameters. In the next stage, the government maximizes agents' utility with respect to those variables under government control, taking as given the behavior rule of agents determined in the first stage and the exogenous parameters.

Because this type of model embodies a two-tiered maximization process, the response of the endogenous variables to change in the parameters is generally very difficult to analyze. Comparative static propositions are quite rare in this literature and recourse is often made to simulation examples (for instance, Atkinson and Stiglitz, 1972). In this section I follow a simulation strategy to indicate possible responses of the average rate and variability of inflation to changes in the parameters of the model.

The utility function used in the simulations is:

$$U[g_\theta, c_\theta] = (g_\theta)^\alpha + (c_\theta)^\beta \tag{8.22}$$

where α and β are constants with $1 > \alpha > 0$ and $1 > \beta > 0$. The specific form of the investment adjustment function employed is

$$C[g_\theta - G] = A(g_\theta - G)^2 \tag{8.23}$$

where A is constant.

Tables 8.2–8.9 give the results of changes in eight parameters. Column 1 indicates the parameter which varies and the values it takes in the particular experiment. Those parameters which are held constant in any experiment take the values:

$$\pi_1 = 0.5 \qquad\qquad A = 0.1$$
$$\alpha = 0.5 \qquad\qquad \beta = 0.5$$
$$\delta_0 = 0.05 \qquad\qquad \delta_1 = 0.2$$
$$y_1 = \bar{y} - \sigma \qquad\qquad y_2 = \bar{y} + \pi_1\sigma/(1 - \pi_1)$$
$$\bar{y} = 30 \qquad\qquad \sigma = 10.$$

An increase in $\bar{y}$ results in a variance-preserving increase in the expected value of y_θ. An increase in σ results in a mean-preserving increase in the variance of y_θ. The heading labeled 'no information' indicates the results for the model of equations 8.13 and 8.19–8.21, and the heading labeled 'full information' gives the results for equations 8.9 and 8.16–8.18.[6]

The following observations can be made about these simulations:

(a)   In all cases, the expected utility of consumers is higher if they do not know the state of nature when deciding on a transactions strategy. This result is consistent with the theoretical results of section 4.

(b)   Decreases in π_1, σ and A all raise the expected utility of consumers.

(c)   Increases in δ_0, δ_1 and $\bar{y}$ all raise expected utility. This effect of an increase in δ_0 and δ_1, the parameters of depreciation on physical stores of value, may seem surprising but has a natural interpretation. Increases in the δ_i make consumers less willing to avoid the inflation tax and enhance the government's ability to provide public goods with less deadweight loss. This observation helps explain why governments undertaking inflation taxation also opt for the widespread interference with the holding of other assets characterized by Shaw (1973) and McKinnon (1973) as financial repression. If one interprets increases in the δ_i as increased repression, this behavior may well be optimal.

(d)   Increases in σ and A both increase the variability of the inflation rate, raising inflation in bad periods and lowering inflation in good periods. It is likely that σ and A are both relatively high in LDCs in comparison to developed economies, helping to account for the relatively high variability observed in LDC rates.

(e)   Increases in π_1 and β both lower the optimal inflation rate in both states of nature.

(f)   Increases in the δ_i and α raise the optimal inflation rate in both states. This effect of the δ_i can be explained as indicated in point (c), above.

(g)   Inflation is high in periods of low income and low in periods of high income. This result contrasts with the prediction of traditional Keynesian macroeconomics, and is an outcome of this chapter's emphasis on production uncertainty, stemming from such factors as the influence of

Table 8.2

Varying parameter $\bar{y}$	No information						Full information					
	EU	$\hat{p}_1$	$\hat{p}_2$	G	g_1	g_2	EU	$\hat{p}_1$	$\hat{p}_2$	G	g_1	g_2
25·000	5·9875	0·123	0·090	1·708	1·345	2·276	5·9810	0·106	0·100	1·598	1·123	2·535
30·000	6·6073	0·121	0·091	2·120	1·768	2·627	6·6004	0·106	0·100	2·002	1·503	2·915
35·000	7·1675	0·120	0·091	2·522	2·185	2·982	7·1605	0·106	0·100	2·398	1·883	3·293

Table 8.3

Varying parameter σ	No information						Full information					
	EU	$\hat{p}_1$	$\hat{p}_2$	G	g_1	g_2	EU	$\hat{p}_1$	$\hat{p}_2$	G	g_1	g_2
5·000	6·6886	0·112	0·097	2·238	2·045	2·469	6·6867	0·105	0·102	2·204	1·895	2·623
10·000	6·6073	0·121	0·091	2·120	1·768	2·627	6·6004	0·106	0·100	2·002	1·503	2·915
15·000	6·4610	0·132	0·085	1·912	1·440	2·757	6·4479	0·107	0·098	1·700	1·113	3·142

Table 8.4

Varying parameter π_1	No information						Full information					
	EU	$\hat{p}_1$	$\hat{p}_2$	G	g_1	g_2	EU	$\hat{p}_1$	$\hat{p}_2$	G	g_1	g_2
0·300	6·6642	0·123	0·097	2·197	1·784	2·433	6·6603	0·107	0·102	2·123	1·490	2·567
0·500	6·6073	0·121	0·091	2·120	1·768	2·627	6·6004	0·106	0·100	2·002	1·503	2·915
0·700	6·5054	0·119	0·080	2·004	1·742	3·028	6·4950	0·105	0·097	1·852	1·513	3·633

Table 8.5

Varying parameter A	No information						Full information					
	EU	$\hat{p}_1$	$\hat{p}_2$	G	g_1	g_2	EU	$\hat{p}_1$	$\hat{p}_2$	G	g_1	g_2
0·050	6·6112	0·115	0·095	2·126	1·676	2·771	6·6088	0·105	0·102	2·068	1·508	2·976
0·100	6·6073	0·121	0·091	2·120	1·768	2·627	6·6004	0·106	0·100	2·002	1·503	2·915
0·150	6·6048	0·126	0·087	2·118	1·829	2·537	6·5929	0·107	0·098	1·948	1·501	2·855

Table 8.6

Varying parameter δ_0	No information						Full information					
	EU	$\hat{p}_1$	$\hat{p}_2$	G	g_1	g_2	EU	$\hat{p}_1$	$\hat{p}_2$	G	g_1	g_2
0·025	6·5030	0·110	0·085	1·731	1·421	2·176	6·4983	0·097	0·093	1·651	1·225	2·400
0·050	6·6073	0·121	0·091	2·120	1·768	2·627	6·6004	0·106	0·100	2·002	1·503	2·915
0·075	6·7146	0·132	0·096	2·541	2·150	3·110	6·7052	0·115	0·105	2·377	1·807	3·459

Table 8.7

Varying parameter δ_1	No information						Full information					
	EU	$\hat{p}_1$	$\hat{p}_2$	G	g_1	g_2	EU	$\hat{p}_1$	$\hat{p}_2$	G	g_1	g_2
0·100	6·4845	0·074	0·058	1·545	1·258	1·957	6·4807	0·066	0·063	1·480	1·092	2·150
0·200	6·6073	0·121	0·091	2·120	1·768	2·627	6·6004	0·106	0·100	2·002	1·503	2·915
0·300	6·7210	0·166	0·119	2·729	2·321	3·325	6·7104	0·145	0·131	2·543	1·945	3·697

Table 8.8

Varying parameter α	No information						Full information					
	EU	$\hat{p}_1$	$\hat{p}_2$	G	g_1	g_2	EU	$\hat{p}_1$	$\hat{p}_2$	G	g_1	g_2
0·300	6·4057	0·097	0·068	1·913	1·643	2·301	6·4014	0·088	0·072	1·796	1·410	2·512
0·500	6·6073	0·121	0·091	2·120	1·768	2·627	6·6004	0·106	0·100	2·002	1·503	2·915
0·700	6·8674	0·126	0·103	2·154	1·708	2·795	6·8631	0·113	0·111	2·080	1·517	3·003

Table 8.9

Varying parameter β	No information						Full information					
	EU	$\hat{p}_1$	$\hat{p}_2$	G	g_1	g_2	EU	$\hat{p}_1$	$\hat{p}_2$	G	g_1	g_2
0·300	4·1389	0·128	0·111	2·114	1·665	2·855	4·1370	0·119	0·118	2·051	1·532	3·022
0·500	6·6073	0·121	0·091	2·120	1·768	2·627	6·6004	0·106	0·100	2·002	1·503	2·915
0·700	11·5219	0·077	0·050	1·657	1·462	1·901	11·5154	0·070	0·052	1·569	1·251	2·043

weather on agriculture. Any realistic attempt at formulating a complete picture of LDC macroeconomic behavior would have to synthesize both approaches.

The results of these simulations emphasize some important possibilities which need to be considered in assessing the inflationary experience of LDCs.

(4) The Optimal Amount of Information

Consider a situation in which the government can reveal or withhold information about the state of nature prior to the agent's choice of a transactions strategy (x). Using a somewhat restricted version of the model of section 2, I establish that it is optimal to conceal all information from the private economy. To begin this analysis, the amount of revenue R, which must be raised is assumed given and independent of the state of nature. This type of restriction could derive from a special form of $u(\cdot)$. Further, only differences between expected utility with complete information (EU) and without any information $(E\bar{U})$ about $\sigma = 0$ are considered. At $\sigma = 0$, $E\bar{U} = EU$ and all inflation rates and xs are equal and I derive conditions on the sign of $E\bar{U} - EU$ for σ slightly greater than zero. Finally, assume $\pi = 0.5$.

First, consider EU. Since R is given, 8.15 is irrelevant and the basic equations determining the $\hat{p}_\theta$ are 8.3 and 8.9, that is,

$$R = \hat{p}_\theta(1 - x_\theta)y_\theta \qquad \theta = 1, 2 \tag{8.24}$$

and

$$\hat{p}_\theta = \delta_1 x_\theta + \delta_0 \qquad \theta = 1, 2. \tag{8.25}$$

Further, EU is given by

$$EU = 0.5\{v_1[c_1] + v_2[c_2]\}. \tag{8.26}$$

For notational simplicity, Φ_θ is defined by $\Phi_1 = 1$ and $\Phi_2 = -1$ with $y_\theta = \bar{y} - \Phi_\theta\sigma$. The following results are valuable in subsequent calculations and follow from equations 8.7, 8.9 and 8.24–8.26, from $c_\theta \geq 0$ and from $\hat{p}_\theta \leq \hat{p}_\theta^*$ given by 8.10:

$$\frac{\partial c_\theta}{\partial x_\theta} = -\hat{p}_\theta y_\theta < 0 \tag{8.27}$$

$$\frac{\partial^2 c_\theta}{\partial x_\theta^2} = -\delta_1 y_\theta < 0 \tag{8.28}$$

$$\frac{\partial^2 c_\theta}{\partial x_\theta \partial \sigma} = \Phi_\theta \hat{p}_\theta \qquad \text{of sgn } \Phi_\theta \qquad (8.29)$$

$$\frac{\partial c_\theta}{\partial \sigma} = -\Phi_\theta \frac{(2\delta_0 + \delta_1^2 - \hat{p}_\theta^2)}{2\delta_1} \qquad \text{of sgn } -\Phi_\theta \qquad (8.30)$$

$$\frac{\partial^2 c_\theta}{\partial \sigma^2} = 0 \qquad (8.31)$$

$$\frac{dx_\theta}{d\sigma} = \frac{\Phi_\theta \hat{p}_\theta (\delta_0 + \delta_1 - \hat{p}_\theta)}{y_\theta \delta_1 (\delta_0 + \delta_1 - 2\hat{p}_\theta)} \qquad \text{of sgn } \Phi_\theta \qquad (8.32)$$

$$\frac{\partial}{\partial \sigma} \left(\frac{dx_\theta}{d\sigma} \right) = \frac{\Phi_\theta}{y_\theta} \frac{dx_\theta}{d\sigma} > 0 \qquad (8.33)$$

$$\frac{\partial}{\partial x_\theta} \left(\frac{dx_\theta}{d\sigma} \right) = \frac{\Phi_\theta}{\delta_1^2 y_\theta} \frac{(\delta_0 + \delta_1 - \hat{p}_\theta)^2}{(\delta_0 + \delta_1 - 2\hat{p}_\theta)^2} \qquad \text{of sgn } \Phi_\theta. \qquad (8.34)$$

These results imply that

$$\frac{dEU}{d\sigma} \bigg|_{\sigma=1} = 0 \qquad (8.35)$$

since $dv_1/d\sigma = -dv_2/d\sigma$ at $\sigma = 0$. It can be shown similarly that

$$\frac{dE\bar{U}}{d\sigma} \bigg|_{\sigma=0} = 0 \qquad (8.36)$$

and that

$$\frac{dx}{d\sigma} \bigg|_{\sigma=0} = 0 \qquad (8.37)$$

in the case where there is no information and $x_1 = x_2 = x$. Thus,

$$\frac{d(EU - E\bar{U})}{d\sigma} \bigg|_{\sigma=0} = 0. \qquad (8.38)$$

To sign $EU - E\bar{U}$ slightly away from $\sigma = 0$, it is necessary therefore, to sign $d^2(EU - E\bar{U})/d\sigma^2$.

Again consider $d^2v_1/d\sigma^2$:

$$\frac{d^2v_1}{d\sigma^2} = v_1'' \left(\frac{\partial c_1}{\partial x_1} \frac{dx_1}{d\sigma} + \frac{\partial c_1}{\partial \sigma} \right)^2 + v_1' \frac{d}{d\sigma} \left(\frac{\partial c_1}{\partial x_1} \frac{dx_1}{d\sigma} + \frac{\partial c_1}{\partial \sigma} \right). \quad (8.39)$$

Now

$$\frac{d}{d\sigma} \left(\frac{\partial c_1}{\partial x_1} \frac{dx_1}{d\sigma} + \frac{\partial c_1}{\partial \sigma} \right) = -\hat{p}_1 \frac{dx_1}{d\sigma} \left(\frac{(\delta_0 + \delta_1)(\delta_0 + \delta_1 - \hat{p}_1)}{(\delta_0 + \delta_1 - 2\hat{p}_1)^2} \right) < 0.$$

$$(8.40)$$

Similarly, the same expression as equation 8.40 evaluated at $\theta = 2$ is also negative. And since $v_\theta'' < 0$, $d^2v_\theta/d\sigma^2$ is negative and so is $d^2EU/d\sigma^2$ at $\sigma = 0$. Next consider $d^2\bar{v}_1/d\sigma^2$, where the bar again denotes no information:

$$\left. \frac{d^2\bar{v}_1}{d\sigma^2} \right|_{\sigma=0} = \bar{v}_1'' \left(\frac{\partial c_1}{\partial x} \frac{dx}{d\sigma} + \frac{\partial c_1}{\partial \sigma} \right)^2 + \bar{v}_1' \frac{d}{d\sigma} \left(\frac{\partial c_1}{\partial x} \frac{dx}{d\sigma} + \frac{\partial c_1}{\partial \sigma} \right).$$

$$(8.41)$$

Using equations 8.13 and 8.37, it can be shown that

$$\left. \frac{d}{d\sigma} \left(\frac{\partial c_1}{\partial x} \frac{dx}{d\sigma} + \frac{\partial c_1}{\partial \sigma} \right) \right|_{\sigma=0} = \left(\frac{\partial c_1}{\partial x} \right) \left(\frac{\partial c_1}{\partial \sigma} \right) \left(\frac{\hat{p}_1}{\delta_1 y_1} \right) \frac{\bar{v}_1''}{\bar{v}_1'}. \quad (8.42)$$

Substituting equation 8.42 into 8.41 and comparing this expression with 8.39 at $\sigma = 0$ shows that $d^2EU/d\sigma^2$ dominates $d^2E\bar{U}/d\sigma^2$ in absolute value. Therefore,

$$\frac{d^2(EU - E\bar{U})}{d\sigma^2} < 0$$

and, since $EU = E\bar{U}$ and $d(EU - E\bar{U})/d\sigma = 0$ at $\sigma = 0$, for a small σ $EU - E\bar{U} < 0$ and it is better to conceal information than to reveal it.

There are a number of important extensions of this result. First, the same result can be proved for unequal probabilities in a similar fashion. Secondly, R need not be given exogenously. The government could choose R (or G) before the realization of θ as in sections 2 and 3. Thus, G would maximize $EU = E(u |G| + v|c|)$. It would still be optimal to conceal *all* information, since it is optimal to do so for any given value of R. In particular, it would increase welfare to conceal information when choosing R^* the optimal R if information were not concealed. Of course, it may be optimal to choose an R different from R^* once the decision to conceal information is made, but this choice would only further increase welfare.

Thirdly, it can be shown by a similar argument that it is better to conceal *all* information about θ, even if the alternative is to reveal only a *little* information. (The government could provide partial information about θ via an indicator variable ϕ. If θ_i actually occurred, ϕ_1 could be announced with probability P_i and ϕ_2 with probability $(1 - P_i)$.)

Fourthly, it should be emphasized that this suppression of all information is optimal because information fulfills no other function than to allow agents to increase the expected deadweight loss of taxation. If agents could use information to make socially profitable decisions, then this result on the optimality of no information would require modification. For instance, early warning of bad weather might not only warn agents of a relatively high future need for revenue by the government, but might also allow an earlier harvest and higher output than otherwise. In this case there would be a trade-off determining an optimal amount of information via an indicator of the type just discussed.[7]

Finally, even within the model of this section, the result that no information is always optimal only holds about $\sigma = 0$. For a large σ, full information may dominate no information. Figure 8.1 can be used to discuss the global properties of this model. First, consider the situation of full information. Two rectangular hyperbolae between $\hat{p}_\theta$ and $(1 - x_\theta)$ are plotted for the different values of y_θ and represent the revenue constraint of 8.24, $\theta = 1, 2$. Equation

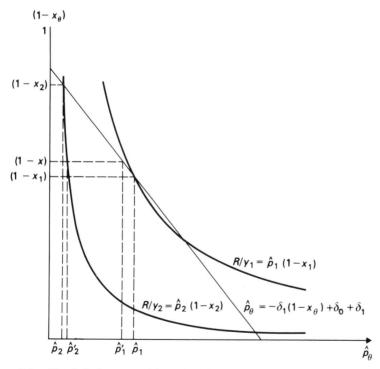

Figure 8.1   *The inflation tax with and without information.*

8.25 is transformed into

$$\hat{p}_\theta = -\delta_1(1 - x_\theta) + \delta_0 + \delta_1. \tag{8.43}$$

The line given by 8.26 cuts each of the hyperbolae twice, once from above and once from below. If the model generates an internal solution for both x_θ, the two upper intersections determine the x_θs and $\hat{p}_\theta$s. The lower intersections yield the same revenue but with higher $\hat{p}_\theta$s and deadweight loss. Note that the low-income state is associated with high inflation.

With no information, a common x-value is chosen according to 8.13. The value of $(1 - x)$ falls between $(1 - x_2)$ and $(1 - x_1)$. In this case the rates of inflation are $\hat{p}_1'$ and $\hat{p}_2'$, which are closer together than $\hat{p}_1$ and $\hat{p}_2$. Whether individuals are made worse off or better off by the concealing of information depends on their risk-aversion and the other parameters of the model. For instance, if individuals are so risk-averse as to act in the presence of uncertainty as though only the worse case were possible, then x would equal x_1, and the deadweight loss of storing $\delta[x]y_\theta$ would increase in state 2 and stay the same in state 1. Consumers would clearly be worse off under no information than under full information.[8]

(5) Conclusions

In the tradition of the inflation tax literature, this chapter has sought the motivation for inflation in the consequent transfer of real resources to the government. The particular contribution of this paper is its emphasis on the interaction of uncertainty with the government's need for revenues to maximize the utility of private agents. An important result is that the government should withhold at least some information on the current state of the economy from private agents. If secrecy is possible, the government can improve the welfare of the average *risk-averse* member of the private economy.

A number of important parameters which affect the average level and variability of inflation were identified. These parameters may vary from country to country and provide guidance on the factors causing different countries to opt for different patterns of inflation. It is in this sense that the chapter emphasizes a synthesis of the structuralist and monetarist approaches to inflation in LDCs. Although the mechanism by which inflation is generated is monetarist, the decisions of the government on the inflation rate are made in response to real factors determining the value and costs of the revenues collected through inflation. Indeed, even the policies of financial repression adopted by LDCs can be rationalized, at least on a theoretical level, as consistent with optimizing behavior. It would seem that any model assuming a government pursuing rational goals with rational means must incorporate some aspects of the structuralist school. On the other hand, it would be extreme to argue that all inflations have been motivated by the rational calculation of optimizing governments.

Chapter 8: Notes

I would like to thank R. J. Arnott, A. Blinder, P. Dasgupta, C. F. Diaz-Alejandro, J. Eaton, V. Shukla, and J. E. Stiglitz for very helpful comments on earlier drafts of this paper.

1   Recent work on the inflation tax includes: Auernheimer (1974), Barro (1972) and Friedman (1978). These papers provide a wide variety of references to the literature. An exception to the emphasis on certainty is the paper by Sjaastad (1976). In his paper the motive for uncertain inflation derives from an ability to systematically fool money-holders by sequentially varying the rate. Besides this reliance on irrational expectations, Sjaastad does not introduce any framework for making utility comparisons of different policies, nor does he consider the optimal provision of information by the public sector to the private sector.

2   Phelps (1973) provides an analysis of the inflation tax in a model with many alternative taxes.

3   This flexibility relative to other taxes is probably most pronounced in LDCs. Another alternative to the inflation tax which is neglected is borrowing by the government in financial markets. Once again, this option is less available in LDCs because financial markets are little developed. To some extent the restricted role of credit markets in LDCs is a result of inflation and the accompanying policies of financial repression (Shaw, 1973; McKinnon, 1973). But it would also seem that a lower level of development implies disproportionately smaller credit markets.

4   For a recent survey which includes a review of structuralism, see Kirkpatrick and Nixon (1976).

5   The inflation rate was measured as the annual percentage change in the CPI as reported in International Monetary Fund, *International Financial Statistics* tapes.

6   To solve for the equilibrium values of the endogenous variables for a given set of parameters, I used the maximization routine of Goldfeld, Quandt and Trotter (1966). All calculations were done in double-precision FORTRAN. Although no analytical proof of the uniqueness of equilibrium could be established, no examples of multiple equilibria were encountered.

7   Marshall (1974) and the authors cited by him discuss situations in which information can decrease traders' utility. This result obtains in the absence of future markets and arises because information, in effect, forces traders to participate in a lottery which need not exist. This result does not involve a deadweight response to taxation and is quite different from the mechanism discussed here. Weiss (1976) analyses situations in which the random taxation of individuals in an otherwise nonstochastic environment can decrease deadweight loss enough to raise expected utility. In his model there is less presumption that less information is better. And clearly his model cannot shed light on the transfer of revenues across states of nature allowed by the suppression of information.

8   A less extreme example is given by assuming that $v(c) = \ln c$. Let $\delta_0 = 0.03$ and $\delta_1 = 0.3$, $y_1 = 2.5$ and $y_2 = 3.5$, and $R = 0.2269$ the maximum revenue in state 1 with full information. Then utility with information is 0.9743 and without information is 0.9684.

Chapter 8: References

Atkinson, A. B. and Stiglitz, J. E., 'The structure of indirect taxation and economic efficiency', *Journal of Public Economics*, vol. 1, no. 1 (1972), pp. 97–119.

Auernheimer, L., 'The honest government's guide to the revenue from the creation of money', *Journal of Political Economy*, vol. 72, no. 2 (1974), pp. 598–602.

Barro, R. J., 'Inflationary finance and the welfare cost of inflation', *Journal of Political Economy*, vol. 70, no. 3 (1972), pp. 978–1001.

Barro, R. J., 'Rational expectations and the role of monetary policy', *Journal of Monetary Economics*, vol. 2, no. 1 (1976), pp. 1–32.

Friedman, B. M., 'Stability and rationality in models of hyperinflation', *International Economic Review*, vol. 19, no. 1 (1978), pp. 45–64.

Friedman, M., 'Government revenue from inflation', *Journal of Political Economy*, vol. 69, no. 3 (1971), pp. 846–56.

Goldfeld, S. M., Quandt, R. E. and Trotter, H. F., 'Maximization by quadratic hill climbing', *Econometrica*, vol. 34, no. 3 (1966), pp. 541–51.

Kirkpatrick, C. H. and Nixon, F. E., 'The origins of inflation in less developed countries: a selective review', in J. M. Parkin and G. Zis, eds, *Inflation in Open Economics* (Manchester: Manchester University Press, 1976), pp. 126–74.

Lewis, W. A., 'Economic development with unlimited supplies of labor', *Manchester School*, vol. 22, no. 2 (1954), pp. 139–91.

Logue, D. E. and Willett, T. D., 'A note on the relation between the rate and variability of inflation', *Economica*, vol. 43, no. 2 (1976), pp. 151–8.

McKinnon, R. I., *Money and Capital in Economic Development* (Washington, DC: Brookings Institution, 1973).

Marshall, J. M., 'Private incentives and public information', *American Economic Review*, vol. 64, no. 3 (1974), pp. 373–90.

Muth, J. F., 'Rational expectations and the theory of price movements', *Econometrica*, vol. 29, no. 3 (1961) pp. 315–35.

Phelps, E. S., 'Inflation in the theory of public finance', *Swedish Economic Journal*, vol. 75, no. 1 (1973), pp. 67–82.

Prest, A. R., *Public Finance in Underdeveloped Countries* (London: Weidenfeld & Nicolson, 1972).

Sandmo, A., 'Optimal taxation: an introduction to the literature', *Journal of Public Economics*, vol. 6, no. 1 (1976), pp. 37–54.

Shaw, E. S., *Financial Deepening in Economic Development* (London: Oxford University Press, 1973).

Sjaastad, L. A., 'Why stable inflations fail: an essay in political economy', in J. M. Parkin and G. Zis, eds, *Inflation in the World Economy* (Manchester: Manchester University Press, 1976).

Weiss, L., 'The desirability of cheating incentives and randomness in the optimal income tax', *Journal of Political Economy*, vol. 84, no. 6 (1976), pp. 1343–52.

Part Two

The Open Economy

9

Unequal Exchange in a Lewis-Type World

PRANAB K. BARDHAN

I

While thanks to Emmanuel (1972), 'unequal exchange' is by now a very popular expression in characterizing the nature of trade between rich and poor nations, its exact connotations have varied from one discussion to another.[1] In particular, its interpretations by Marxist (and neo-Ricardian) value theorists have often been quite different from those by development economists in the tradition of Prebisch (1950) and Singer (1950).[2] In this chapter I address myself to the question of unequal exchange in the sense in which it has been a persistent theme in the writings of Arthur Lewis, first, in his most well-known paper on unlimited supply of labor (1954), then in his Wicksell Lectures on tropical trade (1969) and then, again, in his recent essay on the international economic order (1978). The only way to explain the problem lucidly and briefly is to quote him:

> A farmer in Nigeria might tend his peanuts with as much diligence and skill as a farmer in Australia tended his sheep, but the return would be very different. The just price, to use the medieval term, would have rewarded equal competence with equal earnings. But the market price gave the Nigerian for his peanuts a 700 lbs. of grain per acre level of living, and the Australian for his wool a 1600 lbs. per acre level of living, not because of differences in competence, nor because of marginal utilities or productivities in peanuts or wool, but because these were the respective amounts of food which their cousins could produce on the family farms. This is the fundamental sense in which the leaders of the less developed would denounce the current international economic order as unjust, namely that the factoral terms of trade are based on market forces of opportunity cost, and not on the just principle of equal pay for equal work. (Lewis, 1978)

This idea has also the important corollary that so long as productivity in the food sector remains vastly different across nations, the problem of unequal rewards of labor in open economies is not a matter of the alleged unfavorable terms of trade for primary products *vis-à-vis* manufactures:

The terms of trade are bad only for tropical products, whether agricultural or industrial, and are bad because the market pays tropical
unskilled labor, whatever it may be producing, a wage which is based on
an unlimited reservoir of low productivity food producers ... If tea had
been a temperate instead of a tropical crop its price would have been
perhaps four times as high as it actually was. And if wool had been a
tropical instead of a temperate crop it would have been had for perhaps
one-fourth of the ruling price. (Lewis, 1978)

The fundamental question for Emmanuel, though couched in terms of a
different value theory, is ultimately very similar:

Are there really certain products that are under a curse, so to speak; or is
there ... a certain category of countries that, whatever they undertake
and whatever they produce, always exchange a larger amount of their
national labor for a smaller amount of foreign labor? (Emmanuel, 1969)

But while Emmanuel starts from exogenously given wages in two sets of
countries and considers the international transfer of value implied by
equilibrium production prices, our focus in this chapter, like that of Lewis, is on
the determination of the wage gap itself.

In order to press home his point, Lewis, first, in his 1954 paper, and somewhat more elaborately, in his 1969 paper, used a model which is remarkable
for its simplicity and clarity. It is a Ricardian constant–costs model with two
countries and three goods (only one of them – food – is commonly produced in
both countries), where productivity in the food sector acts as an ultimate determinant of the factoral terms of trade. It is clear, however, that the derivation of
his results in the model crucially depends on the assumption of constant costs
or the linearity of the transformation curve, and also that in a fuller general-
equilibrium re-formulation of his model he cannot ignore demand factors.[3] A
major purpose of this paper is to formulate a Lewis-type, two-country, three-
goods (with 'food' again as the commonly produced good) general-equilibrium
model, where demand plays an important role and transformation curves are
nicely concave to the origin. We attempt to show that even in terms of this
more general model the basic insight of Lewis, pinpointing the key role of food
productivity in determining factoral terms of trade and the relative inequality in
labor rewards between the two trading nations, remains valid. In particular, we
show that while productivity changes in t..e nonfood export (primary products
or manufactures) sector of the poor country are unimportant in influencing the
relative inequality of real rewards of labor between the rich and the poor
country, a productivity improvement (decline) in the food sector of the poor
country reduces (increases) this relative inequality. In section II we lay out the
basic model and in section III grind out the comparative-static results. In
section IV we briefly discuss aspects of productivity changes, not captured in
our model, which might also go toward explaining the unequal rewards

problem. In section V we go back to the Lewis explanation in terms of the low productivity of the food-producing sector in poor countries and try to place this, in the spirit of Lewis and particularly of Marx, in the historical perspective of the interaction of social classes and technology, of the 'relations of production' and 'forces of production' in poor agrarian economies.

II

There are two countries in the world. The rich country A produces 'food' (denoted by subscript f) and 'cars' (denoted by c), the poor country B produces 'food' and 'textiles' (or 'tea',[4] denoted by t). Consumers in either country demand all the three commodities, f, c and t. Country A exports 'cars' in exchange for imports of 'textiles' from B. Food is assumed to be neither exported, nor imported.[5] Labor is the only input in production, so that output is given by:

$$Q^j_i = A^j_i F_i(L^j_i), \qquad \begin{matrix} i = f, c, t \\ j = A, B \end{matrix} \qquad (9.1)$$

where Q is output, L is labor used, A is a multiplicative technical progress parameter, the superscripts refer to the country and the subscripts to the commodity. For simplification, we shall assume the F_i function to have a constant elasticity σ_i, with $1 > \sigma_i > 0$.

We do not directly talk about capital; stocks of capital are given in each sector (and, therefore, suppressed in our equations) and are immobile, both inter-sectorally and internationally. This is a deliberate departure from Emmanuel's model, where unequal exchange crucially depends on international mobility of capital equalizing profit rates. Our primary concern in this chapter is with the unequal labor rewards between a very rich country (say, the USA) and a very poor country (say, India) and it is well known that private capital inflow in a very poor country from rich countries is relatively small,[6] particularly in comparison with private foreign capital inflow in rich and middle-income countries. International migration of labor is also assumed away, but labor is mobile inter-sectorally.

We assume that in the poor country B food is produced on family farms, where income is shared and any labor not employed in the commercial textiles sector is residually absorbed on the family farm. The producers in the textiles industry maximize profits and the price they have to pay to hire labor is, à la Lewis, the value of the *average* product of labor on the family farm. We can, thus, write:

$$P_t A^B_t F'_t(L^B_t) = W^B = |P^B_f A^B_f F_f(L^B_f)|/L^B_f \qquad (9.2)$$

where P_t is the international price of textiles, P^B_f is the domestic price of food in country B. W^B is the textile wage rate in country B and single primes denote first derivatives.

Straightforward producer profit maximization in country A gives us:

$$P_c A_c^A F'_c(L_c^A) = W_c^A \tag{9.3}$$

$$P_f^A A_f^A F'_f(L_f^A) = W_f^A \tag{9.4}$$

where P_c is the international price of cars, P_f^A is the domestic price of food in country A and W_c^A and W_f^A are the wage rates in car and food sectors, respectively. In one variant of the model we would like to take into account a parameter for unionization of labor in the car industry (jacking up its wage rate) in the rich country, so that we write:

$$W_c^A = \gamma W_f^A, \ \gamma \geq 1. \tag{9.5}$$

In either country the total labor force, which is fully absorbed in the two sectors (no 'open' unemployment), is given. We ignore the effects of population growth.

In general the domestic demand for each commodity in either country is given by

$$D_i^j = D_i^j(P_t, P_c, P_f^j, Y^j), \qquad \begin{aligned} i &= f, c, t \\ j &= A, B \end{aligned} \tag{9.6}$$

where Y^j is national income in the jth country.

Now the commodity market equilibrium conditions:

$$D_f^B = Q_f^B \tag{9.7}$$

$$D_f^A = Q_f^A \tag{9.8}$$

$$D_t^B + D_t^A = Q_t^B \tag{9.9}$$

Equilibrium in the domestic food markets given by 9.7 and 9.8, coupled with Walras's Law ensures trade balance in the international markets; equilibrium in the traded textiles market, given by equation 9.9, ensures market equilibrium in the other traded good, cars. There are four commodity prices in the system, that is, P_t, P_c, P_f^A and P_f^B, that are to be determined by the three equilibrium conditions 9.7, 9.8 and 9.9. We shall set P_f^B equal to unity and let the other prices be determined by the system.

As the reader may have already suspected, unlike in the standard two-by-two model where there is in effect only one equilibrium equation, any comparative static exercise in our model is going to be quite cumbersome. In our pursuit for qualitative results, while keeping the operations manageable, we find it necessary to narrow down the specification of our rather general demand functions in 9.6. In particular, we use the following specific demand function for food and textiles in either country:

$$D_i^j = k_i^j |Y^j/P_i^j|^{e_i}, \qquad \begin{matrix} i = f, t \\ j = A, B \end{matrix} \qquad (9.10)$$

$$k_i^j > 0, \, e_i > 0.$$

This implies that income elasticity of demand e_i is constant and is equal to the (positively defined) *own* price elasticity of demand (so that, by a standard property of demand systems, cross-price elasticity is zero) in either country. While this is undoubtedly restrictive, it does not seem to throw away any of the most essential properties we want to preserve for the problem at hand.

III

Now to comparative statics. We want to find out the impact of variations in different parameters in the model on the relative real rewards of labor in the two countries. Let us define ω as the ratio of the wage (in terms of food) in the two countries, that is,

$$\omega = \frac{W_c^A/P_f^A}{W^B}. \qquad (9.11)$$

Note that we take money wages in the car industry in the rich country and the textile industry in the poor country and deflate them by their respective domestic food prices.

Logarithmically differentiating in equations 9.1–9.5 and using the full-employment conditions and after some standard manipulations, we get:

$$\begin{aligned}
\text{d} \log \omega = &-\alpha_1 \, \text{d} \log A_f^B - (1 - \alpha_1) \, \text{d} \log A_t^B + \alpha_2 \, \text{d} \log A_f^A \\
&+ (1 - \alpha_2) \, \text{d} \log A_c^A + \alpha_2 \, \text{d} \log \gamma - (1 - \alpha_1) \, \text{d} \log P_t \quad (9.12) \\
&- (1 - \alpha_2) \, \text{d} \log P_f^A + (1 - \alpha_2) \, \text{d} \log P_c
\end{aligned}$$

where

$$\alpha_1 \equiv \frac{(1 - \sigma_t)}{(1 - \sigma_t) + (1 - \sigma_f)(L_t^B/L_f^B)} \quad \varepsilon |0, 1|$$

and

$$\alpha_2 \equiv \frac{(1 - \sigma_c)}{(1 - \sigma_c) + (1 - \sigma_f)(L_c^A/L_f^A)} \quad \varepsilon (0, 1|.$$

Now we have to express the commodity prices in terms of the technical progress parameters (As) and the unionization parameter γ.

Logarithmically differentiating the price-determining market equilibrium equations 9.7–9.9, using the specific demand and production equations 9.10 and 9.1, respectively, solving for labor allocation in each sector from the full employment conditions and the factor price equations 9.2–9.5, and taking national income in either country as the value of total output of that country, we get after a lot of cumbersome derivations,

$$M \begin{bmatrix} d \log P_t \\ d \log P_f^A \\ d \log P_c \end{bmatrix} = b \qquad (9.13)$$

where M is a 3×3 matrix and $b = (b_1, b_2, b_3)$ is a column vector. The different elements of the M matrix are:

$$m_{11} = |\sigma_f(L_t^B/L_f^B)(1 - e_f) + e_f\{1 + (L_t^B/L_f^B)\}(1 - \Pi_f^B)|/q^B$$

$$m_{12} = m_{13} = m_{31} = 0$$

$$m_{21} = -[\sigma_t + e_t|(1 - \sigma_t) + (L_t^B/L_f^B)\{1 - \sigma_f(1 - \beta)\} - \beta(1 - \Pi_f) \\ \{1 + (L_t^B/L_f^B)\}|]/q^B$$

$$m_{22} = [e_t(1 - \beta)|-\sigma_c + \Pi_f^A\{1 + (L_c^A/L_f^A)\}|]/q^A$$

$$m_{23} = [(1 - \beta)e_t|-\sigma_f(L_c^A/L_f^A) + (1 - \Pi_f^A)\{1 + (L_c^A/L_f^A)\}|]/q^A$$

$$m_{32} = -m_{33} = -|e_f(1 - \Pi_f^A)\{1 + (L_c^A/L_f^A)\} + \sigma_f(1 - e_f)(L_c^A/L_f^A)|/q^A$$

The new terms used in describing the elements of the M matrix are Π_f^j, which is the share of the food sector in national income of country j, and β, which is the proportion of total textile output in country B that is domestically consumed, and q^B is $|(1 - \sigma_t) + (1 - \sigma_f)(L_t^B/L_f^B)|$, and q^A is $|(1 - \sigma_c) + (1 - \sigma_f)(L_c^A/L_f^A)|$.

The elements of the column vector b are:

$$b_1 = d \log A_f^B|(1 -)e_f\Pi_f^B\{1 + (L_t^B/L_f^B)\} - \sigma_t(1 - e_f)|/q^B - d \log A_t^B(m_{11})$$

$$b_2 = -d \log A_f^B|\sigma_t(1 - \beta e_t) + \beta e_t\Pi_f^B\{1 + (L_t^B/L_f^B)\}|/q^B \\ + d \log A_t^B|\{1 + (L_t^B/L_f^B)\}\{1 - \beta e_t(1 - \Pi_f^B)\} - \sigma_f(1 - \beta e_t)(L_t^B/L_f^B)|/q^B \\ + d \log \gamma \; |(1 - \beta)e_t|\sigma_c(1 - \Pi_f^A) - \sigma_f\Pi_f^A(L_c^A/L_f^A)|/q^A \\ - d \log A_f^A(m_{22}) - d \log A_c^A(m_{23})$$

$$b_3 = d \log \gamma \; |\sigma_f(1 - e_f\Pi_f^A)(L_c^A/L_f^A) + e_f\sigma_c(1 - \Pi_f^A)|/q^A \\ + d \log A_f^A|(1 - e_f\Pi_f^A)\{1 + (L_c^A/L_f^A)\} - \sigma_c(1 - e_f)|/q^A + d \log A_c^A(m_{32}).$$

The determinant of matrix M is

$$|M| = -(m_{11})(m_{32})e_t(1 - \beta) > 0 \qquad (9.14)$$

under the plausible assumption, which we shall make, that income elasticity of demand for food is less than unity.

Using Cramer's Rule, we get from 9.13:

$$d \log P_t = |M_1|/|M| \qquad (9.15)$$

$$d \log P_f^A = |M_2|/|M| \qquad (9.16)$$

$$d \log P_c = |M_3|/|M| \qquad (9.17)$$

where M_1 (M_2 or M_3) is the derived matrix of M with its first (second or third) column replaced by b.

Going back to equation 9.12 we shall now look at the impact on the inter-country relative real wage ω of changes in one parameter at a time. Let us, first, take changes only in the parameter A_f^B. From 9.12, 9.15, 9.16 and 9.17,

$$\frac{d \log \omega}{d \log A_f^B}|M| = -\alpha_1|M| - (1 - \alpha_1)|M_1| - (1 - \alpha_2)|M_2| + (1 - \alpha_2)|M_3|.$$
$$(9.18)$$

When only A_f^B changes,

$$|M_1| = -(m_{32})e_t(1 - \beta)|(1 - e_f \Pi_f^B)\{1 + (L_t^B/L_f^B)\} - \sigma_t(1 - e_f)|/q^B$$
$$> |M| > 0$$

and

$$|M_2| = |M_3|.$$

Putting these back in 9.18, it is easy to see that

$$\frac{d \log \omega}{d \log A_f^B}$$

is negative. In other words, *an improvement in productivity in the food-producing sector in the poor country reduces the inter-country real-wage inequality.*

Contrast this with the impact of an improvement in productivity in the nonfood exportable producing sector. From 9.12, 9.15, 9.16 and 9.17,

$$\frac{d \log \omega}{d \log A_t^B} |M| = -(1 - \alpha_1)|M| - (1 - \alpha_1)|M_1| - (1 - \alpha_2)|M_2| + (1 - \alpha_2)|M_3|.$$

(9.19)

When only A_t^B changes,

$$|M_1| = (m_{11})(m_{32})e_t(1 - \beta) = -|M|$$

and

$$|M_2| = |M_3|.$$

Putting these back in 9.19, it is easy to see that

$$\frac{d \log \omega}{d \log A_t^B}$$

is zero. In other words, *an improvement in productivity in the nonfood export-able producing sector in the poor country keeps the inter-country real-wage inequality unchanged.*

Take now the parameters relating to the rich country. Let us, first, change the parameter A_f^A. From 9.12, 9.15, 9.16 and 9.17,

$$\frac{d \log \omega}{d \log A_f^A} |M| = \alpha_2|M| - (1 - \alpha_1)|M_1| - (1 - \alpha_2)|M_2| + (1 - \alpha_2)|M_3|.$$

(9.20)

When only A_f^A changes,

$$|M_1| = 0$$

and

$$|M_3| - |M_2| = |M| = (m_{11})e_t(1 - e_f)(1 - \beta) > 0.$$

Putting these back in 9.20, it is easy to see that

$$\frac{d \log \omega}{d \log A_f^A}$$

is positive. In other words, *an improvement in productivity in the food-producing sector in the rich country increases the inter-country real-wage inequality.*

Again, the impact of an improvement in productivity in nonfood exportable producing sector in the rich country stands in contrast. From 9.12, 9.15, 9.16 and 9.17,

$$\frac{d \log \omega}{d \log A_c^A} |M| = (1 - \alpha_2)|M| - (1 - \alpha_1)|M_1| - (1 - \alpha_2)|M_2| + (1 - \alpha_2)|M_3|.$$

(9.21)

When only A_c^A changes,

$$|M_1| = |M_2| = 0$$

and

$$|M_3| = -|M| < 0.$$

Putting these back in 9.21, it is easy to see that

$$\frac{d \log \omega}{d \log A_c^A}$$

is zero. In other words, *an improvement in productivity in the nonfood exportable producing sector in the rich country keeps the inter-country real-wage inequality unchanged.*

Let us now change the parameter γ, representing the wage-enhancing power of unions in the car industry in the rich country. From 9.12, 9.15, 9.16 and 9.17,

$$\frac{d \log \omega}{d \log \gamma} |M| = \alpha_2|M| - (1 - \alpha_1)|M_1| - (1 - \alpha_2)|M_2| + (1 - \alpha_2)|M_3|.$$

(9.22)

When only γ changes,

$$|M_1| = 0$$

and

$$|M_3| - |M_2| = (m_{11})e_t(1 - \beta)|\sigma_f(1 - e_f \Pi_f^A)(L_c^A/L_f^A) + e_f \sigma_c(1 - \Pi_f^A)|/q^A > 0.$$

Putting these back into 9.22, it is easy to see that

$$\frac{d \log \omega}{d \log \gamma}$$

is positive. In other words, *the larger is the wage-enhancing power of unions in the car industry in the rich country, the larger is the inter-country inequality in real wages.*

At this point let us note that our real wages have been defined as money wages deflated by domestic food prices. This may be quite appropriate for the poor country, but for the rich country nonfood items may dominate the worker's consumption budget and one may like to take a different deflator. Suppose one continues to deflate the money wage in the poor country by its domestic food price, but decides to deflate that in the rich country by the price of the other produced good, cars, so that the relative real wage of the rich country is now

$$\bar\omega = \frac{W_c^A/P_c}{W^B}.$$

It can be shown from our basic results, that productivity improvements in the food-producing sector in the poor country reduce the inter-country real-wage inequality and that productivity improvements in the nonfood exportable producing sector in the poor country do not change this inequality, remain intact. Also remaining intact is the result in the case of changes in the unionization parameter. However, in this case a rise in A_f^A in the rich country reduces the real-wage inequality and a rise in A_c^A increases this inequality, in contrast to the earlier case.

In this chapter our focus is on real-wage inequality between the rich and the poor country, and not on the commodity terms of trade. But let us, in passing, note the changes in the commodity terms of trade with variations in different parameters in the model. The commodity terms of trade of the rich country are given by $T = P_c/P_f$. Since $\log T = \log P_c - \log P_f$, all we have to do is to solve for the two prices from 9.15 and 9.17. Evaluating $|M_1|$ and $|M_3|$ when only A_f^B changes, we can show after some manipulations, that

$$\frac{d \log T}{d \log A_f^B}$$

is positive. In other words, a productivity improvement in the (nontraded) food-producing sector in the poor country leads to a decline in its commodity terms of trade. However, when only A_f^A changes, we can show that

$$\frac{d \log T}{d \log A_f^A}$$

is positive under the sufficient condition that $1 \geq \gamma\sigma_f$. This suggests an interesting asymmetry. Productivity improvement in the (nontraded) food-producing sector in the poor country necessarily worsens its terms of trade, but a similar productivity improvement in the rich country does not necessarily worsen the latter's terms of trade and may, in fact, improve them.

There is again an asymmetry in the effects of productivity improvements in the nonfood exportable sector on terms of trade. When only A_c^A changes,

$$\frac{d \log T}{d \log A_c^A}$$

is unambiguously negative, but when only A_t^B changes

$$\frac{d \log T}{d \log A_t^B}$$

is not necessarily positive (it *is* positive for $1 \geq e_t$, that is, when the exportable of the poor country is an income-inelastic good) and may, in fact, be negative (if the income elasticity of demand for the exportable textiles is high and the proportion of output exported is small). Thus, a productivity improvement in the nonfood exportable sector necessarily worsens the terms of trade of the rich country, but a similar productivity improvement in the poor country does not necessarily worsen the latter's terms of trade and may, in fact, improve them. An increase in the wage-enhancing power of the unions in the exportable sector of the rich country, represented by parameter γ, is unambiguous: it necessarily improves its terms of trade, as emphasized in Prebisch-type models.

IV

Going back to our main issue of inequality of real wages in a trading world of two countries, our analysis in section III has yielded some results about the effects of technical progress (or lack of it) in different sectors. There are, however, some other aspects of productivity changes, not captured in our model, which may have important bearings for the problem at hand.

First, by assuming competitive commodity markets, we have ignored the impact on wage inequality of the market structure[7] often associated with technological changes. A large part of process innovations, and especially product innovations, are introduced in the market by companies in rich countries which enjoy monopoly rent from the new technology for varying lengths of time and there exist several legal institutions and other devices for protecting this rent for a sustained period. This monopoly rent, in which Big Labor in rich countries has a share, is continuously regenerated from one product cycle to another and is, thus, an important source of the wage gap between rich and poor countries.[8]

Secondly, by assuming labor to be the only variable factor of production, we have ignored the possible effects on wage inequality of differential technological gaps between rich and poor countries in industries with different capital intensities. Sectoral differences in capital intensity provide the starting point of a large part of current international trade theory.[9] The Heckscher–Ohlin–Lerner–Samuelson model, based crucially on these differences, puzzles out all the assumptions sufficient to yield the perfectly counterfactual result of full factor-price equalization between trading countries. Technological gaps between countries are ruled out by assumption in this model. It is, however, possible to introduce patterns of inter-country technological gaps in this model and derive results about inter-country wage gaps under free trade. Let us briefly illustrate. Retain all the assumptions of the standard 2 × 2 × 2 trade model, except that now country A is technologically more advanced than country B. Let us suppose the technological gap between A and B is wider in the labor-intensive industry than in the capital-intensive industry. If factor prices between the two trading countries were to be the same, the labor-intensive commodity will be relatively cheap in the more advanced country A. But under free trade, all commodity prices have to be equal between the two countries. So factor prices have to adjust: only by letting labor be more expensive in the more advanced country can the market under free trade keep the advanced country producing the labor-intensive commodity at the same post-trade price as the other country.[10] Thus, with this particular pattern of technological gap between the rich and the poor country, one can explain a consistent wage gap under free trade in an extended version of the standard model of trade theory.

One may pause to ponder how plausible is this presumption of the technological gap between the rich and the poor country being wider in the labor-intensive industries. Rigorous quantitative work on sectoral differences in production functions across countries is rather scanty, but there exists some econometric support for the presumed pattern of technological gap in Arrow *et al.* (1961), Diaz-Alejandro (1965) and Clague (1967). In a poor country usually the more 'modern' sector of the economy is relatively capital-intensive, the gap with the advanced country is relatively small, machines and blueprints in both countries embody relatively new technology, engineers working in this sector in both countries are probably trained at similar Institutes of Technology, and so on. Whereas the labor-intensive sector in the poor country is usually the 'residual' sector, the 'hold-all' for anybody who could not be absorbed elsewhere, it has a long 'tail' of inefficient enterprises peopled with the army of the 'diguised' unemployed scrounging for survival. In addition, this particular sectoral pattern of inter-country technological gap is perpetuated by transfer of technology through trans-national companies. Problems of private appropriability of benefits of technological improvements are usually more acute on labor-intensive production techniques and, hence, trans-national companies are more interested in developing and transferring technology to the more capital-intensive sector.

V

Let us now revert to the Lewis idea – confirmed by our model in sections II and III – of the key role of productivity in the food-producing sector in explaining the problem of unequal rewards of labor between rich and poor countries. This idea becomes particularly important when put in the historical context of movements in agricultural productivity in rich and poor countries. The present average level of agricultural productivity per man in most of Africa and Asia (representing the overwhelming majority of the world's poorest people) is considerably below the level attained by the rich countries, even at the start of their industrial revolution in the first half of the nineteenth century.[11] In recent years, particularly since the 1940s, productivity in agriculture has increased very rapidly in the rich countries, indeed noticeably faster than in their manufacturing industries. In contrast, average agricultural productivity has declined to some extent over the last half-century in the Afro-Asian poor countries. At the beginning of the 1970s, agricultural productivity in France was about twenty-five times that in India (not to speak of the USA, where it was more than eighty times that in India). The persistent and ever-widening wage gap has to be understood in this context.

If the root of the unequal rewards problem lies in the relative agricultural stagnation of poor countries, one has to understand the socioeconomic history of this stagnation and its causes. Simply to point the blaming finger at the indisputable technological fact of low agricultural productivity or to the equally indisputable demographic fact of high population pressure on land in poor countries is inadequate to the point of being misleading. Yet even to begin to do justice to the problem of explaining agricultural stagnation in these countries over, say, the last 100 years in terms of an interpretative framework that is sufficiently coherent and at the same time capable of handling the important variations from one country case to another, is clearly beyond the scope of the present chapter. It is, however, necessary to point out, at the risk of inevitably distorting oversimplification, that such an interpretative framework has to involve the prevailing mode of production, the social-class structure and the nature of class control of the state apparatus.

Over a long period, up until very recently, in most of these countries the predominant mode of surplus extraction in agriculture in the form of rent and forced labor was certainly not conducive to improvements in labor productivity. Any introduction of new methods and organizations of production, would have required more intensive management and supervisory efforts and surplus reinvestment than the frequently absentee landlords were prepared to make. Land was often just one low-risk item in their portfolio largely dominated by their other interests, in usury, trade, or urban professions. Given their social control over the agricultural population, they found it easier to squeeze surplus by means of rack-renting and extra-economic coercion, and to create through subinfeudation a whole hierarchy of extortionary rights delegated down the line. This social control by the landed elite was fortified by their political alliance with the colonial administration in countries which were colonies, and with the comprador class even in countries which were not colonies, but were integrated in the world commercial network, in both cases retarding the bourgeois transformation of the economy.[12]

An equally, if not more, important factor behind the perpetuation of agricultural stagnation was the nature of state policy toward agriculture and the class interests it served. Most of the poorest people in the world live and till the soil in areas where provision and control of water supply for agriculture is crucial for any attempt at productivity improvement. The state of agricultural technology is, thus, inextricably linked with the hydraulic role of the state. Yet a major failure of the colonial governments in these countries (except in regions where water management for some export crops like cotton was important) was precisely in the area of public investment in irrigation and drainage, in control of floods and soil salinity, and in maintenance and repair of old water networks. The role of the state is also important in the generation of new plant and livestock breeding and pest-control technology through public research institutions and in its promotion and diffusion through public credit and extension services. The governments in these countries had largely neglected this role. This neglect and failure of government policy is not inconsistent with the class interests of the landed oligarchies and the plantation plutocracies. Public research and development in primarily land-saving biochemical technology would have threatened the land monopoly[13] of the rentier gentry; public credit institutions would have threatened their territorial monopoly in usury; and, in general, improvements in agricultural productivity would have raised the wage costs for recruits in plantations and mines.

The unequal-rewards problem is, thus, not simply a matter of 'exploitation' through international trade or one of antagonism of interests of one geographical area against another, emphasized in the proliferating literature on 'dependency' or theories of 'development of underdevelopment'. It is deeply embedded in the relations of production in agriculture and their interaction with the development of the forces of production. External connections are important primarily in so far as they influence this interaction.[14]

Chapter 9: Notes

Leonard Cheng provided valuable research assistance. Thanks are also due to the National Science Foundation for partial research support under Grant No. SES-7804022 A01.

1 For a Marxist analysis in terms of three different meanings of unequal exchange ('disjunctive', 'asymmetric' and 'nonequivalent' exchange), see Andersson (1976).

2 For an attempt to couch Emmanuel's problem in an extended Prebisch–Singer framework, see Bacha (1978).

3 For criticisms of the Lewis model on both these points, see Findlay (1978).

4 We say 'textiles' or 'tea' to indicate that for the purpose of our model it does not matter whether it is a primary product, or a manufacture, as long as it is produced in a commercialized sector different from the traditional or 'subsistence' food-producing sector.

5 In his 1954 paper Lewis has this assumption, but in the model of his 1969 paper he assumes food to be internationally traded. We do not take into account foreign trade in food for two

reasons: one, it is somewhat unusual for a poor country (barring exceptions like Burma and Thailand) to have food produced largely in family farms or in the 'subsistence' sector and yet for it to be traded in international markets. Secondly, as for food imports, up until recently the very poor countries (with exceptions like Egypt) have not been significant net importers of food on a sustained basis.

6 Except, in cases like Zaire, where private foreign investment for the sake of resource extraction has been significant.

7 Other aspects of the market structure which tend to widen the wage gap involve (a) effective rates of protection in rich countries being biased against labor-intensive manufactured exports of poor countries, and (b) international marketing and distribution chains being often under control of trans-national companies originating in rich countries.

8 For a very simple modeling of the wage gap determined by the rate of introduction of 'new' goods in rich countries and the 'imitation lag' in technological adoption in poor countries, see Krugman (1979).

9 In the real world, where final goods use in production a whole complex of intermediate goods, sectors may not always be distinguishable in a definite pattern in terms of their total (direct plus indirect) capital intensities. This is one of the major lessons of the so-called Leontief paradox.

10 For an algebraic and geometric proof of this result see Bardhan (1965) and Bardhan (1970), ch. 1 appendix, respectively.

11 See, for example, the data on agricultural productivity put together in Bairoch (1975).

12 Even if one takes the more well-documented history of preindustrial Europe and explores the origins of the agricultural revolution that preceded the first industrial revolution, one finds that two specific historical processes paved the way for its first taking place in sixteenth–seventeenth-century England: one was by which serfdom was dissolved (which English landlords, unlike their counterparts in contemporary Eastern Europe, were unable to prevent largely due to peasant resistance in the late medieval period), thus precluding forcible squeezing of the peasantry as the form of surplus extraction by landlords; and the second was the way in which small peasant proprietorship (which emerged at the fall of serfdom in large parts of Western Europe, notably in France) was short-circuited or undermined by English landlords, who gained control over large consolidated blocks of land, thus opening the way for accumulation and technological transformation brought about by an agrarian capitalist class. For more details on this line, see, for example, Brenner (1976).

13 For a study of the effects of social-class structure on the nature of technical change in Argentine agriculture, see De Janvry (1978).

14 For recent viewpoints that put the process of *production*, rather than the process of *circulation*, back at the center of Marxist theories of development, see Laclau (1971) and Brenner (1977).

Chapter 9: References

Andersson, J. O., *Studies in the Theory of Unequal Exchange between Nations* (Abo, Finland: Abo Akedemi, 1976).

Arrow K. J., Chenery H. B., Minhas B. S. and Solow, R. M., 'Capital labor substitution and economic efficiency', *Review of Economics and Statistics*, vol. 43, no. 2 (1961), pp. 225–50.

Bacha, E. L., 'An interpretation of unequal exchange from Prebisch-Singer to Emmanuel, *Journal of Development Economics*, vol. 5, no. 4 (1978), pp. 315–30.

Bairoch, P., *The Economic Development of the Third World Since 1900* (Methuen: London, 1975).

Bardhan, P. K., 'International differences in production functions, trade and factor prices', *Economic Journal*, vol. 75, no. 297 (1965), pp. 81–7.

Bardhan, P. K., *Economic Growth, Development and Foreign Trade: A Study in Pure Theory* (New York: John Wiley, 1970).

Brenner, R., 'Agrarian class structure and economic development in pre-industrial Europe', *Past and Present*, no. 70 (February 1976), pp. 30–74.

Brenner, R., 'The origins of capitalist development: a critique of neo-Smithian Marxism', *New Left Review*, no. 104 (July–August 1977), pp. 25–92.

Clague, C., 'An international comparison of industrial efficiency: Peru and the United States', *Review of Economics and Statistics*, vol. 49, no. 4 (1967), pp. 487–93.

De Janvry, A., 'Social structure and biased technical change in Argentine agriculture', in H. P. Binswanger and V. W. Ruttan, eds, *Induced Innovation: Technology Institutions and Development* (Baltimore, Md: Johns Hopkins University Press, 1978), pp. 297–323.

Diaz-Alejandro, C., 'Industrialization and labor productivity differentials', *Review of Economics and Statistics*, vol. 47, no. 2 (1965), pp. 207–14.

Emmanuel, A., *Unequal Exchange: A Study of the Imperialism of Trade* (New York: Monthly Review Press, 1972).

Findlay, R., 'The fundamental determinants of the terms of trade', paper presented at the Conference on the Past and Prospects of the Economic World Order, Stockholm, Sweden, August 1978.

Krugman, P., 'A model of innovation, technology transfer, and the world distribution of income', *Journal of Political Economy*, vol. 87, no. 2 (1979), pp. 253–66.

Laclau, E., 'Feudalism and capitalism in Latin America', *New Left Review*, no. 67 (1971), pp. 19–38.

Lewis, W. A., 'Economic development with unlimited supplies of labor', *Manchester School*, vol. 22, no. 2 (1954), pp. 137–91.

Lewis, W. A., *Aspects of Tropical Trade, 1883–1965* (Stockholm: Almqvist & Wiksell, 1969).

Lewis, W. A., *The Evolution of the International Economic Order* (Princeton, NJ: Princeton University Press, 1978).

Prebisch, R., *The Economic Development of Latin America and its Principal Problems* (New York: United Nations, 1950).

Singer, H., 'The distribution of gains between borrowing and investing countries', *American Economic Review*, vol. 40, no. 2 (1950), pp. 473–85.

10

Protection and Growth in a Dual Economy

RONALD FINDLAY

The reciprocal influences between international trade and economic development, considered in both their historical and theoretical aspects, has characterized all of Arthur Lewis's seminal contributions to our discipline. His most influential single contribution has undoubtedly been the famous model of economic development with unlimited supplies of labor. This model, however, at least in the form in which it has been most popular, is a closed one in which international trade is not explicitly introduced. It is true that the second part of the Lewis (1954) article does contain a most ingenious and interesting trade model, but it is a basically different construction, a static three-commodity, two-country Ricardian system, rather than an 'opening up' of the dynamic analysis of capital accumulation in a dual economy that constitutes the first part.

The Ricardian model of the second part of the 1954 paper, amplified and applied in the Lewis (1969) Wicksell Lectures, and its relation to the dual economy model of the first part, raise some fascinating issues that I have examined elsewhere.[1] My intention in this chapter is, first, to briefly sketch how the dual economy model can be extended to an open economy, and then to investigate the question of how protection affects the rate of growth in this context. This seems to me to be a question of major interest, if we believe the dual economy model applicable to at least a good part of the developing world, in view of the extensive controversy on 'inward-looking' versus 'outward-looking' strategies of development and the considerable empirical research that has been devoted to this issue.

Formal Structure of the Dual Economy Model

It is convenient to begin by quickly outlining the formal structure of the dual economy model. The output of the 'modern' sector, denoted $Q(t)$, depends upon inputs of capital and labor according to the production function

$$Q(t) = F[K(t), L(t)] \qquad (10.1)$$

with the stock of capital $K(t)$ and flow of output $Q(t)$ considered as being measured in the same physical units, so that output is a composite good that can be used for either consumption, or investment. Assuming constant returns to scale, we have:

$$q(t) = f[k(t)] \qquad (10.2)$$

after conversion of the production function to an intensive basis. The real wage at which labor is available from a 'peasant hinterland', otherwise outside the model, is fixed at a level $\bar{w}$. Profit maximization in the modern sector requires

$$f(k^*) - f'(k^*)k^* = \bar{w}. \qquad (10.3)$$

At any moment the total stock of capital $K(t)$ will be given by history, so that the level of employment will be determined in conformity with the profit-maximizing capital–labor ratio k^*. In view of the linear homogeneity of the production function, k^* also determines the rate of profit on capital as

$$r = f'(k^*) \qquad (10.4)$$

which has the dimensions of a pure number per unit time. With workers consuming the entire wage, the common growth rate of capital, employment and output is

$$g = sr \qquad (10.5)$$

where s is the fraction of profits that are saved. Looked at in this way, it is clear that what we have is a one-sector von Neumann model so long as the real wage is not driven up by exhaustion of the surplus labor pool. The model as presented is that of a closed, self-contained system. We now indicate how international trade can be introduced without altering the basic structural properties of the model.[2]

The 'Small' Open Dual Economy

The simplest way in which this can be done is to regard the economy as facing exogenously given relative prices on world markets for any number of commodities. If the individual production functions for all these goods have constant returns to scale, then the assumption of fixed relative prices on world markets permits aggregation into a single Hicksian 'composite commodity'. Assuming no nontraded goods or tradeable goods in which the domestic economy has external market power, the unit in which Q, K and $\bar{w}$ are all defined can be taken as this composite commodity. The production functions for the individual goods and the pattern of world relative prices determine the aggregate production function for the composite commodity, which will also display homogeneity of the first degree. Given $\bar{w}$ the profit-maximizing capital–labor ratio can be determined as before and this will also determine the efficient pattern of commodity specialization. The disposition of the income so generated determines the composition of consumption, investment, exports and imports. The growth rate, as before, is equal to $sf'(k^*)$.

In spite of its extreme simplicity, this model of a small open dual economy would seem to be quite helpful in interpreting cases of rapid expansion based on manufactured exports, such as South Korea or Taiwan, for example. Here, the combination of modern industrial technology and relatively low real wages and a highly elastic labor supply produces a high rate of profit, translated into a high growth rate by the generous ploughback of profits. Foreign capital is also attracted by the high profit rate, thus providing a further source of capital accumulation and growth. Initially, at least, such countries do not face an external market constraint, once they have overcome the initial difficulties of finding appropriate channels and outlets for their goods.

The eventual rise in the real wage does not necessarily choke off this process, though it may slow it down somewhat, since technological progress is occurring at the same time, keeping up the rate of profit and, hence, the rate of growth. The polar-limiting case is of course the small open neoclassical economy, in which the composite technology is the same but in which it is employment that is exogenous and the real wage that is a variable. Hong Kong and Singapore, the other members of the celebrated 'Gang of Four', may conform more to this limiting case. With free immigration from their respective hinterlands, however, both these economies could then be transformed to the Lewis model, with higher growth of capital and employment and a slackening in the rise of the real wage.

Expansion on the basis of a more or less constant real wage would not tend to be accompanied by changes in technique or in the efficient pattern of specialization. A rising real wage, however, would lead to specialization in newer, increasingly capital-intensive lines. The 'Gang of Four' have, thus, largely moved out of the traditional labor-intensive manufactures into more capital-intensive and technologically progressive sectors, leaving the original field more open to countries where the evolution of the real wage has been less rapid, or perhaps even stagnant.

The model as presented so far assumes that all goods are tradable at constant relative prices on world markets. Monopoly power in primary commodities, like Brazilian coffee or Malaysian rubber, can however be introduced. Nontraded goods also can be incorporated into the model of an open dual economy which, thus, has a very flexible and adaptable structure, well suited to the analysis of a wide variety of problems in the trade and development field.[3]

Protection and the Rate of Growth

The effect of protection on the rate of growth of an open economy is a question of obvious relevance and analytical interest but one on which there has been a dearth of results or insights. The extensive empirical literature on the effects of trade restrictions in developing countries has been confined to the conventional static measures of consumption and production loss arising from the distortionary effect of tariffs and quotas on the allocation of resources. One 'dynamic' argument for protection that has been lurking in the literature for some time relates to the effect of a tariff on saving via its effect on income distribution. A tariff on capital-intensive imports by a labor-abundant country will increase profits and reduce wages by the familiar Stolper–Samuelson theorem. If the propensity to save out of profits is higher than out of wages, this will raise the proportion of national income saved and, hence, the rate of growth of capital. The protected economy could, thus, eventually have a higher level of consumption than the free-trade economy, once the capital stock becomes sufficiently larger to offset the restriction of the gains from trade caused by the tariff, though total utility over the infinite horizon would be higher along the free-trade path.

In his 1954 paper Lewis advances what is essentially the Manoilesco argument for tariffs in the context of the dual economy. Capitalist industry pays labor its marginal product, while labor is remunerated at its average product in peasant agriculture, thus preventing the Paretian efficiency condition of equal marginal products from being fulfilled. Tariffs on manufactures could offset the excessive labor cost and so move the economy closer to the Paretian optimum, though the first-best intervention would be a wage-subsidy to industry equal to the gap between average and marginal product in agriculture. All this is now familiar from the recent literature on optimal intervention in the presence of domestic distortions. Again, the entire context of the discussion is purely static. The rest of this chapter is devoted to analyzing the effect of protection on the rate of growth of a two-sector 'small' open dual economy.

The constant returns to scale production functions are

$$q_i = f_i(k_i) \quad i = 1, 2 \tag{10.6}$$

with the usual properties

$$f_i'(k_i) > 0, f_i''(k_i) < 0$$

where the subscripts 1 and 2 refer to the consumption and capital-goods sectors, respectively. The capital-goods sector is more capital-intensive than the consumer-goods sector at any common factor–price ratio. The relative price of the consumer good in terms of the capital good on world markets is fixed and denoted $\bar{p}$. The fixed real wage is $\bar{w}$, measured in units of the consumption good.

Profit maximization determines a capital–labor ratio k_1^* that equates the marginal product of labor in the consumer goods sector to the wage, so that we have

$$f_1(k_1^*) - f_1'(k_1^*)k_1^* = \bar{w}. \tag{10.7}$$

The rate of profit in the consumer-goods sector under free trade would be

$$\bar{r} \equiv \bar{p}f_1'(k_1^*) \tag{10.8}$$

which has the dimension of a pure number per unit time.

In the capital goods sector let $\hat{k}_2$ denote the capital–labor ratio at which

$$f_2(\hat{k}_2) - f_2'(\hat{k}_2)\hat{k}_2 = \bar{p}\bar{w}. \tag{10.9}$$

We assume that

$$f_2'(\hat{k}_2) < \bar{r} \tag{10.10}$$

which means that it will not be profitable to produce the capital good under free trade, since the maximum rate of profit obtainable in that sector at the wage $\bar{p}\bar{w}$ is less than the rate obtainable in the consumer-goods sector $\bar{r}$. The entire capital stock will, therefore, be devoted to the consumer-goods sector, so that the dual economy would specialize completely on this sector under free trade. Employment at any moment will be determined by the capital stock and the profit-maximizing condition 10.7, while capital, employment and output will all grow at the rate $s\bar{r}$ under free trade, with imports providing the entire flow of investment at each instant.

Let a tariff be introduced just high enough to induce production of the capital good, with the real wage in terms of consumer goods still equal to $\bar{w}$. The internal relative price of consumer goods in terms of capital goods is now

$$p^* = \frac{\bar{p}}{(1 + \tau)} \tag{10.11}$$

where τ is the appropriate tariff level. Since $\bar{w}$ is unchanged, k_1^* remains the profit-maximizing capital–labor ratio in the consumer-goods sector, but the rate of profit now falls to

$$r^* = p^*f_1'(k_1^*) = \frac{\bar{r}}{(1 + \tau)}. \tag{10.12}$$

In the capital-goods sector we have

$$f_2(k_2^*) - f_2'(k_2^*)k_2^* = p^*\bar{w} \tag{10.13}$$

where $k_2^* < \hat{k}_2$, since

$$p^*\bar{w} = \frac{\bar{p}\bar{w}}{(1 + \tau)} < \bar{p}\bar{w}.$$

The rate of profit in the capital goods sector is

$$f_2'(k_2^*) = r^*. \qquad (10.14)$$

Since $f_2'(k_2^*) > f_2'(\hat{k}_2)$, the effect of the tariff is to raise the rate of profit in the capital-goods sector and lower it in the consumer-goods sector until a common rate is achieved.

The relationships that we have been considering could be further elucidated by means of Figure 10.1. The axes in the right-hand panel are the rate of profit, which is a pure number per unit time, and the real wage measured in units of the capital good, denoted by m, which is equal to the product of the fixed wage in terms of consumer goods $\bar{w}$ and the price of consumer goods in terms of capital goods, denoted by p. The downward-sloping curve, marked WR, in the right-hand panel is the factor-price or wage–profit frontier for the capital-goods sector. For each value of m, there is a corresponding value of k_2 that makes the marginal product of labor equal to m and also determines the marginal product of capital in the capital-goods sector $f_2'(k_2)$, which is equal to the rate of profit in that sector. The wage–profit frontier WR depends purely upon the properties of the production function $f_2(k_2)$.

The left-hand panel of Figure 10.1 indicates how the rate of profit in the consumer-goods sector depends upon the relative price p. The rate of profit in this sector is equal to $pf_1'(k_1^*)$ and k_1^* is determined uniquely by w, so that the rate of profit in the consumer-goods sector is directly proportional to p. To

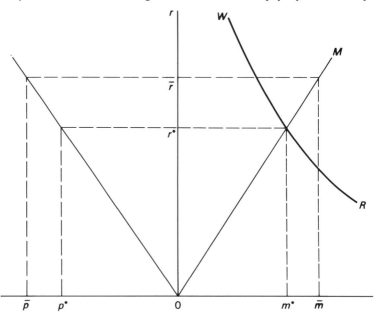

Figure 10.1   *Equilibrium values of the real wage, the rate of profit and the relative price.*

each value of p, there consequently corresponds a value of the rate of profit in the consumer-goods sector $pf'_1(k^*_1)$, and of the real wage measured in units of the capital good, $m = p\bar{w}$. The ray from the origin OM in the right-hand panel indicates the values of r and m corresponding to each value of p. The linearity of this relationship follows from the fact that $\bar{w}$ and $f'_1(k^*_1)$ are constants.

At the given world price ratio $\bar{p}$, the rate of profit in the consumer-goods sector is above the rate of profit in the capital-goods sector corresponding to the wage of $\bar{m} = \bar{p}\bar{w}$. Production of the capital good is, therefore, not viable under free trade. The intersection of OM and WR determines r^* and p^*, the only price ratio at which the profit rates in the two sectors will be equal, given $\bar{w}$. The required tariff rate τ can now be determined by the relation $\tau = \bar{p}/p^* - 1$. The effect of the tariff is, therefore, to reduce the rate of profit in the consumer-goods sector, which is the only viable sector under free trade, and raise the profit rate in the capital-goods sector until the two are equal at r^*.[4]

The levels of output and employment in each sector can now be determined. The fixed wage and constant returns to scale give the model a linear structure, which implies that there is an indeterminacy in the level of output of the capital-goods sector, which can be at any positive value up to the autarky level. The linearity of the model implies that the tariff which is just high enough to induce any production at all of the capital good is also high enough to be prohibitive of any capital-goods imports. The fraction of the demand for capital goods that is met by domestic production is therefore a policy variable, which is assumed to be set at some value a between zero and unity, and then left constant over time.

The demand for capital goods (investment) will depend upon the disposition of the tariff revenue in addition to saving out of profits. The main assumption to be considered in relation to the proceeds of the tariff is that it is returned as a subsidy to profits. The consequences of two alternative assumptions, that it is spent entirely by the government on import of capital goods and that it is returned as a subsidy to wages will also be briefly noted.

The revenue from the tariff, measured in terms of the consumer good, is $\tau(1 - a)I$ divided by $\bar{p}$. Evaluated at domestic relative prices, this corresponds in terms of capital goods to p^* times this amount. Since $p^*/\bar{p} = 1/(1 + \tau)$, the revenue in terms of capital goods is $\tau/(1 + \tau)$ times $(1 - a)I$. The demand for investment can, therefore, be written as:

$$I(t) = s[p^*f'_1(k^*_1)K(t) + \frac{\tau}{(1 + \tau)}(1 - a)I(t)]. \tag{10.15}$$

Dividing both sides of this equation by $K(t)$ we obtain:

$$g^* = \frac{1}{1 + [1 - s(1 - a)]\tau} \cdot s\bar{p}f'_1(k^*_1) \tag{10.16}$$

as the growth rate of the capital stock and, hence, of the entire system under the regime of protection with tariff proceeds distributed as a subsidy to profits.

It is apparent that the effect of protection is to reduce the growth rate obtainable under free trade, since g^* is equal to the latter multiplied by a coefficient that is always less than unity, except when s is equal to one and a is equal to zero, that is, capital goods are not produced domestically, though on the borderline of profitability and the entire tariff revenue is spent on capital-goods imports. The growth rate varies inversely with τ, whenever a is positive, and inversely with a itself for any given value of τ, reaching a minimum value of sr^*, when a is equal to unity.

The reader can readily verify that g^*, when all the tariff revenue is spent by the government itself on capital-goods imports is given by 10.16, with s in the denominator replaced by unity. Thus, the growth rate when the tariff revenue is invested by the government is always higher than when it is given as a profits subsidy, except of course when s in the private sector is itself equal to unity. If s in the private sector is less than unity, and a is equal to zero, the growth rate is equal to the free-trade rate of $s\bar{p}f_1'(k_1^*)$ when the government invests all of the tariff proceeds. The free-trade growth rate can, thus, never be exceeded under protection, even when the private sector's propensity to save is less than unity and the government spends all of the tariff proceeds on importing capital goods.

If the tariff revenue is distributed as a subsidy to wages, the second term on the right-hand side of 10.15 does not appear and the growth rate under protection becomes equal to the minimum value of sr^*. It is interesting to observe that this result is independent of the value of a. The reason is that in this case it is immaterial whether the economy completely specializes on the consumer good, with the whole investible surplus spent on capital goods at the domestic price p^*, or produces all the capital goods demanded at home, at an opportunity cost in terms of consumer goods equal to p^*, which from 10.12 and 10.13 is equal to the ratio of $f_2'(k_2^*)$ to $f_1'(k_1^*)$. The rate of growth under all the protectionist regimes considered is, therefore, bounded below by sr^* and above by the free-trade rate $s\bar{r}$, the magnitude of the range being measured by the factor $1/(1 + \tau)$.

To complete the analysis, it is necessary to indicate how the allocation of the capital stock between the two sectors and, hence, the overall ratio of capital to total labor employed is determined. We, first, note that

$$Q_2(t)/K(t) = ag^*. \qquad (10.17)$$

Multiplying both sides of 10.17 by the capital–output ratio in the capital-goods sector $k_2^*/f_2(k^*)$, we obtain λ, the fraction of the capital stock allocated to the capital-goods sector as

$$\lambda = \frac{k_2}{f_2(k^*)} \frac{as\bar{p}f_1'(k_1^*)}{1 + [1 - s(1 - a)]\tau}. \qquad (10.18)$$

The overall ratio of the capital stock to the labor force employed, can be determined as the value of k, which satisfies

$$\frac{\lambda}{k_2^*} + \frac{(1 - \lambda)}{k_1^*} = \frac{1}{k}. \tag{10.19}$$

The impact effect of the tariff is, therefore, to reduce the level of employment, since the capital stock is a predetermined state variable and $k_2^* > k_1^*$. The profit rate is reduced from $\bar{r}$ to r^* and the growth rate from $\bar{g}$ to g^*. The capital stock and employment will, therefore, be increasingly below the levels they would have attained on the free-trade growth path, at each subsequent instant of time. This is the *dynamic* cost of protection, distinct from though of course related to the conventional concept in terms of static welfare economics. The conventional 'production cost' of the tariff can be seen at any instant in the reduction in the value of GNP at international prices induced by the tariff in diverting capital to the inefficient domestic capital-goods sector. In addition, there is an 'employment cost' in this dual economy model that does not appear in neoclassical models that assume full employment, since employment falls as capital is switched to the more capital-intensive sector. The conventional 'consumption cost' of the tariff in this case is an 'investment cost', since the higher domestic relative price induced by the tariff is for capital goods rather than consumer goods. Capital, employment, consumption and real income are, thus, all increasingly reduced over time as a result of the tariff.

Recent research has demonstrated fairly conclusively that the growth of both output and employment has been significantly higher in the more 'open' developing countries than in those that have followed import-substitution strategies behind protective barriers. Krueger (1980) finds no theoretical propositions in the literature to account for this, since it does not necessarily follow from conventional Neoclassical doctrine. The model presented here, overly simple and stylized though it is, might therefore help to fill this important gap in the trade and development literature, to which Arthur Lewis has contributed so much.

Chapter 10: Notes

The first draft of this paper was written at the Institute of Southeast Asian Studies, Singapore. I am grateful to the Director, K. S. Sandhu, and the staff of the Institute for their kind hospitality. I would also like to thank N. Saavedra-Rivano for pointing out a mistake in an earlier version and S. Wellisz for correcting it. Responsibility for remaining errors is, of course, my own.

1 See Findlay (1980).
2 On dual economy models with international trade, see Bardhan (1970); Brecher (1974); Findlay (1973); and Hornby (1968).
3 See Findlay (1973), for some extensions along these lines.
4 If the trade pattern were reversed $\bar{p}$ would be less than p^*, requiring the tariff to be placed on the consumer good. It can be seen from Figure 10.1 that the rate of profit would be reduced in this case also.

Chapter 10: References

Bardhan, P. K., *Economic Growth, Development and Foreign Trade* (New York: Wiley, 1970).

Brecher, R., 'Minimum wage rates and the pure theory of international trade', *Quarterly Journal of Economics*, vol. 88, no. 1 (1974), pp. 98–116.

Findlay, R., *International Trade and Development Theory* (New York: Columbia University Press, 1973).

Findlay, R., 'W. Arthur Lewis' contributions to economics', *Scandinavian Journal of Economics*, vol. 82, no. 1 (1980), pp. 62–79.

Hornby, J. N., 'Investment and trade policy in the dual economy', *Economic Journal*, vol. 78, no. 309 (1968), pp. 96–107.

Krueger, A. O., 'Trade policy as an input to development', *American Economic Review*, vol. 70, no. 2 (1980), pp. 288–92.

Lewis, W. A., 'Economic development with unlimited supplies of labour', *Manchester School*, vol. 22, no. 2 (1954), pp. 139–91.

Lewis, W. A., *Aspects of Tropical Trade, 1883–1965* (Stockholm: Almqvist & Wiksell, 1969).

11

Lessons of Experience under Fixed Exchange Rates

ARNOLD C. HARBERGER and SEBASTIAN EDWARDS

Introduction

In the course of an extended study[1] of inflation and monetary instability throughout the world we have examined in some detail (a) the world inflation as such, (b) the phenomena of chronic and acute inflation and (c) certain attributes of countries that have been subject to exchange-rate crises. The present paper takes our work in this latter area several steps beyond what has previously been reported.

In the main body of our work on inflation we have concentrated on three economic policy indicators, which we believe help explain differences among countries in the rate of monetary expansion. These variables are:

β = net increase, during the year, of banking system credit to the public sector, expressed as a percentage of the year's GDP. Thus, if the public sector's borrowings from the banking system stood at 200 at the beginning of the year, and went to 300 by year's end, the net increase would be 100. If GDP of the year were 800, then β would be 12·5 percent (= 100/800).

γ = fraction of total banking system credit going to the public sector. Thus, if at the beginning of the year total bank credit were 400, and if at the end it were 500, then (using public-sector credit figures from above) γ would be 0·50 (= 200/400) at the beginning of the year and 0·60 (= 300/500) at the end. In the tables presented in this chapter γ is always measured from end-of-year data. Whenever the public sector is a net lender to the banking system, γ is simply recorded as <0.

λ = percentage increase during the year in total domestic credit of the banking system. This, with the figures just presented, would be 25 percent $|=(500/400) - 1|$.

Table 11.1 shows how different groups of countries have behaved with respect to these variables and the rate of inflation. Part A of the table compares acute inflations (sharp spurts averaging 80 percent per annum or more for two or more years) and chronic inflations (at 20 percent or more for at least five consecutive years), with a control group of stable countries that managed successfully to maintain fixed exchange rates *vis-à-vis* a chosen major

Table 11.1   *Comparison of Inflationary Experience by Classes of Countries*

		Median Values (%) of			
		π^*	β	γ	λ
(A)	*Groups of countries*				
	Acute inflation countries†	124	3·7	0·467	120
	Chronic inflation countries‡	27	2·3	0·316	34
	Control group – stable countries§	2	0·5	0·249	14
(B)	*Recent inflation countries*				
	(i) during recent inflation‖	29	5·4	0·315	43
	(ii) during earlier control period¶	5	1·2	0·287	18
(C)	*Devaluation crises countries*				
	(i) in year of crisis**		1·8	0·350	15.0
	(ii) in year before crisis		1·9	0·350	16·8
	(iii) in control period***		0·9	0·260	14·0

Notes:

*Annual rate of inflation.

†Argentina, 1974–6; Bolivia, 1952–9; Chile, 1971–6; Indonesia, 1965–8; Paraguay, 1951–3; South Korea, 1950–55; Uruguay, 1965–8 and 1971–4.

‡Argentina, 1949–74; Brazil, 1957–76; Chile, 1952–70; Uruguay, 1958–75.

§Taiwan, 1960–72; Honduras, 1954–70; Haiti, 1954–70; Jamaica, 1954–65; Iran, 1960–70; Thailand, 1954–70; Portugal, 1954–70; Guatemala, 1954–70; El Salvador, 1954–70; Greece, 1954–70; Sri Lanka, 1954–65; Burma, 1954–69; Mexico, 1954–70; Dominican Republic, 1954–70; Morocco, 1960–70; Iraq, 1954–70; Nigeria, 1960–70; Malaysia, 1954–70; Sudan, 1954–70; Trinidad/Tobago, 1954–65.

‖Ghana, 1974–8; Zaire, 1974–8; Nigeria, 1975–7; Portugal, 1974–7; Colombia, 1973–7; Turkey, 1975–6; Peru, 1974–8; Israel, 1974–7.

¶Ghana, 1956–60; Zaire, 1969–72; Nigeria, 1957–9; Portugal, 1966–9; Colombia, 1961–71; Turkey, 1969–72; Peru, 1969–73; Israel, 1966–70.

**Bolivia, 1972; Burma, 1975; Colombia, 1957; Costa Rica, 1974; Ecuador, 1970; Egypt, 1962; Finland, 1957, 1967; Ghana, 1967; Greece, 1975; Iceland, 1960, 1967; India, 1966; Indonesia, 1968; Israel, 1962, 1971; Italy, 1976; Korea, 1960; Mexico, 1976; New Zealand, 1967; Pakistan, 1972; Peru, 1958, 1967; Philippines, 1962, 1970; Rwanda, 1966; Spain, 1958; Sri Lanka, 1967; Venezuela, 1964.

***Bolivia, 1964–6; Burma, 1961–2; Colombia, 1954–5; Costa Rica, 1966–7; Ecuador, 1964–5; Egypt, 1954–5; Finland, 1963–4; Ghana, 1959–60; Greece, 1961–2; Iceland, 1955–6, 1963–4; India, 1961–2; Indonesia, 1974–5; Israel, 1957–8, 1964–5; Italy, 1961–2; Korea, 1975–6; Mexico, 1964–5; New Zealand, 1958–9; Pakistan, 1962–3; Peru, 1955–6, 1962–3; Philippines, 1956–7, 1965–6; Rwanda, 1969, 1972; Spain, 1954–5; Sri Lanka, 1959–60; Venezuela, 1959–60.

Source:
International Monetary Fund, *International Financial Statistics*.

currency. The message from this part of the table is clear: all three explanatory values are ordered, as between groups of countries as we would expect on the hypothesis that they are potentially causal correlates of inflation.

In part B of Table 11.1 we introduce a number of countries whose inflationary experiences have in certain recent years diverged significantly from the world's 'norm.' These are compared with the same countries' experiences in an earlier control period. Again the three variables (β, γ and λ) behave in such a way as to confirm the hypothesis that they are linked to the rate of inflation.

Part C of Table 11.1 is really the starting point for this chapter. It reports on twenty-nine situations of devaluation crisis. In order to qualify for inclusion in this part of the analysis, a country's devaluation had to be at least 20 percent, and the devaluation year had to be preceded by at least four consecutive years of exchange-rate stability. In this way the devaluation crisis is distinguished from systems of managed float, crawling peg, institutionalized minidevaluation, and so on. We consider that devaluation crises, as we have defined them, were typically an undesired outcome of a policy that had as one of its significant objectives the maintenance of a fixed exchange rate. We consider these devaluation crises, therefore, to be simply another set of manifestations of the inflationary disease, side by side with the cases of chronic, acute and recent inflation reported on in parts A and B of Table 11.1.

In this light the results reported in part C of Table 11.1 confirm that, particularly with regard to β and γ, devaluation-crisis countries behave in crisis years like chronic-inflation countries, while in the control period they behave like the control group of stable countries. Also of interest is the fact that the danger signals represented by relatively high values of β and γ tend to be present also in the year prior to devaluation. They, thus, provide a means of alerting the analyst (or the policy-maker, for that matter) to the likelihood of an impending crisis.

The remainder of this chapter is devoted to exploring in some depth the nature of the differences between devaluation-crisis countries and those that have been successful at maintaining fixed exchange rates. To aid in this examination, we introduce in section 1 an indicator of monetary policy. Using this indicator we then proceed to explore, in section 2, the international-reserves policies of the crisis group and the stable group, respectively, as well as the monetary policies that they pursued in given circumstances with respect to international reserves. In section 3 we scrutinize more closely the relationship between reserves and monetary policy. We find in particular, in that section, that the devaluation crisis countries are significantly less prudent than the stable countries, *both* when they are losing reserves, *and* when they are gaining reserves. The only situation in which they appear to exhibit greater prudence (if it may be called that), than the stable countries is in the periods when reserves are low, and a turning point is brought about. In such periods one can discern the importance of conscious policy measures on the part of the crisis countries.

(1) An Indicator of Monetary Policy

One can discern in the literature of monetary economics two canonical types of policy. The first, associated with 'the rules of the game' of the gold standard or other fixed exchange-rate arrangement, entails a country's expanding bank credit when reserves (gold) flow in, and contracting bank credit when reserves (gold) flow out. Under this set-up, there would be a tendency for short-run movements in domestic credit to be in the same direction as short-run movements in international reserves. It is quite different when the objective of monetary policy is to achieve a certain target level (or target rate of growth) of the money supply. Here, if there is an increment of reserves (particularly an unexpected one), it will have to be offset by a corresponding cut in domestic credit.

These observations suggest an indicator which has, say, the change in the international reserves of the banking system in the denominator, and the change in the consolidated banking system's domestic credit in the numerator. If this ratio of changes is positive, it reflects a 'rules of the game' policy or a *reserves target*, while if the ratio of changes is negative, it reflects a *monetary target*.

Our indicator μ is based on this line of thought. However, because a very small change in reserves could cause the ratio $\Delta D/\Delta R$ to be extremely large, we opted for a definition that kept μ bounded between $-1\cdot0$ and $+1\cdot0$. This is accomplished by defining μ as being the smaller in absolute value of $\Delta D/\Delta R$ or $\Delta R/\Delta D$, where D is domestic credit and R is international reserves. Since the smaller of the two ratios above must always be ≤ 1 in absolute value, we thus succeed in placing bounds on our indicator.[2] The indicator μ can be defined for an individual bank, a group of banks, or the consolidated banking system as a whole. In our own work we have at times used it to refer to the consolidated banking system and at other times to refer to the central bank alone. In this chapter we shall restrict it explicitly to the consolidated banking system of a country.

(2) The Behavior of International Reserves in Crisis and Successful Countries

In this section we examine the reserves behavior of crisis countries and successful countries, first, with respect to their typical reserves levels (in relation to the total banking system portfolio, $R + D$), and then in terms of the types of monetary policy pursued at different international reserves levels. For this exercise, crisis countries continue to be defined as those experiencing a devaluation of at least 20 percent after a period of at least four years of exchange-rate stability. On the other hand, successful fixed exchange-rate countries were defined as those countries that have maintained their exchange rate within a limit of annual variation of 2 percent for at least ten consecutive years. The period considered for the analysis was 1954–78, but as this analysis compares devaluation crisis situations with the successful maintenance of a fixed exchange rate, we have for each country excluded episodes characterized by floating exchange rates, crawling pegs, minidevaluation policies, and the like.[3]

Table 11.2 shows the frequency distribution of the reserves ratio for the two sets of countries, both in relative (part A) and absolute (part B) terms. It is clear from part A that there is a substantial difference in behavior. But even

Table 11.2 *Reserve Ratios in Crisis Versus Successful Countries*

	Interval for Reserve Ratio $[R/(R + D)]$				
	less than 0·1	0·1–0·2	0·2–0·3	0·3–0·5	0·5 and over
(A) *Percentage of Cases (Quarterly Observations) in Interval*					
Crisis countries	0·464	0·362	0·122	0·034	0·018
Successful countries	0·230	0·282	0·207	0·179	0·102
(B) *Number of Cases (Quarterly Observations) in Interval*					
Crisis countries	432	337	114	32	17
Successful countries	258	317	233	201	114
From B, $\chi^2(4) = 263\cdot36$					
$\chi^2_{0\cdot001}(4) = 18\cdot47$					

Source:
International Monetary Fund, *International Financial Statistics.*

after observing the differences in part A, most readers are likely to be astonished by the size of the χ^2 emerging from a test of homogeneity derived from the absolute frequencies given in part B.

A second body of evidence concerning differential reserves behavior of the two groups of countries is drawn from a recent paper by Edwards (1980). In that paper Edwards fitted a single demand function for reserves to data for forty-one countries over a period of nine years (1964–72). Using slightly different criteria from those of the present chapter, Edwards divides the forty-one countries into eighteen crisis countries and twenty-three successful ones. Tests were then made made on the residuals of the two groups of countries from the common, fitted-reserves demand function. The fitted function was:

$$\log R = -0\cdot56 + 1\cdot19 \log Y + 1\cdot47 \log API + 0\cdot46 \log \sigma$$
$$ (0\cdot28) \quad (0\cdot03) \qquad\quad (0\cdot09) \qquad\qquad (0\cdot05)$$
$$[R^2 = 0\cdot80; F(3, 365) = 484\cdot6]$$

where the numbers in parentheses below the coefficients are their respective standard errors. Here R represents level of international reserves (in dollars), Y is national income (also expressed in dollars), API is the country's average propensity to import (taken as a variable to reflect the relative degree of openness of the economy) and σ is the coefficient of variation of international reserves around their trend for the past fourteen years. The residuals from this function had a mean of $-0\cdot114$ for the crisis countries. This was significantly negative, since its standard error was $0\cdot051$. In contrast, the residuals from the successful countries had a positive mean of $0\cdot09$, which was also (with a standard error of $0\cdot042$) significantly different from zero.

This evidence, thus, clearly confirms the message derived from Table 11.2, indicating a distinct tendency on the part of crisis countries to hold lower reserves than successful ones. What has been done here is to demonstrate that this proposition holds not just for the raw data, but also after correcting for such variables as the various countries' economic size, degree of openness and degree of vulnerability to balance of payments shocks.

The third body of evidence focuses on the times when the two sets of countries were pursuing reserves-target policies. After identifying the years in which our policy indicator μ took on values greater than or equal to 0·1, we derived for these years the distribution of the reserves ratio $[R/(R + D)]_{-1}$ for both sets of countries. Key attributes of this distribution are set out in Table 11.3. The table reveals a very clear result: the critical ratio (of the banking system's international reserves to its total portfolio) that triggers a reserves policy in successful countries is substantially higher than the critical level in crisis countries. If we compare columns 1 and 2 of Table 11.3, we can see that the median of $[R/(R + D)]_{-1}$ for crisis countries during the total period (0·103) is smaller than even the first quartile (0·137) for the successful countries. Similarly, the third quartile (0·180) for crises countries is smaller than the median (0·220) for the successful countries. These results tell us that the crisis countries reacted later than successful countries to the erosion of the level of international reserves, and that they only began to take measures to rebuild these reserves after a lower ratio of reserves to money had been reached.

Column 3 of Table 11.3 shows the distribution of $[R/(R + D)]$ for 31 December of the year previous to the devaluation in the crisis countries.[4] Comparing this column with column 2 we can see that the year before the devaluation the reserves ratio is even lower than the critical level (column 2) that 'normally' triggers a reserves-target policy for the same crisis countries. In general, we can say that crisis countries have devalued when they 'ran out of reserves', and the fact that the distribution of $(R/R + D)_{-1}$ is significantly lower the year previous to a devaluation (column 3) than the year prior to a reserves-policy measure (column 2), suggests that in a sense devaluations are used as a last-resort measure, after the reserves ratio has fallen to a level too low to allow a reserves policy to be a viable solution.

The present section has demonstrated that the crisis countries tend to hold lower international reserves than the successful ones. This is true for the raw data, as well as for residuals from a common regression designed to explain variations in the reserves of different countries. It is also true as a description of

Table 11.3   *Distribution of* $(R/R + D)_{-1}$ *for Successful and Crisis Countries When a Reserves Policy Is Being Pursued*

	Successful Countries (1)		Crisis Countries (2)		Crisis Countries Year Before Devaluation (3)
First quartile	0·137	>	0·050	>	0·010
Median	0·220	>	0·103	>	0·085
Third quartile	0·402	>	0·180	>	0·110
$n =$	82		132		20

the circumstances under which the countries appear to pursue reserves-target policies. The crisis countries appear to enter with reserves-oriented policies only after the reserves ratio has fallen to levels far below those that typically trigger such policies on the part of the successful countries.

(3) Choices of Policy in Given Reserves Settings

In the preceding section we examined the overall distribution of reserves, and the choice of reserves under given circumstances (as determined by a cross-section-cum-time-series regression in one case, and by the apparent existence of a reserves-target policy in the other). Here, we shall look at the matter the other way round, delineating the circumstances by reference to what is happening to reserves, and inquiring into the policy choices of the successful *vis-à-vis* the crisis countries in what are apparently similar situations.

In classifying different reserves situations we took into account both the level of reserves and their direction of movement. We consider, first, in Table 11.4 situations where the reserves ratio $[R/(R + D)]$ is falling. As is there indicated, a dramatic difference in behavior exists between the successful and the crisis countries. Regardless of whether the reserves ratio was very low (less than 0·1), or merely quite low (between 0·1 and 0·2), the crisis countries were much less prone to pursue reserves-oriented policies than were the successful countries.

What does this result mean? We can safely work on the presumption that when the reserves ratio is falling, the absolute level of reserves is most of the time going to be falling as well. Thus, the situations of reserves policy are likely to be situations in which credit is restricted during a period when reserves are falling, precisely for the purpose of stemming the fall in reserves. This is the prudent policy to follow for countries attempting to maintain a fixed exchange rate. Our evidence, then, is that the successful countries, at both levels of reserves investigated, tend to behave much more prudently in the face of declining reserves ratios than do the crisis countries. Moreover, the difference in policy choices as between the two groups of countries, is striking. In both cases the hypothesis of homogeneity is rejected at the 0·001 level (of χ^2) with great ease. And for the most dangerous situation (that with $[R/(R + D)] < 0·1$) the strength of the statistical test is truly remarkable.

Table 11.5 deals with situations of a rising reserves ratio. At first glance, it appears to tell a story dramatically opposed to that of Table 11.4. For whereas in Table 11.4 the crisis countries were shown to be less prone to pursue reserves policies while the reserves ratio was falling, Table 11.5 shows them to be more prone than the successful countries to pursue reserves policies when $|R/(R + D)|$ is rising.

The anomaly is only apparent, however. The key to understanding what is happening is the recognition that when reserves are still at low levels, and are rising, a policy of expanding domestic credit in response to the rise in reserves can be quite risky. The prudent use of credit expansion in response to rises in

Table 11.4   Policy Choices under Falling Reserves Ratios (number of quarters that countries in the group pursued given policies in the indicated situation)

Reserves Situation	Policy Target	Country Group successful	crisis	Total
$[R/(R + D)]$ Below 0·1 and falling	Monetary ($\mu < 0$)	121	219	340
	Reserves ($\mu > 0$)	29	5	34
	Total	150	224	374
	$\chi^2(1)$ = 29·76 $\chi^2_{0·001}(1)$ = 10·83			
$[R/(R + D)]$ Between 0·1 and 0·2 and falling	Monetary ($\mu < 0$)	132	103	235
	Reserves ($\mu > 0$)	52	12	64
	Total	184	115	299
	$\chi^2(1)$ = 12·33 $\chi^2_{0·001}(1)$ = 10·83			

reserves is (so to speak) to 'blow away' unwanted excess reserves. It is difficult to imagine that there would be important situations of unwanted excess reserves when the reserves ratio is less than 0·2 (recall that this is approximately the median reserves ratio for the successful countries). Hence, the greater propensity of the crisis countries to pursue reserves policies under these conditions is to be seen as a greater willingness to run risks. Once again, the levels of statistical significance of the χ^2 tests are such as to clearly warrant our rejecting any notion of homogeneity of behavior as between the two groups of countries.

The single place where the crisis countries appear to exhibit more forceful policy behavior than the successful countries is in bringing about lower turning

Table 11.5   Policy Choices under Rising Reserves Ratios (number of quarters that countries in the groups pursued given policies in the indicated situation)

Reserves Situation	Policy Target	Country Group successful	crisis	total
$[R/(R + D)]$ Below 0·1 and rising	Monetary ($\mu < 0$)	41	8	49
	Reserves ($\mu > 0$)	67	143	210
	Total	108	151	259
	$\chi^2(1)$ = 41·69 $\chi^2_{0·001}(1)$ = 10·83			
$[R/(R + D)]$ Between 0·1 and 0·2 and rising	Monetary ($\mu < 0$)	39	19	58
	Reserves ($\mu > 0$)	94	105	199
	Total	133	124	257
	$\chi^2(1)$ = 6·42 $\chi^2_{0·01}(1)$ = 6·64			

points in the ratio of international reserves to the total portfolio of the consolidated banking system. This is exhibited in different ways by Table 11.6. In this table we look to either a reduction in domestic credit, or a devaluation, as the device for bringing about an improvement in the reserves situation. We define the 'event' Z_t as taking place with respect to quarter t whenever there has been either a devaluation, or a contraction of credit (from beginning of quarter to end of quarter) during either quarter t, or quarter $t-1$. Correspondingly, we define the event O_t as occurring whenever there has been neither a devaluation, nor a quarterly contraction of credit, in either of the quarters t or $t-1$.

The homogeneity tests of Table 11.6 ask, for the two classes of countries, respectively, whether there is a significantly different incidence of policy actions Z_t in the quarters t and $t-1$ leading up to turning points, than there is in other situations. Turning points here are defined as those taking place when the reserves ratio is less than 0·1 (they are dated to the first quarter in which a rise of the reserves ratio occurs). Thus, they are quarters in which in some sense policy-makers should be interested in turning the trend of reserves around. In addition, turning points have been defined as major ones, so as to exclude minimal wiggles in the graph of the reserves ratio through time. The results of Table 11.6 are especially interesting in that it is the crisis countries that seem to have consciously used policy measures to bring about turning

Table 11.6 *Policy Initiatives and Turning Points (homogeneity test: turning points versus other quarters for each group of countries)*

Event	Quarter of Reference		Total
	Lower Turning Point of Reserves $[R/(R+D) < 0·1]$	Other Quarters	
Crisis Countries			
Policy initiative (Z) (credit restriction or devaluation in t or $t-1$)	17	278	295
No policy initiative (O)	8	441	449
	25	719	744
	$\chi^2(1) = 7·506$		
	$\chi^2_{0·01}(1) = 6·635$		
Successful Countries			
Policy initiative (Z)	7	479	486
No policy initiative (O)	11	739	750
	18	1,218	1,236
	$\chi^2(1) = 0·042$		
	$\chi^2_{0·10}(1) = 2·706$		

points in the reserves ratio. The successful countries' behavior around turning points is truly no different ($\chi^2 = 0.042$) from what it is at other times.

This is in a sense not surprising. All the countries in question have somehow served as viable economies. To do this, requires a certain amount of responsibility and discipline. What we seem to have observed is that the successful countries exercise this responsibility and discipline on a more or less continuing basis. Thus, when they encounter a period of low and falling reserves, they may well be able to convince their actual creditors and their potential lenders that there is no cause for alarm. Their reserves ratios will ultimately turn around as a consequence of continuing prudence in economic policy.

By way of contrast, when the crisis countries encounter falling reserves, when their level is already low, actual and potential creditors are likely to take a different attitude. If these countries are rarely prudent or cautious, either when reserves are falling or rising, something special must be done to surmount a crisis situation. Sometimes, creditors may insist on such action as a condition for a roll-over of old loans or an extension of new ones. At other times, international lenders may simply refuse additional credit assistance, leaving the country to struggle through the crisis on its own. This is the type of scenario, then, that is suggested by our examination of the behavior of crisis and successful countries.

(4) Conclusions

There are some simple conclusions to be drawn from the exercises on which we have here reported. There can be no doubt, we feel, concerning the behavior of crisis countries *vis-à-vis* successful ones. The two sets of countries exhibit notably distinct patterns of behavior. The crisis countries hold less reserves, and also, at any given level of reserve holdings, follow more risky monetary policies. It would, thus, be quite wrong to think of the crisis countries as the unlucky pawns of a malevolent fate. They should quite clearly, we think, be recognized as being less responsible in their policy choices than the successful countries *under given circumstances*. And the cure, if one is to be found, for their malaise is more to be sought in the realm of modified norms of policy than in wishful hopes for favorable changes in the underlying constraints that their economies confront.

Chapter 11: Notes

Acknowledgement and thanks are due to the National Science Foundation. The work referred to in the introduction was done under Grant No. SOC 76-11189, that reported in the body of the paper under Grant No. SOC 79-06778. This paper was presented at the first Latin American Meetings of the Econometric Society, Buenos Aires, Argentina, July 1980.
1   The first paper in this sequence was A. C. Harberger (1978) (lecture delivered at Ohio State University, 9 March 1978). The second paper was A. C. Harberger (1981).

2 Our examples up to this point have taken as the autonomous element in the picture an unexpected increment of international reserves, where it is quite clear that a monetary target policy will correspond to $\mu < 0$ and a monetary reserves target policy to $\mu > 0$. The situation changes slightly when the initial shock is an unexpected movement of demand for credit. If, say, market interest rates go up, the banking system will try to expand domestic lending at the expense of international reserves. If the central bank is pursuing a monetary target, this sort of reshuffling in bank portfolios will be perfectly feasible, and there will therefore tend to be a negative relationship between movements in domestic credit and movements in reserves. However, if the central bank is pursuing a reserves target, it will resist the loss of reserves implied above. In this case the resulting ΔR would tend to be zero, with μ also zero. Taking both types of disturbances together – namely, credit shocks as well as reserves shocks – we, thus, have that the expected sign of μ tends to be always negative when a monetary target is being followed, and to be ≥ 0 when a reserves target is being pursued.

3 Our devaluation crisis situations are Bolivia, 1972; Colombia, 1957; Costa Rica, 1974; Ecuador, 1970; Ghana, 1967; Greece, 1975; Iceland, 1960, 1967; India, 1966; Israel, 1962, 1971; Korea, 1960; Mexico, 1976; New Zealand, 1967; Pakistan, 1972; Peru, 1958, 1967; Philippines, 1962, 1970; Sri Lanka, 1967. Data for these countries (as crisis countries) come from the following years. Bolivia, 1968–78; Colombia, 1954–72; Costa Rica, 1954–78; Ecuador, 1954–78; Ghana, 1954–78; Greece, 1972–6; Iceland, 1954–72; India, 1954–72; Israel, 1954–75; Korea, 1954–78; Mexico, 1972–8; New Zealand, 1954–72; Pakistan, 1954–72; Peru, 1954–77; Philippines, 1954–78; Sri Lanka, 1954–75. The successful countries are Bolivia, 1959–68; Burma, 1954–69; Dominican Republic, 1954–70; El Salvador, 1954–78; Greece, 1954–71; Guatemala, 1954–78; Haiti, 1954–78; Honduras, 1954–78; Jamaica, 1954–65; Iran, 1954–78; Iraq, 1954–74; Malaysia, 1954–72; Mexico, 1954–72; Morocco, 1954–72; Nigeria, 1954–72; Portugal, 1954–72; Sri Lanka, 1954–65; Sudan, 1954–78; Taiwan, 1954–78; Thailand, 1954–78; Trinidad, 1954–65. Quarterly data are only available on a more or less systematic basis starting with the first quarter of 1957. Hence, when we report on exercises using quarterly information, the data series begin at this point, except for specific countries whose quarterly series, as reported in *IFS*, start later.

4 Note that by choosing 31 December of the prior year as the date for this variable, we avoid the confusion that might be caused by the automatic effect of a devaluation in raising the value of R (and therefore the ratio of $R/R + D$), when all variables are expressed in domestic currency.

Chapter 11: References

Edwards, S., 'Exchange rate crises and the demand for international reserves: the case of LDCs, 1964–72', unpublished paper (University of Chicago, June 1980).

Harberger, A. C., 'A primer on inflation', *Journal of Money, Credit, and Banking*, vol. 10, no. 4 (1978), pp. 505–21.

Harberger, A. C., 'In step and out of step with the world inflation: a summary history of countries, 1952–76', in M. J. Flanders and A. Razin, eds, *Development in an Inflationary World* (New York: Academic Press, 1981).

12

Currency Baskets and Real Effective Exchange Rates

WILLIAM H. BRANSON and LOUKA T. KATSELI

Introduction and Summary

With the major currencies continuously moving (if not floating freely) against each other, a country that does not choose to float must decide what to peg to. If it pegs its currency to one of the major currencies, it floats against the others. If it pegs to the SDR, it floats against all currencies. Thus, in the system begun in the early 1970s the very concept of a fixed exchaege rate is unclear.

In this situation many countries have chosen to peg their currencies to a basket, or a weighted average of other currencies. This trend was noted by Arthur Lewis in his Per Jacobssen lecture at the IMF:

> It is now the conventional wisdom that the currencies of the developed countries should float, but the currencies of the less-developed (LDCs) should not; that is to say that each LDC should choose a more developed country (MDC) as a partner – or the SDR – and tie itself in a fixed relationship. (Lewis, 1977, p. 33)

Since the SDR weights are not particularly relevant for any single country, many countries compose their own basket.

Generalized floating (or dirty floating) raises problems of measurement. What is meant by 'the' exchange rate in a floating, multiple-currency world? The answer that has appeared in the literature is an 'effective' exchange rate, which is generally some trade-weighted index of changes in the home currency price of various foreign currencies. The IMF now publishes data on effective exchange rates. These are based on the IMF's multiple exchange-rate model (MERM), described by Artus and Rhomberg (1973). It will be shown in this chapter that this is only one of a possible number of definitions for an 'effective' exchange rate that depends on the implicit choice of a target for exchange-rate policy. In an earlier paper (Branson and Katseli-Papaefstratiou, 1981), presented at a conference in Stockholm in 1978, we derived weights for currency baskets that would eliminate the effects of other countries' nominal exchange-rate fluctuations on various home-country policy targets. There we considered the problem of choosing a currency basket in the presence of third-country exchange-rate fluctuations, holding prices constant. Here, we extend that discussion in several ways.

First, in section 1, we focus our analysis on fluctuations in real exchange rates and show that pegging to a currency basket is the same as holding constant a real effective exchange rate that uses a specific set of weights depending on the chosen policy target. We also show that the optimal weights of the earlier paper can be used for currency baskets defined across real exchange-rate fluctuations. The underlying model of trade prices and quantities is similar to the one in Branson and Katseli-Papaefstratiou (1981) and is summarized in the appendix to this chapter. The model of section 1 differs from others in the recent literature in two respects. First, a partial equilibrium approach is adopted as opposed to the general equilibrium model of Flanders and Helpman (1979). This affects the exact composition, but not the general form of the weights. Secondly, we derive weights that insulate policy targets from third-country real-exchange-rate fluctuations. The alternative in the literature is to adopt a variance-minimizing approach for a portfolio or a vector of targets. Examples are Flanders and Helpman (1979), de Macedo (1979) and Lipschitz and Sundararajan (1980). They derive weights which differ from ours in form, being functions of the variance–covariance structure of movements in real exchange rates.

In sections 2 and 3 we discuss several problems involved in choosing and computing optimal weights or the equivalent real effective rate. In section 2 it is shown that the index formula itself aggregates countries that are in a currency area, so that monetary authorities should use weights based on trade with countries rather than on currency denomination of trade. In section 3 optimal weights are combined with a crawling peg against the basket. Finally, in section 4 we report on an initial empirical investigation of pegging practices in Greece, Portugal and Spain. These are all countries that have moved to basket pegs, with geographically diversified trade. We present initial estimates of the implicit weights in their baskets, and find that all three countries experienced real appreciation relative to the basket during the 1970s.

(1) Real Effective Exchange Rates and Optimum Weighting Schemes

The objective of this section is to extend our previous work on the choice of weights for currency baskets and to develop further the theoretical framework for analyzing the construction of and role of real effective exchange rates in the exercise of exchange-rate policy. It is easiest to begin with a definition of a real effective exchange rate, and then go on to show how different currency basket weights define alternative real effective rates. Table 12.1 gives a complete listing of the symbols that will be used throughout this chapter.

Table 12.1   *Symbols and Definitions*

$I =$	real effective exchange-rate index of the home country
$i =$	index over N countries, $i = 1, \ldots, N$. We study the 0th country. The Nth country is the numeraire
$w_i =$	weights for 0's basket peg
$T_i =$	units of 0 currency per unit of i currency
$J_i =$	units of numeraire ($) per unit of i currency
$r =$	units of 0 currency per unit of numeraire ($); $T_i = J_i \cdot r$
$q_i =$	foreign country's cost index and foreign exchange ($) prices of goods competing with 0th country exports and imports; for simplicity, it is assumed that $q_{xi} = q_{mi} = q_i$
$p_0 =$	home country cost index and price of nontraded goods
$\hat{Z} =$	dZ/Z, for any variable Z
$e =$	exchange rate of 0 in the aggregate model of the appendix to this chapter; units of 0 currency per unit of foreign exchange; $p = eq$
$p_x, p_m =$	home (0th) country prices of exports and imports
$X, M =$	export and import quantities of country 0
$\alpha_i, \beta_i =$	0's export and import shares from/to country i
$d_x, s_x =$	price elasticities of export demand and supply in 0
$k =$	$d_x/(d_x - s_x)$, an inverse index of export market power of country 0
$d_m, s_m =$	price elasticities of import demand and supply of country 0
$k' =$	$s_m/(s_m - d_m)$, an inverse index of import market power of country 0

Movements in a real effective rate index for the home country (country zero) are given by

$$\hat{I} = \sum_1^N w_i(\hat{T}_i + \hat{q}_i - \hat{p}_0); \quad \Sigma w_i = 1 \tag{12.1}$$

where the weights w_i remain to be chosen. Noting that the bilateral exchange rate of the home country 0 against country $i(T_i)$ can be decomposed into the home-country price of an arbitrarily chosen numeraire r, and the numeraire price of the currency i, J_i, the numeraire can be factored out of the index in equation 12.1 as follows. Substitute $J_i r$ for T_i, and add and subtract $\hat{q}_N$ to obtain

$$\hat{I} = \sum_N w_i(\hat{J}_i + \hat{r} + \hat{q}_i - \hat{q}_N + \hat{q}_N - \hat{p}_0).$$

Since the weights sum to unity, the real exchange rate *vis-à-vis* the numeraire can be factored out to give

$$\hat{I} = (\hat{r} + \hat{q}_N - \hat{p}_0) + \sum_N w_i(\hat{J}_i + \hat{q}_i - \hat{q}_N). \tag{12.2}$$

In equation 12.2 the first term represents the home-country real exchange rate against the numeraire, and the second term is the weighted sum of the numeraire's real rate against all other countries.

Now, consider a policy rule that moves the nominal exchange rate against the numeraire r to hold I constant:

$$\hat{r} + \hat{q}_N - \hat{p}_0 = -\sum_N w_i(\hat{J}_i + \hat{q}_i - \hat{q}_N), \quad \text{or} \quad \hat{I} = 0. \tag{12.3}$$

This policy rule *both* stabilizes the effective real exchange rate I defined by w_i *and* pegs the real rate in terms of the numeraire to the currency basket across all N currencies (including the numeraire) defined by the same weights w_i. Thus, if the home-country real exchange rate *vis-à-vis* the numeraire is held equal to the basket real exchange rate defined by a given set of weights w_i, the real effective exchange rate defined by those weights is held constant. In nominal terms, this was noted by Crockett and Nsouli (1977, p. 131).

The weights w_i in equation 12.3 can be chosen to insulate one of a number of targets for movements in third-country exchange rates *vis-à-vis* the numeraire. Examples of such targets from Branson and Katseli-Papaefstratiou (1981) are (a) the terms of trade p_x/p_m, (b) the balance of payments $p_x X - p_m M$ and (c) the price ratio of traded to nontraded goods. In principle, these optimal basket weights may be calculated for a variety of policy targets. Flanders and Helpman (1979) and Lipschitz and Sundararajan (1980), for example, derive optimal basket weights for some of these, as well as other policy targets.

The policy targets can, in turn, be expressed as combinations of trade prices and quantities. In the appendix to this chapter changes in trade prices and quantities are expressed as functions of movements in (a) the home country's real exchange rate against the numeraire $\hat{r} + \hat{q}_N - \hat{p}_0$ and (b) the numeraire's real exchange rate against third countries $\hat{J}_i + \hat{q}_i + \hat{q}_N$. These can be combined to give an expression for movements in the chosen target variable, which can, in turn, be set equal to zero to solve for the weighting scheme w_i that insulates that particular combination of trade prices and quantities from movements in third-country real exchange rates.

Balance of Trade Weights

The balance of trade is given by $BT = p_x X - p_m M$. If we index p_x and p_m to unity initially, so $p_x = p_m = 1$, differentiation of this expression for the trade balance yields

$$\mathrm{d}BT = (\hat{p}_x + \hat{X})X - (\hat{p}_m + \hat{M})M. \tag{12.4}$$

Here, X and M are the initial levels of trade. Substitution from equations A10–A13 in the appendix to this chapter for $\hat{p}_x$, $\hat{p}_m$, $\hat{X}$ and $\hat{M}$ gives us the following expression for the change in the trade balance, in home currency terms:

$$
\begin{aligned}
\mathrm{d}BT = {} & (X - M)\hat{p}_0 \\
& + [Xk(1 + s_x) - Mk'(1 + d_m)](\hat{r} + \hat{q}_N - \hat{p}_0) \\
& + Xk(1 + s_x) \sum_N \alpha_i(\hat{J}_i + \hat{q}_i - \hat{q}_N) \\
& - Mk'(1 + d_m) \sum_N \beta_i(\hat{J}_i + \hat{q}_i - \hat{q}_N).
\end{aligned}
\tag{12.5}
$$

The first term is the effect of home price changes with a given initial balance; the second term gives the effect of changes in the real exchange rate against the numeraire; the term in brackets is the Marshall–Lerner condition. The last two terms give the effects of changes in third-country real exchange rates on export and import values, respectively.

To obtain the weights for the currency basket that would stabilize the trade balance, we set $\mathrm{d}BT = 0$ in 12.5, and solve for the real effective exchange rate index:

$$
\hat{r} + \hat{q}_N - \hat{p}_0 = \frac{X - M}{Xk(1 + s_x) - Mk'(1 + d_m)} \hat{p}_0 - \sum_N w_i(\hat{J}_i + \hat{q}_i - \hat{q}_N)
\tag{12.6}
$$

with weights w_i given by

$$
w_i = \frac{Xk(1 + s_x)\alpha_i - Mk'(1 + d_m)\beta_i}{Xk(1 + s_x) - Mk'(1 + d_m)}.
\tag{12.7}
$$

These are the same as the balance of trade weights 12.37 in Branson and Katseli-Papaefstratiou (1981), and are essentially the same as the IMF's effective MERM weights. If initially $X = M$, the results of 12.6 for real exchange rate against the numeraire N is given by

$$
\hat{r} + \hat{q}_N - \hat{p}_0 = - \sum_N w_i(\hat{J}_i + \hat{q}_i - \hat{q}_N).
$$

The nominal rate should be moved to make movements in the real rate equal to movement in the weighted average of thi. J-country real rates, with weights given by 12.7. These define a currency basket stabilizing the balance of trade; they also define an effective rate I with reference to stabilizing the trade balance.

Terms of Trade Weights

We could derive weights insulating the terms of trade p_x/p_m from third-country real exchange rates from equations A10 and A12 in the appendix to this chapter. However, given the balance of trade weights in 12.7, we can proceed more directly. Assume $X = M$ initially, and eliminate quantity effects from the balance of trade weights by assuming $s_x = d_m = 0$. Then those weights become the terms of trade weights:

$$w_i = \frac{k\alpha_i - k'\beta_i}{k - k'}. \tag{12.8}$$

These are the same as 12.28 in Branson and Katseli-Papaefstratiou (1981), and they define a currency basket or effective rate that would stabilize the terms of trade. As noted in Branson–Katseli-Papaefstratiou in the small-country case, where $k = k' = 1$, exchange-rate policy cannot influence the terms of trade; weights 12.8 are relevant only when $k \neq k'$.

Weights Stabilizing the Relative Price of Traded Goods

Equation 12.7 gives weights for a currency basket aimed at stabilizing the trade balance. These are essentially defined as weights for *the* effective exchange rate in the IMF literature. See, for example, Artus and Rhomberg (1973). On the other hand, as early as 1976, Stanley Black derived weights aimed at stabilizing the relative price of traded versus nontraded goods. These define an alternative effective exchange rate oriented toward relative prices. In Branson and Katseli-Papaefstratiou (1981) the Black weights were shown to be the small-country case of a more general scheme, as we now see.

Movements in the price of traded goods can be written as

$$\hat{p}_T = z_x \hat{p}_x + z_m \hat{p}_m \tag{12.9}$$

where z_x and z_m are weights of exports and imports in total trade in value terms and $z_x + z_m = 1$. Substitution from equations A10 and A12 in the appendix to this chapter for $\hat{p}_x$ and $\hat{p}_m$ yields

$$\begin{aligned}
\hat{p}_T = \hat{p}_0 &+ (z_x k + z_m k')(\hat{r} + \hat{q}_N - \hat{p}_0) \\
&+ z_x k \sum_N a_i(\hat{J}_i + \hat{q}_i - \hat{q}_N) \\
&+ zk' \sum_N \beta_i(\hat{J}_i + \hat{q}_i - \hat{q}_N).
\end{aligned} \tag{12.10}$$

Movements in the price of nontraded goods are given by domestic cost conditions, represented by $\hat{p}_0$. To hold p_T/p_0 constant, we thus have the solution

$$\hat{r} + \hat{q}_N - \hat{p}_0 = - \sum_N w_i(\hat{J}_i + \hat{q}_i - \hat{q}_N) \tag{12.11}$$

with the weights w_i given by

$$w_i = \frac{z_x k\alpha_i + z_m k'\beta_i}{z_x k + z_m k'}. \tag{12.12}$$

These are the same as in Branson and Katseli-Papaefstratiou (1981, equation 32), and they provide an effective exchange rate or currency basket stabilizing the relative price of traded versus nontraded goods as third-country real exchange rates fluctuate. In the small-country case, these simplify to total trade weights:

$$w_i = z_x \alpha_i + z_m \beta_i.$$

These are Black's (1976) preferred weights.

The weighting expressions in equations 12.7, 12.8 and 12.12 give alternative weights for currency baskets, or definitions of real effective exchange rates, for alternative targets of exchange-rate policy. The important points here are that, (a) as in our earlier work (Branson and Katseli-Papaefstratiou, 1980; 1981), each weighting system defines an effective exchange rate that corresponds to a chosen target, but (b) the weights here, as opposed to the model in the above reference, are used to define an index across real exchange rates. Even though the analysis is a straightforward extension of the earlier model, it is an important extension in that it permits us to consider the cases of *PPP* and of independent variations in prices and exchange rates as extreme cases of one general framework. Next, we turn to some comments on the application of weighting schemes in the exercise of exchange-rate policy.

(2) Issues in Calculating Optimal Weights

The weighting schemes of section 1 use trade weights α_i and β_i, and they are aggregated to the point where each country has a single import-competing price disturbance $\hat{q}_i$ and all countries have the same elasticity of demand d_x for the export good. Two kinds of questions have been raised in considering how to apply any of these schemes. One is whether trade weights, or currency weights, are appropriate. The second is how to disaggregate in general across commodities. Two examples of the disaggregation question are whether to use trade or current account weights, and how to adjust for the commodity composition of exports across, for example, agriculture, mining and manufacturing. In this section we will consider these two kinds of questions in turn.

Trade Shares Versus Currency Shares
Up to this point, we have noted the small-country special case in passing. But we have left for separate discussion a problem that generally appears as one of two seemingly different questions. These are as follows. How should trade weights be modified, if trade is denominated in a world currency? For example, Zambia's copper exports are stated in sterling as determined on the London metal exchange. Should we not use shares of currency denomination in the α_i and β_i weights, rather than direction of trade? The first question was first raised at a seminar at Columbia University, USA, 19 April, 1978. The second

was raised by Lipschitz (1979) and, again, in discussions at the Finance Ministry in New Delhi and the Monetary Authority of Singapore, 9 and 28 January, 1980. Here, we show that these questions are essentially the same, that they are really the question of the smallness of third countries, and that they are already answered in the formulation of the real exchange rate in the weighting schemes of section 1.

Consider, first, the question of using currency area weights instead of trade weights in the calculations. Suppose a subset H of the third countries denominate their trade with the home (zero) country in dollars, as an example. Then it seems intuitively plausible to argue that those countries should be included in a 'dollar area', and that their weights should be combined with that of the USA in calculations. This is not quite correct, though.

The true importance of the fact (if, indeed, it is a fact) that a country h prices its trade in dollars is the implicit assumption that country h's prices move with US prices, adjusted for the movements in h's dollar exchange rate J_h. This is the assumption that h is a small country relative to the USA. In this case the real exchange rate of h vis-à-vis the USA is constant, and the term $J_h + \hat{q}_h - \hat{q}_N$ in the weighting calculations is zero.

The implications of this for the use of the weighting schemes can be seen by concentrating on the example of the export price index for country 0 from the appendix to this chapter:

$$\hat{p}_{x0} = \hat{p}_0 + k(\hat{r} + \hat{q}_N - \hat{p}_0) + k \sum_N a_i(J_i + \hat{q}_i - \hat{q}_N). \qquad (12.13)$$

Suppose the US dollar is chosen as numeraire, so N is the US. Consider, first, a case in which all other countrys' prices are independent of the US. Then a q_N impulse will raise p_{x0} by

$$\hat{p}_{x0} = k\hat{q}_N + k \sum_1^{N-1} a_i(-\hat{q}_N) = ka_N\hat{q}_N.$$

The summation in the third term of 12.13 runs across all N countries. Thus, the $\hat{q}_N$ impulse is entered with a weight of unity in the term giving the movement in the real exchange rate of the home country against the numeraire, but it is taken out with a weight $\Sigma_1^{N-1}a_i$ by the term giving the movement in third-country real exchange rates.

Now, consider a case in which some subset of H countries $(1, \ldots, h, \ldots, H)$ have prices that move with the dollar, so that for each of these the real exchange rate vis-à-vis the dollar is constant. This is the case in which the h countries are small relative to the US dollar, and one would wish to integrate them into a dollar currency area. Now, the effect of a q_N impulse on p_{x0} is given by

$$\hat{p}_{x0} = k\hat{q}_N + k \sum_{H+1}^{N-1} a_i(-\hat{q}_N) = k(a_N + \sum_1^H a_i)\hat{q}_N.$$

Thus, the aggregation of countries that are truly in a currency area in the sense that their real exchange rates are constant *vis-à-vis* each other is accomplished by the weighting index. If countries price their trade in the same currency, but their prices move independently, they will not and should not be aggregated. But if their prices move together, they automatically will be.

The problem of a country which is selling a commodity priced in a numeraire on the world market is essentially the same. If copper trades at one world price, then all the relevant q_i for a copper exporter will move together, and be aggregated by the indexes into one world market. At this level, the appropriate aggregation is again automatically achieved by the index. The real problem for a commodity exporter will come with commodity disaggregation within the importing countries. This takes us to the disaggregation question.

Levels of disaggregation

While the indexes of equations A10–A13 in the appendix to this chapter will perform the aggregation of the world market for a single-commodity exporter, they do not take into account the probability that in each country i, the demand price for the commodity moves somewhat independently of the average import-competing price. This example raises one question of disaggregation. The formulas in equations A10–A13, and the subsequent weighting schemes, treat each country i as importing a single good with demand elasticity d_x. To implement the weighting schemes ideally, one would want to use for q_i the internal demand prices in country i for the particular exports and imports of the home country zero, and apply to them the appropriate disaggregated elasticity and share parameters. Thus, for a country exporting only copper, one would ideally use movements in copper prices in the various i countries, combined with estimates of elasticities relevant for copper, and the exporter's trade shares. This would then give the correct index for that country's $\hat{p}_x$, and so on, and the proper calculation of weights. Another major example of the disaggregation issue is the choice between current account and trade shares for α_i and β_i. The effective weighting schemes of the IMF (see, for example, Artus and Rhomberg, 1973) and the portfolio weights of Kouri and de Macedo (1978) and de Macedo (1979) use current-account shares.

In general, we would expect the services components of the current account to have different elasticities than the trade component. For example, if migrant workers determine the value of their remittances in terms of foreign exchange, k is effectively unity. If they fix the value in terms of their home currency, k is effectively zero. Thus, ideally, the shares should be current-account shares, and the elasticities should be averages of the trade and services components. Consistency would suggest not using trade elasticities with current-account shares.

The broad point here is that the formulas of section 1 are highly aggregated, with elasticities implicitly given as weighted averages of the relevant trade and services components. One can obtain a first aggregate approximation for the weighting schemes by using trade or current-account shares α_i and β_i and the corresponding average elasticities. But more precise calculation would require appropriate disaggregation of both shares and elasticities.

(3) Adjustment of the Real Exchange Rate and Choice of Optimal Weights

The optimal weighting schemes of section 1 give alternative sets of weights for real exchange rates, which have the following property: if the home-country real exchange rate *vis-à-vis* the numeraire follows the path of the real basket rate, effects of third-country fluctuations in real rates will not affect the chosen target. Thus, if the nominal rate r is manipulated to maintain

$$\hat{r} + \hat{q}_N - \hat{p}_0 = - \sum_N w_i(\hat{J}_i + \hat{q}_i - \hat{q}_N)$$

with the appropriately chosen weights w_i, the target is insulated from movements in real rates $(\hat{J}_i + \hat{q}_i - \hat{q}_N)$.

In the case of the balance of trade weights, this movement in the real rate will maintain trade or current-account balance, depending on whether the w_i include trade or current-account weights. On the other hand, the terms of trade weights and the weights stabilizing the ratio of prices of traded to nontraded goods (p_T/p_0) will not in general meet a balance of payments target. If those weights are chosen, there will still remain the need for adjustment of the real rate relative to the basket to hold the balance of payments near its target. One way to achieve this adjustment would be to adopt a crawling basket peg such as

$$\hat{r} + \hat{q}_N - \hat{p}_0 = - \sum_N w_i(\hat{J}_i + \hat{q}_i - \hat{q}_N) + F(B, R) \tag{12.14}$$

where B is the balance on current account or overall payments, and R is reserves. This is the real-rate equivalent of the basket crawl formula 4 in Branson and Katseli-Papaefstratiou (1981).

The adjustment function F in equation 12.14 gives the speed at which the home-country real rate is adjusted relative to the basket real rate. This is also the speed of adjustment of the real effective rate defined by w_i. The arguments of $F(\cdot)$ are the external-balance indicators used to adjust the real effective rate. Obvious choices for these indicators would include flows such as the current-account balance, or stocks such as reserves relative to a target level. These are represented by B and R, respectively, in 12.14. The optimal weighting of these indicators is analyzed in Branson and de Macedo (1980).

Since adjustment of the real effective rate, perhaps using a crawl formula, can be used to maintain payments balance, it would seem sensible not to choose the trade-balance weights for the currency basket. One can use, for example, the traded versus nontraded goods (p_T/p_0) weights to eliminate variance in that ratio, and combine this with a basket crawl to maintain payments balance. This combination would, of course, give a nonzero trend in the p_T/p_0 ratio as the real rate versus the numeraire moves relative to the basket, that is, when $F(\cdot) \neq 0$. This would be the trend in p_T/p_0 needed to meet the external balance target chosen for the F adjustment function. However, the choice of weights 12.12 for p_T/p_0 would reduce the *variance* around that trend.

To summarize, adjustment of the real effective rate can be used to maintain external balance. This means that the weights for the currency basket can be oriented toward a target other than the trade balance, namely, toward one of the relative-price targets. Use of one of those weighting schemes will then stabilize the chosen target around the trend dictated by the necessary adjustment of the real effective rate.

(4) Application to Exchange-Rate Experience in Southern Europe

Three countries in southern Europe, Greece, Portugal and Spain, have experimented with versions of basket pegs since exchange rates began to float in the early 1970s. In this section we briefly examine their experience, to see whether their choice of weights roughly conforms to the analysis above. We begin with a brief description of their experience. Next, we discuss choice of targets for these countries, and finally we examine the evidence.

Experience Since 1971

Following the breakdown of the Bretton Woods system of fixed parities, Greece, Portugal and Spain each sought to pursue a more flexible exchange-rate policy. Given the fact that the major currencies exhibited substantial fluctuations *vis-à-vis* each other, pegging the exchange rate to any single one of them meant substantial and continuous realignments *vis-à-vis* the others. Since all three countries have geographically diversified trade (see Table 12.2, below), this implied that each would experience analogous movements in the home-currency price of traded commodities, if not of the terms of trade.

As early as the third quarter of 1971, Spain and Portugal abandoned the dollar currency area and followed the Deutsche mark (DM) in its upward trend against the dollar. This continued until the middle of 1975 when both countries, hit by rising prices and appreciating effective real exchange rates, started devaluing in nominal terms *vis-à-vis* both hard currencies. The escudo's devaluation against the dollar has continued since; the devaluation against the DM halted around the end of 1979. The Spanish authorities, probably sensitive to the inflationary consequences of further nominal devaluations against as major a trading partner as Germany, reversed that trend at the third quarter of 1977 and attempted to stabilize the rate around 36 pesetas/DM. This lasted approximately until the end of 1979.

Greece followed the dollar in its downward movement *vis-à-vis* the other hard currencies for a much longer period than either Spain, or Portugal. The rate was held at 30 drachma/dollar until the middle of 1975, when a basket peg was adopted and the drachma started devaluing *vis-à-vis* the basket. It is only toward the end of the decade, with rapid inflation of import prices and the CPI, that the rapid depreciation *vis-à-vis* the European currencies was slowed. This policy shift was also prompted by increased trade prospects with the European Economic Community in light of the imminent entry into the EEC, and the expected movement towards harmonization of monetary and exchange-rate policies.

The experience of the three countries during the 1970s can be, thus, subdivided into three roughly comparable periods. In the first period, mid-1971–mid-1975, Spain and Portugal maintained rough parities *vis-à-vis* the Deutsche mark and appreciated substantially *vis-à-vis* the dollar; in the case of Greece the opposite held true. In the second period, which lasted to 1977 in the case of Spain, and until the end of 1979 in the other two countries, all three countries experienced substantial effective nominal devaluations *vis-à-vis* all major trading partners. Since that time, monetary authorities have attempted to maintain rough parities with the European currencies.

Choice of Targets for the Currency Basket

Currency baskets aimed at stabilizing three different policy targets were discussed in section 1, above. The targets are the trade balance, the terms of trade and the ratio of the price of traded goods to nontraded goods p_T/p_0. Which target would be most appropriate for Greece, Portugal and Spain?

In section 3 we argued that the effective real exchange rate can be varied to meet a balance of trade target. This implies movement of the home-currency real rate against the numeraire *relative* to the basket real rate, as illustrated in equation 12.14. In Table 12.3 we see that over the 1970s the effective real rate appreciated, on average, in all three countries. In Table 12.4 we see that, at least in the cases of Portugal and Spain, there is evidence that the effective real rate was responsive to an external-balance target. Thus, the choice of weights for the currency basket itself comes down to terms of trade versus p_T/p_0 weights.

Exchange-rate policy can affect the terms of trade only in countries with nonzero net market power; $(k - k')$ in equation 12.8 must be nonzero. In Branson and Katseli-Papaefstratiou (1980) we estimated indexes of market power on the export side and the import side for 101 countries. Greece, Portugal and Spain have relatively low values of the market power index, suggesting that the small-country assumption may be a good approximation in these cases. Thus, the terms of trade weights in equation 12.8 are probably not appropriate.

On the other hand, there is evidence that in these countries exchange-rate fluctuations do move p_T/p_0. Equations explaining quarterly movements in the consumer price index (CPI) for several countries were estimated in Katseli-Papaefstratiou (1979). These include movements in export prices and import prices in dollars, and in the exchange rate as independent variables. The maximum estimated one-quarter elasticities of the CPI with respect to a traded-good price are: Greece, 0·26 (export price); Portugal, 0·37 (import price); and Spain, 0·09 (import price). If these elasticities are close to the shares of traded goods in the CPI, the implicit elasticity of the ratio p_T/p_0 to changes in p_T is close to unity. Given the smallness of these countries, this means that a given change in the exchange rate moves p_T/p_0 more than it moves the terms of trade. Thus, the scanty evidence that is available suggests that the p_T/p_0 weights of equation 12.12 above would be most appropriate for Greece, Portugal and Spain. If we assume that the three countries are small, which is consistent with the Branson–Katseli-Papaefstratiou (1980) calculations, these weights reduce to total trade weights, as noted at the end of section 1.

Evidence from Greece, Portugal and Spain

Table 12.2 shows the direction of trade for the three countries in the 1970s. In all three, the EEC is the largest trading partner, with a share around 50 percent. For Greece, Germany is the largest among the EEC countries; the United Kingdom dominates for Portugal; and Germany and France come out about even in Spain. The US share varies from 5 percent of Greek exports to 15 percent of Spanish imports. The trade shares of Table 12.2 are the α_i and β_i of the optimal weighting formulas.

In Tables 12.3 and 12.4 we show the results of regression estimation of the weights in equation 12.14 in section 3, above. The dependent variable is the quarterly percentage change in the country's real exchange rate relative to the US dollar $\hat{r} + \hat{q}_{us} - \hat{p}_0$. The independent variables are the percentage changes in the real exchange rates of the dollar against the other major currencies $\hat{J}_i + \hat{q}_i - \hat{q}_{us}$ ($i \neq$ US); thus, the signs of the coefficients should be negative. The implicit US weight is one minus the absolute value of the sum of the estimated weights for $i \neq$ US; $w_{us} = 1 - \Sigma w_i$. In Table 12.3 a constant term is included for the average movement of the real effective rate over the period; a negative coefficient indicates real appreciation. In Table 12.4 we add the level and rate of change of net foreign assets F and $\hat{F}$ as indicators of external balance.

In general, the equations for Portugal and Spain seem reasonable; those for Greece are more difficult to interpret. This is probably due to the fact that Greece's currency basket was defined across nominal, rather than real, exchange rates. As has been shown in Katseli (1981), in the case where the basket is defined across nominal rates, the estimated weights are roughly the same as those of Table 12.3 but the explanatory power of the regression is markedly higher ($R^2 = 0.28$). In Table 12.3 all the constants are negative, indicating real appreciation relative to the basket. In Table 12.4 the level of net foreign assets has a significant negative coefficient for Spain, and both F and $\hat{F}$ seem to play a role in Portugal.

The patterns of coefficients giving currency weights permit us to draw several tentative but interesting conclusions:

(a)   The estimated weights seem reasonable as a description of actual experience. They do not, however, correspond particularly closely to our p_T/p_0 weights.

(b)   Over the whole period of the 1970s the weight of the dollar in the basket was markedly higher in the case of Greece than in either Portugal, or Spain. This is hard to explain in terms of the Greek trade shares (Table 12.2), but can be understood in light of the inertia of the early

Table 12.2 Direction of Trade: Percentage of Country's Total Exports (and Imports)

	Greece Exports			Greece Imports			Portugal Exports			Portugal Imports			Spain Exports			Spain Imports		
	1973	1975	1979	1973	1975	1979	1973	1975	1979	1973	1975	1979	1973	1975	1979	1973	1975	1979
Industrial countries	70·6	62·9	59·4	76·3	70·5	67·3	78·6	78·8	81·8	76·3	70·0	71·1	70·2	63·2	62·3	70·4	60·4	56·7
USA	6·5	5·1	5·5	8·3	7·4	4·8	9·8	7·2	6·0	8·2	12·4	11·8	13·9	10·5	7·2	16·1	15·9	12·5
Japan	1·2	1·6	1·1	7·0	8·3	9·5	1·7	0·9	1·1	4·3	3·4	2·6	1·5	1·2	2·0	2·6	2·4	2·3
EEC	54·9	49·7	49·1	50·1	42·5	44·3	48·6	50·1	56·9	45·4	40·3	41·6	47·8	44·7	48·0	42·9	34·7	35·9
France	6·6	7·3	6·1	7·6	5·9	6·3	5·1	6·6	10·0	6·9	7·6	8·3	12·7	13·6	16·1	10·3	8·3	9·7
Germany	21·5	21·1	19·3	19·5	15·9	15·9	7·6	10·2	12·7	14·5	11·4	12·4	11·7	10·7	10·3	13·6	10·3	9·6
Italy	9·5	8·3	9·8	9·1	8·2	9·3	3·2	3·3	6·0	5·2	5·0	5·1	5·3	3·4	6·5	6·0	5·1	5·6
United Kingdom	7·1	4·9	5·2	5·6	4·8	5·7	23·7	21·2	18·1	11·8	8·7	9·1	8·0	7·6	7·2	6·3	5·3	5·1
Oil-exporting countries	3·3	12·6	14·7	6·7	10·7	11·7	0·6	1·9	1·6	3·2	10·8	15·0	6·2	10·5	10·9	11·8	21·7	24·9
Nonoil-developing countries	16·3	14·5	17·3	12·5	14·1	15·2	19·7	16·6	13·9	19·0	13·7	10·5	20·5	20·4	22·0	15·3	13·6	15·5

Source:
IMF, Direction of Trade Yearbook, 1980.

Table 12.3 Movements of Real Home-Currency Price of the Dollar Relative to Real Dollar Price of Selected Currencies (quarterly data 1970II–1980II percentage change)

	C	$\frac{\$}{DM}\cdot\frac{CPIWG}{CPIUS}$	$\frac{\$}{Y}\cdot\frac{CPIJ}{CPIUS}$	$\frac{\$}{£}\cdot\frac{CPIUK}{CPIUS}$	$\frac{\$}{L}\cdot\frac{CPIIT}{CPIUS}$	$\frac{\$}{FF}\cdot\frac{CPIFR}{CPIUS}$	$\frac{\$}{P}\cdot\frac{CPISP}{CPIUS}$	US wt w_N	R^2	D–W
Greece										
$\frac{D}{\$}\cdot\frac{CPIUS}{CPIGR}$	−0·003	−0·228	0·071	−0·049	−0·132	0·082	—	$w_N=0.580$	0·078	2·2
	(0·5)	(1·1)	(0·5)	(0·3)	(0·4)	(0·3)				
	−0·002	−0·204	—	−0·041	−0·159	0·105	—	$w_N=0.491$	0·073	2·2
	(0·4)	(1·0)		(0·2)	(0·5)	(0·4)				
Portugal										
$\frac{E}{\$}\cdot\frac{CPIUS}{CPIPO}$	−0·004	−0·652	0·057	0·045	−0·500	0·329	0·007	$w_N=0.279$	0·389	2·4
	(0·6)	(3·2)	(0·4)	(0·3)	(1·6)	(1·2)	(0·0)			
	−0·004	−0·634	—	0·051	0·524	0·348	−0·013	$w_N=0.228$	0·387	2·3
	(0·6)	(3·2)		(0·3)	(1·8)	(1·3)	(0·1)			
Spain										
$\frac{P}{\$}\cdot\frac{CPIUS}{CPISP}$	−0·009	−0·161	−0·053	−0·043	−0·441	−0·024	—	$w_N=0.278$	0·320	1·8
	(1·7)	(0·9)	(0·4)	(0·3)	(1·8)	(0·1)				
	−0·009	−0·179	—	−0·049	−0·421	−0·042	—	$w_N=0.309$	0·317	1·7
	(1·8)	(1·1)		(0·3)	(1·8)	(0·2)				

Note:
1. *t* statistics in parentheses.

Table 12.4 *Movements of Real Home-Currency Price of the Dollar Relative to Basket*

	C	$\bar{F}$	F^1	$\dfrac{\$}{DM}\cdot\dfrac{CPIWG}{CPIUS}$	$\dfrac{\$}{\bar{Y}}\cdot\dfrac{CPIJ}{CPIUS}$	$\dfrac{\$}{£}\cdot\dfrac{CPIUK}{CPIUS}$	$\dfrac{\$}{FF}\cdot\dfrac{CPI1T}{CPIUS}$	$\dfrac{\$}{FF}\cdot\dfrac{CPIFR}{CPIUS}$	$\dfrac{\$}{P}\cdot\dfrac{CPISP}{CPIUS}$	US w_N	R^2	$D-W$
Greece $\dfrac{D}{\$}\cdot\dfrac{CPIUS}{CPIGR}$	-0·002 (0·4)	0·048 (1·9)	—	-0·118 (0·6)	0·004 (0·0)	-0·054 (0·3)	-0·727 (1·6)	0·358 (1·1)		$w_N = 0.453$	0·15	1·98
	-0·002 (0·7)	-0·050 (0·0)	-0·0001 (0·3)	-0·111 (0·2)	0·022 (0·2)	-0·071 (0·2)	-0·775 (0·5)	0·374 (0·5)			0·16	1·98
Portugal $\dfrac{E}{\$}\cdot\dfrac{CPIUS}{CPIPO}$	-0·002 (0·3)	-0·012 (1·6)	—	-0·705 (3·3)	0·044 (0·3)	0·093 (0·5)	-0·424 (1·4)	0·339 (1·2)	-0·079 (0·4)	$w_N = 0.252$	0·44	2·4
	0·001 (0·1)	-0·008 (1·0)	-0·0002 (1·6)	-0·671 (3·2)	0·098 (0·6)	0·040 (0·2)	-0·481 (1·6)	0·341 (1·5)	-0·099 (0·5)		0·49	2·7
Spain $\dfrac{P}{\$}\cdot\dfrac{CPIUS}{CPISP}$	-0·009 (1·7)	-0·002 (0·4)	—	-0·162 (0·8)	-0·056 (0·4)	-0·066 (0·4)	-0·462 (1·8)	-0·002 (0·0)		$w_N = 0.268$	0·34	1·7
	0·007 (0·8)	0·0003 (0·1)	-0·0001 (2·2)	-0·138 (3·2)	-0·179 (1·3)	-0·040 (0·3)	-0·500 (2·1)	-0·059 (0·2)			0·42	1·9

Note:
1. In billions of home-currency units.

period and preoccupation of the Greek authorities with balance of payments considerations.

(c)   The weight of the Deutsche mark is highest in the case of Portugal (0·63). Here, again, the explanation is probably historical relationships and possibly a domestic inflation target. Maintaining a relatively stable rather than declining home-currency value of emigrant remittances, might also be an important aspect of that choice.

(d)   In all three cases the share of the Italian lira is quite high. This probably reflects the preoccupation with competitive export positions in third markets.

(e)   For all countries there was a nominal devaluation and real appreciation of their currency relative to the basket. The nominal devaluation was strongest in Portugal (8 percent on an annual basis) compared to Greece (approximately 4 percent) and Spain (less than 1 percent) (Katseli 1981). On the other hand, the real appreciation *vis-à-vis* the basket was strongest in the case of Spain (around 4 percent).

(f)   Inclusion of the current-account balance and the level of foreign assets as potential determinants of the adjustment *vis-à-vis* the basket seem to improve both the Spanish and Portuguese results. This is especially true for the stock of foreign assets, which proves to be an important determinant of the authorities' reaction to third-country exchange-rate movements. Inclusion of these two variables seems to make little difference in the case of Greece.

These results suggest a general pattern: confronted with inflationary pressures in the mid-1970s from both domestic and foreign origins, the monetary authorities in all three countries attempted to safeguard their competitive position internationally through a process of nominal effective devaluations. These policies produced a relatively small real effective exchange-rate appreciation in the face of domestic inflation rates, which at least in Spain and Portugal exceeded 20 percent by 1977.

Thus, by the end of the 1970s these countries found themselves caught in the classic dilemma associated with exchange-rate policy, namely, the conflict between balance of trade and domestic inflation targets. The econometric evidence, however sparse, seems to suggest that in small open economies the effects of exchange-rate movements on the price ratio of traded to nontraded goods is higher than the effect on the terms of trade. The experience of these countries in the 1970s and the switch in policies in the early 1980s seem to substantiate that claim.

Appendix: A Log-Linear Trade Model with Real Exchange Rates

Here, a simple partial-equilibrium model is developed that provides the framework for the choice of weights for currency baskets or effective exchange rates. The model is essentially the same as that developed in Branson and

Katseli-Papaefstratiou (1981, section IV). There independence of movements in exchange-rates and price levels was implicitly assumed. Here, the model is developed in terms of real exchange rates. It is a log-linear supply-and-demand model for exports and imports which includes the exchange rate as the translator between home and foreign prices. We begin with the simple two-country version, and then disaggregate to many countries and a numeraire.

Movements in Aggregate Trade Prices and Quantities

Let us begin by concentrating on the export side. Export supply prices are assumed to be stated in home-currency units p_x, while foreign import demand prices are given in foreign exchange units q_m. The supply function is written as

$$\ln p_x = \ln p + s_x^{-1}\ln X. \tag{A1}$$

Here, p is a shift parameter representing the domestic cost of production of exportables and s_x is the price elasticity of export supply. We assume that p is also the home-currency cost of production of import substitutes and non-tradeables. Equation A1 gives export supply X as a function of the relative home-currency supply price p_x/p. The demand function giving the foreign currency price of exports is

$$\ln q_x = \ln q + d_x^{-1}\ln X. \tag{A2}$$

Here, q is a shift parameter representing the domestic cost of production of import-competing goods in the foreign country, and export demand depends on the relative price q_x/q. Again, we assume that q is also the cost of production of exports in the foreign country. For the analysis in a case where domestic costs of production in the various sectors move differently, see Branson and Katseli-Papaefstratiou (1981). The exchange rate e links p_x and q_x:

$$p_x = eq_x. \tag{A3}$$

Substitution of A3 into A2 for q_x and total differentiation yields the expressions for percentage changes in export prices and quantities:

$$\hat{p}_x = k(\hat{e} + \hat{q}) + (1 - k)\hat{p} \tag{A4}$$

$$\hat{X} = ks_x(\hat{e} + \hat{q} - \hat{p}) \tag{A5}$$

where $k \equiv d_x/(d_x - s_x)$; $0 < k \leq 1$. As noted in Branson and Katseli-Papaefstratiou (1980; 1981), k is an index of market power on the export side. In the small-country case $d_x \to -\infty$ and $k \to 1$.

The analogous model on the import side yields the equations for percentage changes in import prices and quantities:

$$\hat{p}_m = k'(\hat{e} + \hat{q}) + (1 - k')\hat{p} \tag{A6}$$

$$\hat{M} = k'd_m(\hat{e} + \hat{q} - \hat{p}) \tag{A7}$$

where $k' \equiv s_m/(s_m - d_m)$; $0 < k' \leq 1$. Again, k' is an index of market power on the import side; for a small country where $s_m \to \infty$, $k' \to 1$.

Disaggregation to Many Countries

To disaggregate the model, we consider a world of $N + 1$ countries, $0, \ldots, N$. Country 0 is the home country whose exchange-rate policy we are analyzing. Country N is the numeraire, arbitrarily chosen. Countries $j(=1, \ldots, j, \ldots, N-1)$ are the other (nonhome, nonnumeraire) countries in the system. The index i runs across *all* countries other than the home country, including the numeraire, thus, $i = j, N$.

The home-country price index p in equation A1 is now p_0. The import-competing price in country i's demand function is q_{mi}, and the export-supply price of country i is q_i. The bilateral exchange rate of the home country 0 against country i is T_i, in units of currency 0 per unit of currency i. This can be decomposed into the home-country price of the numeraire r, and the numeraire price of the currency i, J_i:

$$T_i = J_i r. \tag{A8}$$

For exposition, we focus on disaggregation of movements in the export price $\hat{p}_{x0}$; disaggregation of $\hat{X}_0$, $\hat{p}_{m0}$ and $\hat{M}_0$ follow easily by analogy. With export weights given by α_i, $\hat{e}$ and $\hat{q}$ in the $\hat{p}_x$ equation A4 are the aggregates

$$\hat{e} = \sum_1^N \alpha_i(\hat{J}_i + \hat{r})$$

$$\hat{q} = \sum_1^N \alpha_i \hat{q}_i.$$

The disaggregated expression for $\hat{p}_{x0}$ is now

$$\hat{p}_{x0} = k\sum_N \alpha_i(\hat{J}_i + \hat{r}) + k\sum_N \alpha_i \hat{q}_i + (1 - k)\hat{p}_0. \tag{A9}$$

This is precisely the same as equation 24 in Branson and Katseli-Papaefstratiou (1981), with slight changes in notation. The analysis there proceeded in terms of *nominal* exchange rates. Here, we wish to continue in terms of movements in *real* exchange rates.

First, let us add and subtract the change in the numeraire's import-competing price $\hat{q}_N$ in the second term of A9:

$$\hat{p}_{x0} = k\sum_N \alpha_i(\hat{J}_i + \hat{r}) + k\sum_N \alpha_i(\hat{q}_i + \hat{q}_N - \hat{q}_N) + (1 - k)\hat{p}_0.$$

Now, remembering that $\Sigma \alpha_i = 1$, we can regroup the terms on the right-hand side into movements in real exchange rates:

$$\hat{p}_{x0} = \hat{p}_0 + k(\hat{r} + \hat{q}_N - \hat{p}_0) + k\sum_N \alpha_i(\hat{J}_i + \hat{q}_i - \hat{q}_N). \qquad (A10)$$

The first term on the right-hand side of A10 is the change in the domestic (zero-country) export supply price due to changes in domestic cost conditions. The second term is the change in the home-country real exchange rate against the numeraire, using export prices. The third term sums the change in the numeraire's real exchange rate against all countries other than the home country, including the numeraire (country N), again using demand prices for exports of the zero country.

Several properties of A10 for $\hat{p}_{x0}$ are worth noting:

(1)　If the home country is small, $k = 1$ and $\hat{p}_0$ drops out of A10; $\hat{p}_{x0}$ depends only on world prices and exchange rates.

(2)　An increase in the demand price q_j in any one of the j (nonnumeraire, nonhome) countries clearly raise p_{x0} by $\hat{p}_{x0} = k\alpha_j\hat{q}_j$, proportional to j's share in home-country exports. The increase in q_j also raises the numeraire's real exchange rate vis-à-vis j.

(3)　An increase in the demand price in the numeraire country alone raises p_{x0} by $\hat{p}_{x0} = k\alpha_N\hat{q}_N$, symmetrically to all the other countries. This results from the summation of the third term in A10 across all $i = 1, \ldots, N$. Thus, the formulation in A10 is completely symmetric across all nonhome countries, with the numeraire chosen arbitrarily.

The disaggregation of the expressions for $\hat{X}$, $\hat{p}_m$ and $\hat{M}$, and their statement in terms of real exchange rates, follow analogously to the development from equation A4 for $\hat{p}_x$ to A10 for $\hat{p}_{x0}$. The disaggregated version of A5 for the change in exports is

$$\hat{X}_0 = ks_x[(\hat{r} + \hat{q}_N - \hat{p}_0) + \sum_N \alpha_i(\hat{J}_i + \hat{q}_i - \hat{q}_N)] \qquad (A11)$$

On the import side, $\hat{e}$ and $\hat{q}$ in equations A6 and A7 disaggregate into

$$\hat{e} = \sum_1^N \beta_i(\hat{J}_i + \hat{r})$$

and

$$\hat{q} = \sum_1^N \beta_i\hat{q}_i$$

where β_i are import weights and $\Sigma\beta_i = 1$. The disaggregated versions of A6 and A7 for $\hat{p}_{m0}$ and $\hat{M}_0$ are then given by

$$\hat{p}_{m0} = \hat{p}_0 + k'(\hat{r} + \hat{q}_N - \hat{p}_0) + k'\sum_N \beta_i(\hat{J}_i + \hat{q}_i - \hat{q}_N) \qquad (A12)$$

$$\hat{M}_0 = k'd_m[(\hat{r} + \hat{q}_N - \hat{p}_0) + \Sigma\beta_i(\hat{J}_i + \hat{q}_i - \hat{q}_N)]. \tag{A13}$$

In equations A12 and A13 the term $(\hat{r} + \hat{q}_N - \hat{p}_0)$ is the change in the home country's real exchange rate against the numeraire, and the term $(\hat{J}_i + \hat{q}_i - \hat{q}_N)$ is the real exchange rate of the numeraire against country i (including the numeraire), using the prices relevant for country zero's imports. Equations A10–A13 give the expressions for changes in export and import prices and quantities in terms of movements in home prices and real exchange rates.

Chapter 12: Note

Thanks go to Ramon Espinosa and Cynthia Arfken, for assisting with research.

Chapter 12: References

Artus, J. R. and Rhomberg, R. K., 'A multilateral exchange rate model', *IMF Staff Papers*, vol. 20, no. 4 (1973), pp. 591–611.

Black, S. W., *Exchange Rate Policies for Less Developed Countries in a World of Floating Rates*, Princeton Essays on International Finance 119, (Princeton, NJ: Princeton Universtiy International Finance Section, 1976).

Branson, W. H. and Katseli-Papaefstratiou, L. T., 'Income instability, terms of trade, and the choice of exchange-rate regime', *Journal of Development Economics*, vol. 7, no. 1 (1980), pp. 49–69.

Branson, W. H. and Katseli-Papaefstratiou, 'Exchange-rate policy in developing countries', in S. Grassman and E. Lundberg, eds, *The World Economic Order: Past and Prospects* (London: Macmillan, 1981), pp. 391–419.

Branson, W. H. and de Macedo, J. B., *The Optimal Weighting of Indicators for a Crawling Peg*, National Bureau of Economic Research Working Paper No. 527, August 1980.

Crockett, A. D. and Nsouli, S. M., 'Exchange rate policies for developing countries', *Journal of Development Studies*, vol. 13, no. 2 (1977), pp. 125–43.

Flanders, J. M. and Helpman, E., 'An optimal exchange rate peg in a world of general floating', *Review of Economic Studies*, vol. XLVI, no. 3 (1979), pp. 533–42.

Katseli-Papaefstratiou, L. T., *Transmission of External Price Disturbances in Small Open Economies* (New York: Garland Press, 1979).

Katseli, L. T., *Macroeconomic Adjustment and Exchange-Rate Policy in Middle Income Countries: Greece, Portugal and Spain in the 1970s*, Yale Economic Growth Center Discussion Paper No. 374, April 1981.

Kouri, P. J. K and de Macedo, J. B., 'Exchange rates and the international adjustment process', *Brookings Papers on Economic Activity*, no. 1 (1978), pp. 111–50.

Lewis, W. A., 'The less developed countries and stable exchange rates', in IMF, *The International Monetary System in Operation* (Washington, DC: IMF, 1977).

Lipschitz, L., 'Exchange rate policy for a small developing country, and the selection of an appropriate standard', *IMF Staff Papers*, vol. 26, no. 3 (1979), pp. 423–49.

Lipschitz, L. and Sundararajan, V., 'The optimal basket in a world of generalized floating', *IMF Staff Papers*, vol. 27, no. 1 (1980), pp. 80–100.

de Macedo, J. B., *Portfolio Diversification Across Currencies*, Yale Economic Growth Center Discussion Paper No. 321, September 1979.

13

Negotiating International Economic Order

GORAN OHLIN

The discussions about comprehensive reforms of the international economic system to create a New International Economic Order have now gone on for so long as to seem almost a permanent and unchanging feature of the life of the United Nations organizations. After all those years, disenchantment is inevitable. As John Lewis (1979, p. 17) noted in his 1979 report as DAC Chairman, 'the specialists in North–South dialoguing find their fora awkward, their constraints cumbersome, and their audiences slipping away'. More serious than the flagging attention of the public is the lack of interest of governments increasingly evident on both sides. How should one explain the failure of this massive political and economic effort? The record of these negotiations and the substantive issues are well known and I shall not restate them here. Briefly, the perspective in which they will be seen is the following.

In one sense the existing international economic order, characterized by the unequal economic relations between the unindustrialized countries in Africa, Asia and Latin America on the one hand and the industrialized world in America and Europe on the other, established itself, as Arthur Lewis (1978, p. 7) has argued, in the last quarter of the nineteenth century when tropical countries entered international trade in a significant way. Its political roots in Western colonialism go even further back.

In another sense, the international economic order is often taken to be the system of rules and institutions created after the Second World War to avoid a repetition of the collapse of the international economy in the 1930s. The economic constitution then laid down for nation states was, for all its imperfections, a new and remarkable achievement. But its political premises were faulted by discord among major industrial powers, which resulted in relaxation of international monetary discipline. Then the developing countries, which had consistently sought changes and amendment in the postwar system, were greatly increased in numbers when Asian and African countries became independent. The pressure for renegotiation of the postwar arrangements and their enlargement to take fuller account of the interests of the developing countries went into a new phase with the creation of UNCTAD in 1964 and were intensified in the 1970s. These efforts have so far yielded very little.

Conflicts of Interest?

The easiest explanation of the general stalemate in North–South talks might seem to be that the developing countries are pressing for such profound changes in the international economic system that they conflict too violently with the national interests of the rich countries to be acceptable to them. The steamy rhetoric that envelops so many North–South encounters fosters this view. The proposals for change are, for instance, called a bid for power which the North is unwilling to surrender, and the diplomatic offensive is made out to be more of a demonstration or a confrontation than a quest for negotiated change.

In actual fact, the core of the proposals to modify the prevailing regimes in international trade and investment, capital flows and other areas are far from revolutionary. Many have their origins in proposals that were part of the Anglo-American plans for the postwar world, such as commodity-price regulation. A great many academic assessments have long concluded that there are extensive mutual interests in proposals for international economic reform. Such views have drawn support from the stagnation of world trade and industrial growth in the 1970s, from the energy crises in rich and poor countries alike, and from the new concerns with global food-supply prospects, ecological and environmental deterioration – all of them issues that can be said to demonstrate the malfunctioning or the inadequacy of the existing world economy to the harm of industrial countries, as well as to the young countries for whom national development is an imperative. The inter-dependence of the world economy, which reveals not only the dependence of the poor countries on the rich ones, but also the opposite, is used to support the claim that the call for a new world economic order is a proposal that the rich cannot refuse, as it is in fact in their own vital interest.

Why, then, do the industrial countries' governments and negotiators fail to recognize this? Economists seeking to press their own conceptions upon recalcitrant policy-makers are frequently inclined to interpret past history in terms of national interests infallibly pursued, while they ascribe to the governments of the present nothing but the most shortsighted and obtuse perception of their own true interests. As Arthur Lewis (1955, ch. 7) noted in his essay on government, 'clearly, good government is very difficult', and those who argue that industrial countries act counter to their own interests in resisting suggestions for world economic reform tend to assume that a preoccupation with serious domestic difficulties or a failure to understand the premises and needs of the postcolonial world are to blame. There may be much in this.

On the other hand, many students of international political economy scoff at 'interdependence rhetoric' and its tendency to brush aside conflicts of interest with exaggerated references to looming catastrophes or to vague claims of mutual gains in an uncertain future (Bergsten *et al.*, 1975, p. 21). It can certainly safely be said that the economic interests of nation states converge in some respects and conflict in others.

The aim here is not to argue where this balance lies in North–South issues, but the premiss is that there is obviously a potential to translate at least some of the mutual interests into mutually satisfactory accords, even if it proves impossible in others.

Now, the peculiarity of the North–South talks that have been going on for so long is precisely that they have led practically nowhere. The contrast with major negotiations of the past is staggering. It took two or three years to prepare Bretton Woods – in very exceptional conditions, to be sure – and even after the war some international agreements have been negotiated successfully in reasonable time. The North–South talks rather lead the mind back to the desultory international economic conferences of the 1920s and 1930s culminating in the World Economic Conference in London in 1933, the failure of which, as Arthur Lewis (1950, p. 68) once observed, marked the end of an era of efforts to cope internationally with the economic problems of the time.

As already noted, some of the North–South issues have been around since long before the NIEO rounds of the 1970s. Gunnar Myrdal (1956, p. 251) was reflecting on the failure of the efforts to stabilize international commodity prices, and his frustration has a modern ring:

> It is a routine experience of every international civil servant that, almost as a rule, government representatives arrive at their meeting with instructions to oppose initiatives ... It is usually realized that there is a common gain to be made and shared, but it is feared that the others get it all and perhaps more than that ... [The] essential difficulty to overcome in intergovernmental negotiations of this type is very simply the restrictiveness of national governments and their suspicions about each other.

But precisely the long record of efforts in the commodity field also suggests another possible explanation than the meanness of governments – that interests are indeed more numerous and complex than appears when the issue is boldly sketched, that technical difficulties are sometimes very great and that the impact of uncertainty about the future make the implications of proposed actions seem risky and unclear. Time and again, international negotiations in the commodity field seem at the brink of success, which shows the awareness of a common interest, but then slide back without quite making it.

Should this be surprising? It is often pointed out that price and income stabilization is considered natural and necessary in the national agricultural markets of industrial countries where governments arbitrate and impose themselves by law. This makes nonsense of their opposition to similar action in the international field when it is based on abstract principle, such as the sanctity of the market. But already in limited groups such as the European Economic Community the Common Agricultural Policy is a chief source of discord and hurdles for negotiators. In a wider international context it has so far, in contrast to the spectacular liberalization of international trade in manufactures, proved impossible to make a dent in agricultural trade or to avoid heated conflict between, for instance, the EEC and the USA.

Myrdal complained of a lack of enlightened generosity, and this is undoubtedly a feature of international negotiation, not least among countries whose governments and negotiators are intensely watched by the many domestic groups whose interests they compromise or enhance by their actions. This is one reason why international negotiation is intrinsically difficult, and the question to be examined in the following is whether the obstacles to negotiation in North–South matters are perhaps so serious that agreement is unlikely even in what appears to be 'positive-sum games'.

Facile references to lacking political will or insuperable conflicts of interest in North–South issues tend to deflect attention from the very special setting and circumstances in which these issues are tackled. This is a pity, as the multilateral diplomacy within which the reforms of the international economic order are discussed, is a novel phenomenon.

Even the general implications of multilateral diplomacy in international organizations are not easily assessed. For major powers it may, for the most part, be a marginal adjunct to classical diplomacy, but to smaller and weaker countries it may offer opportunities they would not otherwise have had. Its greatest contribution has perhaps been to provide new forms for settlement of disputes that arise between states. The belief implicit in the schemes for postwar international economic organization that the time had come for universal systems of rules and international law has taken some knocks, especially in the monetary field. Although based on charters internationally negotiated, it is far from clear whether multilateral diplomacy as presently practiced in international organizations is suited for, or even capable of, reforms that would set new and different rules for governments.

Size and Diversity

It is too obvious to be denied that it must be very much more difficult to engineer agreement among 150 states than among the fifty or less that reached at least partial agreement on the postwar system for international cooperation. And at the time conditions were peculiar indeed. The participants were allied in an on-going but victorious war. American or Anglo-American leadership was readily acquiesced to, and it was exercised with rare vision and openmindedness. In the monetary and financial discussions extraordinary personalities like Keynes and Harry Dexter White dominated the proceedings. The present situation is obviously different on all counts. Apart from the addition of close to 100 new states, there has been a great diffusion of power frequently commented upon, and the complexity of negotiation has been compounded.

In an interesting analysis of the failure of the international monetary reform negotiations in 1971–4, John Williamson (1977, ch. 7) has argued that the new complexity of the world was not the decisive obstacle. He pointed to the great advance in economic negotiation techniques in the postwar years which made possible such things as the GATT liberalization rounds or the relative success of the SDR negotiations. He found a certain truth in the charge of inadequate will to make concessions, but he suggested that considerable political will had been invested in launching the talks at all and, therefore, believed that if technical solutions could have been arrived at, politicians would have been pleased to take credit for them. He was thus inclined to look more to the conduct of the negotiations and concluded that the secretariat should have more actively pursued technical solutions with a potential for agreement and compromise instead of drawing up options for ministers in the hope of a great political horsetrade at some point in the negotiations.

This does not, of course, invalidate the observation that a large and heterogeneous participation makes agreement elusive, especially in matters that have not reached the degree of serious technical negotiation of the Committee of Twenty.

International Organizations as Negotiating Forums

It was the control of the agenda of the United Nations that made it possible for developing countries to force talks about these matters against the reluctance of major industrial countries. The latter have frequently recalled that the United Nations is a deliberative body only, and that its proceedings should not be described as negotiations in any proper sense.

Everyone recognized that declarations adopted by international organizations will not necessarily be abided by, even by states that vote for them, let alone by those who oppose them. When such declarations are none the less pursued, it is presumably because they are expected to have an impact on world opinion, to exercise some pressure on reluctant governments, and to guide the course of future diplomatic efforts. That they are of some importance, must be the view also of governments which invest considerable effort in forestalling the adoption of declarations and pronouncements which they oppose.

Such conflicts, the portentous and extensive statements, and the massive machinery of documentation and meetings, lend to contemporary international assemblies an aura of importance and seriousness, even when it is widely known that at best only insignificant results are to be expected. The solemnity of the proceedings may appear as little more than a celebration of the fortunate circumstance that there is a shared will to confer and consult, which probably serves a role of its own and to some extent takes the place of the binding treaties often aspired to which are, after all, not the only means of ordering relations among states.

Too much has, perhaps, been made of the voting rights of the United Nations that enable countries contributing less than 5 percent of the budget to take decisions with a two-thirds majority. It threatens the very survival of the organizations if declarations are voted through in a discordant manner, but it is not a reason why genuine negotiation could not take place under the auspices of the United Nations. There are a few instances of such negotiation, but there are many grounds for suspecting that the North–South dialogue will not be crowned by grand settlements arising out of the profusion of meetings that now succeed and repeat one another in New York and Geneva.

Neither governments and delegates, nor the secretariats, are committed to seeking agreements that would have to involve concessions on all sides. It is hardly even envisaged, and government instructions are not framed as negotiating mandates. It is widely recognized that the present financial disorder, the alarming food prospects, the precarious energy-supply arrangements and many other aspects of the world situation call for a far greater measure of international cooperation, but in the proceedings of the international organizations, the impulses to joint action are mostly ground asunder.

The permanent secretariats of those organizations are not necessarily well suited to drive proceedings toward positive conclusions. They have a vast range of administrative and technical tasks. They operate in a heavily bureaucratized and politicized environment, leaving little scope for active and flexible brokerage, and their perception might well be swayed by their interest in survival and enlargement of their organization and its responsibilities. The qualities that lead to promotion to high posts are not, and should perhaps not be, those wanted in a group servicing negotiations that aim at quick and forceful action. In standing bodies, with permanent delegates and secretariats, negotiations tend to become permanent, too.

The Group System

The division between rich and poor countries in the United Nations had become established long before UNCTAD I, and the emergence of the group system was probably inevitable, especially after the setting up of an *ad hoc* working party at the OECD in 1963 in order to prepare a joint strategy for the forthcoming Geneva meeting in 1964. The only surprising thing is that it was then possible to maintain the unity of such a large and diverse body as the Group of Seventy-Seven. There has been much complaint about the inherent tendency of the group system to widen rather than narrow the gaps in positions, as each of the two groups strives for agreement by yielding to its hardliners.

In games and bargains among more than two participants coalitions will always be of decisive importance, and if such coalitions become too rigid, the chances of reaching agreement will be very small. Unless the consequences of failure are perceived as so disastrous or costly as to seem worth much concession, a coalition marked by widely divergent interests might well exhaust its negotiating capacity internally and have no room for bargaining with outsiders.

Negotiators from industrial countries sometimes complain that this is precisely the trouble with the Group of Seventy-Seven and that it, on its side, attributes to Group B a unity of interests and attitudes which barely exists. Southern negotiators believe that industrial countries coordinate their policies effectively in such bodies as the OECD and the EEC, and many think that if the Third World had a secretariat of its own, it would make for better negotiation. It is, perhaps, significant that this proposal has not gained wide adherence.

In bargaining about concrete and tangible matters the group system breaks down. In specific commodity markets many Group B countries are producers and exporters which aligns them with individual members of the Group of Seventy-Seven. In the Law of the Sea Conference similar North–South alliances frequently arose. But in general discussions about global arrangements the group system has become institutionalized in most international organizations, except the IMF and the World Bank, where the structure of decision-making bodies and the weighted voting make for a different environment.

The adoption of the group system as a quasi-constitutional feature has contributed an element of structure that conferences of 150 states badly need. Third World nonalignment, of which the Group of Seventy-Seven can be seen as a manifestation, has also been a contribution to international political stability. But this has been at the cost of effective multilateral negotiation. As a seasoned Swiss diplomat (Jolles, 1979, p. 14) has concluded,

> the consultations within the respective caucuses must not be allowed to monopolize the time of international conferences to the point of relegating the real negotiating process between the groups to the eleventh hour. This has frequently happened in the past. Much more time has been spent on elaborating common platforms than on narrowing down the differences between them and on seeking to solve specific issues across the negotiating table.

The North–South dichotomy in international organizations also mesmerizes many political commentators into thinking that it is also the expression of a worldwide confrontation and stalemate in political and economic relations outside of these assemblies, and it has led to extravagant speculations about future stratagems of North and South that wildly exaggerate the will and capacity of both groups to pursue united policies. There is more to the world than that, and the consequence of sustained failure to progress through multilateral diplomacy is more likely to be that it is bypassed by events and that elements of international order grow on less overarching bilateral and regional links.

Lack of Individual Leadership

It is undeniable that personal qualities matter greatly in international negotiation. In postwar development cooperation the vitality, determination, and charisma of some outstanding personalities is recognized to have been of decisive importance in overcoming the inertia of governments and rallying them to greater commitments in the joint interest. Robert McNamara has obviously enhanced the standing and capacity of the World Bank. In North–South relations Dr Raoul Prebisch played a singular role as a supplier of ideas, militant leader and persuasive mediator.

With the routinization of North–South talks, they seem to have lost towering personalities who might incarnate the will to achieve what is possible and necessary and help to lead the way out of the stalemate. That is not to say that there is a lack of able and talented negotiators. The spectacular growth of multilateral diplomacy raises a great demand for delegates and negotiators, and it is understandable that governments may be reluctant to spare their best negotiators for such blocked situations. Especially for smaller and poorer countries, the strain and expense of covering the sprawling agendas of current international conferences and meetings is quite unreasonable. In view of all this, it is remarkable how much ability is still invested in these Byzantine proceedings.

But the circumstances do not favor the emergence of personalities commanding general respect and confidence. The task of conciliating the groups internally requires able diplomacy, and occasionally delegates from minor countries who have received no precise instructions may attain considerable influence by their freedom to maneuver (Gosovic, 1972, p. 278). But the institutionalized distrust is hard to overcome, and prolonged immersion in the rarefied atmosphere of those talks is likely to impair the sense of their role.

The Issue of Nonreciprocity

From the outset North–South discussions have been couched in terms that could not be conducive to negotiations in a traditional sense. As Ambassador K. B. Lall of India remarked at the occasion of UNCTAD II, a negotiating technique based on mutual concession could not easily be applied to economic development (Gosovic, 1972, p. 320).

The basic difficulty that little or nothing could be expected to come out of strategy based on unilateral demands was recognized by Prebisch, who at the end of the 1960s attempted to promote a doctrine of 'convergence' under which developing countries would pledge themselves to certain policies of development which the rich countries would in return commit themselves to support, in the interest both of international solidarity, and ultimately of their own welfare. This doctrine had little impact and many Third World negotiators remained convinced that reciprocity was alien to these proceedings either because developing countries were too poor to have anything to offer, or because they were only asking for rights and dues that should not be bargained for.

That the group system also made it more difficult to offer concessions than to make demands is obvious. However, in the GATT where negotiation along group lines has been less suitable and less common, developing countries have also tended to refrain from offers and, thus, from active participation in genuine negotiation. And in the monetary field John Williamson (1977, p. 174) argues that individual developing countries in the Committee of Twenty were so aware that their own actions had a negligible feedback on the international monetary system that they failed to realize that this was not true of them collectively, and that they would therefore be expected to accept the obligations and disciplines of the proposed SDR standard if they were to collect the benefits, and that they were thus reduced to an attitude of 'all asking and not bargaining'.

The failure or unwillingness to put North–South issues in a negotiable form may have been welcome to those who did not want the talks to turn serious. Mahbub ul Haq (1980–81) has argued that in retrospect it is clear that mistakes were indeed made on both sides, that the call for a New Order should not have been launched as a 'demand' of the developing countries, but with more emphasis from the start on the global needs of the world economy and more attention to the interests of the North – and that the North should similarly have been wiser and more farsighted. Such things bear saying, and the Brandt Report is an elaboration on that theme, but the trouble is that by now the habits and postures have become engrained and encrusted.

The Prospects of World Order Talks

After reviewing these handicaps of multilateral diplomacy, one must conclude that the chances of negotiating substantive change through such channels are not very great. The setting for the negotiations is so stained with failure, and the conduct of them is so cumbersome and flawed, that they are heavily biased against agreement. Even such shifts in attitudes and political will as can reasonably be expected in North and South would not be likely to survive the crunching treatment of the negotiating system which has become an engine of frustration. If the mere continuation of such talks, in global rounds or in other forms, will not lead anywhere, what are then the prospects?

Many both in North and South have seen the need for a facelifting of the agenda to make it more appropriate to the present and future needs of the world, which do not today appear quite the same as when North–South talks started. One such view was expressed by Peter Jay (1979, p. 513) in an appeal to the USA, where he was then British Ambassador:

There is scope indeed for an imaginative approach. It must start from the indivisibility of the globe, from the need for nations to coexist peacefully on it; from the threat to that posed by extreme inequality and absolute poverty; and from the enlightened self-interest of the developed countries in tackling poverty and extreme inequality in ways that are politically acceptable to the beneficiaries ... the West will also have to identify more clearly with the general and specific goals of the Third World. It will have to offer a world political and economic order that makes small countries feel secure, poor countries confident of development, aggressive countries fearful of retribution, and all countries properly independent within their necessary interdependence. The order must offer better prospects than disorder.

The Brandt Commission with its large and heterogeneous membership of prominent political personalities agreed on a similar view of world needs and proposed, as an attempt to mobilize the political will and the mutual interests necessary to meet the many signs of crisis and disorder, a limited North–South summit. Such a meeting should not be expected to strike at once a global bargain. But if approached in general awareness of the need for greater trust it could go a long way toward installing that notion of a compact which Prebisch once thought of as an 'international commitment to development'. The Brandt Commission, alarmed by the present trends of disorganization and mounting conflicts in a nuclear world, even saw it as a commitment to survival. On the political foundation of a shared determination to turn the trends, multilateral diplomacy might again serve the great historical purposes that were hoped from it at its inception.

What if this does not happen? Some possibilities may be sketched. One is that the present paralysis of multilateral diplomacy is gradually overcome. The world is changing rapidly. The economic dynamism of some parts of the Third World, the financial and geopolitical role of the oil-exporters and the participation of China have not yet been fully reflected in multilateral diplomacy. With new and more numerous foci of power, the possibility of more flexible and shifting alliances might restore a greater degree of mobility. Whether it would then be possible to resume the global economic constitution building of the early postwar years, which has dominated the minds in the discussion of a New Order, is an open issue. Events in the monetary field have already marked a retreat from schemes for universal rules, and the monetary nonsystem may be a portent of the general shape of things to come. Already several years ago, Richard Gardner (1974, p. 558) suggested that

> the hope for the foreseeable future lies, not in building up a few ambitious central institutions of universal membership and general jurisdiction as was envisaged at the end of the last war, but rather in the much more decentralized, disorderly and pragmatic process of inventing or adapting institutions of limited jurisdiction and selected membership to deal with specific problems on a case-by-case basis, as the necessity for cooperation is perceived by the relevant nations.

This building of world order 'from the bottom up rather than from the top down' is already under way and breaks through North–South barriers in the forging of vertical links, as in the Japan–ASEAN–Australia nexus in the Western Pacific basin, the European Lomé connection and many messier and more confusing ones. That this development conflicts with the plans for global order drawn up in international organizations is not a serious objection. The issue is whether this decentralized approach suffices to meet the needs of a world economy in which mutual dependence is already global in so many ways. Will it enhance the risks of conflict and tension, will it leave global needs unmet, or will it make it possible to achieve the necessary trimming of national sovereignty more smoothly than the direct reach for global order? And would the Third World lose its bargaining power in a more pluralistic world, as many fear? The conflict is probably more apparent than real. Multilateral global diplomacy would, in any case, stand to gain from paring its agenda down to essentials, which would restore its capacity for the double task of political dialogue and technical negotiation.

Chapter 13: References

Bergsten, C. F., Keohane, R. O. and Nye, J. S., 'International economics and international politics: a framework for analysis', in C. F. Bergsten and L. B. Krause, eds, *World Politics and International Economics* (Washington, DC: Brookings Institution, 1975), pp. 3–36.

Gardner, R. N., 'The hard road to world order', *Foreign Affairs*, vol. 52, no. 3 (1974), pp. 556–76.

Gosovic, B., *UNCTAD: Conflict and Compromise* (Leiden: Sijthoff, 1972).

ul Haq, M., 'Negotiating the future', *Foreign Affairs*, vol. 59, no. 2 (1980–81), pp. 398–417.

Jay, P., 'Regionalism as geopolitics', *Foreign Affairs*, vol. 58, no. 3 (1980), pp. 485–514.

Jolles, P. A., 'Thoughts and reflections on the future of the North–South dialogue', in *Centre for Applied Studies in International Negotiations, Seminar on North–South Dialogue* (Geneva: CASIN, Autumn 1979).

Lewis, J. P., *Development Cooperation: Efforts and Policies of the Members of the Development Assistance Committee* (Paris: OECD, 1979).

Lewis, W. A., *Economic Survey, 1919–1939* (London: Allen & Unwin, 1949).

Lewis, W. A., *The Theory of Economic Growth* (London: Allen & Unwin, 1955), pp. 376–429.

Lewis, W. A., *The Evolution of the International Economic Order* (Princeton, NJ: Princeton University Press, 1978).

Myrdal, G., *An International Economy: Problems and Prospects* (New York: Harper, 1956).

Williamson, J. H., *The Failure of World Monetary Reform, 1971–1974* (New York: New York University Press, 1977).

Part Three

Cost Benefit and Planning

14

General Equilibrium Theory, Project Evaluation and Economic Development

T. N. SRINIVASAN

Introduction

Among Arthur Lewis's varied contributions to the theory of economic development and the practice of development policy, one of the earliest was his book on *The Principles of Economic Planning*, published in 1950 *prior* to his justly celebrated paper on 'Economic development with unlimited supplies of labour'. He returned to this theme sixteen years later in his book *Development Planning*. Another important strand of his work is his historical as well as theoretical studies of foreign trade. In his work on planning and on the theory of economic growth he drew attention to the possible divergence between market prices and social (or shadow) prices of goods and factors. This chapter is devoted to a survey of recent contributions to a field in which the many areas of Lewis's interest, namely, development planning, development practice, foreign trade theory and policy, as well as the derivation and use of shadow prices, appear to converge. This field is social cost–benefit analysis, or more narrowly, project evaluation or appraisal.

Recent contributions to this topic involve analytical insights from the theory of international trade, general equilibrium theory and development planning. Another area of development economics that has attracted analytical attention and empirical work is that of computable models of development. Indeed, Tjalling Koopmans (1977), in his Nobel lecture, drew attention to some of the earlier work in this area as examples in which two strands of optimization models, one consisting of applications to enterprise decision-making and the other to determining the aggregative future growth of an economy are combined and merged. At present there are several general equilibrium models available and equilibria computed for a number of developing countries: Adelman and Robinson (1978); Bacha *et al.* (1977); Dervis and Robinson (1978); Goreux (1977); Goreux and Manne (1973); and Lysy and Ahluwalia (1977). Some work has already been done and more is in progress in designing and computing 'global' general equilibrium models (Ginsburgh and Waelbroeck, 1978).

It is fair to say, that while a number of contributions have been made by economists working in public finance, trade theory and programming to the literature on these two topics, a consensus is yet to emerge on the analytical basis for many of the project-appraisal techniques. Nor is there agreement on the utility of computable general equilibrium models either in understanding the development process, or in devising development policy. Yet some project-appraisal technique or other is being used to decide on project choice by many governments and for project lending by international agencies. Some national planning commissions, for instance in India, have established project-appraisal divisions within the Commissions. Substantial human and financial resources are being committed by national and international agencies in using these techniques and models for planning. It is necessary, therefore, to examine in some depth the analytical issues and policy-makers' practice.

No new results are offered in this chapter. Instead, it brings together the diverse results, coming from analysts working in different traditions and with different tools and perspectives. It relates them to policy-makers' specific practices, and to the practical recommendations contained in some of the recent 'do-it-yourself' books for bureaucrats written by economists. The underlying approach to this broad survey is of Neoclassical general equilibrium theory. Project appraisal will be examined first in some detail, followed by a discussion of computable general-equilibrium models. In the concluding section some open issues will be raised.

Project Appraisal Techniques

The Institutional Framework
Before turning to project appraisal, a few words about the economy in which the technique is to be applied are in order. It is a mixed economy in which production takes place both in the private sector, consisting of producers responding to market signals, and in the public sector. It is also an open economy trading with the rest of the world. The government controls the public sector directly and the private sector indirectly through taxes levied (and subsidies granted) on commodities and on incomes of individuals, profits of firms, and so on. The government may also have the power to prohibit outright activities in the private sector that it deems not to be in the social interest. It is also assumed that the government evaluates the consequences of its exercise of any instrument of policy through an individualistic social-welfare function that incorporates 'equity' considerations. In applications to developing countries additional institutional constraints may be involved that result in market imperfections. Producers and consumers will otherwise be assumed to operate in purely competitive markets.

A Project and its Evaluation
A project is an activity which produces a vector of outputs from a vector of inputs.[1] The inputs and outputs will also be distinguished by the time period of

their use or availability. The government has to decide whether to go ahead with any project proposal in the public sector. In those countries where government controls capacity creation through licensing arrangements, it has to evaluate the private sector proposal as well in order to decide on issuing such a license. A private producer in a competitive environment would, of course, value the inputs and output at their going market prices and only calculate his net profit. He will undertake the project, if this is positive. The government in evaluating the same project is to value the inputs and outputs using 'shadow' prices that reflect social valuations of inputs and outputs.

Shadow Prices

The rationale for using shadow prices is that the social valuation of a commodity *may* differ from the price that is received by private producers and/or paid by consumers in the market. Consumer or producer prices may differ due to commodity taxation. Indeed, taxation and public production are instruments of public policy through which the government can bring social considerations to bear on private decisions. It is not surprising, therefore, that the project appraisal literature had close connection with that on public finance.

In deriving shadow prices the government is assumed to maximize social welfare subject to a set of constraints. In a mixed economy the constraints will include the fact that private producers and consumers respond to market signals. The shadow prices for a commodity would then reflect the change in the social-welfare maximum brought about by the change in the use of the commodity in the economy by one unit. The optimization exercise also would yield a set of optimum taxes and subsidies, so that the social-welfare optimum can be viewed as a (decentralized) market equilibrium. If, however, some of the socially optimal policies are either infeasible (because some relevant constraints were ignored in the optimization), or are not pursued for whatever reason, one could take as a point of departure an existing equilibrium that reflects these nonoptimal public policies and define the shadow price of a good as the change in social welfare resulting from a change in the use of that good by one unit at the *existing* equilibrium. A slightly different approach is to assume that levels of some instruments of public policy are specified and the maximization of social welfare is in respect of those instruments of policy not so restricted.

Since many forms of taxation involve 'deadweight' losses, attempting to achieve improvements in social welfare through such taxation can result in a trade-off between equity and efficiency. A convenient point of departure, therefore, is the ideal case where such a trade-off does not arise and, indeed, where market prices and shadow prices coincide.

Second Fundamental Theorem of Welfare Economics and Market Optimum

Such a case can be characterized by appealing to the so-called second fundamental theorem in welfare economics for closed economies. This theorem states that given a private-ownership economy, in which the production set of each producer is convex, and each consumer has a continuous and convex preference ordering defined over his convex consumption set, any Pareto-optimal allocation can be sustained as a competitive equilibrium, provided lump-sum transfers between individuals are feasible and no consumer is on the boundary of his survival set, so to speak (Koopmans, 1957). It is then clear that, as long as social welfare is individualistic and respects the Pareto criterion, a social-welfare optimum can be sustained as a competitive equilibrium, with, of course, suitable lump-sum transfers. The important point to note is that, even though 'equity' considerations have been introduced explicitly through the maximization of social welfare, the fact that it can be sustained as a competitive equilibrium implies that production efficiency obtains. As is well known, even apart from the strong assumptions about preferences and technology, the informational requirements for the computation of the required lump-sum transfers are severe. In the absence of full information transfers that are truly lump-sum may be difficult to devise without causing problems, as has been suggested by Hammond (1979) and others.[2] It is natural, then, to consider other instruments of public policy such as commodity taxation and public production. While all the models to be discussed in this context assume a mixed economy and an individualistic social-welfare function that respected the Pareto criterion, they differ in specifying the constraints on the government's tax and other policy instruments. One such elegant model for a single consumer economy (or equivalently for an economy with many identical consumers) is due to Boadway (1975).

Optimal Taxation: Diamond–Mirrlees Economy

Diamond and Mirrlees (1971) derive public production and tax policies that maximize social welfare. Assuming convexity, nonsatiation, and continuity of preferences, and convexity of production sets, they demonstrate that aggregate production efficiency may sometimes be traded off against equity. But in a variety of circumstances, as long as taxation (including differential taxation of profits of private production in so far as such production is subject to diminishing rather than constant returns to scale)[3] is optimal, production efficiency can be shown to be desirable by adding some mild restrictions on demands if necessary. An implication of aggregate production efficiency is that the 'shadow' prices of goods and factors for public production are the same as private-sector producer prices; the common set of prices being derived from the supporting hyperplane to the convex aggregate production set at the optimal point. A particularly elegant and general derivation of this result is by Roberts (1978).

The result that private and public-sector *production* decisions are to be based on the same set of producer prices has important implications for project appraisal. Since, given the same producer price vector, both public and private sector will evaluate the project the same way, there is no further need for intervention by the government to decide whether the project should be accepted or not. The need for project appraisal as such disappears altogether as long as aggregate production efficiency is optimal. The government needs only to set the correct producer prices. However, one can also argue that public-sector production has no special role to play, since in this 'convex' economy there are no increasing returns or externalities inherent in public production. The optimal choice of this common producer price vector becomes particularly simple for an open economy in which all goods are traded at *fixed* relative prices. In such a case, since trading is merely another way of transforming one good into others, efficiency implies that relative producer prices are the same as world prices, barring production specialization to a subset of commodities at an optimum.

Nonoptimal Taxation

One can go a bit further, if public production efficiency is optimal,[4] even though optimal taxes are not being levied, that is, some taxes are set at levels, from which a departure could improve social welfare. Diamond and Mirrlees (1976) show that in an economy where some price-taking private[5] producers maximize profits, given constant returns to scale technologies, shadow prices for government production must be such that the profits of constant returns to scale industries calculated at these shadow prices equals zero. The essence of the argument is that scaling down a constant return to scale production activity slightly and transferring the released resources to the public sector does not change aggregate supplies. Since the public sector is assumed to transact with the private sector at producer prices, and since for a constant return to scale activity the profit from released resources is zero at the initial prices, public-sector profits at private producer prices are unchanged by the transfer. And hence, by the assumption made on consumer demands and profit taxation, producer prices do not change. Thus, if the initial production plan (given the constraints on taxation) was optimal, the transferred resources cannot change welfare. This means that the value of the resources at public-sector shadow prices must be zero. Since the transferred resources amounted to a *proportion* of the resources used in constant returns to scale activity, this implies that the profit of the activity evaluated at public-sector shadow prices is zero.

Two special cases of this result are worth noting. First, if *all* commodities can be traded internationally at fixed relative prices, any pair of them can be viewed as a constant returns industry, using (that is, exporting) a unit of one commodity as input and producing (that is, importing) λ units of the second commodity, where λ is the world relative price of the second commodity in terms of the first. Thus, the relative shadow prices for government production become the relative world prices.

The second special case is one in which the constant returns activities span the commodity set: that is, if there are in all n commodities and at least $(n-1)$ linearly independent activities y^j $(j = 1, \ldots, n-1)$ in the constant returns sector, then by denoting the producer price vector by p and government shadow price vector by s, we have $py^j = sy^j = 0$ for $j = 1, 2, \ldots, n - 1$, implying that $p = s$. In other words, the shadow prices for the public sector are the same as producer prices for the private sector. This also means that not only is there production efficiency in the public and private sectors separately, but in the aggregate as well, in spite of nonoptimal taxes.

An interesting combination of the two special cases is the following. Suppose the $n = 2m$ commodities fell into two mutually exclusive and collectively exhaustive categories: the first m being goods traded internationally at fixed relative prices and the remaining m being primary factors of production. Suppose further each of the m traded commodities are produced by domestic constant returns to scale activities using primary factors. Then using $(m - 1)$ 'production' activities consisting of, say, exporting a unit of the first commodity in exchange for importing an amount of each of the other $(m - 1)$ traded commodities equal to its relative world price along with the remaining m constant return production activities, we can span the commodity set consisting of all the $2m$ commodities. Thus, the given world prices for traded commodities determine *all* shadow prices.

It is not entirely clear how significant the above results are from the point of view of project appraisal. Given the premiss of an initial situation that, among other things, is characterized by the efficiency of public production, *public-sector* shadow prices can be determined from the slopes of the supporting hyperplane to the convex public production possibility set at the initial production point on its frontier. In this sense, the above results are essentially alternative characterizations of the same set of shadow prices. Given that aggregate production efficiency is not being achieved because of nonoptimality of taxation, producer prices in the private sector presumably do not reflect social valuation of commodities. Supposing that the government can prevent a socially undesirable project from being implemented in the private sector (because of its private profitability) through licensing arrangements, the interesting question is: what are the shadow prices for evaluating private projects which by definition are worthwhile at going producer prices in the private sector? Of course, any project that is socially desirable but privately unprofitable can always be implemented in the public sectors. It would seem that the public-sector output ought to use the same set of shadow prices for evaluating public or private projects, but whether this is so is not entirely clear from the analysis. Dasgupta and Stiglitz (1974) in their comprehensive analysis study the case where all commodities are tradeable at fixed (world) relative prices and the only restriction on government is that private profits cannot be taxed. They show, that while the government should use world relative prices in evaluating a public project, the *same* project, if it is in the private sector should only be evaluated differently, to the extent that the social cost of private profits have to be taken into account. However, unlike Diamond and Mirrlees (1971), they assume no restrictions on commodity taxes.

Shadow Prices for Traded Goods

In an economy where *all* goods are tradeable at fixed relative prices in the world market, the one robust result that seems to hold under a variety of circumstances, though not necessarily universally, is that the shadow prices for evaluation of public-sector projects are world prices. The logic of this result can be simply stated. As long as the only constraint in which quantities traded in world markets appear is the balance of trade constraint, at the initial optimal situation (subject to whatever constraints on taxes) the marginal rate of substitution (in social welfare) of any two traded goods will equal their relative price in world markets. But this marginal rate of substitution of the same two goods also equals (assuming efficiency and that both goods are being produced in positive amounts) their marginal rate of transformation in *public* production, provided the only constraint on public production is its transformation function. This yields the result on public-sector shadow prices. When there is aggregate production efficiency, then marginal rate of transformation in private production equals that in public production, and the world prices become the relevant shadow prices for evaluation of private-sector projects as well. The role played by there being only one restriction, namely, balance of trade, on the quantities traded in deriving this result is crucial.

It follows readily that when there is a binding import or export quota or when there is a government budgetary constraint[6] or when import tariffs on a commodity depend on the level of imports of the same or some other commodity the above result does not go through, as has been noted by Dasgupta and Stiglitz (1974), Bhagwati and Srinivasan (1981) and Blitzer *et al.* (1981). In the first case this is so for the obvious reason of the binding quantity constraint, in the second because of the revenue effects of the quantities traded and in the third because the quantity imported of a commodity determines the tariff, and the tariff so determined need not be optimal.

Monopoly Power in Trade

Life is made simple if all commodities are tradeable at fixed relative prices in world markets. It gets a bit more complicated if we allow the relative prices to vary with the volume of trade, while still maintaining the assumption that all goods are traded. This is the so-called 'monopoly power in a trade' situation of trade theory. This is relevant for those developing countries which supply a substantial share of some primary commodities. The simplest way of introducing this notion is to assume that there is a commodity, say, tea, in which the country in question has a substantial share in world markets, while in all other commodities it is a price-taker. Thus, the price relative of any two of the set of commodities, excluding tea, is fixed, while the price of any commodity relative to tea depends on the volume of tea exported. Denoting the exports of tea by z_1, and net exports of other commodities as $z_i (i = 2, \ldots, n)$, and with the nth commodity as numeraire, one can write the balance of trade constraint as:

$$\phi(z_1) - \sum_{i=2}^{n} p_i z_i = 0$$

with $p_n = 1$. What this says is that exporting z_1 units of tea fetches $\phi(z_1)$ units of numeraire in world markets which can be spent on other commodities at fixed prices p_i in terms of numeraire. As before, if the only constraint in the social-welfare optimization problem in which traded quantities enter is this balance of trade constraint, then the social value or shadow price (in numeraire terms) of a unit of i (other than 1) at the *optimum* is p_i and that of 1 is $\phi'(z_1)$ or the marginal export revenue $\phi'(z_1)$. For reaching this optimum in the situation where tea is produced by atomistic price-taking producers, government intervention in the form of an optimum export tariff would be required. Bhagwati and Srinivasan (1981) have shown, however, that, if the quantity of tea exported is not optimal in the initial situation, then the marginal export revenue at the nonoptimal export level would not be the shadow price of tea, though the shadow price of other traded commodities will continue to be their world prices (in terms of numeraire). Unfortunately, this distinction between optimal and suboptimal initial situation is not made in manuals on project appraisal which typically recommend the use of marginal revenue in place of average revenue when monopoly power in trade is present.

Nontraded Goods

Introducing nontraded goods leads to further complications. The literature appears to be less than perfectly clear on the derivation of shadow prices for nontraded goods. Dasgupta and Stiglitz (1974) unarguably state that the shadow price of a nontradeable (in terms of social utility as numeraire) is the loss in production of a traded good that would be incurred if an additional unit of the nontraded good were produced, the loss being valued by the utility numeraire price of that traded good. But this, of course, means that one has to know the price of a traded good (it does not matter which good) in terms of *utility* numeraire, whereas the project evaluator may know only the price of a traded good in terms of another *traded* good as numeraire (that is, world market relative prices). Only by solving the entire optimization exercise could one know the price of a traded good in terms of social utility. Little and Mirrlees (1974, p. 167) suggest that, since the shadow price of a commodity would equal its shadow cost of production (that is, value at shadow prices of the bundle of inputs needed to produce a unit of that commodity), and since there are as many such equations as prices, 'it can be confidently asserted that these equations have a solution'. The difficulty with this assertion is seen clearly if we start with assuming constant returns to scale in production and there being n_1 traded goods (with an index set I), and $n_2 + m$ nontraded goods,[7] the latter consisting of m primary factors (index set F) and n_2 produced goods (index set II), and denoting the initial equilibrium input–output coefficient matrices by $A_{I,I}$, $A_{I,II}$, $A_{F,I}$ etc. The Little–Mirrlees assertion amounts to calculating (local) shadow prices p_{II} for nontraded goods for p_F for primary factors, given the shadow price (that is, world prices) $\bar{p}_I$ for traded goods by solving (primes indicating transposition of a vector):

$$\bar{p}'_I(I - A_{I,I}) - p'_{II}A_{II,I} - p'_F A_{F,I} = 0$$

$$-\bar{p}'_I A_{I,II} + p'_{II}(I - A_{II,II}) - p'_F A_{F,II} = 0.$$

Unfortunately, we have here $(n_1 + n_2)$ equations in $n_2 + m$ unknowns. But there is one case, considered at length in Bhagwati and Srinivasan (1981), in which things do work. If the number of factors m equals the number of traded goods, so that $A_{F,I}$ is a square matrix, and if there is no linear dependency in the factor-intensity vectors in traded-goods production. (That is $A_{F,I}$ is non-singular), then we get:

$$p_{II} = |(I - A'_{II,II}) + A'_{F,II}(A'_{F,I})^{-1}A'_{II,I}|^{-1}|A'_{I,II} + A'_{F,II}(A'_{F,I})^{-1}(I - A'_{I,I})|p_I$$

$$p_F = (A'_{F,I})^{-1}|(I - A'_{I,I})p_I + A'_{II,I}p_{II}|.$$

Indeed, the so-called Little–Mirrlees rule of decomposing nontradeables and primary factors would amount to just this. This analysis is analogous to the unique determination of factor prices and factor input coefficients by the *market* prices for *traded* goods in the fundamental model of Samuelson (1953). Given the factor prices and production technology, the *market prices* for nontraded goods are determined. The demand conditions determine the outputs of nontraded goods. As long as the market prices for traded goods remain unchanged because, say, they are determined by fixed *ad valorem* tariffs over fixed world prices, then the technical coefficients also remain unchanged. Thus, the above procedure for computing the *shadow* prices (in terms of a traded good) of nontraded goods goes through.

Mirrlees (1977a) also derives shadow prices for nontraded goods in a model with commodity taxation that may not necessarily be optimal but with 100 percent taxation of pure profits. His procedure, to begin with, assumes that the shadow price (in terms of social utility as numeraire) of government revenue (or equivalently of a tradeable good) is exogenous and at the second stage 'estimates' it on the basis that additional government revenue is uniformly distributed as lump-sum income among individual consumers. Thus, by equating the change in social welfare brought about by increasing each consumer's lump-sum income by one unit to the product of shadow price (in terms of social utility) of a tradeable good and the cost of meeting additional demands generated (each good being valued at its shadow price in terms of that tradeable good), he obtains the shadow price of the tradeable good in terms of social utility. Since this procedure is not based on conditions characterizing the relevant social optimum, one can judge the closeness of the shadow prices yielded by it to the true shadow prices at the social optimum only by computing both in some well-specified examples.

We may summarize the above discussion as follows. (1) In an economy satisfying the assumptions of the second fundamental theorem of welfare economics, including in particular the feasibility of lump-sum transfers among individuals, there is no need for project evaluation and shadow pricing. But then, the problem is really evaded by transforming it into one of calculating optimal lump-sum transfers to achieve maximal social welfare. The informational requirements for making such calculations are severe, not to speak of incentive-incompatibility problems. (2) In a Diamond–Mirrlees economy, in which consumer preferences and production sets (public and private) satisfy the assumptions of the theorem, but only commodity taxation is feasible and lump-sum transfers are not, as long as aggregate production efficiency obtains at the social welfare optimum (achieved through optimal commodity taxation), the need for project evaluation disappears again since optimally chosen producer prices (common to public and private sectors) reflect the social-welfare valuation of all commodities. Again, the problem of project evaluation is transformed to one of calculating optimal taxes or equivalently optimal producer and consumer prices. (3) If all commodities are tradeable internationally, and the only constraint in which quantities traded enter is the balance of trade constraint, then the relative valuation of the commodities for project evaluation (public and private) is their marginal contribution to the trade balance. In the particular case, where the country is a price-taker in world markets, this amounts to using world relative prices as shadow prices. In so far as private profits are not entirely taxed away, the social cost of such profits also have to be taken into account in the evaluation of private projects. (4) The problem of shadow-pricing a nontraded good (in situations with nonoptimal taxation) involves some rather *ad hoc* and unrealistic assumptions, perhaps no more so than in any applied welfare analysis.

Srinivasan and Bhagwati (1978; 1981), Blitzer *et al.* (1981), Boadway (1975; 1976) and Mirrlees (1977a) (discussed earlier) view a 'small' project as a perturbation of an initial equilibrium in which there are distortionary taxes. They examine whether such a project will improve social welfare. Boadway's approach is to allow for distributive effects of policy changes by using what he calls a 'distribution characteristic' of each good, rather than its equivalent of weighting the income gains and losses to different individuals. The distribution characteristic of good *i* is the average of the marginal contribution to social welfare of an additional consumption of a unit of the numeraire good by each consumer, weighted by his share in total consumption of good *i*. While this way of rewriting the expressions for policy-induced change in social welfare is illuminating, from an informational and computational point of view it provides no particular advantage.

The approach to shadow prices by treating a project as a perturbation of an initial equilibrium is no different from the approaches discussed under the headings optimal and nonoptimal taxation, unless the initial equilibrium has some features, such as sticky wages (sector-specific or general), and so on, that make it different from a standard competitive equilibrium modified by taxes and transfers. A part of the contribution of Bhagwati and Srinivasan (1981) is devoted to the sticky-wage problem.

Shadow Prices of Primary Factors

Many of the models discussed so far do not treat nonproduced factors of production explicitly. Since the consumer budget constraint is written in these models as $q'c \leq$ lump-sum income + share in profits after tax (if any), where q is the vector of consumer prices and the consumer's factor endowment is subsumed in c. First, this means that the consumer has to pay the relevant commodity tax, even when he consumes out of his own initial endowment, including, in particular, his labor. Secondly, in models in which *all* commodities are tradeable, the implication is that labor, land, and so on, are also tradeable internationally. Alternatively, one could have assumed that all nonproduced factors of production are specific to production units and any returns to such factors being included in the unit's profits. However, the straightforward thing to do would be to divide the commodities into tradeable goods and nontradeables, the latter including primary factors as well.

Shadow-pricing of primary factors (capital and labor) in an economy with distorting trade taxes or quotas but free of any other distortions is the focus of the works of Findlay and Wellisz (1976), Bhagwati and Srinivasan (1981), Srinivasan and Bhagwati (1978) and Bhagwati and Wan (1979). Using the traditional two-factor, two-commodity, constant returns to scale production, general equilibrium model (with full employment of all factors) of trade theory, and (subsuming distributional considerations by employing a Bergson–Samuelson social utility function) Srinivasan and Bhagwati (1978) show the shadow price of a factor (in terms of a traded good) is the change in output of traded goods (valued at fixed world relative prices) with respect to a change in the endowment of that factor by a unit, if tariffs are the only distortions. If an optimum tariff is being levied to exploit monopoly power in trade, when it exists, then the changes in output are to be valued at marginal terms of trade. In the case of a quota, which is being enforced through a production tax-cum-subsidy, leaving consumption to take place at world prices, again world prices are the shadow prices for valuing the change in outputs. If the quota is enforced by permitting domestic prices (common to producers and consumers) to deviate from world prices to the required extent, then the *market* wages and rentals also happen to be their shadow counterparts, the reason being that the economy at the margin becomes a closed economy.

Bhagwati and Srinivasan introduce a third nontraded good which is produced under constant returns to scale and, thus, work with a model in which market prices of factors and the nontraded good are uniquely determined by traded-goods prices. In such a model all shadow prices (in terms of a traded good) are determined from the world prices of traded goods. They briefly note that in a model where the number of traded goods differs from the number of factors, the shadow price of a factor will still be the value at world prices of the change in output of traded goods induced by the availability of an extra unit of that factor, provided nontraded-goods prices are kept constant through appropriate tax-cum-subsidy policies.

Tax Reform

One of the usual arguments for project evaluation is that an initial equilibrium of an economy is often subject to *unremovable* tax distortions, and through the selection of appropriate projects, the government can mitigate the distortionary effects of taxes. A version of this argument is that, if the government cannot tax the rich and subsidize the poor, it can accept projects that directly help the poor and reject those that help the rich. I am not convinced that this is a good theory of government or politics: a government that is unable to exercise its fiscal instruments in desired ways is unlikely to get away with accepting projects that have similar effects. A more realistic view is that for historical reasons or inertia some distortions get built into the system, and given this, one tries to mitigate the effects of distortions while at the same time trying to eliminate them. It is, therefore, worthwhile to look at tax reform (as contrasted with optimal taxation or project selection) as an instrument of improving social welfare.

The issue addressed in this body of literature is whether a tax reform that reduces distortions in some specified fashion improves welfare as in Bruno (1972), Dixit (1975), Foster and Sonnenschein (1970), Kawamata (1974), Hatta (1975; 1977a; 1977b) and Rader (1976). This literature can be related to Hotelling's (1938) work and to many of the traditional partial-equilibrium public-finance and cost–benefit theories (Harberger, 1971). The contributions to the analysis of tax changes in a general-equilibrium framework are also relevant, in particular, Guesnerie (1975; 1977; 1979), Shoven and Whalley (1973; 1977) and Whalley (1975).

Many of these contributions assume that there is only one consumer in the economy. Distortion is defined (except in Bruno) as the difference between the vector of marginal rates of substitution in consumption (with one of the commodities as numeraire) and marginal rates of transformation along the production-possibility frontier, though in deriving many of the propositions this frontier is assumed to be a hyperplane. In Bruno (1972) the distortion arises from the difference between the common producer and consumer price vector and an exogenous *constant vector* of shadow prices. The main result of these studies is that a simultaneous reduction by the same proportion in the distortions (relating to each good, other than the numeraire – for which the distortion is zero by definition) increases the welfare of a single consumer, assuming that there is a unique equilibrium corresponding to each level of distortion and all goods are normal in consumption. The latter assumption is weakened somewhat in Hatta's and Bruno's papers. Kawamata (1974) shows, in a model with many consumers with strictly convex preferences and producers with strictly convex production possibility sets, that even if there are multiple equilibria corresponding to a given distortion, corresponding to any of these equilibria, one can find *an* equilibrium corresponding to a equi-proportionate reduction in all distortion which is Pareto-superior. Dixit (1975), and in some of his propositions Hatta (1977a) also, consider nonequi-proportionate reduction in distortions as well.

The relationship between project evaluation and these propositions on tax reforms is seen most clearly in Bruno's work. His constant shadow-price vector is best interpreted, as he himself does, as corresponding to the given world prices for traded goods (assuming all goods are tradeables) faced by a 'small' price-taking economy. Then his result that reducing all distortions proportionately leads to an increase in output evaluated at shadow prices (and welfare) could be reinterpreted in terms of project evaluation, if we identify the change in output vectors in the two situations as constituting a project.

Project Evaluation in Developing Economies

Most of the models discussed so far do not appeal to any institutional or other aspects of an economy that could be called specific to a developing economy. However, the two major 'do-it-yourself' kits on project evaluation by Little and Mirrlees (1974), Dasgupta *et al.* (1972) and a variant from the Little–Mirrlees cuisine by Squire and van der Tak (1975) are specifically addressed to less developed countries. All three assume an economy, presumably in an equilibrium, subject to various distortions, socially nonoptimal taxes, and so on, with some resources, such as labor, not being employed to the extent of their availability. The distribution of wealth among individuals is considered socially nonoptimal. Since most of the models discussed so far had many of these features, one may wonder what distinguishing features are brought in by considering a developing economy. One apparent difference is in the social-welfare function: the models discussed so far defined social welfare on an individualistic basis, so that the project affected social welfare only through its impact on individuals' utilities.[8] The manuals on project analysis for less developed countries, on the other hand, implicitly define social welfare as a function of individual utilities, as well as some aggregate variables (termed 'merit wants' in Dasgupta, *et al.*, 1972), such as total employment of unskilled labor (reflecting that employment is socially desirable over and above its contribution to incomes of individuals), balance of payments excluding induced balancing flows (reflecting the social objective of self-reliance), and so on. Another difference is in the models discussed so far, a complete set of markets in the Arrow–Debreu sense is assumed to exist, so that time-discounting, risk and locational preferences are implicit. The practitioners of project analysis for less developed countries explicitly take into account these aspects in deriving some key shadow prices, such as the shadow wage rate for unskilled labor, the social rate of discount or equivalently the shadow price of investment in terms of consumption (with public investment and consumption sometimes distinguished from private investment and consumption) and net foreign-trade deficit.

Noneconomic or Extra-Economic Objectives

The introduction of objectives, such as self-reliance, employment in specific industries, and so on, for their 'social' value over and above their contribution to private welfare is not entirely new. For instance, Bhagwati and Srinivasan (1969) derive, using a social-utility function, optimal fiscal interventions to achieve such objectives (which they term noneconomic) in the traditional two-commodity, two-factor model. If their optimal tax subsidy policies were being followed and if any other distortions present were being tackled optimally, then the shadow prices would, of course, be the relevant tax–subsidy-corrected market prices. This would also mean that a project evaluator would, first, have to determine whether the existing set of taxes and subsidies are being levied to achieve some social objective or other before he decides to adjust for them in his shadow-price calculations. Indeed, Little and Mirrlees (1974, p. 224) explicitly state this. More generally stated, a commodity tax is 'distorting' only if it is nonoptimal from the point of view of social-welfare maximization. As such, a given tax may or may not be considered 'distorting', depending on whether the project-evaluator takes it to reflect an optimally exercised instrument to achieve an appropriate social objective. This has led some to conclude that almost any project can be claimed to be worthwhile from a social-welfare point of view, by correcting some and not correcting other market prices. In this context that the robustness of the result that world relative prices are the shadow prices for traded goods even in the presence of noneconomic objectives is particularly appealing.

Derivation of 'Key' Shadow Prices from Macromodels

The manuals of project evaluation derive two 'key' shadow prices, that of labor and investment from an explicit or implicit aggregate optimal growth model, in which aggregate output is produced with fixed capital and labor (or several categories of labor as, for instance, in Little and Mirrlees). This output is divided between additions to capital stock (investment) and current consumption. The latter depends on employment and on other constraints, if any, such as consumption floors. Little and Mirrlees (1974) argue that 'the optimization problem must, therefore, be solved as a whole, perhaps for an infinite horizon, if we are to know what ARI (accounting rate of interest or equivalently the shadow price of capital) and SWR (shadow wage rate) ought to be in the immediate future'. They continue: 'The moral is, that optimum growth calculations in solvable models are the only satisfactory way of telling at what level current accounting (i.e. shadow) prices should be put.' They conclude (p. 304) that 'in the absence of adequate guidance from computed models, presumably one should be able to make fairly sensible guesses about the general long-term development of the economy, and work backwards from these guesses to estimates (of shadow prices) . . . in the present'.

It is by no means obvious that the two-stage procedure of deriving some key shadow prices (that of capital and categories of labor) from a macrooptimizing model can be grafted on to another model (optimizing or otherwise) for determining the remaining shadow prices so as to have a complete set of shadow prices for project evaluation. Further, as Rudra (1972) and Hammond (1978) point out, once a large optimizing model has been solved to provide *all* shadow prices in one fell swoop, what is the role of project evaluation? After all, project selection itself could be part of such an optimization exercise.

Project Appraisal as a Planning Procedure

It would be going too far to reject any macroframework whatever for project appraisal. The need for such a framework becomes clear in the context of planning economic development. Any plan, almost by its very definition, is a collection of projects. By the same token, a plan cannot be an arbitrary collection of projects. However, it is unlikely that one could devise an all-purpose optimizing model that would produce *the* optimal plan, the associated set of projects, and a set of shadow prices to evaluate projects that have not yet been proposed and evaluated as part of the optimization exercise. In such a context, a macromodel (of a multisector kind) may be useful not for project selection, but for checking mutual consistency of sectoral plans and for generating broad development alternatives. In such a context one can see the role of project appraisal as that of selecting among projects proposed for meeting sectoral targets. The techniques used for appraisal should ensure that an accepted project is feasible and leads to social-welfare improvement.

The application of the first of the two criteria, namely, feasibility, is not difficult to meet, if a project is 'small', so that it has negligible impact on the aggregate demand for those inputs it uses. A large project leads to difficulties in several ways: first, because of its nonnegligible impact on the economy through its input demands (and output supplies), its feasibility may have to be checked as part of the macroconsistency exercise itself. Secondly, the shadow prices for inputs and outputs cannot be assumed to be unaffected by project choice, if the project is sufficiently 'large'. This nonstationarity of shadow prices is investigated in depth by Bhagwati and Wan (1979), and by Baumol (in this volume). The latter shows that a linear approximation to a nonlinear programme (a frequent practice) can yield shadow prices which do not come anywhere near to the true shadow prices, and what is even worse, it can impute a positive (zero) shadow price to a truly free (scarce) input! However, it is not simple to specify and solve even a moderate-sized nonlinear programme. Thirdly, if the largeness of the project implies indivisibility and increasing returns to scale, then most of the shadow-price derivations that depend crucially on the convexity of the production sets lose their meaning. Setting aside the issue of large projects, we still have to address the criterion for choosing projects that improve social welfare. The question is: can we derive shadow prices that will enable one to determine whether a project provides welfare improvement without solving a full-blown optimizing model?

An analogy from linear programming is helpful. The values of the dual variables at the optimal solution of a linear-programming problem correspond to the shadow prices associated with solving the full-blown model. But the simplex algorithm also yields a set of prices at each iteration, which has the property that *at these prices* (1) all activities in the basis break even, and (2) bringing into the basis any activity that is outside the basis but yields a 'profit', would increase aggregate 'profits'. The analogy is complete, if we identify aggregate 'profits' as social welfare and a 'project' as an activity that is outside the current basis. The only problem may be that an activity ('project') rejected at one iteration may come back into the basis at a later iteration. This back-and-forth movement can in principle happen several times. One could argue, of course, that this is not a problem in that a project could indeed be socially worth while at one set of shadow prices and not at another. Be that as it may, an approach to project appraisal that comes closest to this is that in which one starts from a full specification of the initial 'equilibrium' of the economy, views the project as a perturbation of this equilibrium and evaluates its effect through the social-welfare function.

It is perhaps fair to say, in conclusion, that the gap between the analytical basis and practical recommendations for project evaluation is yet to be narrowed sufficiently. While the modern literature on public finance as well as optimal growth has provided valuable insights, these cannot yet be translated into procedures that can be confidently recommended for application by a project-appraisal bureaucracy in a developing country. Yet these procedures are far from useless. Indeed, by forcing the project formulations and evaluators to specify in detail the probable impact of a project, on particular socioeconomic groups, decisions are likely to be made on a more informed and possibly consistent basis than would otherwise be the case. But there is also the danger that project-evaluators may become the economic counterparts of witch-doctors.

Computable General-Equilibrium Models and Development

Computable general-equilibrium models had their antecedents in the comput-able 'planning' models of the 1950s and 1960s for developing economies, most of which in no way could be characterized as 'planned economies'. Nevertheless, whether they were relatively simple macromodels of the Harrod–Domar–Mahalanobis–Feldman variety or the more elaborate mul-tisector consistency models or even multisector optimizing (of a target year or inter-temporal variety) models, they were mainly useful (and used!) for check-ing mutual consistency of macrotargets (income growth, savings, employment and foreign-capital inflow), and for delineating alternative growth patterns and their macropolicy implications. Indeed, in India, a country in which some of the earliest planning models for a developing country were built, they were viewed essentially as relatively economical and efficient ways of generating and studying alternative growth paths, by changing the parameters of the objective function or the constraint set. The model runs were intended only as diagnostic devices for locating critical bottlenecks or isolating critical parameters and not for either drawing up a national development plan, or to track the economy's progress. This is not to say that there were no enthusiasts who contemplated the use of the dual of the programming exercise in deriving shadow prices for project appraisal and other decisions. They did not get very far, partly because of the instability of the shadow prices (to which a reference was made earlier) with respect to even minor perturbations of the parameters of the model.[9] The continuous substitution possibilities (in production and consumption) that are a feature of the computable general-equilibrium models are intended in part as a response to the instability problem.

In spite of their many drawbacks (most of which were known to some of the model-builders), these models were useful conceptual devices through which development economists thought out many crucial policy issues in *quantitative* terms. In some respects they represented a practical quantitative formulation of many issues addressed in the theory of the second best, though some went too far in accepting many a market distortion as unremovable and underplayed the role of the market in the allocation process. These models were sometimes used to generate project-selection criteria (particularly in respect of projects in the foreign-trade sector), such as domestic-resources cost (of earning or saving) of foreign exchange (DRC).[10] In a context where foreign-exchange availability was considered a major constraint on growth, the estimation of shadow price of foreign exchange from these models and the use of DRC in project selection were important applications of policy significance.

The state of the art in building and using such models was reviewed in Blitzer *et al.* (1975). In his systematic survey of the theoretical basis of economywide planning models for this volume Lance Taylor concluded: 'If we had a better theory of prices and economic power than the Walrasian one, model builders would clearly use it. At the moment ... all that can be said is that a |linear programming| model is likely to be a poor facsimile of a Walrasian economy, while a nonlinear constant returns model will be a better one. If competition is basically the only game in town, you might as well play it with elegance' (p. 100). Mirrlees (1977b) seems to share this emphasis on using the competitive equilibrium framework for analyzing public policy because, in his view, this would avoid debate about 'dubious relationships of disequilibrium macro-economics or oligopoly theory, and concentrate on essentials'.

By the late 1960s and early 1970s, concern was being expressed by academics, policy-makers, aid-donors and international agencies that the fruits of growth had not trickled down to the poor in developing countries. It was force-fully argued that distributional considerations besides aggregate income growth have to be taken into account in devising policies (Chenery *et al.*, 1974).

The model-builders have responded to this by concentrating on the endogenous determination of the distribution of income (among socioeconomic groups within an economy) and the structure of relative prices. It is natural to turn to the Walrasian general-equilibrium framework for this purpose, since in such a framework, the distribution of income among individuals or groups is the distribution of the market valuation of the returns to their initial endowments as modified by any fiscal interventions of the government. The problem of income distribution is then transformed into one of computing the equilibrium structure of relative prices. It cannot be denied that a manageable model that computes the equilibrium-relative prices is at once elegant and intellectually satisfying, even though as Scarf (1973) points out, 'Walrasian model of competition ... is far from being the exclusive analytical framework for the study of micro-economic problems'. The question is whether such an exercise helps in evaluating projects and illuminates the *process* of development. There are several reasons for some skepticism on this count, even if we ignore the criticisms of Kornai (1971).

First, the computable models assume that a set of markets exist and these operate smoothly except for whatever policy restrictions are imposed, such as price floors or ceilings, together with rationing, and so on. But an important, if not the most important, aspect of development is the evolution of the system, in terms of integration of existing fragmented markets, coming into being of new markets, new products, new technologies, and so on. These models, operating solely on an undoubtedly important aspect of reality, namely, the mutual adjustment of quantities and prices at each point in time, have little to say on the evolution of the system. This is particularly unfortunate in models that cover long periods into the future.

Secondly, one of the stylized facts about many a developing economy that is said to distinguish it from any developed economy is that of 'dualism', one manifestation of which is the phenomenon of differential rewards to the same mobile factor in different sectors or locations (rural and urban) that are not explainable in terms of sector or location-specific factors. The theoretical and computable models incorporate this dualism in a mechanistic way by postulating, for instance, an exogenously specified wage differential between sectors or locations, resulting in excess supply of labor and unemployment in a location. This is made consistent with equilibrium by assuming a labor-migration mechanism that keeps the unemployment at such a level that a potential migrant to the high-wage location is indifferent between migrating and not migrating, the indifference arising from the fact of expected wage allowing for unemployment in the high-wage location equals the actual wage in the low-wage location. As Arrow (1967) points out, the question why such wage differentials persist is of first importance and just assuming it to be exogenous tells us nothing about development.

Thirdly, the time structure of these models is one of a sequence of equilibria, in which the productive capacity in any period is limited by inherited capital stocks (including inventories) and periods are linked by investment activities. The market clearing prices in any period are determined given either a sectoral investment (including stock changes) determination mechanism that was independent of future prices, or that depended on expected future prices which, in turn, are linked to current and past prices through an adaptive price-expectation mechanism. There is no doubt that a temporary equilibrium approach is useful for analyzing some short-period problems. But it would appear bizarre to derive a dynamic path for a developing economy as a sequence of such equilibria, in which an equilibrium (in the sense of all markets clearing) is established in each period through an unspecified process!

Fourthly, the main motivation of constructing many of these models was to improve our understanding of the process of income distribution and of poverty. The computable models can at best trace the 'functional' distribution of income, though in terms of a larger number of functional categories than just labor and capital shares. But the phenomenon of poverty at a point in time is linked to the distribution of income across households at that time and an essential aspect of the dynamics of poverty is what happens to *cohorts* of households and not just to household categories. Though, for instance, in a model for the Philippines (Rodgers *et al.*, 1977), an attempt is made not only to map functional distribution into household income distribution as is done in other models, but also to model the process of household formation and its functioning through its existence. It is fair to say that this attempt is rather mechanical. It is not simple to incorporate the impact of political power (and the dynamics of power groups) on income distribution. The exercise of power can change the rules of the game, that is, the way the economy functions. It is possible that the work of Aumann and Kurz (1977) and Kurz (1977) provide the beginnings of a fruitful line of inquiry. But in their framework the government is invisible: the rules of the bargaining game, coupled with the political rule that a majority (simple, two-thirds, weighted, or unweighted) decides, determine the outcomes.

Fifthly, the particular advantage of the ability to compute numerically the equilibrium prices and quantities (ignoring uniqueness issues) is that it enables one to analyze the (comparative static) impact of government policies on such an equilibrium, without resorting to techniques (such as those used in project analysis) that require the policy changes to be 'small'. This tool, as applied to a context where the unspecified process of movement from the equilibrium before policy change to the one after is supposed to be completed within each period, is likely to be very misleading.

Finally, some of these models (in particular, Adelman and Robinson, 1978, p. 185) claim to have incorporated monetary effects in a general equilibrium model. These attempts appear faulty and certainly have not succeeded where theorists have failed in satisfactorily incorporating money in general-equilibrium theory. Since some of their policy simulations are sensitive to changes in aggregate price level (that is, determined through the introduction of money), their results have to be viewed with caution.

Some Open Issues

One would not wish to suggest that the computable general equilibrium models have come to a dead-end as far as analyzing the growth of a developing economy. Nor would one like to be accused of what Arrow and Hahn (1971) call the 'vulgar mistake' of supposing that the analysis of competitive equilibrium has nothing to teach us about an economy, developed or developing. But for the research resources spent, probably far more useful lessons can be learnt by deeper analysis of specific markets, such as those for labor, land, agricultural resources and credit. The institutional framework within which such markets operate is important. For instance, in many agrarian societies, a landlord and his tenant farmer enter into several transactions at the *same* time: in land (supplied by the landlord), in labor (supplied by the tenant), in other purchased inputs for which an agreement is struck in the sharing of costs, in credit (for production and tenant's consumption needs) supplied by a landlord and in marketing services (for output) supplied by the landlord. It has been alleged that, in such a context, a landlord may not be interested in introducing new varieties of crop or methods of cultivation that will increase the yield of land. The argument is that, though he will gain from higher yields, he will lose income from loans to his tenant, in so far as the tenant may borrow less because his income goes up with the yield increase. This has been offered as an explanation why in some parts of India the new technology of agriculture ushered in by the green revolution of the late 1960s did not take root. The logic of this argument is not entirely persuasive. Transaction costs alone do not explain why the same pair of individuals exchange goods and services across a spectrum of markets. There are other interesting issues to analyze as well: why do we observe active rental markets for mechanical power (tractors, pumps, and so on) but not for animal power (bullocks)? Why is there an active market for tenancies (that is, land rental market) but a thin one for land? A multisector general-equilibrium model with all of agriculture aggregated into a simple sector as is often done is not suitable to pose such questions. And without understanding the functioning of allocation and accumulation processes in agriculture, very little of substance can be said of effects of policies to promote development or alleviate poverty in South Asia, if not in other areas of the less developed world.

Sectoral models are useful in planning investment and its time-phasing in some key industries in which scale economies are important. An extensive literature on this has emerged since Alan Manne's (1966) early work. Of course, inconsistencies can arise from the fact that separate industry or sector models do not take into account interdependencies that a general-equilibrium model fully articulates. This is not a serious problem, once it is realized that the consistency of the general-equilibrium model is bought, in any case, at great cost in terms of untestable assumptions and compromises to fit available data into a computable model. There is no better way to conclude this chapter than to quote the words of Arrow (1967),' the problems of developing countries remind us dramatically that something beyond, but including, neoclassical theory is needed'.

Chapter 14: Notes

An earlier version of this paper constituted the author's Walras–Bowley lecture at the summer meetings of the Econometric Society at Boulder, Colorado, USA, 22 June, 1978. Valuable comments on various drafts from Bela Balassa, William Baumol, Clive Bell, Jagdish Bhagwati, Alan Blinder, Charles Blitzer, J. Marc Boussard, Michael Bruno, Hollis Chenery, Partha Dasgupta, Peter Diamond, Roger Gordon, Ian Little, Bagicha Minhas, Graham Pyatt, Hugo Sonnenschein, Nicholas Stern, Lance Taylor, Jean Waelbroeck and Robert Willig are gratefully acknowledged. The author is solely responsible for any errors or misrepresentations that still remain. The research for the paper was completed while the author was on the staff of the Development Research Center of the World Bank. Views expressed should not be attributed to the World Bank or its affiliated organizations.

1 One could consider *any* intervention such as a regulation, a tax, or an expenditure in an initial equilibrium as a project in a general sense. Project appraisal in such a context becomes general social cost–benefit analysis. Much of the literature reviewed here is relevant for this as well.

2 The incentive incompatibility problem arising out of incomplete information is a feature not merely in the context of computing lump-sum transfers, but of almost all information-exchange-based resource allocation planning mechanisms.

3 Diamond and Mirrlees (1971) assume constant returns to scale production function.

4 It must be noted that the optima corresponding to different sets of constraints on public instruments need not be the same; nor need any of these optima belong to a set of Pareto-optimal allocations that the resources, technology and consumer preferences would permit. Finally, nonuniqueness problems can arise.

5 Other producers including public producers face convex (rather than convex cone) technology sets. In this model supply depends only on producer prices, while consumer demand depends on consumer prices and profits.

6 In a model in which Walras's law ensures that government budget constraint is met whenever every other agent meets his or her budget constraint, this constraint is to be interpreted as applying to a part of the budget. Such a situation may arise, for instance, when a limit is set by law on the extent to which public-enterprise losses can be met from general revenues.

7 This should really be understood as characterizing the initial pattern of production, so that there are goods that the economy could have produced but is not producing. The rest of the argument is based on the assumption that this pattern of specialization is unchanged by the introduction of the project.

8 However in Diamond and Mirrlees (1971) social welfare is defined as a function of individual consumption vectors, so that at any given m-tuple of consumption vectors by the m consumers, the *social* marginal rate of substitution in consumption of two commodities by individual i can differ from i's *own* marginal rate of substitution.

9 Of course, given the linear activity-analysis framework of these models, the problem of primal-dual instability was to be expected.

10 The related concept of Effective Rate of Protection spawned a large volume of empirical or theoretical studies. But most of these are partial-equilibrium studies.

Chapter 14: References

Adelman, I. and Robinson, S., *Income Distribution in Developing Countries* (Oxford: Oxford University Press, 1978).

Arrow, K. J., 'Samuelson collected', *Journal of Political Economy*, vol. 75, no. 5 (1967), pp. 730–37.

Arrow, K. J. and Hahn, F., *General Competitive Equilibrium* (Amsterdam: North Holland, 1971).

Aumann, R. and Kurz, M., 'Power and taxes', *Econometrica*, vol. 45, no. 5 (1977), pp. 1137–62.

Bacha, E. and Taylor, L., 'Foreign exchange shadow prices: a critical review', *Quarterly Journal of Economics*, vol. 85, no. 2 (1971), pp. 197–224.

Bertrand, T. J. and Vanek, J., 'The theory of tariffs and subsidies: some aspects of the second best', *American Economic Review*, vol. 61, no. 5 (1971), pp. 925–31.

Bhagwati, J., 'The generalized theory of distortions and welfare', in J. Bhagwati, ed., *Trade Balance of Payments and Growth* (Amsterdam: North Holland, 1971), pp. 69–90.

Bhagwati, J. and Srinivasan, T. N., 'Optimal intervention to achieve non-economic objectives', *Review of Economic Studies*, vol. 36, no. 105 (1969), pp. 27–38.

Bhagwati, J. and Srinivasan, T. N., 'The evaluation of projects at world prices under trade distortions: quantitative restrictions, monopoly power in traded and non-traded goods', *International Economic Review*, vol. 22, no. 2 (1981), pp. 385–99.

Bhagwati, J. and Wan, H., Jr, 'The "stationarity" of shadow prices of factors in project evaluation, with and without distortions', *American Economic Review*, vol. 69, no. 3 (1979), pp. 261–73.

Blitzer, C., Dasgupta, P. and Stiglitz, J., 'Project appraisal and the foreign exchange constraint', *Economic Journal*, vol. 91, no. 361 (1981), pp. 58–74.

Blitzer, C., Taylor, L. and Clark, P. B., *Economy-Wide Models and Development Planning* (London: Oxford University Press, 1975).

Boadway, R. E., 'Cost benefit analysis in general equilibrium', *Review of Economic Studies*, vol. 42, no. 131 (1975), pp. 361–74.

Boadway, R. E., 'Integrating equity and efficiency in applied welfare economics', *Quarterly Journal of Economics*, vol. 90, no. 4 (1976), pp. 541–56.

Bruno, M., 'Market distortions and gradual reform', *Review of Economic Studies*, vol. 39, no. 119 (1972), pp. 373–83.

Chenery, H., Ahluwalia, M. S., Bell, C., Duloy, J. and Jolly, R., *Redistribution with Growth* (London: Oxford University Press, 1974).

Dasgupta, P., Sen, A. and Marglin, S., *Guidelines for Project Evaluation* (New York: United Nations, 1972).

Dasgupta, P. and Stiglitz, J., 'Benefit–cost analysis and trade policies', *Journal of Political Economy*, vol. 82, no. 1 (1974), pp. 1–33.

Dervis, K. and Robinson, S., *An Industry-Focused General Equilibrium Model of the Turkish Economy* (Washington, DC: World Bank, 1978, mimeo.).

Diamond, P. and Mirrlees, J. A., 'Optimal taxation and public production, I: production efficiency; and II: tax rules', *American Economic Review*, vol. 61, nos 1 and 3 (1971), pp. 8–27, 261–78.

Diamond, P. and Mirrlees, J. A., 'Private constant returns and public shadow prices', *Review of Economic Studies*, vol. 43, no. 133 (1976), pp. 41–8.

Diewert, E., 'Optimal tax perturbations', *Journal of Public Economics*, vol. 10, no. 2 (1978), pp. 139–77.

Diewert, E., 'Cost–benefit analysis and project evaluation from the view point of productive efficiency', Technical Report No. 316 (Palo Alto, Calif.: Stanford University Institute for Mathematical Studies in the Social Sciences, 1980).

Dixit, A., 'Welfare effects of tax and price changes', *Journal of Public Economics*, vol. 4, no. 1 (1975), pp. 103–23.

Findlay, R. and Wellisz, S., 'Project evaluation, shadow prices and trade policy', *Journal of Political Economy*, vol. 84, no. 3 (1976), pp. 543–52.

Foster, E. and Sonnenschein, H., 'Price distortion and economic welfare', *Econometrica*, vol. 38, no. 2 (1970), pp. 281–397.

Ginsburgh, V. and Waelbroeck, J., 'A general equilibrium model of trade', in V. Ginsburgh and J. Waelbroeck, eds, *Activity Analysis and General Equilibrium Modeling, Contributions to Economic Analysis* (Amsterdam: North Holland, 1978, forthcoming).

Goreux, L. M., *Interdependence in Planning: Multilevel Planning Studies of the Ivory Coast* (Baltimore, Md: Johns Hopkins University Press, 1977).

Goreux, L. M. and Manne, A. S. (eds), *Multilevel Planning: Case Studies in Mexico* (Amsterdam: North Holland, 1973).

Guesnerie, R., 'On production of the public sector and taxation in a simple model', *Journal of Economic Theory*, vol. 10, no. 2 (1975), pp. 127–56.

Guesnerie, R., 'On the direction of tax reform', *Journal of Public Economics*, vol. 7, no. 2 (1977), pp. 179–202.

Guesnerie, R., 'Financing public goods with commodity taxes: the tax reform viewpoint', *Econometrica*, vol. 47, no. 2 (1979), pp. 393–422.

Hammond, P. J., 'Cost benefit analysis as a planning procedure', in J. Artis and A. R. Nobay, eds, *Contemporary Economic Analysis* Vol. 2 (London: Croom Helm, 1978), pp. 221–50.

Hammond, P. J., 'Straightforward individual incentive compatibility in large economies', *Review of Economic Studies*, vol. 46, no. 142 (1979), pp. 263–82.

Harberger, A., 'Three basic postulates for applied welfare economics', *Journal of Economic Literature*, vol. 9, no. 3 (1971), pp. 785–97.

Harberger, A., 'On the use of distributional weights in social cost benefit analysis', *Journal of Political Economy*, vol. 86, no. 2, pt 2 (1978), pp. S87–S120.

Hatta, T., 'Radial change in distortion and choice of numeraire', *Econometrica*, vol. 43, no. 3 (1975), pp. 519–20.

Hatta, T., 'A theory of piecemeal policy recommendations', *Review of Economic Studies*, vol. 44, no. 136 (1977a), pp. 1–22.

Hatta, T., 'A recommendation for a better tariff structure', *Econometrica*, vol. 45, no. 8 (1977b), pp. 1859–70.

Hotelling, H., 'The general welfare in relation to problems of taxation and railway utility rates', *Econometrica*, vol. 6, no. 3 (1938), pp. 242–69.

Kawamata, K., 'Price distortion and potential welfare', *Econometrica*, vol. 42, no. 3 (1974), pp. 435–60.

Koopmans, T. C., *Three Essays on the State of Economic Science* (New York: McGraw-Hill, 1957).

Koopmans, T. C., 'Concepts of optimality and their uses', *American Economic Review*, vol. 67, no. 3 (1977), pp. 261–74.

Kornai, J., *Anti-Equilibrium* (Amsterdam: North Holland, 1971).

Kurz, M., 'Distortion of preferences, income distribution, and the case for a linear income tax', *Journal of Economic Theory*, vol. 14, no. 2 (1977), pp. 291–8.

Lal, D., 'Methods of project analysis: a review', Occasional Paper No. 16 (Washington, DC: World Bank, 1974).

Little, I. M. D. and Mirrlees, J. A., *Project Appraisal and Planning for Developing Countries* (London: Heinemann, 1974).

Lysy, F. and Ahluwalia, M. S., *A Price Endogenous Model of Malaysia: Some Static Experiments* (Washington, DC: World Bank, 1977, mimeo.).

Manne, A. S. (ed.), *Investment for Capacity Expansion – Size, Location and Time Phasing* (London: Allen & Unwin, 1966).

Marglin, S., *Value and Price in the Labor Surplus Economy* (Oxford: Clarendon Press, 1976).

Mirrlees, J. A., 'Optimal tax theory: a synthesis', *Journal of Public Economics*, vol. 6, no. 4 (1976), pp. 327–58.

Mirrlees, J. A., *Social Benefit–Cost Analysis and the Distribution of Income* (Oxford University, 1977a, mimeo.).

Mirrlees, J. A., 'The theory of optimal taxation', *Handbook of Mathematical Economics*, in K. J. Arrow and M. Intrilligator, eds (1977b, forthcoming).

Pyatt, G., *Income Distribution and Endogenous Prices in Development Planning Models* (Washington, DC: World Bank, 1978, mimeo.).

Rader, T., 'Welfare loss from price distortions', *Econometrica*, vol. 44, no. 6 (1976), pp. 1253–7.

Roberts, K. W. S., *On Producer Prices as Shadow Prices* (Cambridge, Mass.: MIT Press, 1978, mimeo.).

Rodgers, G. B., Hopkins, M. and Wery, R., *Economic-Demographic Modelling for Development Planning: BACHUE – Philippines* (Geneva: International Labor Office, 1977).

Rudra, A., 'Use of shadow prices in project evaluation', *Indian Economic Review*, vol. 7, no. 1 (1972), pp. 1–15.

Samuelson, P., 'Prices of goods and factors in general equilibrium', *Review of Economic Studies*, vol. 21, no. 1 (1953), pp. 1–20.

Scarf, H., *Computation of Economic Equilibria* (New Haven, Conn.: Yale University Press, 1973).

Schwartz, H. and Benney, R., *Social and Economic Dimensions of Project Evaluation* (Washington, DC: Inter-American Development Bank, 1977).

Shoven, J. and Whalley, J., 'General equilibrium with taxes: an existence proof and a computational procedure', *Review of Economic Studies*, vol. 40, no. 124 (1973), pp. 475–90.

Shoven, J. and Whalley, J., 'Equal yield tax alternatives: general equilibrium computational techniques', *Journal of Public Economics*, vol. 8, no. 2 (1977), pp. 211–24.

Squire, L. and van der Tak, H., *Economic Analysis of Projects* (Washington, DC: World Bank, 1975).

Srinivasan, T. N. and Bhagwati, J., 'Shadow prices for project selection in the presence of distortions: effective rates of protection and domestic resource costs', *Journal of Political Economy*, vol. 86, no. 1 (1978), pp. 97–116.

Taylor, L., Bacha, E., Cordoso, E., and Lysy, F., *Models of Growth and Distribution for Brasil* (London: Oxford University Press, 1980).

Tinbergen, J., 'Some refinements of the semi-input–output method', *Pakistan Development Review*, vol. 6, no. 2 (1966), pp. 243–7.

Tinbergen, J., *Development Planning* (London: World University Library, 1967).

Warr, P. G., 'On the shadow pricing of traded commodities', *Journal of Political Economy*, vol. 85, no. 4 (1977), pp. 865–72.

Whalley, J., 'A general equilibrium assessment of the 1973 United Kingdom tax reform', *Economica*, vol. 42, no. 166 (1975), pp. 139–61.

Whalley, J., 'Uniform domestic tax rates, trade distortions and economic integration', *Journal of Public Economics*, vol. 11, no. 2 (1979), pp. 213–21.

15

The Economics of Pollution Control

PARTHA DASGUPTA

Introduction

Environmental problems can usually be identified with the inter-temporal mal-utilization of resources which are at the same time potentially self-regenerative and in principle exhaustible. There is, of course, more to such problems than the characterization that has just been offered. But for our purposes here it is as well to note that such a characterization is very much consistent with common parlance. Resources such as minerals and fossil fuels do not fall into this category, for they are not renewable. They are a pristine example of exhaustible resources. The act of extracting and utilizing a unit of such a resource reduces the total stock by precisely that amount. There are no means by which the total stock can be increased. Improvement in technology (for example, enabling one to drill offshore or engaging in recycling) can, of course, increase the quantity that can be used. But this is a different matter. Then again, discoveries of new deposits will increase the *known* available stock. But this too is a different matter. Note as well that we do not usually regard the *depletion* of an exhaustible resource as an environmental issue, except in so far as the act of extraction and use in production has 'environmental effects'. Thus, to take two examples, the burning of fossil fuels increases the mean surface temperature, and the smelting of ores is a common source of atmospheric pollution. The environmental issues here pertain not to the fact that the world's supply of fossil fuels and mineral ores is being reduced, but rather the fact that such activities have a deleterious effect on the earth's atmosphere.

The kinds of resources that fall within the characterization that has just been offered are those that are capable of regenerating themselves as long as the 'environment' in which they are nurtured remains favorable. Animal, bird and fish populations are typical examples. Arable and grazing land are yet another class of examples, though they may not appear to be so at first blush. So long as a piece of agricultural land is utilized carefully, and so long as there are no natural calamities, it regenerates itself over the annual cycle. But if utilized in excess over a period of time – that is, cultivation without either natural, or artificial, augmentation of soil nutrients – the quality of the soil will deteriorate. Indeed, if such a period of excessive utilization is long enough, the land can become valueless for agricultural purposes, having been reduced to barren wasteland. Both water (be it a lake or an aquifer) and the earth's atmosphere generally undergo a natural self-cleaning process as pollutants are deposited in them. But the effectiveness of such natural cleansing processes (that is, the rate at which the pollution disappears) depends both on the nature of the pollutant, and on the rate at which they are deposited. If the rates of deposit are unduly high over a period of years, it may take a long time for the resource to regenerate itself.

Underground reservoirs of fresh water display yet another characteristic. Often enough the issue is not one of depositing pollutants in them. Under normal conditions, aquifers are recharged by natural seepage and underground flows over the annual cycle. But if as a result of excessive extraction of fresh water the groundwater stock is allowed to fall to too low a level, then, in the case of coastal aquifers, there can be a salt-water intrusion thereby resulting in the destruction of such basins. Resources, such as fish, in their natural environment can normally survive as a species indefinitely, so long as the stock is not depleted below a certain level by human encroachment. But excessive rates of catch, leading to the bio-mass falling below the species' threshold level, result in the permanent destruction of the stock. The social cost – in terms of the value of forgone catch – therefore rises dramatically when the stock falls within a small range round the threshold value.

Each of the foregoing, without doubt, represents the kind of resources one has in mind when one reflects on environmental issues. Each also highlights a feature which did not appear in the characterization of environmental resources with which I began, namely, that the stock of such a resource can, even in the best of circumstances, never exceed a certain level. This last is of central importance, for it is a direct consequence of the earth being of finite size. To be sure, this upper bound to the stock size can be large; so large, in fact, that for a long while one may not really be in a position to monitor the fact that the resource is being encroached upon. Thus, if the rate of utilization of such a resource has in the past never been very great, the stock, for all intents and purposes, may be treated as unlimited. It could then be regarded as a free good. And it is most often so regarded. With the passage of time, it can happen that a society's need for the resource rises and the stock is allowed to fall to noticeable levels. Meanwhile, it is still regarded as a free good. There is then a presumption that the resource, being free, is being excessively exploited. In traditional terminology the lack of market for a common property resource results in each user conferring an external diseconomy on others. It is then that the society becomes conscious of a 'problem' and wants to know what stock size it ought, collectively, to aim toward.

The earth's atmosphere is a good example of this. Its capacity to absorb pollution, while large, is clearly finite. Despite its limited carrying capacity, it was reasonable to treat it as a free good until recently; for our capacity to pollute was even more limited. So much that even twenty-five years ago atmospheric pollution was not a major item in any discussion of resource utilization. Today it is a serious item in the agenda for research. On the other side of the coin is the question of waste disposal into rivers, lakes and the seas. Until recently the carrying capacity of many such resources could have been viewed as limitless. Not so today. Moreover, for most societies such 'sinks' are much too costly to exploit effectively. For it requires a well-developed sewage system to carry wastes to them. For poor societies, the option often is to rely on rain water, air and sunlight to degrade urban pollution. But in many cases they provide society with too slow a regenerative process for the need at hand. On occasion the concentration (of clean environment) falls to such a low level that it cannot provide society with its needs. This results in the outbreak of diseases, such as cholera and the plague. These days many call them 'crisis situations'. In fact, such situations have been with us always.

Related to this is the fact, greatly emphasized by ecologists in recent years, that the capacity of common property resources, such as the atmosphere and the seas, to absorb pollutants is far less than one would suppose at first blush. Filter-feeding animals, such as oysters, can concentrate poisons to levels far higher than those in their surrounding environment. So too along food chains, where the concentration of toxics, such as DDT, tends to increase from one trophic level to another. Such systems act as what ecologists call *biological amplifiers*. Thus, the *average* content of pollutants in the seas, *on its own*, is no index of the damage that is caused by their presence.

I began by noting that environmental problems usually concern the inter-temporal mal-utilization of potentially self-renewable resources. Such resources may be of direct use in consumption (fisheries), in production (plankton, which serve as food for fish species), or in both (drinking and irrigation water from underground basins). Often though, environmental problems are thought to arise as a consequence of the excessive production of pollution. It is usually most convenient, when discussing the optimum control of pollutants, to focus attention on the pollutants themselves and this is precisely what I shall do in this essay. But conceptually it is useful to bear in mind that the emission of pollutants, in effect, means a *reduction* in the *quality* or *size* (or both) of the stock of a renewable resource – the resource being the sink into which the pollutants are being deposited. This is worth keeping in mind, because it enables one to place the problem of pollution control in the more general context of the problem of utilizing renewable resources. In particular, it enables us to recognize that there are many environmental problems whose origins have little to do with the production of pollution, as the term is normally understood.

Pollutants can have an impact on welfare either as a stock, or a flow or both. Persistent pollutants, such as detergents (for example, ABS), pesticides (for example, DDT) and industrial inputs (for example, PCB) have an effect both as a stock, and as a flow. DDT as a flow is useful in agriculture as an input. As a stock it is hazardous for health. Likewise, PCBs as a flow are useful, because they are an important ingredient in the production of plastics, paints and hydraulic fluids. About as nondegradable as DDT, they have damaging conse-quences as a stock in water. They appear to be fatal to the larger types of phytoplankton, which are microscopic plants. A decrease in their numbers affects the food supply of the zooplankton, the slightly larger herbivorous animals that feed on the tiny plants. The zooplankton, in turn, are normally consumed by tiny fish that are consumed by larger fish caught by fishermen. Thus, PCB as a stock affects a vital part of the marine food chain, and thereby indirectly affects the supply of food fish in any specific area. This dual feature is fairly typical of nondegradable pollutants. The stock is detrimental, either because of its direct effect on consumption, or because it has deleterious effects on production; while the flow is beneficial, either because it is useful in production, or because it is an unfortunate byproduct of production which can be made harmless only by the expenditure of resources. Stocks of persistent pollutants may display 'threshold' effects; again, rather like self-renewable resources. For example, the effect of small deposits of toxins may well be negligible and this may be true over a range. Beyond this range the deleterious effects often rise rather rapidly as, for example, would appear to be the case with DDT concentration in human body fat.

In this chapter I shall present a prototype model of pollution control and indicate what would appear to be the main policy options. It will also enable me to bring together various strands in the environmental debate undertaken over the past decade and a half – not only as regards the broad alternative strategies that various groups of people have advocated, but also the mode of implementing such strategies. Since my concern here is with inter-temporal issues, I shall ignore uncertainty, a crucial feature of such problems. For an extended discussion of the treatment of uncertainty in these problems, see Dasgupta (1982).

(1) A Simple Classification of Pollutants

Ecologists have found it useful to construct a two-way classification of pollutants in accordance with whether they are *qualitative* pollutants, or *quantitative* ones.[1] The first category (which includes chlorinated hydrocarbon pesticides, such as DDT; industrial chemicals, like the PCBs; and certain herbicides) consists of synthetic substances that are produced and released into the biological environment solely as an outcome of human activity. The latter, on the other hand, consists of substances, such as mercury, nitrates, phosphorus and radiation, that are naturally present in the environment, but whose presence, either as stocks or as flows, are augmented by human activity.

For economic analyses of pollution management, this particular two-way classification is, perhaps, not very helpful. However, the ecologist's motivation behind the two-way classification mentioned above is clear enough. Many qualitative pollutants are biologically active: they stimulate physiological activity in ecological systems. But since, by the definition of qualitative pollutants, organisms have had no experience with them, these substances are often not biodegradable. They are among the most tenacious of molecules, and several of them are suspected of causing serious long-term damage.

In the economics literature on pollution management it has been customary to focus attention on the concentration of pollutants themselves, and to regard them directly as economic 'bads'. This is a perfectly reasonable procedure. But it is conceptually useful to bear in mind, as we have noted, that the emission of pollutants into an ecological system results in a *reduction* either in the *quality*, or in the *size* (or both), of resource stocks that are positively valued. Eutrophication of lakes is an example containing elements of both. The discharge of nitrogen and phosphorus (for instance, in the form of inorganic fertilizers) into aquatic ecosystems leads to the growth of various algae. This, in turn, results in the generation of foul odor and taste in drinking water. It can at the same time lead to a depletion of dissolved oxygen, and thereby to loss in fish stocks. In very many instances, though, it is only the quality of a valued resource which is affected by the emission of pollutants. Ambient air-quality standards are based on quality indices of the air. For water, a quality index much in use is the dissolved oxygen level, which is related to the biochemical oxygen demand (BOD) via what is known as the Streeter–Phelps equation. But since such quality indices, by their definition, reflect the concentration of pollutants of various kinds that are present in the resource in question, one may as well focus attention on the pollutants themselves in the construction of formal models.

Pollutants are created as byproducts of production, consumption and as intermediate products in the process of production.[2] A good example of the first is provided by the pulp and paper industry. Cigarette smoke is an oft-cited example of the second. Pesticides, herbicides and chemical fertilizers are obvious examples of the last. Here, we wish to introduce the kinds of considerations that must typically be taken into account in the analysis of economic problems arising from pollution. A general formulation would, therefore, be helpful for our purposes here, so that it can incorporate a wide variety of features. At the same time, it is sensible to keep the formulation as uncomplicated as possible. In doing this I begin by supposing that the pollutant appears as a byproduct of production. Subsequently, we shall note that the formulation can absorb the case where the pollutant is an intermediate good in production.

(2) The Emission–Output Ratio

Let us suppose that we are concerned with production at a participation location. Let Y_t denote an aggregate index of output at t, whose production is under scrutiny. If P_t is the *rate of discharge* of pollutants associated with this output, then we may suppose that

$$P_t = \alpha Y_t \tag{15.1}$$

where α is the emission–output ratio. Presumably, this ratio can be influenced by choice of technology. Thus, for example, in the case of coal-based electric power plants one may introduce stack-gas scrubbers to remove the sulphur dioxide (SO_2) produced during coal combustion.[3] Likewise, sewage-treatment plants, designed to raise the quality of household and industrial sewage to a level suitable for discharge into rivers, lakes and coastal waters, are among the most important examples of the model we are constructing here; although, strictly speaking, household waste ought to be regarded as a by-product of consumption. Alternatively, one may look for different input mixes in the production of Y_t which generate less pollution; for example, switching to solar energy for the generation of domestic heating and, thereby, reducing SO_2 emission; or, in the case of crop production, substituting the use of pesticides by alternative techniques which involve, among other things, special planting combinations, the use of repellents and hormones, and the introduction of beneficial insects. In the former case pollutants are produced as a byproduct of production (or consumption), but are treated before being discharged into the atmosphere. In the latter case choice of a suitable mix of inputs reduces the amount of pollution that is generated – something that is often called the choice of a 'clean technology'. In either event, the idea is that the emission–output flow coefficient α can be reduced by the expenditure of resources.[4]

We are concerned here with the flow of pollutants discharged into the surrounding medium. Thus, we suppose that with each technique of production there is an associated value of α. We now use an accounting device which will prove most useful for exposition and which will not diminish the generality of the formulation. We shall suppose that, if there is no attempt at pollution control, there is a best technology for producing the output. That is to say, this is the technology which the producer will choose, if he is not constrained either by emission charges, or by emission standards. To produce a given flow of output Y_t using this technology, involves a stream of costs. This cost stream we keep in the background for the moment. But we now suppose that to *reduce* the emission–output coefficient from the level associated with this technology involves an *additional* flow of costs which we discount at the consumption rate of interest (or the social rate of discount) to arrive at a capitalized figure. This additional investment outlay we call I, and we suppose that the emission–output ratio is a function of I. Thus $\alpha = \alpha(I)$. Again, to have an interesting problem we take it that α is a declining function of I (that is, $d\alpha/dI < 0$), to capture the fact that the emission–output ratio can be reduced by increasing investment. Note in particular from our accounting convention that $I = 0$ is associated with the production technology that would be chosen by the producer in the absence of any environmental consideration. By this convention the emission–output ratio associated with this technology is $\alpha(0)$. In Figure 15.1 I have drawn a stylized version of the function $\alpha(I)$. The diagram displays the phenomenon of *increasing marginal cost* of pollution control (that

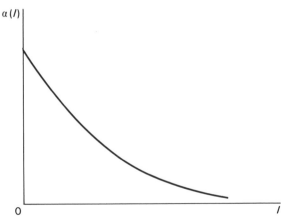

Figure 15.1   *The relation between abatement investment and the emission-*
output ratio.

is, $d^2\alpha/dI^2 > 0$); a feature which appears to be fairly pervasive (see Kneese and
Schultze (1975), chapter 2).[5]

(3) Clean-Up Costs and the Natural Rate of Pollution Degradation

I now proceed to characterize the manner in which the pollution concentration
changes with time. I denote the concentration level in the medium under study
by S_t at date t. Thus, for example, if it is the stock of SO_2 in the air which is
under discussion we may measure S_t by the number of micrograms of SO_2 per
cubic meter at t. Ignoring seasonal variations and exceptional local
circumstances, and taking the discharge of *other* pollutants into the medium as
given, we may take it that the net rate of change of the stock of the pollutant in
question is a function solely of the rate of discharge P_t and the concentration
level itself. This we write as $H(P_t, S_t)$ and, therefore, that

$$dS_t/dt = H(P_t, S_t).^6 \qquad (15.2)$$

It is appealing to simplify the functional form H and suppose that it is 'additive
separable' in P_t and S_t. This is often a good approximation, and so I assume
that $H(P_t, S_t) = G(P_t) + J(S_t)$, where G and J are known functions.[7] Thus, the
growth equation 15.2 reduces to the form

$$dS_t/dt = G(P_t) + J(S_t). \qquad (15.3)$$

In what follows I shall suppose solely for expositional ease that $G(P_t) = P_t$,
and therefore that the natural rate of degradation of the pollutant depends
solely on the concentration level. There are important cases where this is not

true. For example, it is judged that about 50 percent of the CO_2 emitted by the combustion of fossil fuels finds itself dissolved in the oceans and causing no harm. Thus, if atmospheric CO_2 content is under study, we would have approximately that $H(P_t, S_t) = P_t/2$; P_t being the emission of CO_2 into the atmosphere at date t. But since nothing crucial hinges on our formalization excepting for ease of exposition, I shall suppose that $G(P_t) = P_t$.

We are concerned with pollutants that are rendered harmless by natural processes with the passage of time. In some important extreme cases the process may be painfully slow, as with chemicals such as the PCBs, and pesticides like DDT and mirex.[8] For these limiting cases, one may approximate and write $J(S) = 0$. Others, such as herbicides like 2,4-D, are degraded by soil bacteria within months. For these, $J(S)$ is negative. Here, I shall consider pollutants and ecosystems whose interaction results in the former being neutralized over time, provided their concentration is not too large. In this case one would suppose that $J(S)$ is *negative* if S is not too large, but is *zero* if S is large enough.

In Figure 15.2 the function $J(S)$, which one may call the *natural deprecia-tion rate* for the pollutant – in the medium in question – has been drawn in a stylized manner. We are considering pollutants that do not multiply once released (unlike, say, harmful bacteria) and so J is never positive. Since J is *not* the percentage rate of depreciation, but the rate of depreciation itself, one supposes that the absolute value of $J(S)$ increases with increasing S, until S is within a neighborhood of the threshold level $\bar{S}$ at which point J increases rapidly to zero. Beyond $\bar{S}$, the stock does not depreciate: at concentration levels in excess of $\bar{S}$, the ecological system characterizing the medium into

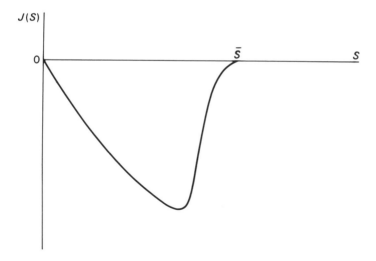

Figure 15.2   *The relation between the stock of a pollutant and its own net rate of decay.*

which the pollutant has been discharged is, to all intents and purposes, destroyed. Therefore, the pollutant does not get degraded. Examples of such interactions abound in the ecological literature.[9]

For those cases where it is judged that $\bar{S}$ is 'large', it is often convenient to ignore the range beyond $\bar{S}$ and to simplify and suppose that the pollutant depreciates at a fixed percentage rate, say, δ, where δ is a positive number. In this case we have

$$J(S_t) = -\delta S_t, \tag{15.4}$$

so that equation 15.3 reduces to the familiar form

$$dS_t/dt = P_t - \delta S_t.^{10} \tag{15.5}$$

In what follows we shall not need to restrict ourselves to the form 15.4. But if the reader finds this special form helpful for conceptual purposes, there is no harm in thinking in terms of it. The point I wish now to formalize is yet another kind of pollution control: namely, neutralizing discharged effluent in the medium in question. Artificial aeration of water bodies with low oxygen content is an obvious example. But this involves expenditure – what are often called *clean-up costs*. Thus, let E_t denote costs incurred at t in reducing the stock of pollutant by artificial means. We may as well incorporate this clean-up cost directly into the 'decay function' J and write it as $J(E_t, S_t)$ – where we must suppose to have an interesting problem that $\partial J/\partial E < 0$, to capture the fact that pollution degradation can be augmented by expenditure. Consequently, the growth equation 15.3 now reads as:

$$dS_t/dt = P_t + J(E_t, S_t).^{11} \tag{15.6}$$

(4) The Social Damages Due to Pollutants

Thus far, a description of the system under study. We now come to the normative issues. To have a nontrivial problem I suppose that the output is valued, but that the pollutant is a 'bad'. I consider the latter first. Recall that the pollutant may be damaging to welfare either as a flow (for example, noise), or as a stock (for example, DDT), or both. It may damage welfare directly (for example, the effect of smog on health, or the contamination of drinking water); or indirectly by being detrimental to production elsewhere (for example, crop reduction due to salinization of irrigation water; and the pollution of fish stocks, or the corrosion of metals by SO_2 in the air). Such a damage function we write as $D(S_t, P_t)$ where, by convention, I suppose D to be a *positive* function (that is, it is a damage function) which we shall subtract from the social benefits associated with output Y_t. Thus, $D(S_t, P_t)$ denotes the *flow* of social damage (or disbenefits) when S_t is the concentration level and P_t is the emission flow at date t.[12] The measurement of such damage poses some of the most difficult problems in environmental economics. There is often not only a great deal of uncertainty about the physical or biological effects of pollutants; there is also the problem of converting these effects into monetary units. This last can raise deep philosophical issues – the evaluation of health damages being a case in point. (For an excellent discussion of these problems, see Maler and Wyzga, 1976.)

It should be noted that the damage function, as has been formulated above, absorbs a wide variety of cases. The costs associated with operating water-treatment plants is a case that merits mention. If the production of the output under study involves the contamination of a source of drinking water, and if measures are taken to treat the *flow* of drinking water, then the damages attributable to the pollutant in the source are the costs of water treatment.

In many important cases damages depend solely on the pollutant stock – noise being a major exception. For expositional ease, I concentrate on such cases. Thus, $D = S(S_t)$. In Figure 15.3 I present a stylized version of such a damage function. For the purposes of illustration, I present the case where due either to threshold effects, or to the phenomenon of synergism, damages as a function of pollution stock display what scientists often call a *nonlinear dose–response relation*. The terminology is unfortunately far less precise than one would have expected from scientists, because the case they wish to emphasize, and which is implicitly caught in Figure 15.3, is a *special* kind of nonlinearity, one for which marginal damage is very large in the neighborhood of a certain stock level $\bar{\bar{S}}$, and is small elsewhere. Thus, for example, below a certain level of pollution trees survive in smog. So do fish in waters in which the dissolved oxygen is above a certain threshold. Neither survives beyond the threshold. Likewise, SO_2 and certain kinds of atmospheric particulates are, together, hazardous for health at concentrations below the levels at which each on its own is dangerous. We might then be considering the case where the particulates are already present in small concentrations and SO_2 is the pollutant being discharged into the atmosphere.

Now, it may be thought that since by definition $D(S)$ is the *flow* of social damages when pollution level is S, Figure 15.3 does not really capture the non-linear dose–response relation scientists are concerned with. For it can be argued that, in highlighting such relations scientists wish to point out (possibly temporary) *irreversibilities* that occur due to the destruction of socially valued resource *stocks* (such as forests or fish) when pollutants exceed threshold levels. Nevertheless, one can confirm that the policy implications arising from the case under study are similar to those arising from a nonlinear dose–response relation. To see this notice from Figure 15.3 that marginal damage is very high in the neighborhood of the pollutant level $\bar{\bar{S}}$. Moreover, the flow of damage beyond $\bar{\bar{S}}$ is large, though *marginal* damage is small. Likewise, for concentrations below $\bar{\bar{S}}$ the flow of damage is small and marginal damage is small. It is, therefore, clear that a socially optimal policy will involve, among other things, keeping the pollution level from ever reaching $\bar{\bar{S}}$, if it can be avoided.

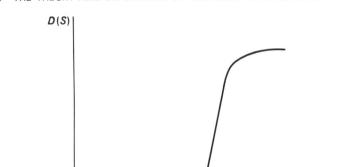

Figure 15.3   *The relation between the stock of a pollutant and damages.*

(5) The Social Benefit from Production

I come finally to the net social benefits associated with the output Y. Since by our accounting convention all costs that are not directed at pollution control have been separated out, they have now to be taken into account. Thus, let $B(Y)$ denote the flow of net social benefits when production flow is Y. Since production costs have been included in the calculation of net social benefits, $B(Y)$ will typically be decreasing at large output levels. In Figure 15.4 a stylized form of the social-benefit function is presented.

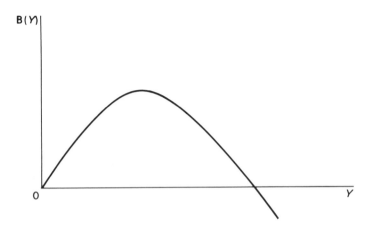

Figure 15.4   *The relation between production flow and net social benefit.*

(6) The Environmental Planning Problem: Alternative Formulations

We are now in a position to piece together the various bits of our construction and pose the planning problem of which the problem of pollution control is only a part. Let r (>0) denote the consumption rate of interest (or the social rate of discount). The variables in our model which a planner can control are clearly:

(a) the capitalized value of pollution-abatement costs I;
(b) the output of the product over the planning horizon Y_t;
(c) clean-up expenditures over the planning horizon, E_t.

The flow of net social benefits at date t is clearly $B(Y_t) - D(S_t) - E_t$, and the present discounted value of this at the initial date is therefore $|B(Y_t) - D(S_t) - E_t|e^{-rt}$. The criterion of welfare is the sum of the discounted present values of net social benefits over the future. Thus, the planner's problem is the following:

choose

$$I, Y_t, E_t \ (t \geq 0)$$

so as to maximize $\displaystyle\int_0^\infty [B(Y_t) - D(S_t) - E_t]e^{-rt}\, dt - I$

subject to the constraints

$$dS_t/dt = \alpha(I)Y_t + J(E_t, S_t),$$

$$I, Y_t, E_t \geq 0$$

where S_0 is given.

$\left.\begin{array}{c} \\ \\ \\ \\ \\ \\ \\ \\ \\ \\ \\ \end{array}\right\}$ (15.7)

Simple though it is, 15.7 would appear to reflect the essential features of problems associated with the economics of pollution control. It is on the basis of such formulations that rules for social cost–benefit analysis of pollution control projects need to be developed. In section 8 I shall highlight the rules for social cost–benefit analysis that problem 15.7 generates. Often enough though, because among other things, of the deep uncertainties that are involved in the estimates of damage functions, shortcuts are undertaken in the manner in which a pollution-control problem is posed. Thus, for example, an upper limit to concentration levels may be selected – say, on the basis of thresholds – and, if the inherited level of concentration is less than this the cost–benefit analysis is then directed at maximizing social surplus subject to the constraint that the

concentration level never exceeds this upper limit. The advantage of this formulation is that one avoids having to introduce damage functions into the
analysis. For the model under discussion, such a formulation would be as
follows: let S^* be the chosen upper limit, and suppose S_0 is less than S^*. Then
the planning problem is:

choose $\qquad\qquad\qquad$ Y_t, I and E_t $(t \geq 0)$

so as to maximize $\qquad\quad$ $\int_0^\infty |B(Y_t) - E_t| e^{-rt}\, dt - I$

subject to the constraints

$$dS_t/dt = \alpha(I)Y_t + J(E_t, S_t)$$

$$S_t \leq S^*, \text{ all } t \geq 0$$

and

$$I, E_t, Y_t \geq 0; \text{ all } t \geq 0$$

where S_0 is given.

$\qquad\qquad\qquad\qquad\qquad\qquad\qquad\qquad\qquad\qquad\qquad$ (15.8)

Problem 15.8 is a reasonable manner of posing a pollution-control problem
if S^* is a threshold level of the kind depicted in Figure 15.3. Indeed, if the
damage function possesses the characteristic of Figure 15.3 in a sharp form
(with $\bar{S} = S^*$) and there is not much difference between the control problems
15.7 and 15.8.

A major source of difficulty arises with this latter approach, if the existing
concentration level S_0 happens to exceed the level S^* that is judged tolerable.
In this case cost–benefit analysis is typically directed at locating the least-cost
mode of attaining the target within a specified period. For our model, the
problem would be posed as follows: assuming that it is feasible, suppose that it
is desired that the target be met within T years. Then the planning problem is:

choose $\qquad\qquad\qquad$ Y_t, I, and E_t $(t \geq 0)$

so as to maximize $\qquad\quad$ $\int_0^\infty |B(Y_t) - E_t| e^{-rt} dt - I$

subject to the constraints

$$dS_t/dt = \alpha(I)Y_t + J(E_t, S_t)$$

$$S_t \leq S^* \text{ for } t \geq T$$

and I, Y_t, $E_t \geq 0$ all $t \geq 0$,

where S_0 is given, and $S_0 > S^*$.

$\qquad\qquad\qquad\qquad\qquad\qquad\qquad\qquad\qquad\qquad\qquad$ (15.9)

The problem with 15.9 is, of course, that T is arbitrarily chosen. In particular, if T is small, maximum social surplus will be small: either I or E_t (or both) will need to be raised dramatically, or output will have to be curtailed in order to drive the concentration level down to S^* by year T. Without engaging in sensitivity analysis, it is not possible to judge how costly one choice of T is as compared to another. One may call the solution of 15.9 a *target-oriented programme*.

(7) The US Environmental Protection Acts: an Illustration

It is worth distinguishing between problems 15.8 and 15.9. In the final section of this chapter I shall report on a simulation exercise on the CO_2 problem which is cast in the form of 15.8. Problem 15.9 is interesting, though, because it is in terms of such a formulation that one can interpret and see the underlying logic in target-oriented environmental programmes that governments occasionally embark on. Thus, for example, the 1970 Clean Air Amendments in the USA considerably expanded the role of the federal government in setting and enforcing ambient air-quality standards by appealing to a level of ambient concentration below which it is judged that no health damages occur. In discussing the Amendments Kneese and Schultze (1975) note that,

> Congress directed the Environmental Protection Agency (EPA) to use scientific evidence to determine threshold values for pollutants assumed to have them, and then to set those values minus 'an adequate margin of safety' as 'primary standards'. These standards, which relate to injury to human health, are to be met first. More rigorous standards, to be met later, relate to public 'welfare' and aims to protect property, crops, livestock, and public transportation from pollutants. The states were to prepare implementation plans assuring that the primary standards would not be violated anywhere in the state after mid-1975. These plans to meet primary standards were supposed to have been completed by the beginning of 1972; deadlines for the secondary standards were more flexible. (Kneese and Schultze, 1975, pp. 51–2)

They then go on to write:

> Perhaps the most striking feature of the new legislation was in the amendments to the National Emission Standards Act ... which established specific emission standards (α in our notation) for automobiles. These include limits on hydrocarbons (HC) and carbon monoxides (CO) for new car models in 1975 and an additional standard for oxides of nitrogen (NO_χ) to be met in 1976 ... the act effectively calls for a 97% reduction, compared with uncontrolled conditions. (Kneese and Schultze, 1975, p. 52)[13]

In the case of water pollution control Kneese and Schultze note that the 1972 Water Pollution Control Act Amendment for the USA begins by asserting two national goals: (1) 'that the discharge of pollutants into the navigable waters be eliminated by 1985', and (2) 'that wherever attainable, an interim goal of water quality which provides for the protection and propagation of fish, shellfish, and wildlife and provides for recreation in and on the water be achieved by July 1, 1983'. In the context of our formulation here it would seem that the first goal states that by 1985 the value of α must be driven to zero, whereas the second goal pertains to a target water-quality level to be attained by 1983. In view of this, it should perhaps not be surprising that Kneese and Schultze (1975) in their excellent monograph, provide a sustained critique of the US pollution-control programme. Their complaint for the most part is that prior to passing the environmental legislations no systematic exercise was performed to calculate the costs involved in meeting stated targets and to conduct sensitivity analyses with a view to computing the amounts that could be saved by relaxing the targets somewhat; for example, by increasing T in our formulation 15.9 – the date by which the target quality standard must be met; or indeed, by reducing the target quality standard; that is, by increasing $S*$.[14] In the following two sections I shall bring out various features of the pollution-control problem as formalized in 15.7 and highlight some of the general properties of the solution to it. In section 10 I report on a simulation exercise due to Nordhaus (1977) on the carbon-dioxide problem, which is cast in the form of problem 15.8.

(8) Some Prototype Policies

While relatively simple, the formulation of the pollution-control problem, as captured in 15.7, nevertheless accommodates a wide variety of considerations that have been aired over the past decade and a half. We discuss them here. In problem 15.7 the social objective is the sum of the present discounted values of the flow of net social surplus. Quite obviously, the nature of the optimal programme depends on the characteristics of the various functions appearing in 15.7 and also the pollution level S_0 that the economy has inherited from the past. In particular, it depends on the availability of 'pollution-free' technologies, the extent to which pollutants ameliorate under natural conditions, the social value of output and the social damages caused by pollution. Without specifying these precisely, one cannot tell what the solution to 15.7 actually looks like. Nevertheless, one can discuss the broad categories of solutions that would emerge under different specifications. Since some of these categories have been discussed extensively in the environmental literature, we mention them below.

It will be recalled that the social objective in problem 15.7 is

$$\int_0^\infty [B(Y_t) - D(S_t) - E_t]\, e^{-rt}\, dt - I.$$

In Table 15.1 below we list four broad categories of policies that would appear to yield a high value to this objective under differing specifications of the various functions in problem 15.7. The first category of policies is characterized by the pursuit of limited economic activity and modest expenditures on pollution expenditure. Limiting output would imply a modest emission of pollutants. Granted that such a policy yields only modest levels of direct welfare $B(Y)$; but it does mean that only a moderate expenditure on pollution control is required to result in low pollution damage $D(S)$.

The second class of policies consists in pursuing vigorous economic activity, from the fruits of which substantial sums are incurred on pollution control, so as to limit the concentration of effluents. It would be misleading to suggest that it is in terms of an advocacy of these two classes of policies that one distinguishes 'environmentalists' from those who are not. Eminent environmental economists, such as Professor Allen Kneese, have supported the latter while commenting on the environmental programmes pursued in the USA (see Kneese and Schultze, 1975, p. 77). What one may infer, though, is that the environmental debate during the past decade and a half strongly questioned the desirability of the third broad class of policies in Table 15.1 which consist of a high level of economic activity together with negligible expenditures on pollution-control programmes – policies that were, in effect, being pursued until environmental problems were placed on the agenda of public debate. However, a glance at problem 15.7 suggests that one cannot tell, *a priori*, whether this third class of policies may not be optimal. For notice that what society loses via social damages $D(S)$ *may* well be more than compensated by gains from large output and low expenditures on pollution control. What the environmental debate does draw attention to, is the suspicion that the social damages are likely to be so vast that this class of policies simply cannot be desirable.[15]

To be sure, I am painting the tension between these views in broad strokes. To be sure also, there have been additional strands in the environmentalists'

Table 15.1

Policy	Output, Y	Pollution-control expenditure, E/I	Level of pollution
Limited growth and modest depollution effort	medium	medium	medium to low
High growth rates and vigorous depollution programmes	high	high	medium to low
High growth rates and negligible pollution-control programmes	high	low	high
Low growth and negligible pollution-control programmes	low	low	?

literature which cannot be captured in as aggregate a model as the one we are discussing here. In any case, for certain types of production in certain locations, one policy may be optimal; not so for others. One simply cannot tell in advance. Nevertheless, the construct we are discussing here can, indeed, support the objections that have been raised to the view that poor societies ought to curb their aspirations for growth, because of the environmental implications – the fourth class of policies in Table 15.1. The point is that, if output is very low, there is simply too little social surplus available for financing programmes that are required for the treatment of even the most common forms of waste which cause serious social damages. We have placed a query regarding the concentration of pollution in this fourth category simply because, while it may involve negligible *industrial* pollutants, it may typically involve suffering both because of low output, and high doses of other forms of pollution. It cannot be emphasized strongly enough that some of the worst forms of environmental degradation are associated with low income, not high. Deterioration of health due to inadequate sanitation, not to mention inadequate diet, is a burden that the poor bear, not the rich. In the face of this, a call for curbing the growth rates that LDCs aspire to appears at the very least as an indication of misplaced human concern.

(9) Cost–Benefit Rules for Optimal Pollution Control

The planning exercise 15.7 is in general difficult to solve analytically. At the technical level the first point to note is that, as Figures 15.2 and 15.3 display, the problem is in general 'nonconvex', so that *marginal* social cost–benefit analysis as a means of *locating* the optimal policy is not a reliable procedure. Often enough, such 'nonconvexities' prohibit the planner from relying exclusively on shadow prices (that is, *pollution charges*) as a mode of decentralization. Where this is the circumstance, there is a clear case for centralized coordination and control by way of *pollution standards*. It is possible to distinguish charges and standards in the context of a planning exercise in which the government has incomplete information about damages and about technology (see Weitzman, 1974; Dasgupta *et al.*, 1980). The point here is different. Here, I have assumed away uncertainty and differential information. The desirability of standards as a mode of control here arises from 'nonconvexities' and not incomplete information.[16] Nevertheless, there are many circumstances where in characterizing the solution to problem 15.7 it is possible, for heuristic purposes, to talk in terms of charges. I do this below. Furthermore, for expositional ease I restrict myself to optimal *stationary policies* where, by definition, the economic variables are constant over time.[17]

Since the pollutant is undesirable, we would expect its shadow price to be negative; that is, we would expect charges to be imposed on them – not subsidies. Let p denote the *emission charge*, where p is positive. We can now obtain the social cost–benefit rule for production Y. It goes as follows: the present discounted value of output at date t is $e^{-rt}B(Y)$; and the present discounted value of the social damages due to this output is the effluent charge associated with this output. This latter is $pPe^{-rt} = p\alpha(I)Ye^{-rt}$. Output at t ought, therefore, to be chosen so as to maximize, not $e^{-rt}B(Y)$, but $e^{-rt}[B(Y) - p\alpha(I)Y]$. It follows that the cost–benefit rule for the production of Y is:

$$dB/dY = p\alpha(I). \quad [18] \qquad (15.10)$$

The rule for clean-up expenditure is likewise simple to characterize. The present discounted value of clean-up cost at date t is $e^{-rt}E$. The social benefit from this expenditure is $-e^{-rt}pJ(E, S)$, the social value of reduced concentration; (this is positive because J is negative; see Figure 15.2). Thus, clean-up expenditure at date t ought to be chosen so as to maximize $e^{-rt}[-pJ(E, S) - E]$. This yields the rule:

$$-p\partial J/\partial E = 1 \qquad (15.11)$$

(unless $E = 0$ is optimal, in which case $-\partial J(E, S)/\partial E < 1/p$ at $E = 0$; that is, marginal cost exceeds marginal benefit at $E = 0$).[19]

The investment rule for pollution control is likewise simple to obtain. An investment outlay I is equivalent to expenditure in perpetuity of rI per period. When p is the emission rate, the *social damage* due to this output is $e^{-rt}pP = e^{-rt}p\alpha(I)Y$. Therefore, the present value of net social loss at date t due to I is $e^{-rt}[p\alpha(I)Y + rI]$. Notice that this entire expression is positive. The aim in undertaking pollution control is to reduce this loss. It follows that the rule determining optimal investment in pollution control is:

$$-pYd\alpha(I)/dI = r \qquad (15.12)$$

(unless $I = 0$ is optimal, in which case $-pYd\alpha(I)/dI < r$ at $I = 0$. Note that $d\alpha/dI < 0$, Figure 15.1). Quite clearly, firms would not undertake pollution-control measures unless emission charges or emission standards were imposed on them.

Next, it will be recognized that the pollutant concentration is a capital stock with negative social value $-pS$. From 15.7, it is obvious that the social rate of return to holding this 'asset' can be expressed as the sum of two terms, $\partial J(E, S)/\partial S$ and $[dD(S)/dS]/p$. The first term denotes the increased rate at which the pollutant disappears, and the second term the damage that is inflicted on future generations from a unit more of concentration – an intergenerational externality.[20] But r is the social rate of discount. Therefore, the optimal programme must be characterized as well by the condition:

$$r = [dD(S)/dS]/p + \partial J(E, S)/dS. \quad [21] \qquad (15.13)$$

Finally, as we are characterizing a stationary state, equations 15.1 and 15.6

yield:

$$\alpha(I)Y = -J(E, S). \qquad (15.14)$$

We are required to solve for *five* unknowns, p, Y, I, E and S from *five* equations 15.10–15.14. If a solution does not exist, it means that even in the long run an optimal policy does not tend to a stationary state with positive values for each of the five variables. For simplicity of exposition, therefore, I suppose that a solution exists. It should then be noted that there may be multiple solutions. The implication of this is curious. For it suggests that the long-run characteristics of the optimal plan – that is, the stationary state to which the plan converges, if it does – may well depend on what pollution level the economy starts with. That is, *history matters.*[22] Notice finally that if the pollutant displays threshold effects – either in terms of the damage inflicted (Figure 15.3), or in terms of the amelioration rate (Figure 15.2) – these threshold levels will typically be avoided along the optimal programme.

(10) The Carbon-Dioxide Problem: An Application

The combustion of fossil fuels results in the emission of carbon dioxide (CO_2) into the atmosphere. It would appear that about 50 percent of this remains there. It is known that CO_2 in the atmosphere produces a 'greenhouse effect', so that other things being the same, an increase in CO_2 concentration results in an increase in the mean global surface temperature. The current concentration of CO_2 in the atmosphere is about 330 parts per million. It is thought that, if the use of fossil fuels grows at about 3–4 percent per year, the atmospheric concentration of CO_2 will rise to a level between 365 and 385 parts per million by the year 2000. In a well-known study Manabe (1971) estimated that, other things being constant, this will result in an increase in the mean global temperature by 0.3–0.6 degC. In a subsequent study Manabe and Wetherald (1975) argued that a doubling of atmospheric concentration of CO_2 would result in an increase in the mean global temperature by 3 degC. Taken on its own, 3 degC, not to mention 0.6 degC, may not appear as a significant increase. Unfortunately, it is thought that even a 0.6 degC increase is sufficiently large to bring about changes in atmospheric circulation and the melting of sea ice; that is to say, it is feared that there is significant *climatic amplification* associated with increase in the mean surface temperature of the earth. The impact on agriculture could be deleterious, and the effect would be worldwide. It is for such reasons that the carbon-dioxide problem is taken very seriously by scholars with varied dispositions.

   In an interesting and important recent study, Nordhaus (1977) has estimated efficient ways of allocating energy resources, so as to ensure that CO_2 concentration in the atmosphere never exceeds a given multiple of the current level. The point is that while alternative energy sources, such as fission and solar energy, are currently more expensive than fossil fuels, they have no significant CO_2 emissions.[23] Nordhaus's simulation study is based on a problem rather like 15.8. He chose a planning horizon of 200 years, a discount rate of 10 percent per year, and his central analysis was conducted on the basis of an upper limit to the concentration level being twice the existing one.[24] It is assumed that there is no effective technology for removing CO_2 from the atmosphere by artificial means. The only way, therefore, that remains for controlling CO_2 emission is a judicious mixture of output control and a move toward more expensive energy sources; that is, in the notation of this chapter, controlling both Y_t and I. It should be noted that since the model does not incorporate a nonconvex damage function, like in Figure 15.3, nor a nonconvex natural amelioration function, like in Figure 15.2, Nordhaus's planning model does not have nonconvexities of the type that prohibit an appeal to shadow prices. In fact the problem, as he poses it, is a linear programming one, and he obtains the inter-temporal structure of CO_2 taxes which could in principle be used for implementing the optimal plan.

We shall not present details of Nordhaus's highly original study. Table 15.2 reproduces his results. The table is self-explanatory and so we merely highlight the more interesting results. Notice, first, from the first two rows that total energy consumption is not significantly constrained by the imposition of the carbon constraint. Indeed, in year 2100 the simulation run projects an *increase* in US energy consumption as a consequence of the constraint from 395×10^{15} Btu to 405×10^{15} Btu. However, from the second pair of rows one notices that CO_2 emissions are severely curtailed in *later* years along the optimal programme when the CO_2 constraint is imposed. This suggests that it is only in later years that the optimal programme is characterized by a major shift to

Table 15.2

	Actual	*1980*	*2000*	*2020*	*2040*	*2100*
Energy Consumption in USA 10^{15} Btu/year						
Uncontrolled CO_2 (that is, $S^* = \infty$)	{71}	76	92	155	250	395
100 percent increase CO_2 ($S^* = 2S_0$)		76	92	142	160	405
Global Carbon Emissions 10^9 ton/year						
Uncontrolled CO_2	{4·0}	6·9	10·7	18·4	40·1	45·4
100 percent increase CO_2		6·9	10·7	16·6	16·0	4·9
Carbon Emission Tax p_t \$/ton at 1975 prices						
Uncontrolled CO_2	{0·00}	0·00	0·00	0·00	0·00	0·00
100 percent increase CO_2		0·14	1·02	8·04	67·90	87·15

Source:
Nordhaus (1977).

costly input mixes. This is readily explainable. The upper limit on the concentration chosen being *twice* the current level means there is a lot more of CO_2 emission than the programme allows. Given that one is discounting future costs, it is quite natural that a move toward expensive but 'clean' sources of energy ought to come some time in the future – in the simulation exercise, in fact, it comes some sixty years from now. The last row of the table is revealing. It shows that the CO_2 emission tax becomes significant only at about the middle of the next century.[25]

We have noted that major impacts of a CO_2 concentration constraint of twice the present level begin occurring about sixty years from now. Not until then. Nevertheless, it is instructive to calculate the social cost of imposing the constraint on CO_2 concentration level. To do this, one computes the maximum value of the social objective in problem 15.8 under the assumption that $S^* = \infty$ (the unconstrained problem) and then subtract from this the maximum value for the case $S^* = 2S_0$. This is a useful exercise to perform precisely because the upper bound to the concentration level is, in any such exercise, somewhat arbitrarily chosen. Nordhaus calculates that at 1975 prices this cost is about US $87 billion. This is not an unduly large figure. But it is arguable that the upper bound has been chosen too generously, given the gravity of the problem and the risks that are involved. For this reason Nordhaus computes the social costs incurred if the constraint on CO_2 concentration is only 50 percent in excess of the current level (that is, $S^* = 3S_0/2$). It is of the order of $540 billion in present value terms. This is a large sum. However, as with all global environmental problems, a central dilemma remains: how is international agreement to be reached among diverse nations?

Chapter 15: Notes

This essay is based on ch. 8 of *The Control of Resources*, to be published by Basil Blackwell, 1982. I am most grateful to Edward Dommen and Jack Stone of UNCTAD and to Yusuf Ahmad of the UN Environment Programme for encouraging me to write the book and to write it in a style quite different from my norm. I have benefited from their comments, as well as those from Ezra Bennathan, Andrew Cornford, Carol Dasgupta, Robert Dorfman, John Krutilla, Karl Maler and Hirofumi Uzawa.

1 See Ehrlich *et al.* (1977, ch. 11, p. 629).
2 We are concentrating our attention on manmade pollution and not 'natural pollutors' such as volcanoes.
3 To give an example of such coefficients, in 1976 the emission standards in force for new fossil fuel-based steam–electric-power plants in the USA consisted, among other things, of 0.80 lb of SO_2 per Btu heat input as a maximum two-hour average emission from the combustion of liquid fossil fuels, and 1.2 lb for those using solid fuels; see Ehrlich *et al.* (1977, p. 551).
4 Another way of reducing α is to divert the effluent to a different medium where it is less harmful. This case, too, is caught in our formulation.
5 Thus, Kneese and Schultze (1975, pp. 19–21) write: 'As a virtually universal phenomenon, the greater the percentage of pollutants already removed from an industrial process, the higher will be the cost of removing an additional amount ... for example, when 30% of the BOD has been removed from the waste discharges of a typical large meat-processing plant, the cost of removing an additional pound is 6 cents. But once 90% of the BOD is removed,

another pound costs 60 cents; above 95%, the cost rises to 90 cents ... In one analysis, the total ten-year cost of eliminating 85 to 90% of water pollution in the United States was estimated at $61 billion. Achieving 95 to 99% freedom from pollution would add *another* $58 billion, bringing total costs to $119 billion, or about 1% of national income. A 100% objective (zero discharge) would demand an *additional* $200 billion.' It is often argued by environmentalists that in many cases there is no need for a trade-off, that technologies exist that are both cheaper *and* cleaner, and that bad practices have resulted in the prevalence of inferior technologies in both these senses. The formulation in the text does not contradict this thesis. It merely supposes that inefficient techniques of production have been disbanded and that we are comparing alternative techniques that *do* involve a trade-off.

6 I am simplifying here considerably for expositional ease. As I have mentioned in the text H depends not only on P_t and S_t, but also on activities elsewhere by possibly other agencies that alter the medium into which the pollutant under scrutiny is discharged. I ignore these complications here by considering these other activities as *given*. The question of *synergism*, is quite something else and will be incorporated in the text below. In certain special cases $H(P, S) = 0$ for all P and S to denote the fact that the stock does not change. This is so for noise pollution, for noise does not accumulate as a stock. The Streeter–Phelps equation, referred to in the text, is an example of equation 15.2.

7 I am considering the deterministic case here. If we wish to introduce uncertainty we may proceed by supposing that $H = H(P_t, S_t, \theta_t)$, where θ_t is a random variable at date t.

8 Under experimental conditions, the persistence of insecticides such as toxaphene have been noted to be as high as 45 percent of the original deposit even after fourteen years in as open a medium as soil.

9 See Ehrlich *et al.* (1977).

10 Keeler *et al.* (1972) use this formulation, as do many others. It should be noted that 15.4 is the functional form of *radioactive decay*.

11 For the radioactive decay case of 15.4, one may simplify and suppose that $\delta = \delta(E)$, with $d\delta(E)/dE > 0$. Thus, 15.5 reads as $dS_t/dt = P_t - \delta(E_t)S_t$, a convenient form with which to work.

12 The damage function may well depend explicitly on time t, to capture, say, the fact that the population in the locality in question is increasing or decreasing. I ignore this here for simplicity of exposition.

13 Expressed in grams per mile, these emission standards (α) were determined to be 0·41 HC, 3·4 CO and 0·04 NO_x.

14 The amounts may well be large. Kneese and Schultze (1975, p. 70), estimate that the cost difference between achieving the less ambitious goals in the earlier legislations in the USA and the ones in the 1970 and 1972 amendments on air and water quality standards may well be of the order of US $250 billion.

15 However, for illustrative purposes economists have developed theoretical models in which such a policy is indeed optimal. See Keeler *et al.* (1972) in which a model of pollution is developed in which this is the case. Keeler *et al.* call this a Murky Age; murky, though optimal!

16 To be sure, there are administrative problems in relying on standards. For a good discussion of this, see Kneese and Schultze (1975). As we are concerned with *analytical* issues here, we ignore such problems.

17 In many such planning problems the solution of problem 15.7 will, in the long run, tend to a stationary state, no matter what the initial concentration level S_0, is. But not necessarily. Though it may look easy enough, characterizing the solution of 15.7 is hard analytically.

18 Unless the optimum is to produce nothing, that is, $Y = 0$, in which case the rule is $dB/dY < p\alpha(0)$ at $Y = 0$. This can readily happen at specific locations, where it may be best not to engage in production of this sort and to move the location of production. Since there is then not much to say about this case, we ignore it.

19 This will be the case when technological possibilities of cleaning up pollutants after their discharge are limited as, for example, with gaseous emissions into the atmosphere.

20 In a different context, Smith (1968) calls this a stock externality.

21 The first term on the right-hand side of 15.13 is positive and the second term is negative.

22 This is a general characteristic of optimal control problems in which stock variables enter the instantaneous net benefit function, as is the case with 15.7. See Arrow and Kurz (1970). In addition, the problem has nonconvexities. Multiple solutions will often emerge.

23 It is not overlooked that nuclear fission poses other environmental problems.

24 In the notation of problem 15.8 in the text, we have $S^* = 2S_0$.
25 In 1975 the prices per ton of carbon or carbon-based fuels were about US \$25 a ton for coal, \$100 a ton for petroleum and \$200 a ton for natural gas.

Chapter 15: References

Arrow, K. J. and Kurz, M., *Public Investment, the Rate of Return and Optimal Fiscal Policy* (Baltimore, Md: Johns Hopkins University Press, 1970).

Baumol, W. J. and Oats, W. E., *The Theory of Environmental Policy* (Englewood Cliffs, NJ: Prentice-Hall, 1975).

Dasgupta, P., *The Control of Resources*, (Oxford: Basil Blackwell, 1982).

Dasgupta, P., Hammond, P. and Maskin, E., 'On imperfect information and optimal pollution control', *Review of Economic Studies*, vol. 47, no. 150 (1980), pp. 857–60.

Ehrlich, P., Ehrlich, A., and Holdran, J., *Ecoscience: Population, Resources, Environment* (San Francisco: Freeman, 1977).

Freeman, A. M., Haveman, R. H. and Kneese, A. V., *The Economics of Environmental Policy* (New York: Wiley, 1973).

Keeler, E., Spence, M., and Zeckhauser, R., 'The optimal control of pollution', *Journal of Economic Theory*, vol. 4, no. 1 (1972), pp. 19–34.

Kneese, A. and Schultze, C. L., *Pollution, Prices, and Public Policy* (Washington, DC: Brookings Institution, 1975).

Maler, K. G. and Wyzga, R. E., *Economic Measurement of Environmental Damage* (Paris: OECD, 1976).

Manabe, S., 'Estimates of future change of climate due to an increase of carbon dioxide concentration in the air', in *Man's Impact on Climate*, W. Matthews, W. Kellogs and G. Robinson, eds (Cambridge, Mass.: MIT Press, 1971).

Manabe, S. and Wetherald, R. T., 'The effect of doubling CO_2 concentration on the climate of a general circulation model', *Journal of Atmospheric Sciences*, vol. 32, no. 1 (1975), pp. 3–15.

Nordhaus, W., 'Economic growth and climate: the carbon dioxide problem', *American Economic Review*, Papers and Proceedings (February), vol. 67, no. 1 (1977), pp. 341–6.

Smith, V. L., 'Economics of production from natural resources', *American Economic Review*, vol. 58, no. 3, pt 1 (1968), pp. 409–31.

Weitzman, M. L., 'Prices vs. quantities', *Review of Economic Studies*, vol. 41, no. 128 (1974), pp. 477–91.

16

Planning and Dual Values of Linearized Nonlinear Problems: A Gothic Tale

WILLIAM J. BAUMOL

Everyone is aware that the world is rarely *perfectly* linear. Yet planning analysis continues to rely heavily on linear models. Linear programming is one of the most attractive tools available for formal planning calculations. Continued reliance upon linear techniques *cannot* be ascribed to unavailability of good calculation algorithms for nonlinear programmes. On the contrary, powerful calculation techniques that work in the nonlinear case have been available virtually from the inception of mathematical programming. Rather, the propensity toward linearization is to be explained in terms of the difficulty of empirical estimation of nonlinear functions, at least in regions not very close to the range of current experience. In a linear world this constitutes no problem. One can determine precisely the shape of an entire hyperplane from its height and partial derivatives at a single point. But where a surface may bend and curve in a manner which the investigator knows he does not know, it is at best dangerous to draw inferences about distant portions of a surface from empirical information about its behavior in a relatively small neighborhood. Apart from that, linear estimation techniques introduce other difficulties: heavier data requirements, more complex identification criteria, and so on. All in all, therefore, even with the best of intentions, the planner generally is unable to determine the shapes of the relevant nonlinear functions. In these circumstances, recourse to linear programming techniques becomes a great temptation.

The analyst may comfort himself by the belief, or at least the surmise, that the nonlinearities involved are realtively minor, though he rarely offers either evidence for this belief, or even a discussion of the degree of nonlinearity that is small enough to be neglected with impunity. This is all the more serious since as was shown elsewhere (Baumol and Bushnell, 1967), even mild nonlinearities in the underlying problem can and characteristically will introduce very serious errors into a linear-programming calculation intended to approximate the solution to the problem. The optimal solution to the linear problem is likely to yield values of the structural variables which differ by orders of magnitude from their true optima and are very different qualitatively as well. The LP 'solutions' can easily be worse than answers that are randomly selected. Moreover, reductions in the 'curvature' of the nonlinear functions in question may produce no noteworthy improvements in the results. If correct, these conclusions should be more than a little frightening to casual users of linear programming.

It has been objected that the primal programming calculation is concerned more with the value of the objective function than with the structural variables; that is, it may not matter if the output levels selected are very far from those that are optimal, provided the resulting yields are close to their maximum; and if the objective function is very nearly a hyperplane, it is argued, the approximation can consequently produce little sacrifice in overall yields. Though the argument seems questionable to me, I will not pursue it here. Rather, it is mentioned only because it contrasts so sharply with the case of a calculation whose main purpose is to evaluate the (dual) shadow prices, and for which the behavior of the objective function is only a secondary consideration.

In economic planning the values of the dual variables can be extremely important. Because they indicate the marginal yields of the different resources which constrain the development process, they can play a key role in determination of expenditure (investment) priorities. But it is, of course, crucial, if they are to be used for this purpose that the calculated values bear some reasonable resemblance to the true magnitudes they are intended to approximate.

I will show here that, unfortunately, a linear 'approximation' to a nonlinear programme can yield dual values which bear not the slightest resemblance to the true values of the shadow prices. Not only are the quantities likely to be seriously erroneous, but *the calculation is likely to make free goods of inputs that are in scarce supply* (that is, which have a positive marginal yield) and, perhaps more surprising, *they seem even more likely to impute scarcity value to inputs that are available in excess*. This last result is surprising because we have been taught to expect LP solution vectors to contain large numbers of zeros, a characteristic frequently not shared by a (well-behaved)[1] nonlinear programme. Yet, we will see that the dual values for such a nonlinear programme can easily be made up of nothing but zeros – the null-vector solution.

The Case of the Interior Maximum to the Primal Programme

As we know, the optimal point for a primal nonlinear programme may well lie in the interior of the feasible region. In particular, the solution of a programme with a nonlinear objective function and linear constraints need not lie at one of the corners of the feasible region. Thus, in Figure 16.1, point m inside feasible region 0abcd is the true optimum, if the true objective function is represented by the hill-shaped surface. On the other hand, the solution to an approximating linear programme, if it is unique, always lies at a corner, say, point c on the diagram, where the plane tangent to the graph of the objective function at T represents the approximating linear objective function.

Consider a particular dual variable v, say, that associated with the constraint represented by line segment bc. Let this constraint be

$$k_1 y_1 + k_2 y_2 \leq k. \tag{16.1}$$

Now, assuming the derivative exists,[2] the shadow price property of v is a consequence of the theorem that (whether the problem is linear or nonlinear) the

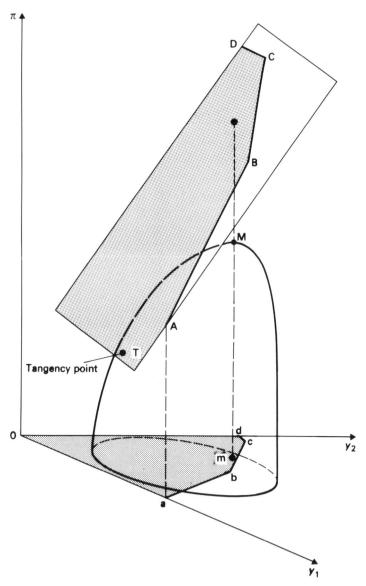

Figure 16.1   *Solution points of the nonlinear program and its linear approximation.*

optimal value $v°$ of the dual variable v, properly defined, must satisfy

$$v° = \partial \pi°/\partial k \qquad (16.2)$$

where $\pi°$ is the optimal value of the primal objective function. What 16.2 tells us is that we can determine the value of $v°$ from our diagram by undertaking

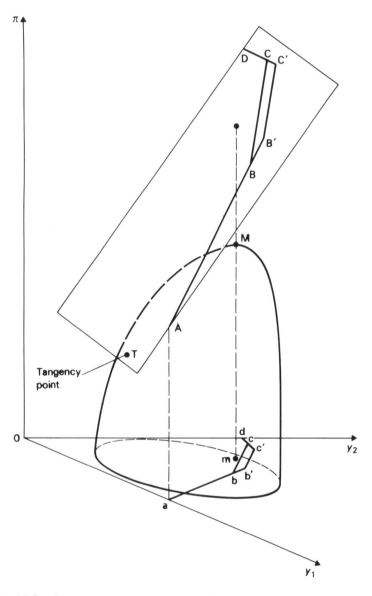

Figure 16.2   *Dual value obtained by a shift in constraint.*

(see Figure 16.2) a small outward shift, from bc to b'c', in the corresponding constraint segment – a shift that leaves its slope unchanged. We then observe how much the value of π° increases as a consequence (it can, clearly, never decrease, since the loosening of the constraint, at worst, will still permit the previous solution). The limit of $\Delta\pi^\circ/\Delta k$ as Δk approaches zero will give us the desired value of v°.

In the case shown in Figure 16.2 in the linear calculation $\Delta\pi^\circ$ is given by the difference in heights between points C' and C on the plane above corners c' and c of the expanded and the initial feasible regions. In that case we must have (letting the subscript l refer to the results of the linear calculation):

$$\partial\pi_l^\circ/\partial k = v_l^\circ > 0 \tag{16.3}$$

and we certainly would expect such a result to be common.

On the other hand, because the true solution point m is an interior maximum, the expansion of the feasible region resulting from the increase in k will not *really* improve matters. The nonlinear maximum will remain precisely where it was so that (letting the subscript t connote true values):

$$\partial\pi_t^\circ/\partial k = v_t^\circ = 0. \tag{16.4}$$

Thus, as asserted earlier, here we have a case in which the input in question is a free good (its true duel value is zero) and yet the linear calculation is likely to assign it a nonzero value. It must be reemphasized that the qualitative difference indicated by 16.3 and 16.4 is not a peculiar result ascribable to any special features built into our illustration. Rather, it is to be regarded as a normal and very likely possibility.

Nonlinear Solutions on the Boundary of the Feasible Region

The immediate source of the qualitative linearization error that has just been described is the interior solution to our illustrative nonlinear programme. However, the solutions to such programmes do not always fall inside the feasible region. One may well ask whether the linear and the true solution cannot be expected to correspond roughly in such a case. For, by hypothesis, the true optimal point must now lie somewhere on the boundary of the feasible region, perhaps at or near a corner point. If the primal solution points for the linear approximation and the underlying nonlinear programme are not far apart and the slope of the linear objective surface is not very different from that of the true surface near those points, we may well expect the values of the $\partial\pi_l^\circ/\partial k$ to be similar to the corresponding $\partial\pi_t^\circ/\partial k$. Unfortunately, there are a number of conditions required for this argument to hold, and as we will see, they may well not be satisfied in practice.

The first source of difficulty is the only one which is quite obvious. Linear approximations are not constructed at the optimal point or, usually, even any-where near it. If one knew the approximate location of the optimal point to begin with, so that one would be able to select an *initial* point known in advance to be nearby, there would be no need for any approximating calcula-tion. A linear approximation is normally constructed on the basis of initial points (such as tangency point T in the figures) for which the required informa-tion happens to be available. Consequently, though the linear surface and the true objective surface may be similar in shape near those initial points, the two may well differ widely near the optimal solution which can be far away. The slopes of the profit function at these points and, hence, the dual values may then also differ substantially.

This difficulty, as already admitted, is an obvious matter and it may be con-sidered a matter of imperfect knowledge which hampers application rather than a fundamental analytical problem. This is, however, certainly not true of the next problem which we will examine. This second problem remains even if the LP and the true solution points are close and the slopes of the two surfaces are very similar. Even then the two partial derivatives of the objective function with respect to k, and hence the two dual values, can well differ substantially.

This second problem arises, because even where the nonlinear optimum lies on the boundary of the feasible region, it may well not fall at a corner point of that boundary. Thus, optimal point m in Figure 16.3 lies in the interior of line segment cb. In our diagram a consequence is that linear profit π_l is bound effectively by two constraint lines, dc and cb, while the true profit π_t is bound by only one. (In a problem with n structural variables, that is, n dimensions, π_l will be bounded by n constraints, while π_t may still be bounded by only one.)

Here, it may be tempting (but incorrect) to surmise that for those derivatives that are nonzero[3]:

$$\partial \pi_l^o / \partial k \leq \partial \pi_t^o / \partial k. \qquad (16.5)$$

This may seem to follow, because additional constraints can only reduce (or leave unchanged) the value of the objective function. However, since we know nothing about the relative *changes* that result in π_l^o and π_t^o, we can infer no relationship such as 16.5 between their derivatives. Letting π' and π'' refer to the optimal value of the objective function before and after the loosening of the constraint by an increase in k, and assuming for purposes of illustration that the linear values are very close to the true values *near the linear optima*, it is clear that we must have

$$\pi_l' \leq \pi_t', \; \pi_l'' \leq \pi_t''$$

that is, the true optimum must always equal or exceed the corresponding linear optimum. But that tells us nothing about the *differences*, that is,

$$\pi_l'' - \pi_l' \gtrless \pi_t'' - \pi_t'$$

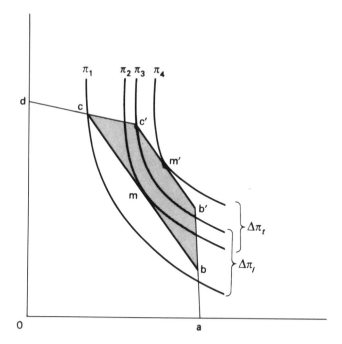

Figure 16.3   *A boundary solution not at a corner.*

since the direction of this inequality clearly depends on the *change* in the loss from linearization before and after the constraint is loosened, namely, on the relative size of $\pi'_t - \pi'_l$ and $\pi''_t - \pi''_l$. The problem is illustrated in Figure 16.3, where the loosening of the constraint represented by cb shifts that line segment outward to c'b', changing the linear optimum from c to c' and the true optimum from m to m'. On the assumption we have adopted for the moment, that near c and c' the linear and true values of π are close to one another, the resulting change in the value of the linear profit function will be $\Delta\pi_l = \pi_3 - \pi_1$ and that in the true profit will be $\Delta\pi_t = \pi_4 - \pi_2$. Clearly, the relative magnitudes of $\Delta\pi_t$ and $\Delta\pi_l$ can vary in virtually any way. For example, if we take $\Delta\pi$ to be proportional to the distance between the pertinent curves, the case shown in the figure will yield a relationship the opposite of that of 16.5. Thus, the true dual value can be either larger, or smaller, than its linear proxy, and there seems to be no way to place *a priori* bounds on the difference between them.

There is another, perhaps more fundamental, reason for which we cannot rely on as loose a relationship as 16.5 to characterize the comparative behavior of the linear and the nonlinear dual. For linear approximations to nonlinear programmes are beset by a third and perhaps even more fundamental difficulty. This stems from the fact that there is, in general, not the slightest reason to expect the two solution points to lie anywhere near one another. For, as will be shown now, the linear solution point depends entirely on the choice of initial point from which the linear approximation is constructed, and has no connection with the location of the true optimum. *By an appropriate choice of initial point, virtually any corner of the feasible region can perhaps be made to serve as the linear optimum.* This, as we will see now, can cause critical problems *even where the nonlinear solution lies at a corner of the feasible region* (though it certainly does not help matters if the true optimum lies at a point that is not a corner).

The nature of the problem is brought out by Figure 16.4. In that diagram the curves labeled π_1, π_2 and π_3 are true iso-profit loci. The true optimum is m, the point of tangency between π_3 and the boundary of the feasible region. The solution point of the linear approximation will lie at one of the corners a, b, c, or d. If it happens to fall at c, or even at b, one may hope that things will not work out too badly.

But the corner point that is selected by the linear calculation is by no means certain to be either b, or c. Rather, it is highly sensitive to the choice of initial point. That is, suppose the linearization is in fact carried out by selecting some initial point and fitting a tangent hyperplane to the true nonlinear surface at that point. Then the linear iso-profit curves will be a set of parallel straight lines tangent to the true iso-profit curve at that initial point. For example, suppose the initial point is r. Then c'b', the tangent to the true iso-profit curve at r, will be one of the linear iso-profit curves. In this case r has been selected so that c'b' happens to be parallel to segment cb of the boundary of the feasible region, and all other points on the curve rsm have been selected similarly. This means

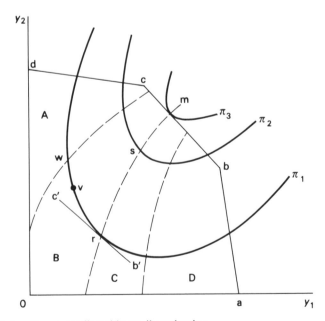

Figure 16.4   *Errors attributable to linearization.*

that for any such initial position all points on cb will be optimal solutions to the linear programme. Similarly, if the initial point is w, the iso-profit curves will be parallel to ba and so any point on that segment will be a linear solution. For the same reason, any point such as v on the arc wr of π_1 will yield point b as its linear solution.

More generally, constructing the other two broken curves as we constructed rsm, we see that they divide the feasible region into four subregions. The one labeled A consists of all points $y^a = (y_1^a, y_2^a)$ such that if y^a is used as the initial point for the linear approximation, the resulting linear programme will select the corner a as its optimum. A similar relationship holds for subregions B, C and D.

We conclude that, if we have no initial information about the location of the true optimum m, we may well happen to utilize an initial point in region D or A, which yields a linear solution very far[4] from m. Thus, suppose now that the nonlinear optimum falls at one corner point, and that the linear optimum falls at another. Then the presence of the other constraint lines at these points will generally lead to very different values for $\partial\pi_l^o/\partial k$ and $\partial\pi_l^o/\partial k$. For example, suppose the true optimum lies at c, while the linear optimum is a (see Figure 16.3). Here, the difference is clear, for we have this time:

$$\partial\pi_l^o/\partial k > 0, \quad \partial\pi_l^o/\partial k = 0$$

since the shift in the constraint line cb to c'b' makes no change in the feasible region in the neighborhood of the linear optimum a. Similarly, if w is the capacity associated with constraint line segment ab, we will have:

$$\partial\pi_l^o/\partial w = 0, \quad \partial\pi_l^o/\partial w > 0.$$

Concluding Comment: Generalization

Our qualitative conclusions may seem from the preceding discussion to depend on the possibility that the linear solution point will lie far away from the true optimum. This may be suggested by the cases in which the true optimum fell well inside the feasible region or at some distant corner. In fact, however, at least the qualitative distortions in the dual values which we have observed arise *inevitably* even where the two solution points are very close, just so long as they do not coincide, because then the two points must be bound by different constraints and the corresponding dual variables must therefore differ accordingly.

In terms of Figure 16.3 let the linear solution fall, for example, at point c. Then, suppose the true solution point y_t is at *any* other point in the diagram, no matter how far from *or how near* to point c. In that case it is necessarily true that either constraint line dc, or constraint line cb (or both) must not be binding at y_t, so the dual values must differ quantitatively and qualitatively from the true magnitudes of the corresponding marginal yields. An investment programme based on linear dual values may, therefore, not serve the community very well.

Chapter 16: Notes

I am very grateful to the Sloan Foundation, whose support greatly facilitated the completion of this paper. This note grew out of discussions at the Friday seminar at the Stockholm School of Economics.

1   By a well-behaved programme, I mean here one that involves diminishing returns, diminishing marginal rates of substitution, and so on, so that conventional methods of solution apply.
2   If the derivative does not exist the value of v will, of course, lie between the values of the corresponding right- and left-hand derivatives, but that changes nothing of importance in our discussion. For the derivation of the theorem, see Balinsky and Baumol (1968).
3   Later we will return to the serious problems associated with the zero-valued derivatives.
4   As a practical matter such a choice may be *forced* upon us by the information that happens to be available. Usually, we do not have the luxury of taking as the initial point any point in the feasible region that happens to appeal to us. Rather, the data are generated by current practice which, so far as we can tell in advance, may be distant from any optimum.

Chapter 16: References

Balinsky, M. L. and Baumol, W. J. 'The dual in nonlinear programming and its economic interpretation', *Review of Economic Studies*, vol. XXXV, no. 3 (1968), pp. 237–56.
Baumol, W. J. and Bushnell, R. C. 'Error produced by linearization in mathematical programming', *Econometrica*, vol. 35, nos 3–4 (1967), pp. 447–71.

Part Four

Economic History and History of Thought

17

Economic Growth and Stagnation in the United Kingdom before the First World War

SIR ALEC CAIRNCROSS

The period before the First World War is full of interest to economists and Arthur Lewis, in particular, has contributed greatly to our understanding of it. He has brought economic theory to bear on the historical evidence, and in doing so has helped to illuminate the complex process of economic development for the benefit of theorists. He is particularly fascinated by the experience of the United Kingdom as industrial leadership passed to other countries; and as this is a fascination I share, it seemed appropriate, in contributing to a volume in his honor, to look back at that experience, concentrating on the twenty years or so before 1914. Arthur Lewis has provided his own answers to many of the conundrums posed by the record of those years, and if I agreed with all his answers, there would be no point in my taking up the subject. Points of disagreement are the natural starting point rather than the wide range of other issues on which I am in full agreement. I shall, therefore, have little to say on the behavior of prices and wages, as developed in chapters 3 and 4 of his *Growth and Fluctuations, 1870–1913,* and will concentrate on chapter 5 on 'The British climacteric' with its rousing concluding paragraph:

> Britain was caught in a set of ideological traps. All the strategies available to her were blocked off in one way or another. She could not lower costs by cutting wages because of the unions, or switch to American-type technology because of the slower pace of British workers. She could not reduce her propensity to import by imposing a tariff or by devaluing her currency, or increase her propensity to export by devaluing or by paying export subsidies. She could not pioneer in developing new commodities because this now required a scientific base which did not accord with her humanistic snobbery. So instead she invested her savings abroad; the economy decelerated, the average level of unemployment increased and her young people emigrated. (Lewis, 1978, p. 133)

These are all arguable propositions, but in my view each of them is only a half-truth and they add up to a distorted picture of the forces at work.[1] It is also not clear to what point in time between 1873 and 1913 the last sentence is intended to apply: the increase in foreign investment, the deceleration of the economy, and the rise in unemployment and in emigration did not operate steadily from decade to decade and there were long stretches of time in which each of these trends was reversed.

The arresting conclusion with which the paragraph ends does not follow in any obvious way from the propositions that precede it. These propositions may explain why the rate of growth was lower than elsewhere or began to decelerate. They would be unlikely to lead to an inadequacy of job opportunities, unless they generated a balance of payments constraint. Such a constraint undoubtedly existed from time to time. But did it operate throughout the period or, as we might expect from the argument, with increasing severity? And if there was an intermittent constraint, is it clear that it derived from a loss of competitive power affecting exports and imports, rather than from a quite different source, such as capital movements, which, on other grounds, could be defended as advantageous to the British economy?

But there is a prior question. Did the economy decelerate, and if so, when and why? If there was no deceleration and if unemployment was no higher at the end of the period than at the beginning, the whole argument falls to the ground. If there *was* a deceleration, it remains to be investigated whether it coincided with a falling-off in job opportunities and a balance of payments constraint. Now there are good grounds for believing that there was some deceleration after 1870. The most thorough and authoritative analysis of the historical record is that of Matthews, Feinstein and Odling-Smee (forthcoming). They put the peak rate of growth in income per head before 1860 and, perhaps, as far back as 1830. Their results can be summarized as in Table 17.1.

The first column shows a long downward swing in the rate of growth of GDP over the nineteenth century. The movement is less continuous when measured in relation to population growth, but still shows a marked falling off in the forty years after 1873 compared with the earlier part of the century. That the falling off was not just in labor productivity but was manifest in total productivity as well appears from the last two columns, which allow for the contribution made by capital investment. The estimates of real disposable income per head show

Table 17.1   *Annual Percentage Rates of Growth in the United Kingdom, 1800–1973*

	GDP	Population	GDP per head	Real disposable income per head	Total factor productivity	Total factor productivity in manufacturing
1800–1860*	2·6	1·3	1·3	1·1	—	—
1856–1873	2·2	0·8	1·4	1·7	0·9	0·8
1873–1913	1·8	0·9	0·9	1·0	0·5	0·6
1951–1973	2·8	0·5	2·3	2·5	2·3	2·5

*United Kingdom.
Source:
Mathews *et al.* (forthcoming, tables 16.1 and 16.6).

an even more drastic slackening of pace after 1873, because the rise in output in the years before 1873 was reinforced by a favorable movement in the terms of trade, and a rapid increase in income from abroad.

It is important to appreciate that such estimates, however careful, are subject to wide margins of error which are larger the further back we go. They create a presumption that there was a falling off in the growth of GDP, but cannot establish it as a fact. No one without experience of the problems of conjuring indices out of the statistical scraps surviving from a century ago can have much conception of the limitations of the data or the resulting indices. This is particularly true of data on production, as Giffen pointed out a century ago and as Arthur Lewis has recently reminded us.[2] It is even more true of productivity, where to the difficulties of measuring outputs are added the even greater difficulties of estimating inputs. In measuring labor input we have to rely on the decennial Census of population, coupled with miscellaneous information on trade union unemployment, hours of work, educational attainment, and so on. As for the input of capital, there is no way of arriving at a really reliable measure of investment in industry and commerce. The indices may tell us what can plausibly be assumed on the basis of other evidence, rather than provide a means of checking or improving on that evidence.

The limitations of the data are even more apparent when we shorten the periods to be compared and move to inter-censal dates. It is commonly believed that there was a marked retardation in the British economy after 1890, or alternatively after 1900. This proposition involves a comparison of successive decades or, if we use Lewis's approach, successive cycles. Take, for example, the table in Aldcroft and Richardson's *The British Economy, 1870–1939* (Table 17.2). These figures come from different sources and are plainly not altogether self-consistent. They do not suggest a very different experience before and after 1890 in respect of industrial production. But they do point to a quite alarming falling off in the growth in industrial productivity starting in the 1880s, if we believe column 2, or after the 1880s, if we believe column 3.

A quite different and more plausible picture emerges from Arthur Lewis's calculations. His indices of GDP and of industrial production, taken together

Table 17.2 *Annual Percentage Rates of Growth in the United Kingdom, 1860–1913*

	Industrial production (including building)	Industrial productivity per man-year	Total output per man-hour
1870–80	2·3	1·2	0·9
1880–90	1·6	0·5	3·8
1890–1900	2·8	0·2	1·3
1900–13	1·6	0·2	0·6

Source:
Aldcroft and Richardson (1969, p. 126)

with Feinstein's (1972, table 60) estimates of employment, yield the following results, measured from peak to peak of the business cycle (Table 17.3) or from decade to decade (Table 17.4). If we begin with the first column in Tables 17.3 and 17.4, it would be difficult to interpret this as clear evidence of retardation after 1873. Lewis, using the same figures but for different periods, shows a steady deceleration in rates of growth from the third quarter of the century (Lewis, 1978, p. 113):

1853–73	1·95
1873–83	1·90
1883–99	1·85
1899–1913	1·70

This may well be a more revealing picture, since there must be some doubt about the contrast between the 1880s and 1890s in Tables 17.3 and 17.4. It is also consistent with the picture given in Table 17.1. But not only do changes in the period compared throw some doubt on the trend: there is no agreement between the three different measures of GDP. For the periods selected by Lewis, we get the following (Feinstein, 1972, table 6), with rate of increase in GDP measured from:

	output data	*expenditure data*	*income data*
1873–83	1·90	2·02	1·45
1883–99	1·85	2·36	2·72
1899–1913	1·70	1·30	1·16

Thus, it is only if one attaches overriding importance to the output data that a steady trend appears. The fact that Lewis's index of industrial production also shows a slight but consistent downward trend does not resolve the matter because this index is an important element in Lewis's GDP estimates from output data. Are there good grounds for attaching more importance to the output than to the income and expenditure data?

This is not an easy question to answer. If one looks at Tables 17.3 and 17.4 and compares the more volatile behavior of the income and expenditure estimates on the one hand, and the greater similarity between changes in the output and the 'compromise' estimates on the other, one is bound to feel rather more confidence in the output data as apparently more plausible and self-consistent. But until we have some rational explanation of the divergences, such a judgment must be distinctly tentative.

Neither the income nor the expenditure data are free from criticism and the two show wide divergences from one another. In 1870 the income estimate is nearly 12·5 percent below the expenditure estimate, and in 1913 the divergence is not much less. Over the whole period, however, there is not a great deal of difference in the rates of growth shown by these two measures – nor, indeed,

Table 17.3 Rates of Growth of GDP, Industrial Production, Employment and Productivity between Peaks, 1870–1913 (percent per annum)

	GDP (output)	Civil employment	GDP per employed worker	Industrial production	Employment in industry	Labor productivity in industry	Labor productivity in manufacturing industry
1873–83	1·89	0·62	1·27	2·23	0·61	1·62	1·66
1883–90	1·66	1·07	0·59	1·81	1·28	0·53	0·69
1890–99	1·98	1·12	0·86	2·37	0·98	1·39	1·61
1899–1913	1·70	0·90	0·80	1·95	1·13	0·82	0·87

Table 17.4 Rates of Growth of GDP, Industrial Production, Employment and Productivity between Census Years 1870–1913 (percent per annum)

	GDP (output)	Civil employment	GDP per employed worker	Industrial production	Employment in industry	Labor productivity in industry	Labor productivity in manufacturing industry
Decade Preceding							
1870–72 (average)	2·07	0·95	1·12	3·03	0·96	2·07	2·31
1880–82 (average)	1·79	0·56	1·23	2·25	0·61	1·64	1·70
1890–92 (average)	1·73	0·97	0·76	1·84	1·28	0·56	0·58
1900–02 (average)	1·98	1·10	0·88	2·24	0·98	1·26	1·42
1910–12 (average)	1·46	0·93	0·53	1·64	1·13	0·51	0·52
1911–13 (average)	1·64	1·00	0·64	2·00	1·13	0·87	0·95

Sources:
Based on Lewis (1978, appendix I), and Feinstein (1972, tables 57 and 60).

by all three – so that we can be fairly confident that the average rate of growth over the forty-three years was about 1·90 percent per annum (taking the 'compromise' estimate). This by itself implies some falling off compared with the earlier part of the century. All three indicators also point to a perceptible falling off after 1900, although whether it was as large as the income, and still more the expenditure, data suggest must be very doubtful.

The conclusion that it seems safest to draw is that there was some falling off in the rate of growth in the last quarter of the nineteenth century but that it was obscured by the fluctuations that took place over that period and was not, in terms of our power to measure such changes, very conspicuous. What does stand out more clearly from the figures is a check to the rate of growth after 1900. This is apparent in the output data but is very much more marked in the income and expenditure data (Table 17.5).

This means that there is something to be explained. Had we confined ourselves to industrial or to manufacturing production this would have been even more apparent. In the late 1860s and early 1870s industrial production seems to have been growing at a rate of over 3 percent per annum, and this rate was never recovered after 1873. The same is true of manufacturing production. But were these checks to output a reflection of lower productivity growth or did they also mean a loss of jobs?

That there was a slowing down of productivity growth in the last quarter of the century can be agreed. But again the changes within that period are not easy to identify. They rest on estimates of employment that are just as much subject to error as the estimates of production. For total civil employment, the most important source of error is likely to lie in the unemployment estimates. But for industry and manufacturing, there are additional difficulties of classification. For example, while Lewis shows an increase in the working population in manufacturing from 4·48 million in 1861 to 4·67 million in 1871,

Table 17.5   *Rate of Increase in* GDP *and in Industrial Productivity in the United Kingdom, 1870–1913*

Rate of increase over preceding decade in GDP *at constant factor cost (percent per annum)*

	Output data	Expenditure data	Income data	Compromise estimate
1870–72 (average)	2·05	—	2·50	2·19
1880–82 (average)	1·81	2·00	1·67	1·83
1890–92 (average)	1·73	1·63	2·09	1·82
1900–02 (average)	1·98	2·57	2·25	2·26
1910–12 (average)	1·46	1·13	1·33	1·31
1899–1913	1·70	1·30	1·16	1·35

Source:
Feinstein (1972, table 6).

Feinstein arrives at corresponding estimates of 4·30 million and 4·70 million, and although these figures may not seem far apart from one another, the increase over the decade in the one is less than half the increase in the other.

With these qualifications if we look back to Tables 17.3 and 17.4, we find an increase in the numbers in civil employment at an accelerating rate in the 1880s and 1890s followed by a rather slower growth in the next decade. These trends apply whether measured from peak to peak, or from decade to decade. Employment in industry followed much the same pattern of growth. The rate of increase was slightly higher than in total civilian employment in each decade except the 1890s and was conspicuously higher in the 1880s. For manufacturing alone, the rate of expansion was slightly *lower* than in total employment in each decade except the 1880s, when it was at its peak. The two most interesting contrasts are in the 1890s and after 1900. In the first of these total employment was still accelerating, while industrial employment grew rather more slowly; and in the second total employment decelerated slightly, while industrial employment accelerated again. The significance of all this will become apparent presently.

These changes in employment imply variations in the growth of labor productivity which are perhaps easiest to follow from Table 17.4. The figures for manufacturing in the final column show a clear deceleration from the 1860s with a marked dip in the 1880s. Industrial productivity follows a similar pattern but at a lower level, because of the inclusion of mining where productivity was beginning to fall. It will be observed that the pattern is by no means the same as for GDP, where the fluctuations are narrower and the improvement in the 1890s is much less pronounced.

What is one to make of these variations in productivity growth? Are they to be explained in sociological terms ('humanistic snobbery')? If so, why the dip after 1900? Or in the 1880s, if it really happened? Do they, perhaps, reflect a failure to invest associated with a high rate of foreign investment in the two decades concerned? This is an attractive hypothesis: was it really possible to invest half the country's savings overseas without detriment to industrial productivity?

The short answer suggested by the figures of domestic investment is that it was. The big swings in investment were in residential construction and town-building, and it was hardly surprising if this fell off in decades when emigration was high. Industrial investment formed a quite limited proportion of the total and did not necessarily fluctuate with it. Moreover, in a period like the first decade of this century when real incomes were depressed by less favorable terms of trade, capital requirements dropped as the domestic market became less buoyant.

If we confine ourselves to investment in manufacturing, there is not much to suggest that inadequate investment played a significant part in the slow growth of productivity after 1900. Measured in terms of gross fixed-capital formation, the average for the decade beginning in 1900 was 70 percent higher than the average for the previous decade and the lowest level touched, in 1907–8, was higher than in any year in the 1890s, except 1898–9. Much the same is true, if comparison is made in terms of net investment.

In distribution and other services the increase in gross investment from one decade to the next was much less and the falling off from the peak in 1903 was much greater. But even if we take an aggregate of the two categories of industrial and commercial investment and look at the immediately prewar years when foreign investment was at its height, there is no sign of a major setback: indeed, manufacturing investment in 1913, measured gross, was as high as it had ever been (Table 17.6).

So much for production and productivity. What about jobs? Did job opportunities lag behind and give rise to unemployment and emigration? Or did emigration take place against a background of full or nearly full employment? We can compare unemployment and emigration by decades only. For Great Britain (Ireland raises different issues), the figures are as in Table 17.7. It will be seen that, while net emigration fluctuated widely between one decade and the next, the average level of unemployment (so far as we are able to measure it by the trade union percentages) was comparatively steady between decades (although not within them). There is very little evidence that unemployment was lower before 1870 than after. There is some slight evidence of higher unemployment when growth was slower, for example in the 1880s and after the turn of the century. And it is true also that the decades when unemployment was highest were decades of high emigration. But the differences in unemployment between one decade and another hardly suggest that the state of the British labor market had much to do with the very large changes in net emigration. The figures for Germany point to common external influences at work on the two countries in every decade except the last; and there is little doubt that the pull of the USA and the Commonwealth was generally much stronger than the push of unemployment. The experience of the 1890s, for example, is striking evidence of the deterrent effect of a severe depression in the USA, Australia and the Argentine. It can easily be shown

Table 17.6   *Gross and Net Fixed Capital Formation in Manufacturing and Distribution in the United Kingdom, 1870–1913 (£ million per annum at 1900 prices)*

	Manufacturing and construction		Distribution and other services		Total	
	Gross	Net	Gross	Net	Gross	Net
1870–79	23·2	10·5	13·1	6·7	36·3	17·2
1880–89	21·1	3·0	8·9	1·1	30·0	4·1
1890–99	32·3	9·8	15·5	6·4	47·8	16·2
1900–09	55·0	24·6	18·7	7·3	73·7	31·9
1910–13	57·3	19·7	11·5	−1·7	68·8	18·0

Source:
Feinstein (forthcoming).

Table 17.7

	Net emigration from Great Britain (thousands)	Unemployment percentage (%)	Net emigration from Germany (thousands)
1861–71	296	4·3	
1871–81	257	3·7	860
1881–91	819	5·3	1320
1891–1901	122	4·4	320
1901–11	756	5·1	105

Source:
Statistical Abstract of the United Kingdom, 76th number, Feinstein, (1972, table 57) and Hoffman (1965, pp. 173–4).

that the time of the outflow coincided with the phase of development *abroad* and that it was the usual experience for migration to be higher at the peak of the business cycle, rather than when unemployment was at its worst.

It seems preferable to approach the fluctuations in emigration and unemployment in terms of the dominant factors in the situation – investment at home and abroad. The bursts of overseas investment impinged on a narrower front of the British economy than purely domestic booms. They brought business to the export industries and this in practice meant manufacturing industry. So when foreign investment was at its peak, manufacturing industry grew faster than the rest of the economy. But not necessarily very fast: for the transfer of funds could also bring pressure on the reserves. Moreover the peaks were liable to be relatively short and sharp. Domestic booms on the other hand tended to affect a wider range of activities – all those involved in town-building – and if accompanied by a drying up of foreign investment could take longer to eat into the reserves, even when the balance of trade was moving into heavy deficit. Thus, the impact on employment was more massive and more prolonged.

In those terms it is easy to understand why net emigration virtually ceased in the very decade – the 1890s – when imports of manufactures were rising fastest and exports grew least. From 1889 to 1899 the growth in exports of manufactures by volume was no more than 10 percent, while the growth in imports was no less than 31 percent. The domestic boom was putting such a strain on labor supplies that exports could not grow. When the strain was relaxed and foreign investment took over, exports responded and grew as fast as in the 1870s but this was not sufficient to make up for the collapse of domestic investment. Similarly, in the 1880s emigration was very heavy in spite of a rapid expansion in exports (30 percent during 1880–89). It was not a collapse in export prospects, nor an abnormal level of importation that brought about the depression of the 1880s; and it is doubtful how far it was depression in the United Kingdom that brought about the high rate of emigration in that decade. The root of the trouble was the difficulty of adjusting quickly to the fading away of a major domestic boom.

It is worth looking a little more closely at the changes taking place in foreign trade over the period to see whether they point in a protectionist direction. Was there a connection between the trends in exports and imports and the supposed slowing down in the rate of growth of the British economy? We are familiar nowadays with the idea that cyclical fluctuations can be aggravated by a deficiency in competitive power which may in this and other ways act as a drag on the level of activity and slow down the rate of growth. We know from recent experience how easy it is to fit the evidence into a model of this kind. But we must be on our guard against misconstruing an earlier period in terms of current controversies.

We have already seen (Tables 17.3 and 17.4) that the rate of growth in GDP did not show a sudden break in trend, except perhaps after 1900. We have also seen reason to doubt whether it is right to interpret emigration from Britain as a form of disguised unemployment. Hence, it is not to be taken for granted that foreign trade was acting as a drag on the level of activity or the rate of growth. By 1913 the more natural accusation – and one made in the pamphlets of the period – was that the expansion in exports had gone too far and was draining away resources that could have been better invested in the United Kingdom.

Let us, therefore, narrow the issue. We can begin from Arthur Lewis's contention (1978, p. 118) that 'in the period 1873–99 the combination of 1·6 percent growth of exports and 4·5 percent growth of imports subjected British manufacturing to a terrible beating for which the term "the Great Depression of 1873 to 1896" does not seem to be inappropriate'. The first thing to be said about this judgment is that it relates not to the period usually represented as the most unsatisfactory in the pre-First World War history of the United Kingdom, but to an earlier period in which the rate of growth is generally viewed more favorably.

Next, we need to look more closely at the composition of exports and imports to understand the changes in progress. In 1873 more than half the total trade in manufactures, exports and imports consisted of textiles. Another important element on the import side was leather, leather goods, furs and skins. Imports of these two groups (at constant prices) rose between 1873 and 1899 from £25·3 million to £69·4 million[3] while all other imports of manufactures rose from £11·1 million to £46·3 million. Exports of manufactures other than textiles and leather goods increased from £47·7 million to £109·5 million. So the fact that net exports of manufactures rose over those twenty-six years by only 10 percent is a reflection of the failure of the textile industries to increase their net exports but is quite consistent with a substantial expansion in the net exports of other industries. The slow growth in textile exports might be thought a healthy adjustment, if balanced by fast growth elsewhere: and it would have been unthinkable to offer the textile industries protection against imports.

If textiles and leather are left aside, and iron and steel also excluded,[4] can it really be said that the rest of British industry took a 'terrible beating' when it trebled the volume of its exports? What leverage on employment would protection have offered it? The complete exclusion of all manufactured imports other than textiles and leather, furs, and so on, would have offered British manufacturers a market worth about £40 million when manufacturing production was running at fifteen times that figure or more.

The period 1873–99 is made up of two very different periods, 1873–89 and 1889–99. The figures of trade by volume in those two periods are given in Table 17.8. While the 1880s were not a particularly prosperous period, any difficulties encountered by British industry could hardly be ascribed to import penetration. Although the volume of imports of manufactures nearly doubled, it remained relatively small and rose by only about one-third of the rise in the volume of exports. Thus, while it is true that imports of manufactures grew at a faster rate than exports over the years 1873–89 and while imports increased their share of the domestic market, it was still possible for manufacturing output to grow quite rapidly. As we have seen, manufacturing employment in the 1880s increased faster than at any other time after 1870.

The fact that emigration increased simultaneously is a reflection of the depression in agriculture far more than of any lasting setback to industry. It was in the 1870s and 1880s that the rural outflow reached its peak and by the 1890s it was already subsiding. The towns were able to absorb most of the outflow in the 1870s but in the 1880s the northern towns, in particular, did not expand fast enough and many of them actually lost population by migration. To the extent that the pace of town-building slackened in the 1880s, it is possible to argue that there is evidence of a failure of the economy to absorb surplus labor. If the trend of previous decades had remained unchanged, there would have been about 500,000 more residents in the towns of the north of England. But it is by no means clear that these emigrants were moved by lack of job prospects or that a faster expansion in exports would have so altered the job market as to result in their employment in Britain.[5]

What is clear is that the situation changed radically in the 1890s. The volume of exports of manufactures remained virtually static, while imports went on rising rapidly. It was in *this* decade that the manufacturer 'took a beating' from imports, in the sense that net exports actually fell. But this did not prevent output from expanding; and it was quite consistent, as explained earlier, with the virtual cessation of emigration and a drop in unemployment.

Table 17.8   *Growth in Volume of Exports and Imports of Finished Manufactures, 1873–1913 (£ million at 1913 prices)*

	1873	1889	1899	1913	*Increase, 1873–89*	*Increase, 1889–99*
Exports of manufactures	179·2	260·9	272·5	396·7	81·7	11·6
Retained imports of manufactures	30·9	58·5	97·6	135·1	27·6	39·1
Net exports	148·3	202·4	174·8	261·6	54·1	−27·6

Source:
Schlote (1952, tables 10, 13 and 16).

The fact is that periods of rapidly expanding exports were invariably also periods of rapidly increasing investment abroad, while booms in domestic investment coincided with periods of low investment overseas. Whether there was a deflationary drag depended not on whether exports were expanding, but on the rate of expansion in foreign investment in comparison with the foreign balance. This in turn was a matter of financial conditions, especially as it seemed possible to play on the capital balance by monetary policy without exercising comparable pressure on domestic investment.

As argued earlier, emigration responded to overseas development. This meant that it was high in periods favorable to exports and low in periods when exports were comparatively stagnant. But this was a phenomenon dominated by external events, not – with the possible exception of the mid-1880s – by the ease or tightness of the British labor market. It is quite true that, as a rule, emigration was highest when unemployment was relatively high. But this means no more than that a domestic boom was a more massive affair than an export boom and exercised a broader influence on domestic industry and employment. Hence, the periods of high foreign investment, although also periods of rapid growth in exports, were less successful in generating additional employment on the scale required by a growing economy than were periods of town-building like the 1870s and late 1890s.

The test of these propositions comes after 1900. For here is a period of which it would be impossible to say that British manufacturers were 'taking a beating' from imports, since net exports of manufactures were growing fast. Nevertheless, it was exactly the kind of period in which British industry failed badly to find the jobs that would have kept emigrants at home and unemployed workers in employment. Is it really possible to maintain that the failures of the period before 1914 were due to rising imports of manufactures and reluctance to resort to protectionist measures to keep them out? It is only too obvious that the emigration, chiefly to North America, had the same origins as the wave of foreign investment in the prewar decade; and that the unemployment was largely associated with the collapse of the building boom, and perhaps also rising interest rates associated with record levels of foreign investment and the resulting pressure on the reserves.

Would a higher growth rate for British exports have served to maintain the growth in GDP and in productivity? This seems a defensible proposition in respect of the 1870s and 1880s but is not very easily argued in relation to the next two decades. Over the period as a whole the balance of payments on current account improved, and it would be difficult to envisage a situation in 1913 with a still-higher volume of British exports unless it were completely offset by higher imports. In the 1890s when emigration was roughly balanced by immigration and unemployment was relatively low, additional exports might well have involved net immigration, unless one assumes that productivity would have gained from a more rapid expansion in demand. Even in the 1880s a faster growth of exports would have meant a quite abnormal rate of expansion in employment in manufacturing.

Arthur Lewis is quite right to put the economic development of the United Kingdom at the end of the nineteenth century in the context of world economic development and to draw comparisons with the performance of other countries in what he calls the 'industrial core' of the world economy. But it seems to me to stand to reason that the United Kingdom could not hope to outdistance these other countries indefinitely, that she was bound eventually to be over-taken and surpassed by larger countries with greater locational advantages, that in the process the cumulative advantages she once enjoyed in the early stages of industrialization would give way in face of the cumulative advantages similarly enjoyed by her competitors, and that there was no escape from this process by retreating within her limited domestic market.

Chapter 17: Notes

1   For example, the trend in money wages did respond over the cycle to the state of the labor market. In any event, since it is part of Lewis's argument in chapter 4 that the movement of money wages in all the industrial countries held to a more or less fixed trend from 1883 to 1913, he can hardly treat failure to change the trend as something peculiar to Britain.
2   'Any index of industrial production or of real output for any country before 1914 must incorporate a great many of the author's assumptions' (Lewis, 1978, p. 251).
3   These are Schlote's figures at constant prices and include re-exports for which no analysis by volume is readily available. Re-exports of manufactures totalled £5·5 million in 1873 and £18·1 million in 1899.
4   Imports of iron and steel goods came to only £3·3 million in 1899 or about one-tenth of exports.
5   The northern towns continued to lose population by migration in the two following decades, though not to any great extent in the 1890s.

Chapter 17: References

Aldcroft, D. and Richardson, H. W., *The British Economy, 1870–1939* (London: Macmillan, 1965).
Feinstein, C. H., *National Income, Expenditure and Output of the United Kingdom, 1856–1965* (Cambridge: Cambridge University Press, 1972).
Feinstein, C. H. (forthcoming).
Hoffman, W. G., *Das Wachstum der Deutschen Wirtschaft seit der mitte des 19 Jahrhunderts* (Berlin: Springer-Verlag, 1965).
Lewis, W. A., *Growth and Fluctuations, 1870–1913* (London: Allen & Unwin, 1978).
Matthews, R. C. O., Feinstein, C. H. and Odling-Smee, J., *British Economic Growth, 1856–1873* (forthcoming).
Schlote, W., *British Overseas Trade from 1700 to the 1930s* (Oxford: Blackwell, 1952).

18

The Cyclical Pattern of Long-Term Lending

CHARLES P. KINDLEBERGER

I

For the most part, Sir Arthur Lewis solves puzzles for us; this time he has reset an old one. In writing on international investment in the period 1870 to 1913, he states: 'The main puzzle which international investment has posed has been its timing' (Lewis, 1978, p. 178). His solution, adding French, German and British capital exports, and subtracting capital imports into the USA to form an overall view of lending is one that I find less than completely satisfactory. To a certain extent, it hides what is taking place, just as the average height of a family of two adults and four children under 10 years of age would do. Aggregation reveals how much net foreign lending from the core is available for investment at the periphery, but it fails to uncover the secret of the cyclical pattern of long-term lending. That secret, in my judgment, calls for the analysis of separate historical patterns of lending by different countries, and by the same country at different periods of time, rather than an aggregative technique. And it is a secret that may be of consummate importance for world economic stability.

Let me return to a paradigm I used some years ago in a textbook, contrasting lending by the United Kingdom from 1870 to 1913, as illuminated by Cairncross, with that of the USA in the interwar periods, studied by Bloomfield (Kindleberger, 1958, pp. 373–75; Cairncross, 1953; Bloomfield, 1950). British lending was anti-cyclical. In boom, foreign lending slowed down; in depression it picked up. At turning points there were brief periods of positive correlation: foreign and domestic lending soared together from 1871 to 1875, and collapsed simultaneously in 1890. There are also peculiarities about 1910–1914, to be discussed below. On the whole, however, foreign lending was counter-cyclical.

The mechanism that produced this result, according to Cairncross, was the terms of trade (the same analysis was developed simultaneously by Rostow, 1948). The terms of trade were regarded as a proxy for relative profitability at home and abroad, as would be true if all changes in the terms of trade emanated from the demand side. High import prices reflect profitability in the production of primary products at the periphery and give rise to faster capital exports; rising domestic and export prices relative to import prices in this analysis mean that domestic production can earn good profits and divert investment from overseas primary production to domestic industry. Sir Arthur himself is partial to this sort of explanation. While I found little evidence that the terms of trade actually behaved in the manner implied, and have serious doubts that they are an adequate measure for the relative profitability of home and foreign investment, it is true that on the whole, British capital moved counter-cyclically. The exceptions are the second half of the 1880s, which Sir Arthur calls 'the real puzzle' (Lewis, 1978, p. 180), and the years 1910–14.

American lending, in contrast, rose and fell in the 1920s and 1930s with domestic investment and the domestic business cycle. The movement at the turning points was anti-cyclical. In 1923 and 1928–9 foreign investment fell because of a pick-up in domestic business that raised interest rates (Lary, 1943, p. 92 ff). In 1930, after the stock-market crash, foreign lending recovered for the first two quarters of the year, actually reaching a ten-year high in the second quarter, as interest rates fell to new, very low levels. It then dried up precipitously as investors lost confidence in the credit worthiness of potential borrowers. The 1924 success of the Dawes loan lifted overall foreign lending in the second half of the 1920s to 1928. And in the depression of the 1930s, long-term capital moved toward the USA, rather than away from it, although direct foreign investment abroad remained barely positive.

My explanation for this contrast, leaving aside the minor issue of the turning points, has been that there are two cyclical models of foreign lending, one emphasizing relative demands for savings, foreign and domestic, the other domestic supply of savings in the presence of constant demands. In the British case a relatively steady flow of savings was directed now abroad, now to domestic industry, depending upon the relative state of the two demands. In depression at home, savings go abroad; in boom, they are directed at the margin to home investment.

In contrast to this 'demand model', the supply model, applying to the interwar USA, assumes unused opportunities for both foreign and domestic investment in something akin to a rationing situation. A rise in the supply of savings permits increases in both home and foreign investment. This model is helpful, particularly after some event that widens investors' horizons and gives them a view of unexploited opportunities. Unexpected successes of particular loans have served to produce such shifts in horizons, especially the Baring loans of 1816–17 to recycle the French indemnity after the Napoleonic War, the Thier *rentes* of 1871–2 to recycle the Franco-Prussian indemnity, the French loan to Russia in November 1887 that enabled Russia to refund its 1878 borrowings from Germany to finance the Russo-Turkish war, and the aforementioned Dawes loan of 1924.

Newly awakened interest of US investors in foreign loans after the success of the Dawes loan – the US tranche being eleven times oversubscribed – both conforms to the supply model of foreign lending, and lends support to the widely held contemporaneous view that London was an experienced lender, the USA an inexperienced one with, in the latter case, deleterious effects on the world economy. Part of the indictment was based on US commercial policy, exemplified in the Fordney–McCumber tariff of 1919 and the Hawley–Smoot tariff of 1930. This is not compelling. One can object to US policies after the First World War on microeconomic grounds of resource allocation, but the suggestion that they made it difficult or impossible for creditors to pay debt service is largely partial-equilibrium analysis unacceptable in a general-equilibrium situation. It is true, however, that old foreign lenders are likely to behave differently than new – to eschew the pejorative expressions 'experienced' and 'inexperienced'. This is not so much learning by doing as it is having settled down to a steady scanning of wider investment opportunities. The German case of the late 1880s to be cited below makes it dangerous to be unduly categorical.

The harm of pro-cyclical lending, of course, is that it destabilizes the world economy. For historical reasons, the argument can be constructed in terms of fixed exchange rates. (To extend it to flexible exchange rates, would require a host of assumptions about exchange risk, speculation, and the like, and is left to the interested reader.) In upswing, US imports rise to stimulate income abroad, and with it, investment opportunities that evoke a flow of capital imports from the USA. Direct investment may, in fact, respond to the accelerator effect of rising exports in foreign countries. When the downturn occurs in the lending country, imports and investments dry up at the same time, dealing a double blow to foreign balances of payments. It was on this account that League of Nations experts in 1945 recommended that capital flows be made counter-cyclical in the postwar world (League of Nations, 1945, pp. 285, 303).

A number of observers have commented that the United Kingdom was not involved in financial crises from 1866 to 1920 – although this may make too little of the Baring crisis of 1890. This is explicable by her anti-cyclical pattern of lending which served greatly to stabilize the world economy. The crisis of 1873 ran mainly between the USA and the Continent, especially Germany and Austria, and was precipitated in the USA by the halt in Central European pro-cyclical lending. In 1907 financial crisis in New York was linked to that in Italy through short-term capital flows passing through London and Paris, though those two centers did not become involved. But the notion that stable British lending helped to dampen fluctuations in the British economy and the rest of the world overlooks the second half of the 1880s, and the burst of lending from 1910 to 1914. This last was pro-cyclical and would have ended up, in my judgment, in a typical pattern of 'overtrading, revulsion and discredit', had the outbreak of war not produced a very different kind of crisis. In the last spurt before the war British foreign lending, notably to Canada, partook exactly of the pro-cyclical, positive feedback, learning variety that fit the USA after the war. It is inappropriate to regard 1913 lending as a norm for postwar comparisons as, for example, Cairncross does in the introduction to *Home and Foreign Investment, 1870–1913* (1953, p. x). 1913 was an outlier, part of a cyclical movement which was sharply at variance with 1870–1910 experience.

A recent paper by Serge-Christophe Kolm also contrasts capital flows that are correlated positively and negatively with domestic business cycles, and uses an analysis extending beyond the demand and supply models above (Kolm, 1979). Three domestic elements affect capital flows: the supply of savings, which works in the direction of positive correlation; the domestic demand for savings, which presses in the counter-cyclical direction; and diminishing returns to scale, which lead to foreign investment as fuller and fuller utilization of domestic capacity is reached and domestic costs rise faster than those abroad. Kolm was seeking to explain that world business cycles under floating exchange rates were becoming positively coordinated and capital movements in the 1970s increasingly pro-cyclical. His analysis was addressed to the possibility of different cyclical patterns of foreign direct investment in a given country at different stages of factor utilization, and is not concerned with horizon shifts or capital-market learning.

Finally, by way of introduction, it should be mentioned that capital (and migrants) flow in channels dug by accumulated information and experience, rather than moving evenly over broad surfaces. In a world of rational expectations and generalized information with similar objective functions and aversion or indifference to risk, French, German and British investors would be expected to respond to the same stimuli in roughly the same ways. In these circumstances it would be appropriate to aggregate their respective capital flows. But French capital exports in the prewar period were directed to Russia, southeastern Europe and Africa, British lending to the Continent was cut off abruptly by the revolutions of 1848 and, apart from some competitive lending in Italy and the Middle East, thereafter went to the USA, the Empire and regions of recent settlement such as Argentina. In 1914 France had 60 percent of its investment in Europe; in 1900 Britain had 5 percent (Pollard, 1974, p. 73). French investments in 1910–13 earned 3·87 percent in Russia, while much safer British foreign investments returned 5·3 percent (Lévy-Leboyer, 1977, p. 113). It is difficult to imagine the British investors lending 1·25 billion francs (£50,000,000) to Russia in April 1906 to save the tsar from bankruptcy after the Japanese defeat and the revolution of 1905 – an expensive French political gesture (Girault, 1977, pp. 251–2). With different patterns of domestic activity, different behaviorial models, capital flowing in different channels to different recipients in turn, the suggestion that there should be one general timing for capital flows of most countries over the world cycle is difficult to accept.

II

More insight can be obtained into cyclical patterns of foreign lending, if we move out from the British (1870–1910)–US (1920–39) comparison to include other periods in the nineteenth century and other countries. Maurice Lévy-Leboyer's masterly essay on the French balance of payments in the nineteenth century has a diagram that shows that vast differences between French and

British patterns, except in the 1850s when both countries followed a modest pro-cyclical pattern (1977, p. 80). On Imlah's figures British lending declined from 1859 to 1861, again in pro-cyclical fashion, and recovered from 1862 all the way to 1872, with the pattern changing from pro- to anti-cyclical during the crisis of 1866 as foreign lending continued upward, while domestic business turned down. The United Kingdom switched patterns once again in 1885, with a pickup in domestic business and foreign lending leading up to the Baring crisis. This last is Lewis's 'real puzzle'. Real income was rising, even though nominal income and the profitability of industry declined. There was something of a stock-market boom at home from a change in the company laws of 1856 and 1863 that led many companies to go public in anticipation of restrictions. In particular, a boom took place in brewing shares as investors anticipated increased profits from the shortage of wine arising from the phylloxera disease attacking French vineyards (Wirth, 1893, p. 200). French lending to Russia picked up in 1887, and especially in 1888 (Girault, 1973; Kennan, 1979, p. 343).

What was particularly interesting at this time was the German anti-cyclical pattern, achieved without much maturing experience during the 1871–9 pro-cyclical period. It resulted from a peculiar mixture of political and economic motives. The political element consisted of steps taken in Bismarck's economic warfare against Russia. The German loan to Russia of 1883 had not gone well. Russian securities were falling in price in Berlin after March 1886. A dubious character by the name of Elie de Cyon suggested that the time had come for Russia to detach itself from economic dependence on Germany and transfer the market for its securities to Paris. In May 1887 Russia confiscated German properties in Russian Poland. In July Bismarck issued an instruction to the Orphans' Courts to discriminate against Russian securities in the portfolios of their wards, and in November the *Lombardverbot*, forbidding banks to lend on Russian securities. The political aim is clear from a quotation of a high German civil servant: 'the intention is to deprive a hostile government of means for the development of armaments against us. Let the Russians, we thought, get money, if they had to, from their friends, the French' (Kennan, 1979, ch. XVIII, esp. p. 343 and note). Beginning in that year Russian bonds coming due on the German market were increasingly converted into French securities (Girault, 1977, p. 253). And in 1888 the great conversion referred to earlier took place. Russian, German and British banks all took part, but the lion's share went to the French, followed by a Rothschild conversion of 1,702 million francs of railroad bonds. The miniscule relation between gross French exports to Russia and French lending to that country (White, 1933) – in defiance of transfer theory – is accounted for by the fact that French lending was for recycling German loans, not provision of fresh capital.

In addition to selling off their Russian bonds to the French, German investors in this same period dumped some Argentine bonds, largely in London, thus contributing to the weak market in Argentine issues that collapsed in 1890. One reason given for these sales was uneasiness over what was taking place in Argentina (Lauck, 1907, pp. 59–60); another was that the investors disapproved of instability of the exchange rate for the Argentine peso (Morgenstern, 1959, p. 523). It is hard to avoid the conclusion, however, that the strong demand for capital inside Germany played a substantial role in inducing German investors to sell the foreign securities they thought weakest, Kolm's diminishing returns as capacity gets used more fully to the contrary notwithstanding. Reduced profits at home in boom from diminishing returns are one possibility; another is higher profits from demand-led expansion. The character of the boom at home may differ from cycle to cycle, as well as the nature of foreign lending. In Germany at this time, the boom in steel, chemicals and electricity was exigent. Gross foreign lending took place, as exemplified in Bleichroeder's elaborate operations in Mexico (Stern, 1977, pp. 427, 433, 442). By 1900 Germany had joined again in the boom in foreign lending, seeking especially to rival the United Kingdom in the Middle East. The decade after 1885, however, led to a sharp reduction in capital exports, and capital imports from France, via Russian recycling, and Britain, via Argentina.

While Britain and Germany for a time after 1885 swapped accustomed lending models, Germany adopting the anti-cyclical one and the United Kingdom the pro-cyclical, they differed in more than their experience in foreign lending. The British had old wealth, the Germans by and large new. Old wealth is risk-averse. Trustee investments grow as a proportion of total traded securities. Widows and orphans, so often mocked in accounts of the defenseless members of society, are the wives and children of men who have accumulated wealth. Safe securities to the French are those appropriate for 'un père d'une famille' ('the father of a family'). Others thought to need a particular brand of safe investments have been noted from time to time as spinsters, retired clergymen, retired merchants, magistrates, civil servants, admirals, even 'young men about to marry' (Kindleberger, 1978, p. 31n). A substantial incentive on the demand side for the British 'financial revolution' of the first half of the eighteenth century (Dickson, 1967) may well have been the rise in the nuclear family, detected by Lawrence Stone as having occurred in the years 1700–1720, calling for new arrangements by heads of families for the protection of their prospective widows and orphans, when less reliance could be put on the extended family to take care of collateral relatives (Stone, 1977). Dutch investment in the United Kingdom in the eighteenth century, largely in East India, Bank of England, South Sea Company shares and government stock (US translation, bonds) took place largely as accumulated wealth sought outlets less risky than mercantile ventures. Many of these investments were made for institutions like orphanages and by (or for) women (Wilson, 1941; Carter, 1975, p. 139). British women subscribers to government stock rose from 18 percent of the total in 1723–4 to 29 percent in 1750 (Dickson, 1967, p. 325), 'partly due to greater longevity, partly to the increasing practice of investing widows' dowers', and spinsters' legacies', but there may also have been changes in practice with respect to the use of nominees.

Foreign securities, and especially foreign government and, in the second half of the nineteenth century, railroad securities, were frequently regarded as more suitable for trustee investments, especially in France, and Commonwealth securities in Britain, guaranteed as to debt service by the Colonial Office after the 1850s. This was not particularly rational in the light of widespread defaults of Latin American countries after the pro-cyclical lending boom of the 1820s, or defaults on the part of individual states of the USA, nine in all, in the depression of the early 1840s, following the boom of the 1830s. Sir Arthur regards the tastes of clergymen, widows and orphans as following a bandwagon effect, since they had little hard information (Lewis, 1978, p. 180) and the diversion of 'trustee' investments from 'risky' domestic investments to 'safe' investments abroad as giving rise to unexploited opportunities (ibid., p. 177). Rational or irrational, the predilection of even professional investors for overseas securities seems to have been a fact.

A further source of trustee investments, to be sure, was the moneys disinvested by owners of businesses, or their heirs, as private firms went public. Not all owners of companies, converted to public form after the incorporation acts of 1856 and 1863, or the wave of the late 1880s, disinvested. In some cases change was one of form, not ownership. But going public gave owners, and especially their heirs, with little appetite or capacity for running the business, a chance to diversify portfolios, with securities thought to be less risky. One can, of course, argue that for every share of a private company sold and the proceeds invested abroad, new savings must be used to buy the same share. The rise of the public company, however, provided means by which these new savings were channeled abroad in domestic depression when new company formation at home was limited, and favored foreign investment through furnishing an escape route for reluctant investors in industry (Jefferys, 1938, pp. 112, 134).

There is one exception to the notion that foreign lending to governments and railroads is less risky than domestic industrial investment. This is the wave of investment in southern and central Europe and in Egypt and Turkey undertaken by the *Crédit Mobilier*, and following it, other French and some British banks in the third quarter of the nineteenth century and some years thereafter. *Crédit Mobilier* and Rothschild investments in infra-structure in Italy, Spain and Austria were competitive and known to be risky. Government guarantees were sought and obtained, where possible. French governmental banks established to aid agriculture and to improve the mortgage market joined in making loans to the Khedive of Egypt (Jousseau, 1884, p. lxv). Some of these were eventually sold off in London in 1879 at a loss (ibid., p. lxxiv). Large profits of banks such as the *Crédit Lyonnais* and the banques d'affaires (established for lending to industry) in the Thiers *rentes* of 1871 and 1872 whetted the appetite for speculation in foreign government bonds, issued at low prices and expected to be bid up as the finances of the country in question improved (Bouvier, 1961, I, pp. 214–17). But the French investor who was sold Russian bonds after 1887 did not have fat profits dangled before him. Commissions for the issuers were high, to be sure, but yields were low. The investor was beguiled into thinking that because the bonds were issued by a government, they were safe like *rentes*. Journalists and the French and Russian governments combined to keep this thought alive.

To the extent that investors in foreign securities were looking for safety – truer, I believe, of old money in France and the United Kingdom than of new money in Germany – the foreign and domestic markets were structurally non-competing. Domestic debt was not rising in France (after 1872) and the United Kingdom. An investor who wanted government or railroad bonds had to go abroad. If the foreign and domestic markets were noncompeting, the notion that foreign lending starved domestic industry – except to a limited extent at the margin – cannot be supported. France, Sir Arthur says, was technologically backward and clearly in need of much larger home investment. 'The case of Britain . . . is more complicated but its failure to invest adequately at home clearly belongs in the area of unexploited opportunities' (Lewis, 1978, pp. 176–7). It is hard to detect a shortage of capital as one contemplates the low interest rates prevalent in France, for example.

There is the possibility that present-day observers are misled by nominal rates of interest up to 1896, whereas real rates of interest were much higher because of falling world prices. It is possible even that there was interest-rate illusion on the part of some borrowers, such as the Russians, who were ignorant of the prospect that they would have to repay French francs borrowed in 1887–96 with francs of much greater value. A recent thesis by L. Dwight Israelsen has disposed of this possibility. Refined econometric analysis shows a perfect foresight real interest-rate model explains Russian borrowing for all major periods, 1800–1914, better than three alternative borrowing models (August 1979, ch. iii and p. 362). Similar analysis indicates that the British lender was fully aware of the Gibson paradox relating real and nominal interest rates (Harley, 1977). But observe in Lévy-Leboyer's table of French and British interest rates that these rates were lower from 1895 to 1904, when prices were rising, than in 1885 to 1894, when prices were falling (Table 18.1). While yields rose in the last period recorded in the table, the level for foreign bonds in both countries is lower in 1900–1904, than it had been in 1890–94. It is also relevant that the spread between domestic and foreign yields was narrower in France than in the United Kingdom.

In Germany domestic industry and foreign borrowers competed more directly than seems to have been true in France and the United Kingdom. This is likely to have been due to the prominent role of the German banks in direct-ing the flow of private savings for the uninitiated public. The conflict between domestic and foreign outlets is clearly visible in banking history: the Deutsche Bank was founded in 1872 for the purpose of competing with the United Kingdom in the finance of foreign trade, but found itself so caught up in the *Grunderjahre* boom that it severely neglected its original purpose for the first decade (Helfferich, 1956, pp. 32–4, 58–66, 111). The width of competition between domestic and foreign investment in Germany, as compared with the United Kingdom, made the anti-cyclical pattern of lending after 1873 far more

Table 18.1   *British and French Yields on Various Securities by Subperiods, 1885–1904 (in percent per annum)*

Period	British		French				
	Railroads	Foreign bonds	Bonds	Shares	Foreign	Suez	Russian
1885–1889	3·29	5·04	3·79	4·27	4·49	3·92	4·93
1890–1894	2·97	4·74	3·25	4·00	4·11	3·72	4·13
1895–1899	2·61	4·38	3·06	3·56	3·80	2·95	3·84
1900–1904	2·98	4·48	3·28	3·91	3·96	3·32	3·92

Source:
Lévy-Leboyer (1977, p. 113).

sensitive than that in the United Kingdom. What is not clear is why with a fairly limited experience in foreign lending in the pro-cyclical vein over 1850–72, the pattern should have reversed itself with the boom after about 1879. How much experience is enough?

III

It may be of interest to observe an analogy in migration in Germany which was anti-cyclical in pattern in the 1850s and again in the early 1890s. Some years ago in a bantering discussion, Per Jacobsson, the Swedish economist, then at the Bank for International Settlements, and I found ourselves on different sides of a debate as to whether migrants to the USA were the more vigorous members of European society, anxious to leave decadent Europe and to strike out in new challenges, or whether they were the riffraff, the anti-social who got into trouble, the shiftless who could not make their way at home, while the vigorous members of society were caught up into the expanding economy at home. Both, of course, are true, with a cyclical pattern at work, as Dorothy Swaine Thomas proved (1941). A steady stream of humanity leaves the European farm. In prosperity it is directed to the city and industry; in domestic depression abroad. Regional differences exist: in the United Kingdom, south of the Trent, the movement was to London or abroad; north, to the Midlands or stay at home.

In Germany the movement off the farm to 'regions of recent settlement' was particularly heavy after 1846, given the potato famine and the Revolution of 1848 in which the dissolution of the guilds played a part; and in the mid-1880s. In both cases it was arrested abruptly, in 1854 and 1893, respectively, as expanding domestic demand for labor diverted excess agricultural population into domestic industry (Walker, 1964, ch. vi; Inoki, 1974, p. 45). In both cases it was late in the cycle; for the first years, the pattern was pro-cyclical as channels were dug, information was spread and a positive feedback mechanism developed, with relatives following pioneers. Some prosperity at home, moreover, was needed to cover the costs of moving which were greater trans-Atlantic than within Germany. Only when the boom became taut did domestic demand pull the migratory movement up sharply. Note in all this that while the French followed the same cyclical pattern, with a peak going abroad (to Algeria) because of the agricultural troubles from 1846 to 1853, the movement was on a highly dampened level. On the whole the French did not emigrate, but stayed in France.

The migratory movement is cyclical in another sense, based on what is happening in the country of immigration. In world depression in the 1930s British subjects returned to the United Kingdom on balance from all over the world, and city dwellers in the USA returned to the farm. It was not necessarily thought that jobs could be found in the United Kingdom or on the farm, so much as that given unemployment, it was desirable to be at home where the marginal cost of maintenance was less than in an independent household. In these cases the push overwhelmed the pull.

An important difference between migration and capital movements is found in migratory lags. ('Man is of all pieces of luggage the most difficult to be removed' – Bagehot, 1880, XI, p. 313.) Another is probably in the supply response after emigration and capital outflows take place. With more room at home, population increase may pick up after emigration, especially in countries that have not experienced Malthusian revolution. It is not clear that savings respond as elastically to the relative rise in the rate on capital as net reproduction rates do to the relative rise in wages and salaries.

IV

The counter-cyclical movement of migrant workers today, viewed from the standpoint of the receiving country has highly negative social consequences, especially for Mediterranean workers in northern and central Europe, whose contracts expired after 1973 and who were returned to their homes. A fixed amount of unemployment should be equitably shared, rather than dumped by the core on the periphery. In the absence of offsetting transfers of aid or investments, the country of emigration is destabilized in terms of employment, income and balance of payments. From present appearances, the pattern is unlikely to continue in future, as the receiving countries, especially Germany, are resolved not to become dependent on imported labor, because of social disadvantages which are thought to outweigh economic benefits.

With capital lending, the counter-cyclical pattern makes for world stability, the pro-cyclical one for instability. The stabilizing effect of broadly anti-cyclical lending by the United Kingdom from 1866 to 1910 has been referred to. More interesting for the position today is the anti-cyclical movement of capital from the Euro-currency market in the recession of 1974–5.

Which of the two models of foreign lending obtains at a given time is probably not open to policy choice. The League of Nations recommendation mentioned earlier was incorporated in the articles of agreement of the International Bank for Reconstruction and Development. Among its purposes were

to 'conduct its operations with due regard to the effects of international investment on business conditions in the territories of its members'. At a very early
stage, the bank asserted that counter-cyclical lending would conflict with its
primary concern for economic development, holding that the responsibility for
anti-cyclical action must devolve on the major industrial countries, on the
International Monetary Fund and on any international agency set up to
stabilize commodity prices (IBRD, 1949). Given the difficulties of formulating
and carrying out domestic discretionary anti-cyclical spending policies,
moreover, it is difficult to reach the conclusion that the bank is wrong. Decision and execution lags probably force discretionary investment policies to
have awkward timing. The primary contribution of the bank, and an important
one, is to keep the flow of project lending steady, or steadily rising, and to
prevent its falling into a pro-cyclical profile.

If it be accepted that governments of industrial countries have the
responsibility of stabilizing the world economy, there is little they can do
through international private lending. Foreign government-to-government aid
is probably like World Bank lending in that the best that can be done is to
stabilize it over time and prevent it from developing a pro-cyclical pattern.
Private foreign lending is much more difficult to regulate cyclically. It can be
restrained; a number of countries have sought from time to time by devices
such as the Capital Issues Committee in the United Kingdom to ration or to
eliminate foreign lending. It is much more difficult to stimulate it at all, much
less differentially over time, as various devices such as investment insurance
demonstrate. To make the foreign investment of a particular country conform
to one particular cyclical pattern rather than another seems hopeless. Foreign
lending responds to shifts of horizon, to learning and to profit opportunities at
home and abroad in ways which thus far do not seem to lend themselves to
policy manipulation.

In the early 1970s the switch from one to the other cyclical model occurred
very rapidly. An anti-cyclical pattern had been in operation in 1971–2, when
the Federal Reserve System lowered interest rates as part of policy steps taken
to bring about an upswing in business prior to President Nixon's candidacy for
reelection in the fall of 1972. This was an example of what Assar Lindbeck
calls the political business cycle. Lowering interest rates at a time when the
Bundesbank was trying to hold interest rates high in Germany to restrain inflation led to an enormous outflow of capital. As economic recovery took place in
the USA, the capital flow continued, converting the model to a pro-cyclical
one. The rise in the price of oil engineered by OPEC in 1973 and 1974 brought
about a sharp recession in the USA. The capital outflow continued, resulting
once again in a switch in cyclical models, back to the counter-cyclical one. In
this instance, with lending taking place through the Euro-dollar market to
developing countries, notably Brazil, Mexico, South Korea and to various
members of the Socialist bloc, it seemed as though the major banking institutions, especially the money-market banks, were continuing to lend less from a
mindless or perhaps better, unconscious pursuit of income, than from a sense

of responsibility for the stability of the world economy. In previous localized recessions in lending on aircraft, on oil tankers and on Real Estate Investment Trusts (REITs), these same banks had kept on lending when planes were mothballed, tankers laid up 'on the mud', REITs had difficulties, to ensure a soft landing rather than crash. The possibility exists that the banks kept on lending because of ample reserves, despite worsening capital–deposit ratios, and in ignorance of rising debt–service ratios among borrowers and growing 'country risk'. An academic observer is in no position to make a definitive judgment, but the evidence on balance seems to indicate that continued lending was a deliberate policy – a sort of lender-of-last-resort, responsible policy to forestall crisis. Slowdown in lending took place only as recovery, especially in the USA, strengthened world commodity prices.

Whether the anti-cyclical pattern of lending can be maintained as a new OPEC price rise takes place in 1979 and the prospect for recession in 1980 becomes increasingly likely is an open question. A serious cutback in lending to the developing countries, however, would seriously threaten to deepen the world depression on the lines of the cutback of lending by the USA in 1829.

V

The conclusion of this exegesis on Sir Arthur's questions about lending in 1885–90 is that there is no one model of the cyclical pattern of foreign lending that can be used to forecast the future and estimate the impact of capital flows on world output and income distribution. Anything can happen and often does. The day of positive economics, useful for prediction, is still some distance away.

Chapter 18: References

Bagehot, Walter, *Economic Studies* (1880), in Norman St John-Stevas, ed., *The Collected Works of Walter Bagehot*, Vol. XI, *The Economist*, London, (1978), eleven volumes.

Bloomfield, Arthur I., *Capital Imports and the Balance of Payments, 1934–39* (Chicago: University of Chicago Press, 1950).

Bouvier, Jean, *Le Crédit Lyonnais de 1863 à 1882, Les Années de formation d'une banque des dépôts* (Paris: SEVPEN, 1961).

Cairncross, Alexander K., *Home and Foreign Investment, 1870–1913* (Cambridge: Cambridge University Press, 1953).

Carter, Alice Clare, *Getting, Spending and Investing in Early Modern Times, Essays on Dutch, English and Huguenot Economic History* (Assen: Van Forcum, 1975).

Dickson, P. G. M., *The Financial Revolution in England, A Study in the Development of Public Credit, 1688–1756* (New York: St Martin's Press, 1967).

Girault, René, *Emprunts russes et investissements français en Russie, 1873–1914*, (Paris: Colin, 1973).

Girault, René, 'Investissement et placement français en Russie, 1880–1914', in M. Lévy-Leboyer, ed., *La position internationale de la France, Aspects économiques et financiers, XIXe–XXe siècles* (Paris: Editions de l'Ecole des Hautes Etudes en Sciences Sociales, 1977), pp. 251–62.

Harley, C. Knick, 'The interest rate and prices in Britain, 1873–1913: a study of the Gibson Paradox', *Explorations in Economic History*, vol. XIV, no. 1 (1977), pp. 69–89.

Helfferich, Karl, *Georg von Siemens, Ein Lebensbild aus Deutschlands grosser Zeit*, abridged edn (Krefeld: Serpe, 1956).

Inoki, Takenori, *Aspects of German Peasant Migration to the United States, 1815–1914*, doctoral dissertation, 1974 (Cambridge, Mass.: MIT Press, to be published).

International Bank for Reconstruction and Development, Press Release No. 134, (11 May, 1949).

Israelsen, L. Dwight, 'The determinants of Russian state income, 1800–1914: an econometric analysis', unpublished doctoral dissertation, 1979 (Massachusetts Institute of Technology).

Jefferys, J. B., *Business Organization in Great Britain, 1856–1914* (LSE, 1938) (New York: Arno Press, 1977).

Josseau, J. B., *Traité du Crédit Foncier*, 3rd edn (Paris: Marchal, Billiard, 1884).

Kennan, G. F., *The Decline of Bismarck's European Order: Franco-Russian Relations, 1875–1890* (Princeton, NJ: Princeton University Press, 1979).

Kindleberger, Charles P., *International Economics*, 2nd edn (Homewood, Ill.: Irwin, 1958).

Kindleberger, Charles P., *Manias, Panics and Crashes: A History of Financial Crises* (New York: Basic Books, 1978).

Kolm, Serge-Christophe, 'The Suicide of Bretton Woods', unpublished paper, 1979.

Lary, Hal B., *United States in the World Economy* (Washington, DC: US Department of Commerce, 1943).

Lauck, W., Jett, *The Causes of the Panic of 1893* (Boston, Mass.: Houghton Mifflin, 1907).

League of Nations, *Economic Stability in the Post-War World* (Geneva: League of Nations, 1945).

Lévy-Leboyer, Maurice, 'La balance des paiements et l'exportation des capitaux français', in M. Lévy-Leboyer, ed., *La position internationale de la France, Aspects économiques et financiers, XIXe–XXe siècles* (Paris: Editions de L'Ecoles des Hautes Etudes en Sciences Sociales, 1977), pp. 75–142.

Lewis, W. Arthur, *Growth and Fluctuations, 1870–1913* (London: Allen & Unwin, 1978).

Morgan, E. Victor, *Studies in British Financial Policy, 1914–1925* (London: Macmillan, 1952).

Morgenstern, Oskar, *International Financial Transactions and Business Cycles* (Princeton, NJ: Princeton University Press, for the National Bureau of Economic Research, 1959).

Pollard, Sidney, *European Economic Integration, 1815–1870* (New York: Harcourt Brace Jovanovitch, 1974).

Rostow, Walt W., *British Economy of the Nineteenth Century* (London: Oxford University Press, 1948).

Stern, Fritz, *Gold and Iron: Bismarck, Bleichröder and the Building of the German Empire* (London: Allen & Unwin, 1977).

Stone, Lawrence, *The Family, Sex and Marriage in England, 1500–1800* (New York: Harper & Row, 1977).

Thomas, Dorothy Swaine, *Social and Economic Aspects of Swedish Population Movements, 1756–1933* (New York: Macmillan, 1941).

Walker, Mack, *Germany and the Emigration, 1816–1885* (Cambridge, Mass.: Harvard University Press, 1964).

White, Harry Dexter, *The French International Accounts, 1880–1913* (Cambridge, Mass.: Harvard University Press, 1933).

Wilson, C. H., *Anglo–Dutch Commerce and Finance in the Eighteenth Century* (Cambridge: Cambridge University Press, 1941).

Wirth, Max, 'The Crisis of 1890', *Journal of Political Economy*, vol. 1, no. 2 (1893), pp. 214–356.

19

Inter-Country Diffusion of Economic Growth, 1870–1914

LLOYD G. REYNOLDS

Economic growth is a national phenomenon. It occurs, or fails to occur, within the boundaries of a national state. Yet the existence and growth experience of other countries is highly relevant. After 1750 there was one country, the United Kingdom, and after about 1830 several countries, which had already embarked on a growth path which served to facilitate growth elsewhere. Since that time there has been a gradual diffusion of growth from leader to follower countries, which continues to the present day and has by now touched a large proportion, though by no means all, of the world's population. This chapter explores some features of this process in the late nineteenth century.

By growth we can mean either *extensive growth*, in which population and national product advance at about the same rate, or *intensive growth*, in which output pulls ahead and raises output per capita. While the latter is perhaps more interesting, the former should not be ignored. In the years since 1950, for example, most of the less developed countries have had population growth rates in the range of 2–3 percent, or even above this level in some Latin American countries. Simply to keep output rising at the same rate and to prevent deterioration of living standards is a substantial achievement.

The first thing one observes in a potentially growing economy, such as the United Kingdom in 1750, France in 1800, or Japan in 1850, is a gradual upcreep of population. This is accompanied for quite a long time by a corresponding increase in output, by a pattern of extensive growth. By itself this increase in scale of the economy will facilitate division of labor, as Adam Smith reasoned, and will tend to raise output per worker. In follower countries one can count also on some diffusion of improved technology, and a further widening of markets through trade.

If domestic conditions are favorable to growth (the meaning of this caveat will be suggested later), one will eventually observe the beginnings of intensive growth. The increase in output per capita may at first be almost imperceptible, but in time will become large enough to be identified and measured. There follows a long period of growth *acceleration*, during which the annual rate of increase in output per capita rises to 0·5 percent, then to 1·0 percent, perhaps eventually to 2·0 percent or more. This is not, as Rostow once suggested, a quick 'take-off' within a span of ten–twenty years. Studies by Kuznets and others suggest that the relevant period is more like fifty–sixty years. This was true, at least, in the older industrial countries, and may turn out to be true also in countries whose growth has accelerated more recently.

Our concern here is with identifying and dating the period of growth acceleration, country by country. When did growth actually begin? Does accelerated growth in Taiwan date from 1950? Or does it date from the early years of Japanese occupation, 1900–1920? Is the 'Brazilian miracle' of recent origin? Or does it date from the mid-nineteenth century? Since we are interested in beginnings, we shall not explore the interesting question of what happens *after* the period of growth acceleration. There is a suggestion in Kuznets that the rate of increase in output per capita follows a logistic curve, which tapers off to a plateau, perhaps followed in the very long run by a decline in the growth rate due partly to individual preferences for leisure as against income. But even if this is the dominant pattern, there are cases, such as Japan, in which the growth rate has continued to accelerate for a century or more and has not yet settled down. There are also cases, such as Argentina, in which the high growth rate of 1870–1914 was reduced over 1914–1950 and fell still lower in 1950–1980. Such cases are intriguing, but we cannot pursue them here.

This approach suggests a classification of economies into: (1) *stationary economies*, in which population and output are not growing, or (more hopefully) are growing at about the same rate. There are probably also at any time some countries which are actually slipping backward in terms of output per capita; (2) *growing economies*, that is, countries which have entered the period of growth acceleration, and in which output per capita has been rising long enough so that growth cannot be dismissed as a temporary boomlet; (3) *mature economies*, in which growth is built into the structure of the economy to a degree which warrants an expectation of continuing growth in the future. These countries have then 'graduated' into the developed country club. This classification, I think, is more useful than one based on relative per capita income at a point in time. The most important thing about a country is not its present standing in the world GNP league, but whether it is growing at a rate which will raise its league standing over the decades ahead.

World economic history since 1750, then, can be viewed as a growth procession, in which one country after another has moved from category 1 to category 2 and eventually, after a half-century or so, to category 3. The mature category now includes a dozen or so countries in Latin America, Asia and Africa, along with the older industrial countries which we may call 'the OECD club'. A good many other Third World countries have entered category 2, though others remain in category 1, with stationary or declining output per capita and uncertain growth prospects.[1]

Growth acceleration in a country typically involves an interaction of external stimuli and favorable domestic circumstances. The fact that some economies are already growing increases the opportunity for others to do so.

As Lewis (1980) points out:

> For the past hundred years the rate of growth of output in the developing world has depended on the rate of growth of output in the developed world. When the developed grow fast, the developing grow fast, and when the developed slow down, the developing slow down.

The channels through which growth spreads among nations – the transmission mechanism – have been extensively studied, and we cannot here recapitulate the large literature of the subject. Economic growth in leader countries increases demand for exports from follower countries, thereby increasing their ability to import materials for their own growth. The presence of advanced countries with superior production techniques provides a 'technology shelf' from which follower countries can borrow., There is also the possibility of international factor movements. Skilled workers, managers and technicians can move from leader to follower countries, carrying advanced technology in their heads. Richer countries can lend to poorer countries through a variety of channels.

We should not deny that these international contacts can also have harmful or 'backwash' effects on follower countries, as Prebisch, Myrdal, and others, have argued. But models in which such effects predominate, and in which international contacts actually prevent or reduce growth in follower countries, are not very convincing. One can make a good case for the view that for a country to be integrated into the world economy is on balance favorable to domestic growth.

On this view, the fact that some countries have already embarked on sustained growth provides a favorable environment for growth acceleration in other countries. But the response is in no way automatic. In whatever time period we examine, we shall find that some countries managed to climb onto the world growth escalator while others did not. Why this should be is a complex and difficult question, but one of fundamental importance. Without anticipating the later discussion, I suggest that clues can be found by looking at agriculture and government. It is almost a truism that, especially in a large country, agricultural improvement is a prerequisite for industrialization. Food output must be kept rising at a rate somewhat above the rate of population growth, to accommodate a high-income elasticity of demand for food and to permit food transfers to the growing urban population. Raising agricultural output at, say, 5 percent a year, which with 3 percent population growth is probably a minimal target, is much harder than building new factories, since it involves landholding systems and farmers' incentives as well as technical progress.

It is obvious also that the quality of political leadership and public administration can aid or block development, though it is hard to reduce this statement to precise terms. Economic growth, especially growth which depends heavily on private initiative, is a rather delicate plant, easily discouraged and prevented. Governments which are indifferent or hostile to growth, or which are simply unable to govern, have been an obstacle to growth in many countries.

The chronology of growth diffusion within the OECD club is well known, thanks to economic historians in these countries and to the statistical labors of Simon Kuznets. The story begins in the United Kingdom around 1750. In the first half of the nineteenth century growth acceleration is visible in the early followers – France, Germany and the USA. Soon after mid-century the process spreads to the Scandinavian countries, Russia, Italy and some other east and south European countries. Japan appears as a major non-Western follower in the 1880s. By 1900 accelerated growth is general throughout Australasia, Japan, North America and Europe.

What about other parts of the world? When economists directed their attention toward economic development around 1950, there was a tendency to regard Africa, Asia and Latin America as consisting of a homogeneous mass of 'underdeveloped countries', in which significant development had not occurred before the First World War. The reasons for this view would form an interesting chapter in the history of economic ideas. But the point to be emphasized here is that the view is wrong. The so-called Third World countries are very heterogeneous – much more so than the OECD countries. They differ widely in past growth experience and future prospects. To average out this experience for all LDCs, or even to make continental averages for Asia or Africa or Latin America, is to omit most of the significant features of reality.

When we look, as we should do, at individual countries, we observe that they have been joining the world growth procession more or less continuously since the mid-nineteenth century. The story can be divided conveniently into three periods, distinguished by sharp changes in the international economic environment:

(1) *1870–1914.* This was a long period of world peace and prosperity, marked by rapid growth of output in the leader countries, an even more rapid growth of world trade, and a sharp reduction in transport and communication costs. We shall argue later that a dozen or so countries, mainly in Latin America and southeast Asia, entered the growth-acceleration phase during this period.

(2) *1914–45.* This is a bleaker period, in which the world economy was shaken by two global wars and an unprecedentedly severe depression. The rate of growth in world output slackened, and world trade grew even more slowly than output. In addition, primary exporters suffered a serious decline in their terms of trade. Despite this unfavorable environment, a number of additional countries joined the growth procession during this period.

(3) *1945–73.* This period saw a world economic boom of unprecedented proportions. The richer countries grew at rates well above those of

1870–1940, and world trade grew even faster than world output. The engine of growth, about which writers of the early 1950s were decidedly skeptical, began to pull with renewed vigor. Growth acceleration occurred in additional countries, including the Asian giants India and China. Countries which had experienced growth acceleration before 1940 grew even faster, and some of these graduated into the mature category.

It will probably turn out in retrospect that this era ended in 1973, partly because of the oil-price explosion. Growth rates in the OECD countries have fallen, and seem unlikely to return to the high 1945–73 level. Among developing countries, the nonoil-producers have been hit by staggering balance of payments deficits, and their growth prospects have been seriously reduced.

In a study now underway I hope to trace the course of events from 1870 to the present day in some detail. But this work is still at an early stage. I limit myself here to some observations on the period 1870–1914,[2] which should be regarded as preliminary and will eventually be amplified and refined. I shall, first, outline key features of world economic development during this period, which provided a favorable environment for growth acceleration in follower countries. Next, I shall outline very briefly the available evidence on early growth in a dozen or so countries. Finally, I shall examine a variety of objections which can be brought against the view advanced here.

The World Economic Environment, 1870–1914

The general nature of this boom period was suggested earlier. We must now examine the evidence in more detail.[3]

Growth Rates in Early Developing Countries

The concepts and techniques which we now use in measuring gross national product were devised by Simon Kuznets in the 1920s, and were not in general use throughout the world until after 1945. But under the leadership of Kuznets and the International Association for Research on Income and Wealth which he helped to establish, statisticians have pushed estimates for the major industrial countries back to the mid-nineteenth century. While these estimates are not precise, they are doubtless of the right order of magnitude.

Two sets of estimates for twelve North Atlantic countries are presented in Table 19.1 (Recall that, in addition to these countries, intensive growth was underway also in Japan, Australasia, South Africa, Russia and some other parts of Eastern Europe.) While these countries were all growing, their experiences were rather different. Population was growing very slowly in France, quite rapidly in Canada and the USA. Population growth mainly accounts for the higher growth rate of total output in the USA and Canada. Their performances as regards output per capita was not notably superior.

The median rate of population growth was about 1 percent per year, much

Table 19.1   *Growth of Population, Total Output and Output Per Capita, Selected Countries, 1870–1913*

	Kuznets* (percentages per decade)			Maddison† (percentages per year)		
	Total output	Popu- lation	Output per capita	Total output	Popu- lation	Output per capita
Belgium	30·5	10·0	18·7	2·7	1·0	1·7
Denmark	32·0	11·2	23·2	3·2	1·1	2·1
France	16·9	1·8	14·9	1·6	0·2	1·4
Germany	33·2	12·4	18·5	2·9	1·1	1·8
Italy	15·0	6·8	7·7	1·4	0·7	0·7
The Netherlands	24·8	15·0	8·5	2·2	1·3	0·8
Norway	23·7	8·3	14·2	2·2	0·8	1·4
Sweden	33·9	7·2	24·9	3·0	0·7	2·3
Switzerland	26·7	11·8	13·4	2·4	0·9	1·3
United Kingdom	24·7	9·2	13·9	2·2	0·9	1·3
Canada	45·1	19·1	21·8	3·8	1·8	2·0
USA	52·7	23·0	24·1	4·3	2·1	2·2
Median	28·6	10·6	16·2	2·55	0·95	1·55

Sources:
*Kuznets (1966, pp. 352–353).
†Maddison (1964, pp. 28–30).

lower than in today's LDCs. This is probably the most significant difference between the two eras. In the West European countries, capital accumulation and improved technology enabled total output to pull well ahead of a sluggish rate of population growth, which after completion of the demographic transition was actually declining. Today's LDCs are faced with high rates of population growth, and just to keep a country's head above water by raising total product at the same rate requires considerable effort.

In terms of demand for primary imports the 'total output' columns of Table 19.1 are doubtless the most significant. While there is a marked difference in country performance, the median growth rate is in the range of 2·5–2·8 percent per year. This may not seem high compared with post-1950 experience, but it opened up substantial possibilities for trade and, as we shall see, world trade expanded even more rapidly than world output.

Transport Facilities and Transport Costs

Rapid economic growth in Europe and North America opened up the possibility of enlarged trade with other continents. But this possibility could scarcely have been realized without an improvement and cheapening of transport. This involved replacement of sailing ships by steam-driven steel ships on ocean routes, extensive building of railways to move goods to and from the ports and a worldwide telegraph network linking would-be sellers and buyers.

A key development in ocean transport was the compound marine engine, introduced in 1854–6, which cut coal consumption per horsepower in half. A second development was opening of the Suez Canal in 1869. In addition to shortening the sea routes to Asia by about 4,000 miles, the canal could be used by metal ships but not by sailing ships. Metal ships have substantial economies of scale. Feasible sail area sets a limit to the size of sailing ships which does not apply to metal ships; and a metal ship can carry about three times as much as a sailing ship of the same displacement.

In 1870 only 12·5 percent of total shipping tonnage was operated by steam. By 1913 replacement of sail by steam was almost complete. The world's merchant fleets grew from 9 million tons in 1850 to 35 million tons in 1910, with the United Kingdom accounting for about 42 percent of this tonnage. Freight rates in 1913 were only about 30 percent of the 1870 level. The homeward rate from Burma or Java to London was around 75 shillings a ton in the 1870s, but only about 20 shillings per ton in 1910–13. This large reduction is important in calculating terms of trade. Import prices usually include freight (c.i.f.), while export prices exclude it (f.o.b.). Thus, calculations of the UK–Argentine terms of trade made in London prices will differ from those made in Buenos Aires prices; and it is quite possible for *both* countries' terms of trade, calculated in this way, to improve simultaneously.

The years 1870–1914 were also the peak of the worldwide railway boom. The greatest development, of course, was in North America which had 356,000 miles of track by 1913, and in Europe which had 216,000 miles at that time. But in Asia railway mileage grew from 5,086 in 1870 to 67,591 in 1913 (more than half of this being in India), in Africa from 1,110 to 27,693 and in South America from 1,770 to more than 30,000. This facilitated and cheapened the movement of primary exports to the ports and the movement of imports inland. At the same time export–import dealings were facilitated by the spread of telegraphic communication. The first successful trans-Atlantic cable was laid in 1866, the first Suez–Bombay cable in 1870. By 1900 major ports throughout the world were linked by a telegraph network.

Trade Flows and Trade Policy

In addition to the trade-stimulating developments already noted, restrictions on trade were substantially reduced around mid-century. The United Kingdom, which had abolished duties on grain imports in 1846, was by 1860 virtually a free-trade country. The Cobden–Chevalier treaty of 1860 substantially reduced tariffs between the United Kingdom and France, and this was soon followed by similar treaties between France and several other European countries. The European powers, predominant in military as well as economic terms, also imposed limits on the tariff rates which could be charged by such countries as Turkey, China and Japan. The United Kingdom largely dismantled its colonial trading system, opening the colonies to trade competition.

There was, to be sure, some movement back toward protection after 1880, because of the depression of 1873–9 which stimulated demands for protection by manufacturers, and the influx of cheap grain from the USA which stimulated a similar demand by European farmers. European tariff rates remained moderate, however, and the protectionist movement was not strong enough to check the growing momentum of world trade.

The leading position of the United Kingdom, and especially its consistent import surplus, were important in aiding development of a multilateral payments system. Other countries did not need to balance bilaterally, but could use surpluses with the United Kingdom to finance purchases elsewhere. Use of the pound as a key currency, maintenance of fixed and stable exchange rates and the role of the London banks as a financial clearing house, all facilitated the growth of trade.

Available estimates of growth in the volume of trade have been assembled and analyzed by Simon Kuznets (1967). These estimates show world trade growing at an average rate of 50·3 percent per decade from 1850–80, and 39·5 percent per decade from 1881–1913. We saw earlier that national product in the advanced economies was growing at a median rate of 28·6 percent per decade from 1870–1913. Considering that output in the less developed countries must have been growing less rapidly than this, and in some countries was not growing at all, it is unlikely that world output was growing faster than 2 percent per year. It follows that the ratio of world trade to world output was rising quite rapidly. Kuznets estimates that by 1913 this ratio had reached 33 percent, and that this was *eleven times* the corresponding ratio in 1800.

Trade was dominated by the countries of Europe and North America, which accounted for 76 percent of combined exports and imports in 1876–80 and 75 percent in 1913. Latin America, Africa and Asia accounted for about 20 percent of trade in 1876–80 and 22 percent in 1913, not far from their proportion in recent decades. Granted that these figures are influenced by inclusion of Japan and South Africa, the implication is that the less developed countries were keeping up with the general pace of world trade. This is confirmed by the investigations of Arthur Lewis (1969), who finds that the volume of tropical exports grew at 3·6 percent per year over 1883–1913. Agricultural exports grew a bit slower than this, but mineral and other exports grew faster. Indeed, during this period total exports from the tropical countries grew at almost exactly the same rate as industrial production in the advanced countries.

LDC exports of this era were, of course, overwhelmingly exports of primary products. These formed 97·6 percent of LDC exports in 1876–80, and 89·1 percent of their exports in 1913. (The modest increase in manufactured exports during this period must have come mainly from Japan and India.) While terms of trade between primary products and manufactures fluctuated somewhat within the period, there was no marked upward or downward trend.

Capital, People and Technology

International capital movements were going on throughout the nineteenth century but, as in the case of trade, there was a marked acceleration after 1870. The total value of foreign investments was about $2 billion in 1820, $6 billion in 1870, $23 billion in 1900 and $43 billion in 1914. Of the 1914 total, about

43 percent came from the United Kingdom, 20 percent from France, 13 percent from Germany and 7 percent from the USA. This investment was almost entirely private, made in response to higher prospective earnings abroad. For example, in 1900–1904, average interest rates in London were 3·18 percent on home issues, 3·33 percent on colonial issues and 5·39 percent on foreign issues.

Private capital flowed most readily to countries in which capital could be most productive. It went to countries which had sufficient political stability and demonstrated growth potential to promise a reasonably secure return. Of the 1914 foreign investment, 27 percent was in other European countries, 24 percent in North America, 19 percent in Latin America, 16 percent in Asia and 9 percent in Africa. There was some difference among creditor countries in this respect. French and German investment was predominantly in Europe, while British investment was mainly overseas – about 47 percent within the Empire, 20 percent in the USA and another 20 percent in Latin America.

This overseas investment went mainly into infra-structure, mainly railways, but including also roads, port facilities, telephone and telegraph construction. There was some direct investment in mining and plantation agriculture, relatively little in manufacturing. In general, investment served to facilitate the flow of primary products from the LDCs to the industrializing countries, and the reverse flow of (mainly) manufactured goods to the LDCs.

Movements of population and technology were also important, but because of space considerations we shall say virtually nothing about them. The migration story is familiar. There was a massive movement of people from the United Kingdom and Europe to areas of new settlement, primarily to North America, but also to Argentina, Brazil, Chile, Australia and New Zealand. There were sizable movements also from Asia – of Indians to Ceylon, Burma, East Africa and South Africa; of Chinese to Malaya, Thailand, Indochina and Indonesia. These migrants provided not only labor power but also, in some countries, the bulk of the merchants, bankers and incipient industrialists. Nor should one overlook the substantial flow of administrators, businessmen, engineers and others from the United Kingdom, France and other European countries to colonial areas in Asia and Africa.

International diffusion of technology was no doubt slower and less significant than it has been in recent decades, partly because the technology shelf was smaller and simpler. In agriculture such transfer as occurred related mainly to plantation crops rather than food production, which almost everywhere continued along traditional lines. The only significant exception is the successful Japanese effort to import chemical-fertilizer technology, as well as to improve domestic rice strains by selection and experiment. In nonagricultural sectors European techniques of mining, building construction, railway building and operation, shipping and port facilities were widely disseminated. But in industry diffusion occurred mainly in textile manufacturing, which even before 1914 had achieved sizable proportions in Japan, India and several Latin American countries.

Growth Acceleration: the Limits of Diffusion

The rapid growth of output in the North Atlantic countries, and the even more rapid growth of world trade, initiated a process of export-led growth in other parts of the world. This was true most notably in the major countries of Latin America, including Argentina, Brazil, Chile, Colombia and Mexico. It was true also in several of the smaller Asian countries, including Burma, Ceylon, Malaya, Indochina and Thailand. Late in the period, around 1900, growth acceleration appeared in several parts of West Africa – Ghana, Nigeria and the Ivory Coast. Developments in these countries will be outlined in the next section. But before doing this, it is useful to ask why the incidence of growth acceleration was so uneven, and why most of the less developed world remained unaffected.

The export boom mainly affected agricultural products, and for a country to participate in the boom required some degree of unused productive capacity – additional land which could be brought under cultivation, additional labor time which could be mobilized from the local population or through migration. This requirement was met in most of the thinly settled Latin American countries and also in many parts of southeast Asia and western Africa. But it was not met in densely populated areas where almost all the available land was already in use, such as Egypt, India, China and Java. In other cases, including Venezuela and the Philippines, unused land existed but was effectively monopolized by large owners and unavailable to smallholders.

Water supply was also important. Tea, coffee, cocoa, rubber, bananas, sugar and oilpalm require a year-round water supply. Where there is only rain for a few months and no irrigation, the range of crops is more limited: coarse grains, manioc, cotton and groundnuts if the annual rainfall is thirty inches or less, plus corn, rice, yams and tobacco if rainfall is more abundant. It is noteworthy that the wet areas of Asia and Africa were in the forefront of the export boom, while areas of low rainfall performed less well.

There were also political and infra-structure requirements. Internal peace is a necessary prerequisite. In the Latin American countries the terminal data of the last major civil war is often the initial date of economic growth. In Africa, which was colonized relatively late, tribal warfare continued in many areas until around 1900. In addition, as noted earlier, roads and railways were needed to link interior areas with the coastal ports. Colonial governments, being relatively credit-worthy, were well situated to borrow for infra-structure development; but some did much more than others. The British did a good deal, while the Portuguese did very little. This was true also among independent countries: Brazil did a good deal, while Afghanistan did nothing. It is not difficult to explain nondevelopment in landlocked areas far from the main arteries of sea commerce. These barriers to growth continue today. They help to explain the gradual entrance of additional countries into the growth procession over the last century, and why many of the so-called 'developing countries' are still not actually developing.

Early Growth Acceleration: Some Country Experiences

Even at the risk of distortion through brevity, it seems desirable to suggest reasons for dating growth acceleration in a dozen or so countries from the 1870–1914 era. We begin with Latin America, proceed to Asia and finally to Africa. A few countries which probably should be included in the survey – Peru, Burma, Indochina and the Ivory Coast – are omitted, because of scanty documentation as well as for reasons of space.

Argentina

The Revolution of 1810 against Spain was followed by some fifty years of political turmoil and civil war. But by the 1860s the country had achieved enough stability to respond to the growth opportunities created by European industrialization and transportation improvements. Growth was export-led, with successive waves of new exports appearing to sustain the momentum. The early exports were mainly hides and tallow; but there were sharp increases in wool exports after 1840, grain exports after 1880 and frozen meat after 1900. Diaz-Alejandro (1970, especially ch. 1) estimates that, from 1865 to 1914, gross domestic product grew at an average rate of 'at least 5 percent'. Because of heavy immigration, especially from Italy and Spain, population grew at an average rate of 3·4 percent. This permitted a substantial rise in output per capita, comparable to the rates being achieved in Western Europe and North America.

By 1914 Argentina was a well-integrated market economy, and also closely integrated into the world economy. The labor markets of Argentina, Spain and Italy were virtually one market, with workers even coming over from Europe for seasonal harvest activity. There was a large inflow of foreign capital, mainly from the United Kingdom, which financed close to half of the investment from 1880 to 1914. Trade linkages were strong, with imports averaging about 25 percent of GDP. Domestic markets for land, labor and capital were quite modern and efficient; and some of the distortions typically found in LDCs were absent. Output per worker, for example, was a little *higher* in the rural sector than in the urban sector. Output per capita in 1914 was slightly below that in Canada and Australia; but the three countries were regarded as comparable, and as having similar growth prospects. Why this expectation did not materialize belongs to a later period of economic history.

Brazil

Brazilian development of this era was dominated by the great coffee boom. The origins of the coffee economy go back to the 1820s when it already formed 18 percent of Brazil's exports, which by 1850 had risen to 50 percent. The original development was around Rio de Janeiro, close to ocean transport and a major domestic market. Later development, however, centered south of Rio in the states of Rio Grande do Sul and São Paulo. Climatic conditions here were favorable, and land was available to smallholders, which was not true in most other parts of the country.

Land was abundant and the main problem was labor scarcity. This was met by internal migration from the northeast and other stagnating areas. But there was also government-promoted immigration, especially from Italy. The number of immigrants to São Paulo alone rose from 13,000 in the 1870s to 609,000 in the 1890s. Many of these people in time became coffee planters, while others were able to use their artisan skills.

Coffee exports from Brazil rose from an average of 4·4 million sacks a year in 1878–82 to 12·5 million sacks in 1908–12. By 1906 Brazil had already established a support price system for coffee, maintained by government purchase of surpluses. This was relatively easy at a time when Brazil dominated the world market. In addition to strong export growth, there was considerable industrialization in this period. By 1913 Brazil was producing more than three-quarters of its consumption of cotton textiles. Other manufacturing industries of this period included chemicals, food processing, clothing and metalworking. There was some tariff protection, but this was incidental rather than deliberate, the tariff being regarded mainly as a revenue source.

The increase in output and output per capita was uneven among regions of the country. In the northeast, whose traditional sugar and cotton exports faced severe international competition, output per capita actually fell. But in the coffee-growing region, Furtado estimates that output grew at 4·5 percent per year during 1872–1900, and output per capita at 2·3 percent. For the country as a whole, he estimates that output per capita grew at 1·5 percent, a rate not very different from that of the USA or Western Europe in the same period (Furtado, 1963, pt IV; Coes, 1970).

Chile

Mamalakis (1976) dates the beginning of sustained growth in Chile at around 1840, commenting that 'progress since then has been virtually continuous'. While there was European immigration to Chile, the flow was smaller than that to Argentina or Brazil, and population grew only at rates of 1·0–1·5 percent per year. GNP estimates for the nineteenth century are, of course, conjectural. An early estimate by Ballesteros and Davis puts the growth rate of output per capita at 1 percent per year. Mamalakis considers this too low, and estimates the rate at about 2 percent per year from 1855 onward.

As regards export sectors, wheat was a major export from 1865 to 1900, but declined after that in the face of low-cost competition from Argentina, Canada and the USA. In addition, accelerated population growth ate into the export surplus and this, combined with lagging agricultural performance in Chile, eventually turned the country into a food importer. Wheat was succeeded by nitrates, which were the major export during 1880–1930, providing about half of government revenue, which came very largely from the export sector. Small-scale, unsophistcated production of copper was important quite early, and

Chile was in fact the largest copper exporter by 1880. The modern copper era, however, began only around 1910 with the appearance of large-scale, foreign-owned mining operations developed by the Braden and Guggenheim interests.

By the end of our period the Chilean economy had assumed the general shape which is still recognizable today: an urban economy with half the population already concentrated in urban areas; a consumption-oriented economy, with low or negative personal saving; government revenue derived largely from the export sector, with the remainder of the economy very lightly taxed, yielding little revenue for public investment; a relatively small agricultural sector, which already by 1907 employed only 37 percent of the labor force; an industrial sector which in 1907 employed 18 percent of the labor force (of whom about two-thirds were essentially artisans in shops with four workers or less), engaged mainly in agricultural processing and light consumer goods; and a remarkably large service sector, employing almost half of the labor force.

Colombia

The Colombian growth story begins somewhat later. The previously chaotic political conditions were somewhat stabilized by the advent of the Nuñez regime in 1884, and still more so after Rafael Reyes in 1904 ushered in thirty years of uninterrupted conservative rule. While the national growth rate of per capita income remained low – Harbison (1970) estimates it at 0·5 percent per year after 1895 – there was strong regional development centered in the province of Antioquia. This can be attributed partly to a less rigid class structure than prevailed in other parts of the country, and to an unusual number of people willing to dirty their hands and marked by David McClelland's '*n*-achievement'. It was these people who went into small-scale coffee-growing and contributed to the export boom which was the central feature of the period. Other favorable factors were a superior educational system and availability of land to smallholders.

Coffee is a good peasant crop, with no significant economies of scale, which can be grown alongside subsistence food crops. It needs a light volcanic soil, at least forty inches of rainfall, and moderate temperatures which at this latitude are found at altitudes of 3,000–6,000 feet. Much of the land in Antioquia meets these conditions. So coffee exports increased elevenfold in thirty-five years, from about 100,000 bags in 1880 to 1,100,000 in 1915, by which time coffee accounted for 55 percent of export earnings. Most of this income went to the cultivators, raising demand for locally produced goods, especially cheap woolen and cotton cloth.

The Colombian government encouraged railroad-building from 1880 on, mainly to get coffee to the coast. Railroad mileage rose from 202 kilometers in 1885 to 1,212 in 1915, reducing the cost of transporting coffee to the coast from $70 a ton to $19 a ton. There was a considerable amount of industrialization, again centered in Antioquia, and assisted by government tariff policies. Industrial output was still small in absolute terms, but a foundation had been laid which could be enlarged in later decades.

Mexico

Mexican population grew during the nineteenth century from some 5·8 million in 1803 to 13·6 million in 1900. The average annual rate of increase was about 0·7 percent in 1803–56, 0·6 percent in 1856–77 and 1·6 percent from 1877–1900. Steady growth of per capita output, however, dates only from the late 1870s, when the country was pacified under the dictatorship of Porfirio Diaz which lasted until 1910. The Diaz regime actively encouraged foreign investment in agriculture, mining, power and railroads. Growth was further promoted by 'reductions in banditry, removal of local customs duties that had hampered internal trade, gradual commercialization of agriculture, expansion of raw material and primary product exports and the creation of economic infrastructure', which gradually knit the pre-existing enclaves into a unified market economy.

There are no overall national income estimates before 1900. Reynolds (1970, ch. 1) estimates that, from 1900 to 1910, GDP increased at 3·3 percent per year, population at 1·1 percent and output per capita at 2·2 percent. He speculates further that 'over the whole Porfiriato, the economic growth rate was perhaps 2·6 percent per annum, compared with a population growth of 1·4 percent'. The growth of this period was led by primary exports. Between 1877–8 and 1900–1901 the mineral and metallurgical industries grew at a compound annual rate of 7·3 percent, and combined agricultural, cattle and forestry exports at 6·1 percent. But there was also a significant development of manufacturing industries, whose output rose at 2·8 percent per year over the period.

This pattern of export-led growth, however, left much to be desired. While the monetized sector expanded rapidly, much of the population remained outside the development process. Mining, power, railroads and banking were foreign-dominated. The export industries and the nascent manufacturing industries provided relatively little employment for the growing population. The external orientation of the economy rendered it increasingly sensitive to international business cycles. These defects may have contributed to the Mexican Revolution, which overthrew Diaz and ushered in a new period of economic history.

Ceylon

The Ceylon story begins with the great coffee boom of the 1850s and 1860s. Coffee here was mainly a plantation crop, though about one-quarter of the output was produced on smallholdings. The appearance of coffee rust, however, had by 1880 reduced coffee output almost to zero. This stimulated a search for a new crop, which turned out to be tea. This was also a plantation crop grown at altitudes of 2,500–6,000 feet. Since picking goes on all year round, it requires a stable labor force. Ceylon at this time was a land-abundant, labor-scarce economy, so recruitment of local Sinhalese labor was unfeasible. The need was met by importing large numbers of Tamil workers from South India.

Falling tea prices and profits from 1882 to 1905 stimulated interest in diversification into other export crops, notably (1) coconuts, whose acreage grew from 200,000 hectares in 1871 to 384,000 hectares in 1913. This was essentially a peasant crop, though there were some large holdings, and it was also a lowland crop which did not compete with tea for acreage. (2) Rubber, which began to grow rapidly around 1900. This was also a lowland crop. Production was expanded partly by tea companies which diversified in this direction, partly by a new Sinhalese capitalist class, and partly by smallholders who had about 20 percent of the rubber acreage by 1913.

Thus, by 1913 exports were quite diversified. Tea contributed about 35 percent, rubber about 26 percent, coconut products 20 percent and other products 19 percent. Total exports grew at a rate of 5·4 percent per year over 1880–1913. Modern sector output at this time was roughly half of national output. So even if we assume no growth of per capita output in the traditional sector-cultivated acreage expanding proportionately to population, and unchanged crop yields – we come out with a GDP growth rate of 3·2 percent per year. Since population growth was about 1·4 percent per year, this would mean per capita growth of 1·8 percent.[4]

Ceylon is sometimes viewed as the purest of 'enclave economy' cases, in which export growth failed to rub off on the local population. But Snodgrass and Craig both argue that this was not so. First, smallholders did participate along with plantations in the export boom. They had about 10 percent of the acreage in tea, 20 percent in rubber and 60 percent in coconuts. About 200,000 peasants were growing these crops, compared with 450,000 traditional rice farmers. Secondly, a Ceylonese planter class developed alongside the foreign plantation-owners, going mainly into rubber and coconuts. Craig comments that 'Ceylon seems to have gone further than any other South Asian country ... in producing a middle class of indigenous agriculturalists'. Thirdly, a good deal of infra-structure was laid down. Road- and railroad-building, while intended initially to move exports, benefitted economic activity in general. Government also increased school enrollment two and a half times in 1890–1910, and by 1911 the male literacy rate had reached 40 percent. Finally, there was considerable industrialization, especially in textiles. Manufacturing employment grew at 2·8 percent per year in 1881–1911, absorbing a growing percentage of the labor force.

Thailand

After being opened to foreigners at the same time as Japan, Thailand developed rapidly into a specialized export economy, exporting predominantly rice, but also tin, teak and somewhat later rubber. There was a striking growth of rice exports, which rose from an average of 1,630,000 piculs (= 60 kilograms) in 1865–9 to 14,760,000 in 1905–9 (Ingram, 1971). The proportion of rice exported rose to 50 percent of the total crop, and remained near that level; but this was accomplished by increased output, and did not encroach on domestic consumption. Increased output came mainly from people settling more land, on their own initiative, with little help from government. The area planted to rice rose from 5·8 million rai in 1850 to 9·1 million rai in 1905–6. There was also an influx of Chinese entrepreneurs, who took over trading and other business functions, while the Thais devoted themselves to agriculture. This symbiotic relationship, which continues to the present, seems never to have generated the tensions associated with Chinese business operations in other southeast Asian countries. The increased income generated by exports was used mainly to buy imported consumer goods, particularly cloth, which tended to displace handicraft and home production. The percentage of textile consumption supplied by domestic production fell steadily from 1850 to about 1920, after which it began to rise again; and some other handicrafts experienced a similar cycle of decline and recovery.

While Ingram presents no GNP estimates, one can make a case for modest growth of income per capita in the 1870–1914 era. Some of the export income was drawn off by middlemen and some was remitted to China. (Thai exports consistently exceeded imports by a considerable margin.) But much of it went into increasing the amount and variety of consumer goods available to Thai farmers. Structural change in the economy, however, was largely absent. The country remained overwhelmingly agricultural, with 85 percent of the labor force in agriculture, forestry and fishing.

Malaya

Malaya is a classic export economy, which has progressed through successive waves of primary exports while importing most consumer goods, including a good proportion of the basic foodstuff, rice. Growth spread out from the Straits Settlements established by the British in Penang, Malacca and Singapore. The United Kingdom provided government administrators for these areas, while China provided large numbers of businessmen and common laborers (Lim, 1967).

The primordial export product was tin. Average annual exports rose from 7,000 tons in the 1870s to 42,000 tons in the 1900s, by which time Malaya produced more than all other countries combined. Tin prices were stable over 1870–90, and declined only about 15 percent by 1900, so that capacity to import rose rapidly. While 20 percent of the tin companies were British, 80 percent were Chinese. Capital and entrepreneurship came from Chinese already settled in the Straits Settlements. Mine labor was also Chinese, coming partly from the Straits Settlements and also from new Chinese immigration. Growth was aided by substantial infra-structive development – roads, railways, clearing of rivers, post offices, schools and hospitals – financed mainly by taxes on tin. The basic infra-structure of modern Malaya was laid during this period.

Tin output leveled off to a plateau after 1900, by which time known deposits were being fully exploited. The export boom was carried forward, however, by expansion of rubber. The first Brazilian seeds smuggled out to London in 1876 had been transplanted in Ceylon and Malaya by 1877. The great expansion of rubber, however, came after 1900, as rising world demand forced prices to astronomical levels. Total rubber plantings in southeast Asia, mainly in Ceylon and Malaya, rose from 5,000 acres in 1900 to 1,000,000 acres in 1910, to which another half-million acres was added in 1911. Rubber cultivation was mainly in sizable (500–5,000-acre) estates, owned about three-quarters by Europeans and one-quarter by Chinese. Labor for the estates was mainly imported from India, though there was some Chinese labor as well. There was also a substantial development of smallholdings, divided about equally between Chinese and Malay ownership. The indigenous Malay population stayed mainly in agriculture, and was largely bypassed by the new developments. For other groups in the population, however, there can be little doubt that per capita income rose during this period.

Nigeria and Ghana

As early as the 1830s foreign traders appeared in western Africa offering attractive goods in exchange for exports of palm oil and palm kernels. These palm products grew naturally, were located near the coast, and were easily harvested and transported. After the slave trade was suppressed, the oil trade tended to increase. Substantial export development, however, had to wait for pacification of these areas under British influence. This occurred in southern Ghana in 1874, while Yorubaland (Western Nigeria) was pacified in 1893. Control had been extended to the north in both countries by around 1900. Rapid export growth, then, dates from the 1890s, and there was only a short period of growth within the time-span considered here.

Palm products were soon reinforced by cocoa, first planted extensively in the 1890s. This is a peasant crop, which can readily be added on to subsistence production by taking up idle land, abundant at this time, and combining this with unused family labor time. The family, in effect, worked a bit harder in order to be able to buy imported cloth and other consumer goods; and food production went on much as before. In addition to oil and cocoa. Ghana had substantial gold exports, which formed one-quarter of the total in 1913.

From a small base, exports grew at a high rate: in Ghana, at 9·2 percent per year in 1882–4 to 1913; in Nigeria, at 12·2 percent per year over 1899–1913. The British administrators gradually pushed rail and road networks inward, so that by 1914 the northern regions of both countries had been incorporated into the economy. They also organized agricultural experiment stations and distributed new seed varieties. Cocoa production was so profitable, and the basic techniques were sufficiently simple, that small farmers needed little urging to go into it, which they did in large numbers. Like the rice farmers of southeast Asia, they demonstrated that illiterate people can respond readily to economic incentives. While exports grew rapidly, they were still a small part of the economy. Helleiner (1966) estimates[5] that as late as 1929 traditional production was still 85 percent of GNP, and that in this large sector there was little increase in output per capita. For the economy as a whole, therefore, the rate of increase in output per capita was low – certainly less than 1 percent per year.

Questions and Qualifications

Despite the evidence just presented, the view that some LDCs began growing more than a century ago, and that primary exports were an effective engine of growth, may still appear odd. This is not the way growth occurs in post-1945 growth models, which emphasize capital accumulation, factory-style manufacturing and import substitution. So we should examine some possible objections to our central thesis.

A first obvious fact is that some of the countries we have discussed were, in fact, not countries but colonies. One can argue that meaningful growth is not possible under colonial rule, and that national sovereignty is a prerequisite. This is true in the sense that an independent government can do things which colonial governments cannot – or at any rate did not – do. They can impose import restrictions which may speed domestic industrialization. They can operate independent monetary and exchange-rate policies. They can limit the operations of foreign enterprises and give preference to domestic enterprise.

But to say that a colony cannot grow seems too extreme. Granted, the intent of colonial governments was to use the colony as a source of raw materials and a market for manufactures. But we should not assume that this interchange was without benefit to the colony. A good part of the export proceeds accrued to peasant producers, and the imported goods which they purchased brought some diversification and improvement of consumption patterns. The infrastructure created initially for military purposes and to speed the export trade could later be turned to other uses.

We should note also that 'colonialism' is not a uniform thing. There were a half-dozen colonial powers, which differed widely in approach and in impact on growth. Japanese colonial policy in Taiwan and Korea was quite different from Portuguese policy in Angola and Mozambique, or British policy in Kenya and Nigeria. It is quite possible to conclude that at some times and places colonial rule blocked domestic growth, while in other places it accelerated growth.[6]

A second reason for possible skepticism about the growth of this period is that it depended so heavily on primary exports. An important current of thought holds that dependence on primary products, and exchange of these for manufactures, places a country in servitude to the industrial countries. The terms of trade, it is argued, are bound to turn against primary products over the long run. But more basically, primary production leads nowhere. It does not get a country onto the industrial track on which eventual affluence depends.

This outlook reflects the anti-agriculture, pro-industry bias of much development writing since 1945, a bias which seems now to be diminishing. It is recognized increasingly that agricultural progress is a necessary ingredient of growth, and that for a country to be able to feed itself and perhaps develop an export surplus strengthens its growth prospects. Exports are clearly helpful in providing foreign exchange which can be used to import materials and capital goods needed for development; and in the first instance, a country must export what it has. This usually turns out to be primary products. Indeed, the sequence from primary exports to gradual industrialization to eventual growth of manufactured exports can be traced in the older industrial countries as well as in more recent developers. There is no reason to scorn the early steps in this sequence.

The terms of trade argument has been going on for a long time. One might well predict, *a priori*, a long-term trend in favor of primary products and against manufactures, on grounds of natural-resource scarcity. The classical economists made such predictions in the early nineteenth century, Keynes repeated this prediction in 1911 and a similar view is implicit in today's 'limits to growth' reasoning. But when one looks at statistics, it is hard to discover any long-term tendency. The apparent stability in terms of trade in 1870–1914 has already been noted.

A third (and legitimate) critique of growth during this period is that it did not extend to the entire population. Thus, a 2 percent per capita growth rate in Ceylon does not have the same meaning as a 2 percent growth rate in Belgium, where virtually everyone participated. But again, one should recognize substantial variation in this respect among LDCs. Increases in per capita income were most widely diffused where the new exports come from small-scale peasant producers, as in Nigeria or Thailand. The spread effects were less in the case of plantation agriculture, and still less in the case of mining and other extractive operations. Further, in areas of new settlement such as Argentina or Chile, a larger proportion of the population was integrated into the national economy than in older countries with a long tradition of subsistence, village-oriented agriculture.

Lewis (1970, ch. 1) suggests that in Asia and Africa only a minority, in the range 25–50 percent, were drawn into the money economy. The majority remained locked into subsistence agriculture; and one could usually find groups whose incomes had actually deteriorated – for example, artisans swamped by low-cost imports of consumer goods. But the incidence of growth is always uneven. Significant improvement for a quarter or a third of the population should not be discounted, especially since such a beachhead is likely to be enlarged in later decades.

Finally, the reality of growth may be questioned because it did not, during this period, lead to substantial industrialization. But growth should not, I think, be identified with any one economic sector. A land-rich country can become affluent while remaining largely agricultural, as the experience of Denmark and New Zealand suggests. Nor should manufacturing be identified with factory-style manufacturing. Every country has a manufacturing sector, consisting in the first instance of handicraft workers plus a good deal of household production. As income levels rise, transport facilities improve, and markets become large enough to permit optimum-scale factory units, household and handicraft production give way gradually to factory production. But this shift in the center of gravity of the manufacturing sector is gradual, a matter of decades rather than years (recall that the English hand-loom weavers finally lost out in the 1840s, when the Industrial Revolution was already a half-century old). Large-scale manufacturing, then, is more properly regarded as a consequence rather than a source of income growth; and it is typically not a prominent feature of the early decades of growth.

Instead of industrialization, one should perhaps speak of *diversification* of production. In most countries, in the period 1870–1914, there was some diversification of export crops. Growing demand for food stimulated agricultural production for home use. An increasing number of people were employed in infra-structure industries and in government, and there was a growing variety of service activities. Factory industry, however, was slow to develop. Only Argentina, Brazil, Ceylon and Colombia had made a significant start by 1913, with the textile industry playing its typical role of early leader. Economic reasons for gradualism were often reinforced by political reasons. Colonial administrators were typically prejudiced against expansion of manufacturing in the colonies, regarding industry as the prerogative of the home country. In Latin America, governments were usually allied with the landowning class, which was indifferent or even hostile to industrialization. Bearing these qualifications in mind, we can still conclude that economic growth during this period was genuine, though still only for a limited number of countries. These countries had taken the first hesitant steps along a course which was to continue, with interruptions and fluctuations, over the decades ahead.

Chapter 19: Notes

1   We should note, however, that the two categories are not static. The number of countries which should be regarded as 'developed', or in my terminology 'mature', has grown from one in 1850 to perhaps thirty or forty today.
2   It is especially appropriate to do this in a volume honoring W. Arthur Lewis, who has done more than anyone else to clarify the events of this period, and on whose work any later writer must heavily depend. See in particular Lewis (1969; 1970).
3   In addition to the Lewis volumes cited earlier, the following general references have proved helpful: Bairoch (1975); Kenwood and Longheed (1971); Latham (1978); Kuznets (1966; 1967); Maddison (1964); Maizels (1963).
4   This estimate comes from Donal Snodgrass (1966); see also J. Edwin Craig, Jr (1970).
5   See also Holmes (1970).
6   For a thoughtful analysis, see Fieldhouse (1971).

Chapter 19: References

Bairoch, P., *The Economic Development of the Third World since 1900* (Berkeley and Los Angeles: University of California Press, 1975).

Coes, D., 'Brazil', in W. A. Lewis, ed., *Tropical Development, 1880–1913* (London: Allen & Unwin, 1970), pp. 100–127.

Craig, J. E., Jr, 'Ceylon', in W. A. Lewis, ed., *Tropical Development, 1880–1913* (London: Allen & Unwin, 1970), pp. 221–49.

Diaz-Alejandro, C., *Essays on the Economic History of the Argentine Republic* (New Haven, Conn.: Yale University Press, 1970).

Fieldhouse, D. K., 'The economic exploitation of Africa: some British and French comparisons', in P. Gifford and W. R. Lewis, eds, *France and Britain in Africa* (New Haven, Conn.: Yale University Press, 1971), pp. 593–662.

Furtado, C., *The Economic Growth of Brazil* (Berkeley and Los Angeles: University of California Press, 1963).

Harbison, R. W., 'Colombia', in W. A. Lewis, ed., *Tropical Development, 1880–1913* (London: Allen & Unwin, 1970), pp. 64–99.

Helleiner, G., *Peasant Agriculture, Government and Economic Growth in Nigeria* (Homewood, Ill.: Irwin, 1966).

Holmes, A. B., 'Gold Coast and Nigeria', in W. A. Lewis, ed., *Tropical Development, 1880–1913* (London: Allen & Unwin, 1970), pp. 147–77.

Ingram, J. C., *Economic Change in Thailand, 1850–1970* (Stanford, Calif.: Stanford University Press, 1971).

Kenwood, A. G. and Lougheed, A. L., *The Growth of the International Economy, 1820–1960* (London: Allen & Unwin, 1971).

Kuznets, S., *Modern Economic Growth* (New Haven, Conn.: Yale University Press, 1966).

Kuznets, S., 'Quantitative aspects of the economic growth of nations, X: level and structure of foreign trade: long-term trends', *Economic Development and Cultural Change*, vol. 15, no. 2, pt II (1967), pp. 1–140.

Latham, A. I. H., *The International Economy and the Underdeveloped World, 1865–1914* (London: Croom Helm, 1978).

Lewis, W. A., *Aspects of Tropical Trade, 1883–1965* (Stockholm: Almqvist & Wiksell, 1969).

Lewis, W. A. (ed.), *Tropical Development, 1880–1913* (London: Allen & Unwin, 1970).

Lewis, W. A., 'The slowing down of the engine of growth', *American Economic Review*, vol. 70, no. 4 (1980), pp. 555–64.

Lim, C. Y., *Economic Development of Modern Malaya* (Kuala Lumpur: Oxford University Press, 1967).

Maddison, A., *Economic Growth in the West* (New York: Twentieth Century Fund, 1964).

Maizels, A., *Industrial Growth and World Trade* (Cambridge: Cambridge University Press, 1963).

Mamalakis, M., *The Growth and Structure of the Chilean Economy* (New Haven, Conn.: Yale University Press, 1976).

Reynolds, C. W., *The Mexican Economy: Twentieth Century Structure and Growth* (New Haven, Conn.: Yale University Press, 1970).

Snodgrass, D., *Ceylon: An Export Economy in Transition* (Homewood, Ill.: Irwin, 1966).

20

Latin America in Depression, 1929–39

CARLOS F. DIAZ-ALEJANDRO

The 1930s are widely regarded as a crucial turning point in Latin American development: it marks the acceleration of import substituting industrialization and the start of public policy clearly committed to growth and other social objectives. The contrast between 'before and after 1929' is often exaggerated, but there is little doubt that the events of the 1930s have profoundly influenced the region's attitudes toward foreign trade and finance. It has been generally recognized that several Latin American countries performed 'reasonably well' during the Great Depression of this century, and different hypotheses have been advanced to explain such behavior. Perhaps the flashiest one has been that of André Gunder Frank, who argues that Latin America in the 1930s demonstrates that contrary to Neoclassical orthodoxy the periphery industrializes and prospers only when the center is weak and unable to maintain its imperial and underdeveloping dominance.[1] Also influenced by the Latin American experience during world wars and depressions, Albert O. Hirschman (1958, esp. pp. 173–74) had earlier noted that fluctuations in foreign-exchange receipts of less developed countries may set in motion certain valuable development mechanisms. Alexander Kafka referred to the Great Depression as an example of growth-promoting disequilibrium under some Latin American circumstances; in a manner similar to Hirschman he conjectured that there is an optimum degree of adverse shock, without implying that an adverse shock is better than a favorable one (Kafka, 1961, pp. 8–14).

In what follows the magnitude of the shock of the Great Depression to Latin America will, first, be documented. Secondly, the policies adopted to cope with the crisis will be discussed. Then the performance of various Latin American economies will be explored, and the sense in which they did reasonably well will be analyzed. Sundry observations will close the chapter.

From the outside Latin American countries may all look the same but the region, even in the late 1920s, contained a variety of open economies some of which were less open and more industrialized than others. Indeed, the 1930s witnessed different economic responses which can be divided between those of small or passive and those of large or active economies. Even though statistical documentation for passive countries is scantier than for active ones, this typological point will be of importance throughout the chapter.

Shocks

For a number of exporters of primary products the late 1920s had been difficult years,[2] but on the whole it is useful to picture that period as one of reasonable balance of payments equilibrium in the major Latin American countries. A series of violent external shocks during 1929–33 disrupted that equilibrium, and much of the economic history for the 1930s can be written around attempts to adjust the balance of payments, and then the domestic economy, to the new environment.

The collapse of the world economy during 1929–33 was transmitted to Latin America first of all by a sharp change in relative prices: dollar export prices fell more steeply than dollar import prices. As can be seen in panel A of Table 20.1, within four years the terms of trade fell by 21 to 45 percent in countries for which comparable data are available.[3] Note that for a country with a ratio of exports to Gross National Product of 30 percent a deterioration of the terms of trade by 30 percent would represent a loss in real income of 9 percent, assuming no change in physical output. As a first approximation the deterioration of the terms of trade during 1929–33, as well as their subsequent evolution in the 1930s may be regarded as primarily exogenous to the Latin American economies.[4]

Table 20.1 *Foreign Trade Indicators for Some Latin American Countries (1928–9 = 100)*

	1932–3	1938–9
(A) Terms of Trade		
Argentina	69	98
Brazil	62	43
Colombia	63	57
Chile	59	60
Ecuador	72	56
El Salvador	55	50
Mexico	63	124
Venezuela	79	47
(B) Export Quantum		
Argentina	85	70
Brazil	93	162
Colombia	100	132
Chile	36	87
Ecuador	78	109
El Salvador	96	115
Mexico	60	49
Venezuela	91	145
Peru	82	108

Source:
Basic data obtained from *United Nations* (1976). The terms of trade are defined as an index of dollar export unit values to dollar import unit values.

Except for the spectacular Chilean case, for the countries shown in Table 20.1 the contraction in the export quantum during 1929–33 was substantially less than the terms of trade deterioration. By the late 1930s the export quantum of several countries had surpassed the 1928–9 level, but for most countries the terms of trade for 1938–9 remained below relative to predepression magnitudes. Latin American exports were predominantly rural and mining products, the former showing a smaller price elasticity of supply than the latter; some rural products, such as coffee and livestock, also followed *sui generis* output cycles rooted in their productive characteristics. External demand conditions were not uniformly negative for all primary products, particularly during the late 1930s; Brazilian cotton, Argentine corn and Peruvian gold are examples of favored staples. Such commodity lottery naturally influenced the pace of recovery. Table 20.2 presents the yearly evolution of the purchasing power of exports, defined as the terms of trade multiplied by the export quantum; this table also includes estimates for Cuba. After touching bottom in 1932 or 1933, recovery sets in culminating in 1936 or 1937, after which a new relapse occurs. By the late 1930s the purchasing power of exports remained between 20 and 50 percent below 1929 levels.

The crisis disturbed the balance of payments also via the capital account. After 1930 gross capital inflows fell sharply. Furthermore, with the dollar prices of exports dropping unexpectedly by around 60 percent, debt repayments rose in real terms, compressing the capacity to import beyond what is suggested in Table 20.2. Therefore, between 1929 and 1932–3 the import quantum fell more than the purchasing power of exports, as may be seen in Table 20.3 (with the exception of Mexico). By 1934 all countries, except Argentina, had suspended normal servicing of the external national debt. Import volumes as a rule recovered much faster than the purchasing power of exports. Private portfolio capital was not to play an important role in the external accounts of Latin American countries until the 1960s.

During the 1920s critics of the prevailing pro-trade orthodoxy within Latin America pointed to signs of growing protectionism at the center. In the United Kingdom imperial preferences were advocated by influential groups; in the USA the 1928 presidential election was accompanied by a protectionist wave. These trends culminated with the passage of the Smoot–Hawley tariff in 1930, the British Abnormal Importations Act of 1931 and the Ottawa Commonwealth preferences of 1932. France, Germany and Japan also reinforced their own discriminatory trade arrangements for areas under their political hegemony. The independent Latin American periphery, unconsulted regarding these measures, could go hang. A North American author writing in 1935 about southern cone countries in Latin America described the situation as follows:

> The trade barriers which have been erected in Europe and the United States against agricultural products and raw materials have placed these countries in the forefront of foreign trade decline ... Nationalistic

Table 20.2 Purchasing Power of Exports, 1928–39 (1929 = 100)

	Argentina	Brazil	Colombia	Cuba	Chile	Ecuador	El Salvador	Mexico	Peru	Venezuela
1928	110	97	111	101	91	114	110	94	—	74
1929	100	100	100	100	100	100	100	100	100	100
1930	67	67	82	68	62	91	60	63	66	110
1931	69	62	80	57	41	64	67	49	48	71
1932	65	54	72	43	16	68	40	35	43	74
1933	58	59	63	45	25	50	77	39	52	48
1934	74	70	85	50	38	82	67	56	71	61
1935	78	71	73	56	42	64	57	68	79	39
1936	86	77	83	67	47	77	60	62	80	55
1937	115	75	85	75	73	73	83	69	82	58
1938	68	67	79	64	48	64	53	67	68	58
1939	76	71	80	67	51	68	70	52	70	58

Source:
As Table 20.1; Cuban purchasing power of exports obtained by dividing indices of the value of exports at current prices by the US wholesale price index. Basic data from Ministerio de Hacienda, *Resumenes Estadísticos Seleccionados* (1959, p. 25) and US Department of Commerce, *Statistical Abstract of the United States* (1965, p. 356).

Table 20.3   *Comparison of Purchasing Power of Exports (A) and Import Quantum (B) (1929 = 100)*

		1928–9	1930–31	1932–3	1934–5–6	1937–8–9
Argentina	A	105	68	62	79	86
	B	98	75	49	59	74
Brazil	A	99	65	57	73	71
	B	100	49	44	60	72
Colombia	A	106	81	68	80	81
	B	109	49	44	70	93
Cuba	A	101	63	44	58	69
	B	99	66	32	51	62
Chile	A	96	52	21	42	57
	B	90	70	18	35	49
Ecuador	A	107	78	59	74	68
	B	100	67	43	76	77
El Salvador	A	105	64	59	61	69
	B	95	50	45	55	54
Mexico	A	97	56	37	62	63
	B	94	61	42	60	73
Peru	A	100*	57	48	77	73
	B	100*	62	39	78	88
Venezuela	A	87	91	61	52	58
	B	90	57	35	31	55

*Refers only to 1929.
Source:
As Table 20.2.

> tendencies are not dominant in these countries. National leaders fully recognize the desirability of a heavy volume of trade ... National self-sufficiency to a greater and greater measure was forced upon these countries by the governmental policies of the United States and European nations. (Phelps, 1935, p. 273)

The emergence of a protectionist and nationalistic center was perhaps the greatest shock to Latin American economies during the early 1930s. The memory of this betrayal of Ricardo would last longer in the periphery than in the center.

Policies

An *ex-post* description of measures taken by a group of Latin American countries during the early 1930s risks attributing to 'autonomous policy' a series of improvisations more or less forced by circumstances. Yet not all countries were in a position to improvise. The largest ones, such as Argentina, Brazil, Colombia and Mexico, were at the forefront of experimentation. The smallest countries, such as Honduras, Haiti and the Dominican Republic, did little but wait for export-led recovery. In between there is an interesting contrast between Cuba, which was dragged down by the crisis as surely as the state of Mississippi, versus Chile and Uruguay, which in spite of their smallness eventually broke away from the orthodoxy of the gold-exchange standard and free trade. Unfortunately, data for those years are scanty, particularly for the small or passive countries. There is enough information, however, to document several of the measures taken by the large or active countries.

By the end of 1931 the active nations were experimenting with balance of payments measures previously regarded as heterodox.[5] As gold reserves dwindled or disappeared, convertibility was abandoned and exchange rates depreciated, particularly those applied to imports. Table 20.4 presents indices of those exchange rates, defined as units of local currency per one US dollar. The rates have been deflated by each country's cost of living index (or other available general index) relative to the US cost of living index. The real depreciations relative to the dollar for the countries shown are in the range 36–87 percent. The depreciation trend appears to have been unaffected by whether a country was politically moving Left (Mexico and Colombia), or Right (Argentina and Uruguay).

As may be deduced from Table 20.5, most of the swing in the real import exchange rates arose from nominal depreciations, which had a surprisingly small effect on price levels. Nevertheless, for all countries shown, price indices for 1935–9 were higher than that of the USA. For the passive countries, one may conjecture that there was no such rapid real depreciation of the import exchange rates. Some of these countries (Cuba and Panama) did not even have a central bank, while others (Guatemala and Haiti) maintained their peg to the US dollar throughout the crisis and, on the whole, remained committed to gold-exchange standard rules.

The real depreciation of the Argentine peso during the 1930s can be documented more fully from three additional angles: when other deflators are used,

Table 20.4　*Average Real Import Exchange Rates (1929 = 100)*

	1925–9	*1930–34*	*1935–9*
Argentina	101·5	137·2	133·2
Brazil	100·2	173·2	186·0
Chile	100·5*	186·7	175·3
Colombia	98·8	145·6	158·6
Mexico	103·0	136·4	140·0
Peru	98·6†	153·8	153·1
Uruguay	101·3	155·8	160·3

*Refers only to 1928–9.
†Refers only to 1926, 1927, 1928 and 1929.
Sources and method:
For definitions, see text; basic data obtained from League of Nations yearbooks and national sources.

Table 20.5   *Cost of Living Indices (1929 = 100)*

	1925–9	1930–34	1935–9
Argentina	100·8	86·4	89·8
Brazil	96·9	74·5	94·0
Chile	99·2*	112·1	155·5
Colombia	101·4	65·9	90·3
Mexico	95·7	87·1	111·4
Peru	106·6†	87·9	93·3
Uruguay	98·7	96·7	98·2
USA	101·4	83·9	81·6

*Refers only to 1928–9.
†Refers only to 1926, 1927, 1928 and 1929.
Sources and method:
As Table 20.4.

with respect to the British pound and for the export rate. Table 20.6 presents these calculations. It may be noted that the real depreciation is smaller when wholesale price indices are used as deflators, a not-surprising result when considering the heavier weight of tradeable goods in that index in contrast with cost of living indices. For 1930–33, the depreciation is larger with respect to the dollar than to the pound; for later years, this is reversed when cost of living indices are used as deflators. After 1933, a gap appears between import and export rates, but the most remarkable fact in the light of later experience is that the real average export rate does *not* appreciate in spite of gloomy world market conditions. Special taxes and trading arrangements became commonplace for traditional exports, but the maintenance of a reasonable real export exchange rate left the door open for new nontraditional exports when external circumstances permitted.

Exchange-rate devaluations were not the only measures undertaken by the active countries to restore balance of payments equilibrium: there were also increased tariffs, import and exchange controls, bilateral clearing arrangements and, as noted for Argentina, multiple exchange rates. Contrary to what would happen in the late 1940s and 1950s, exchange-rate and protectionist policies reinforced each other as import-repressing mechanisms. Indeed, by the mid-1930s in many of the active countries there may have been some redundancy in this formidable battery of measures; Ellsworth (1945, p. 67) has argued this point in his valuable study of Chile in depression.[6] For the Colombian case, Chu (1977, pp. 19–20) has argued that most of the change between 1927 and 1936 in the price of imported nontraditional manufactures was due to the devaluation of the peso, rather than tariff increases. This does not deny that for some industries increases in effective protection played an important stimulative role; examples for Colombia include cement, soap and rayon textiles.

The small passive countries appear to have been as impotent regarding protection as with nominal exchange-rate management. Cuba actually lowered tariffs in 1934, undoing much of the protectionist effect of the anomalous Tariff Act 1927. This action was undertaken as part of the Reciprocity Treaty of 1934 with the USA; the USA lowered tariffs for 35 Cuban products, while

Table 20.6 Argentine Average Real Exchange Rates, 1925–39 (1929 = 100)

| | Dollar | | | | Pound Sterling | | | |
| | Cost of Living | | Wholesale Prices | | Cost of Living | | Wholesale Prices | |
	Imports	Exports	Imports	Exports	Imports	Exports	Imports	Exports
1925–9	—	101·6	—	99·5*	—	102·3	—	101·5*
1930–33	—	135·1	—	112·9	—	126·7	—	100·7
1934–6	139·7	124·2	117·9	105·0	160·7	143·1	115·8	103·1
1937–9	131·3	120·0	109·2	100·4	147·6	135·4	113·1	103·9

*Refers to 1926–9 only.
Source:
Diaz-Alejandro (1980, tables 1 and 2).

Cuba granted reductions on 426 items. The US Jones–Costigan Sugar Act of 1934 imposed quotas on imports from Cuba, although setting a premium over the prevailing world price to assure deliveries and protect producers in the USA. The Cuban share of the US sugar market was 52 percent during 1926–30, falling to 29 percent in 1935–39. The US share in all Cuban imports rose from 60 percent in 1926–30 to 68 percent in 1935–9 (Dominguez, 1978, p. 60; Ministerio de Hacienda, 1959, p. 24). Even larger countries were pressured into reversing some of their early tariff increases; wielding the threat of Commonwealth preferences and import quotas on meat, the United Kingdom obtained tariff concessions from Argentina under the controversial Roca–Runciman treaty of 1933. Argentine tariff revenues expressed as a percentage of the value of merchandise imports, which had increased from 17 percent in 1929 to 29 percent in 1933, fell to 22–23 percent in subsequent years (Diaz-Alejandro, 1970, p. 282).[7] Several Latin American countries, on the other hand, met Japanese competition in textiles with a vigorous use of import duties and quotas.

Abandonment of convertibility stemmed the decline in money supplies, which occurred even in active countries during the early stages of the crisis. By the late 1930s, money supplies in active countries exceeded 1929 levels. Table 20.7 contrasts the Cuban case, where money supply shrank by about 40 percent, with those of Argentina, Brazil, Chile, Colombia, Mexico and Uruguay. Interest rates for 1935–9 appear lower than those registered at the height of the crisis (1930–32), and lower than those of the late 1920s. In Argentina, for example, interest rates on ninety days' time deposits were 6 percent at the end of 1929; averaged 4·3 percent during 1930–32; and oscillated at 2–3 percent for the rest of the decade. Active countries also managed to avoid major bank failures.

Table 20.7   *Nominal Money Supply (1929 = 100)*

	1925–9	1930–34	1935–9
Argentina	100·0*	90·6	110·8
Brazil	91·9	108·8	175·0
Uruguay	97·7	103·2	130·4
Chile	97·8†	109·0	213·4
Colombia	111·0	92·6	159·0
Mexico	86·1	97·1	211·2
Cuba	107·6	56·7	60·9
USA	98·5	83·0	117·0

*Refers only to 1926, 1927, 1928 and 1929.
†Refers only to 1928–9.
Sources and method:
Cuban data from Henry C. Wallich (1950, pp. 38–76, 152); Chilean data from P. T. Ellsworth (1945, p. 171); US data from Milton Friedman and Anna Jacobson Schwartz (1963, appendix 17, table 17-1); Mexican data from Leopoldo Solis (1970, pp. 104–5); others from national sources. Data refer to money supplies at the end of the year; definitions of the stock of money vary slightly from country to country; definitions used are closest to M_1.

There has been some controversy as to whether the active countries followed, during the early 1930s, fiscal policies which could be characterized as 'Keynesianism-before-Keynes'. The argument has been most lively for Brazil, and centers on the magnitude of planned fiscal deficits and their financing. In his pioneering work Celso Furtado argued that domestic coffee price-support programmes led to fiscal deficits having an expansionary effect on aggregate demand. Later research noted that much of this expenditure was financed either by new taxes, or foreign loans.[8] Nevertheless, 35 percent of coffee purchases were financed essentially by money creation (Silber, 1977, p. 192). Even in Brazil the authorities remained committed to the rhetoric of fiscal orthodoxy, certainly during the early 1930s. Large fiscal deficits financed by money creation occurred, but typically as a result of unusual circumstances, such as political turmoil in Chile during late 1931 and 1932, including a short-lived socialist government; the war between Peru and Colombia over Leticia in 1932; and the Second Chaco War between Bolivia and Paraguay, also in 1932. In Brazil, the São Paulo rebellion in 1932 and severe drought in the northeast added to the deficits generated by the coffee-purchase programme. In some countries fiscal orthodoxy was buttressed by memories of massive public works and deficit-financing during the 1920s by corrupt governments, such as the dictatorship of Leguia in Peru and Machado in Cuba.

Even if there is little evidence outside Brazil that the full-employment fiscal surplus was reduced to maintain aggregate demand, in most activitist countries public expenditures seem to have been reduced by less, or expanded more, than private expenditures. The share of government in GNP rose in all active countries during the 1930s. On the revenue side there were important changes with the share of custom taxes falling, as may be seen in the following data for Argentina and Brazil (custom revenues as percentage total current revenues):[9]

	Argentina	*Brazil*
1925–9	58	51
1930–34	44	43
1935–9	33	42.

Both Argentina and Brazil witnessed a remarkable expansion in noncustoms current public revenues, which by 1932 (Argentina) and 1933 (Brazil) exceeded the levels reached in 1929, at current prices.

One may conjecture that fiscal policy in active countries exerted at least a modest balanced-budget-multiplier type of expansionary effect on aggregate demand during the early 1930s. The authorities were certainly wise in not seeking a balanced budget under the conditions of those years. During the second half of the decade such an effect was reinforced by a cautious increase in domestically financed deficits, a process encouraged by increasingly self-confident cheap-money policies isolated from the rest of the world by exchange controls.

The rising share of public expenditure in GNP had more than Keynesian significance. Governments became committed to promoting both growth, and structural transformation. The Lazaro Cardenas administration (1934–40), for example, accelerated the land-reform programme of the Mexican Revolution, and in 1938 nationalized the petroleum industry. Governmental regulatory functions expanded; the 1930s also witnessed the strengthening and creation of public institutions granting medium and long-term credits, although the large-scale public involvement in industrial credit was to wait until the 1940s. In an interesting conjecture, Fernando Henrique Cardoso and Enzo Faletto have argued that in countries where the export economy was controlled by national groups that had succeeded in forming an important industrial sector before the crisis, domestic policies took on a more pro-private-enterprise cast, while in countries where exports where controlled mainly by foreign-owned enclaves, the state took a more active role after the crisis relative to private enterprise. But the private sector was not excluded from economies where state participation was preponderant, nor was the public sector absent in the initial stages of import-substituting industrialization, even in countries of liberal tradition (Cardoso and Faletto, 1978, pp. 127–8). Governments and public opinion showed a keener interest in increasing the national share in value added by foreign-owned activities; those enterprises also came under closer scrutiny and supervision by host countries. Some traditional export activities witnessed a rise in the share owned by domestic capitalists; that was the case, for example, for Cuban sugar.

We can now summarize the automatic and policy-induced mechanisms of adjustment triggered by the exogenous shocks Latin America received during 1929–33. The higher level of the international price of manufactures relative to that for primary products, which was expected to continue for the foreseeable future, by itself encouraged the expansion of domestic manufacturing at the expense of rural activities. But besides manufactured importables and primary exportables, the Latin American economy of the 1930s had a third category of goods which may be called nontraded. Regardless of the exchange-rate policy followed, a small country subject to an exogenous worsening of its international terms of trade will witness *over the long run* a decline in the price of its nontraded goods relative to the price of importable goods, further encouraging a movement of resources toward the import-competing sector. Under a gold-exchange standard with fixed rates and with collapsing international prices for both imports and exports, nontraded prices will have a long way to fall; such deflation is likely to be protracted and painful. Countries willing and able to devalue their exchange rate can move toward the new constellation of relative prices speedily, limiting both price and monetary deflation. This is what the active Latin American countries managed to do by 1931 at the latest, while passive countries allowed price and monetary deflation to run its course. The real exchange rates shown in Table 20.4 can be taken as proxies for the domestic price of importable goods relative to the nontraded goods price. It is only a proxy because it does not take into account increments in protection, due either to tariffs or quantitative restrictions, while using the US cost of living as an indicator of international prices for Latin American importable goods.

While the neglect of protection underestimates the increase in the relative price of importables, the second consideration probably contributes toward over-estimation. Policy-makers who permitted budget deficits induced by economic and political circumstances, abandoned gold convertibility and allowed the exchange rate to depreciate, did so, on the whole, moved by survival instincts rather than inspired by the writings of economists either defunct, or living. But in some countries the institutional structure was compatible with those actions, while in others it was not.

Performance

The 1930s belong to the prenational accounts era. Table 20.8 pulls together available *ex post* estimates for GDP growth during the 1930s and 1940s. The four largest Latin American countries (Argentina, Brazil, Colombia and Mexico) do register growth rates superior to those of Canada and the USA for the 1930s. Neither the absolute GDP growth for the 1930s, nor its level relative to the growth achieved during the 1940s, however, are impressive. In the cases of Argentina and Colombia GDP seems to have expanded during the 1920s at clearly faster rates than those shown for the 1930s. For Brazil, the source used in Table 20.8 indicates an annual GDP growth rate higher for 1919–29 than for 1929–39; for Mexico, the opposite is the case, comparing 1921–9 with 1929–39.

Measurements of GDP do not take into account losses of real income arising from deteriorating terms of trade. If these were taken into account, the aggregate Latin American performance during the 1930s would look worse relative to those within the region for the 1920s and 1940s, as well as in comparison with the industrialized countries during the 1930s. In the case of Brazil, for example, 1929–39 growth corrected for terms of trade drops to 3·2 percent per annum, while for 1919–29 growth increases to 7·3 (Haddad, 1980, pp. 36–7).

Table 20.9 subdivides the evolution of GDP into four plausible periods: crisis (1929–33), recovery (1933–9), war (1939–45) and postwar (1945–9). It can be argued that in several Latin American countries recovery started before 1933; data, however, do not warrant much preoccupation at this stage with turning points. Table 20.9 indicates that for the four largest Latin American countries neither the crisis, nor the recovery, were as sharp as those in Canada and the USA. It should be borne in mind that value added in rural activities made up a large share of GDP in those days; even for Argentina, the country with the highest per capita income, rural activities made up nearly one-quarter of GDP in 1929, according to the major source used in Tables 20.8 and 20.9.

Economic performance during the 1930s for at least the largest Latin American countries looks more impressive when attention is focused on manufacturing. While manufacturing growth during the 1940s exceeded that for the 1930s in most countries, as shown in Table 20.10, the Latin American

Table 20.8　Real Gross Domestic Product at Factor Cost (average annual percentage rates of change)

	1929–39	1939–49
Argentina	1·6	3·0
Brazil	4·3	4·8
Chile	0*	3·3§
Colombia	3·8	3·7
Honduras	−1·0	3·8
Mexico	2·1	5·9
Uruguay	1·0†	3·4
USA‡	0·3	4·5
Canada‡	0·5	5·5

*Refers to 1929–40.
†Refers to 1930–39.
‡Refers to Gross National Product.
§Refers to 1940–49.
Sources:
Basic data for Argentina, Chile (1940–49), Colombia, Honduras, Mexico and Uruguay (1939–49) obtained from United Nations (1978); basic data for Uruguay (1930–39) obtained from Millot *et al.* (1972, p. 251); basic data for the USA obtained from Council of Economic Advisors (1974); basic data for Canada obtained from Urquhart and Buckley (1965, pp. 132, 475); basic data for Chile (1929–40) refers to an index for 'aggregate' output, made up by five basic sectors which during 1950–57 made up about one-half of Chilean GNP, see Ballesteros and Davis (1963, pp. 152–77); basic data for Brazil obtained from Haddad (1980, pp. 25–6).

Table 20.9　Real Gross Domestic Product at Factor Cost (total percentage changes)

	1929–33	1933–9	1939–45	1945–9
Argentina	−9·7	29·2	13·2	18·9
Brazil	7·7	40·9	21·9	30·9
Colombia	9·9	31·6	16·8	23·3
Honduras	−8·6	−2·0	23·1	18·6
Mexico	−10·3	37·2	43·3	24·0
Uruguay	n.a.	n.a.	10·4	26·1
Chile*	−36·9	50·6	33·3	9·9
USA†	−30·5	48·0	69·6	−8·8
Canada†	−29·8	50·0	63·1	5·1

*Until 1945, Chilean data refers to the Ballesteros–Davis (1963) index for 'aggregate' output, made up by five basic sectors which during 1950–57 made up about one-half of the Chilean GNP.
†Refers to Real Gross National Product.
Source:
As Table 20.8.

Table 20.10 *Real Manufacturing Output at Factor Cost (average annual percentage rates of change)*

	1929–39	1939–49
Argentina	3·1	3·5
Brazil	6·4	7·2
Chile	3·3†	4·8
Colombia	8·8	6·7
Honduras	1·4	6·1
Mexico	4·3	7·5
Uruguay	5·2‡	5·7
Cuba	−1·6§	4·8
USA*	−0·6	6·1
Canada*	0·8	7·5

*Refers to Index of Total Manufacturing Output.
†Refers to 1927–39.
‡Refers to 1930–39.
§Refers to 1930–39.
Sources:
Basic data for Argentina, Colombia, Honduras, Mexico and Uruguay (1939–49) as Table 20.8; basic data for Uruguay (1930–39) and Brazil (1929–39) also as Table 20.8; basic data for Chile obtained from Munoz (1968, pp. 160–61); basic data for the USA and Canada as Table 20.8; basic data for Cuba obtained from Perez-Lopez (1977, table 3-7, p. 52); the index refers to total industrial production; basic data for Brazil (1939–49) obtained from United Nations (1978).

growth rates clearly exceed those of Canada and the USA for the 1930s.[10] In the important case of Brazil manufacturing growth during the 1930s was significantly higher than during the 1920s (6·4 percent per annum versus 5·2); Colombian industrialization in the 1930s could not have been much behind the pace of the 1920s, if at all.

It is generally accepted that pre-1929 Latin American manufacturing grew, *pari passu*, with the rest of the basically export-oriented economy. Beyond some moderate protectionism, public policy departed little from a neutral attitude toward industry. Important segments of manufacturing relied directly on the export of (slightly) processed primary products; examples include meat-packing plants in the River Plate and sugar mills in several countries. Growth of manufacturing during the recovery phase of the 1930s relied overwhelmingly on import substitution, defined in the usual 'accounting' sense, which focuses on output rather than installed capacity. Comparing Tables 20.11 and 20.9 it may be seen that manufacturing expansion far exceeded that of GDP during 1933–9; note that this was not the case for Canada and the USA. Also in contrast with those two industrialized countries, manufacturing growth during 1933–9 for most Latin American countries shown in Table 20.11 exceeded that achieved during the war.

If there was an engine of growth in Latin America during the 1930s, that engine was import-substituting industrialization. Not surprisingly, the uneven

Table 20.11   *Real Manufacturing Output at Factor Cost (total percentage changes)*

	1929–33	1933–9	1939–45	1945–9
Argentina	−6·5	44·7	23·5	14·6
Brazil	6·9	74·2	36·0	47·4
Colombia	24·8	86·0	34·8	42·0
Honduras	−13·2	32·5	31·8	37·2
Mexico	−7·9	65·3	71·0	20·8
Uruguay	n.a.	n.a.	22·6	41·6
Chile	−6·4	37·7	34·7	18·5
Cuba	−50·0†	73·4	29.0	23.7
USA*	−38.6	53.6	98.3	−9.2
Canada*	−33.2	61.5	90.8	7.6

*Refers to Index of Total Manufacturing Output.
†Refers to 1930–33.
Source:
Basic data for Argentina, Brazil, Colombia, Honduras, Mexico and Uruguay as Table 20.10; basic data for Chile obtained from Munoz (1968, pp. 160–61) for 1939–49, and from Ballesteros and Davis (1963, pp. 160–61) for 1929–39; basic data for USA and Canada as Table 20.8; basic data for Cuba as Table 20.10.

performance by different sectors implied by such a proposition can also be found within manufacturing. Even as some manufacturing activities closely dependent on pre-1929 export-oriented prosperity were shrinking, other activities (sometimes a handful) made dramatic output advances during the 1930s. Such leading sectors typically included textiles, building materials (especially cement), petroleum-refining, tires, pharmaceuticals, toiletries and food-processing for the home market. Among these activities, textiles appear as quantitatively the most important, often providing more than 20 percent of the net expansion of value added in manufacturing and growing at annual rates above 10 percent during the 1930s. The main exception seems to have been Brazil, where earlier industrialization in the consumer-goods sectors of textiles, shoes, clothing and foodstuffs meant that during the 1930s the most rapidly growing industries were those producing intermediate and capital goods.[11]

The industrialization drive of the 1930s seems to have been quite labor-intensive and based on small and medium-sized firms, many newly created. It has been estimated (de Barros and Graham, 1978, p. 12), for example, that in 1930–37 total industrial employment in São Paulo grew at a rate of 10·9 percent per year; the output elasticity of employment was about 1. Real wages appear to have been relatively constant in most countries, with the stagnant primary sector providing an ample reservoir of workers and also, on the whole, an elastic supply of foodstuffs. This view is consistent with the changes in relative prices noted earlier, with both the prices of exportable and nontraded goods falling relative to those of importable goods, with prices for exportable goods falling the most.

The industrialization drive squeezed installed capacity; there are frequent reports of textile mills working two and three shifts even in the early 1930s. In the Brazilian and Peruvian cases the 1920s left substantial excess capacity; large investments had taken place in the Brazilian cement industry during the late 1920s, for example. Statistics do not show an upsurge in imports of machinery and equipment, although one may conjecture that there were substantial changes in the composition of these imports between the 1920s and 1930s. There are indications that the import-substituting drive relied heavily on new entrepreneurs, including fresh immigrants from the troubled Europe of the 1930s. There was direct foreign investment in import substitution,[12] but its role seems relatively smaller than what was to be in later years.

Internationally comparable data are available for the cement industry, which in some ways can be taken as representative of the 1930s industrial success stories (although it was more capital-intensive and foreign-dominated than the textile industry). Table 20.12 presents apparent cement consumption, first; on the whole, it confirms the hypothesis that larger and active countries performed better than North America and than smaller and passive Latin American countries, even if the implied annual growth rate of apparent consumption is far from spectacular. What *is* spectacular is the evolution of the share of consumption supplied domestically, shown in the last two columns, and the implied growth rates in cement production from 1928–9 to 1937–38. During those nine years cement output multiplied by more than fourteen times in Colombia, by more than six times in Brazil and by almost four times in Argentina. By 1937–8 the large and active Latin American countries had become practically self-sufficient in cement.

Changes in income distribution during the 1930s are unclear. In the industrial sector higher prices for import-competing goods combined with a

Table 20.12   *Cement: Consumption and Output*

	Apparent cement consumption in 1937–8 (1928–29 = 100)	Domestic output as percentage of apparent consumption 1928–9	1937–8
Argentina	153	37	92
Brazil	112	16	91
Chile	114	43	99
Colombia	118	6	74
Mexico	148	88	97
Peru	136	46	66
Uruguay	77	81	90
Cuba	34	93	93
Dominican Republic	74	0	0
Haiti	58	0	0
Central American Republics (six)	100	12	11
Canada	51	—	—
USA	63	—	—

Source:
Basic data in physical magnitudes obtained from the European Cement Association (1974); apparent consumption refers to cement production plus imports less exports.

fairly elastic labor supply must have generated large profits. Yet important redistributive structural changes occurred in the rural sectors of a number of countries, partly induced by the weakening of traditional land-intensive exports. Thorp and Bertram (1978) note that in Peru with the decline of the landowners' authority there was an increase in the equality of the distribution of rural income; a similar trend appears to have taken place in Cuba. The acceleration in the Mexican land reform has already been noted; in Brazil many coffee plantations were parceled away; in Colombia the Alfonso Lopez administration carried out less dramatic, but significant, land and tax reforms[13].

To summarize regarding performance: during the 1930s large and active Latin American economies showed an impressive capacity to transform, generating new leading sectors within manufacturing. By the late 1930s those economies had become more self-reliant; in spite of GDP growth, import volumes (with $1928-9 = 100$) by $1938-9$ had dropped to seventy-two in Argentina, seventy in Brazil, eighty-seven in Colombia, fifty-six in Chile and seventy-two in Mexico (data as Table 20.1). The performance of small and passive economies seems to have been poorer. Even though traces of response to the new constellation of international prices can also be seen in those economies, and although they appear to have also engaged in some import substitution (even in Cuba import-replacing activities such as milk-processing and cotton cloth expanded rapidly), those efforts were weak relative to both the depressive forces originating in their primary sectors, and to the industrialization drives of the active and large countries. In those small countries with a large and flexible subsistence sector, as in Central America, the welfare consequences of this involution were better than in Cuba, where the rural sector provided little room for those unemployed in export and related activities. It may also be noted that some small countries which were then outright colonies, such as Jamaica, Puerto Rico and the Philippines benefited from 1930s metropolitan protectionism. Thus, Puerto Rican and Philippine sugar exports rose, while those of Cuba sank, and Jamaican banana exports to the United Kingdom gained at the expense of those from Central America.

There is truth in the assertion that the Latin American countries which performed reasonably well during the 1930s were those which had large domestic markets and some pre-1929 industrial base, as in the cases of Argentina, Brazil, Colombia and Mexico. But this fails to explain the contrasting performance of Chile and Uruguay, on one side, versus that of Cuba. These three countries in 1929 had reached roughly similar levels of population and income. In contrast with Chile and Uruguay, however, Cuba did not have a central bank during the 1930s and maintained its currency rigidly pegged to the US dollar; and as already noted, actually lowered tariffs in 1934. One may conclude that a minimum size in the domestic market *plus* a minimum degree of autonomy regarding the exchange rate, fiscal and monetary policies were necessary conditions for industrialization during the 1930s in Latin America.

Final Observations

The key role given in this chapter to the exchange rate as a variable which can stimulate growth and avoid monetary deflation may be found in the literature both for Latin America, and elsewhere. Milton Friedman and Anna Jacobson Schwartz have noted that over 1929–31 China was hardly affected internally by the crisis; China had a silver standard, which was equivalent to a floating exchange rate with respect to gold-standard countries. During 1929–31 its currency luckily depreciated, a situation reversed when the United Kingdom and then the USA abandoned the gold standard (Friedman and Schwartz, 1963, pp. 361–2, 489–90). The silver standard had served well countries adhering to it in an earlier Depression; during 1873–94 income grew significantly more rapidly in silver-standard countries than in those adhering to the gold standard (Nugent, 1973, pp. 1110–35). The good performance of the Swedish economy during the 1930s has been credited in part to the large depreciation of the krona in 1931 (Lundberg, 1957, p. 107). Dudley Seers used a typology similar to that used in this chapter to discuss Latin American economic performance during 1929–58, grouping together eleven countries following a dollar exchange standard, which consistently had high dollar or gold backing for the local currency and little exchange control. He also notes that governments of these countries made only sparing use of import quotas or tariffs, partly because the application of trade controls was restricted by various reciprocal agreements with the USA.[14] Celso Furtado also stressed the key role of the exchange rate, when analyzing the Brazilian industrialization of the 1930s (Furtado, 1963, chs 32 and 33).

Most mainstream economists, whether of the 1930 or 1980 vintage, would be inclined to give Latin American countries policy advice based on international trade and finance models using the small-country assumption. Trade theory asserts that a truly small country facing perfectly elastic demands and supplies for its exports and imports, respectively, should follow the same trade policy, that is, free trade, regardless of what is going on in the rest of the world. Uncertainty as to the terms of trade will not change matters much, unless one is willing to attribute to government insights unavailable to the private sector. International finance theory adds that a small country will (and should) have little control over exchange-rate and monetary policy; pegging to a key currency and following 'gold-exchange-standard' monetary rules, including free convertibility, are the usual prescriptions for the small, regardless of external circumstances.

Like Walrasian auction markets, smallness in foreign trade and finance is a powerful theoretical construct which may be more insightful in some circumstances than others. In a world of trade quotas, convertibility restrictions or foreign tariffs which are imposed depending on the success of one's export drives, it could be that not even Andorra is small. Optimum currency-area theory, stimulating as it is, gives little practical guidance for drawing the line between small-peggers and large-flexers. The Latin American experience of the

1930s shows that smallness in foreign trade and finance is not an intrinsic and permanent characteristic of a country, but a result of specific conditions in the world economy and changing domestic circumstances. Foreign trade and payments policy for a Latin American-type economy should depend on what is expected to happen in (and on unexpected shocks coming from) the rest of the world.

The fine tuning of international trade and financial policies could lead to extreme protectionism and the loss of 'moneyness' for the national currency. Many Latin American countries during the 1940s and 1950s carried to excess policies initiated during the 1930s, even as world markets became more buoyant. But the advice that developing countries should design their trade and financial policies as if the state of the world economy did not matter (or as if they were small at all times), suggests evangelical fervor rather than scientific analysis or historical knowledge.

Chapter 20: Notes

I gratefully acknowledge comments from Edmar Bacha, Marcelo Cavarozzi, Stanley Engerman, Albert Fishlow, Charles Kindleberger, Paul Krugman, Arthur Lewis and Jose Antonio Ocampo. Cynthia L. Arfken generated most data found in this paper and Virginia Casey efficiently typed it. They cannot be blamed for the opinions and possible errors in the paper.

1 See, for example, André Gunder Frank (1972, ch. 7). The decline in the role of foreign trade and capital after 1929, Frank (1972, p. 75) argues, also reduced 'the transfer of satellite investment resources to the metropolis'. See also A. G. Frank (1969, p. 148–50). The weakening of ties between metropolis and satellite, he argues, will lead to the satellite's involution, which may be toward an isolated subsistence economy or toward a more or less autonomous industrialization, as during the Great Depression.

2 See Kindleberger (1973, ch. 4). External conditions had been unfavorable for Cuban sugar during the late 1920s; the Peruvian and Brazilian economies had been sluggish before the Great Depression struck. The Brazilian control over the international coffee market was slipping badly during the 1920s and even without the Great Depression the Brazilian economy would have required significant reorientation. Competition from synthetic nitrates hurt Chilean export earnings throughout the 1920s.

3 Such a steep fall in terms of trade, however, was not unprecedented. The Argentine terms of trade, for example, fell by 37 percent between 1916–17 and 1921–2; see Diaz-Alejandro (1980, table S-5).

4 Qualifications to that first approximation are necessary. For example, Kindleberger (1973, p. 103) argues that the devaluation of the Argentine peso during 1930 contributed to the decline in the dollar price of wheat in international markets. Brazil attempted to influence world coffee prices since the beginning of this century, and Cuba undertook similar attempts for sugar in the late 1920s. In the unusual Bolivian case the major domestic producer of tin (Patino) had enough influence over the world market to enforce a kind of commodity stabilization scheme, see Whitehead (1972, pp. 66–7).

5 Breaking from orthodoxy was not easy. In Argentina authorities who remembered the inconvertible paper standard of the late nineteenth century feared that a departure from the gold standard would lead to inflation (their fears did not come true until the 1940s). For the hesitations in the Chilean case, see Albert O. Hirschman (1963, pp. 178–83). Hirschman (1963, p. 179) writes: 'In contrast to such countries as Brazil, Argentina, Uruguay and Mexico which pragmatically opted for or stumbled on "reflationary" techniques, Chile followed the famous "rules of the game" strictly until mid-1931.'

6 In the preface to his book, Ellsworth (1945, p. vii) remarks that his interest in Chile was aroused while teaching mechanisms of adjustment to balance of payments disturbances. In

the United Kingdom tariffs had been advocated before the abandonment of the gold standard as an alternative to depreciation; after 1931 *both* tariffs, *and* a depreciated pound (with respect to the US dollar), coexisted.

7 The United Kingdom percentage share in the value of Argentine merchandise imports evolved as follows (Diaz-Alejandro, 1970, p. 46):

1927–9:	18·9
1930–33:	21·4
1934–6:	24·9
1937–9:	21·0.

8 For a review of the controversy, and new interpretations, see Albert Fishlow (1972). See also Eliana Anastasia Cardoso (1979, ch. II). Fishlow and Cardoso argue that the new taxes (or the exchange-rate appreciation generated by foreign loans) improved the Brazilian terms of trade. It may be noted that during the 1930s (and before) Colombia expanded her share in the international coffee market taking advantage of the Brazilian export taxes and quotas.

9 Data from Diaz-Alejandro (1970, p. 490); Villela and Suzigan (1977, pp. 346–9, tables 117 and 118).

10 Another interesting comparison involves Argentine versus Australian performance. Between 1928 and 1938 the GDP of both countries grew approximately at the same rates; Argentine manufacturing, however, grew significantly faster than that of Australia between those years.

11 See Albert Fishlow (1980). For an excellent case study documenting the acceleration of import substitution by the Argentine textile industry during the 1930s see Alberto O. Petrecolla (1968, esp. ch. 4). Import substitution was especially fast for cotton-yarn fabrics. Petrecolla attributes the increased profitability of the Argentine textile industry to higher tariffs on final goods and the depreciated exchange rate, on the one hand, and to lower prices for raw cotton and wool, on the other. Money wage rates in the textile industry in 1936–7–8 were about 5 percent below those of 1929, and the importation of textile machinery remained free. Alberto Petrecolla (1968, p. 61) notes that during the 1930s in Argentina the increase in the number of textile firms accounted for approximately 65 percent of the increase in spindles held by the industry.

12 See the fascinating book of Phelps (1936).

13 See Rosemary Thorp and Geoffrey Bertram (1978, ch. 9); Ramiro Guerra y Sanchez (1944, esp. prologue to 3rd edn); Hirschman, (1963, ch. 2).

14 Seers (1962, pp. 183–4). The eleven countries are Venezuela, Cuba, Guatemala, Dominican Republic, Ecuador, Costa Rica, El Salvador, Nicaragua, Panama, Haiti and Honduras. Seers (1962, p. 185) argued: 'The eleven countries . . . were politically better able than the remaining republics of Latin America to face stagnation or decline in domestic incomes, such as is involved for countries on the dollar-exchange standard if their exports stagnate or decline. Profits of foreign companies in export industries absorb a high proportion of export fluctuations, a big fraction of the labour force is in the subsistence sector (or can return to it), and the working classes have little political power.'

Chapter 20: References

Ballesteros, M. A. and Davis, T. E., 'The growth of output and employment in basic sectors of the Chilean economy, 1908–1957', *Economic Development and Cultural Change*, vol. 11, no. 2, pt 1 (1963), pp. 152–77.

de Barros, J. R. M. and Graham, D. H., *The Economic Recovery and Market Deconcentration of the Paulista Textile Industry during the Great Depression: 1928–1937* (Ohio State University, March 1978, mimeo).

Cardoso, F. H. and Faletto, E., *Dependency and Development in Latin American* (Berkeley, Calif.,: University of California Press, 1978).

Cardoso, E. A., 'Inflation, growth and the real exchange rate: essays on economic history in Brazil', Ph.D thesis (Massachusetts Institute of Technology, February 1979).

Chu, D. S. C., 'The Great Depression and industrialization in Colombia', *RAND Paper Series*, P-5015 (January 1977).

Diaz-Alejandro, C. F., *Essays on the Economic History of the Argentine Republic* (New Haven, Conn.: Yale University Press, 1970).

Diaz-Alejandro, C. F., *Exchange Rates and Terms of Trade in the Argentine Republic, 1913–1976* (New Haven, Conn.: Economic Growth Center Discussion Paper, January 1980, mimeo.).

Dominguez, J. I., *Cuba: Order and Revolution* (Cambridge, Mass.: Harvard University Press, 1978).

Ellsworth, P. T., *Chile: An Economy in Transition* (New York: Macmillan, 1945).

European Cement Association, *World Cement Market in Figures* (Paris: European Cement Association, 1974).

Fishlow, A., 'Origins and consequences of import substitution in Brazil', in Luis de Marco, ed., *International Economics and Development* (New York: Academic Press, 1972), pp. 311–65.

Fishlow, A., 'Brazilian development in long-term perspective', *American Economic Review*, vol. 70, no. 2 (1980), pp. 102–8.

Frank, A. G., *Capitalism and Underdevelopment in Latin America; Historical Studies of Chile and Brazil* (New York: MR Modern Reader, 1969).

Frank, A. G., *Lumpenbourgeoisie; Lumpendevelopment. Dependence, Class and Politics in Latin America* (New York: Monthly Review Press, 1972).

Friedman, M. and Schwartz, A. J., *A Monetary History of the United States, 1867–1960* (Princeton, NJ: Princeton University Press, 1963).

Furtado, C., *The Economic Growth of Brazil* (Berkeley, Calif.: University of California Press, 1963).

Haddad, C. L. S., 'Crescimento economico do Brasil, 1900–76', in P. Neuhaus, ed., *Economia Brasileira: Uma Visao Historica* (Rio de Janeiro: Editora Campus, 1980), pp. 21–43.

Hirschman, A. O., *The Strategy of Economic Development* (New Haven, Conn.: Yale University Press, 1958).

Hirschman, A. O., *Journeys Toward Progress; Studies of Economic Policy Making in Latin America* (New York: Twentieth Century Fund, 1963).

Kafka, A., 'The theoretical interpretation of Latin American economic development', in H. S. Ellis, ed., *Economic Development for Latin America; Proceedings of a Conference held by the International Economic Association* (London: Macmillan, 1961), pp. 1–29.

Kindleberger, C. P., *The World in Depression, 1929–1939* (Berkeley, Calif.: University of California Press, 1973).

Lundberg, E., *Business Cycles and Economic Policy* (London: Allen & Unwin, 1957).

Millot, J., Silva, C. and Silva, L., *El Desarrollo Industrial del Uruguay, de la crisis de 1929 a la posguerra* (Montevideo: Universidad de la Republica Instituto de Economia, 1972).

Ministerio de Hacienda, Direccion General de Estadistica, *Resumenes Estadisticos Seleccionados* (La Habana: Ministerio de Hacienda, 1959).

Munoz, G. O., *Crecimiento Industrial de Chile, 1914–1965* (Santiago: Universidad de Chile Instituto de Economia y Planificacion, 1968).

Nugent, J. B., 'Exchange-rate movements and economic development in the late nineteenth century', *Journal of Political Economy*, vol. 81, no. 5 (1973), pp. 1110–35.

Perez-Lopez, J. F., 'An index of Cuban industrial output, 1930–58', in J. W. Wilkie and K. Ruddle, eds, *Quantitative Latin American Studies, Methods and Findings* (Los Angeles: UCLA Latin American Center Publications, 1977), pp. 37–72.

Petrecolla, A. O., *Prices, Import Substitution and Investment in the Argentine Textile Industry (1920–1939)*, Instituto Torcuato Di Tella (November 1968, mimeo.).

Phelps, D. M., 'Industrial expansion in temperate South America', *American Economic Review*, vol. 25, no. 2 (1935), pp. 273–83.

Phelps, D. M., *Migration of Industry to South America* (New York: McGraw-Hill, 1936).

y Sanchez, R. G., *Azucar y Poblacion en las Antillas* (La Habana: Cultural SA, 1944).

Seers, D., 'A theory of inflation and growth in underdeveloped economies based on the experience of Latin America', *Oxford Economic Papers*, vol. 14, no. 2 (1962), pp. 173–96.

Silber, S., 'Analise da politica economica e do comportamento da economia Brasileira durante o periodo 1929–39', in F. R. Versiani and J. R. M. de Barros, eds, *Formacao Economica do Brasil; A Experiencia da Industrializacao* (São Paulo: Saraiva SA, 1977), pp. 173–208.

Solis, L., *La Realidad Economica Mexicana: Retrovision y Perspectivas* (Mexico, DF: Siglo XX, 1970).

Thorp, R. and Bertram, G., *Peru 1890–1977; Growth and Policy in an Open Economy* (New York: Columbia University Press, 1978).

United Nations, *America Latina: Relacion de Precios del Intercambio*, Cuadernos de la CEPAL (Santiago: UN, 1976).

United Nations, *Series Historicas del Crecimiento de America Latina*, Cuadernos de la CEPAL (Santiago: UN, 1978).

Urquhart, M. C. and Buckley, K. A. H. (eds), *Historical Statistics of Canada* (Cambridge: Cambridge University Press, 1965).

US Council of Economic Advisors, *Economic Report of the President* (Washington, DC: US Council of Economic Advisors, 1974).

US Department of Commerce, *Statistical Abstract of the United States* (Washington, DC: US Department of Commerce, 1965).

Villela, A. V. and Suzigan, W., *Government Policy and the Economic Growth of Brazil, 1889–1945*, IPEA, Rio de Janeiro, Brazilian Economic Studies No. 3 (1977).

Wallich, H. C., *Monetary Problems of an Export Economy: The Cuban Experience, 1914–1947* (Cambridge, Mass.: Harvard University Press, 1950).

Whitehead, L., 'El impacto de la Gran Depresion en Bolivia', *Desarrollo Economico*, vol. 12, no. 15 (1972), pp. 49–80.

21

Indian Industrialization before 1945

IAN M. D. LITTLE

The allegedly evil effects of the impact of Britain on Indian industry are very widely cited[1] as the outstanding example of the manner in which colonialism and/or trade with capitalist countries could destroy indigenous manufacture and lock the dominated economy into the subservient position of supplying the materials for capitalist expansion. Some Marxists would not agree to any distinction between the evils of colonialism, and those of trade with the capitalist West. For those economists and politicians who do not accept this article of faith, the distinction is of great importance. A colonial power has many means at its disposal to exact tribute and to manipulate the economy of the colony in what it believes to be its own interest, means which are not open to a trading partner, however powerful. Government by foreigners may also have inhibiting effects apart from any deliberate exercise of influence.

For those who are openminded, and wish to assess the benefits and possible costs and dangers of trade with capitalist countries, and the receipt of private investment and aid from them, there may be something to learn from history if we can find out what actually happened in the colonial era, and separate out the effects of trade and investment from those of being ruled by foreigners. In the case of India I shall concentrate most on the cotton-textile industry because it is the *cause célèbre*, and by far the most important industry in the time of the British Raj. But other industries, especially those founded before the First World War, will also be discussed.

Indian handicrafts were famous in the eighteenth century, including not only cloth and clothing, but also jewelry and metalware including weapons. There are no figures to indicate how important they were to the economy, but Maddison (1971) guesses 6·5 percent of national income, of which 1·5 percent was exported. There seems to be some difference of opinion as to how far this was purely a luxury trade, but it is difficult to believe that handicrafts exported to the rest of Asia could, given the high cost of transport, have spread far down the income scale. Most of this production was lost. The causes were, however, complex. Indian demand itself declined as an indirect result of British rule, which eliminated much of the local aristocracy. Demand for Indian cottons and silks declined in the USA, continental Europe and Arabia, as well as in the United Kingdom. The fall in exports to the USA appears to have been as large as that to the United Kingdom (Dutt, 1976, p. 205). Part of this was also due to tastes, but much must have been due to the competition of Lancashire.

Lancashire received heavy infant industry protection, but costs were reduced so fast by new techniques that it is reasonable to doubt whether the protection made much difference to British imports for long. Moreover, however reprehensible the protection, it can surely have made little difference to the total fall in Indian exports. It is notable that British duties were substantially reduced over 1824–32, but Indian exports still fell steeply (Dutt, 1976, p. 203). India's export trade in handicrafts was killed by the Industrial Revolution, not by the British Raj.

But what of the domestic market? Here, the power of colonialism comes in. During 1814–59 the Indian tariff on cotton piece-goods was 5 percent, and 3·5 percent on yarn (Harnetty, 1972, ch. 2). While the purpose was revenue, these duties were protective; but, of course, only very slightly so. Undoubtedly, an independent government would have protected far more, and might even have tried to bargain its duties against those of Europe and North America, where modern textile industries were in the making. Imports into India do not seem to have amounted to much until after the Napoleonic wars, when they began to grow rapidly, and contributed to the decline of high-quality spinning and weaving in India. To the extent that Lancashire flooded the Indian market over say, 1821–49, this was partly satisfying an increasing demand which went hand in hand with rising consumption. Thus, Dharma Kumar (1972) quotes J. B. Barpujari, as claiming that Indian handloom production, but not spinning, *rose* from around 1830 despite a large rise in imports of cotton piece-goods. It is also worth noting that the value of Indian exports rose quite fast from 1834–5 to 1850–5, by 5·25 percent per annum in a period of falling prices (Tooke, 1971, table G).

Before turning to the period after the mid-1850s which saw (a) the beginning of more reliable figures, (b) the founding of a modern factory-textile industry in India, it is worth reflecting on the fate of the spinners and the weavers in the first half of the nineteenth century. Spinning was normally a part-time occupation for women. They appear to have earned very little from it. [2] All agree that hand-spinning gradually ceased over the course of the century, and some of this was probably a clear loss in so far as women could find no other earnings. There was still some spinning at the turn of the century, but apparently a day's spinning earned only 1 anna – perhaps a little more than 100 years earlier.

The hardest time for the handloom weavers was probably the 1820s, the scanty evidence suggesting that there was no decline in output in any other period,[3] but this does not necessarily mean that there was no decline in earnings. Weaving is a low-caste occupation in India, despite the skills involved. In the early years of the nineteenth century it does not appear that coarse-cloth weavers earned more than laborers. In Dutt (1976) (again quoting Dr Buchanan's survey of northern India) there are some scrappy figures. In one district earnings of R. 28 per loom (worked by a family of three) can be compared with a ploughman's earnings of R. 16–22. In another earnings per loom were estimated at R. 20·75, but this was disbelieved since minimum subsistence for a family was reckoned at R. 48. In a third district, earnings per loom were estimated at R. 20–32: in a fourth at R. 23·5 – but here again Dr Buchanan disbelieved his estimate, presumably since it was below subsistence, and suggested R. 36. Weavers of fine cloths and silks evidently earned much more, up to around R. 100 per loom. Jumping a century, we quote A. K. Bagchi, who sums up a discussion of weaving wages in the early years of the twentieth century '. . . before the First World War, generally speaking, weavers were just a cut above common labourers in urban centres as regards wages; while the lower limit of weaver's wages was reached by common labourers, the upper was not' (Bagchi, 1972, p. 225). Their relative position so far as very scanty evidence goes, seems not to have changed in 100 years. But the situation was almost certainly worse in the 1820s or early 1830s. This is the period when contemporary accounts most strongly insisted on the distress caused by imports (including the oft-repeated statement, 'The Governor-General reported 1834–35: "The misery hardly finds a parallel in the history of commerce. The bones of the cotton-weavers are bleaching the plains of India"'[4]). There is no reason to suppose that weavers could not be and were not absorbed into agriculture, and most weavers would not have had a significantly reduced standard of living by becoming agricultural workers. However, distress is always caused by the adjustment required of those with skills which are no longer in strong demand. In a better world the transition would surely have been eased, if not by protection, then by adjustment assistance; but it is questionable whether there should still be such protection of hand-weaving (and spinning) after another 160 years.

Let us turn back to the mid-nineteenth century. Imports of cotton piece-goods had reached about £5 mn. (37 percent of total imports) and yarn and twist about £3 mn. This suggested import substitution. The first Bombay mill was founded in 1853. This as well as subsequent development was almost entirely Indian, on the part of Parsis and Gujeratis (only much later Marwaris), both in conception and financing; but management, to a considerable extent, was European, and remained so for a long time. Tariffs were 5 percent on cloth and 35 percent on yarn. Development was probably delayed by the American Civil War, which caused an enormous rise in cotton prices and made exporting highly profitable (Lidman and Domrese, 1970, p. 323). In 1871 there were eleven factories, and thereafter growth was rapid (Harnetty, 1972, p. 33). In 1880–1900 employment in the mills rose from about 40,000 (in 58 mills) to 156,000 (in 194 mills), a growth rate of over 7 percent per annum (Lidman and Domrese, 1970, table 12b). This was a period of pure free trade, since all import duties were removed in 1882,[5] and protection was not to be revived until 1917 (new import duties in 1894 and 1896 were matched by equal excise duties). The new mills did much, of course, to reduce the growth of imports. Over 1850–70 the sterling value of imports of cotton yarn, twist and piece-goods rose at a rate of 6·6 percent per annum. During 1870–1900 they rose at only 0·6 percent per annum (no doubt this owes something to a rise in prices in the first twenty years, and a fall in 1870–1900, but unfortunately, we have no quantity figures for imports for this period, nor production figures).

The position in 1900 was that imports of piece-goods still accounted for 64 percent of total supplies, handloom for 22 percent and mill products for 14 percent (Bagchi, 1972, table 7-I). It has been observed that there was rather little direct competition between Lancashire and India. Lancashire supplied the finer end of the market, and also bleached and printed goods, while India supplied coarse grey cloth: by this time actual competition lay more between the mills and the handlooms. The insistence of the secretary of state in 1894 and 1896 on an excise tax on mill output, is more accurately to be regarded as an insistence on protecting the handlooms from the mills than it is to be regarded as a refusal to protect the mills from Lancashire though, of course, the participants in the debate did not see it like that. This is not to deny that more rapid penetration of the finer counts by the mills might have been achieved, if there had been significant protection or other encouragement in the last quarter of the nineteenth century.

Progress was quite rapid up to 1913–14. The mills began to extend their product range in this period. From 1900–1901 to 1913–14, mill production rose at an annual rate of 8·2 percent, imports 3·8 percent and handloom production 3·6 percent. Import substitution and handloom substitution was proceeding, under free trade for the mills and slight protection for handlooms. 1913–14 was in absolute terms the peak year for imports, but their share in total supply had fallen to 58 percent. The mills now accounted for 22 percent and handlooms for 20 percent. Exports remained very small.

In yarn the line of demarcation between Lancashire and India was even clearer. Only 6 percent of yarn production was in counts over twenty-four, and almost none of this was exported. Over 95 percent of yarn imports were in counts over twenty-five. In the years 1899–1901 only 6·5 percent of yarn supplies were imported, and 16 percent was exported. The imports were presumably for those few handloom weavers who were still producing fine cloth. Exports were of coarse yarns to China and Japan. This trade may have benefited to the extent that free trade imposed on China and Japan under the 'unequal' treaties delayed the latter's factory spinning industry. But India began to lose this trade to Japan around 1905. Thus, yarn exports almost halved during 1905–11.

Over 1913–38 mill piece-good production rose at an annual rate of 4·9 percent, imports fell (from their peak) at a rate of −6·1 percent and handloom production rose at 2·1 percent per annum.[6] Mill production in 1938 accounted for 63 percent of supplies, imports for 10 percent and handloom for 27 percent. Exports remained very small. Imports at the beginning of the period were almost all British; at the end they were more than half Japanese. London had become less firmly anti-protectionist after the First World War and was more ready to let India protect against Japan than Lancashire, especially as Japan exported coarse cloth. There was quantitative protection during the First World War, and duties were raised to 7·5 percent in 1917 (with no increase in the excise on mill production of 3·5 percent). Handloom production suffered seriously from the reduction in yarn imports, almost halving in 1913–19.

Japanese imports began to grow rapidly, to exceed the British by 1935. Import duties on cloth were raised again to 11 percent in 1921, and the excise duty was removed in 1925.[7] Duties were raised again and again in 1930–33 to reach 75 percent on non-British goods, after which quotas were introduced for Japanese goods and the duty lowered to 50 percent (25 percent for the United Kingdom). After the war, the Indian mill industry fell rapidly behind that of Japan in efficiency. The Japanese industry had started twenty years later than the Indian, also under near-free trade. High protection became necessary for survival, even though it very probably itself contributed to perpetuate the inefficiency.[8] The considerably lower rate of growth of mill output of piece-goods over 1913–38, compared with 1900–1913, is notable. It corresponds to a much lower rate of growth of apparent consumption, 0·7 percent per annum in the latter period against 4·6 percent in the former. The size of this difference seems a little hard to believe. Estimates of national income suggest only a slight fall in the rate of growth. However, the relative price of cotton goods did rise substantially, which helps to explain the difference (Bagchi, 1972, p. 246).[9]

There seems to be only spotty anecdotal evidence (known to me) on the other handicraft trades. Some undoubtedly suffered in the nineteenth century, as a result of imports and later from indigenous factory production, but there were also those which gained; for instance, metalworkers probably gained by the decline of smelting and importation of cheaper and better metal. Production of small-scale industry (which, however, includes more than handicrafts) was probably a fairly constant proportion of national output from the late nineteenth century onwards (Lidman and Domrese, 1970, p. 323). Any earlier destruction of indigenous manufacturing can only have been quantitatively insignificant as compared with textiles – for instance, imports of metal manufactures (excluding machinery) came to only 6·3 percent of imports of cotton manufactures in 1849–59 (Dutt, 1976, vol. II, p. 116).

Turning to factory industry other than cotton textiles, jute manufacture developed as early, and within twenty years of its establishment in Dundee. This was, of course, a new industry and almost wholly an export industry, processing local material. Costs were lower than in Dundee. But if the United Kingdom had not been free trade, it might not have developed, or anyway not as fast, since tariff structures usually result in high effective protection for later stages of processing, as was indeed the case in the USA and Europe. Employment grew from 27,500 in 1880 to 216,000 in 1914 (a growth rate of 6·25 percent per annum). Unlike cotton, the industry was started and managed entirely by the British, and remained in British hands until after the First World War, when the Marwaris entered the industry, Birla building his first jute mill in 1915 (Timberg, 1978, p. 64). Reasons for this difference will be looked at below. Since jute was an export industry the question of protection did not arise, although exports and the industry suffered badly in the Great Depression. Up until then it did well, net output rising in 1900–1929 at 3·4 percent per annum and employment at 4 percent per annum (Sivasubramonian, 1977, table 7).

Other agriculture-based industries include tea and sugar. The tea industry was promoted by the government and, of course, thrived in the free-trade period; but sugar, a traditional industry, which exported to the United Kingdom early in the nineteenth century could not survive, as an export industry, against lower-cost producers under free trade. Nevertheless, indigenous production supplied the domestic market until the end of the nineteenth century, when imports rose rapidly following on large cost reductions from improved methods (both in growing and processing) taking place elsewhere in the world. Exports of other producers were also subsidized, and so India was permitted countervailing duties. The domestic industry, both indigenous and white sugar, suffered but survived and began to grow after 1905. Ordinary import duties were raised rapidly after the First World War up to levels of 50 percent in the 1920s, and nearly 200 percent in the 1930s. Although the objective was primarily revenue, the effect was highly protective, compensating producers for falling import prices as productive efficiency rose in other countries. It was only in the 1930s that output responded greatly, white-sugar production overtook khandarsi and imports fell away – eventually to zero.

Paper was another industry founded in the nineteenth century under free trade, which was apparently profitable, and progressed slowly in the period up to 1914 assisted by the relaxation, after 1875, of the restrictive rules for the purchase of government stores. [10] This permitted the government to buy almost half the local output, without which its grass-based production might have been eliminated by competition from imports based on woodpulp. Cement production also began before 1914, but the market was small, and did not begin to rise rapidly until after the First World War when excessive investment took place with resultant overcapacity. Cement is heavy stuff, and there was no protection.

Coal-based iron production began in India in 1875, with the Barakar ironworks, which became the Bengal Iron and Steel Co. This limped along with occasional government support (as often withdrawn as given), but it eventually showed that pigiron production at least could be very profitable in India. The Tata steelworks which began steel production in 1913, with a capacity of about 150,000 tons, received definite encouragement from the government, with a contract for 20,000 tons of rails. Iron and steel production from the first Tata works was profitable without protection. There was, it appears, very little engineering industry before 1914, although some engineering stores for the railways, including wagons, were made.

Most industries which had started and survived, even thrived, without protection before the First World War, seemed to require protection after it. Protection to a number of industries was given before a system of discriminatory protection was instituted under the Indian Tariff Board in 1923. This is true of cotton textiles, sugar, iron and steel, paper and some engineering. Specific reasons for specific industries can be adduced. Thus, the far more rapid increase of efficiency of Japanese than Indian textiles, and the former's organized and aggressive export policies is the main explanation for textiles. In the case of sugar technical-production improvements in other countries, and also the better organization of peasants' cane-growing and its integration with factory production (for example, as in Taiwan), were reasons. In paper the development of woodpulp-based paper production was a reason. Of course, improvements elsewhere always go on. A certain lack of, or slowness of, adaptability on the part of Indian industry is suggested, and there was certainly contemporary criticism, especially of cotton-textile managements, on this score. In other cases, such as sugar, lack of government promotion (needed to solve problems of efficient cane production) can also be pointed to. In iron and steel the main specific reason seems to have been different, and was that the major expansion of the Tata plant was badly timed, taking place when equipment and machinery prices were exceptionally high.

But it was not only old industries that now needed protection. A number of new ones were started under the aegis of the Tariff Board, such as tin-plating, wire, screws and nails (some others it refused to support). All apparently required protection, [11] even against the United Kingdom, although, of course, imperial preference reigned after the Ottawa Agreements of 1932. Some more general reasons seem to be needed. It is no coincidence that British industry was relatively depressed in the 1920s, and that sterling was overvalued. There is a good case for saying that the rupee was also overvalued (even though there was no balance of payments problem). As soon as we come to the Great Depression of the 1930s, protection becomes part and parcel of the attempt, which was worldwide, to stimulate demand by reducing imports. One cannot think of protection in the 1930s as holding lessons for long-term development, or for an appraisal of protection as a mode of industrialization in more normal times.

Let us summarize the above discussion in a preliminary way. First, free trade did not destroy the indigenous textile industry. At no time, except perhaps for fifteen to twenty years after Waterloo, did hand-weaving output decline. Reliable figures are available only from 1900 on, and show that output rose; and it probably rose from the 1830s onwards. Hand-spinning did decline, probably from early in the nineteenth century. It would anyway have declined rapidly, as soon as mill production started in India in the 1850s. By 1900 yarn imports were only 7 percent of Indian mill production. There is also no evidence to support a contention that free trade harmed other handicraft industries in the aggregate, although doubtless some suffered. Secondly, free trade did not fully exist at any time. There were always so-called revenue duties on things made in India. But protection was certainly minimal until the First World War. The cotton mills did operate under pure free-trade conditions for twenty years (1894–1914), because of the countervailing excise duty (which protected handlooms), but they clearly needed no protection from Lancashire at this time. Factory industries which began between 1850 and 1914 include jute, wool, sugar, cement, paper, iron and steel, and a very little engineering. After the First World War, protection increased rapidly, becoming heavy in the 1930s.

Table 21.1   *Manufacturing Growth Rates: Value Added*

	(1) Factory Manufacturing	(2) Small- scale Manufacturing	Total of (1) and (2)	Cotton	Sugar	Paper	Wool
1900–1913	6.0	4.7	4.7	6.5	2.8	1.5	3.6
1919–39	4.8	2.3	3.3	3.9	8.5	6.4	4.2

The second point above does suggest a comparison. How well did industry grow in the near-free-trade period 1900–1913 (earlier there is insufficient information even to make a rough quantitative comparison) as compared with the interwar period? Rough value-added (at constant domestic prices) comparisons can be made using Sivasubramonian's (1977) figures. Table 21.1 shows the estimated growth rates of real value added for various aggregates and industries.[12] One could split the second period, the reason being that protection was heavier in the 1930s especially after Ottawa, but this is likely to be tendentious as the result depends heavily on the years chosen. There are, in any case, no inter-censal figures for small-scale industry, and Sivasubramonian's figures derive from the assumption that employment moved parallel with that of organized industry. However, inspection of the run of figures suggests that:

(1)   Indian factory production suffered only a slight fall in the two years 1930–31 and 1931–2; and recovery became continuous from 1934, which already exceeded 1929.

(2)   Indian white-sugar production 'took off' in 1930–31 under the influence of very high tariffs (more strictly, variable levies depending on the price of imports from Java) (Bagchi, 1972, table 12.3 and pp. 369–81). The traditional industries of khandarsi and gur suffered, especially the former (ibid., pp. 377–80).

(3)   Paper production began to grow noticeably only after 1924–5 when tariff protection (of about 15 percent raised to 20 percent in 1932, but not on all kinds of paper) began. But this was more due to rising demand than protection, in the sense that imports increased their share.

Comparisons can also be made in terms of investment and employment. Bagchi has estimated the real value of imports of machinery and millwork (excluding agricultural machinery) for the period 1904–5 to 1939–40. Since there was almost no local production of machinery even after the First World War, this can be taken as a rough indicator of fixed investment in plant and equipment. The average annual figure at 1904 prices for 1904–5 to 1913–14 was R. 50·4 million, and for 1919–39 it was R 61·2 million, 22 percent higher after an average lapse of twenty and a half years, showing a growth rate of less than 1 percent per annum – not significantly different from that of real national income. It appears that investment was no more buoyant in the protection period than it was before 1914 (Bagchi, 1972, table 32).[13]

Turning to employment, from 1902–3 to 1913–14 factory employment rose at 4·3 percent per annum (Sivasubramonian, 1977, table 2),[14] the fastest growth being shown in food, drink and tobacco, chemicals, wood, stone and glass, and miscellaneous. From 1919–20 to 1939–40 factory employment rose at 2·3 percent per annum, the only industries whose employment grew at more than 3·5 percent per annum being food, drink and tobacco, and chemicals. If we split the latter period at 1929–30, we find a slow down from 2·4 percent per annum.[15] The very slow growth in engineering is notable in all periods. Despite the rise in value added in small-scale industry, Sivasubramonian's figures indicate a slight fall in employment in the twentieth century. From 1900–1901 to 1913–14 the figures show a fall of 0·37 percent per annum. Real earnings rise, because the real wage shows a growth of 2·2 percent per annum. From 1919–20 to 1939–40 the numbers rise by 0·27 percent per annum, while real wages rise by 2·0 percent per annum. The figures calculated from Sivasubramonian (1977, table 18) are, however, very chancy and it would be unwise to build any argument on them.

The fact that Indian industrial output grew faster in the free-trade period than in the interwar period does not, of course, prove that industrial protection is bad for *industrial* growth. Although this is possible in the long run, it could hardly be so in a period when simple import substitution could take place. The interwar period was a more difficult period, because agricultural output and incomes grew more slowly than pre-1914. We cannot go into the reasons for this. The Great Depression had some effect, although less effect on agricultural output in India than in many other countries; mostly because the proportion of output exported was smaller. The depression, of course, had some direct effect on industry, though this was probably limited to the textile industries. But protection began in the 1920s when, as we have seen, it was very largely protection of old industries which were in difficulties because of greater technological progress elsewhere. This applies to cotton textiles, paper, sugar and, perhaps, steel and some engineering. Infant industries were rarer – matches and some engineering are cases in point. Protection was, thus, more defensive than offensive. Industries were saved, and in the 1930s the effects of the world depression were mitigated. Long-run dynamic effects are not very apparent, except that the Tata Iron and Steel Co. again operated without protection after 1934. Finally, it must be said that even when rapid growth results from protection, as in the case of sugar, this by no means proves that the policy was right. Protection had to be very high indeed to compete with Java. It is probable that social loss resulted, and that it would have been better to grow something other than sugarcane in many areas. This remained true thirty years later (Lal, 1972).

Tariffs, or their lack, were of course only one aspect of British policy affecting industrialization. An important distinction has to be drawn between free trade and *laissez faire.* The modern theory of international trade strongly supports the view that protection is the worst way of encouraging industry. It takes no position on the question whether industry should be specially encouraged relative to agriculture or services. But assuming that it should be, then subsidies (or bounties, as they used to be called) in one form or another, and perhaps promotion via government initiatives in the field of education, research and development, or institutional development to improve markets or alleviate problems which transcend the possible field of operation of an individual business, constitute the right methods. If one believes this, then one believes in free trade, but not *laissez faire.*[16]

British policy toward Indian industry is sometimes described as one of *laissez faire.* This is not quite correct. Occasional positive interventions were made. Examples are the encouragement of steel and paper production by guaranteeing a market; there are some others. However, it is true that any positive encouragement was both unsystematic, and unusual.[17] Sins of omission can be multiplied depending on one's view of what an optimal policy would have been. The government is also often charged with sins of commission. This should mean that active steps were sometimes taken to prevent or discourage some development. Nationalist historians must have searched hard for such incidents, but nothing very definite is ever cited.

This does not mean that colonial rule did not dampen and even frustrate initiative in many ways, which cannot easily be documented. Whether or not it did is of some importance to our argument. We have shown that industrialization was proceeding quite well before 1914, under free trade. Nevertheless, the pace was slow compared with what anyone would regard as satisfactory nowadays, and slow compared to Japan (also virtually under free trade up to 1911). Moreover, it is important to know whether purely Indian industry (as opposed to British industry in India) was doing well. Finally, the ultimately most important question is whether Indian industry would have grown much faster (say, as fast as Japan), if there had been no discrimination either by government, or more generally in the social and business environment, between Indians and foreigners; and if the government had encouraged industry in what would nowadays be regarded as all the normal ways, though excluding protection or outright subsidization. Needless to say, we cannot give a definite answer to this last very difficult question. But the answer could possibly be 'yes'.

What were the dampening and frustrating effects of colonial rule both for British industry in India, and Indian industry? So far as the British were concerned, it has been alleged that business groups in the United Kingdom would have discouraged any British enterprise which might compete with British exports to India. There seems to be no direct evidence for this, and the argument supposes that British interests could harm the putative enterprise by denying it inputs, or that markets in India might be denied, or that entrepreneurs are guided more by supposedly patriotic instincts than by the dictates of money and success. It might be thought that the fact that the initiative was taken by Indians in the case of cotton and steel is indirect evidence.

On the other hand, British interests did enter the Bombay cotton industry later, and the Indian industry never had difficulty in obtaining machinery or managers and skilled personnel from the United Kingdom (Bhagwati and Desai, 1972, ch. 2). But this does not prove that there was no nonmarket influence; indeed, it might well be argued that the very limited and late British participation was itself evidence.

Although most British enterprise was in export industries or crops, there was also some production for the home market, for example, paper, sugar, matches and engineering. But it is true that almost none of this would have displaced British imports. Finally, in one most important case, jute manufacture, the largely Scottish Calcutta mills competed directly with Dundee. In sum, however, one cannot exclude the possibility that there was some inhibition about starting industries to compete with the United Kingdom – although there was certainly no overt 'colonial system' which precluded it.

What were the discouragements to purely Indian industry which were peculiar to colonial rule, or to the business and social environment created by that rule? Many are alleged. There was difficulty of access for more than very few to suitable formal education, and on-the-job experience was denied by the British prejudice against employing Indians at high levels whether in business, or government. The exclusiveness of British producers and trading associations, and clubs, made contact and access to information more difficult. British banks would favor British interests, and in general, British firms would prefer to deal with each other. Overt discrimination by government is alleged in buying government and railway stores in India (after 1883). In the 1920s discrimination by the Tariff Board has also been alleged (Kidron, 1965, pp. 13–14). Some answers can be made to some of these points. There were Indian banks (but, like British banks, they did not offer long-term industrial finance). There were also Indian business associations, and firms could and did belong to both British and Indian ones. There were some joint ventures, with mixed Indian and British directors, and so on. Yet, even if overt discrimination is exaggerated, there can be little doubt that it took more determination and more courage for an Indian to start manufacturing than for an Englishman or a Scot. The business environment was surely less welcoming. At the same time the indignity of having to face the constant assumption of British and white superiority is unlikely to have produced an entrepreneurial reaction in any but the rarest spirits.

What do events tell us? We have already seen that cotton and steel were started by Indian entrepreneurship and finance. The fact that foreign management, supervision and skilled labor was used is not surprising, and points mainly to the fact that there was no adequate educational background, and that these were indeed new industries. The Japanese, and all late-developers, have always, and for many years, chosen to call on foreigners in similar ways. In most other pre-1914 industries (including plantation export crops) the British seem to have pioneered, while Indians followed shortly afterwards – indigo, tea, sugar, matches and some engineering. Initiatives in paper and cement seem to have been more or less contemporaneously British and Indian. There is nothing here which suggests that indigenous entrepreneurs were discouraged by foreign controlled or financed industry – indeed, the opposite is suggested.

But there seems to be one big exception which is puzzling, and that is the jute-manufacturing industry. Founded by Scotsmen at the same time as the cotton-textile industry, there was no Indian mill until that of Birla in 1919, two-thirds of a century later. A cultural explanation is the most obvious, and cannot be rejected. The cotton industry was started by Parsis, with Gujeratis coming later. These two groups, plus the Marwaris, who entered manufacturing from banking and trade only after the First World War, account for an extraordinarily high proportion of Indian entrepreneurs. At the same time Bengali manufacturers are rare – and this was as true of East Pakistan as of India. There could be many reasons for this, including the fact that Bengalis had been longest dominated by the British[18]. The Marwaris had established themselves in jute-trading and speculation as early as 1870. It was they, not Bengalis, who eventually entered jute-manufacturing. Why the Marwaris took so long to begin manufacturing does not seem to be explained (Timberg, 1978; or Bagchi, 1972, ch. 6). It could be argued that they needed the growing protection of the 1920s and 1930s to stir them. But this is not a wholly satisfactory explanation, since the Marwari 'assault' on industry began before protection, and since they entered unprotected industries, such as jute.

As we have seen, in the interwar period, both output and employment grew more slowly than before 1914. But output did become more diversified (there were quite a number of new engineering ventures, both Indian and British). Also the Indianization of industry accelerated (Kidron, 1965, pp. 40–45). While it is possible that this was caused by increased protection (although it has been claimed that this new protection discriminated against Indians), it seems more reasonable to believe it to be caused by such factors as: (1) the improvement in the political climate, so that Indians could believe that the days of the Raj were numbered, (2) a similar belief on the part of British investors, and (3) the large growth in the accumulation of capital by Indian traders and businessmen during the First World War. All of these factors would, unlike tariffs, tend to have a *relatively* stimulating effect for Indian business.

During the Second World War, Indian businessmen were convinced that wartime controls were operated in a discriminatory manner in favor of British enterprises. This was part of the reason for the hostility by the Indian business community to foreign enterprise in the immediate postwar period. But the main reason was probably simply the fear that they could not compete with foreign enterprise. They wanted protection as much against foreign enterprise in India, as against imports (Kidron, 1965, pp. 65–9). This lack of confidence on the part of native entrepreneurs is probably widespread in developing countries.

Sir Arthur Lewis has done a great deal to undermine the myth that developing countries made no progress in the colonial era. They did, especially from 1870–1913, primarily as a result of rising agricultural exports. After 1913, progress deteriorated as a result of the First World War, slow European growth in the 1920s and world recession in the 1930s. This is all also true of India. We have concentrated on industrialization. Modern Indian industry started in the 1850s, probably earlier than in any other of the present developing countries, and some twenty years before Japan. Factory employment grew at some 6–7 percent per annum in 1880–1900. By the standards of the time, this was fast. From 1900–1913 it slowed down to about 4·3 percent and in 1919–39 to 2·3 percent. A rapid and sustained growth of industry can occur only in one or both of two ways: (a) as a result of a rapid growth of agriculture, and (b) by taking advantage of foreign trade. The latter can itself be divided into import substitution, or an increase in exports as a proportion of GNP. Relative to her size, India could not sustain much modern industry by import substitution, simply because she was and is too poor. The domestic consumption of manufactures is small. Even by 1975, after more than a century of import substitution, when imports of manufactures are only about 3·5 percent of GDP, about 2·5 percent of the labor force is employed in factories. The very slow growth of agricultural output and incomes is at the heart of the slow growth of industry. India did not – perhaps, could not – take enough advantage of the increased demand for tropical products which made the period 1880–1913 relatively good for other tropical countries (for, even then, India was among the slow-growers). In critizing the British Raj the emphasis should be on the failure to promote agricultural extension, education and research (not to speak of land and tenure reform), not on the failure to protect industry.

The other escape route into rapid industrial growth is, of course, by manufactured exports. Except for jute products (not counting tea as a manufacture), the record was very poor. Lidman and Domrese argued that the great missed opportunity was in exports of iron and steel manufactures. Thus, they write (1970, p. 335): 'Overpopulation called for a government which would meet overpopulation by vigorously promoting industrialization for an export market, on the basis of India's coal and iron resources. Instead India was at this time ruled by a government wedded to a laisser-faire philosophy, and sensitive to the vested interest of its home industrialists.' This seems to me to put too much stress on iron and steel. Similarly, Sir Arthur Lewis (1978, ch. 8) argues of Brazil: 'If Brazil had had the right kind of coal it would by 1913 probably have been well on the way to becoming a major industrial power.' The danger is that the steel-using engineering industries may well be handicapped by a domestic steel industry, if the latter produces at high cost and prices, or produces inferior steel, especially if, as is usually the case, imports of steel are consequently controlled. Of course, this will not happen if the steel is competitive. It is interesting that 'the Indian Engineering Association, representing the large engineering concerns of India wanted protection to be given to the steel industry but only in the form of bounties' (Bagchi, 1972, p. 336). They were right. Engineering industries are surely more important than steel both from the point of view of employment, and of externalities.

Even if the stress on iron and steel is doubtful, the importance of exports is not. Here, the poor performance of the cotton (and, much later, synthetic) textile and clothing industry is of great importance. The inability to match Japanese costs led to protection, and subsequent stagnation. The official mentality in the post-Second World War period was that the textile industry was for the home market only, and the investment required to produce cloth for export was refused or subject to impossible conditions. At the same time, the poor quality of Indian cloth, and import controls, had the result that the enormous market for readymade clothing in North America and Europe was left to Korea, Taiwan and Hong Kong. Cloth is an intermediate good as far as the big markets are concerned. The really appropriate labor-intensive industry is clothing. Except for the Indian domestic market, cloth is to clothing as steel is to engineering.

Chapter 21: Notes

1 For example, Paul A. Baran (1968, pp. 277–85). Joan Robinson (1971, p. 5) wrote: 'The primitive industry was destroyed and modern industry hampered by rigid insistence on free trade, to the benefit of British exports.' But many non-Marxist writers accept the same thesis. For example, in a work which attacks Marxist theories of imperialism, B. J. Cohen (1973, p. 157) writes 'prior to the arrival of the British, a flourishing textile industry had long been in existence. The industry was soon ruined by a flood of cheaper woven products from the power looms of England', citing Baran. K. B. Griffin (1969, p. 35) writes 'The English destroyed the Indian textile industry and then proceeded to supply India with cotton goods from Great Britain', and again (1969, p. 39), 'Industrial decay was complete by the 1880s'. These views largely stem from Indian nationalist and Marxist historians, especially R. C. Dutt and Palme Dutt. Other citations could be made, all clearly implying that the textile industry was virtually eliminated. What else does one make of words like 'destroy'? Unwary readers might think this inconsistent with the widely known fact that the Indian factory-textile industry was started in the 1850s, and grew rapidly. One has to get used to the fact that 'industry' is tendentiously or unwittingly used by such writers to mean handicrafts. It should also be noted that 'deindustrialization' has become a term of art and abuse among Marxist writers. It does not mean that industry as a whole (or even handicraft industry) declines. The original definition proposed by Daniel Thorner (1962) equated it to the *proportion* of the population dependent on secondary industry. He rejected the hypothesis for the period 1881–1931. More recently, A. K. Bagchi (1979) has accepted the hypothesis for 1811–1901 for six districts in Bihar. He also claims an absolute decline in these districts, a claim vigorously contested by Marika Vicziany (1979). (References to this literature are in the *Indian Economic and Social History Review*, April–June 1979.) I am not here concerned with this, to my mind, irrelevant discussion. It is easy to imagine a pattern of growth of 'deindustrialization' from which almost everyone soon benefits. Finally, it should be noted that others have contested these sweeping claims for deindustrialization, notably Macpherson (1972) and M. D. Morris (1963).

2 R. C. Dutt (1976, Vol. I, ch. XIII) gives figures, quoting Dr Buchanan's survey of 1808 (for northern India), of R. 1·5–4·5 per annum, to be compared with a subsistence level for a family of R. 48, and a ploughman's wage of R. 16–22. These figures contrast strongly with some given by A. K. Bagchi (1979, pp. 154–5), whose original source is also Dr Buchanan (for the Purnea district of Bihar). Here, an average spinner was said to earn R. 7·75 per annum, and a ploughman 10·75, while the subsistence level was put at R. 24. The former figures are consistent with spinning being a part-time supplement, while Bagchi uses the latter to support an argument that spinners could be said to be dependent on secondary industry. This was required for his argument that the proportion of people dependent on secondary industry declined during the nineteenth century.

3 This does not, of course, preclude an absolute decline in some districts. It is also possible that there was a small fall in numbers in the twentieth century, as productivity rose.

4 The quotation is from Karl Marx, *Capital.* Morris D. Morris reports, however, that these sentences do not appear in Lord William Bentinck's report or other papers (Morris, 1969, p. 165).

5 Import duty on coarse cloth – all that Indian mills made – was actually removed in 1879.

6 A. K. Bagchi (1972, table 7.1). But J. Krishnamurty (1979) makes a lower estimate of the growth of handloom production, and suggests that the numbers of workers fell, there being some rise in productivity.

7 It was introduced again after independence, both for revenue reasons and to protect handloom weavers, who were also subsidized in other ways.

8 Some of the reasons for Indian inefficiency are discussed by Bagchi (1972, ch. 7, ss. 4 and 5).

9 The above story, since 1900, is based on Bagchi (1972, ch. 7).

10 Relaxation from the rule of purchasing in the United Kingdom began in 1875 and was completed in 1914.

11 Of course, some duties were required, once steel was protected, in order that effective protection should not be negative. But effective protection was in fact positive, since the Tariff Board seems to have understood well enough the theory of effective protection.

12 We use all Sivasubramonian's (1977) results, where comparison of the two periods is possible, except that jute is not included as an industry since protection is irrelevant in this case.

13 The figures are deflated only by a price index of cotton-textile machinery. Bagchi thinks the 1930s figures may be an underestimate, because the price of sugar machinery, imports of which are large in 1932–5, may have fallen more than those of cotton-textile machinery. This, however, could hardly alter the conclusion in the text.

14 Owing to a change of definition of factories, figures for 1900–1901 and 1901–2 are not fully comparable, and are not split down by industry.

15 A comparison with the postwar period is of some interest – for instance, over 1961–77 factory employment grew at 2·9 percent per annum. This was a little better than the interwar period, but investment was far heavier. The Indian capital–labor ratio has surely been rising since 1914.

16 It is tedious, but perhaps necessary in self-defense, to add the tautological qualification that, if a country can exert monopoly power in its trading relations, then it should do so, unless it can gain some other compensating advantage as a result of *not* exercising this power. We cannot here go into the fiscal problem of subsidization. Suffice it to say that protection is a form of subsidization paid for entirely by a tax on the good in question; it would be very rare that that was the best way of paying for the subsidy; and also unusual that a production subsidy would be the best form of subsidy.

17 Systematic promotion was adumbrated by the Indian Industrial Commission in 1916–18. But, for complex reasons, the follow-up was very feeble; see Clive Dewey (1979).

18 It has been suggested that the areas of permanent settlement did not produce entrepreneurs, because the British were all too successful in creating a breed of country gentlemen.

Chapter 21: References

Bagchi, A. K., *Private Investment in India, 1900–1939* (Cambridge: Cambridge University Press, 1972).

Bagchi, A. K., 'A reply', *Indian Economic and Social History Review*, vol. 16, no. 2 (1979), pp. 147–62.

Baran, P. A., *The Political Economy of Growth* (New York: Monthly Review Press, 1968).

Bhagwati, J. N. and Desai, P., *India: Planning for Industrialization* (London: Oxford University Press, 1972).

Cohen, B. J., *The Question of Imperialism* (New York: Basic Books, 1973).

Dewey, C., 'The government of India's "new industrial policy", 1900–1925: formation and failure', in K. N. Chaudhuri and C. J. Dewey, eds, *Economy and Society: Essays in Indian Economic and Social History* (Delhi: Oxford University Press, 1979), pp. 215–57.

Dutt, R. C., *The Economic History of India*, Vols I and II (New Delhi: Government of India Ministry of Information and Broadcasting, 1976).

Griffin, K. B., *Underdevelopment in Spanish America* (London: Allen & Unwin, 1969).

Harnetty, P., *Imperialism and Free Trade: Lancashire and India in the Mid-Nineteenth Century* (Manchester: Manchester University Press, 1972).

Kidron, M., *Foreign Investment in India* (London: Oxford University Press, 1965).

Krishnamurty, K. J., 'The distribution of the Indian working force, 1900–1951', in K. N. Chaudhuri and C. J. Dewey, eds, op. cit., pp. 258–62.

Kumar, D., 'Economic history of modern India', *Indian Economic and Social History Review*, vol. 9, no. 1 (1972), pp. 63–90.

Lal, D., *Wells and Welfare* (Paris: OECD Development Centre, 1972).

Lewis, W. A., *Growth and Fluctuations, 1870–1913* (London: Allen & Unwin, 1978).

Lidman, R. and Domrese, R. I., 'India', in W. A. Lewis, ed., *Tropical Development, 1880–1913*, (London: Allen & Unwin, 1970), pp. 309–38.

Macpherson, W. J., 'Economic development in India under the British Crown, 1858–1947', in A. J. Youngson, ed., *Economic Development in the Long Run* (London: Allen & Unwin, 1972), pp. 126–91.

Maddison, A., *Class Structure and Economic Growth* (London: Allen & Unwin, 1971).

Morris, M. D., 'Towards a reinterpretation of nineteenth-century Indian economic history', *Journal of Economic History*, vol. 23, no. 4 (1963), pp. 606–18.

Morris, M. D., 'Trends and tendencies in Indian economic history', in M. D. Morris, T. Matsui, B. Chandra and T. Raychaudhuri, eds, *Indian Economy in the Nineteenth Century: A Symposium* (Delhi: Indian Economic and Social History Association, 1969), pp. 101–70; reprinted from *Indian Economic and Social History Review*, vol. 5, no. 1 (1968).

Robinson, J., 'Going into Europe – again?' (symposium), *Encounter*, vol. 36, no. 4 (1971), pp. 5–6.

Sivasubramonian, S., 'Income from the secondary sector in India, 1900–1947', *Indian Economic and Social History Review*, vol. 14, no. 4 (1977), p. 427–92.

Thorner, D. and Thorner, A., *Land and Labor in India* (Bombay: Asia Publishing House, 1962).

Timberg, T. A., *The Marwaris* (New Delhi: Vikas Publishing House, 1978).

Tooke, T., 'A history of prices, and of the state of the circulation during the nine years 1848–56, vol. VI (1857), Appendix XXIII', in K. N. Chaudhuri, ed., *The Economic Development of India under the East India Company, 1814–58: A Selection of Contemporary Writings* (Cambridge: Cambridge University Press, 1971), pp. 168–89.

Vicziany, M., 'The deindustrialization of India in the nineteenth century: a methodological critique of Amiya Kumar Bagchi', *Indian Economic and Social History Review*, vol. 16, no. 1 (1979).

22

The Rise and Decline of Development Economics

ALBERT O. HIRSCHMAN

Development economics is a comparatively young area of inquiry. It was born just about a generation ago, as a subdiscipline of economics, with a number of other social sciences looking on both skeptically and jealously from a distance. The 1940s and especially the 1950s saw a remarkable outpouring of fundamental ideas and models which were to dominate the new field and to generate controversies that contributed much to its liveliness. In that eminently 'exciting' era, development economics did much better than the object of its study, the economic development of the poorer regions of the world, located primarily in Asia, Latin America and Africa. Lately it seems that at least this particular gap has been narrowing, not so much unfortunately because of a sudden spurt in economic development, but rather because the forward movement of our subdiscipline has notably slowed down. This is of course a subjective judgment. Articles and books are still being produced. But as an observer and longtime participant I cannot help feeling that the old liveliness is no longer there, that new ideas are ever harder to come by and that the field is not adequately reproducing itself.

When scientific activity is specifically directed at solving a pressing problem, one can immediately think of two reasons why, after a while, interest in this activity should flag. One is that the problem is in fact disappearing – either because of the scientific discoveries of the preceding phase, or for other reasons. For example, the near-demise of interest in business-cycle theory since the end of the Second World War was no doubt due to the remarkably shock-free growth experienced during that period by the advanced industrial countries, at least up to the mid-1970s. But this reason cannot possibly be invoked in the present case: the problems of poverty in the Third World are still very much with us.

The other obvious reason for the decline of scientific interest in a problem is the opposite experience, that is, the disappointing realization that a 'solution' is by no means at hand and that little if any progress is being made. Again, this explanation does not sound right in our case, for in the last thirty years considerable advances have taken place in many erstwhile 'underdeveloped' countries – even a balance sheet for the Third World as a whole is by no means discouraging (see, for example, Morawetz, 1977). In sum, the conditions for healthy growth of development economics would seem to be remarkably favorable: the problem of world poverty is far from solved, but encouraging inroads on the problem have been and are being made. It is, therefore, something of a puzzle why development economics flourished so briefly.

In looking for an explanation I find it helpful to take a look at the conditions under which our subdiscipline came into being. It can be shown, I believe, that this happened as a result of an *a priori* unlikely conjunction of distinct ideological currents. The conjunction proved to be extraordinarily productive, but also created problems for the future. First of all, because of its heterogeneous ideological makeup, the new science was shot through with tensions that would prove disruptive at the first opportunity. Secondly, because of the circumstances under which it arose, development economics became overloaded with unreasonable hopes and ambitions that soon had to be clipped back. Put very briefly and schematically, this is the tale I shall tell – plus a few stories and reflections on the side.

A Simple Classification of Development Theories

The development ideas that were put forward in the 1940s and 1950s shared two basic ingredients in the area of economics. They also were based on one unspoken political assumption with which I will deal in the last section of this chapter. The two basic economic ingredients were what I shall call the rejection of the *monoeconomics claim*, and the assertion of the *mutual-benefit claim*. By rejection of the monoeconomics claim I mean the view that underdeveloped countries as a group are set apart, through a number of specific economic characteristics common to them, from the advanced industrial countries and that traditional economic analysis, which has concentrated on the industrial countries, must therefore be recast in significant respects when dealing with underdeveloped countries. The mutual-benefit claim is the assertion that economic relations between these two groups of countries could be shaped in such a way as to yield gains for both. The two claims can be either asserted, or rejected, and as a result, four basic positions exist, as shown in Table 22.1.

Even though there are, of course, positions that do not fit neatly just one of its cells, this simple table yields a surprisingly comprehensive typology for the

Table 22.1   *Types of Development Theories*

		Monoeconomics claim	
		asserted	*rejected*
	asserted	Orthodox economics	Development economics
Mutual-benefit claim	*rejected*	Marx?	Neo-Marxist theories

major theories on development of the periphery. In the process it makes us realize that there are two unified systems of thought, orthodox economics, and neo-Marxism; and two other less consistent positions that are therefore likely to be unstable: Marx's scattered thoughts on development of 'backward' and colonial areas on the one hand, and modern development economics on the other. I shall take up these four positions in turn, but shall give major attention to development economics and to its evolving relations with – and harassment by – the two adjoining positions.

The orthodox position holds to the following two propositions: (a) economics consists of a number of simple, yet 'powerful' theorems of universal validity: there is only one economics ('just as there is only one physics'); (b) one of these theorems is that, in a market economy, benefits flow to all participants, be they individuals or countries, from all voluntary acts of economic intercourse ('or else they would not engage in those acts'). In this manner both the monoeconomics, and the mutual-benefit claims, are asserted.

The opposite position is that of the major neo-Marxist theories of development which hold: (a) exploitation or 'unequal exchange' is the essential, permanent feature of the relations between the underdeveloped 'periphery' and the capitalist 'center'; (b) as a result of this long process of exploitation, the political-economic structure of the peripheral countries is very different from anything ever experienced by the center, and their development cannot possibly follow the same path – for example, it has been argued that they cannot have a successful industrialization experience under capitalist auspices. Here, both the mutual-benefit claim and the monoeconomics claim are rejected.

A cozy internal consistency, bent on simplifying (and oversimplifying) reality and, therefore, favorable to ideology formation, is immediately apparent in both the orthodox and the neo-Marxist positions. This is in contrast with the remaining two positions. It should be clear why I have placed Marx into the southwesterly cell (mutual-benefit claim rejected, monoeconomics claim asserted). Writing in *Capital* on primitive accumulation, on the one hand, Marx describes the process of spoliation to which the periphery has been subject in the course of the early development of capitalism in the center. Thus, he denies any claim of mutual benefit from trade between capitalist and 'backward' countries. On the other hand, his well-known statement, 'the industrially most developed country does nothing but hold up to those who follow it on the industrial ladder, the image of its own future', coupled with the way in which he viewed England's role in India as 'objectively' progressive in opening the way to industrialization by railroad construction, suggests that he did not perceive the 'laws of motion' of countries such as India as being substantially different from those of the industrially advanced ones. Marx's opinions on this latter topic are notoriously complex and subject to a range of interpretations, as is indicated by the question mark in Table 22.1. But to root *neo*-Marxist thought firmly in the south*east*erly cell took considerable labors (which involved, among other things, *uprooting* an important component of the thought of Marx). The story of these labors and revisions has been told elsewhere (Sutcliffe,

1972, pp. 180–86; Singer, 1977, pp. 50–56)[1] and my task here is to deal with the origin and dynamics of the other 'hybrid' position: development economics.

It is easy to see that the conjunction of the two propositions – (a) certain special features of the economic structure of the underdeveloped countries make an important portion of orthodox analysis inapplicable and misleading, and (b) there is a possibility for relations between the developed and underdeveloped countries to be mutually beneficial and for the former to contribute to the development of the latter – was essential for our subdiscipline to arise where and when it did: namely, in the advanced industrial countries of the West, primarily in England and the USA, at the end of the Second World War. The first proposition is required for the creation of a separate theoretical structure, and the second was needed if Western economists were to take a strong interest in the matter – if the likelihood or at least the hope could be held out that their own countries could play a positive role in the development process, perhaps after certain achievable reforms in international economic relations. In the absence of this perception it would simply not have been possible to mobilize a large group of activist 'problem-solvers'.

The Inapplicability of Orthodox Monoeconomics to Underdeveloped Areas

Once a genuinely new current of ideas is firmly established and is being busily developed by a large group of scholars and researchers, it becomes almost impossible to appreciate how difficult it was for the new to be born and to assert itself. Such difficulties are particularly formidable in economics with its dominant paradigm and analytical tradition – a well-known source of both strength and weakness for that social science. Accordingly, there is need for an explanation of the rise and at least temporary success of the heretical, though today familiar, claim that large portions of the conventional body of economic thought and policy advice are not applicable to the poorer countries – the more so as much of this intellectual movement arose in the very 'Anglo-Saxon' environment which had long served as home for the orthodox tradition.

Such an explanation is actually not far to seek. Development economics took advantage of the unprecedented discredit orthodox economics had fallen into as a result of the depression of the 1930s and of the equally unprecedented success of an attack on orthodoxy from within the economics 'establishment'. I am talking, of course, about the Keynesian revolution of the 1930s, which became the 'new economics' and almost a new orthodoxy in the 1940s and 1950s. Keynes had firmly established the view that there were *two* kinds of economics: one the orthodox or classical tradition – which applied, as he was wont to put it, to the 'special case' in which the economy was fully employed; and a very different system of analytical propositions and of policy prescriptions (newly worked out by Keynes) that took over when there was substantial unemployment of human and material resources.[2] The Keynesian step from one to two economics was crucial: the ice of monoeconomics had been broken and the idea that there might be yet another economics had instant credibility – particularly among the then highly influential group of Keynesian economists, of course. Among the various observations that were central to the new development economics and implicitly or explicitly made the case for treating the underdeveloped countries as a *sui generis* group of economies, two major ones stand out, that relating to rural underemployment, and that stressing the late-coming syndrome in relation to industrialization.

(1) Rural Underemployment

The early writers on our subject may have looked for an even closer and more specific connection with the Keynesian system than was provided by the general proposition that different kinds of economies require different kinds of economics. Such a connection was achieved by the unanimous stress of the pioneering contributions – by Kurt Mandelbaum, Paul Rosenstein-Rodan and Ragnar Nurkse – on *underemployment* as a crucial characteristic of underdevelopment. The focus on rural *under*employment was sufficiently similar to the Keynesian concern with *un*employment to give the pioneers a highly prized sensation of affinity with the Keynesian system, yet it was also different enough to generate expectations of eventual independent development for our fledgling branch of economic knowledge.

The affinities were actually quite impressive. As is well known, the Keynesian system took unemployment far more seriously than had been done by traditional economics and had elaborated a theory of macroeconomic equilibrium with unemployment. Similarly, the early development economists wrote at length about the 'vicious circle of poverty' – a state of low-level equilibrium – which can prevail under conditions of widespread rural underemployment. Moreover, the equilibrium characteristics of an advanced economy with urban unemployment and those of an underdeveloped economy with rural underemployment were both held to justify interventionist public policies hitherto strictly proscribed by orthodox economics. The Keynesians stressed the task of expansionary fiscal policy in combating unemployment. The early development economists went further and advocated some form of public investment planning that would mobilize the underemployed for the purpose of industrialization, in accordance with a pattern of 'balanced growth'.

In these various ways, then, the claim of development economics to stand as a separate body of economic analysis and policy derived intellectual legitimacy and nurture from the prior success and parallel features of the Keynesian revolution. The focus on rural underemployment as the principal characteristic of underdevelopment found its fullest expression in the work of Arthur Lewis. In his powerful article 'Economic development with unlimited supplies of labour' he managed – almost miraculously – to squeeze out of the simple proposition about underemployment a full set of 'laws of motion' for the typical underdeveloped country, as well as a wide range of recommendations for domestic and international economic policy.

With the concept of rural underemployment serving as the crucial theoretical underpinning of the separateness of development economics, it is not surprising that it should have been chosen as a privileged target by the defenders of orthodoxy and monoeconomics (see, for example, Viner, 1957, pp. 345–54). For example, Theodore W. Schultz devoted a full chapter of his well-known book *Transforming Traditional Agriculture* (1964) to an attempt at refuting what he called 'the doctrine of agricultural labor of zero value'.[3] This suggests an interesting point about the scientific status of economics, and of social science in general. Whereas in the natural or medical sciences Nobel prizes are often shared by two persons who have collaborated in, or deserve joint credit for, a given scientific advance, in economics the prize is often split between one person who has developed a certain thesis and another who has labored mightily to prove it wrong.

At the outset of his celebrated article, Lewis had differentiated the underdeveloped economy from Keynesian economics by pointing out that in the Keynesian system there is underemployment of labor as well as of other factors of production, whereas in an underdevelopment situation only labor is redundant. In this respect, my own work can be viewed as an attempt to generalize the diagnosis of underemployment as the characteristic feature of underdevelopment. Underdeveloped countries did have hidden reserves, so I asserted, not only of labor but of savings, entrepreneurship and other resources. But to activate them, Keynesian remedies would be inadequate. What was needed were 'pacing devices' and 'pressure mechanisms'; whence my strategy of unbalanced growth.

My generalization of the underemployment argument may have somewhat undermined the claim of development economics to autonomy and separateness. As the work of Herbert Simon on 'satisficing' and that of Harvey Leibenstein on 'X-efficiency' were to show, the performance of the advanced economies also 'depends not so much on finding optimal combinations for given resources as on calling forth and enlisting . . . resources and abilities that are hidden, scattered, or badly utilized' – that was the way I had put it in *The Strategy of Economic Development* for the less developed countries (Hirschman, 1958, p. 5). A feature I had presented as being specific to the situation of one group of economies was later found to prevail in others as well. Whereas such a finding makes for reunification of our science, what we have here is not a return of the prodigal son to an unchanging, ever-right and ever-righteous father. Rather, our understanding of the economic structures of the West will have been modified and enriched by the foray into other economies.

This kind of dialectical movement – first comes, upon looking at outside groups, the astonished finding of otherness, and then follows the even more startling discovery that our own group is not all that different – has of course been characteristic of anthropological studies of 'primitive' societies from their beginning, and has in fact been one of their main attractions. In the field of development economics something of this sort has also happened to the ideas put forward by Arthur Lewis. The dynamics of development with 'unlimited' supplies of labor, which was supposed to be typical of less developed countries, have in fact prevailed in many 'Northern' economies during the postwar period of rapid growth, owing in large part to massive immigration, temporary or permanent, spontaneous, or organized, from the 'South' (Kindleberger, 1967). One of the more interesting analytical responses to this situation has been the dual labor-market theory of Michael Piore and others. This theory is easily linked up with the Lewis model, even though that connection has not been made explicit as far as I know.

(2) Late Industrialization

I have suggested in the preceding pages that the concept of underemployment achieved its position as a foundation-stone for development economics because of its affinity to the Keynesian system and because of the desire of the early writers on our subject to place themselves, as it were, under the protection of a heterodoxy that had just recently achieved success. There was, moreover, something arcane about the concept, often also referred to as 'disguised unemployment', that served to enhance the scientific aura and status of the new field.

Along with the mysteries, however, the common sense of development also suggested that some rethinking of traditional notions was required. It became clear during the depression of the 1930s and even more during the Second World War that industrialization was going to hold an important place in any active development policy of many underdeveloped countries. These countries had long specialized – or had been made to specialize – in the production of staples for export to the advanced industrial countries which had supplied them in return with modern manufactures. To build up an industrial structure under these 'late-coming' conditions, was obviously a formidable task that led to the questioning of received doctrine according to which the industrial ventures appropriate to any country would be promptly acted upon by perceptive entrepreneurs and would attract the required finance as a result of the smooth working of capital markets. The long delay in industrialization, the lack of entrepreneurship for larger ventures, and the real or alleged presence of a host of other inhibiting factors made for the conviction that, in underdeveloped areas, industrialization required a deliberate, intensive, guided effort. Naming and characterizing this effort led to a competition of metaphors: 'big push' (Paul Rosenstein-Rodan), 'take-off' (Walt W. Rostow), 'great spurt' (Alexander Gerschenkron), 'minimum critical effort' (Harvey Leibenstein) and 'backward and forward linkages' (Albert O. Hirschman). The discussion around these concepts drew on both theoretical arguments – new rationales were developed for protection, planning and industrialization itself – and on the experience of European industrialization in the nineteenth century.

In the latter respect, the struggle between advocates and adversaries of monoeconomics was echoed in the debate between Rostow and Gerschenkron.

Even though Rostow had coined what became the most popular metaphor (the 'take-off'), he had really taken a monoeconomics position. For he divided the development process into his famous five 'stages' with identical content for all countries, no matter when they started out on the road to industrialization. Gerschenkron (1962, p. 355) derided the notion 'that the process of industrialization repeated itself from country to country lumbering through [Rostow's] pentametric rhythm' and showed, to the contrary, how the industrialization of the late-coming European countries such as Germany and Russia differed in fundamental respects from the English industrial revolution, largely because of the intensity of the 'catching-up' effort on the part of the late-comers. Even though it was limited to nineteenth-century Europe, Gerschenkron's work was of great importance for development economics by providing *historical* support for the case against monoeconomics. As industrialization actually proceeded in the periphery, it appeared that Third World industrialization around the mid-twentieth century exhibited features rather different from those Gerschenkron had identified as characteristic for the European late-comers (Hirschman, 1968). But for the historically oriented, Gerschenkron's work supplied the same kind of reassurance Keynesianism had given to the analytically minded: he showed once and for all that there can be more than one path to development, that countries setting out to become industrialized are likely to forge their own policies, sequences and ideologies to that end.

Subsequent observations strengthened the conviction that industrialization in the less developed areas required novel approaches. For example, modern, capital-intensive industry was found to be less effective in absorbing the 'unlimited supplies of labor' available in agriculture than had been the case in the course of earlier experiences of industrialization. Advances in industrialization were frequently accompanied by persistent inflationary and balance of payment pressures which raised questions about the adequacy of traditional remedies and led, in Latin America, to the 'sociological' and 'structuralist' theses on inflation, which, interestingly, have now gained some currency in the advanced countries, usually without due credit being given.[4] Also the vigorous development of the transnational corporation in the postwar period raised entirely new 'political economy' questions about the extent to which a country should attract, restrict, or control these purveyors of modern technology and products.

The Mutual-Benefit Assumption

The new (far from unified) body of doctrine and policy advice that was built up in this manner was closely connected, as noted earlier, with the proposition that the core industrial countries could make an important, even an essential, contribution to the development effort of the periphery through expanded trade, financial transfers and technical assistance.

The need for large injections of financial aid fitted particularly well into those theories advocating a 'big push'. It was argued that such an effort could only be mounted with substantial help from the advanced countries, as the poor countries were unable to generate the needed savings from within. Here, the underlying model was the new growth economics, which, in its simplest (Harrod–Domar) version, showed a country's growth rate to be determined by the propensity to save and the capital–output ratio. Growth economics had evolved independently from development economics, as a direct offshoot of the Keynesian system and its macroeconomic concepts. While devised primarily with the advanced industrial countries in mind, it found an early practical application in the planning exercises for developing countries that became common in the 1950s. These exercises invariably contained projections for an expansion of trade and aid. Their underlying assumption was necessarily that such enlarged economic relations between rich and poor countries would be beneficial for both. Now this proposition fits nicely into orthodox monoeconomics, but it might have been expected to arouse some suspicion among development economists and to mix rather poorly with some of the other elements and assertions of the new subdiscipline. For example, so it could have been asked, why are the countries of the South in a state where, according to some, it takes a huge push to get them onto some growth path? Why are they so impoverished in spite of having long been drawn into the famous 'network of world trade',[5] which was supposed to yield mutual benefits for all participants? Is it perhaps because, in the process, some countries have been *caught* in the net to be victimized by some imperialist spider? But such indelicate questions were hardly put in the halcyon days of the immediate postwar years, except perhaps in muted tones by a few faraway voices, such as Raúl Prebisch's. Of that more later.

Action-oriented thought seldom excels in consistency. Development economics is no exception to this rule; it was born from the marriage between the new insights about the *sui generis* economic problems of the underdeveloped countries and the overwhelming desire to achieve rapid progress in solving these problems with the instruments at hand, or thought to be within reach, such as large-scale foreign aid. A factor in 'arranging' this marriage, in spite of the incompatibilities involved, was the success of the Marshall Plan in Western Europe. Here, the task of postwar reconstruction was mastered with remarkable speed, thanks, so it appeared at least, to a combination of foreign aid with some economic planning and cooperation on the part of the aid recipients. It has often been pointed out that this European success story led to numerous failures in the Third World, that it lamentably blocked a realistic assessment of the task of development, in comparison with that of reconstruction.

But the matter can be seen in a different light. True, the success of the Marshall Plan deceived economists, policy-makers and enlightened opinion in the West into believing that infusion of capital helped along by the right kind of investment planning might be able to grind out growth and welfare all over the globe. But – and here is an application of what I have called the 'principle of the hiding hand' – on balance it may have been a good thing that we let ourselves be so deceived. Had the toughness of the development problem and the difficulties in the North–South relationship been correctly sized up from the outset, the considerable intellectual and political mobilization for the enterprise would surely not have occurred. In that case, and in spite of the various 'development disasters' which we have experienced (and which will be discussed later in this chapter), would we not be even further away from an acceptable world than we are today? In sum, one historical function of the rise of development economics was to inspire confidence in the manageability of the development enterprise and thereby to help place it on the agenda of policy-makers the world over. The assertion of the mutual-benefit claim served this purpose.

The Strange Alliance of Neo-Marxism and Monoeconomics against Development Economics

Predictably, when the path to development turned out to be far less smooth than had been thought, the hybrid nature of the new subdiscipline resulted in its being subjected to two kinds of attacks. The Neoclassical Right faulted it for having forsaken the true principles of monoeconomics and for having compounded, through its newfangled policy recommendations, the problem it set out to solve. For the neo-Marxists, on the other hand, development economics had not gone far enough in its analysis of the predicament of the poor countries: so serious was their problem pronounced to be that nothing but total change in their socioeconomic structure and in their relations to the rich countries could make a difference; pending such change, so-called development policies only created new forms of exploitation and 'dependency'. The two fundamentalist critiques attacked development economics from opposite directions and in totally different terms: but they could converge in their specific indictments – as they indeed did, particularly in the important arena of industrialization. Because the adherents of Neoclassical economics and those of the various neo-Marxist schools of thought live in quite separate worlds, they were not even aware of acting in unison. In general, that strange *de facto* alliance has hardly been noted; but it plays an important role in the evolution of thinking on development and its story must be briefly told.

Doubts about the harmony of interests between the developed and underdeveloped countries arose at an early stage among some of the major contributors to the new subdiscipline. There was widespread acceptance of the view that the advanced industrial countries could henceforth contribute to the development of the less advanced, particularly through financial assistance, but questions were raised in various quarters about the equitable distribution of the gains from trade, both in the past and currently. In 1949 Raúl Prebisch and

Hans Singer formulated (simultaneously and independently) their famous 'thesis' on the secular tendency of the terms of trade to turn against countries exporting primary products and importing manufactures.[6] They attributed this alleged tendency to the power of trade unions in the advanced countries and to conditions of underemployment in the periphery. The argument was put forward to justify a sustained policy of industrialization. Arthur Lewis was led by his model in a rather similar direction: as long as 'unlimited supplies of labor' in the subsistence sector depress the real wage throughout the economy, any gains from productivity increases in the export sector are likely to accrue to the importing countries; moreover, in a situation in which there is surplus labor at the ruling wage, prices give the wrong signals for resource allocation in general and for the international division of labor in particular; the result was a further argument for protection and industrialization.

Both the Prebisch–Singer and the Lewis arguments showed that, without a judiciously interventionist state on the periphery, the cards were inevitably stacked in favor of the center. On the whole, it looked as though this was the result of some unkind fate rather than of deliberate maneuvers on the center's part. Critics from the Left later took Arthur Lewis to task for viewing unlimited supplies of labor as a datum, rather than as something that is systematically *produced* by the colonizers and capitalists (Arrighi, 1970). Lewis (1954) was, of course, fully aware of such situations and specifically notes at one point that in Africa the imperial powers impoverished the subsistence economy 'by taking away the people's land, or by demanding forced labour in the capitalist sector, or by imposing taxes to drive people to work for capitalist employers'. For Lewis, these practices were simply not a crucial characteristic of the model – after all, a decline in infant mortality could have the same effect in augmenting labor supply as a head tax.

It appears nevertheless that the debate among development economists in the 1950s included the canvassing in some antagonistic aspects of the center–periphery relation. The theories just noted attempted to show that the gain from trade might be unequally distributed (perhaps even to the point where one group of countries would not gain at all), but did not go so far as to claim that the relationship between two groups of countries could actually be exploitative in the sense that trade and other forms of economic intercourse would enrich one group *at the expense* of another – an assertion that would be unthinkable within the assumptions of the Classical theory of international trade. Yet, even this kind of assertion was made at a relatively early stage of the debate. Gunnar Myrdal invoked the principle of cumulative causation (which he had first developed in his *American Dilemma*), in seeking to understand the reason for persistent and increasing income disparities *within* countries; but the notion was easily extended to contacts between countries. Myrdal's argument on the possibility of further impoverishment of the poor region (or country) was largely based on the likelihood of its losing skilled people and other scarce factors, and also on the possible destruction of its handicrafts and industries. Independently of Myrdal, I had developed similar ideas: Myrdal's 'backwash effect' – the factors making for increasing disparity – became 'polarization effect' under my pen, whereas his 'spread effect' – the factors making for the spread of prosperity from the rich to the poor regions – was named by me, 'trickling down effect'. (Optimal terminology is probably achieved by combining Myrdal's 'spread' with my 'polarization' effects.) We both argued, though with different emphases, that the possibility of the polarization effect being stronger than the spread effect must be taken seriously, and thus went counter not only to the theory of international trade, but to the broader traditional belief, so eloquently expressed by John Stuart Mill,[7] that contact between dissimilar groups is always a source of all-around progress. Anyone who had observed the development scene with some care could not but have serious doubts about this view: in Latin America, for example, industrial progress was particularly vigorous during the world wars and the Great Depression when contacts with the industrial countries were at a low ebb. To me, this meant no more than that *periods* of isolation may be beneficial and I saw some alternation of contact and isolation as creating optimal conditions for industrial development (Hirschman, 1958, pp. 173–5 and 199–201). In any event, both Myrdal and I looked at the polarization effects as forces that can be opposed and neutralized by public policies; and I tried to show that, instead of invoking such policies as a *deus ex machina* (as I thought Myrdal did), it is possible to see them as arising out of, and in reaction to, the experience of polarization.

A strange thing happened, once it had been pointed out that interaction between the rich and poor countries could in certain circumstances be in the nature of an antagonistic, zero-sum game: very soon it proved intellectually and politically attractive to assert that such was the essence of the relationship and that it held as an iron law through all phases of contacts between the capitalist center and the periphery. Just as earlier those brought up in the Classical tradition of Smith and Ricardo were unable to conceive of a gain from trade that is not mutual, so did it become impossible for the new polarization enthusiasts to perceive anything but pauperization and degradation in each of the successive phases of the periphery's history.[8] This is the 'development-of-underdevelopment' thesis, put forward by André Gunder Frank, and also espoused by some of the more extreme holders of the 'dependency' doctrine. Given the historical moment at which these views arose, their first and primary assignment was to mercilessly castigate what had up to then been widely believed to hold the promise of economic emancipation for the underdeveloped countries: industrialization. We are now at the mid-1960s, at which time real difficulties and growing pains were experienced by industry in some leading Third World countries after a prolonged period of vigorous expansion. This situation was taken advantage of in order to characterize all of industrialization as a total failure on a number of (not always consistent) counts: it was 'exhausted', 'distorted', lacked integration, led to domination and exploitation by multinationals in alliance with a domestic 'lumpen bourgeoisie', was excessively capital-intensive and therefore sabotaged employment, and fostered a more unequal distribution of income along with a new, more insidious kind of dependency than ever before.

At just about the same time, the Neoclassical economists or monoeconomists – as they should be called in accordance with the terminology of this chapter – were sharpening their own knives for an assault on development policies that had pushed industrialization for the domestic market. In contrast to the multiple indictment from the Left, the monoeconomists concentrated on a single, simple, but to them capital, flaw of these policies: misallocation of resources. By itself this critique was highly predictable and might not have carried more weight than warnings against industrialization emanating from essentially the same camp ten, or twenty, or fifty, years earlier. But the effectiveness of the critique was now greater, for various reasons. First of all, as a result of the neo-Marxist writings just noted, some of the early advocates of industrialization had now themselves become its sharpest critics. Secondly, specific policies which in the early stage had been useful in promoting industrialization, though at the cost of inflationary and balance of payments pressures, did run into decreasing returns in the 1960s: they achieved less industrialization at the cost of greater inflation and balance of payments problems than before. Thirdly, the practice of deliberate industrialization had given rise to exaggeration and abuse in a number of countries and it became easy to draw up a list of horrible examples that served to incriminate the whole effort. Fourthly, a new set of policies emphasizing exports of manufactures from developing countries became attractive, because of the then rapid expansion of world trade, and the possibilities of success of such policies was demonstrated by countries like Taiwan and South Korea. Under these conditions, the Neoclassical strictures became more persuasive than they had been for a long time.

The target of the complementary neo-Marxist and Neoclassical writings was not just the new industrial establishment which, in fact, survived the onslaught rather well; on the ideological plane the intended victim was the new development economics which had strongly advocated industrial development and was now charged with intellectual responsibility for whatever had gone wrong. The blows from Left and Right that fell upon the fledgling and far-from-unified subdiscipline left it, indeed, rather stunned: so much so that the most intrepid defense of what had been accomplished by the postwar industrialization efforts in the Third World came not from the old stalwarts, but from an English socialist in the tradition of Marx's original position on the problem of backward areas, the late Bill Warren (1973; 1979).

The Real Wounding of Development Economics

It would, of course, be silly (just as silly as the German proverb *Viel Feind, viel Ehr*[9]) to hold that any doctrine or policy that is attacked simultaneously from both Left and Right is, for that very reason, supremely invested with truth and wisdom. I have already noted that the Neoclassical critics made some valid points, just as the neo-Marxists raised a number of serious issues, particularly in the areas of excessive foreign control and of unequal income distribution. But normally such criticisms should have led to some reformulations and eventually to a strengthening of the structure of development economics. In fact, however, this was not to be the case. No new synthesis appeared.

Several explanations can be offered. For one thing, development economics had been built up on the basis of a construct, the 'typical underdeveloped country', which became increasingly unreal as development proceeded at very different rates and took very different shapes in the various countries of Latin America, Asia and Africa. Lenin's law of uneven development, originally formulated with the major imperialist powers in mind, caught up with the Third World! It became clear, for example, that, for the purpose of the most elementary propositions of development strategy, countries with large populations differ substantially from the ever-more-numerous ministates of the Third World,[10] just as there turned out to be few problems in common between petroleum exporters and petroleum-importing developing countries. The concept of a unified body of analysis and policy recommendations for all underdeveloped countries, which contributed a great deal to the rise of the subdiscipline, became in a sense a victim of the very success of development and of its unevenness.

But there was a more weighty reason for the failure of development economics to recover decisively from the attacks it had been subjected to by its critics. It lies in the series of political disasters that struck a number of Third World countries from the 1960s on, disasters that were clearly *somehow* connected with the stresses and strains accompanying development and 'modernization'. These development disasters, ranging from civil wars to the establishment of murderous authoritarian regimes, could not but give pause to a group of social scientists who, after all, had taken up the cultivation of development economics in the wake of the Second World War not as narrow specialists, but impelled by the vision of a better world. As liberals, most of them presumed that 'all good things go together' (Packenham, 1973, pp. 123–9) and took it for granted that if only a good job could be done in raising the national income of the countries concerned a number of beneficial effects would follow in the social, political and cultural realms.

When it turned out instead that the promotion of economic growth entailed not infrequently a sequence of events involving serious retrogression in those other areas, including the wholesale loss of civil and human rights, the easy self-confidence that our subdiscipline exuded in its early stages was impaired. What looked like a failure to mount a vigorous counter-attack against the unholy alliance of neo-Marxists and neoclassicists may well have been rooted in increasing self-doubt, based on mishaps far more serious than either the 'misallocation of resources' of the neoclassicists, or the 'new dependency' of the neo-Marxists.

Not that all the large and gifted group of development economists which had in the meantime been recruited into the new branch of knowledge turned suddenly silent. Some retreated from the position 'all good things go together' to 'good economics is good for people'.[11] In other words, rather than assuming that economic development would bring progress in other fields, they thought it legitimate to operate on the basis of an implicit Pareto-optimality assumption: like plumbing repairs or improvement in traffic control, the technical efforts of economists would improve matters in one area while at worst leaving others unchanged, thus making society as a whole better off. Economic development policy was here, in effect, downgraded to a technical task exclusively involved with efficiency improvements. An illusion was created and sought that, by confining itself to smaller-scale, highly technical problems, development economics could carry on regardless of political cataclysms.

There was, however, another reaction that was to have a considerable impact. Experiencing a double frustration, one over the appalling political events as such, and the other over their inability to comprehend them, a number of analysts and practitioners of economic development were moved to look at the economic performance itself with a more critical eye than before. In a Freudian act of displacement they 'took out' their distress over the political side on the weaker aspects of the economic record. Within countries with authoritarian regimes, the displacement was often reinforced, unintentionally of course, by the official censorship that was much more rigorous with regard to political dissent than in matters of economic performance.

It was, in a sense, an application of the maxim 'all good things go together', *in reverse*. Now that political developments had taken a resoundingly wrong turn, one had to prove that the economic story was similarly unattractive. Some economists were satisfied, once the balance between political and economic performance had been restored in this fashion, be it at a wretchedly low level. But others were in a more activist mood. Impotent in the face of political injustice and tyranny, yet feeling a faint sense of responsibility, they were attempting to make amends by exposing *economic* injustice. In doing so, they paid little attention to John Rawls (1971, p. 61), who argued at just about that time in *A Theory of Justice* that 'a departure from the institutions of equal liberty ... cannot be justified by, or compensated for, greater social or economic advantage'. But perhaps it was fortunate – and a measure of the vitality of the development movement – that the disappointment over politics led to an attempt at righting at least those wrongs economists could denounce in their professional capacity.

Here, then, is one important origin of the concern with income distribution which became a dominant theme in the development literature in the early 1970s. Albert Fishlow's (1972) finding, on the basis of the 1970 Census, that income distribution in Brazil had become more unequal and that some low-income groups may even have come to be worse off in absolute terms, in spite of (because of?) impressive growth, was particularly influential. An alarm based on this and similar data from other countries was sounded by Robert

McNamara, the President of the World Bank, in his annual address to the board of governors' meeting in 1972. A large number of studies followed, and an attempt was made to understand how development could be shaped in accordance with distributional goals, or to formulate policies that would combine the objectives of growth and distribution.

Before long, attention was directed not only to the relative aspects of income distribution, but to the absolute level of need satisfaction among the poorer groups of a country's population. Thus was born the concern with *basic needs* – of food, health, education, etc. – that is currently a principal preoccupation of development economics. Just as the construct of the 'typical underdeveloped country' gave way to diverse categories of countries, each with characteristics of its own, so did the heretofore unique maximand of development economics (income per capita) dissolve into a variety of partial objectives, each requiring consultation with different experts – on nutrition, public health, housing and education, among others.

There is of course much to be said for this new concreteness in development studies, and particularly for the concern with the poorer sections. Nevertheless, development economics started out as the spearhead of an effort that was to bring all-around emancipation from backwardness. If that effort is to fulfill its promise, the challenge posed by dismal politics must be met rather than avoided or evaded. By now it has become quite clear that this cannot be done by economics alone. It is for this reason that the decline of development economics cannot be fully reversed: our subdiscipline had achieved its considerable luster and excitement through the implicit idea that it could slay the dragon of backwardness virtually by itself or, at least, that its contribution to this task was central. We now know that this is not so; a consoling thought is that we may have gained in maturity what we have lost in excitement.

Looking backward, the whole episode seems curious. How could a group of social scientists that had just lived through the most calamitous 'derailments of history' *in various major economically advanced* countries entertain such great hopes for economic development *per se*? Here, I can perhaps offer some enlightenment by drawing on my recent work in the history of ideas. In *The Passions and the Interests* I showed that the rise of commerce and money-making activities in the seventeenth and eighteenth centuries was then looked upon as promising for political stability and progress; and I stressed that such optimistic expectations were not based on a new respect for these activities, but rather on *continuing contempt* for them: unlike the passionate, aristocratic pursuit of glory and power with its then well recognized potential for disaster, the love of money was believed to be 'incapable of causing either good *or evil* on a grand scale' (Hirschman, 1977, p. 58). A similar perception may have been at work in relation to the less developed countries of Asia, Africa and Latin America of the twentieth century. The Western economists who looked at them at the end of the Second World War were convinced that these countries were not all that complicated: their major problems would be solved, if only their national income per capita could be raised adequately. At an

/r

earlier time, contempt for the countries designated as 'rude and barbarous' in the eighteenth century, as 'backward' in the nineteenth and as 'underdeveloped' in the twentieth had taken the form of relegating them to permanent lowly status, in terms of economic and other prospects, on account of unchangeable factors such as hostile climate, poor resources, or inferior race. With the new doctrine of economic growth, contempt took a more sophisticated form: suddenly it was taken for granted that progress of these countries would be smoothly linear, if only they adopted the right kind of integrated development programme! Given what was seen as their overwhelming problem of poverty, the underdeveloped countries were expected to perform like wind-up toys and to 'lumber through' the various stages of development singlemindedly; their reactions to change were not to be nearly as traumatic or aberrant as those of the Europeans, with their feudal residues, psychological complexes and exquisite high culture. In sum, like the 'innocent' and *doux* trader of the eighteenth century, these countries were perceived to have only *interests* and *no passions*. Once again, we have learned otherwise.

Chapter 22: Notes

The present paper is, of course, a highly selective review. In particular, it does not treat the development of our factual knowledge about the development process which has often included the testing of theories; here the main debt is owed to such figures as Simon Kuznets and Hollis Chenery. A number of other surveys of the sort here attempted have appeared recently. See, in particular, Streeten (1979) and Cardoso (1977). The author is grateful to Geoffrey Hawthorn for a close critical reading of an early draft of this paper.

1 On the complexity of Marx's views, even in the preface of *Capital* where the above-cited phrase appears, see Albert O. Hirschman (1981, pp. 89–90).

2 Dudley Seers (1963) leaned on this established terminological usage with his article 'The limitations of the special case', in which he pleaded for recasting the teaching of economics, so as to make it more useful in dealing with the problems of the less developed countries. The 'special case' that had falsely claimed generality was, for Keynes, the fully employed economy; for Seers, it was the economy of the advanced capitalist countries, in contrast to conditions of underdevelopment.

3 His principal empirical argument was the actual decline in agricultural output suffered when the labor force suddenly diminished in a country with an allegedly redundant labor force in agriculture, as happened during the 1918–19 influenza epidemic in India. Arthur Lewis pointed out later that the consequences he had drawn from the assumption of zero marginal productivity in agriculture would remain fully in force, provided only the supply of labor at the given wage in industry exceeds the demand, a condition that is much weaker than that of zero marginal productivity (Lewis, 1972).

4 See Hirschman (1981).

5 This was the title of a well-known League of Nations study stressing the benefits of multilateral trade, which were being threatened in the 1930s by the spread of bilateralism and exchange controls. Its principal author was Folke Hilgerdt, a Swedish economist. In the immediate postwar period, Hilgerdt, then with the United Nations, noted that trade, however beneficial, had not adequately contributed to a narrowing of income differentials between countries. With Hilgerdt coming from the Heckscher–Ohlin tradition and having celebrated the contributions of world trade to welfare, this paper, which was published only in processed form in the proceedings of a congress (I have not been able to locate it), was influential in raising questions about the benign effects of international economic relations on the poorer countries.

6 An extended account of the emergence of this thesis is now available in Love (1980). See also

my earlier essay, 'Ideologies of economic development in Latin America' (Hirschman, 1961). The latest review of the controversy and evidence is in Spraos (1979; 1980).

7 'It is hardly possible to overrate the value, in the present low state of human improvement, of placing human beings in contact with persons dissimilar to themselves, and with modes of thought and action unlike those with which they are familiar ... Such communication has always been, and is peculiarly in the present age, one of the primary sources of progress' (Mill, 1965, bk III, ch. 17, para. 5).

8 This view has been aptly labeled 'catastrofismo' by Anibal Pinto.

9 'Many enemies, much honor.'

10 This is stressed, for example, by Clive Y. Thomas (1974).

11 An expression attributed to Arnold Harberger, in an article in the *New York Times*, 7 February 1980.

Chapter 22: References

Arrighi, G., 'Labour supplies in historical perspective: a study of the proletarianization of the African peasantry in Rhodesia', *Journal of Development Studies*, vol. 6, no. 3 (1970), pp. 197–234.

Cardoso, F. H., 'The originality of a copy: CEPAL and the idea of development', *CEPAL Review* (second half of 1977), United Nations Commission for Latin America, UN Publications E.77.II.G.5, pp. 7–40.

Fishlow, A., 'Brazilian size distribution of income', *American Economic Review*, vol. 62, no. 2 (1972), pp. 391–402.

Gerschenkron, A., *Economic Backwardness in Historical Perspective* (Cambridge, Mass.: Harvard University Press, 1962).

Hirschman, A. O., *The Strategy of Economic Development* (New Haven, Conn.: Yale University Press, 1958).

Hirschman, A. O., 'Ideologies of economic development in Latin America', in Hirschman, ed., *Latin American Issues – Essays and Comments* (New York: Twentieth Century Fund, 1961), pp. 3–42.

Hirschman, A. O., 'The political economy of import-substituting industrialization in Latin America', *Quarterly Journal of Economics*, vol. 82, no. 1 (1968), pp. 1–32; reprinted in Hirschman, *A Bias for Hope: Essays on Development and Latin America* (New Haven, Conn.: Yale University Press, 1971), pp. 85–123.

Hirschman, A. O., *The Passions and the Interests* (Princeton, NJ: Princeton University Press, 1977).

Hirschman, A. O., 'A generalized linkage approach to development, with special reference to staples', *Economic Development and Cultural Change*, vol. 25, Supplement (1977), reprinted in Hirschman, *Essays in Trespassing: Economics to Politics and Beyond* (Cambridge and New York: Cambridge University Press, 1981), pp. 59–97.

Hirschman, A. O., 'The social and political matrix of inflation: elaborations on the Latin American experience', in Hirschman, *Essays in Trespassing*, op. cit., pp. 177–208.

Kindleberger, C. P., *Europe's Postwar Growth: The Role of Labor Supply* (Cambridge, Mass.: Harvard University Press, 1967).

Lewis, W. A., 'Economic development with unlimited supplies of labour', *Manchester School*, vol. 22, no. 2 (1954), pp. 137–91.

Lewis, W. A., 'Reflections on unlimited labor', in L. E. DiMarco, ed., *International Economics and Development: Essays in Honor of Raoul Prebisch* (New York and London: Academic Press, 1972), pp. 75–96.

Love, J., 'Raúl Prebisch and the origins of the doctrine of unequal exchange', *Latin American Research Review*, vol. 15, no. 1 (1980), pp. 45–72.

Mill, J. S. (ed., J. M. Robson), *Principles of Political Economy*, (Toronto: University of Toronto Press, 1965), p. 594.

Morawetz, D., *Twenty-Five Years of Economic Development, 1950–1975* (Washington, DC: World Bank, 1977).

Packenham, R., *Liberal America and the Third World* (Princeton, NJ: Princeton University Press, 1973).

Rawls, J., *A Theory of Justice* (Cambridge, Mass.: Harvard University Press, 1971).

Seers, D., 'The limitations of the special case', *Bulletin of the Oxford University Institute of Economics and Statistics*, vol. 25, no. 2 (1963), pp. 77–98.

Singer, P., 'Multinacionais: internacionalizacão e crise', Caderno CEBRAP No. 28 (São Paulo: Editora Brasiliense, 1977).

Spraos, J., 'The theory of deteriorating terms of trade revisited', *Greek Economic Review*, vol. 1, no. 1 (1979), pp. 15–42.

Spraos, J., 'The statistical debate on the net barter terms of trade between primary commodities and manufactures', *Economic Journal*, vol. 90, no. 357 (1980), pp. 107–28.

Streeten, P., 'Development ideas in historical perspective', in *Toward a New Strategy for Development*, Rothko Chapel Colloquium (New York: Pergamon Press, 1979), pp. 21–52.

Sutcliffe, B., 'Imperialism and industrialization in the Third World', in R. Owen and B. Sutcliffe, eds, *Studies in the Theory of Imperialism* (London: Longman, 1972), pp. 180–86.

Thomas, C. Y., *Dependence and Transformation: The Economics of the Transition to Socialism* (New York: Monthly Review Press, 1974).

Viner, J., 'Some reflections on the concept of "disguised unemployment"', in *Contribuições à Análise do Desenvolvimiento Econòmico* (Essays in Honor of Eugênio Gudin) (Rio de Janeiro: Agir, 1957), pp. 345–54.

Warren, B., 'Imperialism and capitalist accumulation', *New Left Review*, no. 81 (September–October 1973), pp. 3–45.

Warren, B., 'The postwar economic experience of the Third World', in *Toward a New Strategy for Development*, op. cit., pp. 144–68.

Publications by W. Arthur Lewis

Book reviews, newspaper articles and the other short pieces are excluded.

Books

Economic Problems of Today (London: Longman, 1940).
Economic Survey, 1919–1939 (London: Allen & Unwin, 1949).
Overhead Costs (London: Allen & Unwin, 1949).
The Principles of Economic Planning (London: Allen & Unwin, 1949).
The Theory of Economic Growth (London: Allen & Unwin, 1955).
Politics in West Africa (Whidden Lectures) (London: Allen & Unwin, 1965).
Development Planning: The Essentials of Economic Policy (London: Allen & Unwin, 1966).
Some Aspects of Economic Development (Aggrey Memorial Lectures) (Accra: Ghana Publishing Co., 1969).
Aspects of Tropical Trade, 1883–1965 (Wicksell Lectures) (Stockholm: Almqvist & Wiksell, 1969).
(Ed.), *Tropical Development, 1880–1913* (London: Allen & Unwin, 1970).
Growth and Fluctuations, 1870–1913 (London: Allen & Unwin, 1978).

Official Papers

Industrial Development in the Caribbean (Port-of-Spain, Trinidad: Caribbean Commission, 1949).
Land Settlement Policy (Port-of-Spain, Trinidad: Caribbean Commission, 1950).
(With others), *Measures for the Economic Development of Under-Developed Countries* (New York: United Nations, 1951).
(With others), *Report on National Fuel Policy* (London: HMSO., 1952).
Report on Industrialisation and the Gold Coast (Accra: Government of the Gold Coast, 1953).
Eastern Caribbean Foundation (Trinidad: Government of the West Indies, 1962).
Proposals for an Eastern Caribbean Federation of Eight Territories (Trinidad: Government of the West Indies, 1962).
(With others), *Partners in Progress* (Pearson Commission) (New York: Praeger, 1969).
Presidential Address on Unemployment to the Board of Governors, Caribbean Development Bank (Barbados: Caribbean Development Bank, 1972).
Some Constraints on International Banking (Barbados: Caribbean Development Bank, 1972).
Presidential Address on the Shortage of Entrepreneurship to the Board of Governors, Caribbean Development Bank (Barbados: Caribbean Development Bank, 1973).

Monographs and Pamphlets

Labour in the West Indies (London: Fabian Society, 1939).
Monopoly in British Industry (London: Fabian Society, 1945).

Aspects of Industrialisation (Cairo: National Bank of Egypt, 1953).

Economic Problems of Jamaica (Kingston: *Daily Gleaner*, 1964).

The Agony of the Eight (Bridgetown: *Barbados Advocate*, 1965).

Reflections on Nigeria's Economic Growth (Paris: OECD, 1967).

Socialism and Economic Growth (Annual Oration) (London: LSE, 1971).

The Evolution of Foreign Aid (David Owen Memorial Lecture) (Cardiff: University of Wales, 1972).

Development Economics: An Outline (Morristown, NJ: General Learning Press, 1973).

Dynamic Factors in Economic Growth (Tata Memorial Lectures) (Bombay: Orient Longman, 1974).

The University in Less Developed Countries (New York: International Council for Educational Development, 1974).

The Evolution of the International Economic Order (Janeway Lectures) (Princeton, NJ: Princeton University Press, 1978).

LDCs and Exchange Stability (Per Jacobsson Lecture) (Washington, DC: IMF, 1978).

Economic Inequality in the United States: An Analysis of Racial Differences in Earnings and Employment (New York: Rockefeller Foundation, 1981).

Chapters in Books

'Recent British experience in nationalisation', in E. H. Chamberlin, ed., *Monopoly and Competition and their Regulation* (London: Macmillan, 1954), pp. 459–70.

'The economic development of Africa', in C. W. Stillman, ed., *Africa in the Modern World* (Chicago: University of Chicago Press, 1955), pp. 97–112.

'The economic and social council', in E. A. Wortley, ed., *The United Nations* (Manchester: Manchester University Press, 1957), pp. 34–46.

'The shifting fortunes of agriculture', in *Agriculture and its Terms of Trade: Proceedings of the Tenth International Conference of Agricultural Economists* (London: Oxford University Press, 1960), pp. 27–34.

'Sponsored growth: challenge to democracy', in M. K. Haldar and E. Ghosh, eds, *Problems of Economic Growth* (Delhi: Congress for Cultural Freedom, 1960), pp. 107–20.

'Economic conditions for greater agricultural output', in *Report of the Annual Meeting of the British Association for the Advancement of Science* (1960).

'Depreciation and obsolescence as factors in costing', in J. L. Meij, ed., *Depreciation and Replacement Policy* (Amsterdam: North-Holland, 1961), pp. 15–45.

'The emergence of West Africa', in H. Cleveland, ed., *The Promise of World Tensions* (New York: Macmillan, 1961), pp. 87–100.

'Science, man and money', in R. Gruber, ed., *Science and the New Nations* (New York: Basic Books, 1961), pp. 24–33.

'Competition and regulation in the West Indies', in C. B. Hoover, ed., *Economic Systems of the Commonwealth* (Durham, NC: Duke University Press, 1962), pp. 501–18.

'Tensions in economic development', in L. B. Pearson, ed., *Restless Nations* (New York: Dodd, Mead, 1962), pp. 68–98.

'Industrialisation and social peace', in *Conference Across a Continent*, Report of HRH The Duke of Edinburgh's Study Conference (Canada: Macmillan, 1963), pp. 46–60.

'Social services in development planning', in *Planning for Economic Development in the Caribbean*, Report of a Caribbean Organization Conference (Puerto Rico: Caribbean Organization, 1963), pp. 156–67.

'Closing remarks', in W. Baer and I. Kerstenetzky, eds, *Inflation and Growth in Latin America* (New Haven, Conn.: Yale University Press, 1964), pp. 21–33.

'Economic development and world trade', in E. A. G. Robinson, ed., *Problems in Economic Development* (London: Macmillan, 1965), pp. 483–97.

'African economic development', in J. Karefa-Smart, ed., *Africa: Progress through Cooperation* (New York: Dodd, Mead, 1966), pp. 115–30.

'Planning public expenditure', in M. F. Millikan, ed., *National Economic Planning* (New York: National Bureau of Economic Research, 1967), pp. 201–27.

'Unemployment in developing areas', in A. M. Whiteford, ed., *A Reappraisal of Economic Development* (Chicago: Aldine, 1967), pp. 1–17.

'International trade and economic growth', in D. Krivine, ed., *Fiscal and Monetary Problems in Developing States* (New York: Praeger, 1967), pp. 350–58.

'Development planning', in *International Encyclopedia of the Social Sciences*, Vol. 12 (New York: Macmillan/The Free Press, 1968), pp. 118–25.

'Economic aspects of quality in education', in C. E. Beeby, ed., *Qualitative Aspects of Educational Planning* (Paris: UNESCO, International Institute for Economic Planning, 1969), pp. 71–88.

'On being different', in *Speeches Made at the 1971 Graduation Ceremonies of the University of the West Indies* (Kingston: University of the West Indies, 1971).

'Objectives and prognostications', in G. Ranis, ed., *The Gap between Rich and Poor Nations* (London: Macmillan, 1972), pp. 411–20.

'Reflections on unlimited labour', in L. E. DiMarco, ed., *International Economics and Development* (Essays in Honour of Raoul Prebisch) (New York and London: Academic Press, 1972), pp. 75–96.

'The development process', in *The Case for Development: Six Studies* (New York: Praeger, 1973), pp. 52–84.

'Development and distribution', in A. Cairncross and M. Puri, eds, *Employment, Income Distribution and Development Strategy* (London: Macmillan, 1976), pp. 26–42.

'The diffusion of development', in T. Wilson and A. S. Skinner, eds, *The Market and the State* (Oxford: Oxford University Press, 1976), pp. 135–56.

'The rate of growth of world trade', in S. Grassman and E. Lundberg, eds, *The World Economic Order: Past and Prospects* (London: Macmillan, 1981), pp. 11–74.

Articles

'The inter-relations of shipping freights', *Economica*, vol. 8, no. 29 (1941), pp. 52–76.

'The two-part tariff', *Economica*, vol. 8, no. 31 (1941), pp. 249–70.

'The economics of loyalty', *Economica*, vol. 9, no. 36 (1942), pp. 333–48.

'Monopoly and the law', *Modern Law Review*, vol. 6, no. 2 (1943), pp. 97–111.

'An economic plan for Jamaica', *Agenda*, vol. 3, no. 4 (1944), pp. 154–63.

'Competition in retailing', *Economica*, vol. 12, no. 48 (1945), pp. 202–34.

'Spare time activities of employees', *Modern Law Review*, vol. 9, no. 4 (1946), pp. 280–83.

'Fixed costs', *Economica*, vol. 13, no. 49 (1946), pp. 231–58.

'The prospect before us', *Manchester School*, vol. 16, no. 2 (1948), pp. 129–64.

'Colonial development', *Transaction of the Manchester Statistical Society, Session 1948–1949* (12 January 1949), pp. 1–30.

'Whither prices?', *District Bank Review* (1949).

'The British Monopolies Act', *Manchester School*, vol. 17, no. 2 (1949), pp. 208–17.

(With F. V. Meyer), 'The effects of an overseas slump on the British economy', *Manchester School*, vol. 17, no. 3 (1949), pp. 233–65.

'Developing colonial agriculture', *Three Banks Review*, no. 2 (1949), pp. 3–21.

'Sur quelques tendances seculaires', *Economie Appliquée*, vol. 2, nos 3–4 (1949), pp. 374–91.

'The price policy of public corporations', *Political Quarterly*, vol. 21, no. 2 (1950), pp. 184–96.

'Food and raw materials', *District Bank Review*, no. 99 (1951), pp. 1–11.

'The future of world trade', *Scope: A Magazine for Industry*, Annual Review (1952).

'World production, prices and trade, 1870–1960', *Manchester School*, vol. 20, no. 2 (1952), pp. 105–38.

'Reflections on South East Asia', *District Bank Review*, no. 104 (1952), pp. 3–20.

'United Nations primer for development: a comment', *Quarterly Journal of Economics*, vol. 67, no. 2 (1953), pp. 267–75.

'Thoughts on land settlement', *Journal of Agricultural Economics*, vol. 11, no. 1 (1954), pp. 3–11.

'Economic development with unlimited supplies of labour', *Manchester School*, vol. 22, no. 2 (1954), pp. 139–91.

'Trade drives', *District Bank Review*, no. 112 (1954), pp. 1–15.

(With P. J. O'Leary), 'Secular swings in production and trade, 1870–1913', *Manchester School*, vol. 23, no. 2 (1955), pp. 113–52.

'Investment policy', *Bulletin of the Oxford Institute of Statistics*, vol. 17, no. 1 (1955), pp. 57–8.

(With A. Martin), 'Patterns of public revenue and expenditure', *Manchester School*, vol. 24, no. 3 (1956), pp. 203–44.

'International competition in manufactures', *American Economic Review*, vol. 47, no. 2 (1957), pp. 578–87.

'Recent controversies over economic policy in the British Labour Party', *World Politics*, vol. 10, no. 2 (1958), pp. 171–81.

Unlimited labour: further notes', *Manchester School*, vol. 26, no. 1 (1958), pp. 1–32.

'Employment policy in an underdeveloped area', *Social and Economic Studies*, vol. 7, no. 3 (1958), pp. 42–54.

'On assessing a development plan', *Economic Bulletin of Ghana*, vol. 3, nos 6–7 (1959), pp. 2–11.

'Education and economic development', *Social and Economic Studies*, vol. 10, no. 2 (1961), pp. 113–27.

'Education for scientific professions in the poor countries', *Daedalus*, vol. 91, no. 2 (1962), pp. 310–18.

'Secondary education and economic structure', *Social and Economic Studies*, vol. 13, no. 2 (1964), pp. 219–32.

'A review of economic development' (Richard T. Ely Lecture), *American Economic Review*, vol. 55, no. 2 (1965), pp. 1–16.

'Unemployment in developing countries' (Stephenson Memorial Lecture), *World Today*, vol. 23, no. 1 (1967), pp. 13–22.

'World trade since the war', *Proceedings of the American Philosophical Society*, vol. 112 (1968), pp. 362–6.

'Black power and the American university', *University: A Princeton Magazine*, no. 40 (Spring 1969), pp. 8–12.

'The economic profile of the American black', *Journal of Religion and Health*, vol. 9, no. 4 (1970), pp. 323–30.

'Summary: the causes of unemployment in less developed countries', *International Labour Review*, vol. 101, no. 5 (1970), pp. 547–54.

'The dual economy revisited', *Manchester School*, vol. 47, no. 3 (1979), pp. 211–29.

'Rising prices: 1899–1913 and 1950–1979', *Scandinavian Journal of Economics*, vol. 82, no. 4 (1980), pp. 425–36.

'The slowing down of the engine of growth' (Nobel Lecture), *American Economic Review*, vol. 70, no. 4 (1980), pp. 555–64.

List of Authors and Their University Affiliations

PRANAB K. BARDHAN
University of California, Berkeley

WILLIAM J. BAUMOL
New York University and Princeton
University

JAGDISH N. BAGHWATI
Columbia University

WILLIAM H. BRANSON
Princeton University

SIR ALEC CAIRNCROSS
St Peter's College,
Oxford University

PARTHA DASGUPTA
London School of Economics
and Political Science

CARLOS F. DIAZ-ALEJANDRO
Yale University

SEBASTIAN EDWARDS
University of California,
Los Angeles

JOHN C. H. FEI
Yale University

RONALD FINDLAY
Columbia University

MARK GERSOVITZ
Princeton University

ARNOLD C. HARBERGER
University of Chicago

ALBERT O. HIRSCHMAN
Institute for Advanced Study

LOUKA T. KATSELI
Yale University

CHARLES P. KINDLEBERGER
Massachusetts Institute of Technology

SIMON KUZNETS
Harvard University

IAN M. D. LITTLE
Nuffield College,
Oxford University

GORAN OHLIN
Uppsala University

GUSTAV RANIS
Yale University

LLOYD G. REYNOLDS
Yale University

MARK R. ROSENZWEIG
University of Minnesota, Minneapolis

T. N. SRINIVASAN
Yale University

JOSEPH E. STIGLITZ
Princeton University

LANCE TAYLOR
Massachusetts Institute of Technology

Author Index

Adelman, I. 229, 247, 249
Ahluwalia, M. S. 229, 245, 250, 251
Akerlof, G. A. 105
Aldcroft, D. 289, 299
Andersson, J. O. 170, 171
Anschel, K. R. 27
Arrighi, G. 382, 389
Arrow, Kenneth J. 19–20, 168, 171, 246, 247, 248, 249
Artus, J. R. 194, 199, 202, 214
Atkinson, A. B. 142, 153
Auernheimer, L. 153
Aumann, R. 247, 249

Bacha, E. L. 170, 171, 229, 249
Bagchi, A. K. 358, 360, 363, 368, 369, 370
Bagehot, Walter 309, 311
Bairoch, P. 171
Balinsky, M. L. 284
Baran, P. A. 369, 370
Bardhan, Pranab x, 8, 10, 13, 41, 171, 181, 182
Barro, R. J. 140, 153
Barros, J. R. M. de 348, 353
Baumol, William xi, 243, 274, 284
Bell, C. 245, 250
Bergsten, C. F. 216, 225
Bertram, G. 350, 353, 354
Bertrand, T. J. 249
Binswanger, H. P. 132, 133
Bhagwati, Jagdish x, 9, 13, 26, 31, 235, 236, 238, 239, 242, 243, 249, 251, 366, 370
Blitzer, C. 235, 238, 245, 250
Bloomfield, Arthur I. 300, 311
Boadway, R. E. 232, 238, 250
Bouvier, Jean 306, 311
Branson, William H. xi, 194, 195, 197, 198, 199, 200, 203, 205, 206, 210–11, 212, 214
Brecher, R. 181, 182
Brenner, R. 171
Bruno, M. 240, 241, 250
Bushnell, R. C. 274, 284

Cairncross, Sir Alec K. xi, 300, 302, 311
Calvo, Guillemo 104, 105
Cardoso, F. H. 344, 353, 388, 389
Carter, Alice Clare 305, 311
Chakravarty, Sukhanoy 13, 23, 27
Cheetham, R. J. 26, 27, 41, 42
Chenery, H. B. 5, 13, 48, 51, 59, 168, 171, 245, 250
Chichilnisky, G. 77
Chu, D. S. C. 340, 353
Clague, C. 168, 172
Clark, P. B. 235, 244, 250

Coes, D. 324, 332
Cohen, B. J. 369, 370
Crockett, A. D. 197, 214

Darity, W. A. Junior 77
Dasgupta, Partha xi, 8, 13, 234, 235, 236, 238, 250, 255, 268, 274
Dervis, K. 229, 250
Desai, P. 366, 370
Dewey, C. 370
Diamond, P. 233, 234, 238, 249, 250
Diaz-Alejandro, Carlos xi, 11, 13, 168, 172, 323, 333, 353, 354
Dickson, P. G. M. 305, 311
Diewart, E. 250
Dixit, A. K. 8, 13, 23, 26, 27, 239, 250
Dobb, M. H. 8, 13
Dominguez, J. I. 342, 354
Domrese, R. I. 359, 360, 368, 371
Duloy, J. 245, 250
Dutt, R. C. 356, 360, 369, 370

Edwards, Sebastian xi, 187, 193
Ehrlich, A. 272, 273, 274
Ehrlich, P. 272, 273, 274
Eicher, C. K. 27
Ellsworth, P. T. 340, 352, 354
Emmanuel, A. 9, 13, 157, 158
Evenson, R. E. 121, 122, 133, 134

Faletto, E. 344, 353
Fei, John C. H. x, 8, 13, 23, 27, 28, 41, 42
Feinstein, C. H. 288, 290, 293, 299
Findlay, Ronald, x, xi, 8, 10, 13, 27, 170, 172, 181, 182, 239, 250
Fishlow, Albert 353, 354, 386, 389
Flanders, J. M. 195, 197, 214
Foster, E. 240, 250
Frank, A. G. 334, 353, 354
Friedman, M. 139, 153, 351, 354
Furtado, Carlos, 324, 333, 351, 354

Gardner, Richard N. 224, 225
Gerschenkron, A. 378, 379, 389
Ginsburgh, V. 229, 250
Girault, René 303, 311
Goldfeld, S. M. 153
Goreux, L. M. 229, 250
Gosovic, B. 222, 225
Griffin, K. B. 369, 370
Guesnerie, R. 240, 250

Hagen, E. 9, 13
Hahn, F. 23, 27, 247, 249
Hammond, P. J. 232, 243–4, 250, 268, 274
Haq, Mahbub ul 223, 225

Harberger, Arnold xi, 104, 106, 173, 192, 193, 240, 250
Harbison, R. W. 325, 333
Harley, C. Knick 307, 312
Harnetty, P. 357, 371
Harris, J. R. 13, 41, 42, 104, 106
Hatta, T. 240, 241, 250
Hayek, Friedrich A. von 15, 18
Heckman, J. 124, 133
Helfferich, Karl 307, 312
Helleiner, G. K. 108, 133, 329, 333
Helpman, E. 195, 197, 214
Hirschman, Albert O. xii, 334, 352, 353, 354, 377, 383, 387, 388, 389
Ho, Y. 26, 27
Hoffman, W. G. 294, 299
Holdran, J. 272, 273, 274
Hopkins, M. 247, 251
Hornby, J. N. 8, 10, 13, 181, 182
Hotelling, H. 240, 251
Huffman, W. E. 117, 133

Inada, K. 10, 13
Ingram, J. C. 327, 328, 333
Inoki, Takenori 308, 312
Israelsen, L. Dwight 307, 312

Jamison, D. T. 133
Janvry, A. de 171, 172
Jay, Peter 223–4, 225
Johnson, H. G. 9, 14
Jolles, P. A. 221, 225
Jolly, R. 245, 250
Jorgenson, D. W. 8, 14, 23, 27
Jousseau, J. B. 306, 312

Kafka, Alexander 334, 354
Kalecki, M. 61, 77
Kao, C. H. C. 27
Katseli, L. T. 194, 195, 197, 198, 199, 200, 203, 205, 206, 210–211, 214
Kawamata, K. 240, 251
Keeler, E. 273, 274
Kelley, A. C. 26, 27, 41, 42
Kennan, G. F. 304, 312
Keohane, R. O. 216, 225
Kidron, M. 366, 367, 371
Kindleberger, Charles P. xi, 8, 14, 23, 27, 300, 305, 312, 352, 354, 378
Kirkpatrick, C. H. 153, 154
Kisley, 121, 133
Kneese, A. 258, 265–6, 267, 272, 273, 274
Kolm, Serge-Christophe 302–3, 312
Koopmans, Tjalling 229, 232, 251
Kornai, J. 246, 251
Kouri, P. J. K. 202, 214
Krishnamurty, K. J. 370, 371
Krueger, A. O. 26, 27
Krugman, P. 171, 172
Kumar, Dharma 357, 371

Kurz, M. 247, 249, 251
Kuznets, Simon x, 32, 39, 42, 47, 59, 122, 320, 333

Laclau, E. 172
Lal, D. 251
Lara-Resende, A. 77
Lau, L. J. 133
Lauck, W. Jett 305, 312
Leibenstein, H. 104, 106
Lerner, A. B. 18
Lévy-Leboyer, Maurice 303, 307, 312
Lewis, John P. 215, 225
Lewis, W. Arthur 1–2, 3, 8, 11, 12, 14, 15–19, 20–2, 24, 27, 31, 38, 39, 133, 135, 154, 157, 158, 170, 172, 173, 176, 214, 216, 217, 225, 229, 287, 289, 290, 296, 299, 300, 301, 306, 307, 315, 320, 331, 333, 368, 389, 390
Lidman, R. 359, 360, 368, 371
Lim, C. Y. 328, 333
Lipschitz, L. 195, 197, 201, 214
Little, Ian M. D. 8, 11, 14, 26, 27, 236–7, 241, 242, 251
Lockheed, M. E. 133
Logue, D. E. 137, 154
Love, J. 389
Lysy, F. J. 77, 229, 249, 251

Macedo, J. B. de 195, 202, 203, 214
McIntosh, J. 26, 27
McKinnon, R. I. 154
MacPherson, W. J. 369, 371
Maddison, A. 356, 371
Maler, K. G. 261, 274
Malthus, Thomas 32, 33
Mamalakis, M. 324, 333
Manabe, S. 270, 274
Manne, Alan S. 224, 248, 250, 251
Manoilesco, M. 9, 14
Marglin, S. A. 8, 13, 77, 241, 250
Marshall, J. M. 153, 154
Marx, Karl 21
Maskin, E. 268
Matthews, Robin C. O. 20, 23, 27, 288, 299
Mill, John Stuart 383, 389
Minhas, B. S. 168, 171
Mirrlees, J. A. 8, 14, 104, 106, 232, 233, 234, 236–7, 241, 242, 245, 250
Morawetz, D. 372, 389
Morgenstern, Oskar 305, 312
Morris, M. D. 369, 371
Muth, J. F. 135, 154
Myint, H. 4, 11, 14
Myrdal, Gunnar 14, 217, 225, 382–3

Nelson, R. R. 107, 133
Nerlove, M. 117, 133
Niho, Y. 26, 27, 28
Nixon, F. E. 153, 154

Nordhaus, W. 266, 270–2, 274
Nsouli, S. M. 197, 214
Nugent, J. B. 351, 354
Nurkse, R. 8, 14, 23, 24, 27
Nye, J. S. 216, 225

Odling-Smee, J. 288, 299
Ohkawa, K. 23, 28
Ohlin, Bertil 22
Ohlin, Goran xi

Packenham, R. 385, 390
Petrecolla, Alberto O. 353, 354
Phelps, D. M. 338, 353, 354
Phelps, E. S. 104, 105, 107, 133, 153, 154
Pollard, Sidney 303, 312
Prebisch, Raoul 10, 14, 157, 172, 380, 381–2
Press, S. J. 117, 133
Prest, A. R. 135, 154
Pyatt, 251

Quandt, R. E. 153

Rader, T. 240, 251
Ram, R. 133
Ramaswami, V. K. 8, 13
Ranis, Gustav x, 8, 13, 23, 26, 27, 28, 41, 42
Rawls, John 386, 390
Reynolds, C. W. 326, 333
Rhomberg, R. K. 194, 199, 202, 214
Ricardo, David 21, 32, 35, 173, 383
Richardson, H. W. 289, 299
Roberts, K. W. S. 232, 251
Robinson, J. 369, 371
Robinson, S. 229, 247, 249, 250
Rodgers, G. B. 247, 251
Rosenstein-Rodan, P. N. 8, 14, 23, 24, 27, 28, 378
Rosenzweig, Mark x, 41, 121, 122, 132, 133, 134
Rostow, Walt 20, 28, 378, 379
Rudra, A. 242, 251

Salop, S. C. 106
Samuelson, Paul 22, 237, 251
Sanchez, R. G. 353, 354
Sandmo, A. 142, 154
Sato, R. 26, 28
Scarf, H. 246, 251
Schlote, W. 297, 299
Schultz, T. W. 107, 132, 134, 377
Schultze, C. L. 258, 265–6, 267, 272, 273, 274
Schwartz, A. J. 351, 354
Scitovsky, T. 11, 14, 26, 27
Scott, M. F. 11, 14, 26, 27
Seers, D. 353, 354, 388, 390
Sen, A. K. 8, 14, 77, 241, 250
Shaw, E. S. 153, 154
Shoven, J. 240, 251

Silber, S. 343, 354
Singer, H. W. 10, 14, 157, 170, 172, 381–2
Singer, P. 375, 390
Singh, S. 117, 134
Sivasubramonian, S. 360, 364, 370, 371
Sjaastad, L. A. 153, 154
Smith, Adam 4, 21, 32, 37, 383
Smith, V. L. 273, 274
Solow, R. M. 168, 171
Sonnenschein, H. 240, 250
Spence, M. 273, 274
Spraos, J. 389, 390
Squire, L. 241, 251
Srinivasan, T. N. xi, 41, 235, 236, 238, 239, 242, 249, 251
Stern, Fritz 305, 312
Stiglitz, Joseph 79, 104, 105, 106, 142, 153, 234, 235, 236, 238, 250
Stone, Lawrence 305, 312
Streeten, P. 388, 390
Sundararajan, V. 195, 197, 214
Sutcliff, B. 375, 390
Suzigan, W. 353, 355
Sylos-Labini, P. 61, 77
Syrquin, M. 5, 13, 48, 51, 59

Tak, H. van der 241, 251
Taylor, Lance x, 77, 229, 235, 245, 250
Thomas, Clive Y. 389, 390
Thomas, Dorothy Swaine 308, 312
Thorner, D. 369, 371
Thorp, R. 350, 353, 354
Timberg, T. A. 360, 371
Tinbergen, J. 251
Tobin, J. 77
Todaro, M. P. 13, 41, 42, 104, 105, 106
Tooke, T. 357, 371
Trotter, H. F. 153
Turnham, D. 13, 14

United Nations 59

Vanek, J. 249
Vicziany, M. 369, 371
Villela, A. V. 353, 355
Viner, J. 7, 14, 377, 390

Waelbroeck, J. 229, 250
Walker, Mack 308, 312
Wan, H. Junior 239, 243, 249
Warren, Bill 384, 390
Weiss, A. 106
Weiss, L. 153, 154
Weitzman, M. L. 268, 274
Welch, F. 107, 132, 134
Wellisz, S. 13, 14, 239, 250
Wery, R. 247, 251
Wetherald, R. 270, 274
Whalley, J. 240, 251

White, Harry Dexter 304, 312
Whitehead, L. 252, 355
Willett, T. D. 137, 154
Williamson, J. G. 26, 27, 41, 42
Williamson, John H. 218–19, 223, 225
Wilson, C. H. 305, 312

Wirth, Max 304, 312
World Bank 49, 59
Wyzga, R. E. 261, 274

Zarembka, P. 26, 28
Zeckhauser, R. 273, 274

Subject Index

agricultural labor force 43; changes, 1950–70 *44*, 57–8; decline in *46*; differentials in per worker production 50–1, *52*, *53*, 54, *55*, 56–7, 58; effects of decline *52*, *53*, 54; G.N.P. and 48, *49*, 50; inequalities in production 50; pattern of decline 43–6, 50; per capita production and 47; share of in agriculture 47, 48, 49

agriculture 70–5, 76, 169–70 *see also* Green Revolution

Argentina 12, 304–5, 322, 323, 331, 332, 336, 338–40, *341*, 342, 343–4, 345, *346*

Atkinson measure of inequality 22

Australia 12

Bangladesh 6

banking 185–6

Bolivia 137

Brandt Commission 224

Brazil 6, 137, 314, 322, 323–4, 332, 336, 338, 342, 343–4, 345, *346*

Bretton Woods 217

Burma 6, 322

Canada 12

capital–labor ratio 4

capital mobility 95–6; equilibrium 96–9, 103–4; optimal wage subsidies 99–100; shadow wages rate 99

capital stock 4

Ceylon 322, 326–7, 331, 332

Chile, 322, 324–5, 331, 339, 342

China 11, 224, 322

Classical economics, 3, 4, 15, 21, 31–41

cliometrics 12, 20

closed economy, x, 23–4, 231–2

Colombia 322, 325, 332, 338, 339, 345, *346*

Committee of Twenty 219, 223

commodity prices 217

consumer price index (CPI) 204, 205

cost-benefit analysis xi, 8, 229

Cuba 339, 340, 342

currency xi, 194; basket 194–5, 197, 199–200, 203–6, 210; floating 194; home *208*, *209*; log-linear trade model 210–14; SDR 194; weighting schemes 200–2

development x, xi, 3, 5, 8, 15, 21–6, 33, 37

development economics 157, 229, 241, 272–3, 375–6; attacks upon 384–8; classification of theories 373–5; economists 33; late industrialization 378–9; monoeconomics 375–9, 381–4;

mutual- benefit assumption 379–81; neo-Marxism 381–4; types of theories *373*; underemployment and 376–8

distortion 240

domestic markets 12, 357, 366, 369

dual economy x, 3–4, 8, 23, 31, 36, 173; behavioristic equations 39; capitalist sector 3–4; 6–7, 33, 36, 39; organizational dualism 33, 36, 38, 39; product dualism 38–9; Ramseyan optimal saving model 8, traditional sector 3–4, 33, 36, 39

dual economy model 173; employment cost 181; formal structure of 173–4; protection and the rate of growth 175–81; small open dual economy 174–5

economic environment-international: capital 320–1; diffusion of technology 321; growth acceleration 322; growth rates 317–18; trade flows and policies 319–20; transport 318–19

economic history x, xi, 12, 314–17

education: in rural India 120–31; investment in 128–31; of rural farmers 107–19

education and technology: adoption 108–17; change 117–19; Green Revolution and 123–5; in India 120–31; risk and cost of capital 114–17; technology bias and the labor market 110–14

efficiency wage-productivity model 78, 79; basic model 80–2; calculation of opportunity cost of labor 85–6; comparative statics 82–4; second-best optimality 84–5

efficiency wage-quality model 78, 80, 86–95

Egypt 6, 16, 322

Engel's Law 34

environment: planning problems 263–5; problems 253, 254; U.S. Environmental Protection Acts 265–6

European Economic Community (EEC) 204–5, 217, 218

exchange rates xi, 194; adjustment of real 203–4; balance of trade weights 197–8; crises of 183; fixed 302; floating 303; fluctuations in 195–200; in Latin America 339, 340; in S. Europe 204–6, 210; log-linear trade model 210–14; real effective 195–7; stability 185; stabilizing weights 199–200; terms of trade weights 198–9

food prices x, 76

France 12, 169, 306–7, *308*, 316

functional distribution of income 35, 36

General Agreement on Tariffs & Trade (GATT) 219, 222–3
general-equilibrium theory 20, 40, 239, 240; computable models 229, 244–8
Germany 6, 12, 32, 304–5, 307, 309, 316
Ghana 16, 322, 329
Giffen, Sir Robert 289
Gini coefficient 22
Great Depression xi, 334–8, 383
Greece 195, 204–6, *208*, 209, 210
Green Revolution 21, 108; adoption of high-yield crops 125–6, *127*, 128; education and 123–5; in India 120–31, 248; investment in education 128–31
Gross Domestic Product (GDP) 288–94, 298, 345, *346*
Gross National Product (GNP) 48–9
growth xi, 2, 5–6, 12, 32, 175, 313–17, 330; acceleration of 313–17, 322, 323–9; Classical model 36; descriptive model 23; functional distribution of income 35; in the 2-Sector model 66–9; modern epoch 34; patterns 60; periodization of 316–17; phases of 33; protection and 175–81; rates in early developing countries 317–18; rate of 76, 313; restricted agricultural 70–3; unrestricted agricultural 73–5

Harris Todaro model 5
Harrod-Domar model 213, 244, 380
Heckscher-Ohlin-Lerner-Samuelson model 168
Heckscher-Ohlin theory 22
historical analysis 15, 20–2
Hong Kong 175

income 35, 60, 100–1
income per capita 1, 50
India xi, 6, 169, 322; Ambassador Lall 222; centralized planning in 16; colonial rule and 364–6; cotton-industry 356–60; domestic market 357, 366, 369; exports 356–7, 366, 368–9; Finance Ministry 201; Green Revolution and 120–31, 248; handloom weavers 357–8; imports 358–9; Indian Tariff Board 361–2, 366; industry in 356, 360–9; Intensive Agricultural District Programme 120, 128, 130–1; investment 363–4; manufacturing growth rates *363*; mills 359–60; planning models 244; project-appraisal divisions 230; protection 362, 364
Indochina 322
Industrial Revolution 11
inflation x, 60, 69–70, 77, 182–4; devaluation crises *184*, 185, *187*, *188*; economic

policy indicators 182; government and 148–52; in Latin-America 136–7; in various countries 183, *184*, 185; inflation rate 136, 142–3, *144–7*, 148; tax 135–6, *151*; model of tax under uncertainty 137–42; parameters of 142–8; statistics on the rate *137*
institutional economics 37, 39–40
Intensive Agricultural District Programme (IADP) 120–3, 128, 130–1
inter-temporal planning models 8
international economic order 215, 216
International Labor Office (ILO) 42, 57, 58
International Monetary Fund (IMF) 194, 198, 199, 202, 221, 310
international reserves 186–92; distribution of reserve ratios *188*; falling reserve ratios *190*; policy choices under rising reserve ratios *190*; policy initiatives and turning points *191*; reserve ratios *187*, 189–92
international trade 17, 21, *207*, 216, 217–18, 319–20
investment x, xi, 76, 300, 303, 304–8, 321
Ivory Coast 322

Jamaica 6
Japan 11, 32, 313, 314
Japan-Asean-Australia nexus 224

Kaldor-Robinson Cambridge theory 4
Keynes, John Maynard 3, 31, 32, 218, 375–6, 378, 380
Korea 6, 11

labor 7, 168, 169–70; markets x; marginal productivity 40; relative productivity 9; shadow price of 79; skilled 4; supply curve 7, 35, 36; transfer of x; unequal rewards 157–8; unlimited ix, x, 4–6, 12, 34–5, 38, 41; unlimited supply-of-labour model 40, 172; unskilled 1, 4–5, 12 *see also* agricultural force
Lall, K. B. 222
land 7, 169
Latin America xii, 322, 351–2; adjustment mechanisms 344–5; cost of living indices 340; development in 334, 350; economic policies 338–50; exchange rates *339*, 340, *341*, 351; export quantum 335; fiscal policies 343–4; Great Depression and 334–8; GDP. growth 345, *346*; industrialization 348–9; inflation in 136–7; manufacturing in 345, 347; manufacturing output *347*, *348*; money supply *342*; protectionism and 336; purchasing power of exports *337*, *338*; statistics on inflation rate *137*; *see also* individual countries

Law of the Sea Conference 221
League of Nations 302
Less Developed Countries (LDCs) x, xi, 1, 3, 7, 9, 10, 11, 12, 36, 58, 103, 330–2; employment in 8; exports 320; government policy in 135–6; investment in 321; peasant sector in 23, 24; project evaluation in 241; transition in 39; wage determination in 101–2; *see also* individual countries and inflation
Lewis, W. Arthur ix, 376, 377, 382; biography of 1–3; centralized planning 16–17; Classicists and 31–41; cliometrics 12; contribution of 1; development theory 37; dual economy 4–6, 33; economic development x, 1; economic history x, 12; historical analysis 15, 20–2; Janeway Lectures, 1978 3, 23, 25; modelling development problems 15, 22–6; modern economic growth 6–8; planning by direction 16, 18; political economy and 15–20; Ricardo–Graham model 9–11; terms of trade model x, xi; trade development nexus 8–9; turning-point thesis 37; unequal exchange 157; unlimited labor ix, 4, 15, 34–5, 38; unlimited supply curve of labor 35; unlimited supply of labor model 40, 172; Whidden Lectures, 1965 3, 18; Wicksell Lecture, 1969 3, 9, 10, 23, 25, 157, 173
Liebermanism 16
linear programmes 243–4, 275–6, 283–4; non-linearities 27–45; nonlinear solutions 279–83; primal nonlinear programmes 276–9
Lomé Convention 224
long-term lending 300–11; American 300–2; anti-cyclical 302, 304–5; counter-cyclical pattern 309–11; Dawes loan 301; demand model 301, 303; loans 301; of Germany 304–5; of United Kingdom 300–1, 305; private 310; pro-cyclical 302, 304–5, 306; Russo-German Loan 304–5

McNamara, Robert 222, 387
Malaya 322, 328–9
market economy 16, 17
Marshall–Lerner condition 198
Mexico 305, 322, 326, 338, 345, *346*
migration 5, 12, 24, 25, 51, 100–1, 308–9
monetary economy 185–6
monoeconomics 373, 375–9, 381–4, 385
monopoly power 235–6
monopoly rent 167
multilateral diplomacy 218–25
multiple exchange rate model 194

NBER 16

Neoclassical economics 3, 4, 5, 6–7, 40; models 40; general equilibrium theory 230
neo-Marxism 381–4, 385
Nepal 6
Neuman model 4
new international economic order 25, 214–18, 223
New Zealand 12
Nigeria 322, 329, 331
nontraded goods 236–9
North–South relations 215, 216–18, 220, 222–5, 381

OPEC 20
Organization for Economic Cooperation & Development (OECD) 8, 16, 220–1, 316–17
output 7, 60, *318*

Pakistan 16
Pareto, V. F. D.: Paretian efficiency condition 176; Paretian optimum 176, 386; Pareto criterion 232; Pareto-optimal allocation 232; Pareto-superior 241
parity xi
Philippines 322
planning xi; centralized 16–17; computable models 244–7; linearization of exercises x, 243–4; by direction 16, 18
political economy 15–20
pollutants 254–5; biological amplifiers 254; classification of 255–6; emission-output ratio 256–8; qualitative 255; quantitative 255–6; rate of degradation 258–60
pollution 252–3; atmospheric 253–4; carbon-dioxide problem 270–2; Clean Air Amendments (USA 1970) 265–6; control 263–5; cost-benefit rules for control 268–70; management 255, 256; control policies 266–8; Water Pollution Control Act Amendment (USA 1972) 266
population 34, 35, 313, 317–18
Portugal 195, 204–6, *208*, *209*, 210
Prebisch, Dr. Raoul 222, 224
price control 18
price mechanism 16, 17
private economy 148–52
product per capita 47
productivity 158; changes in 167–8; comparative-static results 161–7; importance of 169–70; in UK 289; Lewis-type model 159–61
project appraisal techniques 229–30; institutional framework 230; 'key' shadow prices 242–3; monopoly power in trade 235–6; non-economic objectives 241–2; nonoptimal taxation

233–4; nontraded goods 236–9; optimal taxation 232–3; projects and evaluation 230–1; as a planning procedure 243–4; in development economics 241; 2nd fundamental theorem of welfare economics 231–2; shadow prices 231, 234, 237–8, 241, 243; shadow price for non-traded goods 235; shadow price of primary factors 239–40; tax reform 240–1
protection 175–81
public-sector production 232

rate of profit 4
real wage 4–5, 6–7, 8, 35, 36, 40–1, 175
resources 252–3
Ricardian model 173
Ricardo–Graham model 9–11

savings 35, 40, 76, 100
Singapore 175, 201
South Korea 175
Spain 195, 204–6, *208, 209,* 210
special drawing rights (SDR) 194, 219, 223
stagnation thesis 33, 35
Stolper–Samuelson theorem 176

Taiwan 6, 11, 175, 314
tariffs 9, 176
technology 168, 321 *see also* education and technology
taxation 230, 231, 232, 240–1, 242; reform 240–1; optimal tax subsidy policies 242
terms of trade x, xi, 8, 9, 10, 12, 24–6, 204, 205; agricultural 60; agricultural productivity and 107; domestic x; growth in the 2-sector model 66–9; Lewis's model 25; of tropical countries 23; short-run model for output and terms of trade 60, 61–6; and inflation 69–70
Thailand 327–8, 331
Third World 1, 32, 221, 224, 225
trade barriers 20–1
transport 318–19

turning-point thesis 37

unemployment x, 5, 34, 79, 80
unequal exchange 157–9, 169–70
UNIDO 8
United Kingdom xi, 12, 32, 299; agricultural depression 297; as industrial leader 287; Baring crisis 302, 304; capital formation *295;* deceleration of economy 288, 289–92; economic growth 313, 316; employment 288, 290, *291,* 292–3, 294–5; exports 296–8; foreign investment 305, *308;* foreign trade and 17, 295, 296–8; GDP 288–94, 298; GDP rates of growth *288, 291,* 292, 296; imports 295, 296–7; India and 356, 359–61, 362; investment 287, 294, 295, 298; lending 300–2, 304–5, 309–10; productivity 289, 292, 293–4; productivity: rates of growth *289, 292*
United Nations 215, 219–21
United Nations Conference on Trade and Development (UNCTAD) 215 220, 222
Uruguay 137, 339
U.S.A. 6, 12, 32, 136–7, 200, 265–6, 300–2, 316
U.S.S.R. 4, 16, 17, 32, 303, 304–5

value theorists 157
Venezuela 322

wages 101; *ad valorem* wage subsidy 79, 86, 99; differentials between rural and urban 78; 102; efficiency wage-productivity model 78, 79, 80–6; efficiency wage-quality model 78, 80, 85–6; labor-turnover model 78, 79; 'optimal' 78; determination in LDCs 101–2; gaps 167–8; wage rates and the Green Revolution 123–5, 128; subsidies 79, 80, 99–100
Walras, M. E. L. 66, 160, 245–6
White, Harry Dexter 218
World Bank 221
world economy xi, 1, 11, 335
World Economic Conference (1933) 217